TELLING TALES

David Blamires (University of Manchester) is the author of around 100 articles on a variety of German and English topics and of publications including *Characterization and Individuality in Wolfram's 'Parzival'*; *David Jones: Artist and Writer*; *Herzog Ernst and the Otherworld Journey: a Comparative Study*; *Happily Ever After: Fairytale Books through the Ages*; *Margaret Pilkington 1891-1974*; *Fortunatus in His Many English Guises*; *Robin Hood: a Hero for all Times* and *The Books of Jonah*. He also guest-edited a special number of the *Bulletin of the John Rylands University Library of Manchester* on Children's Literature.

THE BASKET OF FLOWERS.

[Christoph von Schmid], *The Basket of Flowers; or, Piety and Truth Triumphant* (London, [1868]).

David Blamires

Telling Tales

The Impact of Germany on English Children's Books 1780-1918

Cambridge
OpenBook Publishers
2009

OpenBook Publishers

40 Devonshire Road, Cambridge, CB1 2BL, United Kingdom
http://www.openbookpublishers.com

@ 2009 David Blamires

Some rights are reserved. This book is made available under the Creative Commons Attribution-Non-Commercial-No Derivative Works 2.0 UK: England & Wales License. This license allows for copying any part of the work for personal and non-commercial use, providing author attribution is clearly stated. Details of allowances and restrictions are available at:
http://www.openbookpublishers.com

As with all Open Book Publishers titles, digital material and resources associated with this volume are available from our website:
http://www.openbookpublishers.com

ISBN Hardback: 978-1-906924-10-2
ISBN Paperback: 978-1-906924-09-6
ISBN Digital (pdf): 978-1-906924-11-9

All paper used by Open Book Publishers is SFI (Sustainable Forestry Initiative), and PEFC (Programme for the Endorsement of Forest Certification Schemes) Certified.

Printed in the United Kingdom and United States by
Lightning Source for Open Book Publishers

*To Roger Paulin
for his persistent encouragement
over several years.*

Contents

Introduction	1
1. The Adventures of Baron Munchausen	9
2. A World of Discovery: Joachim Heirich Campe	23
3. *Elements of Morality*: Salzmann and Wollstonecraft	39
4. Musäus and the Beginnings of the Fairytale	51
5. Discovering Germany	63
6. *The Swiss Family Robinson*	79
7. Moral, Didactic and Religious Tales	95
8. Friedrich de la Motte Fouqué: *Undine* and *Sintram*	121
9. Adelbert von Chamisso's *Peter Schlemihl*	135
10. The Fairytales of the Brothers Grimm	147
11. The Fairytales of Wilhelm Hauff	181
12. The Folktale Tradition in Germany	205
13. E. T. A. Hoffmann's *Nutcracker and Mouse King*	223
14. Lesser Fairytales Authors	245
15. Clemens Brentano's Fairytales	263
16. Learning about German History	275
17. The Thirty Years War	291
18. Historical Tales and Adventure Stories	309
19. Picture Books	321
20. Siegfried and the *Nibelungenlied*	353
21. The Franco-Prussian War	371
22. German Books for Girls	395
23. Children's Books and the First World War	409
Primary Texts	423
Select Bibliography	441
Index	449

Illustrations

                                                                                                        Page

Cover: Wilhelm Busch, *Max and Moritz. A Story in Seven Tricks* (Munich: Braun & Schneider; London: A. N. Myers & Co., c. 1892). p. 12.

Frontispiece: [Christoph von Schmid], *The Basket of Flowers; or, Piety and Truth Triumphant. Translated from the original German Edition. With Numerous Coloured Illustrations* (London: Frederick Warne & Co., [1868]).   ii

1. *Adventures of the Renowned Baron Munchausen, Containing Singular Travels, Campaigns, Voyages, and Adventures* (London: Thomas Tegg, 1811). Frontispiece by Thomas Rowlandson.   8

2. *The Life and Exploits of Baron Munchausen. Who Outdid All Other Travellers. Related by Himself* (Glasgow: Richard Griffin & Co., 1827). Title-page.   17

3. *Baron Munchausen.* Webb, Millington and Co.'s Penny Pictorial Library, no. 6. (London: Yorkshire J. S. Publishing and Stationery Co. Limited, c. 1865). Hand-coloured frontispiece.   19

4. J. H. Campe, *The New Robinson Crusoe; an Instructive and Entertaining History, for the Use of Children of Both Sexes. Translated from the French. New Edition* (London: John Stockdale, 1811). Frontispiece by John Bewick.   29

5. J. H. Campe, *The Discovery of America; for the Use of Children and Young Persons* (London: J. Johnson, 1799). Frontispiece by J. Burney.   32

6. C. G. Salzmann, *Elements of Morality, for the Use of Children; with an Introductory Address to Parents. Translated [by Mary Wollstonecraft] from the German. A New Edition* (London: J. Johnson, 1805). Title-page.   44

7. J. K. A. Musäus, *Legends of Number Nip. Translated by Mark Lemon*

Illustrations   ix

(London: Macmillan & Co., 1864). Illustrated by Charles Keene.   57

8. Isaac Taylor, *Scenes in Europe, for the Amusement and Instruction of Little Tarry-at-Home Travellers*. Second edition (London: J. Harris, 1819). Copper-engravings.   72

9. *Travels with Minna and Godfrey in Many Lands. From the Journals of the Author. The Rhine, Nassau, and Baden* (London: Smith, Elder & Co., 1839). Copper-engraving of the Drachenfels, Rolandseck and Nonnenfels, opposite p. 84.   74

10. *The Swiss Family Robinson* (London: Frederick Warne & Co., [by 1883]), opposite p. 145.   91

11. [F. A. Krummacher], *The Little Dove: a Story for Children, Founded on Fact. New Edition*. (London: Charles Gilpin, c. 1854). Title-page and frontispiece.   100

12. [Franz Sales Meyer], *Little Swiss Seppeli; or Confidence in God Rewarded. A True Story Translated from the German* (London: Harvey & Darton, 1829). Title-page and frontispiece.   100

13. Christopher von Schmid, *The Flower-Basket. A Moral Tale. Translated by William E. Drugulin. With illustrations by Julius Nisle* (Stuttgart: J. B. Müller, 1848). Title-page and frontispiece.   110

14. C. G. Barth, *The Young Tyrolese. Translated by Samuel Jackson* (London: Darton & Clark [1838]). Title-page and frontispiece.   116

15. Friedrich de la Motte Fouqué, *Sintram and his Companions. Illustrations by H. C. Selous* (London: Edward Lumley, n.d.), p. 1.   130

16. [Adelbert von Chamisso, wrongly attributed to Lamotte Fouqué], *Peter Schlemihl. With Plates by George Cruikshank* (London: G. and W. B. Whittaker, 1824), opposite p. 44.   141

17. *Unlucky John and his Lump of Silver. A Juvenile Comic Tale. Translated into Easy Verse by Madame Leinstein* (London: A. K. Newman & Co., c. 1825). Hand-coloured engravings. Title-page and frontispiece.   156

18. [George Nicol], *An Hour at Bearwood. The Wolf and the Seven Little Kids*. Second edition (London: Wright, 1839), opposite p. 17.   158

19. Brothers Grimm, *Household Stories. Newly Translated. Illustra-*

tions by Edward Wehnert. 2 vols. (London: Addey & Co., 1853), opposite p. 134 (illustration to 'The Musicians of Bremen').   164

20. W. Hauff, *Longnose the Dwarf, and Other Fairy Tales. Translated by Percy E. Pinkerton. With 14 Plates and 19 Woodcuts* (London: Swan Sonnenschein & Allen, 1881). Frontispiece (illustration to 'The Stone-cold Heart').   188

21. Ludwig Bechstein, *The Old Story-teller: Popular German Tales. Illustrations by Ludwig Richter* (London: Addey & Co., 1854). Title-page and frontispiece.   208

22. *A Picture Story-book* (London: George Routledge & Sons, n.d.). Illustrations by Bertall to [E. T. A. Hoffmann/Alexandre Dumas], *The History of a Nutcracker*, p. 156.   239

23. *The King of the Swans and Other Tales, with Four Lithographs* (London: Joseph Cundall, 1846). Title-page and frontispiece (Rudolphi's 'The King of the Swans').   248

24. *Fairy Tales from Brentano, Translated by Kate Freiligrath Kroeker. Illustrations by F. Carruthers Gould* (London: T. Fisher Unwin, 1884), p. 3.   268

25. Julia Corner, *The History of Germany and the Austrian Empire. New edition, Revised and Enlarged* (London: Thomas Dean & Son, c. 1854). Copper-engraving by Davenport, after Gilbert, opposite p. 170.   280

26. [Robert B. Paul], *A History of Germany, from the Invasion of Germany by Marius to the Battle of Leipzic, 1813. On the plan of Mrs. Markham's histories. For the use of Young Persons* (London: John Murray, 1847), p. 276.   282

27. *Scenes and Narratives from German History* (London: Society for Promoting Christian Knowledge, n.d.), opposite p. 132, 'Gustavus Kneeling in front of his Army'.   284

28. *Little Lily's Alphabet. With Rhymes by S. M. P. and Pictures by Oscar Pletsch* (London: Frederick Warne & Co., c. 1865). W for Winter.   329

29. Heinrich Hoffmann, *The English Struwwelpeter. Pretty Stories and Funny Pictures for Little Children*. Fifteenth edition (Leipzic: Friedrich Volckmar; London: Agency of the German Literary Society,   336

c. 1858), p. 8. 'The Story of Fidgedy [sic] Philip'.

30. *The Heroic Life and Exploits of Siegfried the Dragon Slayer. An Old German Story. With Eight Illustrations Designed by Wilhelm Kaulbach* (London: Joseph Cundall & David Bogue, 1848), opposite p. 108. 359

31. *Golden Threads from an Ancient Loom. Das Nibelungenlied. Adapted to the use of young readers by Lydia Hands. Engravings by Julius Schnorr, of Carolsfeld* (London: Griffith & Farran, 1880), p. 72, 'Criemhild's Frenzy'. 365

32. [Hesba Stretton], Max Krömer. *A Story of the Siege of Strasbourg* (London: The Religious Tract Society, [1871]). Title-page and frontispiece. 375

33. Ottilie Wildermuth, *Nurse Margaret's Two St. Sylvester's Eves* (London: Society for Promoting Christian Knowledge, [1871]). Title-page and frontispiece. 401

Introduction

The boundaries between children's literature and literature for adults are difficult to determine. Until books were written specifically for children – first of all to teach them their letters and instruct them in the rudiments of religion and social behaviour and only later to amuse them – they would read whatever came to hand from other sources. In the eighteenth century animal fables and chapbooks would be their most likely reading material. But other more demanding books might also attract their attention. In this way such classics as Defoe's *Robinson Crusoe* (1719) and Swift's *Gulliver's Travels* (1726) were adopted by children, and the texts were quickly adapted to suit their needs. Stories from the *Thousand and One Nights*, which first appeared in French between 1704 and 1717 and was widely translated into other languages, were also much read by children, as Wordsworth indicates in the first book of *The Prelude*.

Many works from the Middle Ages and early modern times were read by children and have only survived in the popular consciousness as children's books, their original forms now being read only by specialists. Germany provided two such books with the stories of Fortunatus and Till Eulenspiegel (or Howleglass, as he was first known in English). Both of them began as works for adults and were adapted in a variety of ways after their initial translation into English. *Fortunatus* became a chapbook in the late seventeenth century and was rewritten for children in several different forms from the middle of the eighteenth century onwards. Its German origin was lost very early along the way.[1] The story was so well known that Dickens could take knowledge of Fortunatus's inexhaustible purse for granted in *Bleak House*. *Eulenspiegel* was also early translated into

---

1   David Blamires, *Fortunatus in His Many English Guises* (Lewiston, Queenston, Lampeter: Edwin Mellen Press, 1996).

English, but the stories were not adapted for children until 1860, when two different selections appeared in the same year.² Chapbook versions of *Doctor Faustus* derived from Marlowe and/or the English Faust-book, circulated widely in the eighteenth and nineteenth century and would have been easily accessible to children, though not as their principal readers. The many translations and adaptations of Goethe's *Faust* eventually eclipsed the chapbook. In addition, *Reynard the Fox* came into English from Dutch through Caxton rather than from Low German, but it too became part of children's literature in the course of the eighteenth century, with its origins equally as forgotten as those of *Fortunatus*. The reception of *Reynard the Fox* in English is tangled and complex and would merit detailed treatment, but I have chosen not to deal with it here.

It is perhaps surprising that Gessner's *Death of Abel* should have formed part of children's reading, but John Clare mentions it as forming part of his library as a boy at the beginning of the nineteenth century.³ The children's books publisher John Harris published editions of it in 1808 and 1814.⁴ Although books specially written to entertain children appear in the early part of the eighteenth century in England, we find books for adults taken over by children throughout the nineteenth century as well as in the eighteenth. Among German books Fouqué's *Undine* and *Sintram* and Chamisso's *Peter Schlemihl* are cases in point.

Most histories of literature are written from a national point of view; they are histories of English, of French or of German literature. Translated works figure only at the margins, if at all. Children's books are less concerned with these national or linguistic boundaries. Foreign material is readily absorbed; indeed it may often be so fully assimilated that the reader is unaware of its origins. Many French fairytales, such as Perrault's 'Cinderella', 'Bluebeard' and 'Puss-in-Boots' and a few tales by Madame d'Aulnoy, have been so thoroughly acclimatized in Britain that they are often thought to be of native stock. To perhaps a lesser extent, this has also happened with some of the Grimms' best known tales.

The Brothers Grimm are the most obvious and prolific German contributors to British children's books. The tales they collected have been

---

2 David Blamires, '*Eulenspiegel* in englischer Sprache', *Eulenspiegel-Jahrbuch*, 29 (1989), pp. 51-66.
3 *John Clare by Himself*, edited by Eric Robinson and David Powell (Ashington: Mid Northumberland Arts Group; Manchester: Carcanet Press, 1996), p. 16.
4 Marjorie Moon, *John Harris's Books for Youth 1801-1843* (Cambridge: Marjorie Moon and Alan Spilman, 1976), no. 314.

more extensively translated into other languages than any other German book, so they are known throughout the world. But there are many other German children's books that have been translated into English too, though few have proved as long-lasting as the Grimms. Fairytales are probably the most significant and enduring contribution of German authors and collectors to British children's books, and this goes back to the late eighteenth century with an anonymous translation of some tales by Musäus. The Grimms pioneered the collection of traditional tales and were followed by many other national and regional collectors, among them Ernst Moritz Arndt and Ludwig Bechstein. The fairytale enjoyed immense popularity among the German Romantics, many of whom turned their hand to composing their own. From the children's point of view the most successful of these authors was Wilhelm Hauff, but for sheer inventiveness and a multilayered narrative E. T. A. Hoffmann's *Nutcracker* surely beats the rest into a cocked hat. These are the highpoints of a tradition that stretches through the whole nineteenth century.

Fairytales, however, were far from being the only kind of German children's reading to be translated into English. Educational, moral and religious stories appeared right at the beginning of the process and became particularly prevalent in the Victorian period. In general, these tales have not worn as well as the fairytales, having virtually disappeared from publishers' lists by the time of the First World War, if not earlier. But as 'reward' books, prizes given for Sunday school attendance and the like, they were distributed in enormous quantities in the latter part of the nineteenth century. Of course, the German tales formed only a small proportion of this material, but one of the most widely circulated was Christoph von Schmid's *The Basket of Flowers*. This archetypal religious tale can usually still be found today in the stock of most second-hand book dealers who keep nineteenth-century books. More than 120 different editions of this story are known in English.

This range of educational, moral and religious material overlaps to a considerable extent with tales of adventure and exploration, since in our period the latter were usually designed to point moral lessons. The deeds of explorers demonstrated heroism, stoic endurance, courage, inventiveness and the need for mutual support in the face of danger. They could also be used to provide lessons in history, geography, botany and zoology, as we find in the various adaptations of *Robinson Crusoe*, especially *The Swiss Family Robinson*.

The last major category of children's literature that Germany provided Britain with was, perhaps surprisingly, the comic. Till Eulenspiegel has already been mentioned as a figure imported into English at a very early date, in the sixteenth century, though not adapted for children until the mid nineteenth century. But the period we are now concerned with saw a German work of comic genius at its outset – *The Adventures of Baron Munchausen* – and added sixty years later another enduring classic of the nursery – Heinrich Hoffmann's *Struwwelpeter*. A couple of decades further on Wilhelm Busch provided a whole series of verse tales with pictures with *Max and Moritz* at their head.

The subjects and literary forms that Germany offered were richly varied. For the most part they took the form of prose narratives, though some verse did manage to find its way in too. The fables of Wilhelm Hey enjoyed a modest popularity, especially as illustrated by Otto Speckter. German illustrators had an important role to play in the production of children's books, but as this book is chiefly concerned with texts they will not be treated as extensively as they deserve. The quantity of literary material that was assimilated from Germany is extensive. There is more than can be dealt with in detail in this book, especially when it comes to moral and religious tales. They will be treated selectively, but I hope all the same to provide a typical cross-section of what exists. Other kinds of texts and authors will be considered at greater depth.

The transposition of German children's books into English was not a straightforward process. Even where books were conscientiously translated, they were frequently subject to excisions and alterations in order to make the material more acceptable to English readers. Cultural differences between Britain and Germany meant that texts were ruthlessly adapted. The important thing was to produce a book that British parents would buy for their children; it was of quite subordinate significance whether it accurately conveyed the meaning of the German text or made German life and culture more comprehensible to the British reader. Of course, translators varied considerably in competence. Some were very skilled, others much less so. Many were given no credit on title-pages or elsewhere for their work. The translation of children's books was poorly regarded and often done by anonymous women. It may surprise some people to learn that quite a few books were not translated directly from their German originals, but from a French version. The number of Britons conversant with German increased substantially during the nineteenth century, but French was still understood by a much larger proportion of the population. The phrase 'translated from the German' on a title-page always needs to be treated with care. In some instances it may, misleadingly, only mean that the original was written in German. In some instances the name of the original author of a story, in addition to that of the translator, may be omitted from the title-page, so it can be difficult to trace the source. The reason for the omission of names may in certain cases relate to matters of copyright, but it may also have to do with the low status accorded to children's authors. Many such writers were credited on title-pages as the author of their best selling book rather than having their own name given.

The history of children's books presents all kinds of bibliographical problems, since publishers often failed to date their publications so that potential buyers would always imagine they were up-to-date. It is thus very useful to find copies of books with dated inscriptions or labels inside them. These may in addition provide helpful information about patterns of readership. Prefaces may give indications of target readership or buyers, but that is not the same as actual readers, whose responses are very difficult to trace.

Of the many children's books that came from Germany to Britain some have proved to be of enduring value. The fairytales of the Brothers Grimm and of Wilhelm Hauff are still part of children's reading today, and new translations and newly illustrated editions keep appearing on the market. The same is true of *Munchausen, The Swiss Family Robinson* and *Struwwelpeter*. These works endure because in some extraordinary way they transcend the particular circumstances of the periods in which they were first put into print. Other works were important in their day, but because social conditions and religious and moral values have changed they have lost their relevance. But even the children's books that endure are subject to adaptation to increase their appeal to new readers. Their texts are never regarded as sacrosanct, and for this reason they exemplify social and cultural changes in a quite fascinating way. Of course, many works are of genuine high literary value in their own right; they need no justification as socio-historical texts. With this variety in subject-matter and treatment the German children's books that made an impact on Britain between 1780 and 1914 provide an appealing area of study.

Translations and adaptations of children's books, however, constitute only part, though the major one, of the impact that Germany had on nineteenth-century British children's literature. Many British educators sought to satisfy curiosity about Germany by providing information in school-books about its geography, topography, history and culture. Some of this, especially at the outset of our period, is rudimentary and second-hand, tending to be anecdotal rather than analytic, but as the years go by gradually a more detailed picture of the country and its long history is built up. Textbooks are supplemented by travel books, and towards the end of the nineteenth century we find history presented also in story form. Illustrations naturally play a significant role in presenting this material.

Linked with books dealing with German history and culture I have included a chapter on Germany's national epic, the *Nibelungenlied*, and its central figure Siegfried. Here we find mingled translations of the high literature of adults and its adaptation for children, the latter of which does not begin until the mid nineteenth century. There is, moreover, a striking combination of German and Norse materials, beginning with Fouqué and reaching its apogee with Wagner's *Der Ring des Nibelungen* (1863). Wagner, however, lies outside the scope of this book, which concentrates on the medieval epic and the works that go with it.

While textbooks generally provide historical accounts going back to the Romans, several British authors wrote novels of their own, focussing on key periods of German history such as the Thirty Years War and the Franco-Prussian War. G. A. Henty is best known for his boys' adventure stories placed in the context of Britain's colonial expansion, but three of his boys' books focus on aspects of German history and contemporary events. Hesba Stretton, one of the foremost writers of evangelically motivated fiction at the end of the century, wrote about the Franco-Prussian War as it affected the lives of a family and their neighbours in Strasbourg. She was followed by several other authors, and it is interesting to note differences of approach and attitude over a period of some thirty to forty years.

While Britain stood politically on the sidelines as far as the Thirty Years War and the Franco-Prussian War were concerned, British armed forces were directly involved in the First World War. For British children this resulted in a plethora of books on current events, contemporary history, adventure stories and political satires based on children's classics such as Lewis Carroll's *Alice* books, Hoffmann's *Struwwelpeter* and nursery rhymes. The First World War marks a fundamental change in British attitudes towards Germany. The positive appreciation of German culture and its signal contribution to British children's books was abruptly shattered. Only classics such as the Grimms' fairytales and *Struwwelpeter* survived unscathed. Christoph von Schmid's incredibly popular *Basket of Flowers* also continued to be published, but without the author's name and with the German place-names changed to Dutch.

The engagement of British children's books with Germany over a period of around 130 years is far more extensive than most people are aware of. Alongside works that have become classics it includes a wide range of books and stories of less enduring interest, some by authors whose names are now known chiefly to specialists, others that have been transmitted anonymously. Several books and authors have a complex reception-history. Many works originally designed for adults were taken over and adapted for a younger readership. If we take school-books into our purview, we can see children's awareness of Germany gradually expanding as the nineteenth century progresses. Ideally, there should have been some consideration of language textbooks, guides to German conversation, grammars and dictionaries, but this is a large field and one that extends far beyond the limits of children's books. Now, however, it is time to look at individual texts, authors and historical and cultural topics.

1. *Adventures of the Renowned Baron Munchausen, Containing Singular Travels, Campaigns, Voyages, and Adventures* (1811). Frontispiece by Thomas Rowlandson.

1. The Adventures of Baron Munchausen

It may seem wayward to begin a consideration of the contribution of Germany to British children's literature with a book that was not really designed for children. But the stories about Baron Munchausen were quickly adopted by children and became a runaway success. They were, moreover, the earliest such children's book to be published in England. Children love fun, adventure and characters that are larger than life, and the tall stories of Munchausen provide all of those things in plenty. The colourful, eccentric Baron has proved an enduringly popular hero for more than two hundred years, and his stories have been expanded and embroidered, diversely illustrated and adapted for all sorts of other media in a way that is hard to beat. What children are likely to encounter today, however, is very different from the book that first appeared in 1785.

Baron Munchausen's Narrative of his Marvellous Travels and Campaigns in Russia was first published in Oxford with the date 1786. No author's name was given. But the book was actually reviewed in December 1785 in the *Gentleman's Magazine* and the *Critical Review*, so it must have appeared late in 1785 and been post-dated. It was a slim duodecimo volume containing just seventeen anecdotes about the Baron's exploits. This core text was subsequently expanded, at first modestly, then increasingly extravagantly, so that the texts which circulated during the nineteenth century were several times the length of the English original.

The core text is based on two collections of anecdotes first printed in German under the headings 'M-h-s-nsche Geschichten' (M-h-s-n Stories) and 'Noch zwei M-Lügen' (Two more M-Fibs) in a Berlin humorous magazine called *Vade mecum für lustige Leute* (Handbook for Fun-loving

People), nos. VIII and X, published in 1781 and 1783.[5] These anecdotes also appeared anonymously, but their author and the author of the English core text have since been identified as one and the same person, namely Rudolf Erich Raspe (1737-94), a German scientist and scholar who was forced to flee from Germany in 1775 as a result of virtual bankruptcy compounded by embezzlement from the art collections of the Landgrave of Hesse-Kassel. Raspe's authorship was proposed in Germany as early as 1811,[6] but it was not until 1857 that an article in the *Gentleman's Magazine* provided evidence in English.[7] Editions of Munchausen, however, continued to circulate the stories anonymously, and Raspe seems not to have been credited as author on a title-page until John Carswell's edition of 1948.[8]

This state of affairs did not obtain in Germany, because there the stories go under the name of the poet Gottfried August Bürger, best known in Britain for his Romantic ballad 'Lenore', which was translated into English by at least five different hands. Bürger translated the third English edition of *Munchausen* into German, and this was published anonymously in 1786 in Göttingen by Johann Christian Dieterich, but with a false London imprint. The *Wunderbare Reisen zu Wasser und Lande . . . des Freyherrn von Münchhausen* (Wonderful Journeys of Baron Munchausen by Land and Sea), first actually credited to Bürger in a Hamburg edition of 1821,[9] enjoyed even greater popularity in Germany than the English version did in the British Isles.

But why all this mystery and skulduggery about the authorship of these tall stories? It was not uncommon in the late eighteenth century for books to be published anonymously, especially when they were not works of scholarship or ambitious poetry. A book of comic tales or anecdotes would not have been considered worthy of literary recognition. In any case Raspe had lost what credit he used to have in London and the universities through being ejected from the Royal Society, to which as a scientist he had belonged. Thereafter he moved around the United Kingdom, working far away in the Cornish tin mines, the Western Highlands of Scotland and in

---

5   Text reprinted in Werner R. Schweizer, *Münchhausen und Münchhausiaden. Werden und Schicksale einer deutsch-englischen Burleske* (Bern und München: Francke, 1969), pp. 36-40.
6   Schweizer, p. 55.
7   John Carswell, *The Prospector. Being the Life and Times of Rudolf Erich Raspe (1737-1794)* (London: The Cresset Press, 1950), p. 185.
8   John Carswell (ed.), *Singular Travels, Campaigns and Adventures of Baron Munchausen, by R. E. Raspe and others* (London: The Cresset Press, 1948).
9   Schweizer, p. 389.

Muckross, Co. Kerry, where he died of scarlet fever in 1794.[10] The scholar and scientist that he was, and still wanted to be recognized as, did not covet, apparently, the notoriety which this casual collection of tales would have heaped on him.

But there was another reason too. In the pretty little town of Bodenwerder, situated on the River Weser a few miles south of Hamelin (of Pied Piper fame), among picturesque wooded hills and rolling farmland, there lived a real baron, Karl Friedrich Hieronymus von Münchhausen (1720-97), who in his latter years was renowned for telling after-dinner tales of palpable absurdities as if they were completely true. As a youth he had been in the Russian service as a cornet with the Brunswick Regiment and had been present in 1737 at the capture of Oczakow in the war against the Turks. In 1740 he became a lieutenant, and in 1750 the Empress Elizabeth promoted him to captain. But after 1752 he was back in Bodenwerder, living in rural contentment, having married Jacobine von Dunten in 1744.

Bodenwerder is no great distance from Kassel, where Raspe worked for the Landgrave of Hesse, or from Göttingen, where he had been a student at the newly founded university. It is possible that Raspe had heard the Baron telling some of the tales himself. When he first published some of these anecdotes in the *Vade mecum für lustige Leute*, he partly identified their narrator as 'M-h-s-n', enough for many readers to identify him satisfactorily, but not naming him outright. With the book publications, however, in both English and German, the Baron was explicitly named. He was mortified at having his private tales thus treated and at himself, a member of the nobility, being made into a figure of fun.

In Britain Raspe was far from Bodenwerder, but for someone in so precarious a social and financial position as he was it was prudent not to reveal himself when making fun of the aristocracy. The King of Great Britain was also the ruler of Hanover, where Raspe was himself born. Perhaps – though this is speculation – the poverty-stricken Raspe also harboured some resentment or jealousy towards the Baron's powerful kinsman, Gerlach Adolf von Münchhausen, who had formerly been the Hanoverian Minister in London and had founded in 1737 the now famous University of Göttingen. Certainly, the original English text of Munchausen contains various satirical sallies against the aristocracy, as the fictional Baron insinuates in his remarks on arriving in St. Petersburg:

---

10 Carswell, *The Prospector*, p. 255, states 'near Killarney', correcting his introduction to *Singular Travels*, p. xliv, where he gives 'Donegal'.

> I shall not tire you Gentlemen with the politicks, arts, sciences, and history of this magnificent metropolis of Russia; nor trouble you with the various intrigues, and pleasing adventures I had in the politer circles of that country, where the lady of the house always receives the visitor with a dram and salute. I shall confine myself rather to the greater and nobler objects of your attention, to horses and dogs, of which I have always been as fond as you are, to foxes, wolves and bears, of which and other game Russia abounds more than any other part of the world, and to such sport, manly exercises, and feats of gallantry and activity as make and show the gentleman, better than musty Greek or Latin, or all the perfume, finery and capers of French wits or hair dressers.[11]

Other passages in the core text and, more especially, in the additions place the Baron's supposed exploits in a real historical and geographical context and make specific satirical references to people and events of the day. For contemporary readers Munchausen's adventures would have had an edge that today is completely lacking. Nothing dates so quickly as topicality. Fortunately, the kernel of the stories has an enduring appeal that transcends these local allusions.

Although the fictional Baron tells his various anecdotes as if they really happened to him and were thus autobiographical, many of them belong to an international stock of traditional tales. Several late medieval or early modern German collections provide manuscript or printed sources, but many of the Munchausen tales, in both Raspe's core text and the later accretions, can be found in the oral literature of Germany and elsewhere. Where analogues can be located, they almost invariably come from continental Europe rather than the British Isles. For example, in the tale about the stag that grows a cherry tree between its antlers after Munchausen has fired cherry stones at it, the reference to St. Hubert would have had little resonance in Britain, but much on the Continent. St. Hubert was a missionary in the Ardennes in the early eighth century. Similarly, the tales involving wolves, bears and boars also posit Continental conditions.

Raspe's core text, beginning with Munchausen's sharing his mantle with a frozen old beggar (a parody of the famous incident attributed to St. Martin) and ending with the tunes being thawed out of the postilion's horn, reflects the history and geography of the real Münchhausen's career. It opens with the Baron's winter journey through northern Germany, Poland, Courland and Livonia (i.e. present-day Latvia) to St. Petersburg. That provides us with the striking episode in which Munchausen has to rest

---

11 Carswell, *Singular Travels*, pp. 9-10.

overnight in deep snow and ties his horse to what he thinks is the stump of a tree, only to find next morning, when the snow has miraculously thawed, that his horse is dangling from the weather-cock on a church steeple. This is followed by the episode in which a ravenous wolf eats Munchausen's horse from the rear and then takes its place in pulling our hero's sledge. The early English editions have a misprint in the location of this latter episode, about which the Baron says he does 'not exactly recollect whether it was in Esthland or Jugemanland'. 'Jugemanland' is a mistake for 'Ingermanland', the area in which St. Petersburg is situated. In Richard Griffin's Glasgow edition of 1827 it is rationalized into 'Judgemanland', and it is omitted altogether from Thomas Tegg's edition of 1809. Neither 'Jugemanland' nor 'Judgemanland' seems to have been understood in Britain, but both forms are to be found in many later nineteenth-century editions. Many editions give 'Esthland' (Estonia) as 'Eastland'. The precise form of these names does not matter particularly for enjoyment of the book, but it is symptomatic of British ignorance that they remain uncorrected.

The episode in which Munchausen's horse demonstrates its skills on the tea-table takes place in Lithuania at the country seat of Count Przobofsky. Most English editions have 'Przobossky', which presumably came about through the 'f' being confused with a long 's'. The Lithuanian horse features in another much illustrated episode: it survives being chopped in two by a falling portcullis, and its front half drinks thirstily at a spring in the marketplace, with the water immediately pouring on to the ground behind it. Not only this, though: the two halves of the horse are sewn back together with sprigs of laurel, the wound heals, and a bower grows out of the shoots, providing the rider later with ample shade. This episode is located in Oczakow (Ochakov), a small port on the Black Sea and the lagoon of the River Dniepr, where the Russians fought a battle with the Turks in 1737. The historical Münchhausen was present at this engagement. However, the area was not annexed to Russia until 1791.

To the Oczakow incident Raspe links a supposed period of Turkish slavery, during which Munchausen experiences adventures told in the folktale that the Grimms published thirty years later as 'Der Dreschflegel vom Himmel' (The Flail from Heaven), a story akin to the English 'Jack and the Beanstalk'. The Grimms got their version of this story through the Haxthausen family, who lived in Bökendorf, near Paderborn, an area not very far from where Raspe had lived and worked. His inclusion of it in the Munchausen tales is valuable evidence of its earlier oral currency.

14   *Telling Tales*

The core text ends with the episode of the frozen horn which, when it thaws, plays the tunes that the postilion earlier could not get out of it. For this we have a much earlier analogue from Castiglione's *Book of the Courtier*, first published in Italian in 1528, with an English translation made by Sir Thomas Hoby in 1561. Raspe probably knew the German translation by Lorenz Kratzer. The geographical context in Castiglione is astonishingly similar to that of the Munchausen story, which, however, is somewhat different in details:

> [A] merchant man of Luca [sic] travailing then with his company toward Moscovia, arrived at the river of Boristhenes, which he found hard frozen like a marble stone, and saw the Moscovites which for suspicion of the warre were in doubt of the Polones, were on the other side, and nearer came not than the breadth of the river.
> So after they knew the one the other, making certain signes, the Moscovites beganne to speake aloude, and tolde the price howe they would sell their Sables, but the colde was so extreme, that they were not understood, because the wordes before they came on the other side where this merchant of Luca was and his interpreters, were congeled in the ayre, and there remained frozen and stopped. So that the Polones that knew the manner, made no more adoe, but kindled a great fire in the middest of the river (for to their seeming that was the point whereto the voyce came hote before the frost tooke it) and the river was so thicke frozen, that it did well beare the fire.
> When they had thus done, the wordes that for space of an hour had beene frozen, beganne to thaw, and came downe, making a noyse as doth the snow from the mountaines in May, and so immediately they were well understood: but the men on the other side were first departed; and because he thought that those wordes asked too great a price for the Sables, he woulde not bargaine, and so came away without.[12]

Munchausen's Russian adventures were all that was printed in the first and second editions of the book. The third edition, also dated 1786, added five new stories and four engravings signed 'Munchausen pinxit'. Carswell thinks these additional stories were also by Raspe and states: 'It is just possible that the four illustrations are also from Raspe's pencil – we know that he prided himself on his draughtsmanship and did in fact illustrate some of his scientific and antiquarian works'.[13] After this the stories always appeared with illustrations, and as the nineteenth century proceeded the enlarged book was illustrated by many distinguished artists. That was

---

12 Baldassare Castiglione, *The Book of the Courtier*, trans. Sir Thomas Hoby (London: Dent; New York: Dutton, 1966), p. 147.
13 Carswell, *Singular Travels*, p. 171.

often the publisher's chief concern.

The five new stories set the tone for the subsequent additions to the core text: they tend to be tales of the fantastic rather than wittily pointed traditional tales. Increasingly, they allude to places in England and to English habits and public figures. They also contain slightly risqué elements, which later editions occasionally remove. For example, in the adventure with the whale that is half a mile long and pulls away the ship's anchor, the ship springs a leak a foot in diameter, which Munchausen is able to plug with an unnamed part of his body 'without taking off my small-clothes'. The fact that the text prints a dash at this point invited the reader to imagine an indelicacy. A similar note is struck at the end of this section with the tale implying that the narrator (in some editions Baron de Tott (1730-93), who distinguished himself in service in the Orient, in other editions Munchausen himself or a friend of his) is the son of an oyster-woman and 'Pope Ganganelli, commonly called Clement XIV'. Another tale concerns Munchausen being swallowed by a large fish while swimming in the Mediterranean, and a third centres on him being carried in a boat into an almond tree in a Nile flood.

Further tales focus on the shooting down in Constantinople of a balloon that has flown from Land's End in Cornwall. In 1784 the Montgolfier brothers had invented the hot air balloon, François Blanchard had crossed the Channel and Vicenzo Lunardi had made the first aerial ascent from English soil, so Munchausen's encounter at the opposite end of Europe has a designedly topical flavour. The next section of 'Further Surprising Adventures' presents explicit acknowledgement of the Montgolfiers when the Baron makes a giant balloon by means of which he is able to lift up the College of Physicians and keep it in the air for more than three months. His comments on the extravagant dining habits of the College shows the satirical aspect of many of the succeeding episodes coming to the fore.

Already the section entitled 'Further Surprising Adventures' by Carswell, which opens with 'the late siege of Gibraltar' and pokes fun at Captain John Phillips's voyage of discovery to the Arctic in 1773, reveals itself to be by a hand other than Raspe's. Munchausen's adventures increasingly display an acquaintance with specific locations and personages in the British Isles, and this true too of the 'Travels in Ceylon, Sicily, the South Seas and elsewhere' that follow. The adventures range far and wide over the globe and even to the Moon. Several are borrowed from Lucian's *True History*, e.g. the physical nature of the inhabitants of the Moon, life inside the belly of a gigantic whale, and the island of cheese in a sea of milk. Although a few episodes capture the mood of the original Munchausen tales – for example, Munchausen's escape from the lion and crocodile attacking him from opposite sides, which ends with the lion's death in the crocodile's gullet – they mainly deal in fantasy for its own sake or indulge a taste for satirical commentary on the events and manners of the day.

Occasionally the satire is disrupted by a remark of unexpected insight, as when Munchausen says, on arriving at Botany Bay: 'This place I would by no means recommend to the English government as a receptacle for felons, or place of punishment: it should rather be the reward of merit, nature having most bountifully bestowed her best gifts upon it'.[14] Botany Bay was discovered by Captain James Cook in 1770, and in 1787 it was chosen as the site of the penal settlement that marks the beginning of white settlement in Australia. Munchausen and his party were driven away by storm after a three-day stay. Not very many years later another group of fictional voyagers will be storm-tossed for six days after leaving Botany Bay, but the Swiss Family Robinson have a tropical and uninhabited island on which to engage in their great didactic adventures, rather than the land of cheese in a sea of milk that is Munchausen's lot. Johann David Wyss wrote his *Schweizerischer Robinson* for his four sons between 1792-98, though it did not make it into print until 1812-13 and 1826-27.[15]

Botany Bay obviously had great symbolic resonance at the turn of the eighteenth century. We shall be looking at the *Swiss Family Robinson* in more detail later.

By the time of the so-called 'third' edition of *Munchausen* of 1786 not only the content of the book, but also its title have been changed. It now reads: *Gulliver Revived, or the Singular Travels, Campaigns, Voyages, and Adventures of Baron Munikhouson, commonly called Munchausen*, following the spoof affirmation of the book's veracity placed in the second edition and signed 'Gulliver X, Sinbad X and Aladdin X'. This 'third' edition is also marked by a change of publisher to G. Kearsley of Fleet Street. The placing of Munchausen's adventures in the context of *Gulliver's Travels* and the tales of Sindbad and Aladdin in the *Arabian Nights' Entertainments* removes our German hero rather unsubtly from contemporary history, real places and events into the realms of fiction. The *Sequel*, first published in 1792,

---

14 Carswell, *Singular Travels*, p. 68.
15 Robert L. Wyss, 'Der schweizerische Robinson. Seine Entstehung und sein Manuskript', '*Stultifera navis*', *Mitteilungsblatt der Schweizerischen Bibliophilen-Gesellschaft*, 12. Jahrgang, Nr. 3/4 (Oktober 1955), p. 125.

2. Title page of *The Life and Exploits of Baron Munchausen. Who Outdid All Other Travellers. Related by Himself* (1827).

underlines this further by having Munchausen encounter Don Quixote at the end of chapter VIII and in the whole of chapter IX.

The *Sequel* began its life as a separate and, initially, a competing publication to *Gulliver Revived* and introduced the characters of Hilaro Frosticos, Lady Fragrantia and the Marquis de Bellecourt. It bears the title *A Sequel to the Adventures of Baron Munchausen humbly dedicated to Mr Bruce the Abyssinian Traveller* (London: H. D. Symonds, 1792). The mocking dedication to James Bruce of Larbert (1730-94), who published his *Travels to discover the Source of the Nile* in 1790, shows how real contemporary explorations in places remote from Europe might seem very similar to the most extravagant imaginary journeys in the imagination of the times. The *Sequel*, which is about the same length as what Carswell terms the *Singular Travels, Campaigns and Adventures of Baron Munchausen*, is full of digs at personalities and ideas of the time, most of which would have been opaque to children. However, the concrete details of the fantasy would still have had an appeal for them. With the *Sequel* and probably also with the 'Travels in Ceylon, Sicily, the South Seas and elsewhere' one can easily envisage the text being read in quite different ways by children and adults. From the beginning of the nineteenth century the *Sequel* is generally included as an integral part of the Munchausen adventures. No reference is made in presentation or chapter headings to its separate origin.

In an exclamation recorded in the first decade of the nineteenth century Robert Southey asked: 'Who is the author of Munchausen's Travels, a book which everybody knows, because all boys read it?'[16] Just what form of the tales Southey was referring to isn't clear, but certainly from the very outset of the nineteenth century there were abridgements of the text and versions specifically designed for children in chapbook format. The Glasgow firm of Chapman & Lang seems to have been first in the field with an abridged form adorned with three engravings in 1802. The Edinburgh publishers W. and J. Deas included a version in their New Juvenile Library in 1809. Many more Scottish and English publishers followed suit – Dean & Munday of London (1810), H. Mozley of Gainsborough (1814) and Derby (1821), W. and T. Fordyce of Newcastle upon Tyne, C. Croshaw of York, Thomas Richardson of Derby, William Cole of London (all the latter undated); the list in not exhaustive. These are concentrated in the first half of the century, as chapbook production tailed off dramatically after about 1850.

A copy of an early undated chapbook is to be found in the Mitchell Library, Glasgow. It bears the title *The Surprising Adventures, Miraculous Escapes, and Wonderful Travels, of the Renowned Baron Munchausen, who was carried on the back of an eagle over France to Gibraltar, &c. &c.* It has no indication of publisher, place or date, but states simply 'Entered according to order'. Its only illustration is a crude woodcut of a man's head on the outside front page. In a mere eight pages it relates several of Munchausen's adventures, beginning with his fight on the back of a giant eagle and ending with his return to Wapping and being shot from a cannon into a haystack, where he sleeps for three months. The episodic form of the original work allows for chapbook compilers to pick adventures at random from the expanded texts without having to follow a coherent narrative structure. This chapbook probably dates from around 1800.

A twelve-page chapbook produced by Webb, Millington and Co. in their Penny Pictorial Library c. 1860 is a late outlier of this kind of production. It has a hand-coloured frontispiece depicting the Baron with the crocodile and the lion, and there are seven further wood-engravings scattered through

---

16 Robert Southey and S. T. Coleridge, *Omniana or Horae Otiosiores*, edited by Robert Gibbings (Fontwell, Sussex: Centaur Press, 1969), p. 95.

3. *Baron Munchausen* (c. 1865). Hand-coloured frontispiece.

the text. The Baron is supposed to have lived in 'the castle of Airreblast, near the town of Laybach, in Carniola'. Laybach (the present Ljubljana, capital of Slovenia) probably also has the punning sense of 'lay back'. The various episodes are picked from here and there in the Baron's adventures, but exclude those in the *Sequel*.

At the very end of the nineteenth century and during the Edwardian era we have a number of versions of *Munchausen* explicitly designed for children. W. T. Stead included *Tales from the Travels of Baron Munchausen* very early in his popular *Books for the Bairns*. It appeared as no. 23, first published in January 1898, price one penny. Like all the books in this series, it had line illustrations on every page, here, as usual, by Brinsley Le Fanu. Stead found it necessary to stress that lying in order to deceive is wrong, but that the kind of lies found in Munchausen's tales were not meant like that, but were 'monstrous whoppers' designed to amuse. However, concerned as he was to emphasize that the tales were 'not true, not a world of them is true', he wrongly claimed that 'Baron Munchausen never existed'. In this he was simply restating the common nineteenth-century view, though in 1895 Thomas Seccombe had provided what is now the standard information about Hieronymus von Münchhausen and R. E. Raspe as the author of his tales.[17] In sixty pages Stead reproduces nineteen tales, including 'The Storm and the Cucumber-Trees', 'The Stag and the Cherry-Tree' and 'The Trip to the Moon'. No tales are taken from the *Sequel*.

The allusions to contemporary events and figures are, naturally, entirely omitted.

In 1902 the London firm of Grant Richards published *The Surprising Travels and Adventures of Baron Munchausen* in a series called The Children's Library. It had four colour illustrations by W. Heath Robinson. The text, however, was scarcely different from the one usually offered, including the *Sequel*, and arranged in thirty-four chapters. There had, of course, been multifarious editions of *Munchausen* in the course of the nineteenth century, with texts offering greater or lesser variations from those of the eighteenth century. Clearly, many of these had been read by children. What is interesting about Grant Richards's edition is its explicit inclusion in a collection for children and its use of colour plates.

Grant Richards obviously saw commercial advantage in their involvement with Munchausen, since in the previous year they had published John

---

17 *The Surprising Adventures of Baron Munchausen*, illustrated by William Strang and J. B. Clark, with an introduction by Thomas Seccombe (London: Lawrence & Bullen, 1895).

Kendrick Bangs's *Mr. Munchausen*, a set of new Munchausen stories for an American readership. These were ostensibly told to two small children called Diavolo and Angelica by the democratized Mr. Munchausen, whom they call Uncle Munch (a neat allusion to the Munchkin's of *The Wonderful Wizard of Oz*, published in 1900), through the agency of a reporter, Mr. Ananias (here a New Testament allusion) of the *Gehenna Gazette*. This is one of the rare occasions after the publication of the *Sequel* when new tales are foisted on to Munchausen, and one can only say that Bangs does it in the spirit of the original and succeeds in making an amusing new book. To my knowledge, however, it has not been reprinted.

Tracing the large number of editions of *Munchausen* through the whole of the nineteenth century up to the First World War would burst the limits of this book. The stories were presented in a large variety of formats, most of which would have been accessible to children, even if they might not have understood all they read. The original illustrations from the eighteenth century were recycled, as were the additions by George Cruikshank. Increasingly, it was the illustrations that sold the new editions, particularly towards the end of the nineteenth century and in the twentieth. To pursue all of this would involve a much fuller discussion of the role of illustrations in children's books than is possible here.

The important thing to remember is that Rudolf Erich Raspe unwittingly and anonymously made one of the most far-reaching contributions to Anglo-German literature that has ever happened. More than two hundred years since Munchausen first made an appearance in England he is still a houehold name, more now for children than he was in his first hundred years. Not only are there new editions and retellings of his unforgettable tales, but there have been the most extravagant of films. With the cultural changes that have occurred through film and television, Munchausen is now much more a visual than a literary figure. The museum at Bodenwerder has a marvellous collection of illustrated editions of Munchausen in English, German and many other languages from all periods of the stories' popularity.

2. A World of Discovery: Joachim Heinrich Campe

The stories of Munchausen reflect the excitement and wonderment of people at the end of a century in which new discoveries and inventions were being made all the time. This wonderment, however, was transposed into a fantasy world of recent history and geographical and technological exploration where surprise and satirical amusement were the order of the day. Only three years after *Munchausen* was first published in English a quite different sort of German book reflecting the fascination of world exploration made its appearance on the British scene. This was Joachim Heinrich Campe's *New Robinson Crusoe* (London: John Stockdale, 1788), a revision of Defoe's most celebrated novel for the benefit of children of both sexes. It was as different from *Munchausen* as one can imagine. Campe was an educationist of a most serious and morally concerned kind, but he also knew how to capture children's attention with interesting subjects and variety of approach. Many of his books, in particular *The New Robinson Crusoe*, continued to be reprinted for much of the nineteenth century.

Joachim Heinrich Campe (1746-1818) was the most influential of the German Enlightenment educationists. He was part of the educational movement known as 'philanthropist' after the Philanthropinum in Dessau, an establishment founded by Johann Bernhard Basedow (1723-90). The movement also contained Christian Gotthilf Salzmann (1744-1811), about whom more will be said in the next chapter. Linked with it was Friedrich Eberhard von Rochow (1734-1805), who was deeply concerned for the education of the rural population and compiled a highly influential reader called *Der Kinderfreund* (The Children's Friend). Although both Basedow and Rochow wrote a good deal, none of their work was translated into

English. The 'philanthropists' wrote a large number of books designed to instruct children, but their concern was moral education rather than principles of Protestant or Catholic Christianity or the rudiments of Latin grammar. They believed that moral education appropriate to the intellectual capacities of children and young people was best given through simple stories about children and their families and through exemplary figures and deeds of history. From our present perspective 'moral education' may sound grave and offputting, but eighteenth-century children will have warmed to Campe's ability to narrate varied events, surprise them with changes of mood and keep them in suspense about what is to happen next.

Basedow is described from the viewpoint of a boy writing to his uncle in Johann Gottlieb Schummel's children's book *Fritzens Reise nach Dessau* (Fritz's Journey to Dessau) (1776):

> Mr Basedow was standing at a desk in his dressing gown right at the back and was writing. You have already seen him, dear uncle, haven't you? Otherwise I will describe him to you straight away. He is not tall, not as tall as you, and not fat either, and I couldn't say that there was anything special about his face; but I don't know, in his eyebrows and in his eyes there is something I can't describe, but it is something quite special. We came at a rather inconvenient time for him, but he was still very kind and said that Papa should not take it amiss, but he had a lot of work to do before tomorrow and that he would visit us in our lodgings towards evening.[18]

Campe spent a year (1776-77) as educational adviser and co-director with Basedow at Dessau, and Salzmann was there for three years (1781-84) as liturgist. Both went on to found similar establishments of their own.

The work of these German educationists was profoundly influenced by Rousseau, whose *Emile* had been published in 1762. They too objected to rote learning and the dinning into children's heads of knowledge in no way adapted to their capacity for understanding. They were opposed to education based on the authoritarianism of superior age. What men like Basedow, Campe, Salzmann and Rochow attempted was respect for children's natural limitations, and an approach to learning that relied on encouragement and stimulation rather than demanding the child's unquestioning obedience, with physical punishment meted out for failure. Their concept of education was holistic rather than subject-orientated. Their approach was Socratic, using the child's natural curiosity as the means to

---

18 Hans-Heino Ewers (ed.), *Kinder- und Jugendliteratur der Aufklärung* (Stuttgart: Reclam, 1980), pp. 402-03, my translation.

increasing understanding of the world. Everywhere they were ready to explain, to demonstrate cause and effect, not only in the world of nature, but in the realms of human behaviour. They show that certain kinds of behaviour have certain consequences, both positive and negative. Reason and natural religion inform the patterns of action recommended. Where reason cannot provide an explanation, as, for example, with innocent suffering or natural disasters, the answer lies in the inscrutable purposes of God. The teacher in the thinking and practice of the philanthropist establishments occupies the role of a benevolent father; his school is an enlarged family, shaped by loving concern for each and every child.

The child in these establishments is guided into a way of life that is characterized by simplicity, naturalness, honesty and mutual consideration. In Schummel's already quoted book Fritz writes in a letter to his brother:

> Be cheerful, jump about and dance: I want to tell you something about the little philanthropists! . . . But first I must describe a little what they look like. They have all short hair, and not one of them needs a wigmaker. The little ones go without a cravat, with an open neck, and their shirt is folded back over their suit; it looks very nice! And Papa says it's much more healthy than the warm, thick neck-cloths that are now the fashion.[19]

Fritz's letter goes on to describe the boys talking Latin and French at table. He is so taken by their friendliness and self-confidence in talking to his father, whom they had never before met, that all his anxieties disappear. This is, then, the context in which we need to look at Campe's life and books.

Campe was born near Holzminden in the principality of Brunswick and studied theology at the universities of Helmstedt and Halle. From 1769-73 he was tutor with the Humboldt family at Tegel, near Berlin, and in 1775 he returned for a year to supervise the studies of the two brothers, Wilhelm and Alexander von Humboldt (1767-1835 and 1769-1859), both of whom remained affectionately attached to him for the rest of his life. Wilhelm became famous as a classical scholar and linguist, friend of Schiller, minister in the Prussian Government and founder of the University of Berlin (1810), which now bears the two brothers' name. Alexander became the celebrated explorer of South and Central America and the leading German scientist in the fields of geology, plant geography, vulcanology and climatology, a man of infinite curiosity about the workings of the natural world. It is tempting to suppose that the foundation for the achievements of the two brothers was laid by Campe. In 1776 Campe joined Basedow's Philanthropin in Dessau,

---

19 Ibid., p. 403, my translation.

leaving in 1777 in order to start his own small educational establishment in Hamburg, where he remained until 1783. In 1786 he became educational adviser in Brunswick and in the following year took over the running of the School Bookshop. In 1807 he became deputy for Brunswick to the parliament of the new Napoleonic Kingdom of Westphalia at Kassel.

Campe was a prolific author: his collected works, published in 1817 just before he died, amount to thirty volumes. Six of his books were translated into English and enjoyed varying degrees of popularity. These were, in chronological order, *Robinson der Jüngere* (1779-80); *Kleine Selenlehre für Kinder* (Little Book of Pastoral Care for Children) (1780); *Die Entdekkung von Amerika* (The Discovery of America), a three-part work beginning with *Kolumbus* (1781), followed by *Cortez* (1782) and *Pizarro* (1782); and *Gemälde des Nordens* (Pictures of the North) (1785). They were not, however, translated in this order into English. It is obvious from this list of titles that British readers were most attracted to Campe's books of discovery and adventure, and among them one in particular stood out.

More than anything, Campe was known in Britain as the author of the famous Robinsonade that went under the titles of *Robinson the Younger* or *The New Robinson Crusoe*. Campe had made his own translation into English with the former title (Hamburg: C. E. Bohn, 1781-82), but it was an anonymous translation made from his French version that first made the book famous in Britain, using the latter title. After this new editions and abridgements were published by Stockdale up to 1827. A different version, probably an abridgement too, was made by the hack writer Richard Johnson and published by Elizabeth Newbery in 1790 and 1797. It may have been this version that was advertised by John Harris, successor to the Newberys, for c. 1803 and 1808, but no copies of either have been traced.

A new edition of *Robinson the Younger* by John Timäus was published by Campe's Schulbuchhandlung in Brunswick in 1800, so clearly there was a market for an English version of the text in Germany, probably as a means of teaching English to German children. This may have been a commercial response to the English-language edition prepared by Professor F. C. Mertens specifically for beginners in the English language and first published in Frankfurt am Main by F. Wilmans in 1799 (second edition 1807, third edition 1824). Meanwhile, Campe's original German edition continued strong, and by 1882 over a hundred editions had been printed.[20]

---

20 Heinz Wegehaupt, *Robinson und Struwwelpeter. Bücher für Kinder aus fünf Jahrhunderten* (Berlin: Deutsche Staatsbibliothek in der Stiftung Preussischer Kulturbesitz, 1991), p. 83, no. 110.

It must have been a mid-century edition that fell into the hands of R. Hick of Woodhouse Hill, Leeds, who undertook a new translation specifically from the German for his own little boys. This appeared with the title *Robinson the Younger; or, the New Crusoe* (G. Routledge & Co., 1855; new edition 1866). It was translated from one of the German editions published after 1802, which were textually revised and from which certain passages were omitted.[21] A variety of English versions of Campe's text were thus available in the British Isles (there is an Irish edition of 1809) and Germany over a period of about eighty-five years.

Campe's book obviously goes back to Defoe, who, nearing the age of sixty when *Robinson Crusoe* was first published in April 1719, could hardly have envisaged what a runaway success it was to become. The book was reprinted three times in the same year, and in August there came a sequel, *The Farther Adventures of Robinson Crusoe*. Since then new editions, adaptations and abridgements have never ceased to appear. A German translation was published as early as 1720. *Robinson Crusoe* was not only a hugely successful book in its own right, but it spawned an extraordinary number of adaptations, imitations and burlesques in several languages. As early as 1722 we find in Germany *Der Teutsche Robinson* (The German Robinson) and *Der Sächsische Robinson* (The Saxon Robinson), followed by *Der Geistliche Robinson* (The Spiritual Robinson) (1723), *Der Moralische Robinson* (The Moral Robinson) (1724) and *Der Buchhändler Robinson* (The Bookseller Robinson) (1728),[22] but there were many others. Three of these German Robinsonades were translated into English and had varying fortunes. Campe's was the first and the model for the rest. The second was Johann David Wyss's *Schweizerischer Robinson* (1812-13, 1826-27), the most phenomenally successful of all Robinsonades in its many English forms with the title of *The Swiss Family Robinson*. The third is something of an anticlimax in this context: it is Christoph von Schmid's *Gottfried, der junge Einsiedler* (1829), of which an English translation was made as *Godfrey, the Little Hermit* (1853). It was never as popular as Schmid's other tales.

Much of the credit for the success of any Robinsonade has to be granted to Defoe. His brilliantly simple tale of adventure and shipwreck, self-reliance, exploration and the utilization of the riches of nature, culminating in the

---

21 Joachim Heinrich Campe, *Robinson der Jüngere*, ed. Alwin Binder and Heinrich Richartz (Stuttgart: Reclam, 1981), pp. 351-53.
22 Reinhard Stach, *Robinson der Jüngere als pädagogisch-didaktisches Modell des philanthropistischen Erziehungsdenkens* (Ratingen, Wuppertal, Kastellaun: Aloys Henn, 1970), p. 89.

ambiguous relationship with Friday, both servant and friend, is a model of human self-realization. It is a story capable of reflecting a multiplicity of concerns – educational, social, ecological, racial. It is significant that Defoe's *Robinson Crusoe* was the first book that Rousseau allowed his Emile at twelve or thirteen years old to read.[23] When we read Defoe nearly three centuries later, we quickly note the differences between his preoccupations and our own, each reflecting culturally conditioned views, but Defoe's basic model remains perennially fascinating. Towards the end of the eighteenth century Campe found Defoe's novel too full of digressions and too old-fashioned in language as well as being defective in certain aspects of morality to be suitable for children. This proved to be the spur for writing his own adaptation.[24]

While Defoe's book was written as a continuous first-person narrative with no divisions into chapters, Campe's *Robinson der Jüngere* has an entirely different format. The story is placed in a new narrative format – that of a father telling it to a small group of children living just outside the gates of Hamburg. The individual children and also the mother comment on aspects of the story, usually prompted by some question from the father. The narrative occupies thirty evenings. This structure breaks the story into manageable units for the child readership or audience, and the presence of father, mother and children within the framework creates a secondary scenario providing an interpretation and commentary on the primary tale of Robinson himself. The children become participants in the story as well as its audience. Campe makes clear in his preface that the interreactions of father, mother and children are designed as a model of what such a family should be like.

The hero of Campe's book is a seventeen year old boy, the youngest son of a family in Hamburg called Robinson, and his name is Krusoe. He is at the opening of the story the sole surviving son of the family. The eldest son, having become a soldier, has been killed in a battle with the French, while the middle son has died of consumption. Krusoe has been spoilt by his parents and thus not been properly brought up. His adventures begin with him taking ship for England without first getting permission from his parents to do so. When, after various intervening disasters, he is shipwrecked on a desert island in the Caribbean, unlike Defoe's Robinson, who has a gun, tools, food and drink to start him off, Campe's Krusoe has

---

23 Jean Jacques Rousseau, *Emile*, trans. Barbara Foxley (London: J. M. Dent & Sons Ltd.; New York: E. P. Dutton & Co. Inc., 1948), book 3, p. 147.
24 Wegehaupt, *Robinson and Struwwelpeter*, p. 83, no. 108.

4. J. H. Campe, *The New Robinson Crusoe; an Instructive and Entertaining History, for the Use of Children of Both Sexes. Translated from the French. New Edition* (1811). Frontispiece by John Bewick.

absolutely nothing to help him. His adventures are divided into three periods. In the first he is alone and has to make shift with just his head and his hands. In the second he gains a companion, Friday, and learns to value human society. Finally, in the third the wreck of a European ship provides him with tools and other things that make for a more civilized life and eventually permit him to return first to England and then to Hamburg, where he is reconciled with his father and finds that his mother has died. In this way Campe creates a miniature history of human development, except for the fact that the shipwrecked Krusoe already has certain spiritual and emotional resources from his earlier life. These are evidenced through his memory of hymns, which help him in his distress. He is also full of deep contrition for his folly in abandoning his home and parents.

Campe's hero satisfies his hunger first by eating oysters, unlike Defoe's Robinson, who seems to enjoy a totally fish-free diet. The problem of opening oyster shells without any tool is not addressed. But from then on he discovers a variety of ways in which to improve his material conditions – using a shell for a spade, making a rope out of flax, building a shelter in a cave, planting saplings in front to provide defence, and so on. The children identify with Robinson's situation and troubles not simply through interjections and questions, but by dressing up like him at the beginning of chapter 5 and by writing letters to him in chapter 7. The narrative thus becomes interactive. The children learn from Robinson's experiences things that are important to themselves in their own development.

Since Campe constantly emphasizes this, the modern reader never doubts that he or she is being instructed as well as being told an engrossing story. Perhaps the most important lesson for Krusoe was: 'Experience had taught him, that in a life of labour nothing helps industry so much as regularity, and a methodical distribution of the work to the different hours of the day'.[25] This is rubbed in further at the end of the book when Robinson, back in Hamburg, is repeatedly asked to speak about his experiences:

> he never forgot to address to the fathers and mothers who heard him the following exhortation, 'If you love your children, I pray you, teach them, in their early years, to be godly, sober, and laborious:' and if there happened to be young persons present, he was careful to give them this wholesome advice, 'My dear children, obey your parents and your teachers; learn diligently whatever you have a capacity to learn; fear God, and be careful – oh, be careful to avoid idleness! it is the mother of

---

25 *The New Robinson Crusoe* (London: John Stockdale, 1811), vol. 1, p. 319 (thirteenth evening).

every vice'.²⁶

By the end of the book Robinson and his companion Friday have established themselves in Hamburg as models of industry and frugality, generosity, humanity and practical piety, so that the children each make the resolution to try to do the same.

At various points in the book Campe interweaves events from Robinson's story with those of the Hamburg children. One of the most striking of these, perhaps rather heavy-handed from a modern viewpoint, occurs at the end of chapter 8 when the father interrupts his narration of Robinson's story, saying that he doesn't want to end the evening by telling the children about a terrible event which might disturb their sleep and cause them to dream about it. Naturally enough, the children are all agog and anxious about what might have happened to poor Robinson, all the more so as the father puts off continuing his story for several evenings. He then promises them a trip to Travemünde (on the Baltic near Lübeck), which they get excited about, only to have their expectations further upset. The father asks the children to release him from his promise, saying that the wind conditions would make it unsatisfactory for the ships, that if they waited four weeks there would be masses of herring, and – most importantly – that their new friends, Mathias and Ferdinand, who are not arriving for another four weeks, would be puzzled why the trip had not been postponed so that they too could participate. The children are reduced to a painful silence by this reasoning, but are persuaded to acquiesce. They learn how important it is to exercise patience and self-control and that pleasure deferred can mean greater enjoyment when it comes. The trip to Travemünde is briefly alluded to in chapter 13 as having taken place, but it is not described.

One of the key incidents in Campe occurs when Robinson stumbles across the human footprint (chapter 14), which causes him immediate terror because of the supposition that the natives of the Caribbean are cannibals. In response to the children's expression of sympathy the father interjects:

> It would have been better for Robinson, had he been accustomed from his childhood not to give way to the impulse of terror, even in the greatest dangers, and had he, at this moment, preserved more coolness and presence of mind. We can all bring ourselves to it, if we will but pay an early and constant attention to the rendering of our bodies, as well as our minds, sound and vigorous.²⁷

---

26 Ibid., vol. 2, p. 306.
27 Ibid., vol. 2, p. 6.

5. J. H. Campe, *The Discovery of America; for the Use of Children and Young Persons* (1799). Frontispiece by J. Burney.

A little further on the text proceeds to a description of the site of the cannibalistic feast, after which the father responds to one of the children calling the savages 'detestable creatures':

> Let us, my dear Charlotte, detest their atrocious manners, and not their persons: they have received no education, no instruction. If you had been so unfortunate as to have received your birth amongst these savage people, you would, like them, run about naked in the woods, without the least shame, stupid and fierce as a brute beast; you would paint your body and your face with various colours, particularly red: you would make holes in your nose and ears, and be very proud to carry in them, for ornament, birds feathers, sea shells, and other trifles: you would, then, make one of the abominable feasts of your depraved relations, and there take your share with as much pleasure as you do now at our best dinners.[28]

One of the boys mentions that there are still such men in New Zealand, about which their father has read them a travel account the previous winter.

Campe's book is cleverly written and full of incident and suspense. Robinson's discoveries and adventures are nicely calculated to engage the emotions, intellect and moral judgements of the eleven to twelve year old children that Campe envisaged as its readers. Its educational aims are transparent, but engagingly realized through the interplay of Robinson's story with that of the children to whom it is being told. It is not surprising that the book was so eagerly read by generations of children for about a hundred years.

Following the success of *Robinson der Jüngere* Campe went on to write more books using material from the world of geographical discovery not only to deal with history, but also to present contrasting and instructive examples of human conduct. In *Die Entdekkung von Amerika* (Hamburg: C. E. Bohn, 1781-82) he was able to build on *Robinson* to discuss deeds of the greatest bravery and heroism as well as the basest and most despicable actions.

This three-part history was translated into English as *The Discovery of America* (London: J. Johnson, 1799), which dealt with Columbus; *Cortes; or, the Discovery of Mexico* (London: J. Johnson, 1800); and *Pizarro; or, the Conquest of Peru* (London: J. Johnson, 1800). These earliest editions provide no indication of the translator's name, but later editions are credited to Elizabeth Helme (d. 1816), the author of several other instructive children's books, including histories of England and Scotland. All three books enjoyed

---

28 Ibid., vol. 2, p. 12.

several reprintings up to the late 1820s in the case of *Columbus* and *Cortes*, up to 1819 in the case of *Pizarro*. A note in the Osborne Collection catalogue (p. 162) indicates that the 1819 edition of the latter is a different translation from that published in 1800. Elizabeth Helme appears to have been working virtually concurrently with this other translator, as her *Columbus* and *Cortes* appeared in 1799 (London: Sampson Low), with *Pizarro* in 1800 (Dublin: P. Wogan, etc.).

Campe was particularly drawn to using voyages of discovery for educative purposes and explains why in the preface to *The Discovery of America*:

> For if there be any thing capable of enlightening the minds of youth, of extending their knowledge of the world in an agreeable manner, of weakening their inclination to romantic views of life, and Arcadian dreams, exhibited in such inviting colours by our fashionable publications; if there be any thing capable of giving them a proper disgust, at that frivolous, affected, mind and body debilitating tattle, with which such books are filled; and, on the other hand, of instilling a desirable taste for more serious and useful employment; – if there be any thing capable of effecting these valuable purposes, it is certainly the perusal of travels in which such care is taken, both with the matter and the manner, as to render them best calculated to engage the attention of youth.[29]

The format of the three American volumes is similar to that of *Robinson*, i.e. a series of chapters in which a father relates the historical events to a small group of children, including their reactions and questions, together with the father's answers. Although the events and characters portrayed reflect historical reality rather than fiction, Campe is no detached surveyor of the scene. He uses his subject-matter to deliver instances of both admirable and despicable conduct, often through the life of one and the same person. The worst of human behaviour in greed, trickery, suspicion, envy and brutality is particularly to the fore in the Spaniards' treatment of the Aztec Montezuma, the Inca Atahualpa and their respective followers, but the courage, resourcefulness and persistence of the conqueror explorers are, understandably, presented as examples to be admired and emulated. The stories involve such a complex of good and bad that it is impossible for either side to be wholly demonized or celebrated, but one cannot help feeling that Campe has greater sympathy for the luckless Americans than for the rapacious invaders. At the opening of *Cortez* he states:

---

29 J. H. Campe, *The Discovery of America; for the Use of Children and Young Persons* (London: J. Johnson, 1799), pp. vii-viii.

> I am grieved, my children, to be under the necessity of informing you before-hand, that the pleasure you promise yourselves from my narrative will often give place to melancholy and disgust. I must bring you acquainted with times, in which men were so degenerate, so savage, that it is difficult to distinguish them from wolves, tigers, and other ferocious beasts.[30]

A few pages further on he characterizes Cortez's expedition against the Mexicans as 'the most unjust war that ever disgraced the annals of history' and declares:

> You see, therefore, my children, that it is possible for the same man to be at once a hero and a robber, generous and cruel, pious and inhuman! It is the natural effect of superstition. It never once occurred to Cortez, that it might be unjust to make war upon a people who could never have injured the Europeans, since they knew not that they existed. The misfortune of these poor people in never having heard that they had a Mediator, was a sufficient reason for persecuting and subduing them![31]

Campe is everywhere a man of reason, so he has the father and the children engage in a discussion of the pros and cons of celebrating or condemning both Cortez and the Americans.

In *Pizarro* one of the children refers back to the *New Robinson Crusoe* when the father embarks on a description of the qualities of the lama (p. 68), and mention is made of the fact that, if transported to Europe, they might thrive in the climate of the Alps or the Blocksberg in the Harz Mountains (p. 71). Pizarro is in many ways less of a hero than Columbus or Cortez. Of his deception of his fellow explorer Almagro Campe writes:

> Learn then from this example, that the most distinguished talents, the most brilliant actions, cannot merit affection or esteem, unless united to probity and generosity. Hypocrisy and chicane fix a disgrace on human nature for which nothing can atone.[32]

Campe's texts are richly informative in addition to pointing up human successes and deficiencies. This is appropriate in that the American trilogy is designed for children who are that much older than when they heard about Robinson the Younger. From what they have learnt elsewhere two of the boys listening to *Pizarro* can fill in illustrative examples from Roman

---
30 J. H. Campe, *Cortez; or the Conquest of Mexico*, trans. Elizabeth Helme (London: Baldwin, Cradock, and Joy, 1819), p. 1.
31 Ibid., pp. 25-26.
32 J. H. Campe, *Pizarro; or the Conquest of Peru*, trans. Elizabeth Helme (London: C. Cradock and W. Joy, 1811), p. 189.

history. These examples show Campe linking his history from the sixteenth century with comparable deeds from ancient Rome and showing how both periods provide examples of conduct to be shunned or to be embraced.

From more recent times Campe mentions the myths of the land of the Amazons, 'female warriors, who governed among themselves without the assistance of men', and of 'El-Dorado . . . which never existed but in the imagination of the adventurers who pretended to have discovered it' (p. 217). In discounting them he specifically names the French explorer Charles-Marie de La Condamine (1701-74), who travelled over the country of the Amazon and found no trace of their existence. La Condamine's *Voyage à l'Equateur* (1751) provided a model to Alexander von Humboldt for writing about his scientific explorations in the same area. Humboldt, rather ironically in view of Campe's assessment, sailed to South America on a ship called the *Pizarro*.

Two further works by Campe were also translated into English, but neither enjoyed the popularity of *The New Robinson Crusoe* or *The Discovery of America* trilogy. The first of these was entitled *Elementary Dialogues, for the Improvement of Youth* (London: Hookham and Carpenter, 1792) and was translated by a Mr Seymour. The title does not correspond directly to that of any of Campe's works in German, but it reads like a typical product of the times. We shall encounter something comparable when we look at Salzmann.

The last work of Campe's to be translated into English was his *Gemälde des Nordens; dargestellt in Jakob Heemskerks und Wilhelm Barenz nördlicher Entdekkungsreise, und den merkwürdigen Abenteuern vier russischer Bootsmänner auf Spitzbergen* (Hamburg: Herold, 1785), which constituted the first volume of a collection of travel descriptions put together for young people. In English it is called *Polar Scenes, exhibited in the Voyages of Heemskirk and Barenz to the Northern Regions, and in the Adventures of Four Russian Sailors at the Island of Spitzbergen* (London: J. Harris & Son, 1821). Further editions are listed for 1822, 1823, 1825 and 1829.[33] This anonymous translation came much later than the others we have looked at, appearing only after Campe's death, perhaps prompted by the Arctic explorations – admittedly in a different region – undertaken by Ross, Parry and Franklin in the period 1819-22.

The main part of *Polar Scenes* deals with the attempt of the Dutchmen

---

33 Marjorie Moon, *John Harris's Books for Youth 1801-1843* (Cambridge: Marjorie Moon and Alan Spilman, 1976), no. 110.

James Heemskirk, William Barenz and John Cornelius Ryp (to give them the anglicized forms of their names) to find a north-east passage to the Far East. They set off in May 1596 from Amsterdam and reached Spitzbergen in late July. There the two vessels separated, Cornelius going north and Barenz south. Barenz's party was marooned for the winter on Nova Zembla, where the men suffered enormous privations, fighting off polar bears being one of their major problems. They managed to free themselves from the ice in mid June 1597 and reached Russian soil in early August. On this arduous voyage two of the sailors – Barenz and Andriff (a misspelling for Andrisz) – died. Amazingly, Heemskirk and Ryp were reunited on the Kola peninsula and returned to Amsterdam, arriving on 1 November 1597. The shorter part of the book recounts a later expedition, beginning in 1743, in which four Russian sailors were wrecked on Spitzbergen and survived there for six years until they were rescued by another ship, which had been blown off course. In the meantime one of the men died of scurvy.

Campe used these heroic struggles as examples of human endurance in the face of disaster. The men were Robinson Crusoes in the most inhospitable of circumstances, but through self-reliance and providential assistance they – for the most part – survived. The book contains information about whaling, polar bears, sea-dogs and sea-cows and also the peoples living in the northernmost stretches of Russia, especially the Samoyeds and Laplanders. But the principal object of Campe's narratives was to contrast the comfortable lives of his readers with the stoic and inventive heroism of the explorers and to make his audience thankful for their own lives and willing to accept what God dealt out to them.

In using the themes of exploration and discovery as the basis of much of his writing, Campe scored well with his readers. His subject-matter was exciting and chimed in with the widespread fascination with contemporary European explorers, who were busy enlarging the European spheres of knowledge, commerce and power. The voyages he dealt with were located in a fairly distant past – some three hundred years before in the case of *The Discovery of America* books – so his concerns were with general questions of human conduct rather than with specific contemporary issues. The application of positive skills and qualities to the understanding of life was the focus of his educational aims. In this endeavour the use of reason was a primary tool, but Campe was always ready to admit that reason cannot explain everything. The ways of God are often inaccessible to human comprehension, as the ways of thoughtful and loving parents often are to their children. But in these books God is the God of natural religion, not of Christian revelation, which is a different field of exploration.

3. *Elements of Morality*: Salzmann and Wollstonecraft

A great deal of eighteenth-century German children's literature is concerned with matters of morality, understood in the wide sense. As we have already seen with Campe, moral issues and rational conduct also underlie stories of exploration and adventure. They form the central concern of Campe's contemporary, Christian Gotthilf Salzmann, whose *Moralisches Elementarbuch* (first edition 1783, new improved edition Leipzig: Siegfried Lebrecht Crusius, 1785) was translated into English by Mary Wollstonecraft as *Elements of Morality* (London: Joseph Johnson, 1790). This translation is noted in virtually all histories of English children's literature, most probably because of Wollstonecraft's name, but very little comment is ever made about the content or the original author.

Salzmann (1744-1811) was born in Sömmerda, not far from Erfurt, studied theology at the University of Jena and became a village parson in 1768. In 1770 he married Sophie Magdalene Schnell and moved two years later to Erfurt. In 1781 he joined Basedow's celebrated Philanthropin in Dessau, but left after three years to found his own educational establishment at Schnepfenthal, near Gotha, in 1784. Here he remained until his death in 1811, teaching and writing. Schnepfenthal's reputation is briefly alluded to by the dramatist August von Kotzebue in his *Travels from Berlin, through Switzerland, to Paris, in the year 1804*:

> The seminary of the able Salzmann at Schnepfenthal (of which I may boast by experience, that it makes and keeps the hearts of young people susceptible of all that is good and excellent) is as flourishing as ever, and its blossoms yield fine ripe fruits in many a country.[34]

---

34 August von Kotzebue, *Travels from Berlin, through Switzerland, to Paris, in the Year*

The *Moralisches Lesebuch* in its improved edition was adorned with 67 etchings by Daniel Chodowiecki (1726-1801), one of the great illustrators of the period. Many critics attribute the book's success to his work, but that is praise at Salzmann's expense and belittles the author unjustifiably.

Salzmann's classic work is a profoundly didactic text case in the form of a simple narrative about the Herrmann family, father, mother, son and daughter. There is no plot as such, but in forty-five chapters Salzmann follows the day-to-day life of this comfortably off merchant's family, their friendship with a modest pastor's family and their contacts with many other people in their immediate locality. Each chapter exemplifies some virtue or vice, which is signalled to the reader by a word or a sentence printed in bold type. The majority of the chapters focus on matters directly concerned with the children's conduct, but some deal with matters between adults. Salzmann was at great pains to show the consequences of certain kinds of behaviour in terms that a child of six to eight (his target audience) could understand. The narrative thus opens with a chapter in which the fact that little Luise has dirtied her dress makes it impossible for her to join a family excursion to visit the neighbouring wealthy Heilbergs. (The surname of the head of this family has an ironic ring – it means 'mount of healing' – but his material wealth is of no avail to him when he is stricken by ill health. Wealth is no comfort when health is lacking.) Much later in the book there is a parallel exclusion for the young son Ludwig: he is prevented from going to a garden-party because his thoughtless chatter and spreading of confidential conversation within the family has led to an unpleasant fracas between his mother and a woman of dubious morals. Consequently, his parents are wary about whether he can be trusted to behave responsibly.

The Herrmanns are a privileged family, but Salzmann makes it clear that wealth brings with it responsibilities to those less fortunate: giving employment, assisting the destitute, comforting and supporting the sick. The children are taught to respect everyone they meet, whatever their social status or outward appearance. When the family's two servants are both away at the same time, the maid having been given permission to go to a fair in a nearby village and the man-servant being occupied looking after his sick father, the children experience at first hand how much they rely on the servants because they now have to fulfil those tasks themselves. Salzmann never simply enunciates a moral principle: it is always demonstrated through an incident.

1804 (London: Richard Phillips, 1804), vol. 1, p. 12.

A large variety of figures are depicted in the book, some admirable, others wicked. Many appear only in one chapter, but others form part of the Herrmanns' circle of friends and acquaintance. Key roles are occupied by father Herrmann himself, his wife Sophie, Magister Helwig, the pastor who finds Ludwig in the forest when he has got lost and is afraid, and also the old schoolmaster, Rektor Gutmann, who is described as having a powerful influence on both Herrmann and his old school-friend Friedrichson, to whom Herrmann gives a home and employment when he is down on his luck. Salzmann united in his own person the roles of father, pastor and teacher, and in his book these adult males are models of the moral values that he wishes to inculcate in his readers. They represent authority, sobriety, industry and benevolence. The schoolmaster's name actually means 'good man', and 'Herrmann' can perhaps be equated with the English 'Masterman'.

Yet the pursuit of goodness is no guarantee of undiluted material happiness: suffering and deprivation have to be accepted too as part of God's mysterious purposes. The Helwig family is smitten with smallpox, and at the very end of the book Sophie dies of an undiagnosed illness, leaving Herrmann a widower and the children bereft of their mother. By this time, however, the children are ready to respond to their father's desire: 'But if you are good, obedient, industrious children, and attend to truth, I shall still find some comfort, even after the loss of your mother'.[35] As they grow up, Herrmann experiences in them the fruits of the good lessons that he and Sophie have given them.

The *Moralisches Elementarbuch* exemplifies the whole gamut of moral values relevant to pre-pubertal children. Like almost all children's books of this period, it is firmly anchored in the experience and expectations of the middle class, comfortably off, but modest in its aspirations, spurning the pretentiousness and airs of the aristocracy, and conscious of its responsibility towards the lower classes. The book is full of incidental information about social life and conditions: children's games, kitchen and ornamental gardens, leisure activities, appreciation of natural beauty, rural poverty, the plight of soldiers disabled through war, times of meals and of going to bed, gestures of affection. Some of these are altered in the English translation, a practice that points up differences between some German and English social customs.

Salzmann uses a considerable number of personal names in the course

---

35 C. G. Salzmann, *Elements of Morality* (London: J. Johnson, 1793), vol. 2, p. 174.

of his narrative. Some of these, as we have seen, suggest the characteristics of the person in question, though these are few in number. The miser who plays such a nasty role in chapters 20 and 41 is given the name Harpax, the Greek and Latin for 'rapacious', while the beneficent advocate in chapter 23 is called Lebrecht ('live rightly'). This latter name may well have been intended as a compliment to Salzmann's publisher, Siegfried Lebrecht Crusius, who also published Basedow. The majority of the names, however, are ordinary German names of the day, and Mary Wollstonecraft alters most of them in her English translation, not generally using their English equivalents. Chapter 31 contains a sympathetic portrait of an elderly Jew who is able to cure Ludwig's toothache. Although the boy is initially suspicious, Salzmann is at pains to show him overcoming his prejudice so as to accept the Jew's help and take on board his firmly stated view that there are good people in all religions. This chapter testifies to the prevalence of popular prejudice against the Jews and the need to counter it.

Salzmann's philosophical position reflects common Enlightenment views. He constantly promotes a belief in goodness and amendment of life. In describing the unpleasant innkeeper in chapter 33 he has Herrmann explain to his children that the man is as he is because from childhood he has always had wicked people around him. Such a person is to be pitied and helped rather than hated. Everywhere Salzmann encourages mutual respect and assistance, and he extends this to the animal kingdom in the incident in which little Erich, a friend of Ludwig and Luise (called James in Wollstonecraft), catches a field-mouse and wants to kill it. Herrmann calls him cruel and tells him to be ashamed: 'He who can torment a little helpless animal, has certainly a bad heart' (vol. 2, p. 67). Similar incidents of children mistreating animals are commonplace in the literature of the period.

As a product of the Enlightenment, Salzmann's religious views are general rather than sectarian. He speaks about God as Creator and the invisible power at work in the universe, not always or necessarily comprehensible to humankind. But because his book is not concerned with revealed religion, it avoids all mention of Jesus. Nonetheless, Salzmann sees his aim as completely consonant with the Christian ethos. The incidents he presents are not conceived in terms of commands and rules, but as examples of kinds of behaviour with particular consequences that children can readily understand. The values he propounds are expressed undogmatically and flow naturally and rationally, in true Enlightenment manner, from the kind of conduct necessary for an interdependent and harmonious society. They include industry, thrift, moderation, patience in adversity, compassion, persistence, gratitude, honesty and a simple lifestyle. Things to be avoided are selfishness, idleness, gossip, slander, cruelty towards animals and lavishness. Salzmann also firmly embraces the belief that wickedness does not win in the end, but is overcome through God's goodness.

Salzmann's book fits easily into a pattern of educational fiction in English, beginning with Sarah Fielding's *The Governess; or, Little Female Academy* (1749) and including Wollstonecraft's *Original Stories from Real Life* (London: J. Johnson, 1788). Both Fielding and Wollstonecraft are concerned with the education of girls, not with academic studies, but with moral and social questions, with how to behave in polite society. Fielding's Mrs. Teachum and Wollstonecraft's Mrs. Mason are both slightly terrifying in the retrospect of two centuries as they confront the deficiencies of their pupils. Mrs. Teachum has nine pupils aged between eight and fourteen, while Mrs. Mason has just two sisters, Mary and Caroline, aged fourteen and twelve. Neither book has anything like a plot, but simply recounts a number of exemplary situations in which the girls acquire the moral discernment necessary for their position in society. They learn from each other as well as from their governess. Fielding diversifies her narrative with inserted tales such as 'The Story of the Cruel Giant Barbarico, the Good Giant Benefico, and the Pretty Little Dwarf Mignon', 'The Story of Caelia and Chloe' and 'The Princess Hebe'. This was a pattern followed by Madame Leprince de Beaumont in her *Magasin des enfans* (1756), of which an English version appeared in 1757. Among other things it included the classic version of 'Beauty and the Beast'. Wollstonecraft's *Original Stories* eschews such fantasies, but gives several edifying accounts of the experiences of persons who figure in the narrative. Tellingly, she refers in the text to Mrs Trimmer's *Fabulous Histories* (1786), later retitled *The History of the Robins*. Mrs Trimmer is noted for her strong deprecation of fairytales, especially for their providing harmful examples of wickedness, terrifying their child readers and encouraging superstition.[36] (The word 'fabulous' in the title refers to animal fables, which since Aesop have been used to tell moral stories.)

As a teacher and writer on education, Mary Wollstonecraft (1759-97) was well equipped to introduce Salzmann to British readers. In 1787

---

36 See Nicholas Tucker, 'Fairy Tales and their Early Opponents: in Defence of Mrs Trimmer', in Mary Hilton, Morag Styles and Victor Watson (eds.), *Opening the Nursery Door. Reading, Writing and Childhood 1600-1900* (London and New York: Routledge, 1997), pp. 104-16.

> ELEMENTS
>
> OF
>
> MORALITY,
>
> FOR THE
>
> USE OF CHILDREN;
>
> WITH AN
>
> INTRODUCTORY ADDRESS TO PARENTS.
>
> Tranflated from the GERMAN of the
>
> Rev. C. G. SALZMANN.
>
> A NEW EDITION.
>
> IN TWO VOLUMES.
>
> VOL. I.
>
> LONDON:
>
> PRINTED FOR J. JOHNSON, IN ST. PAUL'S
> CHURCH-YARD.
>
> 1805.

6. Title-page of C. G. Salzmann, *Elements of Morality, for the Use of Children; With an Introductory Address to Parents. Translated [by Mary Wollstonecraft] from the German. A New Edition* (1805).

she had written *Thoughts on the Education of Daughters*, following it with *Original Stories*, which was reprinted a number of times up to 1807. In 1789 she contributed to Mr Cresswick's *The Female Reader, or, Miscellaneous Pieces, in Prose and Verse*, an anthology for girls, and in 1790 she adapted and 'improved' a translation of Madame de Cambon's *De Kleine Grandisson*, a children's counterpart in Dutch to Richardson's *Sir Charles Grandison*, which appeared with the title *Young Grandison*. All these books were published by Joseph Johnson (1738-1809). Johnson was one of the most notable publishers of the late eighteenth century and had on his list books by such important figures as Cowper, Thomas Paine, Joseph Priestley, William Godwin, Erasmus Darwin, Wordsworth, Coleridge, Richard and Maria Edgeworth and Anna Laetitia Barbauld. He became the official distributor for the Unitarians.[37] William Godwin, Wollstonecraft's eventual husband

---

37 See Robert Woof, Stephen Hebron and Claire Tomalin, *Hyenas in Petticoats. Mary*

and biographer, informs us that 'The translation of Salzmann produced a correspondence between Mary and the author; and he afterwards repaid the obligation to her in kind, by a German translation of the Rights of Woman'.[38]

Elements of Morality, for the Use of Children; With an Introductory Address to Parents was illustrated with numerous copperplates, sixteen of which were engraved by William Blake on the model of Chodowiecki.[39] The translation was successful enough for Johnson to publish further editions in 1791, 1792, 1793, 1799 and 1805. From at least 1793 illustrations were no longer included. A Dublin edition appeared in 1798 (William Porter), and Oliver & Boyd produced a 'new and improved edition' in Edinburgh in 1821. Various American editions can be cited between 1795 and 1850. The book clearly satisfied a great need, which only abated when Evangelical sentiment required a specific commitment among educationists to its demands.

Apparently Wollstonecraft came across Salzmann's book when she was beginning to learn German, and she made her translation as a kind of exercise.[40] It would be interesting to know how she found the book; perhaps it was through a German governess or language-teacher in London at the time. What German grammar or dictionary she used is unknown. There were certainly grammar books available. John James Bachmair's *A Complete German Grammar* had already appeared in a third edition (London: G. Keith, etc., 1771), and Gebhardt Friedrich A. Wendeborn's *An Introduction to German Grammar* went into a third edition with additions in 1797, so presumably an earlier edition would have been available to her. As far as dictionaries go, she is likely to have used Christian Ludwig's *Teutsch-Englisches Lexicon*, the first German-English dictionary to be published. Its first two editions were published anonymously by Thomas Fritsch of Leipzig in 1716 and 1745, but Wollstonecraft probably used one of the later editions published in 1765 and 1789. Another possibility would be the same lexicographer's *A Dictionary English, German and French* (Leipzig: Fritsch, 1706), from which the *Teutsch-Englisches Lexicon* was derived, and of which

---

Wollstonecraft & Mary Shelley (Grasmere: The Wordsworth Trust, 1997), pp. 2-4.
38 William Godwin, *Memoirs of the Author of a Vindication of the Rights of Women* (London: J. Johnson; and G.G. and J. Robinson, 1798; reprinted Oxford and New York: Woodstock Books, 1993), p. 65.
39 Judith St. John, *The Osborne Collection of Early Children's Books. A Catalogue* (Toronto: Toronto Public Library, 1975), vol. 1, p. 295.
40 Woof, Hebron and Tomalin, *Hyenas in Petticoats*, p. 119.

subsequent editions appeared in 1736 and 1763 (the 1791 edition would have been too late for Wollstonecraft).[41] By the beginning of the nineteenth century more grammars and bilingual dictionaries were being issued all the time, but Ludwig's work dominated the eighteenth century.

Wollstonecraft's translation follows Salzmann relatively closely, but not wholly accurately. She omits occasional words and phrases, particularly at the ends of chapters, though she keeps to the general sense. In a few instances her chapters do not correspond to Salzmann's, though it is hard to see why she has made the changes. Half of Salzmann's chapter 7 becomes Wollstonecraft's chapter 8 and sets up a sequence that is not corrected until she has a second chapter 40, which corresponds to Salzmann's chapter 40.

Understandably, Wollstonecraft's translation of Salzmann adapts the text to fit English circumstances. The various characters are renamed wholesale, only a very few retaining an English form of the original German name. So Herrmann and his wife Sophie become a Mr. and Mrs. Jones from Bristol, and their children Ludwig and Luise become Charles and Mary. Magister Helwig becomes Mr. Benson, the unfortunate Friedrichson Mr. Noel, the cook Dorothee the more familiar Betty (Betty is a servant's name in *Original Stories* too). The miser Harpax is turned into Mr. Skinpenny, Graf Rheinfeld into Lord Smooth-tongue. Ramboldchen, the name of the Helwig family's dog, is changed to Pompey (also in *Original Stories*), which may have reminded English readers of Sir Francis Coventry's satirical *History of Pompey the Little; or, the Life and Adventures of a Lap-dog* (1751). One of Wollstonecraft's changes requires some comment, given her later *Vindication of the Rights of Woman* (1792). Salzmann gives Herrmann's wife the name Sophie, which he frequently uses in referring to her in the text (it was, in fact, the name of Salzmann's own wife). Very rarely, she is called 'Madame Herrmann'. More often, it is 'Mutter' (mother). Wollstonecraft turns her into Mrs. Jones without any first name. Since Salzmann refers to characters of lower social standing almost always by first names, while giving those of equal or higher status titles and surnames, Wollstonecraft's transformation of Madame Herrmann or Sophie into Mrs. Jones can be interpreted as raising her status to that of equality with her husband. In the vast majority of instances Salzmann calls the father – the most important figure in the book – simply 'Herrmann', though he has various characters

---

41 See Timothy Buck, 'Breaking the Ice: Christian Ludwig's Teutsch-Englisches Lexicon, the First German-English Dictionary', in John L. Flood et al. (eds.), *'Das unsichtbare Band der Sprache'. Studies in German Language and Linguistic History in Memory of Leslie Seiffert* (Stuttgart: Hans-Dieter Heinz, 1993), pp. 237-51.

address him as 'Herr Herrmann'. We never learn what his first name is.

The translated narrative is firmly situated in the English landscape. Salzmann is rather vague in his geography, saying merely that the family lived in the town of N. near the banks of a river. The only place that he mentions is Stendal, from where Friedrichson hails and where Gutmann was a tutor. Wollstonecraft converts this into Yorkshire, and Mr. Goodman is described as being an usher at an academy in Bath. In the German text his son is about to study at an unnamed university, whereas in the English he is to go to Oxford.

As far as the general flow of the narrative is concerned, Wollstonecraft keeps close to Salzmann, but her translation is free rather than exact, perhaps especially in the 'Introductory Address to Parents'. She makes judicious substitutions in order to make the details of an incident fit English expectations. For example, when Mr. Benson (Magister Helwig in the German) rescues the lost little boy Charles (Ludwig) in the forest, the illustrative story that Salzmann gives about a peasant hussar, who is similarly terrified in the forest and is wounded by his enemies, is transferred to the American wars. Wollstonecraft, however, gives the episode a twist of her own, as the wounded soldier is tended by 'one of those men, whom we Europeans with white complexions, call savages' until he recovers from his injuries. The 'savage' 'prayed the Great Spirit to take care of him, and conduct him safe to his own country' (vol. 1, p. 24). One could imagine Salzmann approving of such a substitution.

The incidents that comprise Salzmann's long narrative are often linked by unexpected turns of events. The author keeps his readers' or hearers' attention by frequent changes of mood and emotion. There are tears a-plenty, fond embraces, kisses, expressions of delight, exuberance and also sorrow and anxiety. There was obviously too much of this for an English readership, for Wollstonecraft tones it down a good deal. This points to clear cultural differences between the Germans and the English. The free expression of the emotions found in German literature in the chronologically overlapping periods of *Empfindsamkeit* (Sentimentality) and *Sturm und Drang* (Storm and Stress) – Goethe's *Werther* immediately springs to mind – was felt to be excessive in England.

Wollstonecraft is content to leave parents and children embracing each other and kissing, but she draws the line at such demonstrations between grown men. When the lost Ludwig (Charles) is reunited with his father, the German text has the father step out of his carriage and fall on Magister

Helwig's (the curate's) neck, for which the English substitutes: 'Mr. Jones stepped out, and taking the Curate's hand, said, as he cordially shook it . . .' (vol. 1, p. 70). Similarly, when Albert, Herrmann's boyhood friend, meets him again, Salzmann tells us that he fell most demonstratively on Herrmann's neck, which Wollstonecraft transposes into 'He caught Mr. Jones by the hand with great warmth' (vol. 1, pp. 127-28). Even more striking are the differences between the German and English texts in regard to the reconciliation of Helwig and his estranged brother, Anselm. The latter falls weeping round Magister Helwig's neck and kisses him, while the unnamed brother in the English version 'timidly took his [brother's] hand' (vol. 1, p. 93). Again, in the German book both Herrmann and Friedrichson kiss their former teacher, Rektor Gutmann, an action completely omitted from the English. By eliminating or toning down such details Wollstonecraft made Salzmann's work more acceptable to her English readers. Some fifty years later William Howitt still remarks on these affectionate relationships between men, which he finds contrary to English habits:

> Young men entertain that brotherly feeling for each other that you seldom see in England. They go, as youths, often walking with their arms about each other, as only school-boys do with us. They put their arms over each other's shoulders in familiar conversation in company, in a very brotherly way. I say nothing of that hearty kissing of each other on meeting after an absence, that to an English eye, in great rough-whiskered and mustachioed men, has something very repulsive in it.[42]

There are a few other details that differentiate the English text from its German source. Salzmann states that twelve o'clock was the time that Herrmann was accustomed to dine, while Wollstonecraft declares that one was the hour when Mr. Jones usually dined. The evening following the quarrel and accident involving the two coachmen was perhaps an exceptional one, as it continued with the return to the Helwigs' house and the incident between the Magister and his estranged brother, but it did not conclude until one in the morning. There is no indication that the children were dispatched to bed earlier. The German text mentions the watchman calling out under the window and telling the company that the clock has struck one. The English version omits any reference to a watchman and states the clock to have struck twelve. The only reason for changes of this kind must be to conform to English habits.

---

42 William Howitt, *The Rural and Domestic Life of Germany* (London: Longman, Brown, Green & Longmans, 1842), p. 200.

Salzmann, in addition to making several references to the children's games and toys, also has the Magister produce a copy of the *Göttingischer Taschenkalender* in which there are pictures that the children look at with pleasure. Probably he is here paying an indirect compliment to his illustrator, Chodowiecki, since the latter provided pictures for it too. Wollstonecraft naturally enough simply refers to 'a little almanack'. In the original Ludwig mentions reading the *Kinderfreund*, a favourite book of his and one that has given him much pleasure. It is not absolutely clear what is meant here. Friedrich Eberhard von Rochow had produced a reader for use in rural schools called *Der Kinderfreund* (The Children's Friend), which was first published in 1776 and reissued in several new editions up to the beginning of the nineteenth century. But around the same time Christian Felix Weisse had also begun to issue a weekly magazine called *Der Kinderfreund*, issues of which were then published in volume form. The first twenty-four parts were published in Leipzig between 1776-82 by Crusius. Since Crusius was Salzmann's own publisher, it is more likely that this is what he was referring to. Wollstonecraft uses the occasion for her own benefit, as she has Charles read *Young Grandison*, thus alluding to her own version of Madame de Cambon's book published by her own publisher, Joseph Johnson.

The educational aims of Salzmann were very close to those of Campe. Their moral values and the means whereby they were to be inculcated show no serious divergence. Their emphasis on the affectionately knit family as the place in which these values and patterns of behaviour were to be learnt enabled their books easily to take root in middle-class Britain. In terms of their assimilation into British children's literature it is noteworthy that their German provenance is of virtually no interest. The opening and closing scenes of *Robinson the Younger* are, of course, located in Hamburg, and other references to Germany do crop up occasionally in the book, but they are allotted no special significance or comment in the English translation. As to Salzmann's *Elements of Morality*, the opportunity to remark on or explain things German is resolutely rejected, as Wollstonecraft systematically assimilates the story to plain English circumstances. So while the importance of these German books is emphatically acknowledged through their being translated, any significant German quality they may possess is underplayed, ignored or eliminated

4. Musäus and the Beginnings of the Fairytale

German fairytales are indelibly linked first of all with the names of the Brothers Grimm, who produced the first edition of their celebrated collection in 1812-15. Other writers had been publishing a variety of fairytales before then,[43] but because they were not scholarly collectors of traditional tales their contributions have not been given much credit. Two names, however, deserve passing mention here. Johann Gottlieb Schummel, whose description of Basedow and the Philanthropin in Dessau we encountered in the chapter on Campe, included four fairytales in his *Kinderspiele und Gespräche* (Children's Games and Conversations) (1776-78); they seem to be the earliest German fairytales specifically designed for children. None of these were translated into English. The second name is Albert Ludwig Grimm – no relative of the famous Jacob and Wilhelm – who produced a book entitled *Kindermährchen* (Children's Tales) in 1809, *Lina's Mährchenbuch* (Lina's Book of Fairytales) in 1816 and *Mährchen aus dem Morgenlande* (Oriental Fairytales) in 1843. A number of his fairytales were translated into English and will be dealt with in another chapter.

It is clear that the Brothers Grimm were not working in a vacuum, but their scholarly approach and Wilhelm's stylistic skill managed to establish a norm of length, language and tone for printing traditional tales that has dominated the field ever since. In the eighteenth century, however, different forms of the fairytale prevailed. The literary fairytale was all the rage. It had begun in France in the 1690s with the verse tales of Charles Perrault, followed by his more famous prose *Histoires ou contes du temps*

---

[43] A summary list is given in David Blamires, 'The Early Reception of the Grimms' *Kinder- und Hausmärchen* in England', *Bulletin of the John Rylands University Library of Manchester*, vol. 71, no. 3, p. 65.

passé (1697), which contained the classic versions of what we know in English as 'Cinderella', 'Bluebeard', 'Little Red Riding Hood' and 'Puss in Boots'. Round about the same time the Countess d'Aulnoy wrote her own fairytales, based in part on traditional plots, but combined and embroidered for the pleasure of the fashionable salons and adolescent girls. Many other aristocratic ladies (and gentlemen) composed fairytales too, becoming increasingly prolix and sentimental, but Madame d'Aulnoy was recognized as 'la reine de la féerie', and her works were translated into English and German and often abridged. Between 1704-17 there appeared Antoine Galland's French version of *The Thousand and One Nights*, which again was quickly translated into other languages and enjoyed enormous popularity. This was the international literary context in which a German author first essayed a major collection of fairytales.

Johann Karl August Musäus (1735-87) was part of the extraordinary flowering of literary culture that characterized the court of the Duchess Anna Amalia at Weimar, a court that included Wieland, Goethe and Herder among its luminaries. Musäus had himself written two satirical novels before he published in 1782-86 his *Volksmährchen der Deutschen* (Folktales of the Germans). To us today the title is misleading, since what Musäus wrote were decidedly literary tales, more like short novels or romances in terms of length, rational and satirical in tone, minimizing or even excising everything to do with magic and the supernatural. We know from his nephew, August von Kotzebue, that he listened to old people telling folktales and used them as a basis for his own tales, but that is really the only sense in which he can be said to have written folktales. These oral tales were the grit that produced pearls in the oyster of his imagination. He called them *German* folktales to distinguish them from the literature that came from France. Musäus's French forbears and contemporaries were on the whole serious in their approach to the fairytale. They might insert the occasional humorous remark, and Count Antoine Hamilton eventually parodied their plots and themes in *Les quatre Facardins*, but they were subverted by Musäus, whose irony, critical spirit and linguistic virtuosity make his tales one of the brilliant, unsung achievements of eighteenth-century German literature. Musäus has suffered at the hands of folklorists because he did not treat his material like the Grimms, and literary historians have neglected him because his attitude towards the folktale was quite different from that of the Romantics. Nonetheless, his tales have survived, sometimes revised or abridged and made suitable for children, who were certainly not the readership that Musäus first intended.

The *Volksmährchen der Deutschen* consists of fourteen pieces (eighteen if the 'Legenden von Rübezahl' (Legends of Rubezahl) are taken as their five separate parts), of which we may discount 'Dämon Amor' (Demon Love) as not being based on a traditional tale. The rest are derived from oral or printed folktale sources. 'Die Bücher der Chronika der drei Schwestern' (The Books of the Chronicles of the Three Sisters) comes from 'The Three Animal Kings' in Giambattista Basile's *Pentamerone*, which Musäus probably knew in the Italian translation of 1769 (there is a copy in the Thuringian State Library in Weimar), and it is likely that he got the inspiration for 'Ulrich mit dem Bühel' (Ulrich with the Hump) from Perrault's 'Ricquet à la houppe' (Ricky with the Tuft). 'Richilde' is an ingenious and unexpected retelling of the Snow-White story from the viewpoint of the stepmother. 'Rolands Knappen' (Roland's Pages), supposedly taken from a *Volksbuch*, ties in loosely with the story the Grimms published later as 'Tischchen deck dich, Goldesel und Knüppel aus dem Sack' (The Magic Table, the Gold Donkey and Cudgel in the Sack). The 'Legenden von Rübezahl' recount rumbustious incidents with a mountain spirit in the Silesian Riesengebirge, while 'Der Schatzgräber' (The Treasure-Seeker) tells of finding hidden treasure in the Harz Mountains. In 'Libussa' we have a series of fairytale tests which lead ultimately to the founding of the city of Prague. 'Die Nymphe des Brunnens' (The Nymph of the Fountain) combines motifs from various sources, but has much in common with elements of the 'Cinderella' tale-type.

A number of the remaining tales centre on the theme of love. 'Der geraubte Schleier' (The Stolen Veil) is a version of the swan maiden story, while 'Stumme Liebe' (Dumb Love) manages to combine a sentimental love-story with the hero's hair-raising encounter with a ghost in a haunted castle, followed by a version of the dream of hidden treasure. Finally, 'Melechsala' is a daring love-story about a *mariage à trois*, based on the medieval legend of the Count of Gleichen. The mere indication of theme shows that several of Musäus's tales are of dubious interest to children, so it is not surprising to discover that they have been very selectively translated into English and adapted. In both German and English Musäus is a prime example of an author who wrote for an adult readership being gradually and very selectively taken over by children. His writings display a detached, ironic spirit that keeps conventional Christianity at a distance. Satire forms a clear part of his literary purpose, but it was kept in check by his deeper devotion to the idyll of domestic harmony.⁴⁴

Musäus made his entry into English anonymously. Neither his name nor that of the translator appears on the title-page of *Popular Tales of the Germans* (London: John Murray, 1791). The translator was until very recently supposed to be William Beckford (1759-1844), the author of *Vathek*, an Oriental fantasy of wild indulgence and cruelty that is his lasting contribution to English literature. However, G. P. Butler has shown on what flimsy grounds this attribution rests. So few of the books in Beckford's enormous library are in German that 'it is hard to believe that, if he indeed read them, he did so unaided or with ease'.⁴⁵ It is thus improbable that Beckford made the translation.

The anonymous translator rendered just five of Musäus's tales into English: 'Richilda', 'The Books of the Chronicles of the Three Sisters', 'The Stealing of the Veil', 'Elfin Freaks; or, The Seven [actually, Five] 'Legends of Number Nip' (i.e. 'Rübezahl') and 'The Nymph of the Fountain'. Only two of the many later translators of Musäus attempted as many stories: the anonymous translator of James Burns's 1845 edition and J. T. Hanstein in 1865. The 1791 translator provides an interesting testimony to his acquaintance with German literature by a reference to both Campe and Salzmann in a footnote to 'The Three Sisters'. He was also conscious that there might be objections on the part of his readers to some of the material he had translated, so he attempted to deflect criticism by providing an introduction in which he presented them in the form of a dialogue between a reviewer and the publisher. In 'Richilde' the apple that is so fateful for Bianca (Musäus's name for the Snow-White figure) is poisoned at the queen's direction by her Jewish doctor, and it is compared by him with both the apple in the Garden of Eden and that in the Garden of the Hesperides. Referring to this, the translator puts into the mouth of the publisher the following words:

> I own I did not myself like his flippant familiarity with the good people of Israel; and having one day, by way of experiment, read *Richilda, or the Progress from Vanity to Vice*, to a very numerous mixed circle, an old lady, a constant frequenter of the neighbouring meeting-house in Blackfriars, vehemently protested against setting Eve's apple on a level with

---

44 Alfred Richli, *Johann Karl August Musäus. Die Volksmärchen der Deutschen* (Zürich und Freiburg im Breisgau, 1957).
45 G. P. Butler, 'Beckford and Musäus: a Likely Pair?', in *Schein und Widerschein. Festschrift für T. J. Casey*, eds. Eoin Bourke, Roisin Ni Néill and Michael Shields (Galway: Galway University Press, [1999]), p. 30.

that of Atalanta, though the latter was of gold purified in the fire; and she declared herself more scandalized by the concluding allusion than she had at any time felt at the lewdest print that ever stared her in the face as she walked along the public streets (pp. v-vi).

This is doubtless an ironic comment, alerting readers to what they can expect from Musäus while simultaneously poking fun at the narrow-minded. The kind of objections that he was alluding to were increasingly voiced by such writers as Hannah More and Sarah Trimmer. It is perhaps indicative of the moral climate that no further translation of Musäus appeared for another thirty-five years.

Differences in social and cultural attitudes between Germany and England clearly play a role in explaining English reactions to Musäus, but the tales pose a variety of problems to translators apart from the actual content. Musäus is a very allusive writer, and while many of his allusions would have been picked up by an educated reader anywhere, some of them refer more particularly to German matters that would have been lost elsewhere. The 1791 translator is excellent at reproducing Musäus's mood and linguistic tenor, but he understandably often omits the more abstruse or local allusions and occasionally inserts one of his own. A good example of this is to be found in the first of the legends of 'Number Nip' (the translation of 'Rübezahl'). The German text has a descriptive passage about fruit-trees, which is translated as follows: ' . . . her eye was delighted by the fruit-trees, which bore ruddy gold-streaked apples, such as neither Mawe's art of gardening, nor Forsyth's renovating past, can now entice from mother nature' (vol. 2, p. 17). The German original, as one might expect, does not refer to either Mawe or Forsyth, but for the German Hirschfeld the translator has neatly substituted up-to-date English equivalents. Mawe is *Every Man his own Gardener*, attributed to Thomas Mawe, but actually by the horticulturalist John Abercrombie (1726-1806), who used Mawe's name out of a sense of diffidence. Forsyth is William Forsyth (1737-1804), superintendent of the royal gardens at St. James's and Kensington from 1784, who published *Observations on the Diseases, &c. of Forest and Fruit Trees* in 1791.[46] The trouble with all such topical references, whether German or English, is that while they make the story sparkle at the time of first publication, they often later become completely opaque.

In 'The Nymph of the Fountain' the translator, rather disconcertingly for those familiar with German geography, converts the Swabian town

---

46 For Abercrombie and Forsyth see entries in *Dictionary of National Biography*.

of Dinkelsbühl into the English Blackpool, wrongly associating the first element 'Dünkel-' (the old spelling of the name) with 'Dunkel' = 'dark'. At the time of writing the Lancashire locality had only some six houses 'appropriated for the reception of company',[47] so it was far from enjoying the reputation that it has today. Later on in this same story is a verse passage in which the heroine Matilda describes her skills. In the German this runs as follows:

> Ich bin eine Waise,
> Mathilde ich heiße,
> Kann plätten,
> Kann glätten,
> Kann nähen und spinnen,
> Auch sticken
> Und stricken
> Und Augen gewinnen,
> Kann hacken und pochen,
> Auch braten und kochen,
> Bin kunstreicher Hand,
> Und flink und gewandt.

The English translation renders this to a treat: 'I am an orphan, Matilda by name: I'm a stout girl, and nimble, can manage the thimble; can spin, card, and knit, and handle the spit; I can stew, bake, and brew; am honest and true, and here to serve you' (vol. 2, p. 232). This is not an exact translation, but in its attention to rhythm and rhyme and the general sense it provides a skilful equivalent. The over-all achievement in translating Musäus is greatly to be applauded.

It is not very likely that *Popular Tales of the Germans* would have been much read by children. Nor would this have happened with the translations of individual tales by Musäus in the late 1820s, which came on the back of growing interest in the German Romantics. 'Stumme Liebe' was translated as 'The Dumb Lover' by Thomas Roscoe in volume 3 of *The German Novelists* (London: Henry Colburn, 1826) and as 'Dumb Love' by Thomas Carlyle in volume 1 of *German Romance* (London: Chapman & Hall, 1827). Carlyle also translated 'Libussa' and 'Melechsala' in the same volume, and all three were reprinted in 1858 and 1897. An anonymous translation of 'Die Entführung' as 'The Elopement' appeared in *The Odd Volume*, part 2 (1826).

Carlyle, who also translated pieces by Fouqué and Tieck in *German*

---

[47] Nikolaus Pevsner, *The Buildings of England. Lancashire: The Rural North* (Harmondsworth: Penguin Books, 1969), p. 68.

Musäus and the Beginnings of the Fairytale 57

7. J. K. A. Musäus, *Legends of Number Nip* (1864). Illustrated by Charles Keene.

Romance, was as free with criticism of Musäus as with praise. Many of his comments were well made, but he constantly belittled Musäus, writing from the changed perspective of forty years on from his subject's death. By this time attitudes towards the genre of fairytale had substantially changed, due in large measure to the work of the Romantics and the Brothers Grimm. Carlyle concluded his introduction with the hope that his three translated tales

> may furnish a little entertainment both to the lovers of intellectual novelty and of innocent amusement. To neither can I promise very much: Musäus is a man of sterling powers, but no literary monster; and his Tales, though smooth and glittering, are cold; they have beauty, yet it is the beauty not of living forms, but of well-proportioned statues.

'Libussa' was translated again in *Tales from the German*, translated by John Oxenford and C. A. Feiling (London: Chapman & Hall, 1844) and later by J. T. Hanstein as *Libussa, Duchess of Bohemia* (London: Macdonald & Neal, 1866), but to my knowledge no one apart from Carlyle has translated

'Melechsala'.

The mid 1840s saw a renewal of interest in Musäus. The publisher James Burns, who had a considerable interest in German literature, issued a volume entitled *Select Popular Tales from the German of Musaeus* (London: James Burns, 1845), which presented seven tales: 'Mute Love', 'The Nymph of the Fountain', 'Peter Block; or, The Treasure-seeker of the Harz', 'The Three Sisters', 'Richilda', 'Roland's Squires' and 'Legends of Rübezahl' (giving only three of the five that Musäus wrote). This increased the number of Musäus's tales available in English. 'Peter Block' and 'Roland's Squires' reappeared in *Popular Works of Musaeus*, translated by J. T. Hanstein (London: J. Neal & Co., 1865), so retrospectively we can identify Hanstein as Burns's unnamed translator. *The Chronicle of the Three Sisters, and Mute Love*, again translated by Hanstein (London: Macdonald & Neal, 1866), reissues two more of the stories. Burns's edition and the later publications in which Hanstein is credited with the translation have a few give-away shared mistranscriptions of names. They also contain various features that point to a possible child readership. Some of the stories have been condensed – not a surprising thing to happen, given Musäus's prolixity – and the *Select Popular Tales* is illustrated with wood-cuts taken from the German edition of 1842. Certain sexually suggestive touches in the original have also been eliminated. For example, in 'Roland's Squires' the passage is omitted in which, in the German, the third of the squires is forced to sleep the night with the ancient witch. Similarly, the ambiguous role of Albertus Magnus in 'Richilda' in helping the eponymous heroine's mother to conceive is truncated. These changes may result from moral anxieties of the age, but in any case they make Musäus more accessible to young readers.

One set of stories above all seems calculated to appeal to children: the 'Legends of Rübezahl'. After the 1791 translation a version of 'The Legends of Number Nip' appeared in part 2 of *The Odd Volume* (1826). Then came a further adaptation in *Legends of Rubezahl, and Other Tales* (London: Joseph Cundall, 1845). Like Burns, Cundall had a particular interest in German literature, and the two of them published quite a large number of German authors and children's books during the 1840s. Their publications may well have set off the train of retellings of Rübezahl stories that begin with Leitch Ritchie's 'Legends of Number Nip' appended to his *Schinderhannes, the Robber of the Rhine* (London: Simms & M'Intyre, 1848). The name 'Number Nip' points to the 1791 translation as the probable source, and that is certainly the case with Mark Lemon's *Legends of Number Nip* (London:

Macmillan & Co., 1864). Both this book and Cundall's are attractively illustrated, which again signals children as the target readers. Lemon was illustrated by Charles Keene (1823-91), one of the many noted artists who worked for *Punch*, of which Lemon was the first editor. The book went into a second edition in 1872.

Other Rübezahl stories, not necessarily deriving from Musäus, were published by George G. Cunningham in *Tales and Traditions chiefly selected from the Literature of Germany* (Edinburgh, London, and Dublin: A. Fullarton & Co., 1854); by Francis Paul Palmer in *Old Tales for the Young* (London: Routledge, 1857); by Mary C. Rowsell in *Number Nip; or, the Spirit of the Giant Mountains* (London: Swan Sonnenschein & Co., 1884); and by Andrew Lang in *The Brown Fairy Book* (London: Longmans, Green, & Co., 1904). These adaptations demonstrate not only the popularity of the stories, but also the permeable boundaries of regional folklore and children's literature. The Rübezahl tales as examples of tales about events and supernatural beings believed to be true go back way beyond Musäus to the seventeenth-century collection of Johannes Prätorius, but in Germany as elsewhere they nowadays function more as a source for children's books. Nonetheless, the local origins were pointed out in the mid nineteenth century in *A Handbook for Travellers on the Continent*: 'The Riesengebirge are the theatre of the exploits of the mischievous spirit called *Rübezahl*, whose name is well translated into English by that of *Number Nip* (i.e. turnip numberer). There is hardly a mountain or a glen in the country without its legend of this popular demon'.[48]

Even more widely diffused than the 'Legends of Rübezahl' was 'The Books of the Chronicles of the Three Sisters', of which versions were included in Cundall's *Legends of Rubezahl* and in Burns's *Select Popular Tales*. In this same year, 1845, a third translation, by A. Sagorski, also saw the light of day, bearing the title *The Enchanted Knights; or, the Chronicle of the Three Sisters* (London: H. Cunningham). The immense popularity of this story must be due to the fact that of all Musäus's tales it is the most like a conventional fairytale. The plot is concerned with the transformation of three princes into the shapes of a bear, an eagle and a dolphin, their marriages to three sisters and their rescue by the sisters' younger brother, Reinald. As mentioned earlier, it was elaborated from a fairytale in Basile's *Pentamerone,* and Musäus obviously enjoyed developing it. It was not until

---

48 *A Handbook for Travellers on the Continent: being a Guide to Holland . . . to Switzerland*, 13th edition, corrected (London: John Murray, 1860), p. 424.

1848 that a pioneering English translation of *The Pentamerone, or the Story of Stories* was made by John Edward Taylor and published by Cundall (reprinted in 1850), but for some reason Basile never became popular in Britain. The availability of a translation of Musäus's source did nothing to detract from what he had made of it. New versions continued to be made.

In 1850 the seventy year old M. G. Kennedy went so far as to produce a verse form of the story: *The Arm! – the Sword! – and the Hour! Or, the Legend of the Enchanted Knights* (London: Longman, Brown, Green & Longmans). This version in four-line stanzas is a light-hearted romp with burlesque touches, especially at the end of the stanzas. A couple of examples show the kind of comic topical allusion that the author makes. In the baron's encounter with the bear near the beginning of the story he shows the bear potatoes that he has in his pouch: 'Potatoes which no Irishman / Would wish to have re-pealed' (p. 22). The punning allusion to Sir Robert Peel may relate to the repeal of the Corn Laws in 1846, but it may also recall the movement for the repeal of the Act of Union in the early 1840s as well as the potato famine. But at this distance in time the comment reads more like a joke than a serious political statement. A couple of pages later Kennedy graces the disappearance of the bear with the comment: 'Quick as a rail-train when express, / Into the thicket sped / The charmed Bear' (p. 24), which is a reminder to us of just how recent was the growth of the rail network when Kennedy was writing.

Another 'free version' of this story, this time entitled *The Three Sons-in-law*, by A. F. Frere, appeared in 1861 and was followed by Hanstein's *Chronicle of the Three Sisters* (London: Macdonald & Neal, 1866). Hanstein, though claiming to follow 'as closely as possible ... the style of the German', excuses himself by declaring: 'In all works rendered from the German into the English tongue, the adoption must lose much of the beauty of the original, the language of this country being too weak to convey to the mind of the reader the delicate metaphor, and redundant sentences of the German' (p. i). This perhaps explains the loss of resonance in the names of the towns founded by two of the disenchanted brothers at the conclusion of the story, where the real towns of Bernburg (in Saxony-Anhalt) becomes the fictitious 'Bearborough' and Aarburg (in Switzerland) 'Eagleborough'. Yet another version of 'The Chronicles of the Three Sisters' was made by Mark Lemon in his *Fairy Tales* (London: Bradbury, Evans, & Co., 1868), illustrated this time, simply, but humorously and prolifically, by Charles Bennett.

This story by Musäus does not seem to have been included in general collections of tales as much as 'Rübezahl'. The only such place that I have found is Alfred H. Miles's' *Fifty-two Fairy Tales* (London: Hutchinson & Co., 1892), in which it appears under the title 'The Story of Reinald, the Wonder-Child' in a translation by Marie Pabke and Margery Deane. In this respect, then, Musäus fares differently from his great successors, the Brothers Grimm and Wilhelm Hauff. His tales are really not easy to incorporate in anthologies because they are so different in scope and tone from the traditional fairytale. Yet, as we have seen, Musäus is a known literary figure throughout the long nineteenth century. He starts clearly enough within the orbit of serious literature in the 1791 translation, but by the middle of the century he has been at least partly claimed for children's reading. This could not come about through total fidelity to Musäus's original text, but only through progressive adaptation and assimilation. We shall see this process operating on many subsequent occasions, as the works of other authors undergo similar changes because of changes in their target readership.

5. Discovering Germany

The earliest connexions between England and Germany were to do with trade rather than with culture. Not only did Germans from the Hanse towns settle in London, but Englishmen and their families also established communities in cities such as Hamburg and Danzig. The main contact was with northern Germany. With the Reformation religion made further connexions, as many of the English reformers visited or took refuge in Protestant Germany, and the newly founded University of Wittenberg attracted scholars anxious to pursue their studies with such men as Luther, Melanchthon and Karlstadt. Wittenberg is where Shakespeare had Hamlet study. Germany now became a country for gentlemen such as Thomas Coryat (c. 1577-1617) and Fynes Moryson (1566-1630) to visit and describe for the benefit of their compatriots. In 1613 the marriage of Elizabeth, eldest daughter of James VI and I, to Frederick, the Elector Palatine, brought into being the dynastic connexion between Britain and Germany that ultimately led to the Hanoverian monarchs of the eighteenth century. It was through the marriage of Elizabeth's daughter Sophia to Ernst August of Braunschweig-Lüneburg that their son succeeded to the throne of Great Britain as George I.

One of the earliest indications of increasing interest in Germany was the production of the first English-language grammar of German, *The High Dutch Minerva*, first published in 1680 and reissued in 1685. Nonetheless, it took almost another hundred years for a more active British interest in German language and culture to develop. This was brought about, not by the dynastic connexion with Hanover, but rather because of the impact that German thinkers of the Enlightenment and German writers of the *Sturm und Drang* were making outside their own country. All the same, it would be true to say that knowledge of Germany as a geographical and political entity was rudimentary at the close of the eighteenth century. It had none of the pull of France and Italy as a cultural phenomenon for the well-to-do traveller. The discovery of the magnificent scenery of the Rhine and Germany's many fashionable spas had to wait for the early nineteenth century and the spirit of Romanticism, in which Wordsworth and Coleridge, Southey and especially Byron had a crucial role to play.

What, then, did British children learn about Germany from the late eighteenth century onwards? There were, of course, geography textbooks, in which Germany figured along with other European countries. There were also travel books and stories in which travel played an important role. In addition, we find passing allusions to Germany in things such as alphabet books and rhymes. The textbooks are, on the whole, the most systematic sources of information, but they vary immensely in what they offer. The later the book, the more detailed, wide-ranging and analytical the information is likely to be. Not only can one see how, through developments in transportation and communication, more factual material becomes available, but one can see how geography as a subject develops from bald and often arbitrary remarks at second hand into a scientific discipline. But the travel books and stories should not be ignored, since they are sources of popular information too.

All these books have one question to confront at the outset, namely, what is meant by the term 'Germany'? It is not exactly the same as the Holy Roman Empire, which included such predominantly non-German-speaking territories as Bohemia and Hungary and which creaked to an end with Francis II's renunciation of the title of Holy Roman Emperor and adoption of that of hereditary Emperor of Austria in 1804. In any case, the Holy Roman Empire was little more than a nominal entity for many years before its collapse, political power being located not only in Austria, but also in the kingdom of Prussia and the many other separate states. Prussia, in any case, straddled the boundaries of the Holy Roman Empire, since its eastern part with its many non-German-speaking inhabitants was not part of the Empire. 'Germany' was not a self-evident entity such as France, Spain or England. Consequently, many of the early textbooks devote most of their space to listing its various constituent political parts. The 1791 edition of Lenglet du Fresnoy's *Geography for Children* (first English edition 1737) deals with Prussia and Germany separately over about eight pages. It explains the difference between Prussia Royal or Polish Prussia and Brandenburg or Ducal Prussia before going on to 'Germany', which it identifies as 'the holy

Roman empire' with boundaries 'on the north, the Baltic sea, Denmark, and the German ocean; on the east, Prussia, Poland, and Hungary; on the south, Italy and Switzerland; and on the west, France, the Spanish Netherlands, and the Dutch seven United Provinces' (p. 57). At this time Germany was divided into a multiplicity of states, which the textbook proceeds to list in summary form. What is given for Lower Saxony may serve as a typical offering:

> Lower Saxony has part of Denmark and the Baltic sea on the north; Westphalia on the west; it borders to the southward on the Upper Rhine and Upper Palatinate; and contains the duchy and electorate of Hanover, the duchies of Brunswick, Lunenburgh, Holstein, Mechlenburgh, Saxe Lawenburgh, Magdeburgh, and Bremen, with the principality of Halberstad, and bishoprics of Hildesheim and Lubec (p. 59).

Given the considerable space that such accounts occupy, Lenglet du Fresnoy contents himself with adding only the names of just under twenty important towns, the chief rivers (Danube, Rhine, Elbe, Oder, Maes and Moselle) and the predominant forms of religion. On physical geography, agriculture, manufacture, commerce and population he is utterly silent.

Changes in the political structure of Germany and the geographical dimensions of its constituent parts meant that textbooks frequently had to be updated on this account. There are considerable differences between, for example, the fifth and the nineteenth editions of *Geography and History, selected by a Lady for the Use of her own Children* (1803 and 1843 respectively). (The Lady identifies herself only by her initials E.R. at the end of her preface; the first edition of her book appeared in 1790.) The 1843 edition, naturally enough, deals separately with the kingdoms of Hanover, Saxony, Bavaria, Wirtemburg (*sic*) and the duchy of Baden. Prussia is dealt with in a separate section in each edition, while Austria is separated from Germany only in the later edition. About Saxony the 1803 edition declares:

> The electorate of Saxony is the richest country in Germany. Dresden is the capital, and a most beautiful city; famous for its mirrors, founderies of bells and cannon, and particularly for the porcelain manufacture called Dresden. It contains about one hundred and ten thousand inhabitants (p. 76).

The 1843 edition elaborates considerably on the kingdom of Saxony, mentioning the related states of Saxe-Weimar, Schwartzenburg, Saxe-Cobourg, Hildeburghausen (*sic*), Saxe-Gotha and Saxe-Meiningen and adding Hesse-Cassel and Nassau for good measure. It then proceeds:

> Dresden is one of the finest cities in Germany; the houses are built of free-stone, and generally of the same height; the streets and broad and well paved, the squares spacious, and the palaces and public buildings numerous and elegant. Here are manufactures of gold and silver lace, jewellery, porcelain, paper-hangings, and dyed stuffs; and it has extensive foundries for balls (*sic*, presumably a misprint for bells) and cannon. The inhabitants amount to 63,000 (p. 100).

In its concluding remarks on Germany the 1843 edition gives the principal rivers as the Danube, the Rhine, the Elbe, the Oder, the Weser, the Moselle and the Mayn. The naming of the most noted lakes as 'those of Constance, Bregentz, and the Chilm-see (*sic*, presumably the Chiemsee), or the lake of Bavaria' allows one, perhaps, a glimpse of the paper foundations of geography textbooks of this period. How much, I wonder, of what is purveyed rests on secure knowledge or personal observation? Updating the text occasionally leads to errors. When the author writes in the 1843 edition: 'This country is said to contain more mineral waters than all Europe besides; those of Spa, Pyrmont, and Aix-la-Chapelle, are well known for their medicinal virtues' (p. 104), she omits to note that Spa is now in Belgium, although she mentions elsewhere the establishment in 1830 of the new kingdom of Belgium.

A number of other geography textbooks circulated during the first half of the nineteenth century. Particularly popular was *A Grammar of General Geography for the Use of Schools and Young Persons*, written by Sir Richard Phillips (1767-1840) using the pseudonym of the Revd. J. Goldsmith (possibly recalling the much more famous Oliver Goldsmith). The book was first published in 1803, but, with later revisions, it continued to be reprinted up to the middle of the century. The information is a little more basic than that provided by A Lady, but the book contains brief descriptions of Berlin, Dresden, Munich and Vienna and engravings of Berlin and Vienna. Even more compact are the accounts offered by John Guy in his *Geography for Children, on a Perfectly Easy Plan adapted for the Use of Schools and Private Families*, first published in 1840 and reaching a 75th edition by 1869. The information given on Germany, Prussia and Austria is very general, but the author permits himself some comments on the people. 'The Prussians in their wars have proved themselves a brave people; the higher classes are well-informed and courteous, while the peasantry and artisans are industrious and well-taught'. Then a contrast: 'The Austrian nobility are considered haughty and oppressive, but the middle classes are moral and industrious, and greatly attached to reading and music'.

Remarks such as these crop up in other books too. They add a human touch to the otherwise rather dry accounts of states and boundaries, principal towns, rivers and mountains, but they represent British attitudes and perceptions rather than objective facts. A chapbook of c. 1825-30 entitled *A Peep at the Various Nations of the World; with a Concise Description of the Inhabitants* (Dean and Munday; and A. K. Newman & Co.) includes 'Prussian' in its mainly alphabetical sequence of nationalities (there is no 'German' or 'Austrian') and declares: 'The Prussians were originally an idolatrous and cruel people; but since their elevation [to a kingdom in 1701], they have become more civilized, and at the present day hold a respectable rank among the nations of Europe'. The sloppy juxtaposition of the original pagan inhabitants of Prussia and the later German colonists is misleading, but is typical of the unreliability of chapbooks. A later textbook, John Olding Butler's *A New Introduction to Geography: in a Series of Lessons for Youth* (London: William Walker, eighteenth edition, 1860), writes simply of the Germans (not dealing separately with Austrians or Prussians):

> The Germans unite gravity and cheerfulness in their character; they are honest and fair in their dealings, hospitable and kind in temper; they have a genius for the sciences and mechanics, and are famous for some singular inventions, among which is the gun (p. 49).

While many attempts at describing national characteristics are vacuous, misguided or off-beam, Butler here is more specific. He actually seems to know something factually and not to be simply reproducing the rhetoric of the conventional testimonial. Elsewhere in his comments he notes the invention of printing about the year 1440 in Mentz (Mainz) and mentions that 'Hockheim (*sic*), seated in the heart of the wine country of Germany, gives name to the wine called Hock'.

The textbooks considered so far present compact information clearly designed to be learnt by heart. To them we can add *Familiar Geography* by the Abbé Gaultier (1746?-1818), first published by John Harris in 1826 and following on the author's earlier *Complete Course of Geography, by Means of Instructive Games*, published by E. Newbery in 1795. *Familiar Geography* consists of a rather dreary catechism of questions and answers about the most basic material, and it is all too easy to imagine the anxious schoolboy trying to memorize its dry lists of states and principalities, chief towns, rivers and so on.

In an attempt counter this dryness Barbara Hofland (1770-1844), the author of very many storybooks for children, wrote *The Panorama of Europe;*

or, a New Game of Geography, first published in 1813. It was reprinted several times, with updated material as required. The book centres on a family of several children and their friends who each take on the role of a particular country, dress up and present an account of it to their father, who asks them further questions. The children's friend Maria appears 'in a large hoop, with a petticoat of rich silk, surrounded by nine rows of ribbons' – these symbolize the nine circles of Upper Saxony, Lower Saxony, Westphalia, Upper Rhine, Lower Rhine, Franconia, Austria, Bavaria and Swabia. She declares her identity as 'Germany, a most magnificent empire, composed of various principalities, dukedoms, and states, combined under one great head, of which Austria is chief'. She is then catechized by the father about her divisions, rivers, medicinal waters, mountains, principal cities, Bohemia, Hungary and other contiguous countries, mines, vines and other products, both natural and manufactured. Previous to this, thirteen-year-old Edward had appeared 'dressed like a Prussian hussar, but with a black crape veil thrown over him'. He declares himself 'really so awkwardly situated, I scarcely know how to describe myself, for if I throw off my cloak, you would see that my arms were chopped off by France within a few years'. He then proceeds to give a history and geography of Prussia up to the Battle of Jena in 1806. In response to his father's query about commerce he lists the manufacture of glass, iron-work, paper, gunpowder, camblet, linen, silk stockings and cloth as well as the export of naval stores, linseed, hempseed, fish, mead, tallow, amber and caviare. Mrs Hofland's presentation of geographical material within the domestic narrative of children's games is part of a didactic tradition that goes back to such eighteenth-century educators as Sarah Fielding, Madame de Beaumont and Madame de Genlis, the latter's *Tales of the Castle* being alluded to in the presentation of France (p. 54). Joachim Heinrich Campe used a similar technique in his *Robinson Crusoe* and elsewhere. Barbara Hofland's narrative costuming of the geographical material is slight, but it certainly makes the information more readily memorable.

Although several general textbooks of geography were issued in a large number of editions during the late eighteenth and the nineteenth century, they were not the only purveyors of geographical information to children. Travel books were also published, and pre-eminent among them were several written by Priscilla Wakefield. *The Juvenile Travellers; containing the Remarks of a Family during a Tour through the Principal States and Kingdoms of Europe* was first published in 1801 and reached a fourteenth edition by 1824.

It was not a first-hand account of travel, but was based on the writings of several well-known travellers adapted for the benefit of children. In her preface Wakefield pointed out that the unsettled state of political affairs had often made it impossible to define the form of government, or even to point out to what sovereign particular states were subject. As is the case with the textbooks, only a small part of the book relates to Prussia, Germany and Austria.

The structure of the book is formed by the journeys of the Seymour family, undertaken to assuage the grief of Mrs Seymour at the death of her own mother. Mr Seymour – naturally for someone able to engage in such extensive travel – is 'a gentleman of easy fortune', and the couple have a son, Theodore, almost fourteen, and a daughter, Laura, who is twelve. Wakefield uses each of the characters adroitly to give different perspectives on their journeys, sometimes narrating in the third person, other times presenting the family's travels in dialogue or epistolary form. The journey opens with their voyage to Hamburgh and brief stay there and in Lubec before going to Denmark. After travelling in Denmark, Sweden, Lapland and Norway they return to Copenhagen and then sail for Dantzic. Then follows a section that takes in Dantzic, Berlin, Wittemburg (sic), Dresden, Leipsic, Magdeburg, Brunswick and Hanover before moving to Holland. Holland is dealt with at much greater length, before the journey up the Rhine via Cologne, Coblentz, Mentz, Manheim, Carlshrue (sic), Strasburg and the Black Forest to Schaffhausen. Much the largest part of the book is taken up with Switzerland, Italy, Sicily, Spain, Portugal and France. Only at the end of the book, which deals with Moscow, Ukraine and Turkey, do we return via Romania, Bulgaria and Hungary to German-speaking territory with a few pages on Vienna, Cracow and Breslaw. This latter section of the book involves only Theodore, travelling with a Dane named Steinbock, with whom he returns via Stettin to Copenhagen. The book is accompanied by a map, on which the various journeys are traced.

Priscilla Wakefield concentrates her descriptions on the cities visited. Theodore comments on the wealth of Hamburgh, and his father responds:

> An extensive trade is carried on here, [. . .] this city serves as a general warehouse, or market, for the natural produce and manufactured goods of all Germany, whence they are sent to different parts of Europe; and articles of various kinds are returned in lieu of them, to supply the Germans with those things which their own country does not afford (p. 6).

The family enjoys the spacious streets and stately brick houses, boating on the Alster and walking on the city ramparts. They find Lubec dull in comparison, and when they get to Cologne they find it 'an ancient, gloomy, disagreeable city, and so dull, that it seemed as if it had been deserted by the inhabitants' (p. 93). Dantzic is also described as having houses that are 'very antique in appearance', and the rows of trees in the streets are declared 'unfavourable to the health and cleanliness of the place, by preventing a free circulation of air' (p. 49). But the most notable point about the city is the use of ferocious dogs at night to secure the property lodged in the warehouses from fire or robbery. Both Berlin and Dresden are lauded, but Laura prefers Dresden and enjoys particularly the museum and the picture gallery. She is impressed by the dress of the postillions, which is smarter than she has seen elsewhere. The company visit the porcelain factory at Meissen and arrive at Leipsic on the first day of the Easter trade fair. Magdeburg is dismissed again as dull in comparison with Leipsic.

After some months' stay in the flat landscape of Holland the Rhine valley delights the travellers: 'Chestnut-groves, vineyards, pleasant villages, and ancient castles on the tops of rising hills, presented a new scene, so full of charms, that they arrived at Coblentz before they supposed they had reached half way' (p. 94). Mr Seymour explains the construction of the 'Flying Bridge', the pontoon between the town and the fortress of Ehrenbreitstein, to Theodore. They admire the striking views, but find the streets of Coblentz narrow, crooked and lacking in footpaths. Mentz does not seem very agreeable, but Manheim is 'a magnificent city' with a noble square, a fine palace belonging to the Elector Palatine, an elegant custom-house and jewellery shops. Carlsruhe impresses them enormously with its royal gardens bounded by a majestic forest. Strasburg's cathedral tower is noted as the highest in Europe. The Black Forest then represents the period's ideal of the picturesque, being 'wild and romantic: mountains rising in every part, and numerous cascades, of the clearest water, rolling down their sides, whilst their tops were covered with thick forest; the whole enlivened by scattered cottages and villages, delightfully situated' (p. 97).

It only remains, then, for Vienna to be celebrated at some length at the end of the book. The core of the city seems disappointing in comparison with the extremely magnificent suburbs, which are interspersed with gardens and splendid palaces. The cathedral, picture collections and the Prater are noted. The inhabitants, we are told, 'generally live in a splendid manner: their tables abound with wines of various kinds; and small chickens, cut into pieces and fried very dry, are a favourite dish' (p. 417). Exhibitions of fire-works are a frequent occurrence.

While Priscilla Wakefield's *Juvenile Travellers* is clearly aimed at intelligent older children, containing a map, but no illustrations, the Rev. Isaac Taylor's *Scenes in Europe for the Amusement and Instruction of Little Tarry-at-home Travellers* was obviously designed for a much younger age-group. It was first published in 1818 by John Harris and is equipped with a small engraving to each of the eighty-four short sections. It takes a quick canter through Europe, providing vignettes rather than structured accounts of the various countries. For Austria, therefore, we have a rather caustic account of a postillion, followed by brief comments on the Prater and Vienna. Germany merits sections on hunting the wild boar, the Fall of the Rhine at Schaffhausen, Aix-la-Chapelle and mineral waters, negative comments on the poor state of the peasantry, and a laudatory sketch of the Prussian capital, Berlin. There is also a chapter on timber floats on the Rhine, a phenomenon that crops up in most of these children's books, being not only visually striking, but also indicating the importance of the timber trade for Germany and of the Rhine as a vital means of commercial transportation.

A similar anecdotal approach to Isaac Taylor's is taken by the American author Samuel Griswold Goodrich in *Peter Parley's Tales about Europe* (c. 1839-40), a book that circulated widely in Britain. He too has paragraphs on the wild boar, Vienna and Berlin, but in addition he manages to take in Dantzic, the wild man discovered living naked in the forest (presumably Peter the wild boy found near Hamelin in 1725), Frederick the Great, the wretched state of German inns, the construction of mechanical toys, and gipsies. Clearly, no attempt is made at giving even a general picture of Germany, but particular items are picked out to capture the interest of young children.

The early nineteenth century witnessed a great growth of English interest in actually visiting Germany. The main focus was the Rhine, especially the section between Cologne and Mainz, and also the various spa towns of central Germany. Frankfurt am Main and Heidelberg were also much visited. A considerable number of books were published in English in Frankfurt and Heidelberg as well as in London. *Bubbles from the Brunnens of Nassau* by Sir Francis Bond Head is specifically mentioned in a couple of children's books, and on the back cover of the Frankfurt edition of 1845 are listed the titles of fifteen other books in English on aspects of

72 *Telling Tales*

8. Isaac Taylor, *Scenes in Europe, for the Amusement and Instruction of Little Tarry-at-Home Travellers*. Second edition (1819). Copper-engravings. Hunting the wild boar; timber floats; Fall of the Rhine at Schaffhausen.

German history, literature, culture and topography. These were books for adults eager to learn more about the places they were visiting. They were based on personal experience and study, so that we are presented with a more reliable picture of Germany. Neither Priscilla Wakefield nor Isaac Taylor ever visited the country, so they were simply transmitting book knowledge. The writers of the mid-century tell a more personal tale, and what they have to say is not systematic or general. Their scope is broader, describing not merely landscape and places, but also patterns of life, types of entertainment, differences in food and so on.

An excellent example of this new approach is given in the anonymously written *Travels with Minna and Godfrey in Many Lands. The Rhine, Nassau, and Baden* (London: Smith, Elder & Co., 1839). This narrative focusses on two children, Minna and Godfrey, who travel up the Rhine valley from Emmerick to Basle with their father and aunt and are instructed in all kinds of useful knowledge as well as enjoying a great variety of towns and scenery. They learn about geology and viticulture, the mineral waters of Nassau, the different kinds of religion, the history of Germany, contemporary German art, and much more in addition to hearing many legends of the Rhine. Fascinating, too, is the description of the long dinner they have in their hotel in Cologne, which consists of soup, bouilli, melon, tongue, potatoes, cabbage, peas sweetened with sugar, cutlets, calf's head, boiled salmon with custard for sauce, fish vol-au-vent, smoking hot crawfish, roast fowl, salad, rabbit, stewed cherries, leg of roast mutton, joint of beef, fruit, confectionery and cakes of various kinds. The children are overwhelmed by it. At a much later stage in their journey they encounter a vegetable that they are then frequently offered and find disagreeable – *Kohl-Rübe* (kohlrabi): 'It is a species of cabbage; the part which is eaten being a bulb of the size of a moderate turnip, growing a few inches above the ground. This is very inferior to the turnip, more compact and of stronger flavour, without its sweetness. It is much prized in Germany as a valuable vegetable, and we believe is comparatively a new one'. Though the didactic element is strong throughout, the book is packed with lively detail about the German countryside and ways of life. It reflects a new kind of curiosity about Europe outside France and Italy, as the growing prosperity of the middle classes made extended travel possible. Despite their interest, it is worth noting that Mr Cavendish, Minna and Godfrey's father, cannot really speak German, but has to rely on French in order to communicate. In this we can see him as typical of his class and period.

9. *Travels with Minna and Godfrey in Many Lands. From the Journals of the Author. The Rhine, Nassau, and Baden* (1839). Copper-engraving of the Drachenfels, Rolandseck and Nonnenfels.

Twenty-odd years later, M. Betham Edwards covers a similar expedition in her *Scenes and Stories of the Rhine* (London: Griffith & Farran, 1863), in which two boys and two girls, their father and uncle journey from Cologne up the Rhine to Mentz, then to Frankfort, Heidelberg, Stuttgart and Worms. Murray's *Handbook for Travellers on the Continent*, which had reached a thirteenth edition by 1860 and provides an amazing amount of topographical and historical information, is frequently referred to. Cologne Cathedral, though still incomplete (it was not finished until 1880), is marvelled at for its intricate architecture, but the city itself is dirty and poorly drained, though not as gloomy and disagreeable as Priscilla Wakefield described it. The Rhine voyage dwells on the traditional towns and sights – Bonn, Godesberg, Rolandseck, Andernach, Coblentz, Ehrenbreitstein, the Lurleiberg, Bingen and Mentz. Everything provides enjoyment, and the Germans are characterized as 'the cheeriest and most agreeable people in the world, if you only waive all ceremony with them; leave English coldness and fastidiousness behind, and take things good-temperedly as they do'. Frankfort provides copious interest with its toyshops, sausage shops and the Römerberg. The Jewish quarter is mentioned in most of the other books, but here we have a couple of pages devoted to the Rothschilds. When the travellers reach Worms at the end of the book, the 800-year-old synagogue and the history of the Jews in the city are given almost as much space as Luther and the Reformation.

By this time in the second half of the nineteenth century the royal connexions between Britain and Germany were being strengthened, so Bonn is significant not only as the birthplace of Beethoven, but also because Prince Albert studied at its university. Victoria and Albert's eldest daughter, the Princess Royal, had already married Prince Frederick William of Prussia in 1858, but the visit to Darmstadt focusses on the very recent marriage of Princess Alice, second daughter of Victoria and Albert, to Prince Louis of Hesse-Darmstadt in July 1862 and describes her sitting in deep mourning in the ducal chapel together with her husband and father-in-law. Her own father, Prince Albert, had died as recently as December 1861. Princess Alice herself died in 1878, while the Prussian connexion became increasingly fraught after the death of Kaiser Friedrich III.

Neither *Travels with Minna and Godfrey* nor *Scenes and Stories of the Rhine* make any pretence of being systematic in their presentation of Germany. They are not textbooks, but rather story-books full of information and attentive to the details of German life. *Scenes and Stories of the Rhine* includes a good deal about German eating habits, and the children are particularly discountenanced by the simple breakfast of rolls and coffee, which contrasts strongly with the more robust meal they are used to in England. The real-life contact with Germany and German people that the two books recount feeds into the textbooks of the late nineteenth century, which are much more comprehensive and professional than those of the earlier period.

George Gill's geographical reader, no. 4, entitled *Descriptive and Pictorial Europe*, published in 1881, represents something of a compromise between the old kind of story-book and the more systematic approach to geography being developed at the time. The narrative is divided into three sections, the first consisting of a cruise from the Arctic Ocean to Constantinople and the Crimea, the second comprising a score of trips by road, rail and river across various parts of the continent, while the third gives brief descriptive sketches of the different countries. As we are now into the era of the separate German and Austro-Hungarian Empires, there is no separate treatment of Prussia. The trips encompass the Upper Rhine, Mayence (Mainz) to Coblentz, Coblentz to Cologne, the Lower Rhine, the Upper and Middle Danube and the Elbe and are presented in a similar form and of with similar content to the narratives of *Travels with Minna and Godfrey* and *Scenes and Stories of the Rhine*, though much more briefly. A number of maps allow these journeys to be traced, and there are engraved illustrations of the Drachenfels, Cologne Cathedral (still unfinished), boatmen and peasants on the Danube and Nuremberg. The account of the German Empire contains such stock features as the timber-rafts floating down the Rhine and the Germans' fondness of the boar hunt, but there is also information about mining in the Erzgebirge and the Hartz, manufactures in the area including Dusseldorf, Elberfeld (misspelled Elberfield), Aix-la-Chapelle and Essen, amber fishing on the Baltic, and the development of the German army. This section concludes with a characterization of the Germans as part of 'the same great family' that the British belong to: 'They are sociable, frank, and hospitable. We might call them a "nation of readers," for it would be difficult to find any people so fond of books. They are very fond of music, too, and every little town boasts an "opera house," and gardens, where the people assemble to listen to the band, and to smoke'. The positive attitude to the Germans is very marked.

Perhaps the most systematic approach to geography of textbooks from the latter part of the nineteenth century is to be found in *A School Geography* by James Cornwell (1812-1902), which reached its seventieth edition in 1882. The author, a Fellow of the Royal Geographical Society, acknowledges his indebtedness to several French and German geographers and obviously had to keep updating his work. The original work dates from 1847, but political changes and economic and demographic developments necessitated alterations in the statistics presented. In the 1882 edition Cornwell presents systematically arranged material for Germany, Prussia and Austria. There are slight variations between them because of their differences, but the underlying procedure is the same. For Germany, for example, he begins with physical features, dealing separately with extent or area, coast, mountains, plains, rivers, climate, soil, wild animals, forests, minerals, mineral springs and race. He then goes on to political facts, looking at divisions of the country, agriculture, manufactures, commerce, exports, ports, internal communications, population, army (fortresses and naval ports), religion, debt, revenue, education, universities, government and town populations. While most of the information is presented in summary form, a few sections are amplified to include historical, cultural or literary material. No other textbook that I have seen is as comprehensive in its coverage of Germany.

The political and economic changes that affected Germany between the late eighteenth and the late nineteenth century are necessarily reflected in the geography textbooks of the period. But during that same period we can also see a growth in knowledge about Germany on the part of the British middle classes. No textbooks deal with Germany alone – conditions were not sufficiently developed for that. At the beginning of the period knowledge about Germany, Prussia and Austria was rudimentary and confined to the barest physical and political facts until improved means of transport through steamships and railways made travel to the Continent possible for much larger numbers of people. There were steamers on German rivers from 1816. People gradually became aware of Germany's considerable achievements in literature, music and philosophy, science and technology as the nineteenth century progressed, but the appeal of the landscape and architecture seems to have been slender in comparison with the attractions of France, Italy and Switzerland. Few travellers were acquainted with more than the Rhine valley, Cologne Cathedral, the capital cities of Vienna, Dresden and Berlin and probably one or other of the famous spas of Ems, Langenschwalbach, Wiesbaden or Baden-Baden. By the end of the century, however, the political ascendancy of the German Empire under Prussia had made Germany a power to be reckoned with on the European scene, and the geography books reflected this in their increasingly detailed accounts of the country. While maps of the early nineteenth century displayed few place-names and very rarely any geographical features apart from the main rivers, being preoccupied instead with state borders, maps of the later period give much more information. In books the illustrations become more varied and less schematic. It is as though the century began with a view through a telescope and ended with one through binoculars.

6. *The Swiss Family Robinson*

With *The Swiss Family Robinson* we come to one of the great classics of children's literature in English. This story of a father and mother and their four sons who were wrecked on a desert island in the tropics, encountered all manner of birds, beasts, fish and reptiles as well as plant life and established themselves comfortably there has enjoyed extraordinary popularity for nearly two hundred years. Its combination of adventure, danger and discovery with paternal instruction in botany, zoology and geography made it irresistible to generations of youthful readers. Though Campe's *Robinson der Jüngere* was by far the most successful Robinsonade in Germany, *The Swiss Family Robinson*, German too in origin, outstripped it in success in its various English guises. Brian Alderson estimates that from the late 1840s 'close on three hundred different editions must have been published in England and America'.[49] The title of the book is known to virtually everybody in Britain even today, yet in Germany and even in Switzerland, where the book originated, it is nowadays scarcely known. The book's success in Britain probably owes a great deal to pride in the achievements of British explorers and colonists in the eighteenth and nineteenth centuries and to the growth and consolidation of the Empire during this period. The book may be concerned with a Swiss family, but its experiences could easily be identified with imaginatively by British youngsters. These excited readers may well have had relatives or neighbours scattered across the colonies. They could revel in the exotic dangers and delights of the desert island, knowing that it connected up with the strange and marvellous realities of far-flung British settlements.

The history of *The Swiss Family Robinson* is extraordinarily complex, and

---

49 Brian Alderson in Bettina Hürlimann, *Three Centuries of Children's Books in Europe*, translated and edited by Brian W. Alderson (London: Oxford University Press, 1967), pp. 111-12.

aspects of it still await detailed investigation. Part of the problem lies in the fact that the earliest English editions do not derive directly from the original German text, but from a version made in French by the Swiss Baroness Isabelle de Montolieu (1751-1832), who made a good many changes and additions to it. The earliest editions of the story in all three languages are now rare items and are difficult to find all in one place. The result is that most statements made about them tend to be made on the basis of secondary literature rather than stemming from examination of the original editions. When it comes to editions published after about 1850 the matter is no less complicated, and generalities abound. It might be thought that this is a task not worth undertaking, but a book that has enjoyed such popularity in English over nearly two centuries deserves this kind of attention from some future scholar.

The origins of the book lie in a story written by the Swiss pastor Johann David Wyss (1743-1818) for his four sons. It was written between 1792-98 and consists of some 841 pages in manuscript, together with illustrations. The manuscript is bound in four volumes and was placed on long-term deposit in the Burgerbibliothek in Bern in 1997.[50] This text was edited and slightly adapted by Johann David Wyss's second son, Johann Rudolf Wyss (1781-1830), and published as *Der Schweizerische Robinson, oder der schiffbrüchige Schweizer-Prediger und seine Familie. Ein lehrreiches Buch für Kinder und Kinder-Freunde zu Stadt und Land*. Herausgegeben von Joh. Rudolf Wyß (Zürich: Orell, Füßli und Compagnie, 1812-13) in two volumes (The Swiss Robinson, or the Shipwrecked Swiss Preacher and his Family. An instructive book for children and their friends in town and country. Edited by Joh. Rudolf Wyss). These two volumes covered only half of the original manuscript; the remainder was not published until 1826-27 in a further two volumes. The title-page of volume 1 actually gives the form 'Schweizersche', though at p. 1 it appears as 'Schweitzerische'. Volumes 3 and 4 have the form 'Schweizerische'. Volume 1 contains a frontispiece by H. Lips portraying an extraordinary tree with large spherical fruits on the left, palm-trees with three monkeys on the right and in the background. Father and one son, both armed with a gun and accompanied by a dog, occupy the foreground. Volume 2 contains at the end a map of the island, which has been reproduced in very many subsequent editions of the book.

---

50 For a detailed account of the manuscript see Robert L. Wyss, 'Der Schweizerische Robinson. Seine Entstehung und sein Manuskript', *'Stultifera navis', Mitteilungsblatt der Schweizerischen Bibliophilen-Gesellschaft*, 12. Jahrgang, Nr. 3/4 (Oktober 1955), pp. 122-35.

An advertisement on p. 335 of volume 1 indicates that it was published 'Auf Jubilate', i.e. the third Sunday after Easter. The text is divided into chapters with descriptive headings. Volume 1 contains fourteen chapters, the last headed 'Neue Beute von dem Wrack. Das Floß. Die Schildkröte' (New booty from the wreck. The raft. The turtle). Volume 2 contains chapters 15-28, the last comprising 'Anlegung einer zweyten Meyerey. Kleine Entdeckungen. Das Brot. Die Klause. Neue Benennungen. Arbeiten in der Felsen-Wohnung' (Establishing a second farm. Small discoveries. Bread. The hermitage. Giving new names. Work in the rock dwelling). The story then breaks off without any conclusion, leaving the family still on the island, living in Felsenheim and with no indication of possible rescue. However, at the end of volume 2 an editorial postscript explains how, three or four years after the family was shipwrecked, an English transport ship called *The Adventurer* returning from New Holland (i.e. the south-east part of what we now know as Australia) was blown by a storm to the island. A boat was sent ashore and took the journal of the Swiss family back to the ship, but was prevented from returning to rescue them. The journal was taken to England and from there to Switzerland. The captain was stated to be determined to return to rescue the family.

This was the text that stimulated Madame de Montolieu to produce a French translation. It was entitled *Le Robinson suisse, ou journal d'un père de famille naufragé avec ses enfans. Traduit de l'allemand de M. Wiss; par Mme de Montolieu. Orné de huit fig. En taille douce.* (Paris: Arthus Bertrand, 1814). It was published in four volumes, and there was a fold-out map at the end. Madame de Montolieu divided her text into thirty-six chapters, each with descriptive headings. The content covers the same material as appeared in the twenty-eight chapters of the German original, but with slightly different divisions and some additions, especially at the beginning and the end. The fact that Montolieu's version occupies four volumes while the German has only two is explained simply by differences in font-size and lay-out in the two books.

Montolieu created in her *avant-propos* a narrative and geographical context for the original story. She placed the island on which the Swiss family was wrecked as situated towards the south-west of Java, near the coasts of New Guinea, and the ship is described as the Russian vessel *The Podesda*, commanded by Captain Kreusenstern. Adam Johann von Krusenstern (1770-1846) was an admiral in Russian service and undertook the first Russian voyage round the world in 1803-06. Madame de Montolieu, in transcribing the details of the German editorial postscript, makes two odd mistakes. She talks about *The Adventurer* returning from New Zealand (rather than New Holland) and passing by 'Otaheïti' (Tahiti) to the east (rather than the west) coasts of North America, collecting a cargo of furs there for China and then returning to England via Canton. Such a route is plainly absurd and must be attributed to misreadings of the German text.

We now need to turn to the first English version. This appeared with the title first given as *The Family Robinson Crusoe: or, Journal of a Father Shipwrecked, with his Wife and Children, on an Uninhabited Island. Translated from the German of M. Wiss. In two volumes* (London: M. J. Godwin & Co., 1814). Each volume contains a frontispiece and one further illustration designed by H. Corbould and engraved by Springsguth. Volume 1 shows the family on board the ship in the storm and the landing of the ass, while volume 2 has engravings entitled 'Shooting the Kangaroo' and 'The Family Congregation'. The translation is conjecturally attributed to William Godwin (1756-1836), but it is only 'Translated from the German' at a remove. The *Oxford Companion to Children's Literature* correctly states that 'it also incorporated some of Mme de Montolieu's additions', but closer inspection reveals that the whole book is dependent on Montolieu and not on the German original. The very title-page gives the game away: Montolieu spells the author's name 'Wiss', while the German gives the editor's full name 'Joh. Rudolf Wyß'. The English sub-title follows the French 'journal d'un père naufragé avec ses enfans', though the translator is sufficiently alert to give the wife's presence some credit. The German sub-title refers to the father as a 'Schweizer-Prediger', while neither the French nor the English mentions here that he is a 'preacher'.

Looking at the actual text, we discover that the number and division of chapters of this first English version correspond exactly to those of the first two volumes of Montolieu's French version. This portion of the narrative covers only thirteen of the fourteen chapters in the first volume of the German original. A comparison of the chapter-headings in German, French and English makes it plain that the English is in every instance a translation of the French. Moreover, both the French and the English divide the German chapters 11, 12 and 13 each into two parts with the result that they have sixteen chapters to the German thirteen. If the English translator had worked from the German edition, it would have been bizarre to translate only thirteen of the fourteen chapters contained in the first volume. The fact that the English text corresponds exactly to the French in its division and

The Swiss Family Robinson 83

numbering of chapters makes the claim to be 'Translated from the German of M. Wiss' utterly disingenuous. The further statement at the end of volume 2 of Godwin's publication is also deliberately misleading: 'As soon as the German copy of the Continuation can be procured, the translation of it shall be made and published'. The second volume of the German text had already been published in 1813 and was thus theoretically, if not practically, available. Presumably Godwin had translated the first half of Montolieu's version and was still waiting for the second half.

One of the problems of *The Swiss Family Robinson* from the pedagogical point of view is the fact that the fauna and flora of the island do not match its supposed location on the globe. Animals, birds and plants are mentioned, usually for their utility to the family, as though anything might be found anywhere regardless of latitude or longitude. One early example is the agouti, a native of South America and the West Indies, which most children will only have encountered through *The Swiss Family Robinson*. However, the Swiss author was not particularly concerned about geographical verisimilitude, and Humboldt's investigations into plant and animal ecology still lay in the future. Wyss's aim was to provide not only a lesson in world zoology and botany, but also a practical, moral and religious education for the four sons who listened eagerly to his story. The trials and discoveries of the shipwrecked family were designed to build up to the establishment of a comfortable and civilized form of life that could be seen as a New Switzerland, an ideal of purity and the enjoyment of honest labour. The island was not a real place, and it became increasingly unreal through the additions made by Madame de Montolieu. The hotch-potch of natural life on the island was criticized by Captain Frederick Marryat, who, in the preface to his own Robinsonade *Masterman Ready* (1841-45), declared that 'it does not adhere to the probable, or even the possible'. This defect, however, does not seem to have affected the continuing popularity of Wyss's book in its many forms.

Among the many geographical impossibilities we find in chapter 6 of Montolieu a small incident in which twelve year old Ernest captures a penguin and says: 'Oui, mon père, je crois que mon gibier est une espèce de pinguoin, qu'on pourrait distinguer par le surnom de stupide'. Godwin's translation reads: 'Yes, father, I believe that the bird which I have caught is a kind of penguin, or we might distinguish him by the surname of Stupid'. The German original has nothing about penguins in the corresponding chapter. There is, however, a brief allusion in chapter 2, where the family is making its first landing on the island: 'Nur das widrige Gekrächz verschiedener Pinguine und einiger Flamingos, die wir theils fliegend, theils ruhend auf den Felsenspitzen an der Einfahrt der Bucht erblickten, verstimmte in etwas die Harmonie unserer civilisirten Musicanten'. (Only the repulsive croaking of various penguins and some flamingos that we caught sight of, some flying, some resting on the points of rocks at the entrance to the bay, grated a little against the harmony of our civilized musicians.) This was presumably the passage that prompted Montolieu's amplification, which then became a firm part of the story. The German text was overtaken in popularity by the French and English versions, and when it was revised by Heinrich Kurz after J. R. Wyss's death for the third edition (1841-42), this new detail was incorporated with a slight modification: 'Ja, Vater! sagte Ernst, ich glaube mein Wildpret ist eine Boobie, oder ein Dümmling' (p. 43) (Yes, Father, said Ernst, I think my game is a booby, or a fool). The booby is a kind of gannet, but it is hardly more plausible than a penguin.

There are many more passages in which the French and English early texts differ from the original German, but the English does have occasional independent additions with no correspondence in Montolieu. Thus, in chapter 5 in the passage dealing with breakfast we find:

> All this succeeded vastly well, and we sat down to breakfast, some biscuits and a cocoa-nut shell full of salt butter being placed upon the ground, round which we all assembled, *and none of us failing from time to time to wish for a fairy's wand, to have enabled us to add a little milk from the cow, or from some cocoa-nuts, to quench our thirst*. We *however* toasted our biscuit, and while it was hot applied the butter, and contrived *without the fairy's wand*, to make a hearty breakfast.

The text is modified in the fourth edition (1820) so that the first italicized passage reads: 'from time to time wishing for a fairy's wand, to procure a little milk from the cow, or from some cocoa-nuts, to quench our thirst'. There is no mention of a fairy in Montolieu, and the reference here to a fairy's wand is quite surprising. Perhaps this comes indirectly from Godwin's wife, Mary Jane, who edited and translated *Tabart's Collection of Popular Stories for the Nursery* (1804), which included a variety of French, Italian and English fairytales.[51] In any case, the words italicized in the above quotation were omitted from later revisions of Godwin's edition, at the latest by the ninth edition (1834).

---

51 Marjorie Moon, *Benjamin Tabart's Juvenile Library. A Bibliography of Books for Children Published, Written, Edited and Sold by Mr. Tabart* (Winchester: St. Paul's Bibliographies; Detroit: Omnigraphics, 1990), p. 122.

In the chapter concerned with the Swiss family's change of abode Montolieu adds a comment on women that is taken over by Godwin as follows:

> Women, for their part, never fail to have more things to carry than there are places to put them in, said I, also laughing: however, let us see how handsomely I shall be able to provide for what belongs to you, my love. Fortunately, I had already thought of making the ass's load as light as possible, foreseeing that it would be necessary to carry our little one [i.e. six year old Francis] a part of the way (vol. 2, p. 49).

This addition has a rather more worldly tone than we find in the austere Swiss original, which has little to say about the female sex as a whole. The mother is basically in charge of domestic life, cooking and sewing, and is treated with courtesy and affection by father and sons, but the fact that Johann David Wyss's own family consisted of four sons and no daughters meant that the story centres on the education and adventures of boys alone. The passage quoted above does not figure in the 1834 English edition.

Godwin published the second English edition in 1818 with the new title *The Swiss Family Robinson*, and this included the rest of Montolieu's first French translation. This extended English version seems to have appeared in a variety of editions up to the early 1850s. Certain revisions to the 1814 text are apparent up to the end of chapter 16. For the most part these consist of abridgements of the religious, moral and philosophical passages that are so frequent and striking in Wyss's original text and the first translations. Some idea of the kind of changes may be gained from looking at what happened to a short passage in the opening chapter. The 1814 edition reads:

> Soon after the evening set in: the tempest and the waves continued their fury; the planks and beams of the vessel separated in many parts with a horrible crash. It seemed impossible for the boats, or any one of the persons they contained, to escape the raging of the storm.
>
> Papa, cried my youngest boy, six years old, will not God assist us soon? Hold your tongue, replied his eldest brother. Do you not know that it is our duty not to prescribe to God, but to wait for his assistance with patience and humility?
> Well spoken, my boy, said I; but you should not have reproved your brother so sharply. The eldest instantly ran and kissed the innocent little creature.

The 1820 edition reduces this as follows:

> Soon after, night set in: the tempest and the waves continued their fury; the planks and beams of the vessel separated in many parts with a

> horrible crash. We thought of the boats, and feared that all they contained must have sunk under the foaming surge.

All the rest is omitted. It is not always easy to see why certain verbal alterations were made. Presumably the adapter supposed the new text read more smoothly or easily. The excision of some religious passages was probably concerned with reducing the Calvinistic tenor of the original. The simplification of technical explanations about zoology, botany and mechanics placed a greater emphasis on the adventure aspect of the narrative, playing down slightly the pedagogical tone of the book in favour of the excitement of making ever more discoveries that improve the quality of the shipwrecked family's material situation.

The extended and revised English translation of Montolieu's first edition does not follow it in every particular. To the original sixteen chapters are added a further sixteen, which take the story up to 'Completion of two Farm Houses. – A Lake. – The Beast with a Bill. – A Boat'. However, these do not correspond exactly to Montolieu, who has a total of thirty-six chapters. Not only are there differences in chapter divisions, but the English text omits Montolieu's chapter 25, 'Nouvelle excursion; le Vin de palmier' (New excursion; palm wine), and chapter 28, 'Origine de quelques arbres fruitiers européens' (Origin of certain European fruit-trees). The reason is probably that alcohol was regarded with disfavour and that the treatise on European fruit-trees was considered an unnecessary digression. The father's journal ends thus:

> Nearly two years have elapsed without our perceiving the smallest trace of civilized or savage man; without the appearance of a single vessel or canoe upon the vast sea by which we are surrounded. Ought we then to indulge a hope that we shall once again behold the face of a fellow-creature? We encourage serenity and thankfulness in each other, and wait with resignation the event!

There then follows the 'Postscript by the editor' explaining about Captain Johnson and *The Adventurer*.

Meanwhile, Madame de Montolieu had not remained idle. She had dedicated her original translation to her three grandsons and two great-nephews, and it appears that their enthusiasm and that of other young French readers led the baroness into penning a continuation of the story. In this way an extended French text by Montolieu actually predates the authentic German continuation that Johann Rudolf Wyss brought out in two further volumes only in 1826-27. This German second edition simply adds these two new volumes to those already published in 1812-13 and appends various editorial comments. In the preface to volume 4 Wyss alludes to the greater popularity of the work in France and England than either Switzerland or Germany and then comments on the Montolieu edition:

> Bey der französischen [Ausgabe] sind die Verdienste der Verfasserin, Frau von Montolieu nicht gering, sie hat die Erzählung mit manchem Zuge bereichert, Einiges hinzugesetzt, den Ton auf die französische Jugend gestellt, und endlich das Ganze mit einer Fortsetzung bedacht, die viel Vortreffliches enthält. (In the French [edition] the merits of the author, Madame de Montolieu, are not small; she has enriched the tale with many details, made additions, adapted the tone to suit French youngsters and, lastly, provided the whole with a continuation that contains many excellent things.)

A little further on Wyss mentions that the English translation is dependent on the French, as was also the Italian. He refers to the fact that the English edition contains notes on natural history taken for the most part from the French. He also observes that they are furnished with more copper-plates than the German edition, but that they all lack scientific illustrations, which actually would be the most useful. In this respect the German edition of 1841-42 (which came after J. R. Wyss's death) was a considerable improvement. Even so, many of the illustrations depict incidents in the story, and those that portray animals, birds, plants, etc. do not identify their subjects by name.

It was not until 1849 that an English version of the second part of the original narrative appeared, ending with the discovery of another castaway, the young Emily, alias Edward Montrose – she is called Jenny in the German text – and the arrival of *The Unicorn*, Captain Littleton and the Wolston family, who provide the means for the oldest and the youngest of the four brothers to sail back to Europe. Judging from the number of chapters and their length, this is probably based on the German edition of 1826-27, since the edition of 1840-41 has fewer, but much longer chapters. When the two parts were published in one volume in 1852, many of the Swiss author's allusions and disquisitions were omitted and the number of chapters was reduced. Both the German and the English texts include the episode of the boa constrictor which kills the family's ass, an episode that is generally credited to Madame de Montolieu.

It is clear from this survey of the early German, French and English editions that Wyss's story was subject to constant textual changes. Naturally enough, personal names were adapted, but only minimally with Ernst and Franz, who became Ernest and Francis, while Fritz and Jack (Jakob) retained their German forms. Perhaps more interestingly the two dogs, Türk and Bill, became Turk and Ponto in 1814, with Ponto being renamed Flora, certainly by the fourth edition. By the time of the sixth edition in 1826 Wyss's name had disappeared from the title-page. It was, of course, a source of future confusions with later publishers that the book was written by J. D. Wyss and edited by J. R. Wyss, so the book may on occasion be attributed to a non-existent J. D. R. Wyss. But the omission of the author's name is a plain enough signal that the story has become the English equivalent of an anonymous *Volksbuch*. What matters here is the story, and that can be manipulated, abridged or amplified, and details can be changed without any consultation with the author. Most English readers of today know the title of the book, but it's doubtful how high a proportion will know the author's name. Indeed, they will be completely unaware of the multiplicity of forms in which the story has circulated. How many will have any idea that in 1869 Mary Godolphin produced a version in words of one syllable? (She did this also for *Robinson Crusoe*.)

Mary Jane Godwin's edition of *The Swiss Family Robinson* was taken over by the firm of Baldwin, Cradock, and Joy by the sixth edition of 1826 (possibly earlier). By the time of the thirteenth edition (1848) it was being published by the combined firms of Simpkin, Marshall, and Co., Whittaker and Co. and Houlston and Stoneman. From the mid century onwards more and more publishers muscled in on the book's popularity and produced a great variety of texts. These included not simply modifications of the well-known version, but also new translations based on material that had not been available to Godwin. A full German text had been available from 1826-27, but new versions in French also played an important role. Because the English forms feed on both German and French versions of varying provenance, the bibliography of Wyss's book continues to be intricate, if not unfathomable, for most of the nineteenth century.

The Halifax firm of Milner and Sowerby even went so far as to have two quite distinct texts of *The Swiss Family Robinson* on its list. One appears to be a hybrid of Wyss and Montolieu and was published in the firm's 'Cottage Library' cheap format in 1859. There may have been an earlier edition.[52] The other, dated 1862, follows the pattern of Wyss's first two volumes,

---

52 Rowan Gibbs, *The Swiss Family Robinson, Book Catalogue* (Wellington, New Zealand: Rowan Gibbs; Smith's Bookshop Ltd, 1997), no. 326.

including the section on palm-tree wine that Godwin had omitted, then giving the 'Postscript by the editor', after which comes the 'Continuation of the journal', consisting of chapters 36-48. This second part derives from Montolieu's continuation, which gives a quite different story from texts based on Wyss's third and fourth volumes of 1826-27. It is more concerned with adventure than with further discoveries in natural history. It focusses first of all on an accident that befalls the mother and on the devotion that the sons display towards her. Later, mother and Francis disappear, but are eventually discovered in the care of missionaries and a tribe of savages. This version concludes with the arrival of a ship commanded by Captain Krusenstern and with the Zurich astronomer Horner on board. Ernest, the most passionate scientist among the four sons, departs with the ship, anxious to make observations concerned with the transit of Venus. The rest of the family remain in contentment on the island. The leader of the missionary team is called Willis, and he provided the focus for a continuation of the story by Adrien Paul called *Le Pilote Willis* (1855), of which an English translation was published in 1857 by C. H. Clarke.

French books continued to provide material for further developments in the history of *The Swiss Family Robinson*. In 1841 Madame Elise Voïart produced a new French translation entitled *Le Robinson suisse*, with an introduction by Charles Nodier (Paris: Lavigne, 1841), which was then translated into English by W. H. D. Adams (London, Edinburgh and New York: T. Nelson & Sons, 1870). The prologue gives the father of the family the surname Starck (German for 'strong') and names the sons as Frederick (15), Ernest (13), Rudly (12) (the diminutive for Rudolph is presumably an acknowledgement of Johann Rudolf Wyss's part in editing the original work) and 'Little Fritz' (8). The shipwreck takes place between Le Havre and Philadelphia round about lat. 40 degrees N., so the island is situated quite differently from that in the German original or the one in *Robinson Crusoe*. That is presumably Madame Voïart's doing. The translation is stated to be unabridged. The book is copiously illustrated with black and white engravings.

A further French translation was made by Pierre-Jules Stahl (pen-name of P. J. Hetzel) as *Le Nouveau Robinson suisse* (Paris, 1864), and this was translated and edited by John Lovell with the customary title of *The Swiss Family Robinson* (London, Paris, and New York: Cassell, Petter, & Galpin, [1869]). The preface indicates that the work has been 'entirely remodelled', largely to cut out things that the editor had learnt that young readers did not like, such as the father's occasionally inadequate responses to the questions of young minds, and the youngsters' cruelty to animals and lack of tenderness towards their mother. It is clear from remarks of this kind that people in the latter half of the nineteenth century were aware that moral positions occupied at the beginning of the century were not necessarily their own and that aspects of the text needed to be altered accordingly. The basic thrust of the book, however, still remained relevant and attractive.

From 1870 onwards new editions proliferated. The German text was adapted by J. Bonnet (Bielefeld: Velhagen & Klasing, 1872), and this was translated anonymously (London: James Nisbet & Co., 1877). The pastor father is given the name Vetli, while the boys differ from their originals in that Ernest is the oldest at 16, Fritz is 14, Jack 8 and Franz 6. An odd connexion with *Robinson Crusoe* is made through Fritz seeing a man's footprint in the sand the day after their arrival. This links up with the end of the book, when Jack is abducted by savages and then rescued by the help of an Italian called Auferi, who had been shipwrecked twelve years previously and had become the chief of a native tribe. Many of the natives are killed in the rescue process. Later, a ship called the *Maritana* arrives and takes Ernest and Jack to Europe, though four years later Ernest returns to the island with a wife.

Among other English versions we have to note new translations by Mrs H. B. Paull (London: Frederick Warne & Co., 1877) and H. Frith (London: Ward, Lock, 1878); edited versions by the noted writer of boys' books W. H. G. Kingston (London: George Routledge & Sons, 1879) and Alfonzo Gardiner (Manchester: John Heywood, 1887); a severely reduced format by Julia S. E. Rae (London: Trischler & Company, 1891); and another edited version by Geraldine Edith Mitton (London: A. & C. Black, 1907). Finally, a text appeared in 'Everyman's Library' (London: J. M. Dent & Sons Ltd; New York: E. P Dutton & Co., 1910) that continued to be reprinted right into the second half of the century. Unsurprisingly (or should it be surprisingly?), this text derives from one of the editions of the 1850s in which the two halves of Wyss's narrative are first combined. It cannot be the Simpkin, Marshall, & Co. edition of 1852, as that does not contain the incident with the bears (beginning of chapter 48 in 'Everyman's Library'), which is present in the German text. Just which edition it comes from is difficult to ascertain. This is an apt illustration of the problems that the bibliography of *The Swiss Family Robinson* involves. Many editions cannot easily be located in public collections, so it often proves impossible to find the information needed

10. *The Swiss Family Robinson* [by 1883].
The donkey and the boa constrictor.

in order to establish the full derivation of a particular text. Publishers of popular children's books are notorious for failing to indicate the origins of their texts (unless they are new) and for omitting dates of publication. Editions of *The Swiss Family Robinson* exemplifying all these problems have continued to be published throughout the twentieth century, but they are outside the purview of this study.

With its proliferation of new editions adapted from both German and French versions of the book, the late nineteenth century was the heyday of English forms of this celebrated Swiss story. It had more or less ousted Campe's *Robinson the Younger,* and the diverse forms in which it was cast were frequently reprinted. Kingston's version seems to have been particularly successful. For us of more than a century later, it requires a considerable effort of the historical imagination to understand just why *The Swiss Family Robinson* was so popular. Geoffrey Trease, writing in 1948, says:

Persistently pious, indigestibly didactic, it should logically have died long ago. Yet Alison Uttley says she read it seven times in succession, and even today, in a poll of 'Most Popular Books' among secondary schoolboys in New Zealand, it comes out above *King Solomon's Mines* and *The Broad Highway*.[53]

Didacticism was a prevalent feature of eighteenth- and nineteenth-century children's books (and it still plays an important role in the twentieth century, though often more subtly), but Trease also said: 'I am not so sure that the didactic story worries the child as much as the adult. Has there ever been a more blatant example than *The Swiss Family Robinson*?'[54] What carries the young reader along is the story with its incidents of adventure and discovery, dangers successfully negotiated and tasks completed that lead to an increasingly comfortable and varied life. But the facts, the discoveries of the abundant resources and variety of the natural world, are integral to the book. The science and geography lessons that it contains are of its essence. If the omniscient father's explanations were too lengthy for some readers, they could be skipped. Certainly, the religious and moralizing passages were subject to abbreviation or omission as, with the passage of time, they no longer corresponded to the views of the new era.

At the core of *The Swiss Family Robinson* there is the family. For the book's young readers the four boys would be the characters with whom they would identify. They are skilfully differentiated. Fritz, the eldest, is 'a handsome, curl-pated (*sic*) youth, full of intelligence and vivacity'. Ernest is 'of a rational, reflecting temper, well-informed for his age, but somewhat disposed to indolence and the pleasures of the senses'; he is the scientist in the family. Jack is 'a light-hearted, enterprising, audacious, generous lad, about ten years old', while Francis is 'a lovely boy six years old, remarkable for the sweetest and happiest temper, and for his affection to his parents' (1834 edition, p. 17). This variety allows for a multiplicity of exploits to suit their ages. Moreover, as the family is able to take or retrieve a mass of tools and equipment from the wrecked ship, they are able to establish dwellings at Falcon's Nest (Falkenhorst), Tent House (Zeltheim) and Rockhouse (Felsenheim). What child could resist the idea of living in a large house up a tree? The family's possession of guns allows them to kill dangerous or even simply inconvenient animals and birds. For modern sensibilities, they are worryingly trigger-happy. Their colonization of the island involves a

---

53 Geoffrey Trease, *Tales out of School* (London: The New Education Book Club, 1948), p. 23.
54 Ibid., p. 63.

conquest of nature; their relationship is one of opposition and exploitation. But if one compares the Swiss family with either Defoe's or Campe's Robinson Crusoe, their positions clearly reflect the difference between early eighteenth-century and early nineteenth-century manifestations of colonial settlement. The family's achievement is to establish an island Arcadia, a self-sufficient economy and life-style, not simply to survive in basic circumstances. Is it any wonder that father and mother elect to stay there when *The Unicorn* provides an opportunity to return to Europe? The island is a romance-free zone, so Fritz has to leave it when the possibility of such a relationship with Jenny (Emily) Montrose arises. Francis, the youngest, leaves because he feels the need for a larger society in which to develop his talents and also because he thinks a member of the family ought to keep the connexion with Old Switzerland alive.

The role of the mother is perhaps the least satisfactory aspect of the book. The father refers to her as 'my excellent wife' and 'my good Elizabeth', but, as in a fairytale, she has no independent existence apart from her two capacities of wife and mother, and it is as a mother-figure that she is most important. As the boys' mother she presides over all their domestic arrangements, and in return the boys show her respect and devotion. The book, after all, centres on their exploits, not hers, though she often produces the solution to practical problems.

The Swiss family's island is the setting for an experiment in living in the smallest kind of community – the family. It is educational rather than true to nature and geography. Increasingly, later versions of the story found it necessary to state in editorial introductions that many features of this tropical island do not correspond to geographical reality. With this they made it explicit that the book was not to be understood simply as a disguised textbook, but rather as a work of imagination with roots in both adventure and exploration. Its moral qualities are a reflection of the age in which it was written and were no more than parents (and perhaps children) expected.

7. Moral, Didactic and Religious Tales

From the end of the eighteenth century to at least the middle of the nineteenth the dominant pattern of children's literature in the British Isles was didactic. Fairytales and traditional chapbook romances were distractingly popular, but the leaders of educational opinion inveighed against them as superstitious, untruthful, pernicious, misleading and immoral. The sober middle classes required their children to be socialized, taught how to behave properly towards other people of whatever status and to internalize the virtues that made for a harmonious and orderly society. As we have already seen, German writers such as Campe and Salzmann formed part of this programme, and Campe's books continued to be read and reprinted during the early part of the nineteenth century. Many more German authors of this kind were translated into English during this period. Some of them were named, but very frequently the title-pages or prefaces of these new books content themselves with the bare words 'translated from the German'. It is thus not always easy or even possible to identify either authors or specific tales. One can only speculate about the reasons that led publishers to be so vague about the sources of their material. Most probably they were attempting to evade copyright and making payment to the German publishers and authors. But they may also have reasoned that the author's name would have meant nothing to the British reader, unless he or she was famous. Nonetheless, the fact that so many books contain the words 'translated from the German' indicates that German authorship was a significant factor in marketing them. No doubt children's books profited from the considerable attraction that Goethe, Schiller, Tieck, Fouqué and many of their contemporaries had for British readers.

Too many German books of a moral or didactic kind were translated into English in the nineteenth century for all of them to be considered or even noted here. Posterity has not dealt very kindly with them. Most simply reflect the social expectations of their day and have no special historical or literary merits that single them out from the mass of well-meaning, but mediocre children's fiction. Books whose chief purpose is to promote a strong line of moral conduct do not generally survive changes in social attitudes. They would need a strong plot, memorable and sympathetic characters and a compelling literary style to transcend such changes. These qualities, however, are not usually in strong supply in our period. The publishing history of many titles points up considerable differences between the perceptions of the nineteenth century and those of our own times. Books which now seem shallow, conventional and over-simplified may have been very popular in their own day.

In 1805 Darton and Harvey published *Tales for Children, in a Familiar Style* by Maria Joseph Crabb. The preface concludes: 'Most of the subjects are taken from the German'. However, there is no indication as to which of the thirty short tales for small children were taken from the German and whether one or more German authors were used. All the stories demonstrate the unfortunate effects of childish disobedience, selfishness or carelessness. These effects constitute the children's punishment, and the parents do not punish their children themselves, but forgive them since they have now learnt their lesson. Though the stories are taken from German sources, the children's names are all anglicized, as they were with Wollstonecraft's translation of Salzmann.

The story entitled 'The New Year's Gift' reflects the traditions of a German Christmas Eve, but has been transposed to New Year's Day to fit in with contemporary English practice. Only a few years later E. T. A. Hoffmann will give a comparable account of German Christmas celebrations in his *Nußknacker und Mausekönig*, but without the didactic elements. Crabb has a further story that can be contrasted with another famous children's tale. 'The Children who Played with Fire' provides an earnest warning to children. Five-year-old James places some pieces of paper on the fire, but as it does not blaze quickly enough his four-year-old sister Charlotte fans it with the corner of her frock, which then catches fire. Charlotte's mother comes in response to the children's screams and rescues her, but the child is badly burnt. Crabb furnishes a daunting description: 'One side of her face was quite without any skin; her hair was burnt almost all off her head; and

Moral, Didactic and Religious Tales 97

one of her arms was all over large blisters' (p. 47). Forty years later Heinrich Hoffmann dealt with the same theme in a comic, but more drastic fashion in his rhyming tale of Paulinchen (in English, Harriet) and the matches. There Paulinchen burns to ashes. It may have been Crabb's source that Hoffmann was parodying, but the worry that parents have about children playing with fire or matches is so prevalent that Hoffmann would not have needed a particular source for his blackly comic verse tale.

Crabb's collection of German moral tales reached a seventh edition in 1831 (London: Darton & Harvey), so its brand of realistic short tale reflecting the day-to-day possibilities of a small child's life clearly enjoyed some popularity, though probably more with parents than with children themselves. Maria Joseph Crabb was the wife of George Crabb (1778-1851), who went to Bremen in 1801 to teach English. He had previously published *A Complete Introduction to the Knowledge of the German Language* (London: C. Whittingham, second edition, 1799) and on his return to England published several further books on German language and literature. The preface to Maria's *Tales for Children* is dated Bremen, April 29, 1809.

The firm of Darton in its various guises published quite a number of children's books taken from German sources. In 1814 Darton, Harvey, and Darton published *Gustavus; or, the Macaw,* which had the subtitle 'A story to teach children the proper value of things'. Neither author nor translator was named in the book, but the author was Gottlob Eusebius Fischer (born 1769) and the book's German title was *Gustav oder der Papagey* (Leipzig: Leo, 1795). This is a story in fifteen chapters centring on Gustavus, the ten-year-old son of a country minister, and his pet macaw. Gustavus's father does not forbid him to buy the macaw, but points out various moral problems: Is it moral to keep a bird in a cage? Is it not an indulgence? Later Gustavus is shamed that he values his macaw more highly than his friend Jacob, who comes to him in distress because he hasn't sufficient money for his school fees. If Gustavus hadn't bought the macaw, he could have helped Jacob instead. Gustavus goes with his father on a walking trip to Leipsic, where they meet a merchant who is so impressed with the minister's educational ideas that he proposes giving him his own son to educate. In their absence the minister's house burns down, but Jacob manages to save the macaw and takes it to the nearest town to sell it. On his return he discovers a purse with a lot of money inside, and coincidentally it turns out to have been lost by the merchant whom Gustavus and his father met in Leipsic. The merchant allows Mr Liebworth, the minister, to dispose of the money, and he reserves it for Jacob, whose father had died while he was away. The minister is helped by his affectionate parishioners, a new house is built for him, and the merchant's son arrives for his education. The story is chock-a-block with episodes that provide Gustavus with moral lessons, the macaw especially being seen as a symbol of reprehensible desires and self-centredness that distract its owner from being supportive and helpful to others.

In comparing the range of moral, didactic and religious tales written by German authors with those by British and Irish writers, it is readily apparent that most of the Germans are male and clergymen while most of the English-speaking authors are female and thus members of the laity. The majority of the German writers were Protestant, but there were Catholic writers too, as we shall see later. The earlier writers were deeply indebted to the thinkers of the Enlightenment and tended to keep their theology in check, restricting themselves to matters of common moral concern. However, with changes in the religious climate, especially the advent of Evangelical ideas and piety, the temper of moral and didactic children's literature was also affected.

One of the earliest German clerical writers to give voice to specifically religious concerns was the theologian Friedrich Adolf Krummacher (1767-1845), whose name and work crop up in a variety of contexts as a writer for children. Krummacher was well known for his *Parables*, brief tales or anecdotes about a variety of topics that children could relate to from their daily lives, the world around them and the Bible. Several selections were published in English up to the 1860s, beginning with a translation by F. Shoberl (London: R. Ackermann, 1824) and another by Miss F. Johnston (London and Brighton, 1839). As late as March 1906 W. T. Stead published a collection entitled *Parables for Little People* as no. 121 of his *Books for the Bairns*. These *Parables* were much more varied and open in character than the writings of his son, Friedrich Wilhelm Krummacher (1796-1845), several of whose sermons and Biblical works were translated into English, apparently for children. Typical of them was one entitled *The Infant Saviour; the Ransomed of the Lord; and the Flying Roll* (London: B. Wertheim, 1837). The section headed 'The Infant Saviour' dealt with the nativity theme under five heads – 'In the Stable and the Manger', 'In the Arms of his Mother', 'In the Glory on the Field', 'In the Message of the Angels' and 'In the Heart of the Poor Sinner'. The younger Krummacher was far more Evangelical than his father.

A further little book by Friedrich Adolf enjoyed comparable popularity to his *Parables*. This was *Das Täubchen* (1828), which was immediately translated into English by Ann Steinkopff as *The Little Dove. A Story for Children, Founded on Fact* (London: Harvey & Darton, 1828). The story is based on episodes from the childhood of the real life Adelbert Count von der Recke-Volmerstein (1791-1878), who, as a result of encountering destitute children after the Napoleonic wars, founded an institution to care for and educate them. This was situated first at his family home at Overdyk, near Bochum, but in 1822 it moved to Düsselthal, near Düsseldorf, and, when visited by an English traveller in 1826, was looking after one hundred and twenty boys and one hundred and seventeen girls. Its fame grew over the years, and a short description of it is included in the 1860 edition of Murray's *Handbook for Travellers on the Continent: being a Guide to Holland, Belgium, Prussia, Northern Germany, and the Rhine from Holland to Switzerland*. In the English book the young count is called Alfred rather than Adelbert, and Volmerstein is omitted from his family name. The incident that gives *The Little Dove* its title centres on the young Alfred's rescue of a baby dove from drowning in a pond, but the little book contains several other episodes that show the boy going to the assistance of poor and distressed families as well as suffering animals and birds. A new edition was published by Charles Gilpin, taken from Dean and Son c. 1854. Another translation, 'by a lady', was published with the title *Alfred and the Little Dove* (Edinburgh: Johnstone, Hunter & Co.; London: Hamilton, Adams, & Co.).

The social circumstances described in *The Little Dove* recur scores of times in nineteenth-century children's books. Honest and hard-working children are afflicted by poverty through the death or illness of parents. They bear their fate as best they can, trusting in prayer and God's mercy, and are helped back on to their feet through the unexpected kindness of a well-to-do person, generally a member of the aristocracy. The message to the poor is 'Be patient and hopeful, be cheerful in adversity and trust in God'. It is the responsibility of the aristocracy and the comfortably off to help those in distress by providing a modicum of financial or material assistance. This pattern is repeated time and again. The heroes and heroines of the stories naturally survive and are happy, but the social conditions brought about by war, disease, exploitation, failure of crops, physical accident and inadequate medical care are never globally addressed. The haphazard kindly acts of individual wealthy people do not seem an adequate response to the ongoing situation. Count von der Recke-Volmerstein's establishment

11. Title-page and frontispiece of *The Little Dove: a Story for Children, Founded on Fact. New Edition* (c. 1854).

12. Title-page and frontispiece of *Little Swiss Seppeli; or Confidence in God Rewarded. A True Story Translated from the German* (1829).

Moral, Didactic and Religious Tales 101

of the Düsselthal Institution, providing education and training for destitute youngsters, was an important step in the right direction, but nineteenth-century children's fiction still concentrated on individual rather than institutional or political responses to the sufferings of the poor, especially the rural poor.

Only a year later, in 1829, Harvey and Darton published another German book with a similar message. This was *Little Swiss Seppeli; or, Confidence in God Rewarded*, presented as another true story. It concerns two brothers, Seppeli and Fridolin, the eldest of nine children, whose parents send them from their home in Toggenburg to try to sell laces to earn money in a time of great scarcity. The children have been taught to pray regularly and trust in God and been told not to stay away longer than a fortnight. Fridolin returns home, but Seppeli decides to look for a job as a shepherd boy. His artless, innocent demeanour makes people treat him kindly, and his fervent sincerity in prayer elicits admiration and assistance. Eventually this leads him to find a home and a different position with a baron and baroness on an island in the Lake of Constance. There he also learns to read. When Seppeli declares his desire to visit his parents, the baron and baroness give him new clothes, provisions and money to take with him. Seppeli's parents are delighted at his good fortune. His father accompanies him on the return journey and is cordially welcomed by the baron and baroness. A warm, supportive relationship between the noble couple and the peasant family thus ensues. Differences of social status are bridged by innocence, simplicity of heart and a profound trust that God will provide. The result is a story that readers found 'striking and affecting', as the opening pages indicate. The original story was written by the Catholic parish priest Franz Sales Meyer (1786-1818), but the English book does not mention the author's name. The events took place in 1817, a year of famine in Switzerland, and Meyer must have written his story immediately since he died the year after.

Before we go on to look at the two major writers of moral and religious tales for children, there is one further book that we need to consider that had an extraordinary impact in both Britain and America. In German it is called *Das Mährchen ohne Ende*, in English *The Story Without an End*, and it was written by Friedrich Wilhelm Carové (1789-1852), a private scholar with particular interests in Catholicism and its relationship to other religious groups. The book has only a tenuous narrative line, focussing on a child who makes his way through a paradisal landscape of flowers, insects, birds and other small creatures. It can be seen as anticipating Hans

Christian Andersen's 'Tommelise' ('Thumbelina') and other tales in which he dilates on the miracles of the natural world, but Carové is a sentimental moralist, not a quirky genius who can mingle humour and melancholy to lasting effect. Carové's little child is at first alone in a hut with simply a bed and a looking-glass. No other children or adults approach him. The birds refer to him as 'our dear little prince', and the dragonfly calls him 'lord and king of all the flowers'. All the flowers and creatures he meets are anthropomorphized (this is also the case with Andersen). In the course of the story various moral lessons are imparted to the young child. The natural world is a source of wonder. Conceitedness and pride are to be avoided, faithfulness, love, contentment and humility to be embraced. No creature should be despised for being different from oneself. With the sky above and water below, the mind carries pictures that are permanent. The child recognizes the importance of light to life and appreciates the silence of the night. Trickery, self-love, jeering and envy are all to be shunned. *The Story Without an End* is a celebration of firm values, life seen through the innocent eyes of a child.

I have not been able to discover when *Das Mährchen ohne Ende* was first published. No separate printing of it is recorded in the *Gesamtverzeichnis des deutschen Schrifttums*. The story was first translated into English by one of the most distinguished translators from German of the day, Sarah Austin, and she dedicated the book to her daughter, who had so enjoyed it and regretted that it was not longer. It was published with illustrations by William Harvey (London: Effingham Wilson, 1834). Further editions with Harvey's engravings were published c. 1840 and 1864, this latter edition by Virtue Bros. Austin's translation then gained its most sumptuous treatment at the hands of the Hon. Eleanor Vere Boyle, who provided the story with fifteen full-page colour illustrations, superbly printed by Leighton Bros. (London: Sampson Low & Co., 1868; reprinted 1874). Eleanor Vere Boyle (1825-1916) worked using simply the initials E. V. B. and took inspiration from the work of Holman Hunt and Millais. *The Story Without an End* is her most famous book, and her pictures certainly complement the gentle dreaminess of Carové's text. Two further editions illustrate the great diversity of publishers' approaches to the story. An edition by Wells Gardner, Darton & Co. in 1899 is a miniature book with monochrome pictures by Aimée G. Clifford, while Duckworth and Co. in 1912 return to full-colour illustrations by Frank C. Papé (1878-1972). While Boyle's pictures of the child, all fully clothed, are of chubby, rather girlish-looking

Moral, Didactic and Religious Tales 103

infants, Papé's mainly portray a naked, somewhat older boy. This seems to be the last treatment of Carové's story. Its late Romantic idyllic view of childhood did not survive the changes brought about by the First World War, though my copy of the Papé edition has inscribed on the title-page 'Mummy loved this tale all her life. 1934'.

The authors that we have so far considered in this chapter have for the most part made their mark on British children's literature through a single book. Of these *The Story Without an End* was clearly the most successful, to judge by the length of time the book was available in several different editions. We now, however, come to a German author of religious tales whose success in Britain and America was phenomenal – Christoph von Schmid (1768-1854).[55] One of his books in particular, *The Basket of Flowers*, is known in more than 125 separate editions,[56] but a considerable number of his other books were also translated into English and widely distributed. He was born Johann Christoph Schmid, the eldest of nine children, in Dinkelsbühl and studied theology at the Episcopal University in Dillingen from 1785 to 1791. After being ordained priest in the Roman Catholic Church he combined school-teaching with parochial responsibilities in Thannhausen an der Mindel, about thirty kilometres west of Augsburg. It was here that he wrote or conceived the ideas for very many of his books for children. In 1816 he moved to Oberstadion, near Ulm, until in 1827 he was inducted as canon of Augsburg Cathedral. In 1837 he was created a knight of the Order of Merit of the Bavarian Crown, an honour which entitled him to use 'von' with his surname.

Schmid published his first book for children in 1797, but his first real success came in 1810 with *Genovefa*, the retelling of a well-known legend. There are at least two American translations of this text (1832 and c. 1872), and Milner and Sowerby published it in Britain in 1859. In 1816 there appeared the story for which Schmid is most celebrated in Germany – *Die Ostereier*, of which an English translation was published as *The Easter Eggs* (1829). Then followed a spate of further children's stories, with *Das Blumenkörbchen* (*The Basket of Flowers*) coming in 1823. A bibliography of his works in German lists some sixty-three separate items published in his

---

55 Most of what follows on Schmid and *The Basket of Flowers* is taken from David Blamires, 'Christoph von Schmid's Religious Tales for Children: German and English Versions', *Bulletin of the John Rylands University Library of Manchester*, 76, 3 (Autumn 1994), pp. 69-82.
56 See Anne Renier, *The Basket of Flowers by Christoph von Schmid: a Checklist of Copies in the Renier Collection* (Stroud: The Thimble Press, 1972).

lifetime. Schmid seems everywhere to have been a greatly loved personality, much concerned with children and a teaching ministry focussed on them. A monument was erected to his memory in Dinkelsbühl in 1859.

By and large Schmid's stories are set in an unspecified past. *Genovefa* is medieval in its retelling of the legend of Genevieve of Brabant, which is actually a christianized version of the secular tale of the Queen of France and the faithless marshal whose amorous advances she repulses, only to find her husband does not believe her. The events of *Gottfried, der junge Einsiedler* (1829; *Godfrey, the Little Hermit*, 1853), which in essence is a Christian Robinsonade, are said to have taken place several hundred years ago. *Wie Heinrich von Eichenfels zur Erkenntnis Gottes kam* (1817; *Little Henry*, translated from the French of M. Lambert, London: J. Harris & Son, 1823)[57] and *Das Blumenkörbchen* recount events from the beginning of the eighteenth century, *Der Weihnachtsabend* (1825; *Christmas Eve*, 1843) from the middle of it. *Ludwig, der kleine Auswanderer* (1834; *Louis, the Little Emigrant*, Baltimore, 1841) is located in the period of the French Revolution and its aftermath.

Schmid's stories for children enjoyed an immense popularity for most of the nineteenth century, and not only in German-speaking countries. Translations of individual tales appeared in most of the languages of Europe, extending to Icelandic, Welsh, Finnish, Romansch and Maltese. Some tales were even translated into Arabic. There were also editions published in German and English in the United States and in Portuguese in Brazil. How are we to account for this widespread success?

Reading a number of Schmid's tales in succession, one quickly becomes aware of recurrent features and patterns of narration. The typical structure presents an initial idyllic situation followed by an unexpected reversal of fortune and a period of suffering or deprivation, in which the protagonist learns to recognize God's goodness even in times of adversity. At the lowest point of expectation the protagonist is rescued from distress, generally by an unforeseen positive response to a spontaneous, unselfconscious act of goodness or bravery by the protagonist. The story then ends with the re-establishment of happiness, in which justice is tempered with mercy, wickedness is banished and forgiveness is the order of the day. The structure is analogous to that of the traditional fairytale, though with Schmid there is no recourse to magic helpers or to miraculous divine intervention. Where coincidence provides a resolution of the story, it is carefully rationalized

---

57 See Andrea Immel, 'Corrigendum to Moon's *John Harris's Books for Youth*: a Translation from Christoph von Schmid', *Papers of the Bibliographical Society of America*, 77 (1983), pp. 473-75.

and made factually plausible. In contrast to the fairytale, the conclusion of the story does not usually put forward a radical change in the protagonist's original circumstances, nor is there a transformation of personality. The kitchen-maid does not marry a prince. The peasant doesn't marry a princess and acquire a kingdom. The social order remains static. The character is changed morally rather than socially.

Despite the occurrence of misfortune, injustice and wickedness, Schmid's tales are always ultimately reassuring and optimistic. He himself was a child of the Enlightenment, so his Christian teaching is infused with the spirit of rational humanism. His characters do not rail at the body-blows life deals them, but are more likely to discern God's goodness in the lesser things they still enjoy. Acts of kindness are always rewarded, though the reward may come unexpectedly after a long period of suffering or destitution. Though Schmid acknowledges the existence of evil and wickedness, his emphasis is Leibnizian in always perceiving a positive lesson in whatever happens. If Henry of Eichenfels had not been abducted by a gipsy woman and not spent his infancy incarcerated in a robbers' cave, he would not have experienced the outside world and nature as the breathtaking marvels he sees when he escapes into the light. He would have taken everything for granted. The plot-structure of *How Little Henry came to the Knowledge of God* is designed so that Schmid can present the child as an innocent observer of the wonders of the world and the strangeness of human behaviour. Through his experience of nature and the assumption of a controlling intelligence behind, for example, the movement of the sun and the clouds, Henry is led by the wise hermit Menrad to an understanding of God as the invisible Creator.

Schmid's presentation of Christianity is remarkable in that it contains little that is specifically Catholic. He is largely unconcerned with dogma or the distinguishing features of Catholicism. The Virgin Mary and the saints play no role in his stories. God the benevolent Creator tends to figure more prominently than Jesus, the Saviour who suffered for humanity on the cross. When Schmid's characters go to church the terminology used is non-specific, e.g. the word *Gottesdienst*, 'divine service', is used rather than *Messe*, 'mass'. Probably the most distinctively Catholic elements are to be found in *The Easter Eggs*, where the heroine Rosalind frequently resorts to a chapel for prayer, and in the figure of the hermit that crops up in a number of tales. We have already encountered the hermit Menrad with *Little Henry*, while the entire story of *Godfrey, the Little Hermit* centres on the hermit life that the shipwrecked boy, Godfrey, is forced to lead. Similarly, the life of the Countess Genevieve and her infant son in the wilderness is equivalent to that of a hermit. Schmid invests the hermit figure with a certain idealized attractiveness. The solitary individual in tune with God and nature, free from the temptations of a worldly life, is a very positive figure for him. At the end of *Little Henry* Menrad cannot be prevailed upon by the Count to stay at his castle, but returns to his hermitage to devote himself entirely to God.

The Christian content of Schmid's stories centres chiefly on piety and morals rather than on matters of belief. Parents bring up their children to thank God for all his gifts and to accept suffering and misfortune without rancour. They should turn constantly to God in prayer, the efficacy of which is demonstrated time and time again. At the opening of *Christmas Eve* (1843) the eight-year-old orphan Antony prays when he is lost in the snowy forest and is swiftly led by the sound of singing voices to the forester's cottage, where he is treated kindly and eventually adopted by the forester and his wife. When in *Godfrey, the Little Hermit* the shipwrecked boy is plagued with thirst as he stumbles among the rocks in the hot sun, he prays to God for help and shortly comes across a cool spring. In *The Basket of Flowers*, after Mary has been thrown out of her lodging by the unpleasant young peasant wife and goes to sit by her father's grave, she asks God if he has an angel to show her which way to turn. Immediately she hears the voice of the young Countess Amelia (in German Amalia), who has been looking for her and wants to make good the injustice Mary has suffered earlier from the Count and his family. These are typical examples of Schmid's belief in the power of prayer. The answers are prompt, helpful and always carefully motivated and explained. They may have the quality of a miraculous response to need, but they depend respectively, in the instances given above, on human generosity to a person in distress, the abundance of the natural world or a set of unsuspected causal connexions.

The Christian values and patterns of behaviour that Schmid propounds are simple and straightforward. Truthfulness, honesty, kindness, patience, prudence, courage and a forgiving spirit are the mark of goodness. These virtues are most often displayed in peasant families who stretch out a helping hand to those worse off than themselves, but it is not confined to the lower classes. Schmid views goodness as a normal human characteristic, not as something that distinguishes the responses of one social class rather than another.

Moral, Didactic and Religious Tales   107

Yet the characters in Schmid's tales all have a clear sense of the distinction between the classes. They know what is appropriate and inappropriate conduct for their particular station. Mary's father, in *The Basket of Flowers*, is wary and anxious about his daughter's growing attachment to the young Countess Amelia. When the Countess gives Mary a discarded, but still serviceable dress in gratitude for the basket of flowers that Mary has given her for her birthday, Mary's father, James, thinks that others may become envious of them and fears that the gift may make Mary vain. Envy has indeed already been shown towards her by Amelia's maid, and the maid's subsequent false witness against Mary, motivated by her envy, results in father and daughter being banished from their home and in their possessions being confiscated.

Christoph von Schmid does not challenge the social order of his time. The peasant can be as happy in his or her position as the nobility in theirs. Indeed, in *Rosa von Tannenburg* the heroine says to poor Gertrud, the charcoal-burner's wife, with whom she takes refuge on being driven out of her castle, that a quiet, peaceful life is better than choice food and drink. This is, of course, all of a piece with the eighteenth-century ideal of rural retirement and closeness to nature, detached from the busyness and artificiality of the court and the city. Schmid does not over-idealize this, since he makes plain the grimness of poverty and the harsh side of nature, the cold, rain, bleakness and lack of shelter, in many of his tales. The role of the peasantry is to work hard, accept their humble lot, be virtuous and show respect. That of the nobility is to rule wisely and alleviate distress by philanthropy. In this stable social situation misfortune is personal and occasional. It is not a consequence of defects in social consciousness and responsibilities.

Schmid's attention is largely confined the individual and the family. His child protagonists are frequently only children. Where there are brothers and sisters, they are never of crucial importance to the story. The most important relationship is that of child to parent, characterized by obedience, docility, helpfulness and affection. Although Godfrey, the little hermit, is described in a very positive way at the outset, he also had faults, the principal being self-righteousness, a desire to domineer over his brothers and sisters and a complaining spirit. One may wonder at the fact that it took three years of life on a desert island to bring such a boy to a proper feeling of respect and gratitude towards God and his parents. However, Schmid was simply following the model provided by Campe in *Robinson*, *the Younger*, whose hero's disregard of his parents led to an even longer period of isolation and separation.

The world of Schmid's stories reflects the hills, forest and fields, the small towns and villages of the borders of Bavaria and Swabia where he spent his life. In the eighteenth century it was a country of multitudinous principalities, many very small, in which the nobility and their subjects were often in easy contact. The place-names that Schmid gives to the settings of his stories relate to his feelings for the natural world and are broadly symbolic, as is the case with the names of many of his characters. Schmid combines the ordinary with the symbolic and distinctive in such a way as to render social and moral distinctions clear, but not crassly obtrusive. The associations of the names are not always apparent to readers of the English translations, and indeed some of them were changed to make them less difficult for the English-language reader to pronounce or understand.

Let us now turn to look in more detail at *Das Blumenkörbchen*, which is one of Schmid's longest tales. It focusses on a miscarriage of justice, its later discovery and the compensation of the innocent victim. (The names given in this account are the original German names.) The gardener's daughter Marie gives the Countess Amalia for her birthday a beautiful basket of flowers that her father has made with Amalia's name and family coat of arms cleverly worked into it. Marie is rewarded with a dress from the young Countess's wardrobe. At the time of her visit a diamond ring vanishes from the castle, and Marie falls immediately under suspicion of having stolen it. Despite her unflinching denials Marie is convicted on the basis of false evidence given by the Countess's jealous maid. Marie and her elderly father, Jakob, are evicted from their home and banished from the Count's lands. Jakob falls ill, and the two are taken in by a peasant couple. On Jakob's recovery father and daughter manage to make themselves useful and earn their keep. But after Jakob dies and the peasant couple hand over their property to their son, the latter's unpleasant wife makes Marie's life a misery. Finally, the theft of some linen (not by Marie) gives her an excuse to throw the girl out of the house. Marie goes for comfort to her father's grave, which she has adorned with the basket of flowers that had been thrown back at her when she and her father were banished. Here she prays for help and is discovered by the Countess Amalia, who has actually been searching for her, for in the interim the lost ring has been found: it had been taken by a jackdaw and hidden in a nest in an old pear-tree that has recently had to be felled after being damaged in a storm. Amalia is now with her parents visiting a neglected hunting-lodge and has heard of the piety and touching way in which a local girl has adorned her father's grave. She recognizes the basket of flowers and is anxious to find Marie in order to beg forgiveness for the injustice done to her. Marie bears the Count and his family no ill-will. She is fêted and taken into the household as Amalia's companion. An additional episode shows the miserable maid poverty-stricken and dying in a garret. She has been punished for her perjury, but of course Marie also forgives her. The story ends with Marie's marriage to the son of the justice who had earlier pronounced sentence on her.

Marie is a heroine of unblemished virtue, industrious, affectionate, generous-hearted and of a forgiving nature. Her father is deeply Christian and a man of the utmost probity. Despite the harsh treatment that he and his daughter receive at the hands of the law, he desires that Marie should conquer any resentment she may feel and be of a forgiving spirit. His self-reliance and integrity are such that he will accept help from the forester Anton, who meets the two exiles as they are leaving the town of Eichburg, only when he is convinced that the money is Anton's to give, and not money properly belonging to the Count. Father and daughter suffer greatly, but their original act of spontaneous generosity – the making and gift of the basket of flowers – is what provides the means for righting the injustice they have suffered. The basket of flowers is all that Marie can place on her father's grave as a memorial – she cannot afford a gravestone – but it is the hallmark of her devotion and the talk of the neighbourhood. Thus, the only act that she can perform at the lowest point of her misery turns out to be the instrument of her rehabilitation. This kind of motif is one that Schmid was fond of. A further example of synchronicity in *Das Blumenkörbchen* occurs when the village clergyman tells how old Jakob on his deathbed had received a consolation that his daughter's innocence would be proved. When the date of this incident is checked, it coincides with the night of the storm in which the old pear-tree is damaged. By such occurrences Schmid expresses his profound belief in the interconnectedness of human life. Good deeds simply and honestly performed without any ulterior motive bring their own reward in God's good time. His characters have a lively sense of God's presence in their lives. They give thanks for small blessings as well as for great ones. They accept suffering and hardship as part of God's plan for themselves, so that when they reach the depths of misery they cast themselves on God's mercy as a natural reaction, and their prayers are answered.

13. Christopher von Schmid, Title-page and frontispiece of *The Flower-Basket. A Moral Tale* (1848).

Das Blumenkörbchen was translated into English not once, but at least five times. As was the case with the first translation of Goethe's *Werther*, the first two translations were made from a French text and not directly from the German original. The British connexion with French culture and language has always been much stronger than that with German. The first translator, however, was an American – the Rev. Gregory Townsend Bedell, D.D. (1793-1834), the greater part of whose ministry took place in the Episcopalian church of St. Andrew, Philadelphia, where he won a considerable following with his preaching, searching pastoral care and concern for children. In his introduction to *The Basket of Flowers* (Philadelphia: H. Perkins; Boston: Perkins & Marvin, 1833) Bedell admits that his translation is 'a very free one; and in many places large omissions are made, and in others considerable additions will be found'. The reasons for this lie in his earlier remark, namely, that 'with some alterations, to make [*The Basket of Flowers*] convey lessons of clear and decided evangelical truth, it would be a very interesting little work for the libraries of Sunday Schools, and every variety of youthful readers'. This desire to alter and make conform to the tenets of Evangelicalism is a commonplace among British translators of German material. Other translators – for example, the Rev. T. M. Ready, LL.B., on

Moral, Didactic and Religious Tales 111

the title-page of *The Rose Bush* (Schmid's *Der Rosenstock*) – indicate that they have 'corrected' Schmid's text.

What do such 'alterations' and 'corrections' amount to? The German text of Schmid's tales on the whole allows the Christian way of life, morals and religious practice to emerge naturally from the narrative. Where overt instruction is given, it is almost always through the mouthpiece of one of the characters personally involved in the action. More rarely, a respected clergyman (the neutral word *Pfarrer* is most commonly used) may comment or preach a sermon. Schmid hardly ever provides an authorial comment that goes beyond what is implicit in the narrative. By contrast, Bedell's translation frequently engages in such authorial nudges, obtrusive assertions and direct addresses to the reader, a practice that is foreign to Schmid and is damaging to his calculated technique. For example, in describing the father at the outset of the book, Bedell adds:

> While he was quite young James Rode had been brought to a knowledge of the truth as it is in Jesus Christ. He had been born again of the Spirit, and these are the reasons why he had been enabled to discharge his duties. . . . No matter how humble the situation any real child of God may occupy, if he is consistent in his walk and conversation, he is witness for the truth of religion which no enemy can be able to gainsay.

In the characterization of the admirable Mary, Bedell declares:

> By all the neighbours she was called a beautiful girl, and sometimes they were indiscreet enough to call her so before her face – a very great mistake, as all children are naturally prone to vanity.

This sort of moralizing gloss figures throughout Bedell's translation. He also inserts a small number of passages of verse and gives occasional Biblical references that Schmid had not deemed necessary.

Bedell's practice was standard in the nineteenth-century treatment of children's books. It is in fact extended in the translation by a person whose identity is hidden behind the initials J. H. St. A. and who also worked from a French text. The earliest edition of this translation would appear to be that of 1857. The translator increases the Biblical references and inserts a good many more verses, mainly anonymous, but there are a couple of quotations each from Cowper and from Coleridge. After Mary has been given the Countess's dress there follows a very strong homily:

> Do you love gaudy dresses and useless ornaments, young reader? Remember that it is an evidence of an uncultivated taste and a vulgar and frivolous mind. If a woman is overloaded with gaudy ornaments

and unsuitable dresses, they do not adorn her – she only bears about upon her person the badge of inward deformity. Learn to understand the real beauty of simplicity. . . . What innumerable evils have been the consequence of a foolish fondness for dress! . . . Mothers, beware of the appearance of such a taste in your children! Foster it not. Strive to check it, as you would strive to check the first symptoms of a fatal disease, the more insidious, because it appears slight and harmless at first.

Such heavily moralizing sentiments and exhortations are more numerous than in Bedell.

James's deathbed advice to his daughter is quite considerably different from Schmid's German text. Jakob does not actually mention the name of Jesus, but puts all his emphasis on a direct relationship with God as Father, the heavenly thus paralleling the earthly. One of Marie's most important guides is her sense of shame. She should never do anything that she would be ashamed for her father to know. By contrast, J. H. St. A.'s version focusses on Jesus, underlines the need for daily prayer and is much more comprehensive in its religious injunctions. Schmid's position is more general, more genial than his translator's. He has a greater faith in human capacity for good, not the Evangelicals' insistence on human sinfulness apart from God's exercise of grace.

While the translations of Bedell and J. H. St. A. were frequently reprinted and dominated the market in the nineteenth century, a much closer translation from the original German had appeared in 1848. This was entitled *The Flower-Basket: a Moral Tale* and came from the hand of William E. Drugulin. It was published in Stuttgart by J. B. Müller, with W. S. Orr of London as co-publisher. This is a rare book; it is not included in the checklist of the Renier Collection, nor is there a copy in the British Library. It is remarkable in being a faithful translation, with no additional material to make it acceptable to Evangelical readers, and containing three illustrations by Julius Nisle. However, it made little impression in Britain, and no reprints are recorded. One oddity of the translation is the fact that it has the young Countess refer to her father and mother quite incongruously as 'Pa' and 'Ma'. The name of the jealous maid varies from translation to translation. In Schmid's original she is called Jettchen, but Bedell calls her Margaret, J. H. St. A. has Juliette, and Drugulin Harriet.

In the mid 1860s a second translation was made directly from the German. This was published by Warne in 1866. Like so many translations it is anonymous. Although it is a careful piece of work, this translator, like Bedell and J. H. St. A., cannot withstand the impulse to improve on

Moral, Didactic and Religious Tales 113

or correct the German original. When James is explaining the emblematic significance of flowers to his young daughter, he reflects on the lily's whiteness by declaring: 'There is a white robe freely offered to all. Blessed are they who have washed their robes and made them white in the blood of the Lamb'. Such a formulation is not, of course, to be found in Schmid. The anonymous translator also appends, at the beginning and end of each chapter, a very wide range of verses from Cowper, Spenser, Hogg, the German Protestant hymn-writer Paul Gerhardt and many other now largely forgotten poets. By the time of the publication of this translation the methods of book illustration have changed. Metal engraving has given way to colour printing, so that the main feature of the new editions' appeal lies more in their attractive and extensive illustration than in the story by itself. The most ambitious of the Warne editions – and there were several in different formats, usually undated – has twenty-four coloured illustrations printed by the leading colour printed of the day, Edmund Evans. Curiously, the artist who produced these attractive designs is not named.

A further anonymous translation, of which Blackie and Son published an edition c. 1900, with a frontispiece by G. Demain Hammond, provides a second rendering untainted by verse and prose additions and religiously motivated alterations. This may perhaps be the same translation as that published by A. Hislop of Edinburgh, in 1869. Blackie's edition contains a couple of pages of historical information about Schmid. When the same publisher produced a new edition, with illustrations by A. A. Dixon dated 1912, presumably during the First World War, Schmid's name was removed from the title-page, the historical introduction was omitted, and the setting was changed from the imaginary German 'Eichburg' to 'a certain little market town in Guelderland' with a 'Count of Terborg'. Jingoistic patriotism could not brook the enjoyment of a story known to be German, even from nearly a century ago.

Surprisingly, new editions of *The Basket of Flowers*, with or without the author's name, continued to be produced up to the 1960s, making Schmid's story one of the most enduring and frequently republished German children's books. The story has its own attractions, as Schmid was a skilful writer, but a large part of its success in Britain is due to the fact that it was an enormously popular reward book given to those attending Sunday Schools. To what extent it was a book that children chose for themselves and wanted to read is a question that is difficult to answer. But it clearly had a great publishing market from around 1850 onwards. There are editions from a large number of firms – Thomas Nelson, Milner and Sowerby, Ward and Lock, Simpkin and Marshall, W. Nicholson and Sons, Frederick Warne, Hodder and Stoughton, Houlston and Sons, Oliphant Anderson & Ferrier, Blackie and Son, Collins and several others. Many of these editions are undated, presumably so that they never looked out-of-date. Sometimes the author's name is given in a semi-anglicized form as 'Christopher von Schmid', but often it is omitted entirely. Since Schmid was dead by the time his book became such a publishing success in Britain, it is unlikely that he or his heirs gained anything financially from it.

Christoph von Schmid was undoubtedly the most important of the German writers of religious tales for children to be translated into English, albeit in a largely Evangelical disguise aimed at counteracting his Catholic roots. We have to remember that the Catholic Emancipation Act came only in 1829 and that Catholics were the focus of a good deal of antagonism for a long time afterwards. No other German religious writer for children had as many individual works translated into English as Schmid. The only person who comes anywhere near him is the Protestant writer, Christian Gottlob Barth (1799-1862), with around a dozen stories or small collections available in English. None of them, however, enjoyed the many reprints that came the way of several of Schmid's tales as well as *The Basket of Flowers*.

Barth was a Swabian, born in Stuttgart, a student in Tübingen, pastor in Möttlingen and later resident in Calw in the Black Forest, where he founded the Protestant Calw publishing firm and later died. This was prime Protestant territory, as was Greifswald in Pomerania, where he gained his theology doctorate in 1838. In addition to his pastoral duties Barth was deeply involved in evangelical missionary concerns and in writing books for children. The *Allgemeine Deutsche Biographie* tells us:

> He had two particular characteristics. On the one hand he combined a very clear, sharp intellect with an absolute faith in the Bible, the latter going so far as to regard the Copernican system without ado as false on account of its not tallying with the Bible. On the other hand he was able to combine a sparkling sense of humour and serene life-style with an attitude towards life and the world that was rooted in a marked pietism.

Barth's clear faith in the Bible, belief in the efficacy of prayer and God's providence made him an obvious candidate for translation into English, though his stories do not reveal much in the way of humour.

Barth's religious tales were first published in English by Darton and Clark in 1838, and they were followed by other publishers into the 1850s.

Moral, Didactic and Religious Tales   115

Some reprints by the Religious Tract Society date from as late as the 1870s, but after this Barth disappears from the British scene. Most of his tales are located in Germany, with events taking place in specifically named areas and towns. In this respect he is more realistic than Schmid, who uses fictitious, vaguely symbolic place-names. Barth's stories range over large areas of German-speaking Europe and almost always have some reference to missionary activity in more distant parts of the world such as India, the West Indies and Labrador. His protagonists also have individual rather than typical names. Although his stories are fictions, Barth wants his readers to feel that the events he relates could actually have happened, even though they often depend on a range of coincidences that exceed plausibility.

Darton and Harvey published *Setma, the Turkish Girl: and Woodrof, the Swedish Boy* in 1838, no translator's name being given. *Setma, das türkische Mädchen* had appeared in 1831 and tells the story of the capture of a Turkish girl in the siege of Belgrade in 1688 and her subsequent conversion to Christianity in Germany, where she does excellent educational work with girls and ends up living at the ducal palace in Stuttgart. Further editions of *Setma* were published by Paton and Ritchie in Edinburgh in 1853 and by the Religious Tract Society in an undated edition. The RTS also published *The Swedish Shepherd Boy* in the 1850s. Unusually, this is a first person narrative about the struggles of a poor boy in rural Sweden to gain an education, become a teacher and finally a missionary in India. It mainly recounts the protagonist's experience of trials, tribulations and eventual acts of kindness, which he interprets as the hand of God guiding him. The whole account shows how conventional church-going is inadequate and that a feeling experience of the Saviour is essential to true Christianity.

Around 1838 Darton and Clark published a translation by Samuel Jackson of *Der Fensterladen* (1834) under the title *The Juvenile Artist*. This was also included in a composite volume of Barth's tales entitled *Winter Evening Stories* (London: Darton & Clark, c. 1844), which in addition contained *The Young Tyrolese* and *The Wanderer*. *Der Fensterladen* appeared in a different translation by R. Menzies with the title *Gregory Krau; or the Window Shutter* (Edinburgh: Paton & Ritchie, 1850; Stuttgart: Müller, 1851). This is a story with two threads, one about Gregory Krau, a man who gets into bad company and deserts his family, but eventually becomes a true Christian in India. The other thread concerns his son Justus (a symbolic name here!), who develops skills as an artist and picture-restorer. In exercising his practical knowledge he discovers that the picture painted

116 *Telling Tales*

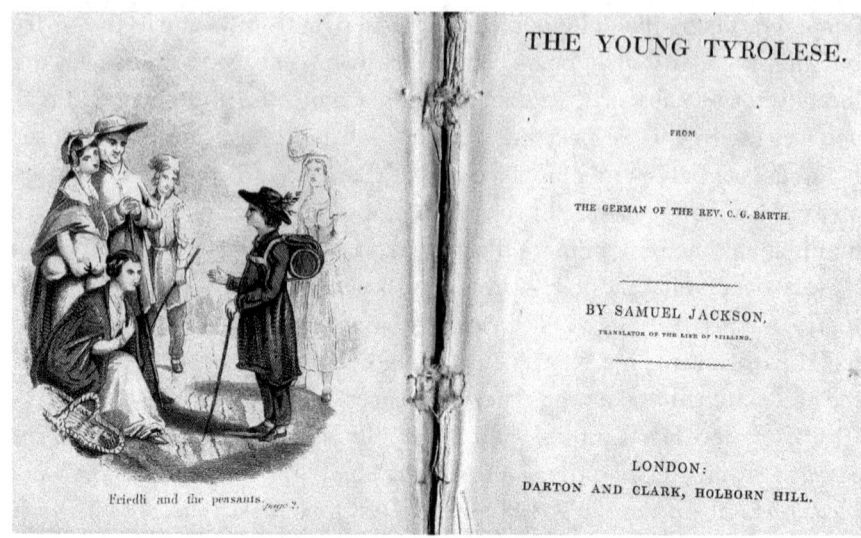

14. Title-page and frontispiece of C. G. Barth, *The Young Tyrolese* (1838).

on an old wooden shutter in their house is a Rubens, which when sold raises the equivalent of 1800 dollars and extinguishes the family's debts. At this point the father, Gregory, returns and is reunited with them. As usual in a story by Barth, there is a lot about trusting in God and about help coming unexpectedly. A short section about missionary work among 'Hindoos' describes them as 'poor deluded creatures' throwing themselves under the wheels of a carriage with a horrible idol. Mention is also made of a man lying on a bed of nails, of the custom of burning widows alive and of 'their senseless Deities'. Like so many other Evangelical writers of this period, Barth gives voice to a self-confidence of religious understanding that is horrified by the different traditions it encountered in other parts of the world.

The Young Tyrolese is a translation of *Der Weihnachtsmorgen oder das Tintenfäßchen* (1836), a story whose title was literally translated in a later edition by R. Menzies as *Christmas Morning; or, the Little Ink Cask* (Edinburgh: Paton & Ritchie, 1851; Stuttgart: Müller, 1852). The hero of this story is a Tyrolese boy, Friedli, who walks to Berlin, selling ink from a cask that his brother has marked with a mill-wheel design and his initials, and is taken in by a gentleman who wants him as a positive role model for his wayward son. Friedli's brother, Ulric, enlists with a Swiss regiment, goes to Holland and eventually, after much illness, gains a place as a footman. The brothers eventually make contact again as a result of Ulric recognizing the ink cask after it has been sent to Esquimaux in Labrador and then returned to Rotterdam. The motif of siblings or close friends being separated through adversity and then finding each other through some stroke of fortune is a commonplace of popular literature. There is a similar occurrence in *Setma*, where the Turkish girl meets her childhood friend Guly as an adult in the service of the Duchess of Wurtemberg. The motif of the token of recognition whereby separated friends or relatives meet each other again also occurs in *The Raven's Feather* (*Die Rabenfeder*, 1832), which the Religious Tract Society published c. 1855 and again in 1878. The raven's feather is also linked with a man called Raven, who provides help to the orphan boy who is the focus of the story.

Barth had a particular regard for the Moravians. *The Young Tyrolese* has among its incidental characters a Moravian missionary who recounts the story of an Esquimau boy from Labrador, and mention is made of the Moravian settlement at Fulneck, near Leeds. In addition, *The Young Artist* contains a brief episode in which the Krau family visits the mother's family in Neuwied, where there was a colony of Moravians among the Jews, Catholics and Protestants who settled there at the invitation of the prince after the Thirty Years War. Barth actually wrote a whole book about the Moravians, which was translated by Samuel Jackson and published by Darton and Clark in 1842. Another edition was published by S. Lingham c. 1845.

Of the remaining stories by Barth that were translated into English *Cuff, the Negro Boy* merits attention on a number of points. It was probably the first of Barth's tales to be translated by the Rev. Robert Menzies (Edinburgh: Paton & Ritchie, 1848). The book is notable for providing a gripping example of the abduction of a three-year-old child by a travelling circus as the result of the failure of the children's attendant to look after them properly. This attendant is given the name Kunigunda, and one can't avoid the suspicion that it may be intended to suggest that she is a Catholic. The book's title suggests that it is the story of a poor black boy, but it turns out that Cuff – for that is his name – is not black in that sense at all, but simply has a blackened skin. He is the abducted middle-class child of only superficially Christian parents, but in his circus captivity he has read parts of the Bible and become a devout Christian. When the circus troupe finally returns to the town Cuff was born in, he finds it vaguely familiar and rediscovers the family house and his parents and siblings. He was originally called Emilius, and his sister Emilia is prompted to a deathbed conversion before dying of 'galloping consumption'. Emilius is now properly educated, and the story ends with him joining a merchant's counting house. The acquisition of a true Christian faith may be the lesson that the book is teaching, but the financial security offered by a counting house clearly doesn't come amiss. When Emilius is successful as a merchant, he gives lots of money for the gospel to be preached to poor blacks in the West Indies. The fact that he himself had suffered and been treated as a black leads him to devote his subsequent wealth to their spiritual benefit. It is an expression of his solidarity with them, even though the difference in their social and financial situations continues to exist.

At the beginning of the nineteenth century moral and religious tales probably gained a broader readership among children than at the end of the century. In the early 1800s children's books had not emancipated themselves very much from the educational, moral and religious didacticism that was everywhere the norm, but by the 1870s there was a mass of books that aimed to entertain rather than instruct children. Middle-class readers certainly had considerable choice. The market for most moral and religious books for children had gradually become more specialized. Many of the books we have looked at were published by the Quaker firm of Darton (with its variety of imprints) in the period up to, say, 1845 and formed part of a much broader output. But from around 1850 we can see religious titles becoming increasingly the province of more specialized publishers such as the Religious Tract Society, Paton and Ritchie of Edinburgh and B. Wertheim of London. Christoph von Schmid was such a popular phenomenon that a whole range of publishers cashed in on him, but he was the exception. The only other author to escape the straightjacket of the Evangelical publishers was Carové with *The Story Without an End*, which attracted the more sentimental section of Victorian and Edwardian middle-class society, especially through the diverse kinds of illustration that it elicited. Schmid at the latter end of the nineteenth century became the province of the working-class Sunday School, and one imagines many more such children received *The Basket of Flowers* as a reward book than actually chose it for themselves.

Most of the books we have considered operate with well-tried formulae. Their protagonists are orphans, the poor, the innocent victims of injustice or economic hardship. They frequently have siblings or parents who go off the rails, but are led back to the straight and narrow through their example of Christian faith. Despite the trials their protagonists undergo the stories are optimistic and end happily. They demonstrate that the world is populated by good and devout people as well as by the wicked and thoughtless. In many ways one can see these tales as the religious equivalent of the fable and the fairytale with ordinary people occupying the roles of fairy, ogre, dwarf, witch and helper, but by the end of the century they had largely lost the general appeal that they previously exerted.

8. Friedrich de la Motte Fouqué: *Undine* and *Sintram*

It often comes as a surprise to modern students of German Romanticism to find out that the author who made the greatest impact on English-speaking readers was Friedrich Heinrich Karl, Baron de la Motte Fouqué. Apart from *Undine* very little of his massive literary output has survived as popular reading. Even by the end of his own lifetime he ceased to be taken very seriously, despite his earlier connexions with Chamisso, E. T. A. Hoffmann and Eichendorff. Fouqué came from a French family that had settled in Germany after the revocation of the Edict of Nantes. Born himself in 1777 in Brandenburg, he early espoused the life of a soldier, but had to retire in 1813 because of ill-health after being wounded in the battles of Lützen and Bautzen. He married twice, the first time unhappily. His second wife, Caroline, was also a popular novelist in her day. Fouqué died in literary obscurity on his estate at Nennhausen, near Rathenow, in 1843.

Fouqué was part of the Romantic trend that enthusiastically embraced medieval literature and culture, identifying with the values of chivalry and romance. He was passionate in his devotion to Norse poetry and sagas and in 1808-10 wrote a dramatic trilogy, *Der Held des Nordens* (The Hero of the North), about Sigurd the Dragon-slayer that stands at the beginning of the nineteenth-century fascination with the figure of Siegfried, a fascination that reached its climax with Wagner's *Ring des Nibelungen*. The ethical and romantic ideals of the medieval knight, whether Norse or German, pervade both *Undine* and *Sintram*, the prose stories that Fouqué published in 1811 and 1814 respectively and that constitute his particular fame in the English-speaking world.

Fouqué was not a writer of works for children, and the earliest

English translations of *Undine* and *Sintram* were clearly aimed at an adult readership that wanted to acquaint itself with the latest products of German Romanticism. Several of his other stories and romances were also translated – *Minstrel Love* (1821), *The Magic Ring* (1825), *Aslauga's Knight* (1827), *The Two Captains* (1843) and *Thiodolf, the Icelander* (1845) – but none were as enthusiastically taken up as *Undine* and *Sintram*. What is interesting here is the way in which the nature of the readership of these two works changed and how, by the end of the nineteenth century, they were clearly considered to be children's books.

Undine was first translated into English in 1818 by George Soane, who also adapted it for the stage as early as 1821. With about a hundred different editions in English up to the present day, published in both Britain and the United States, it proved a runaway success. Fouqué's work was translated many times. Some editions were illustrated, others appeared as a plain text. It was made accessible to a wide readership and stage public and was commented on by several men of letters and critics including Coleridge and Edgar Allan Poe. Some girls were even given the name of Undine.

Fouqué's romance became deservedly famous. With extraordinary skill, never saying too much, Fouqué explores the predicament of the knight Huldbrand, torn between the passionate love of the elemental Undine and the calmer, more predictable affection of the completely human Bertalda. The antitheses of earth and water, courtly castle and rural simplicity, Christian values and dark malevolence overlap in disturbing ways. Huldbrand is first of all impressed by Bertalda when he sees her at a tournament, but his attraction quickly diminishes, and it is as a joke that he requests one of her gloves. Bertalda then demands that he should undertake a dangerous expedition into the forest before he can be rewarded, and thus is set in motion the fateful course of Huldbrand's life. His dangerous encounter with the shape-shifting Kühleborn, Undine's guardian uncle, gives way to an idyll with Undine and the fisher couple who are her supposed parents on their island apart from the rest of the world. Here, through marriage at the hands of the priest symbolically named Heilmann, the water-sprite Undine gains a soul. Kühleborn remains a threatening presence around Undine's new life after the couple leave the island and go first to the ducal palace and then to Ringstetten, Huldbrand's own castle, together with Bertalda. Meanwhile, Undine reveals that Bertalda is the real daughter of the fisher couple who have been entrusted with Undine in her place. Tensions quickly invade the relationships between Huldbrand, Bertalda and Undine. The latter's supernatural origins and associations become a focus of suspicion and recrimination. The fluidity of emotions correlates with the danger that running water – whether well or river – represents to the couple's marriage. Finally, in a quarrel between the three on the River Danube, Kühleborn seizes Undine and takes her back to the realm of water from which she came. After Huldbrand has recovered from the shock, his plans to marry Bertalda are resisted by both her father, the old fisherman, and Father Heilmann. However, despite disturbing dreams Huldbrand determines to go ahead. Bertalda has the well in the castle courtyard reopened in order to get water to wash away the freckles that betray her lowly origins, but Undine reappears out of it and embraces Huldbrand with the kiss of death.

This bald summary cannot do justice to Fouqué's achievement in *Undine*. Neither the language nor the narrative technique is particularly complex, but the blend of apparently detached narration with occasional authorial comment, the skilful mingling of concrete observation and symbolic insinuation, exercise a potent charm on the reader. The German reader will note the symbolism and associations of the names, which get lost in English. Undine derives from the Latin *unda*, 'wave', while the first syllable in Huldbrand signifies 'grace, favour' and the whole name is modelled on the pattern of Hildebrand, the name of the hero in the earliest surviving German heroic poem. Kühleborn means 'cool fountain', while *Heil* in Heilmann relates to 'healing' or 'salvation'. The location of the story in the south-west of Germany near the source of the Danube removes it as far as possible from Fouqué's native heath, but the name of Huldbrand's castle, Ringstetten, seems to allude to 'la Motte' in Fouqué's own family name. Bertalda, fittingly enough, is the only ordinary name in the story. Fouqué's literary inspiration was a slender work on sylphs and other strange creatures by the sixteenth-century scholar Paracelsus, but from it he created an extraordinary romance of divided loyalties, of love and death. As it was accessible on a number of levels, it is not surprising that it was so successful in the nineteenth century.

Among the many early English editions of *Undine* those published by James Burns are significant in that he published several other German authors who wrote for children or whose works were taken over by children. Burns's *The Seasons* of 1843, which included both *Undine* and *Sintram* along with *Aslauga's Knight* and *The Two Captains*, used, without acknowledgement, the translation made by the American Thomas Tracy and included illustrations by an unknown artist. However, in 1845 he published another edition using a new, but still anonymous translation and eleven new illustrations by John Tenniel, who later achieved lasting fame as the classic illustrator of Lewis Carroll's two *Alice* books. These illustrations for *Undine* were his first commission for a full book. Burns's books were later reissued by Edward Lumley in the 1850s and 1860s, so they had a longer life than many of the other editions of both *Undine* and *Sintram*. Their duodecimo format and use of engravings must have made them attractive to youthful as well as adult readers.

The 1850s saw the production of four more stage versions of *Undine*. These were pantomimes by Edward Blanchard (Marylebone Theatre, London, December 1852), J. Courtney (Adelphi Theatre, Liverpool, December 1852), J. B. Buckstone (Theatre Royal, Haymarket, London, February 1858) and an unknown writer (again at the Theatre Royal, December 1858). Clearly, the story of *Undine* provided very congenial material for pantomime entertainment – a beautiful heroine, an intrepid hero, a supernatural villain, and the opportunity for a variety of theatrical effects including the obligatory transformation scene – though the original tragic ending could not be allowed to stand. More burlesques and extravaganzas followed in 1873 (Halifax), 1883 (Margate and Great Yarmouth).

Although there were several new editions and translations of *Undine* in the latter part of the nineteenth century, their paucity or complete lack of illustration marked them as designed for adult readers. But the Burns/Lumley editions and the stage versions surely helped to prepare the way for the explosion of lavishly illustrated editions at the end of the century and for the new focus on the young as the key readership. The sumptuous edition illustrated in full colour by Julius Höppner (London: Griffith, Farran, Okeden & Welsh; New York: E. P. Dutton & Co., 1885) was clearly aimed at the upper end of the art-loving market, while that illustrated in black and white by Heywood Sumner (London: Chapman & Hall, 1888) envisaged a less affluent, but still an adult readership.

The first edition to appeal directly to a younger readership is a combined edition of *Sintram and his Companions* and *Undine* with an introduction by Charlotte M. Yonge (London: W. Gardner, Darton & Co., 1896). This edition was reissued several times in Britain and America up to 1930. The translation is an adaptation of Tracy, and it is accompanied by five full-page monochrome reproductions of paintings by Gordon Browne (1858-1932) together with a number of line-drawings. Charlotte M. Yonge (1823-1901), the celebrated author of *The Heir of Redcliffe* and many other books and stories for children, focusses in her introduction on the topic of folk-beliefs about water-spirits. She has less sympathy with *Undine* than with *Sintram* – the moral concerns of the devout children's writer break in here – when she goes on to say:

> But Undine's freakish playfulness and mischief as an elemental being, and her sweet patience when her soul is won, are quite original, and indeed we cannot help sharing, or at least understanding, Huldbrand's beginning to shrink from this unearthly creature to something of his own flesh and blood. He is altogether unworthy, and though in this tale there is far less of spiritual meaning than in *Sintram*, we cannot but see that Fouqué's thought was that the grosser human nature is unable to appreciate what is absolutely pure and unearthly.

It is worth remembering that Yonge was well over seventy when she wrote this.

In the same year of 1896 the firm of Lawrence and Bullen produced a new edition of *Undine* with dark, brooding illustrations by W. E. F. Britten obviously designed for an adult readership. The translation was by Sir Edmund Gosse, and it was reissued in 1897, but with new illustrations by Florence M. Rudland, who trained at the Birmingham School of Art under Arthur J. Gaskin. They are entirely different in character from Britten's, decorative rather than atmospheric. Yet another edition and translation was published in 1897, this time by Macmillan. Its chief merit lies in the more than sixty illustrations by Rosie M. M. Pitman and the generous layout of the book. These are very much in the *art nouveau* style with an emphasis on sinuous line and decoration, and they express in their delight in nudity or semi-nudity an eroticism that is little in evidence at an earlier period. These editions of the 1890s reflect an astonishing preoccupation with Fouqué, but the peak of achievement was yet to come.

In 1909 an adaptation of *Undine* by W. L. Courtney was published in London by Heinemann and in New York by Doubleday, Page and Co. It contained fifteen full-page illustrations after watercolours by Arthur Rackham (1867-1939), then at the peak of his career as an illustrator of much sought-after gift books. In the same year Constable published his superb illustrations to the *Fairy Tales of the Brothers Grimm*. Rackham's fifteen pictures for *Undine* range from the extreme delicacy and sensitive colour of 'A beautiful little girl clad in rich garments stood there on the threshold smiling' to the sombre terror of 'Bertalda in the Black Valley'. The grotesques that Rackham is often remembered for are here restrained, though they make stronger appearances in the black and white head-pieces to several chapters. The impact of the artist's visits to Germany and Switzerland can be seen in the depiction of medieval buildings and mountain scenery, and the picture of Undine on horseback with Kühleborn and Heilmann at her side is compositionally related to Dürer's engraving *The Knight, Death and the Devil*, of which Rackham had a reproduction on his dining room wall. The language of the translation is full of deliberate poetic archaisms such as one finds in William Morris's verse and saga translations, but Rackham's illustrations are modern, subtle in their colours and moods and wonderfully expressive of Edwardian elegance. It is hardly surprising that when Dame Barbara Cartland was asked to write a newspaper article about the six most romantic novels she had ever read she opened the list with *Undine*. As a child she had, she declared, read fairy stories 'until I believed that I saw Fairies amongst the breath-taking pink-and-white blossoms of the plum trees in Pershore where we lived'. However, at the age of twelve (that is in 1913) she was given *Undine* with the Rackham illustrations. It 'bridged the gulf between the Fairy Stories and the love I expected in real life'.

During the 1890s and the Edwardian era we can see a considerable number of versions of *Undine* presented in forms likely to appeal to both adults and adolescent girls. W. L. Courtney, who provided the text for Rackham, had himself adapted Fouqué's story for the stage in what he subtitled 'a dream play'. The prose dialogue was interspersed with songs in verse. The play was staged twice – once in 1903 in Liverpool, the second time in 1906 at the Criterion in London. It keeps to the broad outline of Fouqué's tale, but strengthens the Christian elements. In the period with which we are concerned it is the last of the many adaptations of *Undine* for the English stage. These dramatic spectacles, studding nearly a century from 1821 to the early 1900s, must have entertained adults and children alike.

During the Edwardian period, however, we find a number of retellings of the story specifically designed for children. These are no longer translations or adaptations, but new narratives targeted at the lower age-range. One of the earliest was written by Mary Macgregor and included in the popular 'Told to the Children' series published by T. C. and E. C. Jack in London and E. P. Dutton in New York in 1907. This series provided children's versions of many classics. *Undine* has delightful colour illustrations by Katherine Cameron (1874-1965). Understandably, given their young readership, they soften and sentimentalize the impact of the original story, avoiding the terrors and the pains, but within these limits they are pretty designs, showing a resemblance to the watercolours of F. Cayley Robinson.

The Story of Undine published by Nelson in 1908 presents a different re-telling, omitting Fouqué's final chapter about Huldbrand's burial. The seven colour plates by E. F. Skinner are in a more adult mode, but with little personal style, competent rather than accomplished. A further children's version, again called *The Story of Undine*, edited by Mary Macleod, was published in 1912 by Wells Gardner and Co. Like the earlier book the same firm had published with Charlotte M. Yonge's introduction, this was illustrated by Gordon Browne.

If these three books with colour plates were not enough to demonstrate the amazing appeal of *Undine* in this brief period leading up to the First World War, we can add two further versions in a different mode. The first is a version by Gladys Davidson, published in 1908 and described as 'told simply for the lower standards'. It is little more than a booklet designed for school use. The other version, entitled *The Story of Undine. The Sprite Maiden*, was published by the indefatigable W. T. Stead in his widely read, pink paperback series *Books for the Bairns*. It was no. 163 and was issued in September 1909. Like most of the books in this series, it was copiously illustrated with fluent line-drawings by Brinsley Le Fanu (1854-1920), which provided a strong pictorial stimulus for reading a highly condensed form of the tale. Although full translations of *Undine* continued to be published during this period, showing that Fouqué had not lost his appeal to adult readers, it is fascinating to see how intensively the story was now marketed for children. This was, of course, happening with many works at this period, particularly with medieval tales and historical romances, but also with other classic works of fiction. *Undine*'s medieval setting and supernatural figures made it a prime target for publishers of children's books. Some brave attempts have been made later in the twentieth century to recoup Fouqué's original story for an adult English readership, but they have enjoyed a very limited success. The Edwardian period seems to have been the last in which figures like Undine could be taken seriously. With the increasing emphasis on social realism that came through the Great War, Neoromanticism slowly ebbed away.

Let us now turn to *Sintram and his Companions*. The German original, *Sintram und seine Gefährten*, was the last of the four stories that Fouqué published in *Die Jahreszeiten*, appearing in 1814. As *Undine* represented spring, so *Sintram* was winter. The whole story shivers with ice, snow, frost and bitter winds. Set in Drontheim and the surrounding mountains in the late Middle Ages, it is a product of Fouqué's deep preoccupation with Norse literature, culture and mythology. While *Undine* has as its central figure a girl, though seen through the eyes of the young knight Huldbrand, *Sintram* focusses on a boy as he grows up to become a knight. When the story opens, Sintram is twelve years old and irrupts into the company of the Northern knights assembled around a massive round stone table, crying that he is being pursued by Death and another person. The whole story reflects the tensions that Sintram is caught in between the cruel paganism of his father Biörn and the ascetic Christianity of his mother Verena, who has entered a monastery. Sintram is at odds with his father, but rarely sees his mother. His closest relationship is with an old retainer, Rolf. Sintram is often a prey to evil or disturbing forces that take strange shapes. One of these is a mysterious pilgrim figure, carrying rattling bones of dead men attached to his clothes. The other is a sinister, ugly dwarf called Kleinmeister (Little Master), who appears in various repellent guises – once like a bear with a crooked horn on his head, another time as a little man wearing a golden-horned helmet – and who can vanish at will.

Sintram's fate has been brought about through his father's swearing, one Christmas time, on the pagan image of a boar that he will kill every German merchant who comes into his power. Soon afterwards two Germans, an old man and his son, arrive looking for shelter, and Biörn orders them to be killed. Verena asks for mercy for them, but Biörn, because of his vow, calls on Death and the devil to help him. Miraculously, the two Germans escape. Biörn receives the name of 'Gluth-Auge' (Fiery Eye) for his stance, while Verena takes the veil. Later Fouqué introduces into the narrative two characters from his novel *Der Zauberring* (The Magic Ring), written in 1811, the Norman lord Folko von Montfaucon and his wife Gabriele. Kleinmeister attempts to enmesh Sintram in a seductive love-relationship with Gabriele, modelling the situation on that of Paris, Menelaus and Helen of Troy. Sintram is sorely tempted, but manages to resist – how could it be otherwise in this struggle between Christian and pagan?

Fouqué links his fictitious narrative with elements of medieval Norse legend through staging a battle on Niflung's Heath and thus invoking the spirit of the *Eddas* and the German *Nibelungenlied*. The story also uses the bear as its most important symbol of pagan might. Biörn's very name means 'bear', Kleinmeister adopts the appearance of a bear in one of his disguises, and it is on a bear-hunt that Folko falls down a precipice while attempting to get a bear's head and claws, booty that Sintram succeeds in gaining for him. Eventually, at another Christmas celebration, Folko smashes Biörn's golden boar's head and gains his submission. Years later Sintram forces Kleinmeister to flee and demonstrates the superior power of Christian faith. The strange figure of Death disappears, and on his deathbed Biörn is reconciled with Sintram. When Sintram is reunited with his mother, she tells him that his vocation is to be a knight, not a monk. The story ends with Sintram being entrusted with the education of the young son of Folko and Gabriele von Montfaucon, whose name, in fitting symbolism, is Engeltram, thus uniting the Germanic element *tram* with the Christian *Engel*, 'angel'.

Fouqué's inspiration for this story was the engraving of *The Knight, Death and the Devil* by Dürer, already mentioned in connexion with Arthur Rackham's illustrations to *Undine*. Most of the details of this complex engraving are worked into Fouqué's story. The dog appears under the name of Skovmaerke in the final chapters, while the castle perched on the top of a distant mountain must have suggested the Stone Fortress on the Rocks of the Moon, to which Sintram retreats in ascetic isolation. The lizard and the skull, the curious object impaled on the knight's lance, the menacing figure behind his horse and the deathlike man on the horse's other side are all incorporated in this strange narrative that sets father against son, paganism against Christianity. This is very much a story for the male adolescent. The role of women is restricted to the remote, virtuous mother, Verena, and the beautiful Gabriele, sexually attractive, but unavailable to the Christian knight that Sintram aspires to be, because she is married. It is the typical situation of courtly love in that the knight's emotions are educated through sublimation and renunciation. The sentiments were appropriate enough for the Romantic era and for the Victorian and Edwardian ages too.

The pattern of translation for an adult readership, followed later by adaptation for younger readers, that we have noted for *Undine* can also been seen with *Sintram*, but there is not quite the same flood of editions. The first translation was made by Julius C. Hare (1795-1855) and published in 1820. Hare went on to become one of the most knowledgeable men in the field of German literature, theology and philosophy and was known already in 1825 as possessing a great collection of modern German books. His library, with its extraordinary range of German Romantic writers, is now held in Trinity College, Cambridge. His translation of *Sintram* was used later in an edition illustrated by Heywood Sumner (London: Seeley & Co., 1883). As we might expect, James Burns published *Sintram* in an anonymous translation in the same format as *Undine*, both separately in

15. Friedrich de la Motte Fouqué, *Sintram and his Companions*. Illustration by H. C. Selous (n.d.), p. 1.

1842 and 1848 and as part of *The Seasons* in 1843. The edition of 1848 presents a different text from the other two, though it is clearly based on the earlier version. It also adds sixteen illustrations by H. C. Selous to the reproduction of Dürer's *The Knight, Death and the Devil* that is included in most of the English editions of *Sintram*. These pick out some of the key episodes of the story and provide a further attraction for younger readers. This edition was reissued by Edward Lumley after Burns had turned away from his earlier publications to devote himself to Catholicism. Another interesting item from this period of the mid nineteenth century is a German-language edition of *Sintram und seine Gefährten* published in London by D. Nutt, Dulau und Comp. und P. Rolandi in 1855 and printed by J. Wertheimer und Comp. in Finsbury Circus. The British Library catalogue indicates a further German edition for 1862. This is a text without illustrations and was perhaps aimed at the growing number of Britons now learning German. David Nutt, who died in 1863, was a publisher and foreign bookseller and was for a time in partnership with Nicholas Trübner, who was probably the conduit for such German books.

The change in target readership for *Sintram* seems to have taken place concurrently with that for *Undine*. The edition illustrated by Heywood Sumner and published in 1883 probably set the trend, but the combined edition of *Sintram and his Companions* and *Undine* with Charlotte M. Yonge's introduction (1896), which we have already noted, makes the youthful readership clear. This was almost certainly the edition that the Bastable children in E. Nesbit's *The Story of the Treasure Seekers* (1899) would have read and that Nesbit expected her readers to know about. The Bastable children are playing in the park when Alice whispers, 'I see the white witch bear yonder among the trees! Let's track it and slay it in its lair'. Noël then pretends to be the bear, Oswald takes on the role of Count Folko of Mont Faucon, Dora wants to be Gabrielle, 'the only one of us who likes doing girl's parts', as Oswald, the ostensible narrator, explains rather dismissively. Alice herself is Sintram, while the eight-year-old H. O. has to be the Little Master. Dicky is the Pilgrim with the bones. Fouqué's story obviously allowed ample scope for imaginative play, even if there wasn't a really good part for a girl.

Over the period from 1896 to the outbreak of the Great War new versions of *Sintram* abounded. Dent reissued the Burns/Lumley translation in 1900 together with *Aslauga's Knight*, but with new illustrations by Charles Robinson (1870-1937). Robinson had achieved great success with his black and white illustrations to Stevenson's *A Child's Garden of Verses* (1895), but the *art nouveau* arabesques and leafy borders that he uses for *Sintram* do not fit well together with the sinister scenes that they enclose. In the same year Fremantle and Co. published a new translation by A. M. Richards with illustrations by Anna Richards. There are head- and tail-pieces to each chapter as well as seven full-page black and white illustrations. These are more atmospheric than Robinson's drawings, but at times an over-use of black creates a rather confusing image. That this was an edition designed for children is made clear by the advertisements for other children's books at the end of the volume.

Whether the translation made by A. C Farquharson, illustrated by Edmund J. Sullivan (1869-1933) and published by Methuen and Co. in 1908 was designed for children is doubtful. Although it is not a gift-book of the Rackham type, the larger format and attention to typography and layout mark the book as more ambitious. Moreover, the twenty full-page pen-and-ink drawings by Sullivan are calculatedly modelled on the style and mood of the engraving by Dürer that was Fouqué's point of departure, and their size gives them an impact denied to Robinson and Richards. However, this was almost certainly the last time that *Sintram* was presented for adult readership.

A plain-text version with a brief introduction was issued for school reading in Blackie's English School Texts in 1905. This goes back to Burns's first translation, anonymous, unacknowledged and probably out of copyright. The story is left to speak for itself, but the edition is hardly one that children would have bought for themselves or that their parents would have bought. Much more agreeable is the version published in 1911 by Wells Gardner, Darton and Co. This was based on the same publishers' earlier edition, in which *Sintram* was combined with *Undine* and furnished with an introduction by Charlotte M. Yonge. The text was edited and shortened by Mary Macleod, but the most pleasing feature of the book was that the cover and three of the full-page plates were reproduced in colour from Gordon Browne's original painted illustrations. Only a small number of Browne's drawings and monochrome plates for the earlier book are utilized, but they add considerably to the attractiveness of the book.

This was the last form in which *Sintram* was presented before the First World War. There had been a drama based on the story written by Helen Leslie in 1901, and another school version, edited by Gordon S. Maxwell, was published by Brodie Books in 1928. Julius Hare's translation was reprinted in 'The World's Classics' collection of Fouqué's four most popular tales, entitled *Undine and Other Stories* (Oxford University Press, 1932), but this seems to have marked the demise of *Sintram* in English. In this book *Sintram* returns to its first English form, the first translation and one intended for adults. Its time as a children's book only covers the period from, say, 1883 to 1911, though children may well have read the mid-century editions published by Burns and Lumley. In the wake of the First World War *Sintram* must have seemed completely out of date. The fearful hero's struggles against symbolic enemies and supernatural powers were an anachronism for children, boys in particular, whose experience included, whether directly or indirectly, the traumas and adventures of modern warfare.

9. Adelbert von Chamisso's *Peter Schlemihl*

In Britain the German Romantic writer Adelbert von Chamisso (1781-1838) is known for one thing only – his extraordinary story of Peter Schlemihl, the man who exchanges his shadow for a purse which, like that of Fortunatus, produces gold coins every time he puts his hand in it. Later in the story Schlemihl acquires a pair of seven-league boots which enable him to travel quickly wherever he wants to go. These are fairytale devices, but *Peter Schlemihl* was not designed as a children's book any more than was Fouqué's *Undine*. In what they enable to happen the gold-producing purse and the seven-league boots correspond to the inexhaustible purse and wishing hat of the late medieval German story of *Fortunatus*, which, though employing various magical devices, is thought of as an ancestor of the modern novel for its realistic accounts of people, events and places. *Fortunatus* unfolds a profoundly moral and thought-provoking view of the world, illustrating the problems that the possession of great wealth is apt to bring and showing how human desires untempered by reason lead to self-destruction. It proved popular both in Germany and abroad. In Germany it circulated as a *Volksbuch* right up to the nineteenth century. In Britain there were translations, a verse play by Thomas Dekker, several chapbooks and adaptations for children from the mid eighteenth century onwards. *Peter Schlemihl*, like *Fortunatus*, has aspects that could appeal to children, but it primarily embodies unsettling questions about alienation and identity that belong indubitably to the province of adulthood. However, some of these anxieties were put back into the sphere of childhood by Hans Andersen in his story 'The Shadow', which was clearly sparked off by Chamisso.

The plot of *Peter Schlemihl* is deceptively simple, but the telling is full of subtle touches that create suspense and make the reader ponder. The story, like Kafka's *The Metamorphosis*, depends on a single event that transgresses reason, before and after which the narrative proceeds in a perfectly matter-of-fact manner until a further element of fantasy – the accidental acquisition of seven-league boots – comes in at the end. Schlemihl, the protagonist of the story, tells in the first person how he went with a letter of introduction to meet a gentleman called Thomas John, from whom he expected to get help. Among the party of people gathered in the garden of John's house he sees a beautiful lady, Fanny, and witnesses how a nameless man in a grey coat produces from his pocket a series of objects, beginning plausibly enough with plaster to bind Fanny's bleeding hand, pricked by a thorn from a rose, then going on to a telescope, a large Turkish carpet, a pleasure-tent and three black horses. No one apart from Schlemihl appears in the least amazed at what happens, yet no one knows who the man is. Schlemihl decides to leave the company, but encounters the mysterious stranger as he departs and is persuaded to part with his beautiful shadow in exchange for a magic purse. Almost immediately Schlemihl discovers that people notice the loss of his shadow, point it out and mock him for it. Wealth, however, eases his path considerably, and he gains the reputation of being a certain 'Count Peter'. He attempts to deflect mockery through avoiding light when outdoors, but every time his lack of a shadow is noted he is ostracized. In this way he loses the hand of his love, Mina, because of her father's suspicions and antagonism. The man in the grey coat keeps reappearing unexpectedly at different stages in Schlemihl's history. On the first occasion, a year and a day after their first meeting, Schlemihl refuses to sign away his soul to the man when it departs naturally from his body. None of Schlemihl's attempts to regain his shadow are successful. The latter part of the story sees him travelling all over the world with the aid of the seven-league boots and devoting himself to scientific work in botany, collecting lichens and algae. He falls ill, faints and on recovering finds himself a patient in an institution called the Schlemihlium, founded in his name, where he is looked after, unrecognized, by Bendel and the widowed Mina. On departing from the hospital he leaves a note, telling them that their old friend is now doing better than previously and that, if he is doing penance, it is the penance of reconciliation. Schlemihl finds his dog again and returns home, finally communicating his strange history to Chamisso.

Chamisso, like E. T. A. Hoffmann in *Nußknacker und Mausekönig* (Nutcracker and Mouse-King), makes great play between levels of fantasy

Adelbert von Chamisso's Peter Schlemihl 137

and reality. The fictive Peter Schlemihl addresses his story in a manuscript to his friend Chamisso, whom he addresses five times as Chamisso and twice as Adelbert in the course of the narrative. The story also refers explicitly to Fouqué's novel *Der Zauberring* (The Magic Ring) of 1813, which Schlemihl dreams is lying on Chamisso's desk along with the works of Haller, Humboldt, Linné and a volume of Goethe. *Der Zauberring* was the latest novel of Chamisso's friend Fouqué, while Albrecht von Haller, Alexander von Humboldt and Carl von Linné were among the leading scientists of the day. Indeed, the various scientific works that Schlemihl declares himself to have written at the end of the book probably represent a kind of homage to Humboldt's explorations and publications in the fields of geography and botany. Schlemihl mentions only the interior of Africa and Asia, the northern polar regions and the eastern coasts of Asia, a complement to Humboldt's concern at this time with South and Central America. The suggestion that Schlemihl's manuscripts will be deposited in the University of Berlin on his death is a graceful acknowledgement of the very recent founding of the University by Alexander's brother, Wilhelm.

Goethe may well represent the synthesis of science and literature with the unnamed volume from his extensive works. We may imagine that volume to be the first part of *Faust*, published in 1808, with its Mephistopheles stalking anonymously through the pages of *Peter Schlemihl*. But the man in the grey coat is more urbane than the figure of the wandering scholar in whose guise Mephistopheles first appears in *Faust*, though his grey coat may recall the diabolical grey monk who first fills that role in the sixteenth-century *Historia von D. Johann Fausten*. But the Devil also appears unbidden in various guises in folktales that were current during Chamisso's own lifetime. The second volume of the Grimms' *Kinder- und Hausmärchen* (1815) has two such tales, in which he appears as a little mannikin ('Des Teufels rußiger Bruder') and as a man in a green coat ('Der Teufel Grünrock', later replaced by 'Der Bärenhäuter') and provides magical gifts in exchange for services of strange kinds. The man in the grey coat offers Schlemihl a choice of typical fairytale devices, among which feature the magic napkin of Roland's squires (referring to a *Volksbuch* that Musäus also refashioned), a mandrake (probably alluding to a story by Fouqué) and the wishing-cap and magic purse of Fortunatus. Chamisso thus cleverly splices the fairytale world with popular literature of the day. The conclusion of the book returns to the subject of scientific enquiry regarding the natural world, and here Schlemihl adverts to another contemporary Romantic author, Ludwig

Tieck, drawing him into this ambiguous world of fact and fiction with an allusion to the satirically titled *De rebus gestis Pollicilli*, i.e. *Leben und Taten des kleinen Thomas, genannt Däumchen* (Life and Deeds of Little Thomas, called Thumbling) (1812), a Tom Thumb play based largely on Perrault's fairytale 'Le petit Poucet' In this way Peter Schlemihl becomes a nexus of both traditional tales and the most up-to-the-minute contemporary literature and scientific research.

The fact that many features of Schlemihl's story reflect key aspects of Chamisso's own life has led to an understandable, but unfortunate emphasis on biographical interpretations of the story, but Chamisso himself was careful to avoid answering questions about the meaning of the story's symbolism. Its continuing appeal derives from the fact that Chamisso, like Kafka, leaves many things open and unexplained while at the same time creating a coherent narrative.

Schlemihl gains access to Thomas John through a letter from the latter's brother, about which John says he will perhaps have time to speak later, if Schlemihl stays. But Schlemihl leaves before any explanation is made and in the process encounters again the man in the grey coat, with results that dictate the remainder of his life. Schlemihl's voyage before arriving in the unnamed port is characterized as both fortunate (*glücklich*) and yet very troublesome (*beschwerlich*) for him, a pointer to the strange events that overtake him. By the end of the first chapter he has exchanged his initial poverty for boundless wealth, but also loses his senses. In his new life he acquires a new identity as Count Peter through the mystification of the King of Prussia using that name as an incognito, and this identity obtains for the central sections of the narrative. Later, after he has seen the fate of Thomas John at the hands of the man in the grey coat – *Justo judicio Dei judicatus sum; justo judicio Dei condemnatus sum* (I have been judged and condemned by the just judgement of God) – and after he has hurled the purse of fortune into the abyss, he experiences a period of wandering that resembles that of the Wandering Jew. This image of the Jew is made explicit as he is reduced to an existence as a mere number, Number Twelve, in the so-called Schlemihlium where he recovers from the extremes of his physical exertions. The name Schlemihl comes from a Hebrew word meaning 'good for nothing' and connotes a persistently unlucky person. Because of his long beard Schlemihl is thought to be a Jew, but was 'not less carefully looked after on this account'. The legend of the Wandering Jew is part of the widespread Christian tradition of hostility towards the Jews as a people for condemning Christ to be crucified, but the narrator's comment seems to hold out a prospect of mercy. Number Twelve presumably suggests the last of the twelve tribes of Israel. At the end of the book Schlemihl returns to his old life of scientific research, aided by the seven-league boots which do not wear out, and he concludes by admonishing Chamisso, the recipient of his story, to respect first the shadow and only afterwards money.

The links between *Peter Schlemihl* and folktales are readily apparent. But we can perhaps also note similarities with *Munchausen* in the travels to Russia and other exotic places, and with *The Swiss Family Robinson* in the geographical and botanical explorations. Despite these features that would surely appeal to children, most of the English translations seem to have adults as their target readers. Up to 1914 there were a dozen editions of *Peter Schlemihl* in English, two of which form part of composite volumes containing items of interest to children. The first was an 1889 volume published by Cassell, which includes Carové's *The Story Without an End* and Novalis's *Hymns to Night* – a rather strange combination of literary works. *The Story Without an End*, a religiose tale for children that enjoyed considerable popularity from much earlier in the century, figures elsewhere in this book. The second composite volume was a copiously illustrated gift book that presents *Schlemihl* alongside Wilhelm Hauff's 'The Cold Heart' (London: Holden & Hardingham, 1914). Both are Romantic tales written within around a dozen years of each other and sit together well in terms of their focus on fantasies of wealth and its dangers.

If we now look at the translations of *Schlemihl* in chronological order, we can see an immediate parallel with the transmission of the Grimms' fairytales. Both English editions were first illustrated by George Cruikshank, and both printed an anonymous translation that has been reissued many times up to the present day. The Cruikshank illustrations to *Schlemihl* were reprinted at least twice in the nineteenth century, but have only been used once, enlarged, in the twentieth in a limited edition (Henley on Thames: Langtry Press, 1992). Cruikshank's eight etchings pick out key stages in Schlemihl's history – the man in the grey coat picking up Schlemihl's shadow; Schlemihl with Fanny in the garden; alone in his room; the man in the grey coat attempting to get Schlemihl to sign the deed; chasing his shadow; on the edge of the abyss; crossing the sea in the seven-league boots; escaping the polar bear. Undoubtedly, these illustrations helped to give Schlemihl a good send-off in his English guise.

Chamisso's German original was edited by Friedrich de la Motte Fouqué and published in Nuremberg in 1814. In consequence the first English translation attributes the work, wrongly though not entirely surprisingly, to 'Lamotte Fouqué'. It appeared in 1824 (London: G. and W. B. Whittaker) in the same format and a year later than the Grimms' *German Popular Stories*. Fouqué's own *Undine* had been published in English in 1818. Clearly, prose works of the German Romantics were making quite an impact in Britain. The translation of *Peter Schlemihl* appeared anonymously, but it stemmed from the pen of Sir John Bowring (1792-1872), as the attribution in later editions makes plain. Bowring was a considerable linguist, writer and traveller and made translations of Goethe, Schiller and Heine. As well as being elected a Fellow of the Royal Society, he received numerous foreign honours.

A notice by the translator in the 1824 edition attributes the impetus for translating Schlemihl to a conversation with Adelung in Petersburgh (Saint Petersburg). This was Friedrich von Adelung (1768-1843), the nephew of the famous grammarian and lexicographer J. C. Adelung, who had been the teacher of Princes Nicholas and Michael, the brothers of Tsar Alexander I, and who in 1824 became Director of the Oriental Institute. After this notice by the translator follows a sonnet, 'To my Friend Wangner', presumably by Bowring. Then comes the author's introduction, i.e. a letter written by Chamisso to his friend Julius Eduard Hitzig, another member of the literary circle in Berlin that included Fouqué and Hoffmann. This letter declares the work to have been put into Chamisso's hands by 'A strange man with a long grey beard, wearing a black, worn-out kurtka, with a botanical case suspended at his side, and slippers over his boots, on account of the damp, rainy weather, [who] inquired after me, and left these papers behind him. He pretended he came from Berlin'. This letter figures in most editions of Chamisso's story and forms part of the playfulness in the story itself, claiming factuality for something that is transparently a fiction. Hitzig, in a letter to Fouqué dated January 1827, describes how, when he first read *Schlemihl* to Hoffmann, the latter 'was beside himself with delight and eagerness, and hung upon my lips till I got to the end'. Hoffmann's reaction not only displays his own affinity to Chamisso as a writer, but is a splendid testimony to the inherent fascination of the story.

Bowring covers himself as a translator by declaring: 'I have not scrupled to introduce a few verbal alterations; but the deviations from the original are very trifling'. His understanding of German is not perfect, so some generally minor mistakes enter the text, but otherwise he follows the

Adelbert von Chamisso's Peter Schlemihl 141

16. *Peter Schlemihl. With plates by George Cruikshank* (1824).

original closely. He makes Thomas John, the man to whom Schlemihl had a letter of introduction, into the more familiar Thomas Jones. One misprint seems to have gone through all subsequent reprints of Bowring. At the opening of chapter 3 in the original Schlemihl describes himself alone in his room, starving despite his gold, as lying like Faffner with his hoard. This appears in English as 'Taffner by his strong hold', and it was never corrected. The *Tarnkappe* or 'cloak of darkness', which allows the wearer to become invisible and which is used by the man in the grey coat in chapter 6 to destroy Schlemihl's prospect of marrying Mina, is misleadingly called a 'wishing cap'. The allusion to Faffner and the *Tarnkappe* links up with Fouqué's dramatic trilogy *Der Held des Nordens* (1808-10), which deals with the legendary figure of Siegfried on the basis of Scandinavian sources, where he is called Sigurd. Presumably the name was garbled in English because it was not recognized and its associations were not understood.

Bowring's translation, together with Cruikshank's plates, was reissued in 1861 (London: Robert Hardwicke) and 1878 (London: Hardwick & Bogue). It was used a generation later, with new illustrations by Gordon Browne, in an edition clearly designed for children (London: Chatto & Windus, 1910). This Edwardian book has a new title – *The Shadowless Man, Peter*

Schlehmihl – though it is new only for this translation, as naming the book *The Shadowless Man* goes back to a different translation of 1843. In this 1910 edition Bowring is explicitly credited with the translation, as he had been with the editions of 1861 and 1878, but the 'note to a new edition', which refers to the translation having been made '[m]ore than twenty years ago' must have been taken from an edition that appeared in the late 1840s. By 1910 Cruikshank's illustrations would have seemed very old-fashioned, hence the new commissions from Gordon Browne (1858-1932), who illustrated a whole host of children's books in the period from the 1880s to just after the First World War. The full-colour frontispiece, sixteen full-page black and white drawings, twelve smaller drawings and numerous headpieces are vigorous and varied, but Browne is more interested in the social satire and comic sides of the story than in capturing its more menacing and unsettling aspects. While the book still contains Bowring's 'To my Friend Wangner' and Chamisso's letter to Hitzig, it sandwiches between them a letter of Fouqué to Wangner (Hitzig seems to be the recipient) and a fuller one from Hitzig to Fouqué, together with Chamisso's poem 'To my old Friend, Peter Schlemihl', dated 1834. All of them are designed to paint the background to the story's original appearance in print in Germany. Literary history thus becomes an increasingly insistent accompaniment to Chamisso's tale, even in an edition targeted at children.

The second and third translations of *Schlemihl* both appeared in the same year, 1843. One was anonymous, the other was by William Howitt. Howitt's translation appeared in a bilingual edition published by Longman and Co. in Nuremberg and London, and it contains six illustrations. William Howitt (1792-1879) had a particular interest in Germany, and he and his wife Mary, a prolific children's author, lived in Heidelberg and travelled around the country from 1840 to 1843. William's solid, richly informative book, *The Rural and Domestic Life of Germany*, had been published by Longman, Brown, Green, and Longmans in 1842 and is based on detailed first-hand knowledge. It is one of the major books in English about contemporary Germany, since Howitt had an enquiring mind and wrote appreciatively, though not uncritically, about what he saw. His translation of *Schlemihl*, however, has a tendency to literalism, perhaps because it was intended as an aid to understanding the German rather than standing as a work on its own. As far as I am aware, it was not reprinted during the nineteenth century, but was used for the Rodale Press edition of 1954, which was designed as a piece of stylish printing to set off Peter Rudland's striking two-colour wood-engravings.

The other translation of 1843 was entitled *The Shadowless Man; or, the Wonderful History of Peter Schlemihl* (London: James Burns) and was reissued in 1845. Around this period Burns was also publishing translations of tales by Musäus, Fouqué and Hauff among others and clearly had a fascination with German literature of the previous sixty to seventy years. When Burns ceased publishing this kind of secular material in 1847, having converted to Rome,[58] his stock was taken over by Edward Lumley, from whom there is a typically undated edition (c. 1860). A Routledge edition with exactly the same title and same number of pages (London and New York: G. Routledge & Sons, [1877]) is almost certainly a further printing of this translation.

Burns's anonymous translator, perhaps the same as he used for other German prose tales, was not a master at the art. He or she was apt to omit occasional sentences, presumably through inability to understand, and there are certainly instances of misunderstanding or simplification that point to an imperfect command of German. These are relatively minor faults, compensated for by helpful explanations elsewhere. Thus, the reference to Faffner is turned into 'like the dragon guarding his treasure', and the *Tarnkappe* is called a 'mist-cap'. Chamisso's original eleven chapters are combined to make five, a process of reduction that Burns used also in his edition of Fouqué's *Undine*. Proper names are kept as in the original apart from Mina (a diminutive of Wilhelmina) being changed to Minna and Schlemihl's appropriately named servant Raskal getting the English spelling for his name. The book is adorned with seven small engravings by an unknown artist.

The Burns/Lumley translation crops up again in a combined edition of *Schlemihl* and Hauff's 'The Cold Heart' (London: Holden & Hardingham, [1914]). Here it is given the title of *The Marvellous History of the Shadowless Man*. An eight-page introduction by A. S. Rappoport sketches in information about Chamisso and the background to the story. However, the main interest of the edition lies in its eleven full-colour plates and six two-colour plates by Forster Robson, for whom the events of the story provide opportunity for a great variety of scenes – picturesque old town, open heath, dark forest, bleak mountain, frozen sea, tropical island, nocturnal settings, a closed room and a romantic dream. This is the full gift book treatment, more chocolate box than individual vision. It is a pity that Rackham never

---

58 Brian Alderson, 'Some Notes on James Burns as a Publisher of Children's Books', *Bulletin of the John Rylands University Library of Manchester*, 76, 3 (Autumn 1994), p. 122.

illustrated the story.

Two other editions were published in the last dozen years of the nineteenth century, paralleling the interest shown in Fouqué's *Undine* and *Sintram* in the same period. The first, an edition of 1889, which printed *Schlemihl* along with works by Carové and Novalis, has already been mentioned. The second is notable for containing illustrations by Sir Philip Burne-Jones and an introduction by the folklore scholar Joseph Jacobs (London: George Allen, 1899).

All of the editions mentioned so far are serious attempts at translating Chamisso's masterpiece into English. They are witness to a fascination with the story over every decade from 1824 to 1914, if we can take the Lumley edition as having been available in the 1850s. They were all aimed at the intelligent middle-class reader. Evidence of a different readership, however, is provided by a little volume entitled *Tales of Fairy Land; or, Legends of the Olden Time*, published 'for the booksellers' in 1852 in a series called 'The Cottage Library'. This is the kind of book that the Halifax firm of Milner and Sowerby and the Wakefield firm of William Nicholson and Sons published during this period and later in the nineteenth century, but this particular volume was printed by Joseph Smith of High Holburn. The preface declares roundly: 'the Germans seem to possess the faculty of invention and contrivance, together with originality of conception and power of execution in such an eminent degree, as to leave the legendary writers of our own, and other countries, at an immeasurable distance'. A little further on it asserts: 'The Romance writer of Germany brings into action such *outre* beings, such legions of Number Nips, such unheard of Demons, Incubusses, Freeshooters, Wild Huntsmen, Bottle Imps, Nightmares, Cocked-hats, and Wooden-legs, as to defy all imitation . . .' This is, thus, just the place to find a curious version of *Peter Schlemihl; or the Man without a Shadow* amidst a variety of poems and prose tales from Ireland, Scotland and Germany.

This is less a translation than an adaptation of Chamisso's story. Indeed, there is no mention of Chamisso as author, still less any indication of adapter. There are several alterations in names. The unnamed place to which Schlemihl sails in Chamisso's original is here called Torrenburg, and Thomas John is oddly rechristened Henric Melthal. The surname may well be taken from the Melctal who figures as the chief supporter of the Swiss patriot William Tell in Florian's retelling of the traditional story. Fanny is given the name Angelina, Schlemihl's servant Bendel becomes Bandel, while Raskal becomes the much less symbolic Bernsdoff (probably a misspelling for Bernsdorff). The forester's daughter Mina, whom Schlemihl is unsuccessful in gaining as his bride, is renamed Maria. The story is given without divisions into chapters and follows the outline of the original up to the middle of chapter 9, when it presents an alternative ending. At the point in the original where Schlemihl thinks that he might find work in a mine he does so, but then experiences such taunts from the other miners that he contemplates suicide. Despairing, he falls asleep and has a dream in which he once more meets his tormentor, the man in the grey coat, refuses to sign his bond and wakes up to find his shadow has been restored. Surprisingly, Bandel greets him outside the mine as the men arrive for their labours. It turns out that Bernsdoff and Maria have not actually married, as Raskal and Mina did in Chamisso's original, so she is not a widow after her husband's criminal execution. Schlemihl can now happily marry her himself and continue with Bandel as his faithful servant. This is, of course, a travesty of the original. It eliminates the episode of the Schlemihlium and removes Schlemihl from the mysterious isolation in which he exists at the end of the story. The happy ending of romance and fairytale has supplanted the solitary life of the scholar and scientist.

Peter Schlemihl is another of those works of German Romantic fiction that were designed for an adult readership, but gradually were also adopted by children. The version included in *Tales of Fairy Land* was certainly in this case, as my copy of this book contains the inscription 'Mary Sumner Willson / A Birthday Present / from Papa'. Though some aspects of the story – its literary and contemporary allusions, for example – may have escaped the attention of youthful readers, the narrative plot is readily accessible. It was illustrated from the start, and Cruikshank's etchings were also used in Germany. The most extensive set of illustrations came from the pen of Gordon Browne nearly eighty years later. Chamisso's story continued to be reprinted and abridged in the period after the First World War, and a new translation was made in 1957. *Schlemihl* did not enjoy quite as high a degree of favour in nineteenth-century Britain as Fouqué's *Undine*, but it deservedly achieved the status of a classic.

10. The Fairytales of the Brothers Grimm

Without a shadow of doubt the single most important German contribution to world literature is the collection of traditional tales made by the Brothers Grimm and first published in two small volumes in 1812-15. It outshines Goethe's *Faust* and such twentieth-century classics as Mann's *Death in Venice* or Kafka's *The Trial* by virtue of an infinitely greater readership. Not only have the tales been translated in whole or in part into virtually every major language in the world, but they have generated countless new editions and adaptations and become the cornerstone of the study of folktales not only in Germany, but throughout the world. Many individual tales, such as 'Snow-White', 'Rumpelstiltskin', 'Hansel and Gretel' and 'Rapunzel', have become a firm part of popular culture. The collection has been the inspiration of some of the finest artists and illustrators from George Cruikshank and Walter Crane to Arthur Rackham, Edmund Dulac, Maurice Sendak and David Hockney, to mention only those who are especially famous in the English-speaking world.

Jacob and Wilhelm Grimm (1785-1863 and 1786-1859) did not set out to produce a children's book that would be unflaggingly popular for nearly two hundred years. Their enterprise was originally a scholarly one: to make a collection of traditional oral tales before they disappeared in the face of increasing literacy. It was all of a piece with the rediscovery of the Middle Ages that was a general western European phenomenon from the latter part of the eighteenth century onwards and particularly among the German Romantics. They did not collect all the tales directly from peasant or local storytellers, but relied on a variety of largely middle-class informants, some of their own acquaintance in the town of Kassel, where they lived, and the surrounding area of Hessen, others from further afield in Westphalia and other parts of Germany. At the outset they received a couple of tales in Low German from the painter Philipp Otto Runge – 'The Fisherman and his Wife' and 'The Juniper Tree' – which seem to have provided a narrative model for the collection as a whole. A small proportion of tales were taken from literary sources. Clearly, the stories were not reproduced verbatim from the mouth of a storyteller; the collectors made summaries that were as accurate as possible, but did not include every word and phrase of what they heard. When the stories were prepared for publication, these summaries were expanded and stylistically improved. For about sixty of the tales included in the volume published in 1812 it is possible to compare the Grimms' original manuscript with the printed text and see the editorial process at work.[59] In half a dozen tales quite significant alterations of content were made, but elsewhere the changes are more to do with presentation, a smoother and livelier style and occasional embellishment. The Grimms' original intention had been to keep more closely to their sources, but as they collected more material they found themselves combining features from different versions of the same tale. In this way they can be said to have created the standard form of many tales.

The two brothers worked together on the first edition of what they called *Kinder- und Hausmärchen* (Children's and Household Tales), and there is no difference in editorial practice or style between them. They also included a few pages of notes in this first edition. But it is little known among English readers that the Grimms went on to produce six further editions of the tales – the second in 1819-22, the third in 1837, the fourth in 1840, the fifth in 1843, the sixth in 1850 and the seventh in 1857. Each of these editions is different from the rest. The major change occurred between the first and second editions, when a large number of tales were eliminated, others added and considerable stylistic and verbal changes were made. Wilhelm Grimm, who bore the responsibility alone for the later editions, continued to make alterations, additions, subtractions and improvements to the collection right to the end. The notes swelled to form a separate volume in 1822, and they too were added to until a third edition appeared in 1856. Under Wilhelm's editorship the tales achieved classic

---

59 Heinz Rölleke, *Die älteste Märchensammlung der Brüder Grimm. Synopse der handschriftlichen Urfassung von 1810 und der Erstdrucke von 1812* (Cologny-Genève: Fondation Martin Bodmer, 1975).

status and eventually overtook the rival collection of Ludwig Bechstein in popularity. Most people nowadays tend to think of the fairytale as the kind of traditional story that the Grimms presented, not perhaps realizing that it is the product of its time and its editors. The Grimms' tales are the epitome of small-town middle-class central Germany, where the values of hard work, thrift, modesty, enterprise and orderliness are underpinned by a simple Protestant faith. They were easy to transpose to Britain, though we shall see that some modifications were necessary for them to acclimatize completely.

When Edgar Taylor made the first translation of the Grimms into English as *German Popular Stories, translated from the Kinder und Haus Märchen, collected by M.M. Grimm, from oral tradition* (London: C. Baldwyn, 1823), the fairytale as a genre was very much in the grip of the French. Of course, such truly English fairytales as 'Jack the Giant-killer', 'Whittington and his Cat', 'Tom Hickathrift', 'Tom Thumb' and 'Jack and the Beanstalk' had circulated in chapbooks, but English tales were not systematically collected until later. It was the fairytales of Charles Perrault, Madame d'Aulnoy and Madame Leprince de Beaumont that dominated the scene. Perrault's 'Little Red Riding-hood', 'Cinderella', 'Bluebeard', 'The Sleeping Beauty in the Wood' and 'Puss-in-Boots' had already become renowned. Madame d'Aulnoy was probably even better known with such tales as 'Graciosa and Percinet', 'The Yellow Dwarf', 'The White Cat' and 'The Blue Bird', while Madame Leprince de Beaumont's fame was to have written the classic version of 'Beauty and the Beast'. In addition, the *Arabian Nights*, introduced to Europe in a French translation by Antoine Galland in the early eighteenth century, had also provided favourites such as 'Aladdin', 'Sindbad the Sailor' and 'Ali Baba and the Forty Thieves'. But it was now the turn of Germany, which was currently enjoying a vogue of novels, stories and plays in English translation, to inject a new range of material into the realm of the fairytale

German Popular Stories (1823), to which a second volume was added in 1826 (London: James Robins & Co.; Dublin: Joseph Robins Junr. & Co.), has several important claims to fame. Not only did it introduce the Grimms to the English-speaking public, but it also set the pattern for fairytales to be copiously illustrated. The Grimms' German original had had no illustrations, but George Cruikshank's twenty-two etchings for the two English volumes were crucial to the books' early popularity and even led to the publication of a German small edition (a selection of fifty tales) illustrated by Ludwig Emil Grimm, Jacob and Wilhelm's younger brother. Ludwig Emil had already provided frontispieces for the two volumes of the 1819 edition, of which the portrait of Dorothea Viehmann, the Grimms' chief informant from the Kassel area, has been much reproduced and imitated in many later editions. Cruikshank's illustrations, brimful of vitality and movement and delighting in the comic and the grotesque, have proved enduringly popular with British readers, so much so that they are still reproduced today, usually with Edgar Taylor's translation.

What kind of picture of the Grimms' collection did Edgar Taylor give?[60] His principal source, the 1819 edition of the *Kinder- und Hausmärchen*, contains 161 tales and nine children's legends, from which Taylor took fifty-seven plus one further tale ('The Nose') that he extracted from the notes in the third volume of 1822. That is about a third of the total then available. Most of these correspond to single tales in the translation, but he combined 'Das Lumpengesindel', 'Herr Korbes' and 'Von dem Tod des Hühnchens' into the one sequence of 'Chanticleer and Partlet' (incidentally taking the names from Chaucer), and 'Der junge Riese' and 'Das tapfere Schneiderlein' were joined to make 'The Young Giant and the Tailor'. Similarly, 'Das kluge Grethel', 'Der gescheidte Hans' and 'Die faule Spinnerin' were turned into 'Hans and his Wife', while 'Vom Fundevogel', 'Der Liebste Roland' and 'Hänsel und Grethel' were transformed into the one story 'Roland and May-bird'. The first volume contained 'The Grateful Beasts', a translation of a story that retained its place in the German editions up to 1850, but was then relegated to the Appendix as no.18 in the 1857 edition. In this same first volume only one of the three tales that form 'Die Wichtelmänner' is retained in 'The Elves and the Shoemaker'.

Taylor's second volume is distinguished from the first in that it contains four tales that do not belong to the Grimms' collection at all. Two of these were taken from J. G. Büsching's *Volks-Sagen, Märchen und Legenden* (1812), namely, 'Pee-wit' and 'Cherry, or the Frog-bride'. 'Peter the Goatherd' is taken from Otmar's *Volcks-Sagen*, probably prompted by the recent publication of Washington Irving's *Rip van Winkle* (1819), which Taylor refers to in his notes and which is a version of the same tale-type. Finally, with 'The Elfin Grove' Taylor provided a much abridged adaptation

---

60 Most of what follows on the translations of Edgar Taylor and John Edward Taylor and that issued by Addey and Co. is taken from David Blamires, 'The Early Reception of the Grimms' *Kinder- und Hausmärchen* in England'. *Bulletin of the John Rylands University Library of Manchester*, 71, 3 (Autumn 1989), pp. 69-77.

of Tieck's mysterious tale 'Die Elfen' (1811). In some ways this could be considered an odd procedure, as there were plenty more of the Grimms' tales that could have been included by Taylor. As it was, it drew attention to the fact that the Grimms were not ploughing a lonely furrow, but had many compatriots working along similar lines or with similar interests. 'Peter the Goatherd' in fact circulated later in the century in another translation by Madame de Chatelain.

It is noticeable that Taylor zealously avoided using any of the Grimms' tales with a religious dimension, so there is no 'Marienkind', no 'Der Schneider im Himmel', no 'Der Gevatter Tod', no 'Bruder Lustig' – the list could be extended. The prevalence of the Devil in the German tales caused Taylor worry, so these tales also were omitted or the Devil was converted into a giant, as in 'The Giant with the Three Golden Hairs'. 'The Fisherman and his Wife' had to be modified slightly at the end. Where in the original the fisherman's wife declares finally that she wants to be 'like God', Taylor tells us that he has 'softened the boldness of the lady's ambition' by indicating that she wants to be 'lord of the sun and moon'. It perhaps hardly needs to be stated that Taylor did not translate any of the children's legends. He probably omitted the 'Märchen von einem, der auszog, das Fürchten zu lernen' on account of its inclusion of ghosts and other beliefs about the dead. Similarly, 'Der singende Knochen' would have seemed unacceptably superstitious.

Violence and cruelty was generally reduced. It is surprising that Taylor actually included 'The Robber Bridegroom' in his selection, though he eliminated the cannibalistic intentions of the robbers, their deliberate murder of the captured maiden, and their chopping off of her finger. These horrifying details are some of the most memorable features of the original German story, and similar ones are to be found in several other tales. 'Aschenputtel' (the Grimms' version of 'Cinderella') ends with the doves picking out the eyes of the wicked stepsisters as the heroine goes to her wedding, but this final paragraph of the German version is excised by Taylor so that the story ends on a happier note. Taylor's second volume ends with 'The Juniper Tree', which he translated rather freely, perhaps because the Low German text was difficult for him, but he cut out the cannibalistic episode in which the father is served up the flesh of his murdered son in a stew. Taylor simply has the father given 'a large dish of black soup' with no implication as to its content. This entails an alteration to the second line of the famous song of the bird – the song that Gretchen sings in Goethe's

Faust – so that instead of 'my father ate me' we have the much milder 'my father thought me lost and gone'. There is still plenty of violence left in the tale, especially at the end where the bird drops the millstone on the stepmother's head and crushes her to pieces, but it is clear that Taylor took pains to reduce the elements of terror and cruelty that he found in the original German.

This first of the translators of the Grimms into English is very concerned about the impact of the stories on his readers. In his introduction he alludes to 'many stories of great merit, and tending highly to the elucidation of ancient mythology, customs, and opinions, which the scrupulous fastidiousness of modern taste, especially in works likely to attract the attention of youth, warned [the translators] to pass by'. This 'scrupulous fastidiousness of modern taste', an expression which may be linked with the growth of Evangelicalism and of prudery that is characteristic of the end of the eighteenth and beginning of the nineteenth century, accounts for Taylor's alterations of religious and other features mentioned earlier, but there are a few others that should be noted too. The original of 'The Fisherman and his Wife' has the couple initially living in a 'Pispott' (chamber-pot), which Taylor changed to a 'ditch', while in his 1839 revision of the text (which I shall come to in due course) he altered it again to a 'pig-stye'. Several later translators settled for a 'hovel'.

There were other places where sexuality was the issue. 'Rapunzel', with its unavoidable implication that the girl and the prince have made love in the tower, was not translated at all. Then there was 'The Frog Prince', the ending of which Taylor drastically altered. Exceptionally here, Taylor was translating from the 1812 text of the story, not the 1819 edition that was the source for all his other tales. This is the opening tale in all seven German editions, and it seems likely that Taylor first encountered the Grimms' collection in the first edition and made at that time a translation of the first tale. When he later got down to serious work on the tales, he then followed the more recent second edition.

In the German original the frog is supposed to sleep with the princess in her bed, but she cannot bring herself to do this, despite the king's insistence that she must fulfil her promise to the frog. This, in translation, is what the 1812 edition says:

> It was no use, she had to do as her father wanted, but in her heart she was bitterly angry. She grasped the frog with two fingers and took him up to her room, got into bed and instead of placing him beside her flung him

smash against the wall. 'Now you'll leave me in peace, you nasty frog!'

But the frog did not fall down dead, but when he came down on to the bed, it was a handsome young prince. He was now her dear companion, and she esteemed him as she had promised, and they fell contentedly asleep together.

Taylor's version – it cannot be called a translation – tells a different set of events:

> ... the princess took him up in her hand and put him upon the pillow of her own little bed, where he slept all night long. As soon as it was light he jumped up, hopped down stairs, and went out of the house. 'Now', thought the princess, 'he is gone, and I shall be troubled with him no more'.
> But she was mistaken; for when night came again, she heard the same tapping at the door, and when she opened it, the frog came in and slept upon her pillow as before till the morning broke; and the third night he did the same: but when the princess awoke on the following morning, she was astonished to see, instead of the frog, a handsome prince gazing on her with the most beautiful eyes that ever were seen, and standing at the head of her bed.
> He told her that he had been enchanted by a malicious fairy, who had changed him into the form of a frog, in which he was fated to remain till some princess should take him out of the spring and let him sleep upon her bed for three nights.

In Taylor's adaptation there is nothing of the prince and princess sleeping together in human form, though he allows the frog to sleep on the princess's pillow for three nights running. He obviously cannot countenance the princess's attempt to kill the frog by hurling it against the wall. The transformation takes place as it were unconsciously, while the princess is asleep, but the transformed frog is not in her bed, as one might have expected from its lying on her pillow, but is 'standing at the head of her bed'. One detail Taylor may have taken from the 1819 text, and that is the emphasis on the fact that the prince has 'the most beautiful eyes that ever were seen'. The 1812 edition has no comparable comment here. In making his alterations Taylor has rendered the princess passive and obedient to her father's commands and thus deprived her of taking her own initiative and responsibility for what follows. In the German original she confronts her own distaste and causes, however unwittingly, the prince's transformation; she does not simply submit to male authority as embodied in the king, her father.

Taylor was an inveterate softener of harsh details that he found in the Grimms' tales. In the story of 'Rumpelstilzchen' the 1819 text has a disturbing conclusion: '"The Devil's told you that! The Devil's told you that!" cried the little man and dashed his right foot with anger so deep into the ground that he went in up to his body, then in a rage he seized his left foot with both hands and tore himself apart in the middle' (my translation). This horrifying ending Taylor modifies and renders harmlessly absurd: '"Some witch told you that! Some witch told you that!" cried the little man, and dashed his right foot in a rage so deep into the floor, that he was forced to lay hold of it with both hands to pull it out. Then he made the best of his way off, while every body laughed at him for having all his trouble for nothing'. With Taylor this has become a childish temper tantrum, whereas the German ending can be seen as an act of self-destruction that removes the threat of Rumpelstilzchen for ever from the queen's life.

Taylor's interferences with the German texts are too extensive to deal with fully here, but they can be characterized as tending to make the stories more reassuring and less disturbing to the children whom he envisaged as readers. This first English translation thus has a markedly different tone from that of the Grimms' text. Yet we must remember that this is a commonplace occurrence in the transmission of fairytales, whether orally or in printed form. Every storyteller puts his or her own mark on the tale told. There is no perfect, uncontaminated 'original' form. The Grimms' own texts were subject to the same process, as a comparison of the manuscript with the printed forms of the seven editions readily demonstrates. Where they used printed texts from the sixteenth to the early nineteenth centuries, the same kind of adaptation and homogenization is also to be seen.

One irritating feature of Taylor's translation is the fact that he gave a few tales titles that are quite different from their German originals. The most misleading is his 'Hansel and Grettel', which is in fact a translation of 'Brüderchen und Schwesterchen' (Little Brother and Little Sister). What he calls 'Snow-drop' is later usually called 'Snow-White', while his 'Rose-bud' appears as 'Briar Rose' or 'Thorn Rose' (the Grimms' version of 'Sleeping Beauty'). 'Die zertanzten Schuhe' (The Shoes that were Danced to Pieces) is renamed 'The Twelve Dancing Princesses'. The translation of titles is a general problem with the transmission of the Grimms' tales, as subsequent translators have often rendered them very differently. At times it can be quite tricky to identify just which tale is being dealt with.

Taylor's two volumes were well received and quickly reissued, but

The Fairytales of the Brothers Grimm 155

in 1839 the translations, together with preface and notes, made a second appearance with the new title *Gammer Grethel; or German Fairy Tales, and Popular Stories, from the Collection of M.M. Grimm, and Other Sources* (London: John Green). This was a quite new book, as the translation was heavily revised and recast and contained a lot of additions in the nature of asides specifically addressed to a child audience. A number of the originally anonymous protagonists of the stories were given names, and some of the titles of the stories were changed. 'The Grateful Beasts', for example, becomes 'Fritz and his Friends', while Otmar's 'Peter the Goatherd' is renamed 'Karl Katz'. Eighteen of the originally translated stories were omitted, and a new one was added – 'The Bear and the Skrattel'. This latter tale, based on a medieval German verse tale, was taken from the third volume of Thomas Crofton Croker's *Fairy Legends and Traditions of the South of Ireland* (London: John Murray, 1828). Croker had himself got it from the Grimms, who had included the tale in the preface to their translation of Croker's first volume of *Fairy Legends*, published as *Irische Elfenmärchen* (Leipzig, 1826). The tales in *Gammer Grethel* were arranged in a completely different sequence from *German Popular Stories* and designed to be read over a dozen evenings, with three or four tales per evening. Cruikshank's etchings were replaced by wood-engravings by John Byfield after Cruikshank's designs. This revised text was reprinted in 1849 (Bohn's Illustrated Library), 1888 and 1897 (George Bell & Sons) and possibly at other times as well.

Meanwhile, the original translation continued to be reprinted. It appeared with stereotype reproductions of Cruikshank's illustrations, issued by John Camden Hotten in 1869, the original two volumes being printed together as one. This contained a ten-page introduction by Ruskin. Chatto and Windus, who purchased Hotten's business on his death in 1873, did another edition in 1884. Taylor's original translation continued to be used for a large number of subsequent editions, right into the twentieth century, though almost always without any indication of his name. In any case his authorship and that of his friend David Jardine was not known until 1898. Further reprints of the 1823-26 translation up to the end of the twentieth century make it, with all its mistakes of translation and manhandling of the texts, the most influential of all English translations of the Grimms' tales. Certainly, it has charm and reads well, but it is a pity that Taylor and Jardine took so many liberties with the German text.

The majority of British translators of the Grimms concentrate on the true fairytales, the tales of magic, and tend to neglect the other kinds of

156 *Telling Tales*

17. Title-page and frontispiece of *Unlucky John and his Lump of Silver. A Juvenile Comic Tale* (c. 1825).

traditional tales that they collected. While Edgar Taylor provides thirty-four tales of magic (well over half the total), he does give eleven animal tales and eight comic tales. The animal tales are mostly of the fable type, but the three making up 'The Adventures of Chanticleer and Partlet', could equally be thought of as nursery tales. 'The Travelling Musicians, or the Waits of Bremen' is the most ingenious and elaborate of the animal tales translated here. The comic tales mainly have foolish peasants as the butt of their humour, but 'Hans in Luck', which Taylor placed first in his selection, is a tale that can prompt reflection as well as laughter. Hans, having taken his wages from his master, returns home to his mother and on the way makes a series of exchanges of what he has for something more attractive and immediately desirable to him, but less valuable in monetary terms. When he finally gets home he has lost everything, but reaches home happy and free of all his troubles. We laugh at Hans's naivety and may feel some sadness at the way in which he so thoughtlessly loses what he had worked seven years to earn, but are we not also invited to see a simple heart, free of the burden of possessions, as worthy of respect?

'Hans in Luck' was one of the earliest of Grimms' tales to be versified in English and published separately. It bore the title *Unlucky John and his Lump of Silver* and was translated from the German into easy verse by Madame Leinstein (London: Dean and Munday, c. 1825). Like many other children's chapbooks of the period it was embellished with hand-coloured engravings. Other editions are known by A. K. Newman and Co. of London and J. Rosewarne of Belper. In the original German Hans has a lump of gold, so Madame Leinstein was obviously using Taylor, who has a lump of silver, as her source. She follows the broad outline of the story, but omits the final episode in which Hans loses the grindstone in a pond and has John return to his 'Granny' rather than his mother. The poem then ends with a moral:

> Good stock of money at command,
> May oft a joy impart,
> Yet, squandered by a thoughtless hand,
> As oft afflicts the heart.

Meanwhile, poor John has had to return to work. The light-hearted spirit of the German tale has been turned into a moral lesson in the English poem. Dean and Munday also published around the same date another versified story from the Grimms – *Wishing; or, the Fisherman and his Wife; a Juvenile Poem* – credited only to 'a lady'. It hardly seems surprising that this is another very moral tale.

A dozen or so years later a versified form of 'The Wolf and the Seven Kids' was made by George Nicol (using the initials G. N.) and published along with 'The Three Bears' and 'The Vizier and the Woodman' (London: W. Wright, 1841). It had appeared separately in 1839 as a second edition, so the original may go back as far as 1837, the date of the preface to 'The Three Bears'. No English translation of the Grimms' original story had been published by this date, so Nicol must have worked from a German text. He follows the original closely in thirty-eight six-line stanzas and appends a satirical discussion by the Three Bears on the story's lack of an obvious moral. A further ironic touch is to be found in the episode describing the wolf's punishment at the end of the story:

> The wolf, 'tis very strange to say,
> During the operation lay
> In slumber deep and still.
> He did not the incision feel,
> The scissors were of such sharp steel,
> And handled with such skill.

158   *Telling Tales*

18. *An Hour at Bearwood. The Wolf and the Seven Little Kids* (1839).
Illustration by George Nicol.

These versifications assimilated a few individual Grimm tales to models of nursery rhymes and tales that were common in England in the early nineteenth century. But by the mid century it became the norm for such individual tales to be in prose. Among them we can note *The Charmed Roe; or, the Little Brother and Little Sister* (London: John Murray, 1847), which had illustrations by the famous German illustrator Otto Speckter (1807-71), and a series of separate tales edited by Madame de Chatelain and published by Darton and Co. c. 1850, which included *The Story of the Charmed Fawn* and *Peter the Goatherd*.

Meanwhile, a number of Grimm tales had been included in collections of German materials published between Taylor's *German Popular Stories* and *Gammer Grethel*.[61] The first of these was George G. Cunningham's *Foreign Tales & Traditions Chiefly Selected from the Fugitive Literature of Germany*

---

61 For information about Cunningham and Thoms I am greatly indebted to Martin Sutton, *The Sin-Complex. A Critical Study of English Versions of the Grimms'* Kinder- und Hausmärchen *in the Nineteenth Century* (Kassel: Brüder Grimm-Gesellschaft, 1996).

(Glasgow: Blackie, Fullarton & Co.; Edinburgh: A. Fullarton & Co., 1828). This included new translations of five tales that had already appeared in Taylor, so it did not introduce new material to the British public. Indeed, Cunningham frequently used Taylor in creating his own, generally more elaborate adaptation of Grimm. More new material was provided by W. J. Thoms in *Lays and Legends of Germany* (London: George Cowie, 1834), which presented fourteen prose tales plus a versified version of 'De Spielhansl' under the title 'The Smith of Apolda'. Of these only two had been translated by Taylor. The others included 'Of One that went forth to Learn to be Afraid', 'The Maiden without Hands', 'Doctor All-wise' and 'The Green Robe' (later entitled 'Der Bärenhäuter' by the Grimms). Thoms also translated two tales about death – 'Gaffer Death' and 'The Little Shroud' – and a tale that presented an awkward treatment of religious matters for some Protestant sensibilities – 'Brother Merry'. Thoms, however, being an antiquary and folklore scholar, was not aiming his work at children, but rather at readers like himself who were interested in different cultural beliefs and practices. Valuable though his work was – and it was carefully translated rather than adapted – it did not have any impact on children. The area of myth, legend, folktale and folklore represents an important aspect of interest in Germany where scholarship and children's literature overlap. It was so for the Grimms themselves, and Edgar Taylor shows in his notes and preface to *German Popular Stories* that he recognized this too. The fascination of legend for both adults and children is clearly demonstrated in the travel books about Germany, and particularly the Rhineland, that were written during most of the nineteenth century.

Edgar Taylor's translations were also used in an extended collection entitled *Household Tales and Traditions of England, Germany, France, Scotland, etc. etc.* (London: James Burns, 2 vols. 1843-45), as Martin Sutton has shown.[62] Burns rarely gave credit to his translators and seems often to have reprinted material with a small number of changes, especially in the opening paragraphs, in order to disguise their origin, as he did here. In this collection he printed forty of the Grimms' tales, only two being additions to the corpus already available in English. These are 'The Old Widow' (one of the children's legends) and 'Little Red Cap; or Little Red Riding-Hood'. Charles Perrault's version of the latter had been current in English and popular since 1729, but the Grimms' version, which contaminates the plot with that of 'The Wolf and the Seven Kids' and provides a happy ending,

---

62 Sutton, pp. 111-36.

now began to compete with it. However, what we have in Burns's edition is not a faithful rendering of the Grimms' tale, but one that attempts to make this very odd story more logical and consistent and in the process creates further problems for the thoughtful reader. Little Red Cap is not eaten by the wolf, because just as he springs out of bed to do so a passing huntsman shoots and kills him with an arrow. He then takes her home and admonishes her: 'See that you never run away from the road again, all your life, nor do what your mother has forbidden you'. The grandmother, however, has been devoured by the wolf and in this version, contrary to the Grimms' text, is not rescued. All the same, Burns's edition does go on to give the repeat story included by the Grimms, in which Little Red Cap encounters the wolf a second time and the wolf falls into a trough and drowns. But since the grandmother is dead, this repeat episode has to replace her with an aunt.

Edgar Taylor's translation was made in the early stages of the development of the *Kinder- und Hausmärchen*, before it had reached its full growth. The next English translation to be made, following Taylor, Cunningham and Thoms, had the advantage of some additions and changes to the collection, though it was still not complete. In 1846 John Edward Taylor published an additional selection of tales under the title of *The Fairy Ring: A New Collection of Popular Tales, translated from the German of Jacob and Wilhelm Grimm* (London: John Murray). It contained twelve illustrations by the up-and-coming artist Richard Doyle (1824-83), who was a regular contributor to *Punch* from 1843 to 1850 and also illustrated *The King of the Golden River* (London: Smith, Elder & Co., 1851), the fairytale that Ruskin composed on the German model. J. E. Taylor's title, *The Fairy Ring*, is symptomatic of the intense interest in fairies that characterized the 1840s and 1850s in Britain, especially in paintings and book illustrations, but also in music and the theatre.[63]

John Edward Taylor was actually a cousin of Edgar Taylor. He was a printer, but also translated eight other books during the period 1840-55. Most important in the context of *The Fairy Ring* is the fact that he translated into English thirty tales from Giambattista Basile's *Pentamerone*, an extraordinary collection of Neapolitan fairytales first published in 1634-36. Taylor's translation appeared in 1848, a couple of years after Felix Liebrecht had first translated Basile into German. Five of the other books he

---

63 Jeremy Maas, Pamela White Trimpe, Charlotte Gere and others, *Victorian Fairy Painting* (London: Merrell Holberton, 1998).

The Fairytales of the Brothers Grimm 161

translated were also by German writers and deal with current affairs and foreign travel. *The Fairy Ring* proved popular enough to go into a revised and enlarged edition in 1847, which was then republished by John Murray in 1857. There were also various American editions between 1851 and 1858.

John Edward Taylor used the Grimms' fifth edition of 1843 for his translation, including a number of tales that made their first appearance in print in that edition. These were 'The Nix in the Mill-pond', 'The Hedgehog and the Hare', 'The Goose-girl at the Well', 'The Spindle, the Shuttle and the Needle', 'The Drummer', 'The True Bride' and 'The Giant and the Tailor'. He also made the first translation of 'Rapunzel', though he gave the heroine the name Violet, with the consequent alteration in the type of plant that the pregnant mother longs for. 'Rapunzel' had given the Grimms problems, as in the first edition the heroine had betrayed the fact that she was pregnant as a result of the prince's visits by asking her guardian why it was that her clothes no longer fitted her. This had caused dismay among adult readers, so from the second edition onwards this detail was changed, and the girl thoughtlessly incriminates herself by remarking that her guardian is much heavier to pull up to the high window than the young prince. It is unfortunately this latter, badly motivated version that has become the standard form of 'Rapunzel' in both German and English.

There are, of course, additional problems for English translators of this story, beginning with the title. While 'rampion' is the dictionary translation of Rapunzel, hardly anybody has the least idea what rampion is or looks like, though it is clearly some kind of salad vegetable. It is not surprising, therefore, that most nineteenth-century translators leave the German name as it stands. J. E. Taylor opted for Violet and thus has the mother longing for sweet-smelling flowers rather than craving something to eat. He follows the standard form of the girl's self-betrayal, but the fact that Violet has given birth to twins is deferred to the very end of the story. Like most nineteenth-century translators he is unable to deal straightforwardly with pregnancy and childbirth. Of course in the Grimms' originals the birth of a child often occurs apparently through some supernatural agency, with the child then being subject to some strange requirement or taboo – he may also be half-human like Hans my Hedgehog, or wholly an animal like the donkey in the fairytale of that name – but the Germans did not have quite the same squeamishness about the natural function of the body as the Victorians.

'Rapunzel' is a story that derives its power from sexual desire expressed in a whole spectrum of ways, beginning with the irrational longings of the pregnant mother that lead the couple into a kind of slavery to the fairy. But the fairy herself is a mother-figure in disguise whose only function appears to be to guard her foster-daughter against sexual contact with the opposite sex. Rapunzel is imprisoned in a tower with no entrance apart from a very high window. But as the nature of the tower defies all reason, so does the length of Rapunzel's hair – an unbelievable twenty yards long. Her sexual attractiveness lies not only in these golden tresses, but also in her beautiful singing voice – its power reminds one of the sirens' song that Odysseus, to escape it, had to have himself bound to the mast of his ship. Similarly, Rapunzel's songs draws the prince day after day back to the tower, and he discovers how to climb up to the window through observing the fairy. It is Rapunzel's voice also that leads the blinded prince back to her, and it is her tears that, falling on his eyes, restores his sight. The disembodied voice represents Rapunzel more powerfully than her hair, since it still attracts the prince after she has lost her hair to the fairy's scissors. However much the English translator tries not to speak about that most female of bodily experiences, pregnancy, the story works against him. As is also the case with 'Briar Rose', no parent can control the sexual maturation of their offspring. Briar Rose's father orders all the spindles in his kingdom to be destroyed, but there is still at the top of an old tower an old lady on whose spindle the princess receives the wound that marks her transition to adulthood. The comparable story for the male protagonist is 'Iron Hans', which was not translated into English until 1853. There it is the hero's mother who has the care of the key that he has to steal in order to regain his golden ball that has rolled into the wild man's imprisoned cage. The wild man then carries the boy away and sets him a series of tests that lead to his acquiring golden hair, a sexual attractiveness that first causes him embarrassment and only much later leads to sexual success. These three stories typify the ways in which the process of growing from childhood to adulthood is dealt with in the Grimms' fairytales. It is one of their most important themes, and their many stories explore it with a wealth of reverberant imagery and motifs.

By the mid nineteenth century the Grimms had become favourites with the reading public, though no edition had printed even a third of what was known in Germany. But in the wake of the two Taylors, Cunningham and Thoms it was now possible to produce a much more comprehensive translation. This began with a new two-volume edition entitled *Household Stories* (London: Addey & Co., 1853). No translators' names are given, but the book has two hundred and forty illustrations by Edward H. Wehnert and proved one of the most popular nineteenth-century editions of the Grimms, being taken over by other publishers and reprinted in various guises up to the present day. It provided translations of 190 tales and six children's legends and was thus much more wide-ranging than anything previously attempted, but it still found it prudent to omit thirteen tales, mainly of a religious character. Yet it is not the religious element as such that caused any given tale to be excluded, since five children's legends are actually incorporated in the translation. It seems to be the element of religious superstition or perceived contravention of Biblical teaching that leads to the omission. The preface in fact states quite baldly: 'The mixture of sacred subjects with profane, though frequent in Germany, would not meet with favour in an English book'.

The quality of the translations is uneven, probably because more than one person was involved. Some occasional awkwardness in word-order may be due to a translator having German as a first language, and Brian Alderson has suggested the anonymous translators may have been members of the illustrator Wehnert's own family, since he had German parents.[64] The translators tend to reduce the amount of violence they found in the original and make other changes as well. Several of the titles they give to individual tales are oddly different from those given in other editions. 'Marienkind' becomes 'The Woodcutter's Child', 'Frau Holle' is turned into 'Old Mother Frost', 'Von dem Machandelboom' is 'The Almond Tree', 'Fundevogel' is called 'Fir-Apple', while 'Allerleirauh' is left as in German but followed in brackets by 'The Coat of All Colours'. 'Die klare Sonne bringt's an den Tag' is mistranslated as 'The Bright Sun brings on the Day', while the Devil is reduced in offensiveness in 'The Evil Spirit and his Grandmother'. Several of the Grimms' titles do present real problems for translators, and those given here reflect prickliness about subject-matter as well as problems raised by the strangeness of personal names or dialect words. As far as the protagonists of individual stories are concerned, the Addey and Co. edition has a mixture of German and English. The name Hans is generally retained, but in the translation of 'Die kluge Else' the German Else becomes the English Alice. However, every English translator except Matilda Davis has 'Faithful John' for 'Der treue Johannes'. Then, apart from Edgar Taylor and Lucy Crane, every English translator gives 'Aschenputtel' as 'Cinderella', thereby aligning the Grimms' story with the much better known one by Perrault.

---

64 Brian Alderson, *Grimm Tales in English* (London: The British Library, 1985).

19. Brothers Grimm, *Household Stories. Newly Translated* (1853). Illustration to 'The Musicians of Bremen' by Edward Wehnert.

The Fairytales of the Brothers Grimm 165

Addey and Co.'s edition, the most extensive collection of the Grimms' tales up to that point, though still not complete, was reissued in a revised version by David Bogue in 1857. An American edition of Addey and Co. was published with the title *German Popular Tales and Household Stories* (New York: Francis, 1853) and reissued by Crosby, Nichols, Lee and Co. of Boston in 1861. But the translation and illustrations achieved their greatest success through being taken over by George Routledge and Co. in 1862. Wehnert's full-page illustrations were made more attractive by the addition of colour printing, and the stories were republished both as a single large volume and as a series of small selections at various dates up to the beginning of the twentieth century. As Routledge had an office in New York as well as London, the book was assured of a wide circulation. From about 1890 the translation was issued by other publishers – George G. Harrap, John F. Shaw, E. P. Dutton and Co., William Collins and Grosset and Dunlap – and it has continued to be used in further reprints up to the end of the twentieth century.[65]

In the decade between 1853 and 1862 four different translations of the Grimms' fairytales were published. In addition to that issued by Addey and Co. in 1853 and George Routledge in 1862, there were three others of very different kinds. None of them presented more than roughly two fifths of the complete corpus of tales, but clearly a variety of publishers wanted to cash in on the popularity that the Grimms now enjoyed. The first of the three was Matilda Davis's *Home Stories* (London and New York: George Routledge & Co., 1855), the second the anonymous *Grimms' Goblins* (London: George Vickers, [1861]), the third *Household Tales and Popular Stories* (London: Ward & Lock, 1862).[66]

Matilda Davis provides new translations of eighty-eight tales from the Grimms, divided into ninety-one in the English. They are presented in the same sequence as in the Grimms' 1850 edition, which makes it look as if she was aiming at a translation of the full corpus, but when Routledge, her publisher, took over the Addey and Co. edition her translation lost out, though it was reissued in 1866 and 1876. Despite this, selections from Davis have been included in several mainly early twentieth-century editions of Grimm. Martin Sutton regards Davis's work as important on two counts: she is the first woman to be named on a title-page as translator of the Grimms, and her translation actually sets new standards of fidelity to her source

---

65 Sutton, p. 183.
66 For much information on Matilda Davis, the Ward and Lock edition, Mrs Paull, Lucy Crane and Margaret Hunt I am again indebted to Martin Sutton.

texts. Although her translations display some of the mid century's tendency to verbosity, she aims at an accurate rendering rather than an adaptation. She is the first person to give accurate translations of the violent details to be found in 'Little Red Cap', 'The Robber Bridegroom' and 'Fitcher's Bird', and she is the first translator at all to venture a rendering of 'Der Schneider im Himmel', entitling it 'The Tailor in Olympus'. She solves the problem of treating religious matters in a humorous way by transposing the figures of God and St. Peter into Jupiter and Mercury. It seems a pity that Davis's translation was not better received. George Thompson's illustrations did nothing to help. Her work was not the commercial success that Routledge obviously found with the Addey and Co. edition. Publishers are not much interested in accuracy or fidelity as values in themselves, if they have something else that they don't have to pay for and sells better.

There are a number of books entitled *Grimms' Goblins*, and they vary a lot in content and presentation. What George Vickers published under this title, probably in 1861, after it had appeared in instalments in magazine format, was a collection of fairytales that included material not only from the Grimms, but also from Perrault, Madame d'Aulnoy, Madame Leprince de Beaumont and Wilhelm Hauff, among others. None of the tales is credited to a particular author, and no translator's name is given. The titles often appear to be chosen to disguise the tales' origins. Of the eighty-four items in the collection, however, sixty-four are from the Grimms, using either the sixth or seventh edition of the *Kinder- und Hausmärchen*. In addition to numerous black and white engravings the book contains forty-two coloured illustrations designed by 'Phiz', i.e. Hablot K. Browne (1815-1882), who is renowned for his illustrations of Dickens. These vigorous illustrations are early examples of the colour printing of Edmund Evans, who became one of the great masters of this art. Phiz concentrates on key moments in the stories and produces splendidly resonant pictures for, among others, 'The Goblin's Gifts', 'Faithful John', 'Jack in Luck', 'The Miller and the Water-Sprite' and 'The Giant Suckling' ('The Young Giant').

In comparison with the source texts the translations are long-winded and full of amplifications and asides. If we compare the opening of 'Faithful John' with the same passage in the Ward and Lock edition of 1862, the difference is immediately obvious:

> Once upon a time, there was a King, who, being old, and happening to fall ill, took it very much to heart, as old gentlemen do, and made up his mind to die, – which, my dear children, you must always remember, is

> half-way towards doing so. So, impressed with this notion, he ordered his attendants to summon to his presence his Faithful John, a favourite servant and friend, whom he kept always about his person, as one who loved him for himself, and not for his grandeur, and could, therefore, be relied upon, whatever might betide. He was called Faithful John, because, all through his life, he had been faithful to his master (*Grimms' Goblins*).
>
> There was once an old king who fell sick – and he thought: 'This bed on which I am lying, will most likely be my death-bed;' so he said, 'send faithful John to me. Faithful John was his favourite servant; and had earned his name from being faithful all his life' (Ward & Lock, 1862).

In reading *Grimms' Goblins* one is always aware of the tiresome narrator, who never ceases to nudge the reader with comments on socially desirable conduct.

The story ends, of course, with the king's son being required to cut off the heads of his twin sons in order to bring Faithful John, now turned to stone as a result of his care for his master, back to life. The king does this, and Faithful John is then able to set the heads back on the princes' shoulders and restore them to life. This gruesome episode exemplifying a belief in the magical power of innocent children's blood is not shirked in either translation, but an earlier incident causes problems. In the German the young king's wife falls into a coma from which she is released by Faithful John sucking three drops of blood from her right breast. This is too indelicate for the translators to follow. *Grimms' Goblins* changes the place on the queen's body to her right shoulder, while the Ward and Lock translation substitutes her finger. No translator before Margaret Hunt (1884) translated this incident completely accurately.

Household Tales and Popular Stories (Ward & Lock, 1862), as we have seen, presents a simpler and more accurate picture of the Grimms' tales than *Grimms' Goblins*. It is thus surprising that the 'advertisement' is inaccurate in its claim about providing certain new stories and that the list of contents omits the titles of several tales included in the selection. What is interesting about this selection is the fact that so many short moral and religious tales are included, so that the emphasis is not overwhelmingly on the tales of magic. Oddly, one tale by Hans Christian Andersen has slipped in – 'The Princess and the Pea' – which was probably taken from a German translation of Andersen and not from the rather different form that Wilhelm Grimm included only in the fifth (1843) edition of the *Kinder- und Hausmärchen*, as Sutton makes clear.

The Ward and Lock editions (1862, 1881 and 1884) contain 35 illustrations (plus two repeats) by the Parisian artist, Bertall, the pseudonym of Charles-Albert d'Arnoux (1820-82), and this gives a clue to the possible origin of this collection. Bertall in fact made forty vignettes for a French edition, viz. *Contes choisis des Frères Grimm*, translated from the German by Frédéric Baudry (Paris: L. Hachette et Cie, 1855), and the Ward and Lock editions print almost all of them from stereotypes. But it is also the case that *Grimms' Goblins* includes thirty from the same set of illustrations by Bertall, though they are not credited to him by name. The two collections have a considerable overlap in their choice of tales, though the actual translations are very different in character from each other. The *Contes choisis des Frères Grimm* is divided into four categories of tale – moral tales, children's legends, tales of magic and comic tales. *Grimms' Goblins* concentrates on the tales of magic, while *Household Tales and Popular Stories* has a particularly large number of moral tales and children's legends. The sequence of tales is different in the two collections, but despite the overlap there is no connexion between them. It was not uncommon at the time for publishers to buy and sell stereotypes of illustrations, Bertall's work certainly being subject to this procedure. His illustrations to Dumas' adaptation of Hoffmann's *Nutcracker* can be found in French, German and English editions printed at various times in the mid to late nineteenth century.

Interest in the Grimms continued unabated. Not only were old editions reprinted, but new translations were made and stories from the Grimms appeared in miscellaneous collections of fairytales. The next new translation to be published was *Grimm's Fairy Tales*, translated by Mrs H. B. Paull (London and New York: Frederick Warne & Co., 1868). Mrs Paull was responsible for translations of *The Swiss Family Robinson* and *Hans Andersen's Fairy Tales* as well as many other works, and her practice, like that of many of her predecessors, was to adapt details of the text of the Grimms where it offended British social and religious norms. She thus changes the figure of the Virgin Mary in 'Marienkind' to the good Fairy Tell True. With 'The Fisherman and his Wife' she has the couple living in a little hut near a lake rather than a chamber pot close by the sea, while at the conclusion of the story the wife wants to be 'equal to the Creator, and make the sun rise' rather than simply be like God. Many stories are given titles that are arbitrarily different from what would be obvious. 'The Golden Goose' is renamed 'The Little Grey Man', 'Snow-white' is called 'The Magic Mirror', 'Rumpelstiltskin' is 'The Gold Spinner'. She calls 'Rapunzel' 'The Garden of the Sorceress', but this is because she has had the bright idea of translating *Rapunzeln* as 'lettuces' and thus calling the girl Letitia or Lettice. With the similarly difficult 'Fundevogel' she gives the boy the name of Birdie, which is more appropriate and adventurous than Bird-Foundling (Burns), Fir-Apple (Addey & Co.) or leaving it untranslated (Davis, Hunt).

Mrs Paull is peculiarly sensitive about relations between the sexes. In what she calls 'The False Bride' (generally known as 'The Goose-girl') the boy who accompanies the heroine in looking after the geese and wants to pull out her hair is changed into a girl, while at the same time being left the name Kürdchen, the diminutive form of Konrad. Clearly, for Mrs Paull it did not do for a boy and girl to be left alone like this, but in making her change she destroyed the significance of the episode as a demonstration of the heroine's gradual recovery of sexual self-confidence and power. Similarly, in 'The Twin Brothers' (the longest of the Grimms' tales by far) Mrs Paull could not countenance the episode in which one twin sleeps in his sister-in-law's bed, being taken as her genuine husband, even though separated from her by a two-edged sword. She mentions nothing at all about the bed or the sword, but says simply that the princess 'thought he was very cold and distant to her'. Again, the point of the episode – the extent of the brother's faithfulness to his twin – is lost. Mrs Paull is not as faithful herself to the Grimms and in the case of 'May Blossom' (her version of 'Briar Rose') she contaminates it with details from Perrault's 'Sleeping Beauty'.

Mrs Paull's edition was printed at least seven times between 1868 and 1888, but in 1893 Warne published a further two-volume complete edition with the titles *Grimms' Fairy Tales and Household Stories* and *Grimms' Wonder Tales* respectively. The translation was credited to Mrs Paull and Mr L. A. Wheatley, the revisions presumably being the latter's work. In 1893 also a selection of 62 tales from this work was issued by Warne with the title *Grimms' Household Stories*. In this selection the story that Mrs Paull, misreading the German Gothic type, called 'The Clever Elfe' (instead of 'Else') was corrected to 'Clever Bess', and various improvements were made to the text.

Meanwhile, other new translations offered competition. Lucy Crane's *Household Stories from the Collection of the Bros: Grimm* (London: Macmillan & Co., 1882) provided fifty-two stories, all familiar from previous collections and taken from nos. 1-93 in the Grimms' complete editions. To her credit she leaves out the two anti-Semitic stories, 'The Good Bargain' and 'The Jew in the Bush' (the latter only omitted by Thoms and J. E. Taylor among previous translators). She makes a blunder in translating *Geißlein* as 'goslings' rather than the correct 'kids' in 'The Wolf and the Seven Kids', and she also wrongly translates 'Von dem Machandelboom' as 'The Almond Tree' instead of 'The Juniper Tree'. But generally her translation is straightforward, lively and true to the tone of the original. Lucy Crane took considerable trouble with the verses to be found in many of the stories. The oddly unrhyming lines in the German original of 'The Frog Prince' she renders very aptly as

> 'Youngest King's daughter,
> Open to me!
> By the well water
> What promised you me?
> Youngest King's daughter
> Now open to me!'

When Aschenputtel calls for help in the task her stepmother has set her, she calls:

> 'O gentle doves, O turtle doves,
> And all the birds that be,
> The lentils that in ashes lie
> Come and pick up for me!
> The good must be put in the dish,
> The bad you may eat if you wish.

However, this edition is noted not so much for Lucy Crane's translation as for her brother Walter's illustrations. Walter Crane (1845-1915) had already made himself quite a reputation with his colour illustrations to children's picture books from about 1865, but he did only black and white illustrations for *Household Stories*. There were head- and tail-pieces for each story and in addition full-page pictures for 'The Sleeping Beauty', 'The Goose Girl', 'Faithful John', 'Rapunzel', 'The White Snake', 'Mother Hulda', 'The Robber Bridegroom', 'The Almond Tree', 'The Six Swans', 'Snow-white' and 'The Golden Bird'. Of these full-page pictures only that for 'Faithful John' does not depict a slim young girl, and only the stories of 'Faithful John' and 'The Golden Bird' have a male protagonist. Although Lucy Crane does have about a dozen fairytales with a male protagonist, they are outweighed by those with females. The disproportion is increased with Walter Crane's pictures, and it is this kind of privileging of tales with heroines that has led to the common perception that fairytales are more for girls than for boys. Certainly, Walter Crane's attention focusses on the more romantic aspects of the tales. *Household Stories* was revised (the goslings were turned back into kids) and reissued in 1886 then again in 1893, 1894, 1923 and 1926. There have also been American reprints, and in 1979 Macmillan issued a facsimile reprint of the 1882 edition.

Two years after the first edition of *Household Stories* came Margaret Hunt's *Grimm's Household Tales* (London: George Bell & Sons, 2 vols., 1884). This was noteworthy on several counts. In the first place, it was the first translation of the full corpus of the Grimms' tales that had been available in German since 1857. Secondly, Hunt aimed at accuracy and fidelity to her sources and only 'slightly softened one or two passages', as she writes in her preface. She does not engage in the kind of adaptations typical of most of her predecessors. Thirdly, she provided a translation of the Grimms' extensive annotations to each individual tale. This feature, together with the scholarly introduction by Andrew Lang, one of the leading folklorists of the day, and the fact that the work contained no illustrations, makes clear the serious nature of Hunt's undertaking. Although Edgar Taylor had used the Grimms' notes in making his own, his principal concern seems to have been with children. With Hunt it was the other way round. Her translation was reissued in Bohn's Standard Library in 1885, then again by Bell in 1892 and 1910. When it was published again in 1944 in one volume (New York: Pantheon Books), the text was revised by James Stern and the notes were removed. Further reprints were published in London by Routledge and Kegan Paul in 1959 and 1975. The loss of the notes in these later editions was probably a marketing strategy and intended to return Hunt's translation to the field of children's books. Hunt's translation had its faults, mainly in an occasional clumsiness of style, but it was indubitably the most faithful of nineteenth-century English renderings of the Grimms.

The 1890s saw a multitude of editions competing for the attention of children and their parents. In addition to Hunt's scholarly translation there were several new editions from Routledge of the Addey and Co. translation with Wehnert's illustrations. Wells Gardner, Darton and Co. also used the Addey and Co. translation, unacknowledged as always, in their *Fairy Tales from Grimm*, first published in 1894 and reaching a fourth edition in 1908. This was plentifully illustrated with lively drawings by Gordon Browne (1858-1932) and equipped with a learned preface on folktales by S. Baring-Gould. Then there was the Paull and Wheatley translation from Warne, and a new edition of Edgar Taylor's *Gammer Grethel* from George Bell and Sons

(1897). These were all reissues of translations that had proved themselves in the market. Two more publishers now sought to take advantage of the Grimms' popularity. First came Ernest Nister, whose main contribution was in the field of large-size illustrated books with superbly printed colour illustrations done in Germany. Then Ward, Lock and Co. entered the field with another 'complete' edition of the tales, translated by Beatrice Marshall (1900). From this point on publishers tend to be far more interested in what illustration can do to sell their books; the matter of translation becomes secondary.

The Nister edition of 1898 (published in New York by E. P. Dutton & Co.) was entitled simply *Grimm's Fairy Tales* (the singular form of the possessive is a commonplace of editions of this period). It was illustrated with numerous black and white drawings by E. Stuart Hardy and others, but its chief attraction was in the ten colour plates by Ada Dennis. These are of the prettily sentimental kind typical of the period, with little girls dressed in pink and white and with long blond hair. Despite the horror that is rarely far to seek in many of the stories, the pictures barely hint at such things. The picture of 'Snow-White, Rose-Red, and the Angel' slips rather easily into sickly religiosity, while that of 'The Princess and the Beggar-Man' from 'King Thrush-Beard' looks more like a pastoral idyll than a punishment for a haughty princess.

This edition contains just thirty-two stories. Nister also published the stories with the same illustrations and colour plates in two separate volumes, one entitled *Hop o' my Thumb's Wanderings and other Fairy Tales from 'Grimm'* (no date). Another, larger edition with fifty-six stories, again simply called *Grimm's Fairy Tales*, was issued in 1910, this time with illustrations by Charles Robinson (1870-1937). Each tale has a head-piece or decorated initial in a kind of post-Beardsley style (probably not by Robinson). The book contains four full-page pictures in rich, subtle colours, two of which focus on brownies in what is here called 'The Cobbler and the Brownies' (more usually 'The Elves and the Shoemaker'. The other two deal with 'The Man of Iron' ('Iron Hans') and 'Mother Hulda' ('Mother Holle'). There is a world of difference between these *art nouveau* illustrations and those of Ada Dennis.

The edition of *Grimm's Fairy Tales* translated by Beatrice Marshall (London, New York and Melbourne: Ward, Lock & Co., Limited, 1900) is more ambitious in scope than their previous editions, but the format closely resembles that of the Routledge and Warne editions with which it was competing. Unfortunately, the illustrations are monochrome rather than in colour, and those taken over from Doré lose impact through being reduced in size. The translation claims to be complete, but Sutton points out that it actually omits 'The Death of the Hen' and 'Going Travelling', while also containing the Andersen tale of 'The Princess and the Pea'. Marshall follows Addey and Co. and Lucy Crane in having 'The Almond Tree' as a title for 'The Juniper Tree', but she is probably the only translator to call 'Herr Korbes' 'Mr Basket' and so provide English readers with a semantically linked name. Elsewhere she dares to break the taboo about the louse by giving 'The Wood-louse and the Flea' as the title of 'Läuschen und Flöhchen'. Margaret Hunt had translated this as 'The Louse and the Flea', but all previous translators had baulked at the term, giving 'spider' or 'ladybird' instead. Marshall had problems with some of the colloquial expressions in, for example, 'Clever Hans', but in general her translation can be called good, though not excellent. In 1912 a selection of 115 tales was issued with the same title and a single monochrome illustration by Henry Austin as a frontispiece. The emphasis lies chiefly on the tales in the second half of the Grimm's collection.

The period between 1900 and 1914 is marked by a great variety of presentations of the Grimms. In addition to the large comprehensive editions already mentioned, there are substantial selections in both new and old translations, alongside which very brief selections were made for small children. John F. Shaw published seventy-four tales c. 1901, using a slightly modified form of the Addey and Co. translation, accompanied by fifty line drawings and a coloured frontispiece. This was an unpretentious book aimed at the lower end of the market. In 1906 Dent issued the first edition of *Household Tales by the Brothers Grimm* in their long-lasting 'Everyman's Library'. This selection of sixty-six tales gave no indication of the provenance of the translations, but a substantial number were taken from *Gammer Grethel*. The illustrations were by Robert Anning Bell (1863-1933). Edgar Taylor was used again by Blackie for their edition illustrated in colour and black and white by Helen Stratton (1903), but this time the text was taken from *German Poplar Stories* with occasional slight changes. This edition had fifty-four stories. In 1909 Grant Richards published another edition consisting of sixty-four tales selected and retold by Githa Sowerby and with twelve illustrations in colour by Millicent Sowerby (1878-1967). Some of the story titles point to Mrs Paull as a source, and the term 'retold' makes it clear that we are not dealing with a new translation.

Among these substantial new selections one in particular stands out – *Fairy Tales of the Brothers Grimm*, illustrated by Arthur Rackham, translated by Mrs Edgar Lucas (London: Constable & Co., 1909). The significant feature of the book is indicated by the illustrator's name preceding the translator's. Arthur Rackham (1867-1939) produced his forty evocative colour illustrations over the same period as he did those for Fouqué's *Undine*, and those for Wagner's *The Rhinegold and The Valkyrie* and *Siegfried and The Twilight of the Gods* came in 1910 and 1911 respectively. The *Grimm* book has fifty-five vigorous black and white drawings too, but it is the colour illustrations that make this edition a collector's piece. Many of them display Rackham's delight in the scenery and picturesque old towns of Germany that he visited frequently between the 1890s and 1930. There are some wonderful studies of birds and animals, for example, the screech owl for 'Jorinda and Joringel', the ducks for 'The Queen Bee' and the goat and kids for 'The Wolf and the Seven Kids'. Rackham is often thought of as a master of the grotesque, but such pictures should be set alongside such delicate portraits as the two illustrations for 'The Goosegirl' to keep them in proportion. But it is the dangerous and suspenseful episodes in fairytales that clamour to be illustrated, and Rackham provides them in plenty. No one else has achieved Rackham's power in suggesting the immense height of the tower inside which Rapunzel was imprisoned. While these colour pictures are the highpoint of this book, the black and white drawings are also immensely skilful. If I draw attention only to one, it would be the illustration to 'The Twelve Dancing Princesses', which with great economy depicts the illuminated castle and, in front of it, the lake gleaming as the boats row their way towards it.

This edition with Rackham's colour illustrations consisted of sixty tales in a new translation by Mrs Edgar Lucas. There was also another edition, undated, in which these illustrations were reproduced in black and white along with those originally done in black and white. This contained three additional tales – 'Faithful John', 'The Three Sluggards' and 'The Three Brothers'. The translation occasionally takes its cue from previous versions, as when the couple in 'The Fisherman and his Wife' live in 'a hovel' and the wife finally desires to be 'Lord of the Universe' rather than simply 'God'. In 'Rapunzel' Mrs Lucas chooses to have 'corn-salad' rather than 'rampion' or 'lettuce'. Elsewhere she makes a straightforward, idiomatic rendering of the tales, though the selection confines itself to the familiar and does not attempt to introduce new stories to the reader.

By the beginning of the twentieth century the Grimms have become such a firm part of the landscape of children's books that much smaller selections and adaptations are being made for younger children and, perhaps, a readership that goes beyond the middle class. Edric Vredenburg edited sixteen tales for Raphael Tuck and Sons in 1900. From this edition we can pretty reliably see what are the most popular tales – 'Hansel and Grethel', 'The Frog Prince', 'Little Red-cap', 'Thumbling', 'The Six Swans', 'The Table, the Ass and the Stick', 'Briar Rose', 'The Valiant Little Tailor', 'Cinderella', 'The Musicians of Bremen', 'Rumpelstiltskin', 'The Goose-Girl', 'The Water of Life', 'Little Snow-White', 'The Little Brother and Sister' and 'The King of the Golden Mountain'. Of these tales only 'Little Red-cap', 'The Six Swans' and 'The Table, the Ass and the Stick' were not included in Edgar Taylor's *German Popular Stories*. The eight colour plates by Eddie J. Andrews are sugar and spice and all things nice, but the black and white drawings by S. Jacobs display more individual character. Vredenburg edited another collection that was illustrated by Mabel Lucie Attwell c. 1914. There was an overlap of eleven tales between the two editions, but the later one included 'The Step-sisters and the Dwarfs' ('Die drei Männlein im Walde'), 'Snow-White and Rose-Red', 'The Travels of Tom Thumb' (replacing 'Thumbling'), 'Dummling and the Three Feathers', 'The Golden Goose', 'The Nose' and 'The Fairy Folk' ('Die Wichtelmänner'). Of these, again, only 'The Step-sisters and the Dwarfs' and 'Dummling and the Three Feathers' were not in Edgar Taylor's collection. Attwell's colour plates feature small, vulnerable children, spindly legged goblins and the odd tiny fairy flitting irrelevantly in the corners of the scene, but her colours are stronger than those of Andrews. Her female figures always look as though they have been taken unawares and are about to burst into tears, if they haven't already done so. Attwell is the epitome of tweeness.

Another selection of comparable size was aimed at older children. *Favourite Stories from Grimm*, re-told by Edward Shirley (London, Edinburgh and New York: Thomas Nelson & Sons, no date) contained fourteen stories, but the 'Cinderella' is by Perrault, not the Grimms. The other tales are 'Hansel and Grethel', 'Rumpelstiltskin', 'The Goose-Girl', 'Little Snow-White, or the Magic Mirror', 'The Golden Goose', 'Briar Rose', 'Hans in Luck', 'The Iron Chest' ('Der Eisenofen', an unusual choice), 'Little Primrose' (an unusually titled form of 'Rapunzel'), 'The Magic Key' ('Fitchers Vogel', another uncommon choice), 'Little Red Riding Hood'. 'The Frog Prince' and 'The Fisherman and his Wife'. The twelve colour plates by

W. H. Margetson (1861-1940) depict older figures than Attwell and do so in a more realistic and complex style. In comparison with Rackham they are very old-fashioned.

Over this same period we find a number of even more compact selections. The well-known 'Told to the Children' series published in Britain by T. C. & E. C. Jack and in America by E. P. Dutton & Co. issued *Stories from Grimm* (c. 1906), told to the children by Amy Steedman and with eight colour pictures by Harry Rowntree (1878-1950). (The artist's name is usually spelt 'Rountree', but here it is as stated.) This contained just ten tales, while Blackie's comparable volume (c. 1912), excerpted from the larger collection illustrated by Helen Stratton, has a mere eight. There is no overlap between the two books. Stratton's illustrations are printed with much more subtle colours than is the case in the large collection.

These developments during the Edwardian period show Grimms' fairytales being presented to the most diverse kinds of reader – the bibliophile, the person interested in folklore, the reader who wants to devour the whole of the Grimms' collection, the whole age-range of children and young people. But alongside faithful translations and careful adaptations in books specifically labelled with the Grimms' name individual tales were also included in general collections of fairytales. Routledge's *Household Tales and Fairy Stories* (1877) included 'The Wolf and the Man', 'Squire Korbes' and 'The Fox and the Cat' among traditional English and French fairytales. Mrs Valentine had 'The Three Soldiers and the Dwarf' ('The Nose'), 'Snowdrop' ('Snow-white') and 'The Giant with the Golden hairs' sandwiched between Perrault and other French literary tellers of fairytales in her *Old Old Fairy Tales* (Frederick Warne & Co., no date). Andrew Lang incorporated a few other items from the Grimms in his *Blue, Red, Green, Yellow* and *Grey Fairy Books* (1889, 1890, 1892, 1894 and 1900 respectively) in translations made by his female collaborators. Finally, W. T. Stead included a few Grimm tales in a number of his *Books for the Bairns* (nos. 7, 123, 144, 153 and 162). This is not an exhaustive list, but it demonstrates clearly enough how thoroughly acclimatized the Grimms had become. In the anthologies the provenance of their tales is generally unacknowledged; they are taken for granted and hardly even thought of as German tales.

The picture of the Grimms that British readers had over nearly a century is extremely varied. It began with Edgar Taylor's renderings, not exact translations, but creative adaptations designed to fit in with the different religious, moral and social preconceptions of the British, and Taylor's choices and stance were still influential at the time of the First World War. Apart from 'Rapunzel', the most popular tales in the period 1900-1914 were all tales that Taylor had included in some form in his 1823-26 collection. Most popular was 'The Frog Prince', then 'Snow-White' and 'Rumpelstiltskin', followed by 'Hansel and Grethel', 'Cinderella' and 'The Elves and the Shoemaker'. After them came 'Faithful John', 'Rapunzel', 'Briar Rose', 'The Golden Goose', 'The King of the Golden Mountain', 'The Golden Bird' and 'The Musicians of Bremen'. All except the last are fairytales in the narrower sense, that is, tales of magic.

By the mid nineteenth century, with the Addey and Co. edition, almost the whole of the Grimms' collection was available in English. Margaret Hunt, Paull and Wheatley and Beatrice Marshall delivered complete or virtually complete translations in the latter part of the century, though they varied in accuracy and readability. Medium-sized selections were to hand from Edgar Taylor onwards and kept being added to. But it was not until the turn of the century that brief selections began to be made, and then there were several within a decade or so. Single tales, occasionally versified and always with illustrations, came from the mid 1820s and probably reached their apogee with Walter Crane's marvellously designed colour 'toy book' version of 'The Frog Prince' (1874). Thomas de la Rue and Co. published a *Rumpel-stilts-kin* illustrated by George R. Halkett in 1882 and a *Clever Hans* illustrated by J. Lawson c. 1884, and during much of the century there were manifold editions of 'Little Red Riding Hood', in which Perrault was often combined with or replaced by Grimm. There was thus something of Grimm to offer every kind of reader, and this range was available from as early as the 1850s.

To an extraordinary extent the image of the Grimms up to the early twentieth century was fixed by Edgar Taylor. It was not simply that his versions continued to be reprinted throughout the period, but that he singled out so many deeply resonant tales for inclusion in his original two volumes. Even where he altered elements of the story he did not undermine their emotional power. Later translators sometimes corrected Taylor's aberrations, but they often also took them over with the result that the commonly accepted English version of the Grimms is rather more proper than the German. The English Grimm tends to focus more strongly on the tales of magic than is the case with the German original. The animal tales, comic, religious and moral tales figure less often in the English selections, though they are of course present in the complete editions. But even among the tales of magic there are some that very rarely appear in the selections. 'The Singing Bone', 'The Girl without Hands', 'Fitcher's Bird' and 'Hans my Hedgehog' are cases in point. Perhaps the cruelty or human distortions that they contain militated against them. The religious tales also had little appeal, reflecting practices and presuppositions alien to the British Protestant mind.

The German edition contains a considerable number of fine tales with male protagonists – 'The Tale of the Boy who set out to Learn about Fear', 'The Devil with the Three Golden Hairs', 'The Knapsack, the Hat and the Horn', 'Bearskin', 'Iron Hans', 'The Master Thief' are just a few – but in the English imagination it is the tales with female protagonists that are most memorable. This may be due to the fact that girls are the more typical readers of fairytales, but it may also be the result of the exclusion of tales more likely to appeal to boys. Several of the tales with female protagonists are famous – 'Briar Rose', 'Ashputtel', 'Little Red Riding Hood', 'Rapunzel', 'The Frog Prince', 'Snow-White', 'The Goose-Girl' – but they tend to be of the beautiful, passive, obedient, long-suffering kind that was the ideal of patriarchal Victorian society. Extreme physical and emotional sufferings may be inflicted on them, ranging from endurance of pointless menial tasks, enforced separation from the family, mutilation, imprisonment, years of enforced silence, the prohibition of laughter, slanderous imputations of wickedness, and so on. Male protagonists may have their courage and physical strength tested, but they do not suffer the degree of pain inflicted on the hapless females. Yet there is always a happy ending: the heroine is rescued and marries the prince of her dreams. The hero too wins his bride and becomes a king, if he is not one already. Yet a story like 'The Robber Bridegroom' contains a second young woman who does not escape from the robber band: she is drugged and killed and has her finger chopped off, so the female reader or listener has an alternative ending to haunt her imagination.

The Grimms' collection as a whole has a striking number of stories featuring siblings of both genders. The most famous are 'Hansel and Gretel', 'Little Brother and Little Sister' and 'Fundevogel', in which a brother and sister (or foster-sister) are abandoned by their parents, undergo a terrible adventure and finally re-establish a supportive family. In these stories the brother first shows initiative, but it is the sister who finally oversees the rescue. Hansel drops the pebbles that guide the children back home, then he drops the crumbs that the birds eat, but Gretel pushes the witch into the oven and makes sure that the siblings ride singly on the duck's back rather than weighing her down with both of them together, as Hansel had wanted. 'The Twelve Brothers', 'The Six Swans' and 'The Seven Ravens' are also crucially concerned with the relationship of siblings and the sacrifices that the sister is prepared to make for her brothers. These stories emphasize the importance of the family unit and of the need for siblings to pull together in mutual support. One can also view Snow-White's housekeeping for the seven dwarfs as part of this pattern. This is a fascinating variation on the negative relationship that siblings of the same gender have with each other. The male protagonist is often the youngest of three and regarded as stupid, while the female protagonist may have older step-sisters. In either case they are faced with victimization or competition rather than getting help. There are thus a number of different patterns to be seen in the tales of magic; they do not all tell the same basic story.

The Grimms' collection is an extraordinary treasure-house. The range of tales is both large and extremely varied. Clearly, the stories came from a pre-industrial society and were rewritten to conform to the bourgeois values of small-town Germany, but they nonetheless transcend their origins. They have a core that is capable of appealing, across historical periods and national affiliations, to the deepest reaches of human experience. It is in the nature of fairytales that they are continually retold and thus refashioned. The Grimms themselves participated in this process, and it continued with the huge number of British translations, adaptations, illustrations and reprints that were issued during the nineteenth century and beyond. During this period the major focus of interpretation had to do with folklore and myth, but what is perhaps most apparent to twentieth-century readers about the tales of magic is their concern with patterns of human maturation. How does the child learn to become an adult? How do girls and boys deal with their feelings about their parents? What do they feel about their siblings? Where does help come from when they feel despair? How does sex relate to love and marriage? What sort of image of themselves do the protagonists of any story have? What fears or anxieties do they have? Each tale tackles questions of this kind. The patterns are inexhaustible.

Note: Since this chapter was first written a virtually unknown collection of German fairytales from the mid nineteenth century has resurfaced, viz. *Papa's Present of Household Stories, from the German* (Darton & Co., 1851). Of the seventeen tales twelve are taken from the Grimms, from either the 1837 or the 1840 or 1843 editions of the *Kinder- und Hausmärchen*. The Grimms' name, however, is not mentioned anywhere in the book. Lawrence Darton, in *The Dartons* (2004), lists an edition under the title *Household Stories* as H722, without any reference to *Papa's Present* or to the Grimms. This translation was not known to Martin Sutton in *The Sin-Complex* (Kassel, 1996). The anonymous translator adds only one new tale to those already published in English by Edgar Taylor in 1823-26, but he or she gives almost all the tales a different title. The translator's command of German vocabulary and idiom is insecure, at times remaining close to the German while at others being quite free and often misunderstanding the original. I propose writing about this collection in more detail elsewhere.

11. The Fairytales of Wilhelm Hauff

Although the Brothers Grimm and Hans Andersen came to dominate the world of fairytales in the second half of the nineteenth century, pushing Perrault and Madame d'Aulnoy from centre stage, they were not the only collectors or authors of fairytales to gain an English-speaking public during this period. Other German collectors of traditional tales are dealt with elsewhere, but of those writers who composed their own tales Wilhelm Hauff heads the list. His *Märchen*, whether published as a book or separately, have kept a firm place in German children's reading from the time of their first appearance right to the present day. Equally, there has been a steady stream of English editions over the same period. During the Victorian and Edwardian periods Hauff's tales were better known than Hoffmann's *Nutcracker* or Brentano's fairytales.

Wilhelm Hauff (1802-27) came late in the development of German Romanticism. Born in Stuttgart and educated at the University of Tübingen, he was tutor to the children of Baron von Hügel before devoting himself full-time to the pursuit of writing. He married early in 1827 and was in the midst of an active literary career when he caught typhoid and died tragically early, just a few days short of his twenty-fifth birthday. He had written several short prose works and a historical novel, *Lichtenstein*, in the wake of Sir Walter Scott, but his lasting claim to fame rests on his fairytales. Literary historians, however, tend to pass over this success with few words, concentrating instead on his writings for adults. This is a pity, as from this point of view Hauff is clearly a lesser Romantic writer, whereas in the annals of children's books he is a major figure.

Hauff's achievement here consists in the stories that he published in three successive years in the form of almanacks or keepsakes – *Die Karawane* (The Caravan) (1825), *Der Scheik von Alessandria und seine Sklaven* (The Sheik of Alexandria and his Slaves) (1826) and *Das Wirtshaus im Spessart* (The Inn in the Spessart Forest) (1827). Each of these collections is presented in the form of a framework story within which other tales are narrated. It is a narrative model that goes back to Boccaccio's *Decameron* and was used most tellingly in the *Arabian Nights*. Hauff was not a collector of traditional tales like the Grimms, but composed his own tales on the basis of a rich fund of traditional and literary sources. He actually incorporated a small number of tales from other authors into the second collection, but these have not usually been included in English editions of Hauff. However, 'Abner, der Jude, der nichts gesehen hat' ('Abner, the Jew, who Saw Nothing') was taken almost literally from Voltaire's *Zadig*, though with changes of names and locations, and 'Die Höhle von Steenfoll' ('The Cave of Steenfoll') is derived from 'The Nicker Holl' in Robert P. Gillies's *Tales of a Voyager to the Arctic Ocean*, which had been translated into German as *Erzählungen eines Reisenden nach dem nördlichen Eismeer* (Leipzig, 1826-27).[67] These two tales do crop up in English, though not very often.

For both the framework and the setting of individual tales Hauff made abundant use of the fashion for things oriental which, as far as literature is concerned, went back to the *Arabian Nights*. New German translations of the *Arabian Nights* by Joseph von Hammer and Max Habicht appeared in 1823-24 and 1825 respectively, so Hauff had an immediate influence. Both the framework and the separate tales of *Die Karawane* are set in the Middle East, while with *Der Scheik von Alessandria* Hauff has one of the slaves tell a story located in his German homeland – this is 'Der Zwerg Nase' ('Dwarf Nose'). *Das Wirtshaus im Spessart* moves the framework to Germany, but includes one oriental tale, 'Saïds Schicksale' ('The Adventures of Saïd'), among the otherwise German and Scottish tales. Many of Hauff's stories have been published separately as well as in their original frameworks. This is the case too with the English versions.

Not all of the stories are fairytales in the sense of tales in which magic plays a key part. Several are adventure stories recounting events that could conceivably have happened. That doesn't mean that they tell ordinary

---

[67] Paul Roggenhausen, 'Hauff-Studien', *Archiv für das Studium der neueren Sprachen und Literatur*, 157 (1930), pp. 163-64.

events, but only that the events, however strange, do not depend on the supernatural. Thus, 'Die Geschichte von der abgehauenen Hand' ('The Story of the Severed Hand'), tells how the narrator was lured into committing a murder on a stranger's behalf, supposing that he was in fact cutting off the head of a dead person so that it could be interred in a family crypt abroad. Similarly, 'Die Errettung Fatmes' ('The Rescue of Fatima') recounts a tale of abduction, treachery and rescue that, however extraordinary, depends on ingenuity of coincidence in the plot rather than on recourse to magic. Both these tales form part of *Die Karawane*.

The Sheik of Alexandria contains a version of a widespread story motif in which the credulous inhabitants of a town, here called Grünwiesel, are led to believe that a dressed-up ape is actually an Englishman. Then, in 'The Story of Almansor' Hauff provides a variation on the well-known theme in which a humble individual encounters and makes friends with the monarch, not knowing who he is, is taken to court to meet him and finally recognizes who his friend is. The theme is perhaps best known in English in the chapbook story 'The King and the Cobbler'. Hauff gives the tale a contemporary twist in that his Egyptian protagonist, Almansor, is taken to the lands of the Franks, where the emperor, never given a name, is known to Almansor as 'Petit Caporal', the name by which Napoleon was affectionately known to his men.

Hauff's final volume, *The Inn in the Spessart*, breathes more the spirit of legends as far as its Western tales go, telling events that reflect folk beliefs, with varying degrees of involvement in the world of magic. However, 'The Adventures of Saïd' is certainly a fairytale in the usual sense.

In all three volumes the individual stories fit comfortably within the framework, whether they appear as first-person narratives and thus make some claim to credibility (as with 'The Severed Hand') or whether they are third-person tales with a greater latitude of subject-matter. Hauff clearly enjoys the play of narrative perspectives, but narrative tone as well as narrative framework is a powerful unifying factor in his writing. His stories have lasted well because they are simply and straightforwardly told and maintain a steady narrative pace. While traditional fairytales avoid superfluous description and concentrate on the basics of the plot, Hauff allows himself more detail and patterns himself more on the style of the novella. His narrative settings are varied, as are his characters, including princes, merchants and slaves from Baghdad, Egypt, Basra and Constantinople as well as townspeople and peasants from Germany, especially the Black Forest, and Scotland. The oriental tales inhabit the periods and milieux of the *Arabian Nights*, while the Western tales reflect the conditions of rural and small-town life on the verge of the Industrial Revolution. In this respect the latter are close to the spirit of the traditional tales, though they are more specific in their settings.

Hauff is a fine story-teller. He knows how to keep his reader's attention as he unfolds his plots, punctuating the action with passages of dialogue and building up the suspense. The tales are varied in length, but all are longer than the norm established by the Grimms. They were designated originally as being for 'sons and daughters of the educated classes', but only a handful seem calculated to appeal to children in terms of their protagonists' ages. Dwarf Nose is twelve years old when his story begins (some editions say he is eight). Almansor is ten when the Franks come to Egypt. Most others are in their mid to late teens. What is also striking, but not often commented on, is the fact that all Hauff's protagonists are male.

Girls and women play only a limited role, and the conventional happy ending of the traditional fairytale with a marriage is largely absent. Exceptionally, Caliph Stork and Princess Owl marry when they have been transformed back into human shape, and similarly, at the end of 'The Rescue of Fatima' Mustapha is married to Zoraida, the girl who had been abducted along with his sister.[68] The female figures that do have a place in some stories play mainly victim roles. As we have noted, Fatima experiences abduction and enslavement before she is eventually rescued; but in 'The Severed Hand' the only female figure is murdered in her sleep. In 'Dwarf Nose' Mimi, the hero's helper in the latter part of the story, has been bewitched into a goose. Many of the females in other stories suffer dreadfully or have witch-like characteristics. Despite all these negative features one can hardly claim that Hauff's male figures, by contrast, have an easy time of it.

The first of Hauff's tales to appear in English was 'The Cold Heart' ('Das kalte Herz'), and it has proved one of the most popular, being printed about a dozen times in a variety of forms up to 1914. In its original German format in *Das Wirtshaus im Spessart* it was divided into two parts, separated by 'Saïds Schicksale' and 'Die Höhle von Steenfoll', but the majority of English versions present it as a continuous story. 'The Cold Heart' was published

---

[68] Hauff is on record as not wanting there to be any love interest in the story by Gustav Adolf Schöll that he included in one collection, and he seems to have regarded love-stories as uninteresting for his intended child readers. See J. Barth, 'Zu Hauffs Märchen', *Wirkendes Wort*, 41 (1991), p. 178.

The Fairytales of Wilhelm Hauff 185

in two different translations in the same year. One was by C. A. Feiling and was included in *Tales from the German, comprising Specimens from the most Celebrated Authors*, translated by John Oxenford and C. A. Feiling (London: Chapman & Hall, 1844). The title and range of material translated indicate an educated adult readership. The other translation appeared in *Popular Tales* (Rugeley: John Thomas Walters; London: J. Burns, 1844), which also printed Karl Spindler's 'S. Sylvester's Night' and Fouqué's 'Red Mantle'. This was volume 4 of 'The Juvenile Englishman's Library', so we have one and the same story being presented from the start to two different kinds of readership. James Burns republished the story in *Select Popular Tales from the German of Wilhelm Hauff* in the following year. The Feiling translation was included in *The Little Glass Man and Other Stories* (New York: Cassell; London: T. Fisher Unwin, 1893). Other translations appeared in 1867 (by M. A. Faber, Leipzig: Tauchnitz), 1881 (by Percy E. Pinkerton, London: Swan Sonnenschein & Allen), 1886 (by S. Mendel, London: George Bell & Sons), 1890 (by Agnes Henry, London: Digby & Long), 1898 (retold by W. T. Stead in *Books for the Bairns*), 1903 (by Cicely McDonnell, London: Dean & Son), 1905 (by Sybil Thesiger, London: James Finch & Co.), 1910 (by L. L. Weedon, London: Ernest Nister; New York: E. P. Dutton & Co.) and 1914 (London: Holden & Hardingham). Those by M. A. Faber and S. Mendel are clearly aimed at adults, but by the end of the century a child readership predominates.

The source for the second part of 'The Cold Heart' is Washington Irving's 'The Devil and Tom Walker' in *Tales of a Traveller* (1824).[69] Hauff, however, tells the story as though it were an authentic legend from the Black Forest, and scholars took him at his word until very recently. When William Howitt was travelling through the Black Forest with his wife and friends, he described these 'wild and primitive regions' with allusions to Hauff's story, mentioning 'the haunts of the spirits Glassmännlein and Holländer Michel', 'the busy wooden clockmakers of Friburg' and 'the timber-floaters preparing their rafts, and setting forth on their voyage to the Rhine and to Holland'.[70] A résumé of the story is included in Hezekiah Butterworth's *Zigzag Journeys to Northern Lands. The Rhine to the Arctic* (Boston: Estes and Lauriat, 1883), pp. 84-91.

The basis of Hauff's tale is simple enough. A young charcoal-burner named Peter Munk attempts to make good financially through encounters

---

69 Barth, pp. 175-77.
70 William Howitt, *The Rural and Domestic Life of Germany* (London: Longman, Brown, Green & Longmans, 1842), pp. 267-68.

with two supernatural denizens of the forest – the good-natured glass manikin and the more sinister giant, Dutch Michael. These two spirits represent the opposition of the Baden and Württemberg sides of the Forest, the charcoal-burners and the lumberjacks. Peter is granted three wishes by the glass manikin, but, as in most stories of this kind, he is foolish in what he asks for and eventually ruins himself through gambling. In the second part of the story he seeks out Dutch Michael and exchanges his living heart for a heart of stone. Because he now has no emotions, whether of sympathy for the plight of others or for any pleasure of his own, he causes suffering all around him till at last he kills his own wife for showing compassion to an aged traveller. The solitude to which Peter is now exposed leads him to seek once more the help of the glass manikin, who gives him a little glass cross and sends him to Dutch Michael to regain his heart. Peter's contrition moves the glass manikin finally to forgive him and restore his wife and mother to life again.

'The Cold Heart' is Hauff's longest tale from the almanacks. It focusses on opposing lifestyles and economic risks.[71] Dutch Michael, the giant, embodies the dangers presented by big commercial interests and the world that stretches down the River Neckar and the Rhine to Rotterdam, where the timber-men get four times the price for their timber than in Cologne. But it is a material that is bought at the cost of the heart. Not only Peter is like this. As he reads the labels on Dutch Michael's bottles of preserved hearts, he discovers that the giant also possesses the hearts of the sheriff in F., of Fat Ezekiel, the king of the dance-floor, the head forester, six corn usurers, eight recruiting officers and three money-dealers. This exploitative world derives from heartlessness and greed, to which everything is sacrificed. But Hauff regards it as reversible: his solution is conservative, a return to the humble life and the values of small-scale society. The glass manikin tells Peter after he has repented of his folly and wickedness: 'If you are true and honest you will honour your trade, and your neighbours will love and esteem you more than if you had ten tons of gold' (Mendel's translation).

Burns's anonymous translator attempts a close rendering of the story, but occasionally omits a sentence or reference that he (or she) thinks distracting for the English reader. There are also occasional additions at the beginning, where there are three short paragraphs describing the Black Forest. The translator appears to have had problems transcribing proper names from

---

[71] Volker Klotz, *Das europäische Kunstmärchen* (Munich: Deutscher Taschenbuch Verlag, 1987), pp. 208-22, especially 216-18, provides a stimulating guide to the economic implications of Hauff's tales.

the German gothic typeface, so 'Ezechiel' appears throughout as 'Eyekiel', 'Winkfritz' shows up as 'Winkfrity', and the neighbours 'Grethe and Bethe' become 'Trethel and Bertha'. Similar mishaps occur in some of the other tales.

C. A. Feiling also published in 1844 a translation of 'Der Zwerg Nase' as 'Nose, the Dwarf'. This was the first of many renderings of this popular story. Later translators had a tendency to convert the simple name into a nickname, for example, 'Nosey' (the Burns translator), 'Longnose' (Pinkerton, Mendel). The story is included in all the larger collections of Hauff's stories in English, and Andrew Lang printed a version in *The Violet Fairy Book* (1901). Butterworth has a summary in *Zigzag Journeys*. The German original was published in *Der Scheik von Alessandria*, but the setting of the story is actually Germany.

The protagonist of 'Dwarf Nose' is a twelve year old boy called Jacob, who is abducted by a nasty old woman, bewitched into slavery as a squirrel for seven years and then escapes, but in the shape of an ugly dwarf with a long nose. He does not realize how much time has passed and, on making contact again with his mother and father, is rejected by them as a charlatan. Eventually he is able to trade on the skills he has learnt with the old woman and becomes a cook in the duke's household. On one of his shopping expeditions he buys a goose, which turns out to be Mimi, the daughter of the enchanter Wetterbock, whom a wicked fairy has turned into a goose. Meanwhile, Dwarf Nose has achieved considerable fame through the excellence of his culinary skills, and is challenged by one of the duke's guests to produce a *pâté souzeraine*, something he has never heard of before. Mimi helps him to find the necessary secret ingredient, the herb Niesmitlust (Sneeze-with-pleasure), which he realizes is the same herb that had released him earlier from his squirrel shape in the hateful old woman's house. He eats the herb and regains his true human form. He and Mimi escape from the duke's palace, and Jacob takes Mimi back to her father, who disenchants her and rewards him with sufficient gifts to buy a shop and become rich and happy. Jacob does not marry Mimi, but returns to his parents (though he must now be about twenty-two years old).

Unlike most traditional fairytales, 'Dwarf Nose' does not end with a radical transformation of the hero's situation. It concludes merely with a heightened version of his status at the beginning of the tale. Jacob was the son of market stall-holders; now he has money for a shop of his own. The relative status of rich aristocracy and ordinary working person remains

188 *Telling Tales*

GLASSMANIKIN.   [*See page* 222.

20. Frontispiece (illustration to 'The Stone-cold Heart') of W. Hauff,
Longnose the Dwarf, and Other Fairy Tales (1881).

intact. There is no revolution, no breaking through class barriers, only a modest improvement in material welfare. Yet Jacob has suffered a great deal to reach this position. It is hard to see him as needing to be taught a lesson, since at his mother's market stall he does no more than scold the horrid old woman for handling and sniffing at the vegetables in such a way as to make other customers unwilling to buy them. Is his behaviour justified or is it to be regarded as impudent? Is it offensive enough for him to lose seven years of his adolescence, be subjugated to the whims of an elderly crone and transformed into the position of a mere animal? Jacob's new life is ambiguous. In being forced by his mother to help the old woman carry her vegetables home he begins the transition from poverty to affluence, for though her house is small and dilapidated from the outside, inside it is all splendour, and the old woman has a multitude of guinea-pig and squirrel servants scurrying at her beck and call. Jacob is physically transformed and can no longer call his life his own, but over seven years he is trained in a variety of ways and finishes by acquiring all the skills of a first-rate cook. Only at this stage does he encounter the magic herb that turns him back into human shape, though badly distorted.

This training and consequent alienation from parents reflects in fairytale terms what must have been, in Hauff's time, a common experience for children put into service or apprenticeship and thus severed from their families. The disagreeable old woman is a projection of all the fears that this kind of training must have held for children. She is the embodiment of the arbitrary power of the employer. She buys six heads of cabbage from Jacob's mother, but by the time they are in her house they have changed frighteningly into human heads. Jacob had thought, when she was at the market stall, that her own head had too thin a neck and might fall off, and he is also disgusted by her long nose. When he is partially disenchanted and escapes from her, it is only to find that he too has a long nose and a head that grows directly from his body without a neck. This deformity of Jacob's expresses symbolically his unease with the change from childhood to adulthood. He has learnt the skills that enable him to earn his living, but he is not yet emotionally independent. The long nose is a metaphor for his sexual embarrassment, as his hunched back exemplifies his inability to stand tall.

The translators of 'Dwarf Nose' had problems with names in the story and with descriptions of food. Lucy L. Weedon, in *Fairy Tales* by Wilhelm Hauff (London: Ernest Nister; New York: E. P. Dutton & Co., 1910), probably had the deftest solutions for the two mysterious herbs *Magentrost* and *Niesmitlust*, which she called 'trencher-man's mint' and 'the cook's delight'. These read so much more suggestively than the literal 'stomach comforter' and 'Sneeze-with-pleasure' of Feiling or 'stomach-hope' and the untranslated 'Niessmitlust' of Burns.

Most translators make a conscientious attempt at rendering the tales faithfully, but J. G. Hornstein's free adaptation in *Caravan Tales and Some Others* (London: Wells Gardner, Darton & Co., Ltd., [1912]) is a complete travesty. The story is renamed 'The Wonder Child', and the setting is transferred to Bagdad, presumably to make it congruent with the other oriental tales. The boy is now simply called 'the Wonder', but the enchanted house and its inhabitants appear as grotesque, unpleasant human beings rather than guinea-pigs and squirrels. The boy doesn't learn different skills during the period of his enchantment, but eventually just manages to totter out of the house. Later he is helped by Habeeba, one of the former female servants of Dame Nose, using the contents of a little casket from the witch's kitchen, to make a meal for the caliph. When they are fetched to see the caliph after having been praised for their efforts, they are magically transformed into handsome people again. The transferral of the story to Bagdad is totally arbitrary, and Habeeba is an unsatisfactory substitute for the goose, Mimi. Hornstein has responded only on a superficial level to Hauff. He completely fails to understand the disturbing symbolism of the story.

The year after 'Dwarf Nose' first appeared in English another of Hauff's most popular fairytales made its entry in a little book entitled *The Christmas Roses and Other Tales from the German* (London: Joseph Cundall, 1845). In German it is called 'Die Geschichte von dem kleinen Muck' and is part of *Die Karawane*. The title presents a problem for English translators because of the negative associations of the protagonist's name in English. The anonymous translator of the Cundall book avoids this in the title, which is 'Story of a Manikin', but calls the hero Midge, probably through a confusion of Muck with the German *Mücke*, 'fly'. The same false association was made by the translator of the Burns *Select Popular Tales*, who called him Little Fly. Other translators provided different spellings for the name, for example Mouck (the Ward, Lock edition, 1862), Mook (Pinkerton, 1881; Hornstein, 1912), Mouk (McDonnell, 1903; Weedon, 1910), though Mendel (1886), Thesiger (1905) and the Cassell/Unwin edition (1893) stick with the German spelling Muck.

The Fairytales of Wilhelm Hauff 191

The 'Story of Little Muck' is a true fairytale in structure, but with features that distance it somewhat from the conventional happy ending of the traditional fairytale. It is set in Nicaea (in Turkey) and has a double framework in that the narrator within the framework of *Die Karawane*, namely, the merchant Muley, presents it as his own father's retrospective account of Little Muck's youth, for at this stage Little Muck is an old bachelor, living alone and coming out of his large house just once a month, only to suffer the mocking attentions of the neighbourhood's naughty boys, including the narrator's. Little Muck's history thus appears as an explanation and retails a supposed real experience. As a boy Muley had been soundly beaten for his treatment of Little Muck before his father told his story.

This is a tale about alienation. Little Muck is, and remains, a physical oddity, the size of a dwarf, but with a head much larger than ordinary. However, at the age of sixteen he still behaves like a happy-go-lucky child. He lives alone with his father, and when the latter dies he is penniless and has to leave home. Upset and hungry after three days' walking, he is eventually taken in by an old woman who feeds all the neighbourhood's cats and makes an exception for this one human being. Later he is blamed for the damage the cats cause in the old woman's absence. One day when she is again away, a little dog leads him into her bedroom and then into a hidden chamber, where he accidentally breaks the lid of a crystal vessel. He feels forced to run away and takes with him a pair of large slippers and a walking stick. These turn out to have magical properties: the slippers carry him swiftly wherever he wishes to be, and the walking-stick is a kind of geiger-counter before its time, being able to locate hidden gold and silver. By means of the slippers Little Muck gains a post as messenger in the king's household, but when he discovers hidden treasure and shares it, his fellow servants take against him and accuse him of stealing from the king's treasury. On being put into prison, Little Muck reveals his secrets to the king, but because he does not reveal all of the conditions needed to use the magic slippers, the king is made a fool of when he tries them out, and he consequently banishes him. Little Muck then discovers magic figs that cause donkey's ears and long noses to grow on those who consume them, together with figs that remove these disfigurements. (This motif is found also in *Fortunatus* and the Grimms' story 'The Nose'.) By selling the first figs, Muck manages to deform the whole royal household. Then, disguised as a doctor, he produces the antidote, regains his slippers and walking-stick from the king, refuses to heal him and escapes. Since then Muck has lived a prosperous, but solitary life, a man whose experience of life has led him to shun humankind.

There is an underlying sadness about this tale. At the outset Little Muck is, in the words of the Burns edition, 'a playful child', 'stupid' and 'silly', but at the end, despite some gains from his magical devices, he is disillusioned with his fellow men. From beginning to end his physical deformity and outsize clothes provoke hostile reactions, teasing and ridicule, though he is cheerful, trustful and generous in deed and mood. Even the old woman who feeds him treats him less well than her cats and dogs: 'Upon the whole, [Muck] lived as lonely a life as in his father's house; for, saving his mistress, he saw nothing but cats and dogs the whole day'. He is accused both by her and by the king's servants of misdeeds of which he is totally innocent. Despite eventually getting the better of the king and taking revenge on him, Muck's success at the end of the story is simply material. It is difficult to know just what Hauff intended by this ending. Was it a condemnation of the generality of people for their inability to treat human difference with sympathy? Is it impossible for those who are different ever to achieve complete happiness? Little Muck is certainly different from the usual simpleton of traditional fairytales who marries a princess and lives happily ever after.

In addition to introducing 'Little Muck' to the British reading public, Joseph Cundall also published 'The False Prince' in another collection, *The King of the Swans, and Other Tales* (1846), of which the title story was by Rudolphi and which contained another tale by A. L. Grimm, a contemporary but no relation of the Brothers Grimm. 'Das Märchen vom falschen Prinzen' is another tale from *Die Karawane* that enjoyed great popularity in English. It tells how an upstart tailor called Labakan uses a fine robe that he has been asked to alter and impersonates a young prince, attempting to win the latter's inheritance. Labakan at first succeeds in convincing the prince's father of his identity, but fails with his mother. The sultaness proposes a test to establish the identities of the rival prince and tailor: each must make a caftan. Naturally, the tailor makes the best, and the prince expostulates that needlework is not a proper test for a prince. The sultaness thereby recognizes him as her son, but the sultan has to be convinced by a second test which a fairy puts forward: the two young men have to choose between two caskets, one bearing the words 'honour and renown', the other 'riches and happiness'. The real prince selects the former, Labakan the latter, and the contents of the caskets confirm the rightness of their choice. The prince finds a golden crown, which grows immediately to fit him, while Labakan gets a large needle and a ball of thread. The prince spares Labakan's life, but forces him to return home. There too he is berated, beaten and sent away. He decides to renounce all ambitions to greatness, sells his casket and sets up again elsewhere as a tailor. The needle turns out to be a magic one that can sew by itself, as a result of which Labakan wins much custom and achieves the riches and happiness that the fairy's casket.granted.

What are the implications of this tale? Like Dwarf Nose, Labakan does not achieve a change of social status at the end of the story, no matter how clever he is in tricking the prince and arriving first at the meeting-place with the sultan. He retains the ambitions of the workman – 'riches and happiness' – rather than adopting the ideals of the aristocracy – 'honour and renown'. His identity is unmasked by the fairy, but he is not over-severely punished for the crisis that his untoward desires cause. He may be banished by the prince and beaten by his master and workmen, but the fairy nonetheless provides him in the end with a magic needle – the fairytale equivalent of the new machinery that was revolutionizing contemporary industrial progress – by means of which he realizes his material ambitions. Labakan is an ambivalent sort of hero: his aspirations are shown to be reprehensible in the stark form in which he envisages them (escaping from the social status into which he was born), but his shrewdness in competing with the aristocracy takes him far enough, given the prince's magnanimity, to improve his own material situation, if only to a moderate degree. He concludes by reflecting that 'honour and renown are often dangerous things'. Labakan's final success is dependent on two things – the fairy's gift (not immediately recognized) and the prince's magnanimity. However, the fact that he achieves his success through secret means, employing no one else, is perceived as dubious and reflects in fairytale terms the suspicion that new machinery provoked in the real world that Hauff was living in.

'The False Prince' circulated widely in English. It actually appeared first in Burns's *Select Popular Tales* (1845), and another version was published in George Vickers's *Grimms' Goblins* (1860-61) with the title 'The Tailor Prince'. It is also found in *Tales of Wonder; or, the Inn in the Black Forest* (London: Cheap Repository Series, 1861), the Ward, Lock editions (1862, 1884), where it is rather freely translated, Mendel's very careful translation (1886, 1914), McDonnell (1903), Thesiger (1905) and Hornstein (1912). Hornstein's version is an elaborated paraphrase of Hauff's original and changes the end of the story, omitting the casket test and turning Labakan's adventures into a dream that he has while falling asleep over working on Prince Selim's robe. The story is thus robbed of much of its original significance. There are two different adaptations of the story in W. T. Stead's *Books for the Bairns*. In no. 57 (October 1900) it is given the title 'The Mad Prince', while in no. 160 (May 1909), in an adaptation by Frank Mundell, it is called 'Prince or Tailor?' Yet another translation was included in Andrew Lang's *Crimson Fairy Book* (1903), this time called 'The Sham Prince'.

Of all Hauff's tales the most popular in English was 'Caliph Stork', which was in fact the first story in *Die Karawane*. Its first appearance in English was in Burns's *Select Popular Tales*, after which it was printed in all subsequent major selections or complete editions. It was also included in *Grimms' Goblins*, Andrew Lang's *Green Fairy Book* (1892) and no. 57 of 'Books for the Bairns'. It recounts how the Caliph of Bagdad and his Vizier acquire the means of transforming themselves into storks, but because they laugh while thus transformed they forget the magic word that will turn them back into human beings. This word is *Mutabor*, the Latin for 'I shall be changed'. An owl that is similarly metamorphosed advises them how to rediscover the word, but only on condition that one of them offers her his hand in marriage and so disenchants her. In this way the Caliph acquires a wife, not through any romantic attachment, but as an exchange for services rendered. Hauff's source was the story of 'König Papagei' (King Parrot) from the German translation of the *Arabian Nights* by Habicht, von der Hagen and Schall (Breslau, 1824).

In Hauff the initial transformation into the form of storks is effected by a black powder and a piece of paper with writing on it in Latin, which the Caliph buys from a pedlar who claims not to know what either is. In the Burns edition of 1845 the pedlar is accurately described as 'a stout little man, with a swarthy face and tattered clothes'. The Ward, Lock edition chooses to add grotesque and unpleasant details:

> He was a little man, dark, and with a hooked nose, and a cunning mouth which displayed two hideous yellow teeth, the only two he had. As soon as he appeared before the Caliph, he bent his forehead to the ground, and in an attempt to smile contracted his face into the most frightful grimace that ever distorted a human visage.

A few lines further on, the translation identifies the man as a Jew, and the passage is revealed as a gratuitous piece of anti-Semitism. None of the other translations do anything of the kind, but stick scrupulously to Hauff's text.

Hauff himself might be accused of anti-Semitism in another of his stories, 'Abner, the Jew who Saw Nothing'. This is a close adaptation of 'Le Chien et le cheval', the third chapter of Voltaire's *Zadig* (1748), in which the man who identifies the tracks in the sand, grass, trees and rocks as a runaway dog and horse is simply an inhabitant of Babylon, an educated young man called Zadig. Hauff changes the location to Morocco and makes the man a Jew, providing an introductory paragraph:

> Jews, as you know, are everywhere; and everywhere there are Jews: their falcon eyes spy out wherever an advantage is to be gained; and the more oppressed they are, the more cunning they become, while they glory in their very cunning. That a Jew, however, may sometime fall into disgrace owing to this very quality, witness Abner, as he one evening took his way through the Morocco gate (Burns edition, 1845).

There was no necessity for Hauff to make these changes (aside from covering his tracks as regards his source), since in the world of the *Arabian Nights* Zoroastrians often play the role of magicians or wise men and likewise often elicit fear and hostility among those envious of them. 'Abner, the Jew who Saw Nothing' was not widely translated into English – it appears only in Burns's edition and Mendel's translation. Its unpopularity is probably due to the fact that the tale contains no fairytale or adventure elements.

Hauff seems fascinated by deformations of the body. Some of them are only temporary, as is the case with Dwarf Nose and Mimi, Caliph Stork, his vizier and Princess Owl, but others are permanent like those of Little Muck and the supposed Englishman in 'The Dancer of Grünwiesel' (also known as 'The Young Englishman'). In addition, the narrator of 'The Severed Hand' explains how he has come to lose his hand; and Peter Munk spends the latter part of his disastrous career without a heart. Hauff's heroes are subjected to many vicissitudes, with varied outcomes. Those who cause a death, whether innocently (as in 'The Severed Hand') or deliberately (as in 'The Ghost Ship'), suffer as a result. The deliberate attempt to change one's economic fortunes is fraught with danger and never succeeds absolutely. The covetous brothers in 'The Stag Florin' destroy their half-brother in attempting to gain his possessions, but fate destroys them too.

One further fairytale of Hauff's also gained wide circulation – 'The Adventures of Saïd', the only oriental tale to feature in *The Inn in the Spessart*. It tells a series of adventures in which the hero narrowly escapes from imminent death, only to be plunged after an interval of calm into another threat. These hair-breadth escapes are implicitly linked to a silver whistle that Saïd's dead mother had been given by a fairy and which Saïd was prematurely given by his father when he was sent to Mecca at the age of eighteen. The tale illustrates the pull between Saïd's mother, who believes in magic, and his rationalist father, who does not believe that fairies can have any effect on human affairs. To begin with, Saïd's escapes, in response to his blowing the whistle and achieving no sound, occur in ways that do not depend on magic, but on coincidence and human agency. However, half-way through the adventures, a lady who helps him in his troubles with the wicked merchant Kalum-Beck, who has virtually enslaved him, turns out to be the fairy friend of Saïd's mother, and from now on the incidence of magic becomes more evident. Saïd's final escape from death occurs in a shipwreck when he is rescued by clinging to the back of a large dolphin, which swims up the river to Bagdad and deposits him by the caliph's palace. Here Saïd is welcomed by the caliph, his grievances against Kalum-Beck are put to right with the latter's punishment, Saïd is reunited with his father, and the two of them are given a palace in Bagdad in which to live. The magical power of Saïd's dead mother and her fairy friend has affinities with that of Aschenputtel's mother in the Grimms' fairytale. It enables the protagonist of the story to overcome extraordinary problems, but once they are solved it vanishes, and ordinary life resumes its place.

English versions of this story begin with Burns's *Select Popular Tales*, which presents a number of divergences from the original. There is some confusion with proper names, and Saïd's father is referred to on several occasions as coming from Aleppo, though at the beginning he is correctly stated to live in Balsora (Basra). Such slips are not uncommon, but there are two deliberate changes of a more serious kind. Saïd's escape on the dolphin is entirely omitted, thus reducing the incidence of magical implausibility; and at the end of the story Saïd marries 'the Grand Vizier's lovely daughter'. In this latter addition the translator is probably picking up the conclusion of 'Caliph Stork', but, as we have seen, Hauff's usual practice was to avoid fairytale marriages at the end of his tales. The other translations follow Hauff's original quite closely, though Hornstein retitles the story 'The Golden Whistle', even though the original has a silver one.

Although Hauff wrote ostensibly for the 'sons and daughters of the educated classes', his tales appeal to children and adults alike. This dual readership is reflected in the variety of English versions of his tales, some of which are specifically aimed at adults, while others equally clearly are designed for children. Hauff first appears alongside other German writers in *Tales from the German*, translated by John Oxenford and C. A. Feiling, and the Walters/Burns edition of *Popular Tales* (both published in 1844). The same is true of Cundall's two children's books of 1845 and 1846. But the Burns *Select Popular Tales* (1845) is devoted wholly to Hauff and prints fourteen of his stories, including one ('The Portrait of the Emperor') which does not come from the three almanacks. Both Burns and Cundall were enthusiasts for German literature. Burns published editions taken from the works of Musäus, Fouqué, Tieck, Lessing, Schiller, Caroline Pichler, Baroness Fouqué, Clauren and Christoph Schmid, dealing with literature for both adults and children. Cundall concentrated more on children's books. Over the period 1845-51 he published Musäus's *Legends of Rubezahl* (1845), A. L. Grimm's *The Two Talismans* (1846), Berthold Auerbach's *Village Tales from the Black Forest* (1846), the Grimm Brothers' *German Fairy Tales & Popular Stories* (1846, i.e. Edgar Taylor's *Gammer Grethel*), Alexander Weill's *Village Tales from Alsatia* (1848), *The Heroic Life and Exploits of Siegfried the Dragon Slayer* (1848), Christoph Schmid's *Christmas Eve, or the Story of Little Anton* (1849), Clara Fechner's *Nut-cracker and Sugar-Dolly* (1849), *Merry Tales for Little Folk*, edited by Madame de Chatelain (1851), *The Comical Creatures from Wurtemberg* (1851) and Theodor Hosemann's *A Laughter Book for Little Folk* (c. 1851). In addition Cundall published a monthly periodical called *The Playmate* (1847), which had a second series in 1847-48, and both included German material. These books represent a remarkable achievement on Cundall's part, as they brought a wide range of German children's books to British readers.[72]

After Burns and Cundall's pioneering editions of Hauff the next British appearance of some of his tales was in *Grimms' Goblins* (1860-61), where adaptations of 'The Caliph Stork', 'Little Mouck', 'The Tailor-Prince' and 'The Magic Whistle' were printed without any indication of Hauff's authorship. All four stories are illustrated with a large vigorous colour wood-engraving after designs by Hablot K. Browne. Then in 1861 we have a selection entitled *Tales of Wonder; or, the Inn in the Black Forest*

---

72 For details see Ruari McLean, *Joseph Cundall. A Victorian Publisher. Notes on his Life and a Check-list of his Books* (Pinner: Private Libraries Association, 1976). The authorship of *Nut-cracker and Sugar-Dolly* is not given by McLean., but appears in Christine Pressler, *Schöne alte Kinderbücher* (Munich: Bruckmann, 1980), p. 152. The information about Schmid's *Christmas Eve* comes from Gumuchian, *Les Livres de l'enfance* (London: The Holland Press, 1979), vol. 1, no. 1737.

(London: Cheap Repository Series). The title substitutes for the little known Spessart (at least outside Germany) the more familiar Black Forest, and the framework is supplied by *The Inn in the Spessart*, while the actual stories are taken from *The Caravan* and *The Sheik of Alexandria*. These are 'The Prophecy of the Silver Florin', 'The History of Caliph Chusid' (i.e. 'Caliph Stork'), 'The Story of Little Muke', 'The Story of the Spectre Ship', 'The Rescue of Fatima', 'Nosey, the Dwarf' and 'The False Prince'. The selection gives a good idea of the varied content and mood of Hauff's stories. There are no illustrations, so perhaps a mixed readership of adults and children was envisaged.

In 1862 Ward, Lock and Co. published a different selection with the title *The Caravan: a Series of Oriental Tales* as the second part of a volume containing *Grimm's Fairy Tales and Other Popular Stories*. This book, profusely illustrated by Bertall, was the first to be published in both Britain and the United States, and it was reissued in 1884. The selection contains 'The Caliph Stork', 'The False Prince', 'The Deliverance of Fatima', 'Little Mouck', 'The Haunted Ship' and 'The Adventures of Saïd'. The first five tales are taken from *The Caravan*, while the last comes from *The Inn in the Spessart*, but the unifying factor, as the subtitle indicates, is the oriental setting of each of the tales. It is interesting to note how much overlap of content there is with these three publications of the early 1860s, but the translations are all different, anonymous and each with its own oddities or mistakes.

The Tauchnitz publication in 1867 of M. A. Faber's translation of 'The Cold Heart' was noted earlier. The volume also contained two other tales by Hauff – 'The Beggar Girl of the Pont des Arts' and 'The Emperor's Picture' – neither of which is a fairytale or included in the three almanacks. After Feiling in 1844 Faber is only the second translator to be identified and credited. The British Library catalogue notes a Mary Anne Faber as the author of *Recollections of Indian Life* (1910), and the two may well be the same person. The next translator identified herself more clearly. This was Elizabeth Still Harrington (i.e. E. S. Stanhope, Countess of Harrington), who brought out a slender volume containing free translations of *The Storks and the False Prince* (London: Henry Sotheran, 1875). These are simplified versions of Hauff's two stories, which remove a good bit of the detail and description, but otherwise follow the plot fairly closely. Hauff's name is not mentioned on the title-page. It is doubtful how widely this slight publication circulated.

By the 1880s it had become the practice to name translators, and in 1881 we find Percy E. Pinkerton credited with a new small selection entitled *Longnose the Dwarf, and Other Fairy Tales*, by W. Hauff (London: W. Swan Sonnenschein & Allen). This was part of an 'Illustrated Library of Fairy Tales' and once more used Bertall's illustrations. In addition to the title story Pinkerton translated 'The History of Little Mook', 'The Caliph turned Stork', 'The Adventures of Said', 'The Stone-Cold Heart' and 'The Story of the Silver Florin'. The first complete translation of Hauff's fairytales was made by S. Mendel and published in 1886 by George Bell and Sons as part of 'Bohn's Standard Library'. It was reprinted in 1914. It is a kind of companion piece to Margaret Hunt's complete translation of *Grimm's Household Tales* (1884), also published by Bell. Neither publication contains any illustrations, so an adult readership can be assumed. Mendel gives the most accurate translation of Hauff not only verbally, but also in the presentation of the stories with the frameworks and in the sequence intended by the author. A further translation probably designed for adult consumption was Agnes Henry's *The Cold Heart* (London: Digby and Long, 1890), which again had no illustrations. It is not the most accurate of renderings, occasionally misunderstanding bits or omitting difficult passages.

In 1893 T. Fisher Unwin published four of Hauff's tales under the title *The Little Glass Man and Other Stories*. Feiling's translations were used, uncredited, for 'The Little Glass Man' itself and 'Nose, the Dwarf', but translations from another, unknown hand were printed for 'Caliph Stork' and 'Little Muck'. The selection is preceded by a rather silly introduction by L. Eckenstein, purporting to tell, by reference to the Blue Fairy and Gogul Mogul, 'How the stories were found'. This is a piece of mere whimsy, providing no factual information whatever.

During the 1890s and 1900s we get a recurrence of the practice of *Grimms' Goblins*, in which individual tales by Hauff are incorporated into general collections of fairytales. Andrew Lang included 'Caliph Stork' in *The Green Fairy Book* (1892), 'Dwarf Long Nose' in *The Violet Fairy Book* (1901) and 'The Story of the Sham Prince, or the Ambitious Tailor' in *The Crimson Fairy Book* (1903). Lang had a whole bevy of female translators for these extensive collections of mainly traditional tales. They included his wife and several other women whose work is acknowledged in his prefaces, but it is generally not clear who translated which particular tale. However, we are told that Miss Blackley translated 'Dwarf Long Nose', and it may be that she translated the other Hauff stories as well. Nowhere is Hauff actually credited with the authorship of the tales, but as Lang's anthologies enjoyed a wide circulation and were often reprinted, these already well-known stories were increasingly understood as part of the vast stockpile of traditional tales. Both 'Caliph Stork' and 'Dwarf Long Nose' gained prominence through the black and white drawings of H. J. Ford (1860-1941), who illustrated all Lang's fairy books and provided appealing, strongly imaginative designs. Lang's books were imitated in a series of anthologies of mainly literary fairytales published by Hutchinson and Co. and illustrated by H. R. Millar. Two of Hauff's tales were included in them. 'Fatma' appeared in *The Silver Fairy Book* [1895] and 'The Adventures of Said' in *The Diamond Fairy Book* [1897], each in a new anonymous translation.

While Lang's books with their colour plates as well as black and white illustrations were aimed at middle-class children, W. T. Stead targeted a less well off readership with his magazine-style *Books for the Bairns*. The first of these pink paperbacks, issued monthly at a penny, was published in March 1896. The series purveyed simplified versions of popular material and usually consisted of sixty-four pages. Each was copiously illustrated with black and white drawings. The series opened with *Aesop's Fables*, but no. 32 (October 1898) presented *Coal-Munk-Peter and his Three Wishes* (i.e. 'The Cold Heart'), and no. 57 (October 1900) had *The Mad Tailor and the Caliph Stork. Two Tales from the East*. Both credited the stories explicitly to Hauff, but they are simplified adaptations rather than faithful translations. Stead actually explains at the beginning of the second part of 'Coal-Munk-Peter' that, while the first part is an abridgement of the original German story, the second has had to be retold from memory, as he lost his first version of it after reading it to his children. The illustrator for 'The Mad Tailor' was Wilfrid Sayers, but both 'The Caliph Stork' and 'Coal-Munk-Peter' were dealt with by Stead's usual collaborator, Brinsley Le Fanu (1854-1920). Rather oddly, Stead published a second version of 'The False Prince' as 'Prince or Tailor?' as no. 160 (May 1909) of *Books for the Bairns*, this being an adaptation by Frank Mundell. Incidentally, it was Allen Lane's memories of reading *Books for the Bairns* as a child that prompted him to launch Puffin Story Books in 1940.[73]

The period from the death of Queen Victoria to the First World War saw a further half dozen editions of Hauff's fairytales, ranging from a reprint of Mendel's translation to the Rev. E. J. Cunningham's comic verse rendering

---

73 For general information see Sally Wood, *W. T. Stead and his 'Books for the Bairns'* (Edinburgh: Salvia Books, 1987).

The Fairytales of Wilhelm Hauff 201

of *The Caliph Stork* (London: Swan Sonnenschein, 1905). This latter is an undistinguished Edwardian children's book with monochrome illustrations by T. C. Gash on most of its twenty pages. At least it is not a version that pretends to enhance the original by turning into verse, as happened with Fouqué's *Undine*. The casual nature of the undertaking is revealed in the concluding lines:

> If a moral you think to see entwined
> In the innocent web of our trifling verse,
> Pray seek it, and possibly you may find;
> If not, why, no matter; you're none the worse.

Both this and Stead's approach in the *Books for the Bairns* show that translators felt no compunction in playing around with Hauff's texts. It isn't that they alter details because of the deeply felt moral and religious considerations of the Evangelicals, but that they don't really grasp Hauff's ambiguities and just want to prettify his tales.

A collection of nine tales, explicitly stated to be 'translated and adapted' by Cicely McDonnell, was published as *Hauff's Fairy Tales* (London: Dean & Son, Ltd., 1903). Rather unusually, it included 'Almansor', which had previously only figured in Burns's 1845 edition and Mendel's complete translation. McDonnell's understanding of German is imperfect, and this is shown at several points in her version of what she calls 'The Dwarf's Nose'. Later in the story she in fact calls him 'Longnose'. Not only does she continually simplify the story, but she converts the heads of cabbage into cauliflowers and refers to the herb (*Kräutlein*) of which the magic soup is made as 'the particular cabbage of which it is made'. The mysterious *Magentrost* and *Niesmitlust* are changed into marjoram and borage. The specks of dust seen in the sun (*Sonnenstäubchen*) which the old woman makes into her bread are rather engagingly, if desperately, translated as 'sunberries'. The book contains forty-one black and white illustrations by Fritz Bergen plus three full-page colour plates and a frontispiece depicting Little Mouk racing in his slippers. The other two plates show the caliph in the process of turning into a stork and Dwarf Nose unwittingly scaring his mother at her market stall.

In 1905 another extensive translation by Sybil Thesiger was published by James Finch and Co. It excluded 'The Haunted Ship', but otherwise was as full as Mendel's. The framework tale of *The Caravan* is presented at the end of that section with the separate title of 'The History of Orbasan, the Robber'. The book is attractively illustrated with sixteen strong black and white pictures by Dorothy Morris, each story being thus covered.

The next edition to appear reverted to colour illustration and was the most ambitious production to date. *Fairy Tales* by Wilhelm Hauff, translated by L. L. Weedon and illustrated by Arthur A. Dixon, was a joint publication of Ernest Nister in London and E. P. Dutton and Co. in New York, appearing in 1910. It printed eleven tales, omitting only 'The Spectre Ship', 'The Severed Hand' and 'The Dancer of Grünwiesel', stories of a particularly grotesque or gruesome nature. It is nonetheless one of the rare publications that include 'The Cavern of Steenfoll'. Lucy L. Weedon, who also translated a selection of *Grimm's Fairy Tales* for Nister and Dutton, produced a fluent and idiomatic, if not always perfectly accurate translation of Hauff. Nister had his sights on a better class of purchaser than Dean and Son. His book is better printed and on a higher quality of paper, the binding is adorned with an *art nouveau* figure, and the book contains six colour plates, twelve full-page monochrome illustrations and many more similar vignettes by Arthur A. Dixon (fl. 1893-1920). The colour plates are taken from watercolour paintings showing a subtle range of hues and depicting a variety of lively scenes.

The title-page of *Caravan Tales and Some Others* (London: Wells Gardner, Darton & Co., 1912), illustrated by Norman Ault, bears the dispiriting line 'Freely adapted and retold by J. G. Hornstein'. The contents present 'Caliph Stork', 'The Death Ship', 'Little Mook', 'The False Prince', 'The Golden Whistle; or the Fortunes of Saïd' and 'The Wonder-Child' (i.e. 'Dwarf Nose'). To these Hornstein adds an invention of his own – 'The Rusty Key'. He keeps to the plots of the first three and 'The Golden Whistle' (though it is a silver whistle in the German), but 'The False Prince' is foolishly altered. At the end of the story the casket test, which sharply brings out the difference between the nobleman and the tailor, is omitted. After the sewing test the court is invaded by Labakan's master and workmen, anxious for revenge on one whose presumption has discredited their calling. Then another twist turns the whole sequence of adventures into a dream that Labakan has had, having fallen asleep when working on Prince Selim's robe. Hornstein's tricks with 'The Wonder-Child' have already been dealt with earlier in this chapter. The book is illustrated with fifteen tipped-in colour plates by Norman Ault (1880-1950), which are carefully composed, but lack distinctiveness. Their small size may have been intended to evoke miniatures, but it robs them of impact.

It seems appropriate that 1914, the year in which the war that changed the face of Europe began, should be marked by two editions that show the divergences in the reception of Hauff. One is a reprint of Mendel's scrupulous, unadorned translation of the full corpus of Hauff's fairytales, first issued nearly thirty years before in 1886 and now reissued in a cheap accessible format for the adult reader. The other is also a book designed for adults, which includes 'The Cold Heart' along with Chamisso's *Peter Schlemihl* (London: Holden & Hardingham). The large format, generously spaced typography and the many colour plates protected by tissue guards mark this out as a gift book. Hauff's story is introduced by a two-page biography by H. Robertson Murray, who was possibly also the translator, though that is nowhere stated. Clearly, the illustrations matter more. They are by Forster Robson and consist of nine plates in full colour, with four more drawings reproduced in two colours. These latter are much more dramatic in impact and adroitly composed. By contrast the full colour plates are rather conventional. 'The Cold Heart' was the first of Hauff's stories to appear in English translation and did so twice in 1844, so it seems curiously appropriate that it should also be the last work of Hauff's to be published before the outbreak of war.

As with so many other German writers, the First World War created a hiatus in the reception of Hauff. A few stories survived the period because Hauff's name was not attached to them, so they continued to be reprinted, for example, in Lang's colour fairy books. As also occurred with Hoffmann's *Nutcracker and Mouse-King*, an adaptation of 'Little Dwarf Nose' and 'The Magic Whistle' by E. Gordon Browne and illustrated by Florence Anderson, again not mentioning Hauff's name, was published shortly after the war (London: J. Coker & Co., c. 1920). Not until the 1940s do we find further editions, and since then they have continued to appear frequently. What is interesting in all of this is the fact that Hauff has ceased to be presented as an author of interest to adults and children alike. He now appears in English only in editions designed for children and accompanied with illustrations in a wide variety of techniques and styles. The tales have nonetheless demonstrated their staying-power and continuing appeal to children and the artists who have illustrated them.

12. The Folktale Tradition in Germany

Although Jacob and Wilhelm Grimm now dominate discussion of folktales and fairytales, they were far from being the only ones concerned with collecting and publishing such material in Germany during the nineteenth century. The Grimms had separated the traditional tales that they were interested in into two broad categories – *Märchen* and *Sagen*. *Märchen* are basically fictional in character and include tales of magic (what we usually call fairytales), comic, religious, nursery and animal tales, while *Sagen* are legends and make some claim to recount incidents that are believed to have actually happened. The Grimms published a large collection of *Deutsche Sagen* in two volumes (1816-18), but this was not translated into English as a complete work until quite recently. Individual tales or small selections were, however, excerpted and included in a variety of British books, as we shall see. Most other nineteenth-century collectors did not categorize their material as strictly as the Grimms and printed fairytales (in the narrower sense) alongside local and historical legends, as British collectors also did. For the most part, they made regional or local rather than national collections of traditional oral tales. Some of this made its way into English and formed part of the growing and widespread general interest in folklore, appealing to both adults and children. As the scholarly work progressed in Germany, various authors used the material for children's books, but little of this was translated into English. The one German writer who followed closely in the Grimms' footsteps, rivalling their attraction to both old and young, and who was also translated into English was Ludwig Bechstein. It is to him that we now turn.

At the beginning of the twentieth century Bechstein, if we judge by the number of editions that his major collections had achieved, was more popular in Germany than the Brothers Grimm. By 1929 his *Deutsches Märchenbuch* (German Fairytale Book), first published in 1845, had reached its seventieth impression, and by 1922 his *Neues Deutsches Märchenbuch* (New German Fairytale Book), first published in 1856, was in its 105th impression.[74] By comparison the Grimms' *Kinder- und Hausmärchen* had only reached its twenty-third impression by 1890.[75] Bechstein was able to build on what the pioneers of folktale scholarship had accomplished. He also collected many tales that do not figure in the Grimms' collection, and he knew how to make them accessible to young readers.

Born in Weimar in 1801, Ludwig Bechstein was the illegitimate son of Johanna Dorothea Bechstein and a French emigré, Louis Hubert Dupontreau. He was taken into the household of his uncle, Johann Matthäus Bechstein, a noted botanist and ornithologist. The young Bechstein studied pharmacy in Arnstadt, Thuringia, but his literary activities brought him to the notice of the Duke of Saxe-Meiningen, who enabled him to study philosophy, history and literature at the University of Leipzig and then appointed him, in 1832, librarian of the ducal library. Bechstein had already published four of his own tales as *Thüringische Volksmährchen* (Thuringian Folktales) in 1823, but from the late 1820s there flowed from his pen a series of literary, historical and folkloristic works that occupied his talents for the rest of his life. He was married twice and died in 1860. While a small proportion of Bechstein's scholarly work is of importance, it is his activity as a collector and editor of folktales and legends that has kept his name alive.[76]

Bechstein was not a field collector of tales in the way that later became the practice among folklore scholars. He took his material from a multiplicity of sources – printed works of all kinds and periods, editions of medieval poems, single folktales published in scholarly journals, *Volksbücher* (chapbooks) and what he refers to in his notes to individual tales as 'oral' sources. Modern scholarship tends to take this last source with a pinch of salt and to assume that Bechstein meant that a story was orally current rather than that he had personally noted it down. Some of his tales are demonstrably reworked versions of tales published by the Grimms.

---

74 Werner Bellmann in *Enzyklopädie des Märchens*, vol. 2, cols. 15-19.
75 *Kinder- und Hausmärchen*, gesammelt durch die Brüder Grimm (Darmstadt: Wissenschaftliche Buchgesellschaft, 1966), p. 840.
76 Walter Scherf in Ludwig Bechstein, *Sämtliche Märchen* (Darmstadt: Wissenschaftliche Buchgesellschaft, 1976), pp. 868-71.

Like Wilhelm Grimm, Bechstein reworked and revised his material. The latest edition of the *Deutsches Märchenbuch* to be published in his lifetime was the thirteenth edition of 1857, which contained eighty tales. The original edition of 1845 had contained another nineteen tales, which were eliminated in the twelfth edition of 1853. In addition the 1853 edition has considerably reworked versions of four of the original tales – 'Das Märchen von den sieben Schwaben' (The Fairytale of the Seven Swabians), 'Die verzauberte Prinzessin' (The Enchanted Princess), 'Die Königskinder' (The Royal Children) and 'Die drei dummen Teufel' (The Three Stupid Devils). The *Neues Deutsches Märchenbuch* provided a further fifty tales that are quite different from those previously published. Bechstein thus has 149 tales compared with the Grimms' 211.

Despite Bechstein's immense popularity in Germany, he did not have anything like the same success in Britain, although a fine selection of his tales was translated into English and published in 1854. The firm of Addey and Co. had published a two-volume edition of the Grimms' *Household Stories* in 1853, illustrated by E. H. Wehnert. This was the most comprehensive translation of the Grimms to date and almost certainly owes its origin to the enthusiasm for fairytales of Joseph Cundall, who was in partnership with Addey from 1849 to 1852. Cundall had previously published a different selection and translation from the Grimms in 1846 as well as their namesake A. L. Grimm, *The Heroic Life and Exploits of Siegfried the Dragon Slayer* and several other German items. It is more than likely that Addey and Co.'s *The Old Story-Teller. Popular German Tales*, collected by Ludwig Bechstein (1854) is a further example of Cundall's German interests.

The Old Story-Teller, like so many similar books, does not name the translators who made Bechstein accessible to British readers. They made versions of fifty-six tales from the *Deutsches Märchenbuch*, using the 1853 edition, since that is the first edition to include 'Der Mann ohne Herz' ('The Man without a Heart'), 'Siebenschön' ('As Pretty as Seven') and 'Der weiße Wolf' ('The White Wolf'), which Bechstein took from Karl Müllenhoff.[77] The tales are accompanied by one hundred illustrations by the celebrated German artist Ludwig Richter. Eight of them are full-page hand-coloured plates and extremely attractive in their evocation of picturesque preindustrial Germany.

What sort of tales were included in this, the only translation of Bechstein to be made in the nineteenth century? Of the fifty-six items eight were

---

77 Ibid., pp. 795, 805, 823.

208 *Telling Tales*

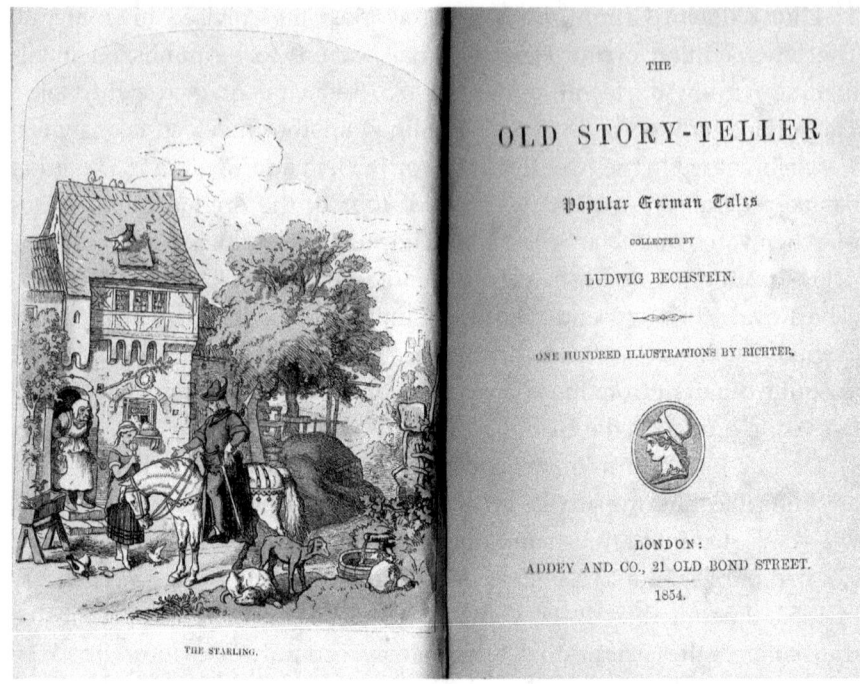

21. Title-page and frontispiece by Ludwig Richter of *Ludwig Bechstein, The Old Story-teller: Popular German Tales* (1854).

actually taken from medieval texts, and a further ten came from an early printed book usually known as the *Buch der Beispiele der alten Weisen* (Book of Exempla from the Wise Ancients), which Bechstein knew in its last popular edition of 1592. This is a German version of the famous Oriental collection known in many languages and with many titles, but generally known in English as the *Fables of Pilpay*, of which the latest edition had appeared in 1818. Two other tales – 'Hop o' my Thumb' and 'Bluebeard' – are closely derived from Perrault. The medieval tales are for the most part moral tales, and those from the *Buch der Beispiele* are chiefly animal fables.

In looking at the character of this selection of what was available of Bechstein's tales at the time, we find that twenty-three have a male protagonist, fourteen a female, and four have them combined, i.e. a brother and sister or a husband and wife. Twelve are animal tales, and two have no protagonist. The German tale 'Das Tränenkrüglein' does not specify the gender of the child that cannot rest in its grave because of its mother's tears, but the English translation, 'The Jug of Tears', makes it a little girl. Many of the tales, like 'Das Tränenkrüglein' ('KHM 109, 'Das Totenhemdchen'),

The Folktale Tradition in Germany 209

have a parallel in the Grimms' collection, that is to say, the tale-type to which the story belongs is also represented in the Grimms. As far as the fairytales (tales of magic) are concerned, readers would not have noticed any obvious difference in tone and length from what they were accustomed to from the Grimms. In his German originals Bechstein does allow himself the occasional personally motivated aside, but these are just the things that the English translators were likely to remove or modify.

The sequence of tales as printed in *The Old Story-Teller* is only loosely related to that of the German original. It opens with 'The Man without a Heart', which reads smoothly but contains a number of mistakes in translation – not things which alter the shape and tone of the story, but blemishes nonetheless. The story concerns an old man who keeps his heart outside his body, turns six brothers and their prospective brides into stone and makes the seventh bride a virtual prisoner. The seventh, youngest brother goes in search of his older brothers, finds the old man's heart, rescues the seventh bride and disenchants the rest. In the course of the story the old man tells the girl his heart is 'in der Bettdecke' (in the quilt). The girl then embroiders flowers on it to please him. The English version has the old man say his heart is 'under my bed-covering', and so the girl gathers flowers on places them on the bed. The old man next says, in the German, that his heart is in the room door ('Stubentür'), which the English mistranslates as 'in the oven'. The youngest brother, on his search, encounters an ox which he invites to share his food. In the German the ox sits down in a leisurely manner ('gemächlich'), which the English renders as 'genteelly'. Whether the extraordinary 'Vogel Greif' that appears a little further on should be translated as 'a large vulture' (as here) or as 'a griffin' (the more usual meaning) is open to debate.

The occasional mistranslations generally concern details and tend not to affect the broad outline of the story. But elsewhere there are deliberate alterations. 'The Two Bones of Contention' ('Der Zornbraten') is both more loosely translated and makes more serious changes. This is a medieval story about how a knight tames an obstreperous mother and daughter who both want to mock and master their respective husbands. It is one of the most extreme examples of a tale calculated to teach women that their role in life is to be subservient to their husbands and fathers. The young knight who solves the situation first kills his falcon, then his hound and his horse for supposed disobedience in order to demonstrate what his new wife can expect from him. This sufficiently tames his wife, but to deal with the mother he has to slice two 'anger-steaks' ('Zornbraten') from her hips. The English changes this to '"two bones of contention", one in each arm', presumably considering the hips a rather too risky and realistic site for the butchery/surgery.

The German original contains several word-plays and allusions that would have made Bechstein's text amusing as well as shocking – humour is one of his hallmarks – but as these can't easily be translated into English, they are omitted or become less specific. In the original, for example, the father upbraids his daughter with the words 'O du böse Chriemhilt!' (you wicked Kriemhild), equating her with the terrible queen in the *Nibelungenlied* who is prepared to sacrifice her own son as well as her brother to gain revenge for the murder of her husband Siegfried. Although there had been two English verse translations of the *Nibelungenlied*, published in 1848 and 1850 respectively, the reference to Kriemhild would have been lost on British children, so it becomes 'Oh, you good-for-nothing girl!' Spoken and written German make frequent and casual reference to the Devil, and one such occurs in this same story when the young bride, following the slaughter of the falcon, hound and horse, thinks the Devil has brought her to this husband. The English translation omits all such allusions. A similar reference in 'Der beherzte Flötenspieler' ('The Courageous Flute-Player') is simply changed to 'some evil spirit'.

A more awkward problem occurs with 'Der Hasenhüter und die Königstochter' ('The Hare-Keeper'), in which a king attempts to test and then try to cheat a shepherd boy, who, through magical help, succeeds in guarding and returning a hundred hares for him. In disguise, the king attempts to buy a hare from the shepherd boy, who says he will only do this if the king kisses the donkey he is riding 'under its tail'. In order to stop the boy from marrying his daughter, the king agrees to this indignity, but the boy whistles with his magic pipe and the hare comes running back to him. The English translator changes the king's task to kissing the ass's tail, something that is merely bizarre rather than demeaning or humiliating.

Bechstein's fairytales were probably too similar to those of the Grimms for them to be serious competition in English translation. Indeed, many of them are only slightly different versions of tale-types already well known from the Grimms. The tales in *The Old Story-Teller* were reissued by John Camden Hotten in 1872 with the new title *As Pretty as Seven and Other Popular German Tales* in a format parallel to Hotten's reissue, now with an introduction by Ruskin, of Edgar Taylor's translation of the Grimms'

German Popular Stories. The Bechstein volume also incorporated nine more tales by the Grimms, taken from the Addey and Co. edition. Chatto and Windus, who purchased Hotten's business after his death in 1873, found sufficient of his stock to sell it in their own binding in 1884.

A very few individual tales of Bechstein's were included in some of Andrew Lang's fairytale collections. Both 'The Three Musicians' and 'The Three Dogs' were incorporated in *The Green Fairy Book* (1892), though they sailed under the name of the Grimms. 'The Man without a Heart' was slipped into *The Pink Fairy Book* (1897) without any indication of provenance at all. All three were new versions of Bechstein, somewhat freer translations than those in *The Old Story-Teller*. Five other tales – 'Millet-Thief', 'The Seven Ravens', 'The Little Cup of Tears', 'The Three Gifts' and 'The Man in the Moon' – were included by Benjamin Thorpe in *Yule-Tide Stories. A Collection of Scandinavian and North German Popular Tales and Traditions* (London and New York: George Bell & Sons, 1892). They were credited to Bechstein and translated afresh. Versions of two other tales – 'Gold Maria and Pitch Maria' and 'The Lost Crown' – were included by Zoe Dana Underhill in her collection of 'fairy tales from all nations' entitled *The Dwarf's Tailor and others* (London: Osgood, McIlvaine & Co., 1897). Again, these are new translations of tales that had already appeared in *The Old Story-Teller*. 'The Lost Crown' was there called 'Golden Hair', and it was taken over by Bechstein from a tale originally written by Justinus Kerner and published in 1813. Neither of them is credited to Bechstein by Underhill; each is simply an 'old German tale'. With these anthologized stories the British transmission of Bechstein seems to have petered out until two new translations were issued in the 1960s.

While Bechstein vied with the Grimms in presenting folktales on a national basis, other collectors focussed on tales from a particular region of the German-speaking lands. Only a few of these made a mark in Britain, but prominent among them is the great German patriot, Ernst Moritz Arndt (1769-1860), who devoted the whole of his adult life to working for a Germany united culturally and politically on the basis of language. Arndt was born on the Baltic island of Rügen, then Swedish territory (a legacy of the Thirty Years War), though German in population. It was Napoleon's invasion of Pomerania in 1806 that sent Arndt into exile in Sweden and developed his ideals of German nationalism. After the defeat of Napoleon he became Professor of Modern History at the newly founded University of Bonn, but his liberal views led to his suspension from office for several years until he was reinstated in 1840. Towards the end of his long life Arndt gave up politics and devoted himself to scholarship. He did not live to experience the united Germany he had worked so hard for.

Shortly after his appointment to the Chair of Modern History at Bonn Arndt published a collection of folktales and reminiscences from his youth with the title *Mährchen und Jugenderinnerungen* (Berlin: Realschulbuchhandlung, 1818). A second edition of the work appeared in 1842-43. The publisher was G. A Reimer, the same man as published the Grimms' *Kinder- und Hausmärchen*. The folktales that Arndt printed in this book are those locally current in Rügen, and they include both fairytales and legends, the latter consisting mainly of stories about encounters with supernatural creatures. Given Rügen's political situation at the time, it is not surprising that some tales have a Scandinavian touch. Three of these stories were translated into English in a little book entitled *Merry Tales for Little Folk*, edited by Madame de Chatelain (London: Cundall & Addey, 1851). The tales are 'The Elfin Plough', 'The Nine Mountains' and 'Johnny and Lisbeth'. The book was reissued in undated editions by Charles Taylor and Crosby, Lockwood and Co., both of London. In my copy of the Taylor edition 'The Elfin Plough' is wrongly credited to Grimm, 'The Nine Mountains' to Arndt and 'Johnny and Lisbeth' left anonymous. The three tales were also reprinted in *Fairy Folk and Wonderful Men*, again edited by Madame de Chatelain (London: Addey & Co., 1852), with no indication of where they came from. Arndt's presence in mid nineteenth-century Britain is thus largely anonymous.

Dinah Mulock included a story called 'Adventures of John Dietrich' in *The Fairy Book* (London: Macmillan, 1863), and this turns out to be an uncredited version of 'The Nine Mountains', but in a different translation. *The Fairy Book* went through eleven editions up to 1913, so that story gained wide circulation. Two other uncredited pieces by Arndt appeared in the Everyman's Library edition of *The True Annals of Fairyland in the Reign of King Cole* (London: J. M. Dent & Sons; New York: E. P. Dutton & Co., 1909). These were two considerably adapted excerpts from 'The Elfin Plough', now entitled 'The Lost Bell' and 'The Wonderful Plough'. It is quite possible that other children's books of the period contain further unacknowledged tales from Arndt's pen. All of these translations and adaptations were in prose, but the American poet John Greenleaf Whittier made a ballad version of the story of John Dietrich and Lisbeth in rhyming couplets with the title 'The Brown Dwarf of Rügen' in 1888. He spells John's surname wrongly as

'Deitrich', but his ballad is a lively, straightforward rendering of Arndt's tale.

We now come to a much fuller collection – the *Fairy Tales from the Isle of Rügen*, by Ernst Moritz Arndt, selected and translated by Anna Dabis (London: David Nutt, 1896). This prints new translations of the tales that were already known, but extends the range of material to a total of seventeen tales. About half the collection consists of tales that centre on the involvement of local people with what Dabis calls 'the underground folk'. This includes the stories edited by Madame de Chatelain and about as much again. Of the remaining eleven tales half a dozen are fairytales in the narrower sense and do not overlap with those of the Grimms. Most deal with figures that have been bewitched and can only be released from their enchantment by the successful completion of a series of difficult tasks. The events described in them take place in a wide area between Sweden, Denmark, Rügen, central Germany, the Alps and India, but the locations are specific rather than general. The other tales recount happenings believed to have taken place in different parts of Rügen and have a variety of named locations and protagonists. Very frequently they involve encounters with supernatural beings and attempt to explain the acquisition or loss of wealth. One rich peasant owes his wealth to meeting and helping the Rat-King one Walpurgis Night, but when his luck deserts him he feels happier in his poverty with God than having riches and being in thrall to the Rat-King ('Birlibi, the Rat-King'). In 'How the Mice are Whistling' the card-player Martin Drews falls prey to the Devil and a fiery mouse and finally has his house burnt down by flaming mice. 'The Story of the Seven Coloured Mice' tells how seven disobedient daughters are turned into mice and their mother into a large stone. They will only revert to human shape if a woman the same age as the mother comes along with seven sons for them to marry.

What is fascinating about Arndt's tales is the way in which the everyday life of the peasantry is fraught with temptations and dangers. The hardness of winning the fruits of the earth is reflected in the encounters with 'the underground folk' and the destruction that can be caused by vermin. In addition, there are dangers to the simple Christian life from the remnants of heathenism (as in 'Princess Svanvitha') as well as from the blandishments of the Devil. Some of the legends demonstrate that these dangers are not always overcome. The tales in general have an immediacy that derives from the fact that their protagonists have 'real' rather than the typical or symbolic names that characterize the Grimms' collection and that the events are carefully localized. Moreover, Arndt informs his readers that he got 'The Nine Mountains' and 'The Hoopoe' from his father's bailiff, Henry Vierk, that his own father frequently told him 'The Story of the Seven Coloured Mice' and that Baltazar Tiers, a farm servant on his father's estate who knew many fairytales, told him 'Birlibi, the Rat-King'.

While Arndt's tales from Rügen are clearly presented in English as part of children's literature, the same cannot be said of the folktales and legends of the region of Germany that is most profusely represented in English – the Rhineland. Books of legends of the Rhine were designed for the tourist trade and published in Germany in English from the 1830s onwards, and travel books often included outlines of legends in connexion with the places they described. Such works as Joseph Snowe's two-volume compendium, *Legends, Traditions, Histories of the Rhine* (Frankfort o. M.: Charles Jugel, 1841) and *Lays and Legends of the Rhine. To which are added: Translations of German Poems and Songs, and a Selection from Grattan's Rhenish Legends* (Frankfort o. M.: Charles Jugel, 1847) were targeted principally, if not exclusively, at the adult reader. Many more similar volumes followed throughout the century, but they belong more to the history of travel and topography than to children's books. A few of the most popular legends are in fact included in the small number of travel books about the Rhineland that were written for children by British authors.

One story, however, enjoyed enormous popularity and was presented to children as well as adults in a wide variety of forms. This was the story of Bishop Hatto of Mainz, whose cruelty towards his people was punished by his being pursued to a tower on an island in the Rhine and eaten by mice. The story was recorded in English as early as 1611 by Thomas Coryat, and this provided the stimulus for Robert Southey to write one of his early stirring ballads, 'God's Judgement on a Wicked Bishop' in 1799. The author of *Travels with Minna and Godfrey in many Lands. The Rhine, Nassau, and Baden* (London: Smith, Elder & Co., 1839) reprinted it after a short prose account of the story. The ballad was reissued in volume 6 of Southey's collected *Poetical Works* (London: Longman, Brown, Green, and Longmans, 1844). The story appears, in a prose version by Gottschalk entitled 'The Mouse Tower', in *The German Novelists*, translated by Thomas Roscoe (London: Henry Colburn, 1826). Another version was included by George G. Cunningham in *Tales and Traditions chiefly selected from the Literature of Germany* (Edinburgh, London, and Dublin: A. Fullarton & Co., 1854). The fact that it is entitled 'The Mausethurm' is perhaps an indication that

German was now sufficiently well understood for it not to need a translation. The most extensive treatment the tale got in English was in *Hatto's Tower: and Other Stories*, by Mary C. Rowsell (London, Glasgow, Edinburgh, and Dublin: Blackie & Son, c. 1870), where it extends to about forty pages. The story of Bishop Hatto clearly enjoyed great popularity, probably because it provided a telling example of cruelty and injustice being subjected to supernatural retribution – a prince of the Church brought low by an army of one of the smallest of God's creatures.

The fate of Bishop Hatto circulated widely in English, but it did not acquire a canonical form. However, the German local legend that is probably best known in Britain – 'The Pied Piper of Hamelin' – owes its name and popularity chiefly to the dextrous rhyming and rhythmic verve of Robert Browning, though he was not the only one to recount it in English. Browning wrote his poem for the son of the actor-manager William Macready when he was ill in bed in the spring of 1842, and it bears the subtitle 'A Child's Story'. It was first published later that year in the collection of booklets known as *Bells and Pomegranates* and was reprinted in 1849 and 1861. Browning's source was not German, but English. He declared that he based himself on the account in Nathaniel Wanley's *The Wonders of the Little World* (1667), but some of the details are almost certainly derived from Richard Verstegen's *Restitution of Decayed Intelligence in Antiquities* (1605) despite Browning's denial that he had consulted it.[78] Verstegen's account is reprinted in Joseph Ritson's *Fairy Tales* (London: Payne and Foss; and William Pickering, 1831), so the story was not completely unknown before Browning made it famous.

Browning dates the events to 1376, like Verstegen, while Wanley has 1284, the traditional date given by the Grimms in *Deutsche Sagen*. Browning further follows Verstegen in describing how one lame boy could not keep up with the rest and so was not swallowed up in the hill to which the piper led them. Again, like Verstegen, he mentions the tradition that connects the German community in Transylvania with Hamelin, suggesting some inexplicable subterranean route between them. There has been much debate about the origins and meaning of the legend, linking it, for example, with the Children's Crusade (1212), but also with other historical feuds and a visitation of the plague, which was carried by rats. The piper's ability to charm both rats and children into following him by playing his magic pipe links him with such folktales as the Grimms' 'The Jew among Thorns',

---

78 John Woolford and Daniel Karlin (eds.), *The Poems of Browning* (London and New York: Longman, 1991), vol. 2, pp. 130-42.

in which the protagonist forces people to dance when he plays his fiddle. The piper is a compelling figure, attractive to children, but suspicious to those in authority. The punishment he metes out to those who refuse to pay him what they have freely promised in order to get rid of their plague of rats is every parent's nightmare – the loss of their children. In essence this legend is a horror story, but somehow in the retelling, perhaps especially in Browning's poem with its joky rhymes, the horror has been displaced by an emphasis on the pictureque and quirky appearance of the piper and by the satirical characterization of the Mayor and Corporation.

Browning's poem quickly became a classic of children literature and was frequently anthologized. It gained a great fillip when it was issued with copious illustrations by Kate Greenaway (London and New York: Frederick Warne & Co., 1888), though her images are a curious mixture of modern and would-be medieval. Another illustrated version of Browning with pictures by T. Butler-Stoney was published by Ernest Nister in 1906. Meanwhile, Robert Buchanan wrote a two-act opera entitled *The Piper of Hamelin*, which was published with illustrations by Hugh Thomson (London; William Heinemann, 1893). This is set in the fifteenth century and follows Browning for the first act, but diverges in the second act to provide a restoration of the children to their parents. Presumably the transposition of the story to the stage and the context of popular entertainment required a happy ending. Browning's poem, however, has not ceased to be the best known form of the story, and the twentieth century has seen many more retellings dependent on it.

In Germany the legend was elaborated by Gustav Nieritz into a children's book typical of the mood of the mid nineteenth century. *Die Wunderpfeife, oder: Die Kinder von Hameln* (Leipzig: Gustav Mayer, 1835) was translated into English by C. W. Heckethorn as *The Ratcatcher's Magic Whistle; or, the Children of Hameln* (London: Ben. George, c. 1873). Nieritz makes the ratcatcher into a much more sinister figure, a magician called Kokerill, and places the emotional weight of the story on the fraught relationship of Tobias, the bailiff's son, and Gilbert, the son of the burgomaster. The children of Hameln are abducted by Kokerill to Siebenbürgen (Transylvania in the early English forms of the legend) and made to work for him, but Tobias, through various magical devices, finds his way there and released them from their underground prison. Kokerill is captured in the shape of a bird and strangled, and the children make their way back home, arriving there after the winter, a year after their disappearance. Gilbert

The Folktale Tradition in Germany 217

and Tobias are reconciled and become friends, and Nieritz ends his story with the moral that Kokerill represents vice, which all children ought to shun. Nonetheless, Kokerill's despotic control of the children, separated from their parents and set to hard work, may also be seen as a reflection of conditions in the nineteenth century to which children were subjected in order to earn a precarious living. It is interesting to note the changes to the original legend that both Nieritz and Robert Buchanan found necessary to make it palatable to nineteenth-century children and their parents.

A considerable number of German legends were published in English from the 1820s onwards, but most of them appeared in books that do not seem to have been designed for children. The second volume of Thomas Roscoe's *The German Novelists* (1826) contains selections from the collections made by Otmar, Gottschalk, Eberhardt, Büsching, the Grimms and Lothar, and Cunningham's *Tales and Traditions* (1854) has a comparable set of offerings. But by the last third of the nineteenth century we have collections, more like Arndt's, that may well have had children among their readers. One of the earliest of these is *Household Stories from the Land of Hofer; or, Popular Myths of Tirol* (London: Griffith & Farran, 1871). It has illustrations credited to T. Green, but no indication of the compiler's name, Rachel Busk (1831-1907), who was proficient in several languages and collected material from many, chiefly printed sources.[79] Like Arndt, she begins with legends about the fairy dwellers in her chosen territory – the Norgs – then proceeding to longer narratives from North and South Tirol, what she calls 'Wälsch-Tirol' (Italian Tirol) and the Austrian province of Vorarlberg. The main item among the Norg myths is a retelling of the medieval German poem whose title she gives as *The Rose-Garden of King Lareyn* (*Laurin*), in which Lareyn, the last of the Norgs, having abducted Simild, the daughter of duke Biterolf, is attacked by her brother, Dietlieb, Theodoric and Wittich in his magic rose-garden. Lareyn has a cloak of darkness that makes him invisible and a girdle that gives him the strength of twelve men, but Theodoric manages to defeat him. After several further exploits Lareyn is defeated and made court fool by Theodoric in his palace at Verona.

Many of the remaining tales in *Household Stories from the Land of Hofer* have analogues in other well-known collections. 'The Wilder Jäger and the Baroness' contains the motif of the protagonist escaping retribution by guessing his supernatural opponent's name, a motif best known in

---

79 Richard M. Dorson, *The British Folklorists. A History* (Chicago: University of Chicago Press, 1968), pp. 381-82.

'Rumpelstiltskin'. 'The Grave Prince and the Beneficent Cat' is a version of the tale-type exemplified by Madame d'Aulnoy's 'The White Cat' and the Grimms' 'The Poor Miller's Lad and the Cat', while 'Klein-Else' is a variant of the 'Cinderella' story. 'Prince Radpot' is a combination of the Grimms' 'The Riddle' and 'King Thrushbeard', and 'Luxhale's Wives' a blending of the Grimm's 'Fitcher's Bird' with motifs from 'The Devil with the Three Golden Hairs'. 'Zovanin senza paura' (Fearless Johnny) is a version of 'The Boy who set out to Learn Fear'. The Tirolean tales are thus clearly part of the well-known stock of European, specifically German, folktales, but have their own character from the mountains and remote valleys in which the stories are located.

A comparable volume dealing with another area was issued a few years later by the same publisher – W. Westall's *Tales and Legends of Saxony and Lusatia* (London: Griffith & Farran; Geneva: The Continental Company, 1877). However, the temper of the majority of tales in this collection is dark and brooding, focussing on family disputes and crimes of passion leading to the destruction of all involved. Three centre in various ways on entanglements with the Devil. In 'The Priest, the Fairy, and Doctor Horn' a mother promises her infant son to the Church if he is spared his life. An angel gives her a talisman to protect him. When the boy grows up and is about to become a priest, he meets a Doctor Horn (the Devil) who tries to dissuade him. But he also meets the fairy Luna, his guardian angel, who helps him in his trials and temptations. Doctor Horn leads him on night rides and adventures reminiscent of Faust's tricks in the *Historia von D. Johann Fausten*, but eventually his soul is saved, though his body is drowned in the fairy's fountain. In 'The Katestone of Annaberg' the Devil is similarly thwarted by Christian sentiments, whereas in 'The Devil's Blacksmith' the eponymous blacksmith, addicted to drink, fails to complete an extraordinary commission he has undertaken and is hauled off to the nether regions in consequence. But while the collection as a whole dwells on the darker side of life, there are occasional lighter touches. 'The Christmas present', for example, tells of a stocking-weaver who can't get any money for a job he has completed for Christmas because the commissioner is absent. On his sad way home he meets a little man who gives him food and goodies, and when he reaches home he finds they have turned into gold and silver. The little man is called Count Carl Kinderfreund (Friend of children), but his action is strangely similar to that of the mountain spirit Rübezahl, who inhabits the Riesengebirge, the chain of mountains separating Silesia and

Bohemia.

Rübezahl is a figure who keeps cropping up in the folktales and children's books of our period. Documentation of his quirky activities goes back to printed sources of the sixteenth and seventeenth century. He appears in a variety of human disguises, tormenting the strong and those in authority and leading them on wild goose chases, while helping the poor and those in distress. We have already encountered him with the English name Number Nip in the 1791 translation of Musäus, and we find that name and Rübezahl (with or without the umlaut) in many subsequent versions of tales told about him. (The German name is commonly interpreted as *Rübe*, '(tur)nip', and *Zahl*, 'number'.) Joseph Cundall's *Legends of Rubezahl* (1845) was taken from Musäus, as was Mark Lemon's *Legends of Number Nip*, illustrated by Charles Keene (London: Macmillan & Co., 1864; reprinted 1872).

Musäus was not the only purveyor of Rübezahl stories, so it is difficult to trace the sources used by each and every British author. Leitch Ritchie briefly retold three legends of Number-Nip as an appendix to his *Schinderhannes, the Robber of the Rhine* (London: Simms and M'Intyre, 1848), and George Cunningham included six, again very briefly, in his *Tales and Traditions* (1854). Francis Paul Palmer also retold some under the heading 'Rubezahl, the Prince of Gnomes' in *Old Tales for the Young* (London: George Routledge & Co., 1857). However, the largest collection of tales in English was made by Mary C. Rowsell in *Number Nip; or, the Spirit of the Giant Mountains* (London: Swan Sonnenschein & Co., 1884). This concludes with a short verse play, presumably designed for children to act. Finally, at the beginning of the twentieth century, we must note another 'Rübezahl' in Andrew Lang's *The Brown Fairy Book* (London, New York and Bombay: Longman, Green, & Co., 1904), where what is the first of Musäus's legends is retold by Mrs Lang. Rübezahl's fame was sufficient for him to be mentioned in *A Handbook for Travellers on the Continent: being a Guide to Holland . . . to Switzerland* (London: John Murray, 13th edition, 1860), where it is claimed 'There is hardly a mountain or a glen in the country [i.e. the Riesengebirge] without its legend of this popular demon' (p. 424). But popular as he was in Britain in the nineteenth century, Rübezahl did not survive very long into the twentieth. Knowledge of him in British children's books vanished after the first decade.

At about the same time there was published the first book in English to deal with folktales from yet another area of Germany. This was Alfred C. Fryer's *Fairy Tales from the Harz Mountains*, illustrated by Alice M Odgers

(London: David Nutt, 1908). The Harz was already well known for its legends and literary connexions. Its highest mountain, the Brocken, notorious as the site of witches' sabbaths, was the setting for the lurid Walpurgis Night scene in Goethe's *Faust*. Another mountain, the Kyffhäuser, was famous as the place where the Emperor Frederick Barbarossa supposedly lay asleep with his knights, waiting for the time that they would be called to save Germany in its hour of need. The story of Peter the goatherd, who stumbles on the scene by accident, had already been translated into English by Edgar Taylor and included in the second volume of the Grimms' *German Popular Stories* (1826). Another version by Madame de Chatelain was published in *Merry Tales for Little Folk, Fairy Folk and Wonderful Men* and also separately. This was not one of Grimms' tales, but was collected by Otmar (pseudonym of Johann Carl Christoph Nachtigall) in an early volume simply entitled *Volks-Sagen* (Bremen: Friedrich Milmans, 1800). Thomas Roscoe provided a further version of the story, together with several others relating to the Harz from Otmar and from Friedrich Gottschalck's *Die Sagen und Volksmärchen der Deutschen* (Halle, 1814), in his *The German Novelists* (1826). A number of other stories from the Harz were included in Cunningham's *Tales and Traditions* (1854). The area was thus by no means neglected as far as British readers were concerned.

Alfred Fryer's collection seems to be the first (and only) book to present a considerable number of tales and legends from the Harz specifically to children. The book is dedicated 'to my godson Bernhard and all other good little men'. Fryer gives no indication of the sources for his twenty-one items, which range from simple anecdotes to quite complex stories. 'Brunhilda' and 'Brunhilda's Golden Crown' spin legends around the rugged gorge of the River Bode, where Brunhilda, the daughter of the king of Bohemia, loses a golden crown in the river as she jumps a chasm in her flight from the giant Bodo, her would-be husband. Another two tales recount legends of Princess Ilse, who gives her name to the River Ilse and the Ilsenstein, a rugged peak nearby. A version of these latter tales had previously been translated by Lady Maxwell Wallace as a separate small book entitled *Princess Ilse* (London: Bell & Daldy, [1856]). Another tale, 'The Three Grey Mannikins', which presents the same story as A. L. Grimm used in 'Tony, the Miller's Son', reflects the importance of mining in the Harz, and 'The Everlasting Lamp and the Magic Spindle' gives voice to some of the superstitions characteristic of the mining community. As we have learnt from the Rübezahl stories in the Riesengebirge, the Harz mountains too have many a legend connected with the discovery of unsuspected treasure.

Collections of legends generally sound a more mysterious and melancholy note than collections of fairytales, and Fryer's *Fairy Tales from the Harz Mountains* certainly follows the accustomed pattern. Several of the legends that he recounts attempt to explain features of the landscape by reference to sinister or romantic events, or they cloak ancient ruins with strange occurrences or characteristics to render them significant. Germany led the way in the systematic collection of local and historical legends, and in the publications that we have looked at we have a fine selection of this material. It is significant that none of the German scholarly collections were translated *in toto* into English during the nineteenth century. What was presented was excerpts, often just a few tales, whether the target readership was adults or children. Only at the end of the nineteenth century do we get full-length books – Rachel Busk's *Tirolean tales* (1871), W. Westall's *Tales from Saxony and Lusatia* (1877), Mary Rowsell's *Rübezahl Tales from the Riesengebirge* (1884), Anna Dabis's selection from Arndt's *Tales from Rügen* (1896) and Alfred Fryer's *Tales from the Harz* (1908). All of these reflect the increasing interest in German books and culture in the period following the Franco-Prussian War.

Legends and accounts of folk beliefs seem to have had an appeal to adults and children alike, and this appeal lasted the whole of the nineteenth century and continues to perhaps a lesser degree today. However, only a few individual tales gained sufficient popularity to be reprinted or retold. None of the big collections enjoyed the reprints that were so common with fairytales. Indeed, when we look at what has survived and is still known today, we cannot cite a great deal more than a couple of new translations of Bechstein's fairytales and Robert Browning's 'Pied Piper of Hamelin'. Legends tend to circulate in less defined, less stable forms than fairytales and works with a known author, so it is not surprising that it took the skill of a leading poet to create an enduring form for the legend of the ratcatcher and the children of Hamelin.

13. E. T. A. Hoffmann's *Nutcracker and Mouse King*

Hoffmann's *Nußknacker und Mausekönig* is an extraordinarily innovative and unusual piece of writing for children, way ahead of its time in its complete abandonment of didacticism and moral instruction. Almost fifty years before Lewis Carroll's *Alice's Adventures in Wonderland* it incorporates its original audience as characters within the story, but whereas *Alice* blends fantasy with parody and comedy the *Nutcracker* displays a less whimsical, perhaps more subtle sense of humour. It is a more realistic kind of fantasy in that the nocturnal events actually unfold in the same place that the children themselves inhabit. Like many of Hoffmann's other tales the boundaries between fantasy and reality are blurred. Not only Marie, the chief protagonist of the story, but also the reader may have difficulty in distinguishing the two.

The German original was first published in 1816 in a volume entitled *Kinder-Mährchen* (Children's Stories), which included tales by Carl Wilhelm Contessa, Friedrich de la Motte Fouqué and Hoffmann himself. The story was later republished in the first volume of Hoffmann's own collection, *Die Serapionsbrüder* (The Serapion Brethren) (1819-20), where its suitability for children is debated. This is a question that is often raised, but the title of the 1816 volume clearly indicates Hoffmann's intention. The question is raised as much as anything because the story operates on more than one level. There are aspects of the story that children would not be expected to grasp (literary allusions, asides, narrative tricks), but most of it is perfectly comprehensible to intelligent children such as those of Hoffmann's friend Julius Eduard Hitzig, for whom the story was written. What is so wonderful about the *Nutcracker* is the fact that it appeals to child and adult alike and that Hoffmann did not 'write down' for his intended child readers. In point of style, themes and narrative technique it is as superbly crafted as any of Hoffmann's other tales. The only difference lies in the fact that the story primarily focusses on children rather than adults. The *Kinder-Mährchen* also includes another children's tale by Hoffmann – 'Das fremde Kind' (The Strange Child) – but this has never enjoyed the same popularity as the *Nutcracker*.

Nutcracker and Mouse King is a Christmas story, and its central character is Marie, the seven year old daughter of Medizinalrat (medical councillor) Stahlbaum and his wife. Marie has a slightly younger brother, Fritz, and a sister, Luise, who is older. Luise plays only a marginal role in the story, but Fritz provides a boy's viewpoint on the events narrated. In some ways he is more down-to-earth, thus contrasting with Marie's absorption in fantasy and make-believe. Father and mother Stahlbaum represent rather starkly the realm of reason. Mother dismisses Marie's account of the battle between the Nutcracker's soldiers and the mice as foolish and berates her for causing her parents anxiety. They are no more understanding at the end of the story. Father accuses Marie of lying and tells her very seriously to cease all her fantasies, otherwise he will throw all her toys, including the nutcracker, through the window. Allied to the medical councillor and his wife is the surgeon Wendelstern, who appears only briefly to deal with the medical consequences of Marie's nocturnal injury.

The most important adult role in the story, indeed the key figure to the whole work, is Pate (Godfather) Drosselmeier, whose Christmas gift of a marvellous toy palace with mechanical figures produces tension between himself and the children because he thinks they do not properly appreciate it. Drosselmeier is an ambivalent figure in the story, a focus of both delight and hostility, mysterious and a little sinister. Not only is he the narrator of the embedded fairytale of Princess Pirlipat, but he is as it were the regisseur of the dramatic production that the entire work embodies. As a skilled man who even knows about clocks, he is the mechanical genius behind everything who directs and interprets events. The scenario is his, and Marie projects on to him all her anxieties and aspirations.

Hoffmann is ingenious in his narrative, since the audience he imagines consists of the very participants in the story he is narrating. However, it is not until the second chapter, 'The Gifts', that he begins to use this device, playfully addressing his 'attentive listener Marie' and pointing out that the heroine of his story, the little Stahlbaum girl, is also called Marie. Later in

E. T. A. Hoffmann's Nutcracker and Mouse King 225

this same chapter he addresses 'honoured reader Fritz' and only a few lines further on exclaims 'listen now, children!' In this way – and it is frequently repeated – Hoffmann engages the separate and combined attentions of his audience, which by implication includes the parents.

The next chapter, 'The Battle', appropriately contains a calculatedly flattering appeal to 'my militarily expert listener Fritz', assuming his acquaintance with the rules of battle. The next address to the audience comes in the tenth chapter, 'Uncle and Nephew', where the narrator is concerned with the painful effects of Marie's having cut herself on the glass of the toy cabinet and invites his audience to sympathize with her. There are many other similar appeals, and each is designed to highlight a particular event or turning-point. The result of such an accumulation of appeals to the audience is rather like a set of Chinese boxes, one inside the other, or of artfully placed mirrors reflecting each other. The child audience, however, has a further dimension that links it with extra-literary reality, in that Hoffmann wrote the story to entertain the Hitzig children, whom he was very fond of visiting. The younger children, Fritz and Marie, aged five and seven respectively, had the same names as in Hoffmann's story, while the older daughter, aged nine, was actually called Eugenie (Luise in the story). The text of the story is ambiguous on Fritz's age, since in the first chapter Hoffmann has him speaking to 'his younger sister', where it is unclear whether this means Marie is younger than Fritz or that she is the younger of the two sisters, in the latter case corresponding to the true ages of the Hitzig children. In the opening sentence of 'The Gifts' Fritz is appealed to by name – 'I turn to you yourself, my dear reader or listener Fritz – Theodor – Ernst – or whatever else you may be called' – but the additional names are in fact Hoffmann's own first two names, and so he includes himself *in propria persona* as part of the audience of the story.

These biographical aspects of the story's composition may be amplified further, although readers outside Hoffmann's intimate circle cannot have been expected to know anything about them. Pate Drosselmeier, the 'wizard' within the story and the narrator of the 'Fairytale of the Hard Nut', occupies the kind of role in this fiction that Hoffmann himself had with the parents and children of the Hitzig family. Ernst Theodor Amadeus Hoffmann (1776-1822) – he replaced his third name, Wilhelm, with Amadeus in homage to Mozart – was a lawyer, theatre director and composer as well as a writer and had just returned to Berlin, where the Hitzigs lived, in 1816. Pate Drosselmeier is a highly placed lawyer, as

Hoffmann also was. But he is described in terms that transmute him into an ambiguous, grotesque figure. For the children he is the year-by-year giver of extraordinary gifts, which are usually taken away from them, but he is also unreliable, surprising in what he says and does, puzzling and even a little sinister:

> Justice Drosselmeier was not a good-looking (*hübsch*) man, but short and skinny with lots of wrinkles in his face. He had a big black patch over his right eye and no hair, for which reason he wore a very beautiful white wig, which was made of glass and very skilfully made. Godfather Drosselmeier was altogether a very skilful man himself and even knew about clocks and had made some himself.

The link between Hoffmann and Drosselmeier belongs to literary history or biography, but that between Drosselmeier and the Nutcracker is at the centre of the story's meaning. Cleverly, Hoffmann does not make the links too explicit. Like Drosselmeier himself, the Nutcracker is shrouded in mystery. He is the last of the Christmas gifts that the children discover, and it is nowhere stated who has given him to the children. He is seen through Marie's eyes, and when she has looked carefully at him her question is not where he has come from, but who he belongs to. Marie compares him in her mind with Pate Drosselmeier because of their odd-looking coats and comes to the conclusion that even if Drosselmeier carried himself as daintily as this little man, he still wouldn't be as good-looking (*hübsch*). This comparison is taken up again at the end of the chapter, after Fritz and Marie have fallen out on account of the Nutcracker and Marie has taken him under her wing. She cannot bear the fact that Drosselmeier is laughing at her actions and gives voice to her thoughts:

'Who knows, dear Godfather, whether you would be as good-looking as he is, if you were to brush yourself up like my dear Nutcracker and had such beautiful little shiny boots on!' This causes Marie's parents to laugh and produces some discomfiture in Drosselmeier that she doesn't understand. This little touch possibly reflects some actual occurrence in Hoffmann's visits to the Hitzig family.

Drosselmeier, in conformity with his ambiguous role in the story, is linked at other points with different figures and seen in different ways. During the first nocturnal battle Marie sees him sitting on top of the clock where the owl should have been, and when Drosselmeier visits her after her accident she scolds him, asks why he didn't help the Nutcracker and accuses him of causing her to be ill and in bed. When he responds with a rhyming account of the battle, Marie thinks he looks much uglier than usual and is waving his right arm about like a marionette. Fritz tells him he is too ridiculous and acting like his *Hampelmann* (jumping jack), which he threw behind the stove a long time ago. The two children's differing reactions show how Drosselmeier plays changing roles in the story and can thus be seen as a trickster figure.

This role and his name recall the figure of König Drosselbart (King Thrushbeard) in the Grimms' fairytale of that name. Both Drosselbart and Drosselmeier are strange in appearance, Drosselbart having a crooked chin that causes the princess to compare it with a thrush's beak, while Drosselmeier, as we know, is bald, wears a wig and has a black patch over his right eye. He thus can see only with his left eye, and there are several more things in the story that link up with this: in the first battle the mouse cavalry attack the left wing of the Nutcracker's army, Marie throws her left shoe at the mice and their king, and Marie's injury is to her left arm. One critic has suggestively interpreted the symbolism of left and right in Jungian terms with the left being associated with the unconscious and the right with the conscious and reason. In the Grimms' tale König Drosselbart adopts a variety of disguises to carry out the tests or humiliations that the haughty princess undergoes, and we can readily see Pate Drosselmeier in this role as controller or organizer of the events in the *Nutcracker*, though they are not designed to punish or teach Marie a lesson.[80] After the series of trials that she undergoes, she does end up with a similar splendid marriage to that of the princess, Pate Drosselmeier being replaced by Nephew Drosselmeier in his guise as the Nutcracker. Hoffmann thus makes use of the fairytale parallel, but adapts it skilfully to his own ends.

Like many of Hoffmann's other tales, the *Nutcracker* moves rapidly and unexpectedly between the everyday and the world of fantasy. What connects the two here is the world of toys and children's imagination. Hoffmann's descriptions of a well-to-do family's Christmas festivities and the children's attitude towards their new and old toys locate the story firmly in the social and cultural reality of the early nineteenth century in Germany. Hoffmann himself was fascinated by movable toys and automata, and the figure of Olimpia, the life-size mechanical doll with which Nathanael in *Der*

---

80 Ronald J. Elardo, 'E. T. A. Hoffmann's *Nußknacker und Mausekönig*. The Mouse-Queen in the Tragedy of the Hero', *Germanic Review*, 55 (1980), p. 5.

Sandmann (The Sand-man) falls disastrously in love, is his most enduring creation in this respect. Pate Drosselmeier's marvellous toy palace with its multitude of walking and dancing figures is the apogee of his mechanical genius, but it has been preceded by earlier gifts to the children of a funny little man whose eyes turn and who can bow, and a box from which a little bird hops out. This range of mechanical toys, stretching from the very simple to the very complicated and ingenious, reflects the achievements of the late eighteenth and early nineteenth century, building on traditions of clock- and toy-making that go back to the late Middle Ages. The more complex devices, involving perhaps years of skilled work, were made for kings and princes and were presented by them as gifts to other rulers. It is this kind of thing, on a smaller scale, that is reflected in Drosselmeier's palace. It would have been comparable to, say, the performing circus engineered by the Tyrolean Christian Tschuggmall (1785-1844), who toured with it as far afield as Poland and Russia.[81] An eighteenth-century wooden clockwork man with moving eyes and mouth, now in the Abeler Museum, Wuppertal, provides a counterpart to Drosselmeier's early gift to the Stahlbaum children.[82] The box with the little bird was probably a by-product of the development of the animated cuckoo in the Black Forest clock-making industry, which is credited to Franz-Anton Schoemwald around 1730.[83] Marie's description of swans swimming on a lake, with golden ribbons round their necks, and singing lovely songs bears strange similarity to the appearance of a life-size silver swan made by the English watchmaker James Cox as part of a larger tableau.[84] It is a nice touch on Hoffmann's part, when Marie recounts that Drosselmeier had told her a little girl feeds swans with marzipan, that he has Fritz interrupt brutally, saying that swans don't eat marzipan. Fritz doesn't doubt the mechanical wonder, but swans eating marzipan is just too ridiculous.

These are the more extraordinary elements in the children's life, but most of what is described in the Stahlbaums' Christmas festivities is typical of middle-class celebrations of the period. Both Marie and Fritz have expectations related to their old toys. Marie's big doll (Mamsell Trutchen) is getting clumsier than ever before and always falling on the floor and damaging her face, so she gets a new one called Mamsell Klärchen. Fritz,

---

81 Mary Hillier, *Automata and Mechanical Toys* (London: Bloomsbury Books, 1988), p. 27.
82 Ibid., fig. 21, p. 28.
83 Ibid., p. 25.
84 Ibid., p. 58, also plate V.

ever preoccupied with his soldiers, knows that his father is well aware that he doesn't have a chestnut horse and is entirely lacking cavalry, but even when Luise rather prissily reminds them that it is Christ who gives them presents through the hands of their parents, Fritz still murmurs to himself that he'd really like a chestnut horse and some hussars. His wish is fully granted.

The Christmas tree is the focus of the occasion, decorated with gold and silver apples, sugared almonds and sweets and a hundred little lights. The two girls have new frocks. The fir-tree was a particularly German manifestation of Christmas and was only adopted in Britain after Prince Albert introduced it to the Royal Family. The parents' decoration of the tree on Christmas Eve in the absence of the children, who are then admitted into the bright splendour from the darkness in which they have been waiting on tenterhooks, seems to be a custom stretching way back in time. Germany, of course, has far more forests than England, and conifers are much more familiar than is the case here. Among the Christmas goodies there are also gingerbread men and women from Thorn, now the Polish city of Torun, but then part of the Prussian dominions. They are a reminder of Hoffmann's own background, since he was born and studied in Königsberg (now Kaliningrad) and worked in Posen (Poznan), Plotzk (Plock) and Warsaw.

The last of the Christmas gifts to be discovered is the Nutcracker, which Father tells Marie is for all the children, for Luise and Fritz as well as herself. Nonetheless, he entrusts the Nutcracker especially to Marie to look after and protect, and the remainder of the story focusses on their relationship. When Fritz is tired of playing with his soldiers, he wants to use the Nutcracker too to crack nuts, and because he gives the Nutcracker the biggest and hardest nuts, three of his teeth drop out and his lower jaw becomes loose. Marie is upset, all the more so as Drosselmeier takes Fritz's side. However, Father comes to her aid and scolds Fritz for wanting to use the Nutcracker again after he has been broken, and reproaches him with transgressing proper military procedures. Although it is nowhere indicated who produced the Nutcracker as a Christmas gift, it is Drosselmeier who mends his jaw while Marie is ill in bed. He replaces the teeth and resets the jaw.

Among the children's other playthings picture books are mentioned a number of times. In the glass-fronted cupboard, in which Pate Drosselmeier's ingenious gifts occupy the uppermost shelf, the picture books come next, with Fritz's soldiers and Marie's dolls on the lower two shelves. That is some measure of their preciousness. Such books had been produced in

Germany since the middle of the eighteenth century, the period in which children were first separately targeted as readers in a more concerted way. They dealt with all kinds of subjects, but quite near in time to Hoffmann's book we have J. A. C. Löhr's *Der Weihnachtsabend in der Familie Thalberg* (Christmas Eve in the Thalberg Family) (Leipzig, 1805), which is similarly slanted to the Christmas theme. Picture books, especially hand-coloured ones, would have been expensive, but certainly within the purchasing power of a medical councillor or lawyer.

The *Nutcracker* is divided into fourteen chapters, perhaps so that it could be read in instalments between Christmas Eve and Epiphany. The central part, chapters 7, 8 and 9, consists of the 'Fairytale of the Hard Nut', which Pate Drosselmeier tells Marie over three evenings while she is recovering from her Christmas injury. She has not been able to play and hasn't had enough concentration to read for herself, so Mother has read to her and told her stories. She has just completed the story of Prince Facardin. This story is one that Hoffmann frequently refers to. It was written by Count Antoine Hamilton (1646-1720), a French writer of Scottish descent, and bears the title *Les quatre Facardins*. It was published posthumously in 1730. The tale is included in two German editions of Hamilton's fairytales that Hoffmann probably encountered in his childhood or youth – *Drei hüpsche kurzweilige Mährlein* (Three Pretty, Amusing Stories), translated by Görg Bider (i.e. W. C. S. Mylius) (Halle: Hendel, 1777) and *Feenmährchen des Grafen Hamilton* (Fairytales of Count Hamilton) (Gotha, 1790) in volume 2 of Friedrich Justin Bertuch's *Blaue Bibliothek aller Nationen* (Blue Library of all the Nations). It is a lengthy and very complicated literary fairytale, written in the wake of Antoine Galland's *Mille et une nuits* (1704-17), the first translation of the *Arabian Nights* into a European language, and has a similar oriental narrative context. Full of the most bizarre adventures located as far apart as Mount Atlas, the Red Sea and Trebizond, it purports to tell the history of four heroes, each of whom bears the extraordinary name of Facardin. However, after some 150 pages the story breaks off with the statement: 'Mais je crois qu'il est bon de remettre le reste du récit que faisoit le prince de Trébizonde, à la seconde partie de ces mémoires'. Then follow the words 'FIN DES QUATRE FACARDINS'. By this time Hamilton has introduced his readers to only three of the Facardins and given little hint as to how the threads of the story might satisfactorily be tied together. One editor has suggested that the tale was intended as a satire on the absurdities of the French literary fairytale, much as Cervantes mocked the customs of chivalry in *Don Quixote*; but it does not have the flair and humour of Cervantes. Hamilton's tale was certainly not written for children as young as the seven year old Marie. Not only would its complicated plot be difficult for a child of that age to follow, but it also contains a number of primly erotic episodes that would baffle a child. Moreover, its exaggerations of traditional fairytale motifs and amazing long-windedness seem calculatedly artificial rather than organic.

What, then, are the aspects of Hamilton's fairytale that we might see as appealing to Hoffmann and relevant to its being mentioned in the *Nutcracker*. Perhaps the first thing to note is the fact that both authors make play with characters bearing the same name. Hamilton has his four Facardins, Hoffmann his uncle and nephew Drosselmeier and the Nutcracker that is mysteriously aligned with each of them, but in different ways. Then there is the fact that Fritz and Marie Stahlbaum have their counterparts in the Fritz and Marie that the narrator constantly appeals to in his telling of the story. Even more oddly, we have in the embedded 'Fairytale of the Hard Nut' a court clockmaker and arcanist called Christian Elias Drosselmeier, the same name as that of Drosselmeier in the framework tale. Hamilton's tale can be seen as providing a literary model for Hoffmann's exploration of the theme of identity. The structure of the *Nutcracker* suggests a sense of multiple identities. The children in their playing with dolls and soldiers adopt identities relevant to their play, as well as having well-defined family and social relationships with their parents and godfather. Marie adds a further dimension to this through the extended nocturnal dream world, which constitutes a greater reality to her than the events within the family. But these worlds are not separate from each other: their personnel, concerns and emotions overlap and intersect.

Les quatre Facardins is also notable for containing an embedded story, when Facardin the Prince of Trebizond meets the second Facardin and listens to an account of his adventures. When this is done the two stories become intertwined. In Hoffmann's tale too the theme and characters of the 'Fairytale of the Hard Nut' are taken into the continuation of the battle between the mice and the toys. It is significant also that the 'Hard Nut', like *Les quatre Facardins*, comes to a halt before the story can be said to have concluded. There is no traditional happy ending: the astronomer simply sees a solution in the stars. The remainder of Hoffmann's story is aimed at achieving that solution through Marie and the Nutcracker. A further link between Hamilton's and Hoffmann's tales comes from the commentary that each author has his story audience make on the embedded tale that they have just heard. With Hamilton this centres on the sultan and female storyteller that he envisages as the listeners to the story of the four Facardins, patterning himself on the *Arabian Nights*. With Hoffmann it is the more closely involved Stahlbaum family.

The reference to *Les quatre Facardins* is not, I would argue, just a casual allusion to a popular literary fairytale. Despite the many differences between Hamilton and Hoffmann in terms of length, artifice and, above all, tone, Hoffmann was obviously stimulated by the French author and adapted some of his ideas and techniques to suit his own purposes.

The main focus of the *Nutcracker* is on the hostilities between the toys and the mice, with the Nutcracker and the mouse King as their respective leaders. Although Marie is explicitly stated not to have a natural aversion to mice, her initial reaction to them as ridiculous rapidly turns into fear and dread. Hoffmann cleverly draws his audience into the emotions he is evoking by suggesting that Fritz, whom he addresses by name, would have run away, jumped into bed and pulled the bedclothes over his head. The Mouse King, emerging from sand, mortar and crumbling brick or stone, is as though driven by a subterranean power. With his seven heads with their seven sparkling crowns, he recalls not only the dragon in one of the most widely diffused folktale-types, 'The Dragon-Slayer', but behind him the dragon representing evil incarnate in the Book of Revelations (12: 3). In the folktale the protagonist is wounded in the battle with the dragon and a false hero attempts to claim the reward, but ultimately the true dragon-slayer is reinstated and marries the princess who was to have been the dragon's victim. In Hoffmann's tale not only is the Nutcracker wounded, but Marie suffers the same fate and faints. A delightful humorous touch occurs just before this when the Nutcracker in desperation echoes King Richard III's dying cry: 'A horse – a horse – my kingdom for a horse!' August Wilhelm Schlegel's translation into German had appeared in 1810, so Hoffmann was pretty topical.

The 'Fairytale of the Hard Nut' contains several elements that link up with Marie's dream, the most obvious being the menacing figure of Frau Mauserinks, the mother of the Mouse King. Here, as in other instances, Hoffmann has made a gender change in the fairytale figure, though the role in the story remains the same. This metamorphosis applies also to Princess Pirlipat, the heroine of the fairytale, who, in a trait that immediately associates her with the Nutcracker, is born with two rows of pearly teeth. The preparation of the royal sausage feast that opens the fairytale parallels the Christmas preparations with which the *Nutcracker* begins. Pate Drosselmeier has promised Marie's mother that his tale will be funny, and indeed it is, at least to begin with. However, the Queen's attempt to propitiate Frau Mauserinks with a little of the bacon used to make the sausage results in the whole mouse tribe appearing and consuming a vast amount of the bacon before they can be shooed away by the chief lady-in-waiting. Consequently the King's enjoyment of the feast is progressively diminished by the lack of bacon in the sausage. When he learns what has happened he vows vengeance on Frau Mauserinks and her seven sons. The job is entrusted to the court clockmaker and arcanist, Christian Elias Drosselmeier, Pate Drosselmeier's namesake. He makes traps in which all Frau Mauserinks' sons and many of her relatives are caught and then killed. Frau Mauserinks warns the Queen to be on her guard with the princess, when for a second time she ruins the King's dinner. At this point Pate Drosselmeier breaks off his narrative, promising to take it up the next evening. Marie asks him whether he really is the inventor of mousetraps. For her the world of the fairytale and that of everyday reality are not separate.

The second section of the fairytale sees Frau Mauserinks' threat carried out. The big ugly mouse is scared away too late from Pirlipat's midnight pillow, for the princess's face and body have already been transformed into a grotesque ugliness. All the blame for this is placed on Drosselmeier (just as Marie has accused her godfather of failing to look after the Nutcracker and of causing her own injury and illness), and the King demands that he shall find a cure for Pirlipat within four weeks or face execution. On the Wednesday of the fourth week Drosselmeier realizes that Pirlipat, with all the sharp teeth she has, is fond of eating nuts. He has the court astronomer cast Pirlipat's horoscope and discovers that she will be cured by eating the kernel of the Krakatuk nut. This nut has to be bitten open by a man who has never shaved or worn boots and then given to the princess with closed eyes, after which he must retreat seven steps and then open them. This cure is announced to the court on Saturday lunchtime, but the nut has still to be found. Drosselmeier and the astronomer are charged with finding it, and advertisements are placed in all the newspapers, including the foreign ones, looking for the man to bite the nut. Again at a critical point in the narrative Pate Drosselmeier breaks off.

The final section has the two searchers coming back to Nuremberg after a fruitless search lasting fifteen years. Going to Drosselmeier's cousin, Christian Zacharias Drosselmeier, who is a toymaker (Nuremberg was famous for its toys), they find he actually has the nut in his possession, having bought it from a stranger seven years previously. When the astronomer peels off its gold exterior, he finds the name 'Krakatuk' engraved on it in Chinese characters. Furthermore, the astronomer discovers that Drosselmeier's cousin's son is the person destined to bite open the nut. The son shows signs of having previously been a *Hampelmann*, a feature that reminds us of Fritz's earlier comparison of Pate Drosselmeier to a *Hampelmann*. But he now only requires a robust wooden pigtail connected to his lower jaw to become the proper Nutcracker to bite the nut for the princess. In fulfilling this task, he restores Pirlipat to her former beauty. However, in stepping back the prescribed seven steps, he treads on Frau Mauserinks, who has just appeared on the scene, and kills her, though not before she has turned him into an ugly misshapen creature and vowed revenge through her seven-headed son. Pirlipat is so shocked at the Nutcracker's changed appearance that she has him driven away, as also happens to the clockmaker and astronomer. The latter now sees in the stars that the Nutcracker will only be transformed if he can kill Frau Mauserinks' son, the Mouse King, and gain the love of a lady. At this point the embedded fairytale ends.

As with *Les quatre Facardins*, the narrative ends without a proper conclusion. Marie thinks Pirlipat ungrateful, while Fritz is sure that the Nutcracker can deal with the Mouse King and regain his former shape. The 'Hard Nut' finds its conclusion in the dream-world of Marie after she has recovered from her injury. In this way a link is made between the inner and outer stories. They are not separate, but intertwined. Two themes weave particularly strong threads through them – physical appearances and food. Is anything just what it seems? Pate Drosselmeier is both grotesque and kind, acting in ways that sometimes seem cruel or unfeeling, sometimes helpful and amusing. He too belongs to both the inner and the outer stories. Similarly, the Nutcracker is both victim and saviour, derided as completely ugly by Drosselmeier, but fallen in love with at first sight by Marie.

After Pate Drosselmeier has finished telling 'The Hard Nut' and Marie has internalized it as part of her dream fantasy of the struggle between the Nutcracker and the Mouse King, Drosselmeier tells her that she, like Pirlipat, is a born princess, that she alone can rescue him and must be steadfast and loyal. Fritz has listened seriously to Marie's account to her parents of what has happened in the night, but he distances himself from it on the grounds that his red hussars would not have behaved like that. None of it is true, he says, but it is not reason that tells him this: it is a different angle on the fantasy.

The remainder of the story focusses on Marie's endeavours to save the Nutcracker, convinced as she now is that he is Pate Drosselmeier's nephew. The 'Fairytale of the Hard Nut' is transposed into Marie's nocturnal anxieties, as the Mouse King reappears and demands the sacrifice of sugar plums, marzipan and tragacanth dolls. The next day the family see how they have been nibbled at by mice. Fritz recommends the baker's cat to deal with the problem, but because Luise can't stand cats Pate Drosselmeier brings a mouse-trap baited with bacon, reminding the reader of his action in the first section of 'The Hard Nut'. On the following night the Mouse King demands further sacrifices – picture books and frock – and in the morning Marie sees a spot of blood on the Nutcracker's neck. He tells her that all he needs is a sword. Fritz, shocked that his hussars acquitted themselves so badly in the fight, gives them a dressing-down and takes a sabre from a pensioned-off colonel. This provides the means for the Nutcracker, in the next night's fight, to kill the Mouse King, whose seven golden crowns he gives to Marie. Playing on Marie's surname Stahlbaum (literally 'steel tree'), he chivalrously declares that she alone is the lady who steeled him with knightly courage and gave his arm strength to vanquish the arrogant creature who dared to show her scorn.

The chapters entitled 'The Realm of Dolls' and 'The Capital City' are conceived extremely theatrically, as Marie follows the Nutcracker up a staircase through the sleeve of Father's fur coat into a kind of Land of Cockayne with a Candy Meadow, an Orange Brook, a Lemonade River, a Lake of Almond Milk, villages called Gingerbread Town and Sweets Houses, and a Honey River. When they come to the Lake of Roses, Marie is delighted at the silver-white swans and the lake that she was expecting Pate Drosselmeier to make for her, but the Nutcracker tells her in an unusual fit of scorn: 'That is something that your uncle can never bring about; much rather yourself, dear Miss Stahlbaum, but let's not bother our heads about it, but take the boat across the Lake of Roses to the capital'. This, then, is in two senses Marie's story: it is a story about her, but it is also the story that she creates in imagination for herself.

Marie is entranced at the reflections she sees in the lake, and once more the Nutcracker has to explain things to her and say that it is not Princess Pirlipat, but always only herself that she sees. The city that they reach is

Konfektburg, the Town of Sweets, where there are handsomely dressed ladies and gentlemen, Armenians and Greeks, Jews and Tyroleans, officers, soldiers, clergymen, shepherds and clowns and every kind of people in the world. Marie may have known them in toy form, but in specifically naming the Armenians, Greeks, Jews and Tyroleans Hoffmann is adverting to contemporary troubles. Both the Armenians and the Greeks were attempting to establish their independence of the Ottoman Empire, while the Tyrolese, under the leadership of Andreas Hofer, had lost their struggle for independence with Hofer's death in 1810. But Marie is dreaming of a peaceable kingdom that exists only in fairytales or the realms of utopian desire. Behind the tumultuous diversity Marie sees is the *Konditor*, the confectioner who is the founder of everything – 'an unknown, but quite uncanny power that people believe can make what it wants out of humankind'.

Although Marie's accounts of what she has experienced are ridiculed by the rest of her family, the images of fairyland still surround her and make her a dreamy child. The end of the story is a wish-fulfilment, but linked as before with a loss of consciousness. This time Marie simply faints while Pate Drosselmeier is mending a clock. When she regains consciousness it is to encounter Drosselmeier's nephew, the Nutcracker, who is to be her bridegroom and who fetches her after the space of a year to be his queen.

It is a common device in tales of otherworldly encounters or visits that they are validated by some physical object that remains when the dream-events are over. In Marie's case this is the Mouse King's seven crowns, which are accounted for by Pate Drosselmeier claiming that he gave them to Marie years before for her birthday. What is odd in the *Nutcracker* is the ending, in which the fantasy replaces everyday reality. Ronald J. Elardo's Jungian interpretation of the story seems stark and inappropriate when he declares: 'In the end, Marie fails to integrate the real and the fantastical. . . For Marie, the hero myth has ended in her loss of consciousness. Her descent into the land of the Confectioner is an end, not a beginning. She has regressed to the level of ego anxiety'.[85] This might be a 'tragedy' if Marie were an adolescent or young adult, but she is a seven year old child! It is not surprising that she is still deep in a world of fantasy. We have to remember that, while there are undoubtedly elements in the *Nutcracker* that make a call on adult sensibilities, the story is suffused with playfulness and was explicitly designed for children.

---

85 Elardo, p. 7.

The *Nutcracker* has had a curious history in English versions. Although there are several translations of other works by Hoffmann from the mid 1820s onwards, its character as a children's book seems to have set it apart and caused translators to avoid it. And, as we have seen, as a children's book it was very much in advance of its time. The first glimpse that we have of it in English was not the whole story, but simply the 'Fairytale of the Hard Nut', which was given the title 'The History of Krakatuk'. It was presented as a separate, complete tale, omitting the narrative context with Marie and Pate Drosselmeier entirely, and thus as a single uninterrupted entity. The translator was the youthful William Makepeace Thackeray (1811-63), and his work has all the charm, liveliness and humour that one could wish for. The translation was published in the *National Standard* during 1833, but it does not seem to have been republished in Thackeray's collected works. It is not listed in Lewis Melville's bibliography to his life of Thackeray, although Melville rescued it for posterity in the collection of *Great German Short Stories* that he compiled with Reginald Hargreaves in 1929.

Thackeray had gone to Germany in 1830-31 and spent six months in Weimar, where he met the aged Goethe. His time in Germany enabled him to get a good grasp of the language, and it provided him with the stimulus for some later writing – *A Legend of the Rhine* (1845) and *The Kickleburys on the Rhine* (1850, under his pseudonym M. A. Titmarsh). A passage in *The Rose and the Ring* (1855), in which the porter Gruffanuff is transformed into a doorknocker and only disenchanted at the end of the story, is reminiscent of a similar incident in Hoffmann's *Der goldne Topf* (The Golden Pot). When Anselmus first goes to archivist Lindhorst's house the doorknocker turns into the grimacing face of the apple woman that he is running away from, and the bell-pull becomes a monstrous snake. Thackeray's use of the idea is comic rather than eerie, not opening up visions of the dark side of the human psyche as in Hoffmann.

Thackeray's understanding of German was not absolutely perfect, but his grasp of sentence-structure and above all the tone of Hoffmann's writing in excellent. Just occasionally he mistranslates a word or phrase or omits something that he does not understand. Thus, he translates 'auf weißen Zeltern' (on white palfreys) as 'under white canopies', gives 'Magenwasser' (stomach salts) as 'cherry brandy' and equates Peterwardein with Petersburg rather than what is now Petrovaradin in Yugoslavia. These are trivial faults in what is otherwise an engagingly readable conversion of Hoffmann into English. It is a pity that Thackeray did not translate the whole of the *Nutcracker* when this first attempt was so successful. It is even more of a pity that the translation fell quickly into oblivion, since the newspaper in which it was published collapsed in 1834.

Some twelve years later a complete version of the *Nutcracker* made an appearance in England, but it was not a translation direct from Hoffmann. It came through an intermediary, Alexandre Dumas the elder's *Histoire d'un casse-noisette* (1845). This was an adaptation, rather than a translation, of Hoffmann, and it was illustrated by the French artist Bertall (pseudonym of Albert d'Arnoux). *The History of a Nutcracker* appeared in two parts and was published by Chapman & Hall in 1847. Bertall's illustrations were taken over and adorn virtually every page, sometimes two to a page. The name of the English translator is nowhere indicated. A later edition was issued by George Routledge and Sons in a volume entitled *A Picture Story Book* (c. 1875).

To judge from this English version, Dumas seems to have closely followed the plot of Hoffmann's story. The English text, however, contains a fair number of allusions to contemporary England, for example, to toy-stalls in Soho Bazaar, the Pantheon and Lowther Arcade, and to the march of the British Grenadiers, which are presumably additions to Dumas. It was the custom in England, as also in France, to give presents on New Year's Day rather than on Christmas Eve, and this difference is noted at the beginning of the English version.[86]

The Dumas version is set from the beginning in Nuremberg. Hoffmann does not name the location, though we may infer it to be Berlin, since that was where the Hitzigs and Hoffmann were living at the time. Dumas presumably took his cue from Drosselmeier being described as having Nuremberg as his home-town. He changed the name of the Stahlbaum family to Silberhaus and made the father a judge rather than a medical councillor. The number of children was reduced from three to two: Luise disappears completely, Fritz we are now told is nine (Hoffmann does not specify his age), while Mary in the English version is seven and a half (as opposed to seven in Hoffmann). The indications of character that Hoffmann allows to emerge from his narrative are developed in the English version into rather obtrusive moralistic differences.

> Fritz was a fine stout boy with ruddy cheeks and roguish looks. He was very impatient, and stamped on the floor whenever he was contradicted;

---

[86] William Hone, *The Every-day Book and Table Book* (London: Thomas Tegg & Son, 1838), vol. 1, cols. 6-16.

22. Illustration by Bertall in [E. T. A. Hoffmann/Alexandre Dumas], 'The History of a Nutcracker', in *A Picture Story-book* (n.d.).

for he thought that everything in the world had been made for his amusement, or to suit his fancy. In this humour he would remain until the judge, annoyed by his screams, or by his stamping, came out of his study, and, raising his fore-finger, said with a frown, 'Master Fritz!'

Those two words were quite sufficient to make Master Fritz wish that the earth would open and swallow him up.

As for his mother, it was no matter how much or how often she raised her fore-finger; for Fritz did not mind her at all.

Hoffmann would not have liked this attack on Fritz's character. By contrast Mary is grossly sentimentalized: 'She was sweet, amiable, bashful, and kind to all who were in sorrow, even to her dolls: she was very obedient to her mamma, and never contradicted her governess, Miss Trudchen; so that Mary was beloved by every one'. There is no governess in Hoffmann's text. The name of Marie's doll Trutchen has been taken over for her. Pate Drosselmeier (now spelt Drosselmayer) has also undergone a transformation, for from being small and dark in appearance he is now about six foot tall, though he stoops, and from being a lawyer he has been changed into 'a great physician and doctor of medicine'. He and the children's father have exchanged professions.

There are a variety of other minor differences between Hoffmann and Dumas in English, some of which may well be due to misunderstanding. It is odd that Princess Pirlipata can only be saved by 'a young man who had never been shaved, and who had always worn boots' when Hoffmann specifies that he should *never* have worn boots. The wearing of boots presumably marks the ritual transition from boyhood to manhood. Dumas has the son of Christian Zacharias Drosselmayer sent to the University of Tübingen at the age of ten, 'where he remained till he was eighteen, without contracting any of the bad habits of his companions, such as drinking, swearing, and fighting'. He is eventually named as Nathaniel, though Hoffmann had left him nameless. Probably the name was lifted from *Der Sandmann*.

Hoffmann made little of the religious associations of his story. He had the elder daughter, Luise, tell the younger children that the Christmas presents came from Christ through the hands of their parents, while the Dumas English version ascribes them to the 'guardian angel who sends and blesses all those fine toys which are given to you'. However, the associations that Hoffmann evoked with the name *Konditor* in the Land of Dolls are reduced in the English version, which translates it, reasonably enough, as 'Confectioner', keeping the main meaning, but losing the religious undertone. The English version introduces the idea of the transmigration of souls through the process of baking by the Confectioner, whereas Hoffmann's text simply talks about his power of being able to make what he wants of humankind.

The Dumas version of Hoffmann's tale has proved much more influential in Britain than the original. It also formed the basis of Tchaikovsky's ballet, first performed at the Maryinsky Theatre, St. Petersburg, on 18 December 1892 with choreography by Marius Petipa. The ballet excludes the 'Fairytale of the Hard Nut', renames the heroine Clara and provides a large number of individual dances for the various toys. Probably most people's knowledge of the *Nutcracker* nowadays stems from this colourful, gloriously entertaining ballet rather than from a book. Performances have become a standard part of Christmas entertainment. Most twentieth-century retellings of the *Nutcracker* in English derive ultimately from Dumas, usually considerably simplified and, as in Walt Disney's *Fantasia*, diverging a great deal from what Hoffmann wrote. Indeed, although Hoffmann's name may be mentioned as the ultimate originator, his literary subtlety of composition is lost sight of.

The first complete translation of the *Nutcracker* directly from the German was made by Major Alex. Ewing as part of *The Serapion Brethren* (London: George Bell & Sons, 1886). This collection of Hoffmann's tales was clearly not designed for children, running as it does to two thick volumes of over 1000 pages and containing no illustrations whatsoever. Major Ewing was the widower of the children's writer Juliana Horatia Ewing (1841-85), author among many other things of *The Brownies, and Other Tales* (1870) and *Old-fashioned Fairy Tales* (1876). Several of Mrs Ewing's books had been published by Bell. Major Ewing's translation was reissued in 1908, and his version of the *Nutcracker* was used as the base for Roberto Innocenti's sumptuously illustrated version (London: Jonathan Cape, 1997). Ewing's translation sticks close to the German and is very readable. It is particularly good at conveying different registers of language, especially colloquial speech. There are a few mistakes or perhaps deliberate alterations made from the German. In the original Fritz says his toy stable is lacking a chestnut horse (*Fuchs*), but Ewing takes this literally as 'a good fox was lacking to his small zoological collection'. He also changes the marzipan that is fed to swans in Marie's fantasy garden into 'shortbread and cake'. Other similar slips do not materially affect one's appreciation of the tale.

Ironically, it was only in the same year that Tchaikovsky's ballet appeared that the first complete translation of *Nutcracker and Mouse King* for children was made from Hoffmann's original. This was by Ascott R. Hope and was published by T. Fisher Unwin in 1892 in his 'Children's Library' series. The book also contained a separate short section entitled 'The Educated Cat', adapted from Hoffmann's novel *Kater Murr*. It took over a small selection of Bertall's illustrations from the Dumas editions. Unwin's 'Children's Library' was a notable, attractively produced collection of both old and new stories for children. It was an international collection, including *Tales from the Mabinogion* and *Irish Fairy Tales* as well as the first English edition of *Pinocchio* (now a rare and costly book) and Wilhelm Hauff's *The Little Glass Man and Other Stories*, so Hoffmann was in very good company. Ascott R. Hope was the name under which Ascott Robert Hope-Moncrieff (1846-1927) wrote a variety of children's books ranging from variations on traditional children's tales, stories for the *Boys' Own Paper* and tales about Red Indians and the heroes of Young America.

Hope's translation of the *Nutcracker* keeps close to the original and is a careful rendering. However, like the majority of translators in his position, his aim is to produce a story that English children will read easily. He does not attempt to explain features of German life that may seem strange to his readers, but instead eliminates them or gives English equivalents. He assimilates Hoffmann's story to English circumstances rather than trying to give his readers a glimpse of Germany at the beginning of the nineteenth century. The children's names are changed to Fred and Mary, while the surgeon loses his surname Wendelstern. Frau Mauserinks becomes Mouseykins (altogether too cosy a name for so terrifying a creature), and Prince Facardin is transmuted into the conventional Prince Charming of Perrault, Madame d'Aulnoy and the English pantomime.

Hope does not credit his readers with any acquaintance with the outside world (outside Britain, that is), for the troops in the first battle against the mice undergo a considerable change. In the English contingents we find 'Gardeners, Highlanders, Japanese, Barbers, Harlequins, Cupids, Lions, Tigers, Baboons, and Apes'. In the German text we have Tyrolese for Highlanders and Tungusians for Japanese. In a later passage the people in Konfektburg include Armenians, Greeks, Jews and Tyrolese, which appear in English as 'Arabs and Greeks, Highlanders and Indians'. Why should Hope have eliminated the Armenians and the Jews?

In Hoffmann's original Marie twice hurts her left arm, and we have noted the significance of 'left'. Hope has her hurt the right arm. This may

E. T. A. Hoffmann's Nutcracker and Mouse King 243

have come about through a hasty reading of the German, which reads: 'Sie fühlte wohl in dem Augenblick einen recht stechenden Schmerz am linken Arm' (At that moment she felt a quite stabbing pain in her left arm). Hope seems to have picked on 'recht' as meaning 'right' rather than 'very' or 'quite' and transferred it to the arm. This, of course, destroys the symbolic significance. The change is accidental, but it illustrates what can so easily happen with translators who are more concerned with the broad outline of the plot than with the patterning of details. Despite these minor changes we have to be grateful to Hope for returning British readers to Hoffmann's original, though sadly most later English versions have reverted to Dumas. The major exception is the Manheim/Sendak edition, in which Hoffmann comes into his own with a splendid translation by Ralph Manheim, the most brilliant of translators from German, and marvellous pictures by Maurice Sendak (New York: Crown Publishers, 1984), but that is way outside our period.

In conclusion, it is worth another step into the twentieth century to see what happened to Hoffmann in the immediate aftermath of the First World War in a new adaptation, again called *Nutcracker and Mouse-King*, with illustrations by Florence Anderson (London: George G. Harrap & Company, 1919). As was the case with other German books at this time, every trace of its German origin was removed. The title-page makes no reference to Hoffmann, only to the adapter E. Gordon Browne. The two children have been thoroughly anglicized as Dick and Molly (the older sister is not mentioned at all), while Pate Drosselmeier has become an Uncle Christopher. No surnames are used anywhere, no locations are geographically specified. Even marzipan is changed into 'sweet biscuits'. Molly's old doll is called Gertrude, and her favourite doll Charlotte, corresponding to Hoffmann's Trutchen and Klärchen. Since the Dumas version calls them Rose and Clara and gives the name Trudchen to a newly invented governess, this adaptation was almost certainly done from Hoffmann. The fact that the Mouse Queen is called Mouseyrink rather than Lady Mouseykins (Ascott R. Hope) or Dame Mousey (Dumas) confirms this. Uncle Christopher's nephew, furthermore, has never (rather than always) worn boots.

The story is resolutely simplified and brought up to date linguistically. The nut Crickcrack, for example, is hard enough for a steamroller to go over without cracking it, while the original speaks of a forty-eight pound cannon. Florence Anderson's four colour plates show an early twentieth-century little girl in dreamy mood and the softest of shades, predominantly pink and pale yellow. While Bertall's engravings capture the angularities and grotesque aspects of Hoffmann's tale, Anderson's drawings as well as watercolour paintings dwell on the pretty side. Yet her line-drawing of Mouseyrink on Princess Pirlipat's pillow conveys the dreadfulness of the episode through the exaggerated size of the Mouse Queen.

The number of English versions of the *Nutcracker* is not as extensive as those of Fouqué's *Undine* and *Sintram,* Chamisso's *Peter Schlemihl* and Hauff's fairytales. One can only speculate on the reasons for this. Although many German children's books were translated into English at an early date, they were exclusively works with a strong educational or moral tendency. *Nußknacker und Mausekönig* did not fit into this category, and it escaped being translated as a work of adult fiction (which was what happened with Fouqué and Chamisso) probably because so many other examples of Hoffmann's work were more obvious candidates. *Der goldne Topf* was translated by Thomas Carlyle in 1827, while *Der Sandmann* appeared in a translation by Lord Albert Conyngham in *The Keepsake* for 1834. Neither of these stories were readily adaptable for children, though *Der Sandmann* reached a much larger and enduring audience through its adaptation into the ballet *Coppélia* (1870) with music by Delibes. The reception of Hoffmann's *Nutcracker* has suffered through contamination with Dumas and Tchaikovsky's ballet, and abridgements of the story for children at the end of the twentieth century still show the marks. Ascott Hope's 1892 translation probably came about through the increased interest in the 1890s in Germany and German books that saw so many new editions of *Undine, Sintram, Schlemihl* and the Grimms' and Hauff's fairytales. Yet it was a one-off affair and did not stimulate further newly illustrated editions in the Edwardian era.

14. Lesser Fairytales Authors

Nineteenth-century Germany experienced a virtual industry in the collecting and writing of fairytales. While the Grimms and Bechstein dominated the field as far as national collections of traditional tales were concerned, many others devoted their efforts to particular regions of Germany. Their work is dealt with in another chapter. But there were also many writers who composed fairytales of their own, sometimes adapting traditional material, but often creating their own tales. Some of them, such as Fouqué, E. T. A. Hoffmann, Brentano and Hauff, gained considerable literary renown, and their fairytales figured prominently in works translated for the educated English reader. In addition, though, there were several writers whose work was recognized as being aimed exclusively at children. They did not necessarily confine themselves to fairytales, but wrote fables, animal tales, moral tales and children's verse as well. The boundaries between these genres were, in any case, blurred. These writers frequently enjoyed considerable popularity in Germany, but were not so successful in Britain. Their names are nowadays scarcely known, but at different periods in the nineteenth century individual tales and even some whole books were translated into English and gained a modest readership. The authors that will be considered here are A. L. Grimm, Robert Reinick, J. J. Rudolphi and Richard von Volkmann-Leander.

The first of these, Albert Ludwig Grimm (1786-1872), is significant on several counts. Firstly, he collaborated with Brentano in collecting material for *Des Knaben Wunderhorn* and, secondly, he himself produced a collection of *Kindermährchen* (Heidelberg: Mohr und Zimmer, 1809) that antedated the *Kinder- und Hausmärchen* of his more famous namesakes. He thus formed part of the Romantics' fascination with folksongs and folktales, but as far as the latter were concerned his attitude towards publication was distinctly different from that of Jacob and Wilhelm Grimm.

A. L. Grimm, like many educated people of the day, believed that one could not reproduce a folktale just as it was presented by its oral narrator, but that it needed some judicious literary improvement. The Brothers Grimm did not believe his tales had turned out very well, and A. L. Grimm in his turn criticized the unpolished form of the tales in the Brothers Grimm's first edition of 1812-15. He was not alone in his criticisms, and indeed the Grimms' second edition of 1819 underwent considerable alterations in content and linguistic style in response to them.

A. L. Grimm spent most of his life as head of the grammar school in Weinheim, being appointed in 1806. From 1829 to 1838 he was mayor of Weinheim and was a deputy to the Baden Diet from 1831. From 1854 he lived in Baden-Baden. In addition to the volume of *Kindermährchen* published in 1809, which reached a fifth edition by 1869, his books for children included *Lina's Mährchenbuch* (Lina's Fairytale Book) (1816), five volumes of *Mährchen der Tausend und Einen Nacht* (Fairytales from the Thousand and One Nights) (1820-24), *Christblumen* (Christmas Roses) (c. 1830) and *Mährchen aus dem Morgenlande für die Jugend* (1843). Of these *Lina's Mährchenbuch* was translated into English as *Fairy Tales, from the German of A. L. Grimm, with illustrations by [Robert] Cruikshank* (London: Charles Tilt, 1827), and *Mährchen aus dem Morgenlande* appeared as *Tales from the Eastern-Land*, translated from the German by H.V. (London: Joseph Cundall, 1847). Joseph Cundall, who published many German works during the 1840s, also published separately in 1846 *The Two Talismans*, one of the four tales contained in *Tales from the Eastern-Land*. This was explicitly credited to A. L. Grimm, but he published *The Water Fairy's Gift and Other Tales* and *The Miller's Son* (both 1846) without any indication of Grimm's name, though they had earlier been credited to him in *The Christmas Roses, and Other Tales*, chiefly translated from the German (London: Joseph Cundall, 1845). Other tales were included in miscellaneous collections and *The Playmate*, a monthly periodical issued by Cundall and later by David Bogue, which also appeared in book form. However, none of Grimm's work was published later than the mid-century book form of *The Playmate*.

The Christmas Roses was a miscellany containing six stories by A. L. Grimm, two by Rudolphi, one by Hauff and one by Ernst von Houwald. Since none of Grimm's tales are included in his 1809 and 1816 fairytale collections, they are presumably taken from *Christblumen*, though I have been unable to check. All have a marked moral tone. In 'The Christmas

Roses', which gives its name to the miscellany, a mother prays to God about her sick son and is given a vase with white flowers which heal him. The story ends with the words: 'Yet the healing virtue and restoring power were imparted to the Christmas roses, only when conveyed by a heavenly visitant to the homes of peace and good-will'. In 'The Gleaner' a farmer's son helps a ragged boy who has been beaten by the squire's son and lost all that he had gleaned in the cornfield. In this way he 'taste[s] a different pleasure'. 'The Hedgehog' is a fable about a fox being driven out of its den by a hedgehog moving closer and closer to him. The hedgehog is interpreted as representing sin. Another example of wrong behaviour occurs in 'Lina', in which the girl of the title is constantly naughty and a tease and is punished by being turned into a cuckoo. 'The Water Fairy's Gifts' follows a common pattern in Grimm's tales. It contrasts a good boy with two bad boys, who set their dog on his sheep and cause a lamb to be drowned. A fairy replaces the good boy's lamb and gives him in addition one with golden wool and another with silver wool, which he then gives to the king's daughter. The king rewards him with the best estates in his kingdom. When the two bad boys attempt to replicate the process, the fairy sends wolves to strangle them and destroy their flock. This same pattern can be seen in Perrault's 'Diamonds and Toads' and 'Mother Holle' by the Brothers Grimm, but with female protagonists.

'Tony, the Miller's Son' is somewhat different in dealing with encounters with 'the little people'. A miller who refuses to yield to requests from the fairies suffers damage to his mill-wheel and the loss of cattle, sheep and pigs. His son, however, secretly helps a little man on another occasion and is rewarded by being led into the mines and given an orange that heals his mother's sickness and a pomegranate that contains diamonds rather than 'pretty pink grains'. The story clearly illustrates the powers for good and evil that the fairies in their various guises were believed to have, but it can be more generally understood as demonstrating the fact that mean-spiritedness creates injury and disharmony while generosity is rewarded in unexpectedly full measure. 'Tony, the Miller's Son' was reprinted once together with 'The Gleaner' in *The King of the Swans, and Other Tales* (London: Joseph Cundall, 1846). Then, after an interval of more than sixty years, it reappeared with the title 'The Little Brown Men' in an adaptation by Frank Mundell in W. T. Stead's *Books for the Bairns* (no. 160, May 1909). There it accompanied 'Prince or Tailor?', an adaptation of Hauff's 'The False Prince', which had also been included in *The King of the Swans*. As far

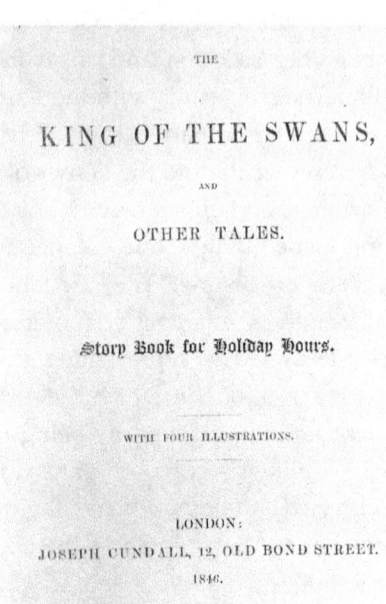

23. Title-page and frontispiece of *The King of the Swans and Other Tales* (1846)

as I can tell, this was the last appearance of a tale by A. L. Grimm in English.

The earliest appearance of A. L. Grimm in English was his *Fairy Tales* (London: Charles Tilt, 1827), which provided three tales taken from *Lina's Mährchenbuch*, namely, 'The Black Guitar; a Fairy Tale, founded on a Dream' ('Die schwarze Zither'), 'The Two Foundlings of the Spring; or, the History of Brunnenhold and Brunnenstark' ('Das Mährchen von Brunnenhold und Brunnenstark') and 'The Story of the Three Brothers; or, the Avenging Cudgel' ('Das Mährchen von dem Knüppel aus dem Sacke'). The latter two items are versions of the tale-types represented by the Brothers Grimm's 'The Two Brothers' (KHM 60) and 'The Table, the Ass and the Stick' (KHM 36). A. L. Grimm's didacticism is very plain at the end of 'The Story of the Three Brothers', since he concludes:

> And long after the magic table had been broken to pieces, and the golden donkey had died, as all donkies must, and Thomas had been buried, and the cudgel itself destroyed, the people of that village continued to warn their children of the cudgel. And the children, when they heard tell the story, grew afraid of the cudgel, and became good children, tractable and obedient.

'The Black Guitar' is nothing like a traditional German fairytale, nor is it a moral tale. It has elements that connect it with the quest tales of medieval romance, the Gothic horror tale and the *Arabian Nights*. The hero, Adelbert, is instructed by his teacher to ask his father for a guitar, at which the latter is enraged. Adelbert then, following a dream, climbs a tower from which beautiful music emerges, discovers a black guitar and rides away with it. He overcomes a dragon by playing the guitar, and the same process allows him to defeat a knight in black armour whom he meets in a tournament. The knight, who is called Otto, tells him a bizarre story about an abducted girl, and the two men engage in fearful adventures searching for her. One night Adelbert enters the pyramid of Cheops, brings a mummy to life and is given a small staff and instructions to travel up river to where it rushes over rocks. The staff when thrown down changes into a snake, which leads them to a cave. They encounter a lion, then six knights in black armour and eventually have to cope with a fence of flames ('"Ho, Ho," cried Adelbert, "is that a hedge like the one which Siegfried rode through?"'). The guitar once more helps them, they rescue the abducted girl, Rosablanka, and take her back home, where she is married to Otto. Adelbert is reconciled with his father and founds a monastery. Later he mounts his horse, playing his guitar, ascends into the sky and vanishes. The story contains several elements that recur in other longer tales by Grimm – the problematic relationship between father and son, the prophetic dream, the magical token or talisman (here the black guitar) and the arduous journeys in the Orient.

Grimm went on to write versions of tales from the *Arabian Nights* in 1820-24, but it was not until 1843 that he published his own *Mährchen aus dem Morgenlande für die Jugend*. This book, together with its steel engravings by J. B. Sonderland, was swiftly taken up by Cundall and published in 1847 with the title *Tales from the Eastern-Land*. It was successful enough to be reprinted by Henry G. Bohn in 1852. Another edition was published by George Routledge and Sons in 1888, so as far as Britain was concerned this was A. L. Grimm's best known work. The book contains four long tales – 'The Merchant of Balsora', 'The Two Talismans', 'The Story of Haschem' and 'The Three Trials'. The German spellings of Arabic names are retained in the English, so we have Jussuf for Yussuf, Haschem for Hashem, and so on. The tales, which all have male protagonists, are full of incident and adventure and modelled on the longer tales from the *Arabian Nights*.

'The Merchant of Balsora' shows its hero tested by two opposing females, one appearing first in the shape of a butterfly and symbolizing the life of pleasure, while the other, Haschanascha, represents inward devotion; her name when spoken always evokes assistance to the hero in times of distress. Haschanascha is black-skinned, and this the hero, Jussuf, finds off-putting, but he can only escape being sacrificed to the sacred serpent of his captors by agreeing to marry her. It takes a long time for Jussuf to accept the values of Haschanascha, but when he finally rejects the butterfly Haschanascha loses her black skin, and Jussuf is married to her. The colour symbolism here applied to human beings reflects the cultural attitudes of the times, and it is reinforced by the frequency with which slaves, in these stories, are referred to as black-skinned too. But it is a feature that makes for uncomfortable reading today. The black and white symbolism is also found in 'The Story of Haschem', where it characterizes two lovers again, but this time without any racial connotations. In 'The Three Trials' the hero has to shoot a white eagle and a black lion in order to be able to open a rusted iron chest, so here one can see black and white as being both necessary for the acquisition of a precious talisman. It is certainly not the case that black is always viewed in negative terms. However, all these 'Eastern' stories embody clear moral values – modesty of lifestyle, the importance of virtuous principles being inculcated in childhood, persistence in times of adversity – but they now emerge from the story rather than being the primary function as in some of the shorter tales.

Two of A. L. Grimm's stories circulated in English apart from the others that were taken from *Lina's Mährchenbuch*. They were translated by Madame de Chatelain (1807-76), who introduced British children to a considerable amount of other German material as well as writing books of her own. 'Little Freddy and his Fiddle' ('Ein lustiges Mährlein vom kleinen Frieder mit seiner Geige') centres on the motif of the fiddle that forces everyone to dance to it, which is probably better known through the Brothers Grimm's 'The Jew in the Thornbush'. 'Never Mind the Laugh of Fools' ('Laß dich der Narren Spott nicht kümmern') is an invented animal fable illustrating the consequences of paying attention to the mockery of those who have no understanding. Both stories were published in the magazine *The Playmate*.

Albert Ludwig Grimm is known in English chiefly through the agency of the publisher Joseph Cundall, and it is Cundall again who provides us with stories by the little known J. J. Rudolphi, the pseudonym of Johann Jakob Rutz, who wrote a collection of *Kindermährchen* (Heidelberg: Winter, 1838), from which Cundall took several items and published them in different books. *The Christmas Roses* contains, first, 'The Tales of the Stork, Fox, and Magpie', which consists of three items. The stork tells how, when he alighted on a ship on his flight back from Africa, he saw the cook slit open a monstrous fish from which a little man escaped. There then follows the little man's account of his adventures à la Tom Thumb, after which the stork carries him back to his parents' home. The fox's tale explains how he escaped being killed as a cub, was trained as a bellows-dog in a smithy, tricked a tom-cat into exchanging places with him, landed in a small menagerie with a lion, helped the lion to escape and joined him in service to a prince, who eventually gave him his liberty. This is a newly invented tale showing the fox in his typical role of trickster. The magpie's tale is a humorous piece about the way in which a huge cabbage is used to simulate, first, the head of a giant and scare away marauding knights and, second, a silent old man, whom the king prefers to all his talkative councillors. Finally, the cabbage is used to substitute for the king when rebels determine to execute him.

The other story by Rudolphi in *The Christmas Roses* is entitled 'The Labyrinth' and follows traditional fairytale structure. In it three brothers go to a castle in quest of a pen that writes by itself, a wheel than can spin itself and a bird that can speak all languages. All fail to find their way back, but are ultimately rescued by their youngest brother. If this were a traditional tale, it would probably include princesses to be rescued or married at the conclusion, but Rudolphi provides no such romantic element. This is also the case with the two stories of his that Cundall published in *The King of the Swans, and Other Tales*.

Both 'The King of the Swans' and 'The Children's Spring' seem designed for quite young children. The first tells how a little girl goes in search of strawberries in winter for her sick friend. She meets a man wearing clothing of swansdown, who directs her to a land where it is summer. Before she can return home she has to make a gift to the King of the Swans and presents him with some of her strawberries. Then, blindfolded, she flies back home, and her friend is restored to health by the strawberries. When she is older the King of the Swans gives her a gold crown of strawberry leaves with rubies, diamonds and amethysts. 'The Children's Spring' seems to have taken its basic motif from Ludwig Tieck's eerie story 'The Elves', of which Edgar Taylor included a condensed version in the second volume of *German Popular Stories*, but Rudolphi's tale is less worrying. In it a little girl, Adelaide, falls through an aperture into an isolated old building and gets wet. A woman with two children finds her dry clothes, and she plays happily with other children there. When she wants to go home, she takes a crystal as a remembrance and is given a basket made of green stone in the shape of acanthus leaves. She is directed along a dark passage and told to follow the star at the end. There she meets her brother, with whom she had been playing at the outset of the story. She is now wearing a dress shining like stars, which is a token of the truthfulness of her experience when she tells her parents about it. Later she sees the scar on her hand that had been caused by her accident, and she remembers being chided for being so curious and decides not to be so curious in the future. This ending is rather odd, as Adelaide has gained precious gifts and no lasting injury from her adventure. The idea that she should desist from being inquisitive is simply part of contemporary notions of undesirable behaviour. Children were trained to be docile and obedient rather than following their own whims and desires.

Rudolphi's tales are pleasant enough, though largely derivative in content and unremarkable in expression. Only Cundall published them, and there were no reprints. However, 'The King of the Swans' was adapted and included in a slender miscellany of fairytales in *Books for the Bairns*, no. 162 (July 1909). Since then Rudolphi has disappeared from print in both Britain and Germany.

The publication in English of our next fairytale author, Robert Reinick (1805-52), also owes a great deal to the interest of Joseph Cundall. His name is nowadays largely forgotten in Britain, but Reinick was one of the most popular authors of children's stories and verses in Germany during the second half of the nineteenth century. According to one authority, his lyrics were, next to those of Heine and Emanuel Geibel, the most often set to music of his period. Certainly, Reinick had a deft touch as a popular writer, but the field in which he excelled – lyric poetry – does not lend itself easily to translation, and there are thus very few English versions of his poems. With his stories and fairytales it is a different matter.

Probably the first of Reinick's stories to appear in English were contained in a book entitled *The Donkey's Shadow and Other Stories*, by various authors (London: Addey & Co., c. 1856). Addey's books reflect Cundall's earlier and contemporaneous productions, so Cundall, who was in partnership with Addey between 1849 and 1852, may well have been the connexion for Reinick's tales. The title story and six others are credited to Reinick, but no indication is given of the translator. The stories are quite varied in character and length. Three are fairytales involving magic or the supernatural, one is a nursery tale, one an animal story, one a humorous anecdote and one a moral tale.

'The Sedge Island' ('Die Schilfinsel') focusses on the danger of contacts between humans and supernatural creatures, as a twelve year old girl is captivated by the song of nixes and later drawn down into the lake where she goes fishing. Three days later her dead body is washed ashore. 'Prince Gold-Fish and the Fishermaid' ('Prinz Goldfisch und das Fischermädchen') also centres on this same motif, but has a happy ending. Here a prince is enchanted by a water fairy into a goldfish and then caught by a fishergirl, Elizabeth. She rejects his invitation to join him in his watery kingdom and throws a stone at him when he is back in the water. After a cry his gold skin rises to the surface of the water and Elizabeth takes it, thinking she will be able to sell it for much-needed money. Later, unknown to Elizabeth, it is announced that the prince has returned and is looking to choose a wife. Coincidentally, Elizabeth attempts to sell the fish-skin there, but is robbed of it by a splendidly attired lady, who claims it is hers and wants to marry the prince. She is the water fairy in disguise, but the prince rejects her and chooses Elizabeth instead. The third fairytale, 'The Forest Mill', also deals with an enchantment. In it a discharged soldier follows a white butterfly to a mill in the forest, which he finds inhabited only by a hen, a cat, a dove and an ass. He is subjected to various tests and disturbances during the night and accused of killing the miller's daughter (i.e. the dove). He declares himself to deserve death, and his eyes are bandaged in readiness for being shot, but once the order has been given to fire he finds himself confronted with the miller, his wife, maid and man, who are the real occupants of the mill and have been under a spell, which he has broken. The miller's daughter lies on the ground before him and has a small red speck on her forehead. The story ends with the soldier marrying her and revitalizing the forest mill. The German original has four more paragraphs, attributing the spell to Oberon, the king of the elves, and explaining that it can only be undone when the one who has killed the dove is ready to give his own life for it.

These fairytales are independent creations of Reinick's, but 'The Fellow-Lodgers' ('Die Hausgenossen') claims to be an adaptation of a Low German tale from East Prussia. In content it is a combination of motifs found also in the Grimms' 'The Mouse, the Bird and the Sausage' and 'Little Louse and Little Flea'. 'Wise Cockscomb' ('Eine Hühnerwirtschaft') is an animal tale derived from elements of the Reynard the Fox stories, in which the fox is finally caught in a trap and killed. 'The Donkey's Shadow' ('Des Esels Schatten') is an amusing anecdote about a man riding from Rome to

Tivoli in the scorching sun on a donkey, and the donkey-driver competing with him in attempting to get a shady rest in the donkey's shadow. The inspiration for this story presumably came from Reinick's visit to Rome and the surrounding countryside in 1838, when he met up with his painter friend Theodor von Oer. The remaining tale, 'Christiana, the Lace-Girl' ('Spitzenchristel'), is set in Dresden and recounts a typical story of a poor girl assisted by a wealthy family, accused by a vicious portress of a theft which she has not committed and, by happy chance, ultimately proved innocent. Tales of this kind abound in nineteenth-century Germany and Britain – Christoph von Schmid's *Basket of Flowers* immediately springs to mind as comparable in plot to 'Christiana, the Lace Girl'. Their reliance on coincidence or a *deus ex machina* to provide a happy resolution to injustice is wearisome to the modern reader, though it probably reassured the philanthropic or Evangelical readers of the day.

As far as I can tell, only one of Reinick's was published in English as a separate book. This was his fairytale 'Die Wurzelprinzessin', which was published as *The King of Root Valley and his Curious Daughter*, with eight illustrations by T. von Oer and R. Reinick (London, 1856). No translator's name is given. Another version was published in the United States a few years later with the title *The Root-Princess. A Christmas Story*, translated by Fanny Fuller (Philadelphia: F. Leypoldt; New York: F. W. Christern, 1865). This attractive fairytale owes a great deal to Hoffmann's *Nutcracker and Mouse-King*, but Reinick's animated Nutcracker is the villain rather than the hero of the piece. The scene is transferred from an urban indoor setting to a hidden valley somewhere off the road from Nuremberg to Leipzig. A coach laden with boxes of toys crashes down a ravine into a stream which has the property of bringing to life everything that falls into it. The Nutcracker thus becomes acquainted with the tiny people no more than a span in height who live in the Root Valley. The Nutcracker marries the Root Princess, but antagonizes the Root people by his arrogance and power politics. War breaks out, and rabbits, moles, lizards and worms are called in to literally undermine the Nutcracker's domain. Eventually, everything is swept away in a storm. The Root people represent a kind of natural, orderly way of life that is innocent and vulnerable to the desire for power of the mechanical, even machine-like invader. The Root Princess falls prey to the Nutcracker and, later, a human bird-catcher, but she is rescued and warns the Root people of the danger, at which they all disappear into the crevices of the surrounding rocks and have never been seen again. While on one level this is a simple fantasy for children, reflecting beliefs about the disappearance of the fairies in the face of human encroachment, it can also be interpreted politically as referring to the self-aggrandizement of Napoleon and his sweeping away of the numerous petty principalities which existed in Germany up to the beginning of the nineteenth century. It is Reinick's lament for the passing of traditional ways.

A few other tales by Reinick find a place in *The Playmate*, but do not add anything substantially different from what we have already looked at. 'The Seven Boys and the Monster', which derives from the traditional tale of 'The Seven Swabians' (the Grimms' *Kinder- und Hausmärchen*, no. 119), was translated by Cundall's half-brother, Lawrence Drake Cundall, who also translated the moral tale 'The Little Pot of Pinks'. Another tale, 'The Hermit', which has affinities with 'The Forest Mill', was translated by Alfred Sothern. It is a pity that we do not know more about the other translators of Reinick's tales. For the most part, his stories were printed only once in English. 'The Forest Mill' and 'Wise Cockscomb' are exceptions in being reprinted in *A Wonder Book of Beasts*, edited by F. J. Harvey Darton (London: Wells Gardner, Darton & Co., 1909). Reinick was of interest to the Victorians as one more German fairytale writer, but he did not become a classic like the Brothers Grimm or Hoffmann.

A few other German writers of fairytales are represented in British collections by the occasional item, but the last author to make a significant impact in the nineteenth century was Richard von Volkmann-Leander (1830-89) with a collection entitled *Dreams by a French Fireside*, translated by M. O'Callaghan (London: Chapman & Hall, 1886). Another translation, by J. Raleigh, appeared with the title *Dreams by French Firesides*, with illustrations by Louis Wain (Edinburgh: Adam & Charles Black, 1890). The German original, *Träumereien an französischen Kaminen*, was first published in Leipzig in 1871 under the pseudonym Richard Leander. The title has an ironic significance, since these tales were written by a leading German army surgeon in his leisure hours during the Franco-Prussian War, especially during the protracted period of the siege of Paris. He sent the sheets of paper on which they were written back to his wife and children, and they were published in book form when he returned. He concluded his preface to the collection with words that embody the feelings of a passionate German patriot:

> So now the little book shall go out into the world as a memorial of that great and glorious time, although the only modest connection with that

time that it can claim for itself is this: that it has grown up out of the love of that for which we fought and struggled; out of love for the German nation and German life. God bless our glorious Fatherland!

These fairytales, born of the love of home and family while far distant from it, enjoyed great popularity. The book went through forty-eight editions in German up to 1913, no doubt because, as one critic writes, 'the collection is defined and permeated by the idyll of middle-class domesticity'. In the twenty-two tales we can see Volkmann-Leander using and adapting fairytale structures and motifs with which he must have been familiar from the Brothers Grimm, Bechstein and Hans Andersen, but which he imbues more strongly with his own social and personal values. These are very much concentrated in the family – in the mutual respect and attachment of husband and wife, the care of parents for children, the preciousness of inner emotions that are often hard to articulate in words.

But while the family is the focus of Volkmann-Leander's tales, it does not exclude other patterns of life. 'The Old Trunk', for example, tells of an old bachelor who possesses a worn trunk containing a secret case that he doesn't want anyone else to touch, inside which a fairytale princess is hidden. As we see here, many of the tales have a readily discernible, but not obtrusively didactic symbolic meaning. 'The Dream Beech' presents a discussion on the nature of marriage, focussing on a crisis in a married couple's life brought about by different understandings on the part of a rational husband and a (for want of a better word) superstitious wife. An old beech tree has the reputation that if anyone has a dream beneath it, not thinking about what he might dream, it will come true. The husband, when he was a poor travelling journeyman, had had a dream of domestic bliss under the beech and, under pressure, told the daughter of the innkeeper that his dream concerned marrying her and some day becoming the landlord himself. In due course then the two marry, have children and are very happy, and on the landlord's death the husband takes over the inn himself. Then, one day another man has a dream under the beech tree, and the husband ridicules his wife's belief that the tree can foretell the future. Despite their happiness she is deeply upset, realizing that her marriage is not a result of destiny following her husband's dream. The husband becomes sad at his wife's emotional withdrawal, sits under the beech and has a repeat of his dream of five years previously. He regards it as merely a dream, but his wife takes it as a sign that they really do belong together.

'God be praised!' she said; 'now everything is right again. I love you so much, so much, far more than you know; and I have been in such misery all these days lest I ought not to love you, and lest God had not destined us for each other. For you did steal my heart, wicked husband, and at first you did deceive me; but now I know that it made no difference, and that although you stole it away from me it would have been yours just the same without that'.

Yet another tale centres on Volkmann-Leander's perception of the intertwining of the miraculous with the everyday. 'The Invisible Kingdom' concerns a young peasant who goes looking for a beautiful princess whom he sees in a dream. On his journey he encounters an old man being severely beaten by two repulsive naked men and manages to drive them away. The old man is the King of Dreams, the naked men are the servants of the King of Reality. Eventually the young peasant finds the princess, marries her and returns to his village as the king of an invisible kingdom, but none of the villagers can recognize his wife as being a princess. This story was also anthologized in *The Diamond Fairy Book* (London: Hutchinson & Co., 1897).

At least two of Volkmann-Leander's tales bear strong resemblances to those of Andersen. 'Goldiekin' ('Goldtöchterchen') is reminiscent of 'Thumbelina', but the heroine here is an ordinary little girl who walks out of the house early one morning and experiences the marvels of nature with a duck and a stork to guide her. When she does not return, her parents search fruitlessly for her, but in the end she is brought home by an angel. The more complex story of 'The Little Blackamoor and the Golden Princess' owes a good deal to ideas in Andersen's 'The Shepherdess and the Chimney Sweep' and 'The Steadfast Tin Soldier'. Andersen makes it clear that his characters are toys or ornaments, but Volkmann-Leander leaves this ambiguous. His blackamoor keeps losing his colour, becoming grey and then white, as it washes off. Yet at an earlier stage in the story, when, as a boy, he qualifies as a chimney sweep and the other apprentices try to wash the colour off him, they are unsuccessful. Our hero then learns to play the violin and after five years becomes a master violinist. At this stage, while he is still grey, he declares his love to a golden princess, who laughs at him. Realizing he has said something stupid, he runs away. Later, he sees her again at a fair, but her gold is now wearing away, leaving brass underneath. She would be prepared to marry him now, but he refuses and instead marries a wife with a golden heart. The golden princess falls into the possession of a huckster. The colour symbolism works well enough with toys in showing that outer appearances often belie inner qualities and that one needs to look below the surface, but for today's reader it is disturbing when applied to a black person. Leander's attitudes towards the blackamoor are very mixed. On the one hand, he registers the injustices he suffers – being trained as a chimney sweep instead of a violinist, being victimized by his fellow apprentices, being left naked afterwards on the street, being mocked for his declaration of love to the golden princess – and with all of this the reader identifies. But on the other hand the blackamoor only succeeds in life to the extent that he loses his blackness – assimilation is the name of the game. The story does not display any sense of the blackamoor as a real person; his blackness is used simply symbolically.

Even where they are overtly didactic Volkmann-Leander's tales have an appealing tone. This is nowhere more evident than in stories where spouses or lovers seek to save their partners. 'The Rusty Knight' was sufficiently engaging that it was used for the title of two twentieth-century collections of Volkmann-Leander's stories. It tells the story of a knight whose wicked conduct is punished by God causing one side of his body to be afflicted with rust. His wife wishes to cure him and is told by a hermit that she must become a beggar, collect a hundred golden guilders and then go with him and put the money in the church poor-box. In trying to accomplish this, the wife undergoes great hardship and also gives birth to a child. Meanwhile, the knight too goes to the hermit and is told to do good and pray in all the churches, if he wants to find his wife again. The wife has only collected two guilders when the knight encounters her and the child and is moved by compassion. He does not recognize her, but puts a purse with more than a hundred guilders in her lap – it is everything he has. The cloak drops from her head, and he sees that he has given the money to his own wife. She puts it in the poor-box, saying she wanted to save him, but he has saved himself. This story has some similarity with the medieval tale of *Der arme Heinrich* (Poor Henry) by Hartmann von Aue, in which a knight who neglects God is afflicted with leprosy and can only be cured by a young girl freely giving her life-blood for him. At the final moment, just before she is to be operated on by a surgeon, Henry undergoes a change of heart, refuses to allow her to sacrifice herself and through that refusal is himself cured. Volkmann-Leander's tale is less extreme in the sacrifice demanded, but the idea that sacrificial love can lead to a godless man's change of heart is just the same.

Clearly, it is impossible to deal separately with all Volkmann-Leander's tales, but to conclude I want to mention 'The Three Sisters with Glass Hearts', since as well as forming part of the complete book it was included in two general anthologies. It appeared with the title 'The Three Sisters and their Glass Hearts', wrongly stated as being 'From the Russian' and without Volkmann-Leander's name, in *The Golden Fairy Book* (London: Hutchinson & Co., no date). A different translation was published as 'The Three Princesses with Glass Hearts' in *The Dwarf's Tailor and Others. Fairy Tales from all Nations*, collected by Zoe Dana Underhill (London: Osgood, McIlvaine & Co., 1897). A king and queen have three daughters with fragile hearts of glass. The first breaks hers looking out of a window and dies; the second cracks hers, but keeps going nonetheless; the third will need a husband who is both a glazier and a king. This latter princess has a very fine page to carry her train and wishes he could fill the part. He trains to become a glazier and then learns that the second condition has been dropped because it has proved impossible to find the combination. The new condition is that he should please the princess and have smooth hands (or 'velvet paws' as it says in the original), so of course he fills the bill. Not only do they marry and have children, but the second princess – the one with the cracked heart – lives on and helps with their education. As the narrator says, articles that are cracked and don't break often survive a long time.

Of the four fairytale authors considered in this chapter Volkmann-Leander has probably dated the least. While several of his tales use traditional fairytale motifs and reveal the influence of Andersen, they are far from being purely imitative. They display a delightful, wry sense of humour as well as common-sense wisdom in the matter of human relationships. Volkmann-Leander writes with subtlety and profound conviction about matters that may appear simple, but are never superficial. His prose is smooth, unshowy and reassuring. Perhaps he was the last person able to write fairytales with such an unstudied optimism. Writers of fairytales in the twentieth century tend to be more ironic, to subvert the genre and infuse it with doubts and questions.

As a tailpiece to this chapter it is not out of place to mention, as an indicator of the impact that German fairytales had on an English writer, one of the most popular of Victorian literary fairytales – John Ruskin's *The King of the Golden River*, first published in 1851 by George Allen of Orpington, but frequently reprinted right into the twentieth century. Ruskin composed this tale in 1841 for the twelve year old Euphemia Chalmers Gray (Effie), whom he married in 1848. At the time of writing Ruskin (1819-1900) was around twenty-two and at the brink of gaining widespread attention with the first volume of *Modern Painters* (1843). *The King of the Golden River*, which first appeared without Ruskin's name, was illustrated by Richard Doyle, who had previously illustrated John Edward Taylor's translation of a selection of the tales of the Brothers Grimm, *The Fairy Ring* (1846). Ruskin was clearly a devotee of the Grimms, and his invented tale follows the typical structure he had learnt from them, but is more expansive and prone to slip occasionally into Victorian verbosity.

The story is set in the mountains of Stiria (Ruskin's spelling) and centres on three brothers, the older two being typically wicked, while the youngest is victimized by them and wholly virtuous. Their names link up with their roles, as the eldest is called Schwartz ('Black'), the youngest Gluck (presumably from German Glück, 'good fortune, happiness'), while the middle brother has the generic name Hans ('Jack'). Unlike the traditional fairytale, Ruskin's does not end with the youngest brother's marriage to a princess; in fact, it has no female characters at all. It is instead a kind of disguised treatise on the values of different kinds of human society. It opens with the older brothers cultivating the Treasure Valley in which they live, destroying birds and animals that do not suit them, exploiting their servants and refusing to pay them. Their lack of care for the world of nature and human beings results in their valley suffering an inundation (an echo of the Biblical Flood) after a visit by a strange gentleman who turns out to be the South West Wind Esquire, as it states on his visiting card.

The brothers then move to a large city where the older two continue their wicked ways, manufacturing gold goods debased with copper. They throw a golden mug belonging to Gluck into their furnace, but later, in their absence, there emerges from it a golden dwarf, who announces himself as the King of the Golden River and tells Gluck that whoever climbs the mountain and casts three drops of holy water into the source of the Golden River will find it turned into gold. The Golden River is the name given to a waterfall the brothers could see from the Treasure Valley glowing golden in the evening sunlight. Curiously, its water does not flow into their valley, but into another one. Each of the brothers attempts to perform the arduous deed, but the older two gain their holy water by theft or deception and fail to give anything to drink to the thirsty dog, small child and old man that they encounter on their ascent of the mountain. Gluck, quite expectedly, succeeds, as he is prepared to help those in need. The dog turns into the King of the Golden River, who picks a lily with three drops of dew on it for Gluck to cast into the torrent. The Treasure Valley is restored to its state of fertility, since, as Ruskin says, 'the inheritance, which had been lost by cruelty, was regained by love'.

The King of the Golden River reflects a peculiarly masculine society; it contains no mother, sister, wife, daughter, witch or fairy, not even a stepmother. But neither does it have any aristocracy apart from the dwarf King of the Golden River himself. (Great Britain had for a long time had only a constitutional monarch, though Queen Victoria's uncle established himself with greater powers when he succeeded to the throne of Hanover as King Ernest Augustus in 1837.) Ruskin's story moves from an oppressive, quasi-feudal agricultural society by way of a corrupt kind of urban industrialism to a paradise or Utopia that is a return to the land, the Treasure Valley, but with a complete transformation of human values. As with the Grimms' story 'The Golden Bird', from which Ruskin seems to have drawn several ideas, the gold is symbolic of the highest value in life. It indicates prosperity and happiness rather than simply economic wealth. The story works well on several levels, but to a modern reader it raises questions that Ruskin may not consciously have been aware of. Given that his marriage to Effie was annulled in 1854 on the grounds of non-consummation, we can perhaps read his omission of any female characters, especially a spouse for Gluck, as indicative of his own unreadiness to deal with the sexual aspect of life. It would be rather unusual, in writing a fairytale for a twelve year old girl, to exclude altogether the idea of a romantic marriage such as we find in 'Aschenputtel', 'Rapunzel', 'Snow-White' or 'Dornröschen', to mention only a few of Grimms' most popular tales. But at this stage in his life Ruskin was more concerned with himself as Gluck and his test with the Golden River. It isn't unreasonable to think of Gluck's climbing of the mountain as equivalent to the intellectual heights that Ruskin was himself in the process of scaling. But given the emphasis on the debased gold forged in the city, we may also understand the gold in the Golden River as indicative of the economic wealth he aimed to accrue through his intellectual endeavours.

However, in the idea of the Treasure Valley Ruskin expresses his antipathy to the industrial city, as, like so many other writers of fairytales, he embraces the potent dream of a fertile and harmonious rural paradise. If we compare the elegiac conclusion of Robert Reinick's *The King of Root Valley and his Curious Daughter* with Ruskin's optimistic ending to *The King of the Golden River*, it isn't a simple matter of Reinick accepting, however reluctantly, the inexorable onward march of history and Ruskin resisting it. Along with his advocacy of a return to the land, Ruskin is demanding a change in the way that human beings behave towards one another.

Schwartz and Hans destroy themselves as they destroy others in their materialistic pursuit of wealth. The future belongs to Gluck, who is pure in heart, truthful and always willing to share what he has with those in need. The brutality of arbitrarily wielded power has to give way to a situation of respect, co-operation and mutual support.[87]

---

[87] For a much fuller discussion of *The King of the Golden River*, with different emphases, see U. C. Knoepflmacher, *Ventures into Childland: Victorians, Fairy Tales and Femininity* (Chicago and London: University of Chicago Press, 1998), pp. 36-72.

15. Clemens Brentano's Fairytales

The fairytales of Clemens Brentano were among the last works of German Romanticism to come to the notice of English-speaking children. Readers were already long familiar with the fairytales of the Brothers Grimm and Wilhelm Hauff, with several of Fouqué's stories, especially his perennially appealing *Undine* and, a little less, the heroic *Sintram*, also with Chamisso's *Peter Schlemihl* and E. T. A. Hoffmann's *Nutcracker*. In addition there were selections from Musäus and their namesake Albert Ludwig Grimm and from their competitor in the field of traditional tales, Ludwig Bechstein. But Brentano's fairytales were a different kettle of fish – leisurely, self-indulgently whimsical and fantastic, written with such shifting focusses of attention that it is difficult to know just who he was writing for, apart from himself. Some of the tales circulated in manuscript during his lifetime, but he was ambivalent about them and could not resist later rewriting and amplifying them. It was only after his death that they were finally published, edited by Guido Görres, as *Die Märchen des Clemens Brentano* (Stuttgart and Tübingen: J. G. Cotta, 2 vols., 1846-47). The opening passage of the 'Rheinmärchen' (Fairytale of the Rhine) and the whole of 'Myrtenfräulein' (Myrtle Maiden) had been published twenty years earlier, without Brentano's name, at the instigation of his friend Johann Friedrich Böhmer in the Frankfurt magazine *Iris* in 1826-27, and plans were then afoot to publish these and other tales properly, but Brentano's desire to rework them resulted in the project running into the sand. Several years later a vastly amplified version of *Gockel und Hinkel* was published separately as *Gockel Hinkel Gakeleia* (Frankfurt: Schmerber, 1838), but succeeding generations have preferred the earlier, rather than the later, versions of Brentano's fairytales.

264 Telling Tales

Clemens Brentano (1778-1842) was born in Ehrenbreitstein, one of the great fortresses on the Rhine, the son of an Italian father and a German mother. He was not cut out for joining the Frankfurt firm of his wealthy merchant father, but became instead one of the leading writers of German Romanticism, publishing poems, plays and prose fiction in profusion. With his friend Achim von Arnim he edited the immensely influential collection of German popular songs and ballads entitled *Des Knaben Wunderhorn* (The Boy's Magic Horn) (Heidelberg: Mohr und Zimmer, 1806-08). He is probably best known today as an outstanding lyric poet, the creator of the Loreley legend with his ballad 'Lore Lay' and the author of one of the most popular Romantic novellas, the *Geschichte vom braven Kasperl und dem schönen Annerl* (1817). This latter was actually the first of Brentano's prose works to be translated into English, some thirty years after it was first published in German, as *Honor; or, the Story of Brave Casper and the Fair Annerl*, translated by T. W. Appell (London: John Chapman, 1847).

It was going on for another forty years before selections from Brentano's fairytales were published in English, so they were not taken up in the same way as the Brothers Grimm or Hauff. That they were translated at all is due to the efforts of the bilingual daughter of the German poet Ferdinand Freiligrath (1810-76), who settled as an émigré in London in 1846 and remained there for twenty years before returning to Germany. Kate Freiligrath Kroeker (1845-1904), was married to a German businessman and played a small part in London's literary life in the 1870s and 1880s, translating her father's poetry and writing articles in the *Athenaeum*.[88] *Fairy Tales from Brentano*, told in English by Kate Freiligrath Kroeker, appeared in 1884 (London: T. Fisher Unwin). This proved popular enough for a second volume to follow in 1887 – *New Fairy Tales from Brentano* – from the same publisher. Both volumes were illustrated by F. Carruthers Gould (1844-1925), who had only recently changed career from working on the stock exchange to being a cartoonist and caricaturist. They enjoyed a number of reprints: *Fairy Tales* in 1890, 1911 and 1925, *New Fairy Tales* in 1902. Kate Kroeker provided a biographical introduction to her first volume and declared herself 'proud to be the first to introduce them to English children'. The fairytales she translated are as follows:

Fairy Tales:

'Das Märchen von den Märchen oder Liebseelchen' = 'Dear-my-

---

88 Rosemary Ashton, *Little Germany. German Refugees in Victorian Britain* (Oxford and New York: Oxford University Press, 1986), pp. 95 and 247.

Soul'
'Hüpfenstich' = 'The Story of Sir Skip-and-a-Jump'
'Dilldapp' = 'The Story of Ninny Noddy'
'Die fünf Söhne des Schulmeisters Klopfstock' = 'The Story of Wackemhard and of his Five Sons'

New Fairy Tales:
'Gockel und Hinkel' (earlier version) = 'The Story of Gockel, Hinkel, and Gackeleia'
'Witzenspitzel' = 'The Story of Frisky Wisky'
'Myrtenfräulein' = 'The Story of the Myrtle Maiden'
'Komanditchen' = 'The Story of Brokerina'
'Märchen von dem Müller Radlof (Rheinmärchen)' = 'The Story of Old Father Rhine and the Miller'

Brentano had been interested in writing fairytales on the basis of traditional plots from the time of his collaboration with Arnim on the *Wunderhorn*, and what he wanted to do then was to rework Italian fairytales for German children. He admired the two Low German tales that the painter Philipp Otto Runge had sent to Arnim and were incorporated in the Grimms' collection, i.e. 'The Juniper Tree' and 'The Fisherman and his Wife'. He also begged copies of tales that the Grimms themselves had collected, so that the oldest extant form of the original core of the Grimms' tales is, in fact, the manuscript copy that they sent Brentano and that eventually turned up among his posthumous papers. But despite Brentano's professed admiration for Runge's two tales, he did not like the sober form in which the Grimms' tales first appeared (the 1812-15 first edition). Likewise, the Grimms did not approve of what Brentano did in his fanciful reworkings of traditional material. They themselves were first and foremost scholars, while Brentano was a poet and creative writer.

The Italian tales that Brentano wanted to retell came from the seventeenth-century collection of tales by the Neapolitan writer Giambattista Basile called the *Pentameron* (1634-36). Basile's fifty tales were recounted within a framework narrative, on the pattern of Boccaccio's *Decameron*. Basile kept close to the pattern of traditional tales as regards plot and length, but he used all the rhetorical devices of a master of Baroque prose and verse to make the tales appeal to the cultivated taste of his day, despite declaring them to be written for children. He composed the *Pentameron* in the Neapolitan dialect, and it circulated mainly in Neapolitan editions until the mid eighteenth century, when editions in Bolognese and Italian began to be produced.[89] Outside Italy it seems that the first translation of any part of the *Pentameron* occurred in the volume of the *Bibliothèque universelle des romans* for September 1777, in which are given three tales ('Peruonto' (I, 3), 'Sapia Liccarda' (III, 4) and 'The Raven' (IV, 9)).[90] This provided the stimulus for Christoph Martin Wieland's verse tale 'Peruonte oder die Wünsche' (Peruonto or the Wishes) in 1778.[91] We might also recall that Musäus's 'Chronicles of the Three Sisters' derives from Basile's 'The Three Animal Kings'. The English-speaking world gained its first taste of the *Pentameron* through Thomas Keightley, who translated 'The Dragon' (IV, 5), 'Gagliuso' (II, 4) (an ancestor of 'Puss-in-Boots') and 'The Goatface' (I, 8) for the first edition of his influential book, *The Fairy Mythology* (1828). He followed this up with two further tales – 'The Serpent' (II, 5) and 'Peruonto' – in his *Tales and Popular Fictions; their Resemblance and Transmission from Country to Country* (1834). A fuller selection of thirty tales appeared in a new translation by John Edward Taylor in 1848.

Brentano was fortunate enough to possess two editions of the *Pentameron* with the Neapolitan text (Rome, 1679, and Naples, 1749). From Brentano's personal copy it appears he intended to rework twenty-five of Basile's tales, but in fact managed to complete only ten.[92] The Grimms, meanwhile, had borrowed Brentano's 1749 edition and had made abstracts of all Basile's tales and included them in the 1822 volume of notes to the *Kinder- und Hausmärchen*. Jacob Grimm had also made a translation of 'The Serpent' (II, 5), which was published in the *Taschenbuch für Freunde altdeutscher Zeit und Kunst* (Pocket-book for Friends of Ancient German Times and Art) (Cologne, 1816).[93] Penzer, in his bibliographical study of the *Pentameron*, goes on to deal with the further complex history of German and English partial editions, revealing their cross-connexions, but he does not mention Brentano's work at all.

The tales of Brentano's translated by Kroeker have their sources in the *Pentameron* as follows. All the plots correspond to standard tale-types in the *Index of Folk-tale Types* by Antti Aarne and Stith Thompson and are identified by AT and the appropriate number:

---

89 N. M. Penzer (ed.), *The Pentamerone of Giambattista Basile*, translated from the Italian of Benedetto Croce (London: John Lane the Bodley Head Ltd; New York: E. P. Dutton & Company, 1932), vol. 2, p. 171.
90 Ibid., vol. 2, p. 222.
91 Ibid., vol. 1, pp. lxvii-lxviii
92 Max Preitz (ed.), *Brentanos Werke* (Leipzig and Vienna: Bibliographisches Institut, 1914), vol. 3, p. 8.
93 Penzer, vol. 2, pp. 225-26.

'Dear-My-Soul' = frame-story
'Sir Skip-and-a-Jump' = 'The Flea', I, 5 (AT 425B)
'Ninny Noddy' = 'The Story of the Ogre', I, 1 (AT 563)
'Wackemhard and his Five Sons' = 'The Five Sons', V, 7 (AT 653)
'Gockel, Hinkel, and Gackeleia' = 'The Cock's Stone', IV, 1 (AT 560)
'Frisky Wisky' = 'Corvetto', III, 7 (AT 1525)
'The Myrtle Maiden' = 'The Myrtle', I, 2 (cf. AT 652)
'Brokerina' = 'Pinto Smalto', V, 3 (AT 425)

The fact that all these tales correspond to standard tale-types means that they are not in essence invented stories of the kind written, in the main, by Andersen or Oscar Wilde, but Brentano treats his sources in such a fanciful and elaborate way that much in his writing may elude the comprehension of younger readers. He writes, in fact, with two different readerships in mind – children for the basic story in terms of its plot, adults for his contemporary references, use of names, ironic asides and amplificatory details.[94]

Some idea of Brentano's procedures may be gained by comparing 'Liebseelchen' ('Dear-my-Soul') with the frame-story of the *Pentameron*. A king has a serious daughter whom he attempts to make laugh by organizing a variety of amusements. In the last of these an old woman's discomfiture causes the princess to laugh, whereupon she is cursed by the old woman not to marry until she finds a certain prince. The princess sets out on the quest and gains three nuts from three fairies (old women) which are to be broken open only in situations of great need. She finds the prince in a marble tomb and has to weep sufficient tears to fill a vessel in order to restore him to life. Exhausted by her efforts to do this, she falls asleep and is thwarted by a black female slave, who fills the vessel and marries the resurrected prince. When the slave becomes pregnant she grows very hostile to the princess, who has remained in the city and attracted the prince's attention. The slave threatens her husband with damaging the baby in her womb, if he does not turn away from the princess. The latter breaks open each of her three nuts in turn, and the magic devices that they contain are instantly coveted and acquired by the slave. The last of these devices is a golden doll, which sparks in her the desire to hear fairytales, for which the prince has to call together ten women, each of whom tells a story on five successive days.

---

94 For the concepts of 'single address', 'double address' and 'dual address' in the target readerships of children's books see Peter Hunt, *An Introduction to Children's Literature* (Oxford and New York: Oxford University Press, 1994), pp. 12-15.

DEAR-MY-SOUL.

HERE once lived an old king who had an only daughter whom he loved very dearly, and so called Dear-my-Soul. But unfortunately she was born under so melancholy a star that she had never laughed once in the course of her whole life. So people used to call her Sad-

24. *Fairy Tales from Brentano.* Illustration by F. Carruthers Gould (1884).

Clemens Brentano's Fairytales 269

At this point the fifty stories of the *Pentameron* make their appearance, and the frame-story is only concluded when the princess herself tells her own story and the prince, despite the slave's pregnancy, has her buried alive and marries the princess.

Basile uses a variety of names in his tales, but they tend to be common names for persons and simple descriptive names for places. Thus, we have here 'a king of Vallepelosa' (wooded valley), which Brentano converts into 'Schattentalien', a combination of 'shady valley' and 'Italy', which Kroeker leaves out altogether. Felix Liebrecht, who translated Basile into German in 1846, translated it as 'Buschtal' (bushy valley). Basile calls the king's laughless daughter Zoza (a diminutive of Lucrezia), while Brentano gives her the descriptive name 'Liebseelchen', adroitly turned by Kroeker into the English 'Dear-my-Soul'. The old woman is nameless in Basile, but Brentano takes a pot shot at the French with his extended caricature of 'Mademoiselle Zéphise la marquise de Pimpernelle' and the two dancing masters who accompany her, and it is the absurdity of French manners that causes the princess to laugh. Mademoiselle Zéphise has a list of clichés with which she operates – amour, plaisir, le coeur, souvenir, bonheur, douceur. Brentano's hostility to the French, which can be seen at several other points in his tales, almost certainly dates from the French occupation of Alsace and the left bank of the Rhine by revolutionary forces in 1793, when he was a boy of sixteen. Brentano calls Basile's nameless slave 'eine häßliche, böse, schwarze Mohrin' (an ugly, wicked, black Moor) and gives her the name 'Russika' with the dual associations of Ruß (soot) and Russian. Kroeker understandably calls her 'Sootica'. The prince who rises from the tomb is called Taddeo by Basile and Röhropp, a dialect form meaning 'stir up', by Brentano, but Kroeker doesn't give him a name.

The English translator of Brentano's fairytales has several problems. With the proper names she tries to find English equivalents for Brentano's jokes and on the whole does this well. She also often looks for English equivalents for descriptions of specifically German characteristics and habits, especially those to do with eating, drinking and clothes. Occasionally things will be omitted where, for example, something taken for granted in Germany might give offence in England. Thus, where Brentano has a verse in which Mademoiselle Zéphise 'Fuhr in die Hölle', Kroeker's rendering avoids the reference to hell. As 'Pimpernelle' and 'hell' are rhymes crying out for each other in English, the avoidance of the word must be deliberate.

Brentano's stories are full of passages in which he suddenly goes into rhyme. Sometimes this is a song, but often it is simply part of the narrative, and as Brentano was a skilful versifier it reads fluently and with considerable charm. These passages, generally in rhyming couplets, present awkward problems for the translator, and while she conveys their surface meaning well enough, her versions often appear banal or clumsy where Brentano has a light and easy touch.

The second story in Kroeker's first volume from Brentano is 'Sir Skip-and-a-Jump, which opens with the death of a queen at the unexpected birth of a daughter. When the king wants to remove his baby daughter from the old woman who is feeding her, he has to promise to pardon the first criminal to offend him and to nourish him as best he can. This turns out to be a flea, which feeds on the king's blood and grows to the size of a calf. In the German original the old woman has the baby 'an der Brust' (at her breast), but Kroeker changes this to 'feeding her from a bottle'. Presumably the idea of breast-feeding was considered indelicate, at least in a children's book, at the period that Kroeker was making her translation.

When it comes to guessing the identity of the extraordinary creature that has been fed with the king's blood – it is stated to be the size of an ox in the German, which Kroeker tones down to a calf – several suggestions are put forward, ending as follows: 'Endlich trat ein Professor auf und behauptete, es sei die Haut eines afrikanischen Buschmanns; der Seelenverkäufer aber behauptete, sie sei von einem Amsterdamer Juden'. The first part of this clearly caused no second thoughts at the time, since Kroeker translates: 'Finally a professor made a very learned speech, in which he proved it to be the skin of an African bushman'. She silently omits Brentano's anti-Semitic jibe: 'the recruiting sergeant, however, asserted it was that of an Amsterdam Jew'. There is a passage in 'Gockel, Hinkel, and Gackeleia' where Kroeker softens another example of Brentano's anti-Semitism. When Gockel has transported the two white mice across a river, he meets three old men who want to buy his old cock in exchange for an old billy-goat, knowing that the cock has in its crop a jewel from the magic ring of King Solomon. Brentano disparagingly refers to them as 'some old Jews who were great natural philosophers; they were taking an old billy-goat and an old, skinny nanny-goat on a rope to the Frankfurt fair'. Kroeker tactfully calls them 'three old Oriental philosophers' and omits the reference to Frankfurt. There was a strong, wealthy Jewish community in Frankfurt, where Brentano's father worked. Its most famous member was Mayer Amschel Rothschild (1743-1812), the founder of the great banking house, who financed the war against

Napoleon. One wonders whether Brentano's unpleasant jibes derive from envy at the Rothschilds' success. The Amsterdam Jew shares a suggestive first syllable with Amschel Rothschild.

In the introduction to her first volume of translations Kroeker had declared that, even in 'its simple and original form', 'Gockel, Hinkel, and Gackeleia' was too full of puns and quips to translate, but she had second thoughts and included a version in her second volume. Despite her title she was actually translating Brentano's early 'Gockel und Hinkel', not the hugely expanded form published separately as *Gockel Hinkel Gakeleia*, which was almost four times as long. We have to keep in mind that she was attempting to make Brentano accessible to English children, not to provide an accurate translation faithful in all details. Children would have been baffled by many of the German names that Brentano uses and that would have been noted more by his adult readers. What Kroeker does is to change Brentano's 'double address' as much as possible to a 'single address', since she is more concerned with providing enjoyment for her child readers.

Both in the original and in the translations Brentano's tales exceed the compass of the traditional fairytale. They are comparable in length to those of Musäus or Hauff, but while Hauff studiously avoided any love interest in his fairytales, the majority of Brentano's have to do with the search for a spouse. Again, while Hauff, the Grimms and Bechstein employ a straightforward, sober style of narration, Brentano's tales are full of winks and nudges, verbal tricks and ironic allusions to contemporary life and events. For example, when he tells how Gockel's ancestral palace was formerly one of the most splendid in Germany, he cannot resist blaming its destruction on the French, 'who are accustomed to doing things like this'. Brentano had lived through a period from 1792 to 1814 when the French had wrought havoc in Germany, while Kroeker, at the end of the nineteenth century, simply says: 'but the enemy had totally wrecked and destroyed it', leaving out any reference to the French. For the most part Kroeker removes the names of petty German states and cities, replacing them with English counterparts. The fact that the 'Rauhgraf von Hanau' becomes the 'Marquis of Dorking' shows how much Kroeker worked at finding an appropriate English association, here, of course, with Dorking hens. Hinkel's ancestors come, punningly, from Hennegau (Hainault), which Kroeker converts into 'the industrious race of the Langshans'. The king who is obsessed with eggs (king of the real town of Gelnhausen in the German) inhabits Eggville and is called Egg-Gorgius in Kroeker (the German is Eifrassius).

She can't everywhere follow Brentano, but in one place at least she inserts an invention of her own. In Brentano's expansive description of the mouse city built of cheese, melons, pumpkins and the like he has half a sentence devoted to the cemetery. Kroeker adds: 'It was built by their famous king, Mousolus I., and hence was called the Mousoleum'. The German language would have allowed Brentano the same pun, but he did not make it. Perhaps he expected his readers to make it for themselves since it is so obvious.

Brentano's 'Dilldapp' (Kroeker's 'Ninny Noddy') is a version of the tale that many will know better from the Grimms' 'The Table, the Donkey and the Stick'. Basile and Brentano, too, have a donkey that provides gold and jewels, but Kroeker changes this to a goose that lays golden eggs. Brentano's tale has a neutral expression to describe the donkey's production of gold, in place of Basile's reference to the donkey's rear, so there was no need for the translator to avoid an impropriety. However, a little later in the story Brentano does have the substitute donkey soil Dilldapp's mother's bed-linen in a nasty way. At the end of the German original Brentano's hostility to all things French is expressed once more. Not only do Dilldapp's sisters all change their allegorical French names to German individual names, but the cudgel also beats everything French out of town. Kroeker omits these matters entirely.

Kroeker deals in a quite similar way with Brentano's 'Klopfstock' (her 'Wackemhard'), but the many allusions and associations in the German text are rather different from those posing problems in 'Dilldapp'. Again, the plot is better known in the Grimms' 'The Four Skilful Brothers'. Kroeker does well with English equivalents for the names of characters, and she even finds a suitable hymn and song to do service for Paul Gerhardt's 'Nun ruhen alle Wälder' (the 'Old Hundredth') and Grimmelshausen's 'Komm Trost der Nacht, o Nachtigall' ('Under the Greenwood Tree') respectively. However, the German text is replete with other allusions, such as that to the hermit episode in Grimmelshausen's great novel of the Thirty Years War, *Simplicissimus*, which would be apparent to the educated adult German reader, though hardly to children. Naturally enough, Kroeker leaves such things out. But even with her omissions of some verse passages and other details the story remains a very long one.

Both 'Frisky Wisky' and 'The Myrtle Maiden' in Kroeker's second volume are shorter tales, more the usual length of a traditional fairytale. These were tales that Brentano composed early and did not rework and embellish. Nonetheless, they both contain humorous and symbolic names

Clemens Brentano's Fairytales 273

of a kind that give Brentano's fairytales an archness or self-regard that some readers find irritating. However, Frisky Wisky is rather too much a nursery tale name in English (cf. Henny Penny, Cocky Locky) and loses the connotations of clever cunning that the German Witzenspitzel conjures up. Brentano's tale 'Witzenspitzel' is a variant of the widespread tale-type 'The Master Thief', of which the Grimms also present an example. This is a comic tale involving a series of incredible tricks, at the end of which the hero wins a bride. Kroeker translated this as 'Frisky Wisky' in *New Fairy Tales from Brentano*, and her version is lively and idiomatic. However, the story is one of the very few by Brentano of which another translation was made. This is to be found in *The Diamond Fairy Book*, with illustrations by H. R. Millar (London: Hutchinson & Co., [1897]), a collection of both traditional and invented fairytales from many countries. This was one of a series, made on the model of Andrew Lang's 'colour' fairy books. Brentano's story is here called 'Wittysplinter', and the translation is anonymous. The German original gives symbolic names to the human and animal figures in the story. The following list gives the German name, followed by Kroeker's and that of the anonymous version: König Rundherum (King Roundabout for both), the giant Labelang (Stretch-Yourself, Sleepyhead), his wife Dickedull (Burst-your-Seams, Thickasmud), the lion Hahnenbang (Shy-Cock, Hendread), the bear Honigbart (Honey-Tooth, Honeybeard), the wolf Lämmerfrass (Lamb's Worry, Lambsnapper), the dog Hasenschreck (Hare's Fright, Harescare), the horse Flügelbein (Wing-legs, Flyinglegs), the neighbouring Queen, Frau Flugs (Queen Nimble, Madam Flosk), her daughter, Princess Flink (Flink for both). The anonymous translation on the whole is a little more formal than Kroeker's, but both convey the original well.

The hero of 'The Myrtle Maiden' is Prince Wetschwuth in German (Wedgwood in English) with a capital Porzellania (Porcelania). The punning or semi-allegorical names are even more obvious in the much longer story of 'Komanditchen' ('Brokerina'), the major part of which is an extended skit on the world of commerce as Brentano had uncongenially experienced it in his youth in his father's business as a wealthy Frankfurt merchant. Only at the end of the tale does Brentano take up his source in the *Pentameron* and describe how Komanditchen, dissatisfied with all those who sue for her hand in marriage, makes and bakes herself an artificial prince out of all kinds of sweet and delicious ingredients. The German tale breaks off before the actual conclusion, but Kroeker provides the ending inherent in the premisses of the plot.

In addition to these Italian tales Brentano also wrote a cycle based on German legends of the Rhine. Kroeker translated part of this as 'The Story of Old Father Rhine and the Miller'. It is a rather rambling narrative based on the popular legend of Bishop Hatto of Mainz, whose cruelty towards his own people in time of famine was punished by his being eaten alive by mice which pursued him to a tower on an island in the middle of the Rhine, where he thought he could escape them. The legend was versified in English by Robert Southey, and it was retold in prose by Mary C. Rowsell in *Hatto's Tower: and Other Stories* (London, Glasgow, Edinburgh, and Dublin: Blackie & Son, 1887), but it was included in virtually every collection of Rhine legends. Brentano substituted a King of Mainz for the Bishop and incorporated the story into a feud between the King of Mainz and the Queen of Trier and a love-story involving a miller and Ameleya, the daughter of the King of Mainz. As we have already noted, Brentano had himself been instrumental in creating the image of the 'Romantic' Rhine with his ballad of the 'Lore Lay', so his 'Story of Old Father Rhine and the Miller' can be understood as part of the same process.

Kroeker's two volumes of translations provide strong evidence of the surge of interest in German literature during the 1880s and 1890s. To them we can add another item – *The Wondrous Tale of Cocky, Clucky, and Cackle*, freely translated from the German of Brentano by C. W. Heckethorn (London: J. Hogg, [1889]), a separate rendering of the long *Tale of Gockel, Hinkel und Gakeleia*. But despite Brentano's fame in Germany, he does not seem to have made a great impact in English. Kroeker's translations were not reprinted after 1925. It is not entirely surprising that, even though both she and Heckethorn had made translations of *Gockel, Hinkel und Gakeleia*, the American writer Doris Orgel was so totally unaware of them that she claimed her *Tale of Gockel, Hinkel & Gackeliah*, illustrated by Maurice Sendak (New York: Random House, 1961) to be translated for the first time into English.

16. Learning about German History

Alongside the many German children's books that were translated into English during the nineteenth century we find a variety of books by British authors that presented aspects of German history to children and young people. Some of these deal with important historical figures. Maria Elizabeth Budden wrote *Hofer, the Tyrolese* (London: John Harris and Sons, 1824) and Charlotte Maria Tucker, who wrote under the initials A.L.O.E. ('A Lady Of England'), produced *The Life of Luther* (London: The Book Society, 1873). This was followed by *The Boyhood of Martin Luther* by Henry Mayhew (London and Edinburgh: Gall & Inglis, c. 1890). Other writers wrote historical fiction set in such crucial periods of German history as the Thirty Years War, the reign of Frederick the Great and the Franco-Prussian War. G. A. Henty was the most notable of these authors, but there were many others. A number of eminent historians concerned themselves with particular periods of German history. Samuel Rawson Gardiner wrote *The Thirty Years' War 1618-1648* (London: Longmans, Green & Co., 1874) and L. Cecil Jane *From Metternich to Bismarck* (Oxford: Clarendon Press, 1910). James Bryce's *The Holy Roman Empire* (Oxford: T. & G. Shrimpton, 1864) covers a large range of German history, but it is hardly aimed at school pupils, so it is outside our purview.

All of these books merit attention, but what is more interesting in the present context is the fairly small corpus of books for children that cover the full range of German history from the period of the Roman Empire onwards. This includes textbooks designed for different age-groups as well as more general works. The books that I have chosen for examination were first published in the period from 1841 to 1913, and several were reprinted

276   *Telling Tales*

many times, often being brought up to date in the process. They are as follows:

> Julia Corner, *A History of Germany, and the Austrian Empire, from the Earliest Period to the Present Time, Adapted for Youth, Schools, and Families* (London: Thomas Dean & Co., 1841. Illustrated)
>
> [Robert B. Paul], *A History of Germany, from the Invasion of Germany by Marius to the Battle of Leipzic, 1813. On the Plan of Mrs. Markham's Histories. For the Use of Young Persons* (London: John Murray, 1847. Illustrated)
>
> Wilhelm Pütz, *Handbook of Modern Geography and History. Part III.* Translated from the German by the Rev. R. B. Paul (London: Francis and John Rivington, 1850. Not illustrated)
>
> Anonymous, *Scenes and Narratives from German History* (London: SPCK, and New York: Pitt, Young, & Co., c. 1858-60. Illustrated)
>
> James Sime, *History of Germany* (London: Macmillan & Co., 1874. Not illustrated)
>
> Charlotte M. Yonge, *Aunt Charlotte's Stories of German History for the Little Ones* (Belfast and New York: Marcus Ward & Co., 1878. Illustrated)
>
> S. Baring-Gould, with the collaboration of Arthur Gilman, *Germany* (London: T. Fisher Unwin, 1886. Illustrated)
>
> H. E. Marshall, *A History of Germany*, with illustrations in colour by A. C. Michael (London: Henry Frowde and Hodder & Stoughton, 1913. Illustrated)

Corner, Paul, Pütz and Sime are clearly textbooks. The little SPCK book consists largely of potted biographies, taken from a whole range of German history and aimed at younger children; it reflects an overt Christian moral purpose. Yonge seems to have been marketed as a children's book, and this is also the case with Marshall. Baring-Gould is a popular history that would also appeal to an intelligent young person. Since each of these books takes the narrative up to the time of writing, it seems appropriate to deal with them in chronological order. As most of them are not readily accessible, I have adopted a descriptive-cum-interpretative mode in considering their content, methodology and underlying philosophy.

All of the books provide a chronological survey from the period at which the ancient Germanic peoples impinge on the Roman Empire right through to just before the date of publication. The emphasis by and large is on kings, battles and the struggle for power, but each author also finds space for occasional anecdotes and comments on aspects of social, cultural and, especially, religious history. All the books except those by Pütz and

Learning about German History 277

Sime are illustrated and thus made attractive to children in a way that Lewis Carroll's Alice would have approved, even though she might have found the content hard going.

The history of Germany is not easy to write. The geographical territory claimed for 'Germany' changes from period to period, and in the Middle Ages the Empire struggled in its fateful involvement with Italy. Both modern France and modern Germany include the Merovingian kings, Charlemagne and Lewis the Pious as part of their respective histories, while the title of Corner's book, *A History of Germany, and the Austrian Empire*, adumbrates some of the problems at the modern end. Corner in fact contains separate sections on Hungary and Bohemia in relation to Austria. Similar problems arise with earlier periods: writing about the Reformation, the Thirty Years War or the Napoleonic era demands a perspective that views Germany as part of Europe and not as a separate country on its own. In any case, despite the existence of the Holy Roman Empire, Germany was for centuries politically fragmented until in the nineteenth century Austria was separated off and Germany was united under Prussia. We need now to look at how our chosen authors tackled these problems.

Julia Corner (1798-1875) produced a barrage of children's history books in the early 1840s. Not only was there one dealing with Germany, but others on England, France, Greece, Rome, Scriptural history, China and India, Holland and Belgium, Poland and Russia, Spain and Portugal, Scotland, Ireland, Italy and Switzerland, Denmark, Sweden and Norway. The 1854 edition of *A History of Germany* takes the story to 1851 and covers in some 270 pages material from the ancient Germans onwards. Corner has a generous view of history, including a considerable amount of social, economic and religious history, many illustrative anecdotes and, for the modern period, geographical descriptions. There is a useful map, a ten-page chronological table of principal events and, as a kind of appendix, forty-one pages of questions related directly to the text. The inclusion of questions of this kind derives from Richmal Mangnall's *Questions for the Use of Young People* (1800), generally known as 'Mangnall's Questions'. Corner herself wrote *Questions on the History of Europe*, which she designated 'a sequel to Mangnall's Historical Questions'.

As is the case with most books dealing with Germany, several of the proper names Corner uses are misspelt. Because English-speakers tend to pronounce the German 'berg' and 'burg' in exactly the same way, we find Weinsberg, Nuremberg, Wurtemberg and Königsberg all wrongly given the suffix 'burg'. 'Schelstadt' on the banks of the Rhine, where Charlemagne had a castle (p. 16), is presumably what the Germans call Schlettstadt and the French (since it is in Alsace) Sélestat. Maximilian is spelt in the French way as Maximilien, which suggests that Corner may have been using a French source here. (There is no indication in her preface as to what she used as source material.) She uses the then current English form Ratisbon for the German Regensburg, but the old German form Mentz for what is now called Mainz (French Mayence). From time to time Corner interrupts her chronological narrative with chapters of social history. Thus, we find the feudal system dealt with in 'Germany in the tenth and eleventh centuries'. In the section on 'Germany in the sixteenth century' the extent of material achievement is illustrated with the famous anecdote about the banker Fugger entertaining the Emperor Charles V and demonstrating his wealth by burning a large fire consisting of cinnamon and consigning the Emperor's bonds to the flames. (The motif of burning spices instead of wood as a demonstration of fantastic wealth is also found in the German *Volksbuch* of *Fortunatus*, first published in 1509 and widely reprinted up to the nineteenth century.)

When Corner comes to the post-Napoleonic period, she outlines the many states which made up the Germany of her day, paying particular attention to the British connexion with Hanover and Saxe-Coburg. She notes the fact that Frederick the Great was the grandson of our George I. She mentions the visit of George IV to his kingdom of Hanover in 1821, and also the Duke of Cumberland's accession to the throne of Hanover in 1837 as Ernest Augustus I. She remarks on the latter's revocation of the constitution granted to Hanover by William IV and on the fact that a liberal constitution was not restored until the revolution of 1848. Three pages are devoted to the House of Saxe-Coburg as the principality from which Prince Albert came and married Queen Victoria in 1840.

Corner's book contains far too much information to analyse in detail. Reasonably enough, about two-thirds of the book is devoted to the period from Charles V to the mid-nineteenth century, but the Reformation is oddly dismissed in less than a page while simultaneously being described as 'the most important event that took place in the time of Maximilien the First' (p. 92). 'Secret tribunals of Westphalia', a sensational, but less important topic, then occupies more than four pages. Corner is not always accurate: she has King Conrad I fight against the Huns (p. 25), when she means the Hungarians. She also wrongly declares the Emperor Frederick II to have founded, in addition to the University of Naples, another one at Vienna; but this latter university was not founded until 1365 by Charles V, the second German university after Prague (1348). Just occasionally Corner adopts a rather reprovingly governessy tone. Commenting on the cruelty of the usurper Henry V towards his father Henry IV – the one who stood a penitent in the snow outside the castle of Canossa, waiting to be absolved by Pope Gregory VII – she says: 'We cannot, however, be surprised that a man [Henry V], who could forget his duty towards his aged parent [Henry IV], should also be capable of insulting a minister of religion' (p. 47). The minister of religion she is referring to was the Pope.

Julia Corner's book continued to be reprinted and brought up to date for many years, but it gained a rival as early as 1847 in *A History of Germany. . . On the plan of Mrs. Markham's Histories*, written by the Rev. Robert B. Paul, who identified himself solely by his initials at the end of his introduction. The 'Mrs. Markham' whose name he gives as providing a model for his work was the pseudonym of Elizabeth Penrose (1780-1837), the successful author of, *inter alia*, histories of both England and France. Paul's book enjoyed considerable success: there were new editions in 1853, 1869 and 1882. The 1847 edition ends with the final defeat of Napoleon and his death on St. Helena, but says nothing about the next twenty-five years.

Paul's history is about twice the length of Corner's. With the same chronological spread he has a pretty even weighting of periods and events, i.e., more recent history is not dealt with at noticeably greater length than earlier periods. Although the structure of the book is formed by the sequence of rulers and struggles for power, there is plenty of room for description of other topics, especially religious matters and occasionally art and literature. Each of the sixty-four chapters is followed by a supplement giving information that does not fit straightforwardly into the chronological narrative.

The ideological viewpoint from which Paul looks at German history is more clearly focussed than is the case with Corner. He writes from an Anglican, anti-Catholic position – the Catholic Emancipation Act was as recent as 1829 – and he gives extensive coverage to religious questions. This can be seen in his treatment of Pope Gregory VII (pp. 93-96) compared with the highly positive account of the Emperor Frederick II (pp. 141-44, 146-49, 156-61). In contrast to Corner's perfunctory treatment of the Reformation, Paul provides an extensive coverage of Luther and the Reformation, including a four-page summary of the articles of the Confession of Augsburg.

MARIA THERESA PRESENTING HER INFANT SON TO THE ASSEMBLED STATES. *Page 170.*

25. Copper-engraving by Davenport, after Gilbert in Julia Corner, *The History of Germany and the Austrian Empire. New edition, Revised and Enlarged* (c. 1854).

A further indication of the author's sympathies occurs in the couple of pages he devotes to the persecution of the peasants in the mountains of Salzburg in the early eighteenth century who, in this Catholic territory, wished to be 'evangelical', and were thus banished by the Archbishop. The end of the book points in the same direction, as Paul eulogizes the accomplishments of Blücher and his role in the defeat of Napoleon. He concludes with Blücher's words to a flatterer whose immoderate praise deeply offended him: 'For what do you commend me? It was my recklessness, Gneisenau's cautiousness, AND THE GREAT GOD'S LOVING KINDNESS' (p. 471).

Paul was also involved as the translator of the German historian Wilhelm Pütz's *Handbook of Modern Geography and History*, of which Part III covers European history from the discovery of America to 1848. The book contains nothing to do with geography; it does not even have a map. Germany is treated as part of the inter-state warfare and politics that characterize so much of European history. No country's existence can be dealt with without reference to others. While this is mainly a political history, reflecting rulers, wars, conquests and treaties, there are two sections that give accounts of religion, arts, sciences and the like, mainly in the shape of lists of names. The aim of the book is to provide objective facts, events and dates with little attention to analysis. Unlike all the other history books under discussion, this one eschews all anecdotes or illustrative examples. Personal prejudice breaks through, however, in comments on the most recent times. Pütz remarks that lyric poetry 'during the last ten years has assumed a polemical character, in the disgraceful writings of Heine, Anastasius Grün, Hoffman (sic) of Fallersleben, Freiligrath, K. Beck and Herwegh' (p. 299). All of these were political poets with aims that rendered them inimical to Germany and Austria's rulers. Heine lived in Paris from 1831 until his death in 1856, while Freiligrath fled to England in 1846 and resided there permanently from 1851 to 1867. Hoffmann von Fallersleben is perhaps best known nowadays as the author of 'Deutschland, Deutschland, über Alles', written in 1841, but more famous since German unification in 1870.

Scenes and Narratives from German History was published by the Society for Promoting Christian Knowledge sometime between 1858 and 1860, to judge from the content. This was designed for younger readers than the previously mentioned books and confines itself to dealing with eight personages or events – Hermann, or Arminius; Otho, the Lion (i.e. Otto the Great); Henry IV; Frederic (sic) Barbarossa; Martin Luther; Wallenstein and the Thirty Years War; the Siege of Magdeburg; and Frederic (sic) the Great. The siege of Magdeburg by Tilly, one of the most terrible devastations of the Thirty Years War, in which the city was razed to the ground and its inhabitants slaughtered, is dealt with through the depiction of the fate of an imaginary family, but the other chapters follow the usual pattern of historical narrative.

The text contains a few odd statement. One edition talks about Hermann (Arminius), victor over the Romans in AD 9 in the Teutoburg Forest, as belonging to 'the great Gothic race to which our Anglo-Saxon forefathers belonged' (p. 9), which a later edition corrects to his being 'one of the direct ancestors of our Anglo-Saxon forefathers'. (The Goths were, in fact, just one of the many Germanic tribes of peoples that rubbed up against the Roman Empire, and Hermann was not a Goth.) Rather bizarrely, the author claims that 'the descendants of Hermann's tribe . . . brought the worship of Hermann with them'. False etymologies are adduced to link the ancient road from London to Lincoln known as Ermine Street with both Hermann and the worship of the Saxon sacred pagan statue known as the 'Irmin-sul' (pillar of Irmin). This is sheer fantasy: the name Ermine Street is derived

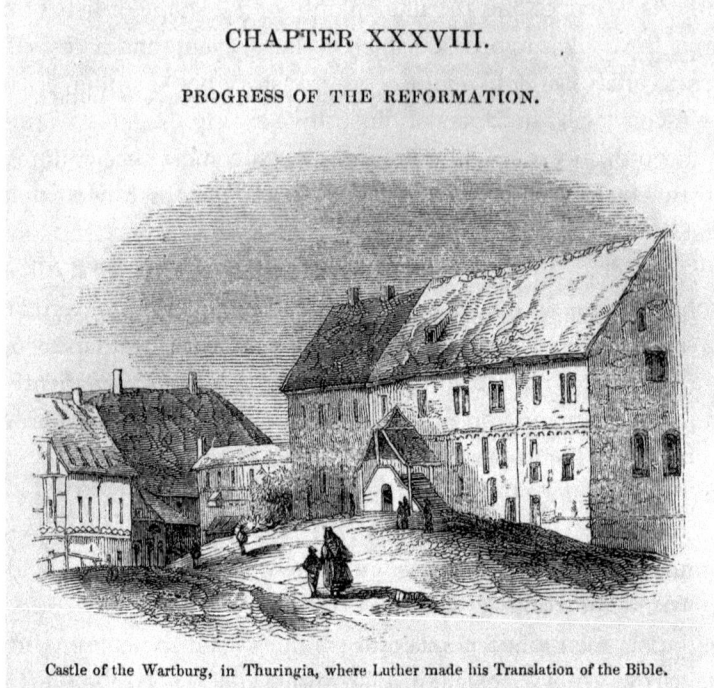

26. *A History of Germany, . . . to the Battle of Leipzig, 1813. On the Plan of Miss Markham's Histories. For the Use of Young Persons* (1847).

from that of the tribe of the Earningas, who have left no other trace of their name.

In a number of places the actions of historical figures are directly related to the expectations placed on the children reading the book. The chapter on Frederic the Great concentrates on his youth and pays less attention to his period as a monarch. The childhood of Henry IV is regarded as a warning: children 'should remember that nothing will help them to become good and useful men and women, so much as learning, while they are young, to do those things which are right, although not pleasant, and learning also to do them because they are right, and in a cheerful manner' (p. 37). Wallenstein is characterized as 'not a good man, and you will soon see that his conduct from this time grew worse and worse. The fact is, that his mind was full of ambition' (p. 124). Frederic the Great is castigated for 'never seeming to think anything of breaking his promise' with regard to Maria Theresa. His promises to other nations were broken too: 'Deliberate, open lying, this was, and it happened no less than four times during the course of the war, in which Prussia was engaged for about five years. Here was the fruit of that friendship with Voltaire, who had taught him to neglect his Bible' (pp. 199-200). History here is seen in terms of examples of good and bad behaviour to be emulated or avoided as appropriate. This is not history as a chronology of supposedly objective facts, but as moral education.

In 1874, in the immediate wake of the Franco-Prussian War, we have the third of the books examined here that was written by a professional historian rather than a writer of children's books or a popular author. James Sime's *History of Germany* forms volume 5 of a 'Historical Course for Schools' edited by Edward A. Freeman. Lucidly written and superbly organized, it presents in twenty chapters the history of Germany from the earliest times right up to the unification under Prussia. The chapters are subdivided into small numbered sections, each with a summary heading for ease of understanding. The period up to the death of Maximilian I occupies just under half of the text, while that from the Reformation to the present has slightly more space. The three chapters dealing with 'The struggle with Buonaparte', 'Revolutionary movements' and 'Recent events' are more detailed in their coverage. There is a six-page chronological table at the beginning of the book, but no illustrations or maps. The reader has the sense that Sime is not merely presenting a series of discrete facts, but documenting and interpreting processes. He marks changes and turning points, and in his account of the nineteenth century he is particularly good at uncovering the real reasons rather than the pretexts for action underlying Prussia's ascendancy. Only three years after the Franco-Prussian War he sums up the feelings of the Germans:

> The German people were displeased that France was allowed to keep Belfort; but on the whole they regarded the results of the war with pride and pleasure. The ancient military fame of Germany had been more than maintained; the Fatherland had been united; and the national sentiment was gratified by the conquest of the long lost provinces of Elsass and Lorraine, which would henceforth form a defence against French attacks. The Austro-Prussian war had raised Prussia to the first place in Germany; the present war raised Germany to the first place in Europe (p. 267).

Sime was obviously writing for an older readership, not requiring the sugared pill of illustrations. Furthermore, he is extremely sparing in his use of anecdote. He refers only to the wives of Weinsberg (pp. 73-74) and Frederick Barbarossa and the Kyffhäuser (pp. 77-78), both briefly (see below). While the thrust of his narrative is concerned with political struggles and developments, he finds space at the end of several chapters

27. Scenes and Narratives from *German History* (n.d.). 'Gustavus Kneeling in front of his Army'.

for comments on literature, the visual arts and music. Sime is surer of himself in dealing with recent events than are most of the other authors. As a professional historian he outclasses both Paul and Pütz. The book was reprinted in 1898 and 1909.

Our next author, Charlotte M. Yonge (1823-1901), was, like Julia Corner, the author of several history books for children. 'Aunt Charlotte's *Stories*' covered English, French, Greek, Roman and American as well as Bible history 'for the little ones'. The German history was first published in 1878 and appeared in an updated edition in 1893. It is a strange and unsatisfactory book. Its opening chapters on 'The ancient Germans' and 'Valhall' are a jumble of German and Norse material. Then we have 'The German Romans', followed by another farrago entitled 'The Nibelonig heroes', based chiefly on the *Nibelungenlied*,[95] of which three English translations were available by this time. Garbled names are a special feature of Yonge's book: she attempts to use German forms, so we get Karl the Great instead of the usual Charlemagne, but many of her names are wretchedly misspelt. However, the use of German forms is deeply significant as indicating a closer feeling towards Germany in the period of the new united monarchy.

The pattern of the book follows the reigns of one or more monarchs at a time, giving facts rather than explaining processes. As no map is provided, the reader is often at a loss to know where the various places are that are mentioned in the text. The hectic unfolding of event after event, often oddly juxtaposed with other titbits of information, is accompanied with nudging emotive adjectives or comments. Since Yonge follows the sequence of Austrian monarchs for her structure, Prussia is not adequately treated. Yonge was, of course, much better known as a novelist than as a historian, and this spills over into her book, which seems to have been written without the proper care for accuracy. As just one example, she describes Tilly, the commander of the Imperial army in the early stages of the Thirty Years War, as 'a Hungarian of peasant birth, brave and honest, but very fierce and rude' (p. 239), whereas Julia Corner, correctly, refers to him as 'a native of Brussels' (p. 120).

The next book to concern us is Sabine Baring-Gould's *Germany*, published in Fisher Unwin's 'History of the Nations' series in 1886. Baring-Gould (1834-1924) was one of the most prolific writers on popular subjects in the Victorian period, and this history of Germany was written as much for the general reading public as for young people. The preface is revealing of the author's brisk, no-nonsense stance:

> The story of such a people as the Germans could not fail to possess intense interest for anyone; but for us of another branch of the Teutonic family, it has the additional charm that it is the history of our blood-relations. On their experience we have built, and to the light of their example we look for guidance; in their triumphs we rejoice; to the grandeur of the genius of their poets and prose-writers, of their scientists and theologians, we look with pride and admiration, congratulating ourselves that we, too, are Teutons (p. iv).

Baring-Gould was an Anglican clergyman of wide, if not always exact learning, self-confident in his judgements and opinions. Following the

---

95 By Jonathan Birch (1848); W. H. Lettsom (1850); A. Forestier [A. A. Woodward] (1877). See Francis E. Sandbach, *The Nibelungenlied and Gudrun in England and America* (London: David Nutt, 1904), pp. 39-54, 72-74.

Franco-Prussian War, Baring-Gould, like Sime and Charlotte M. Yonge, refers to Alsace as Elsass, though Aix-la-Chapelle remains in its French form. He is a great Germanophile, but he can still write in conclusion: '. . . though the empire of Germany is a splendid power, it is also a very crushing power to the people, and though the nation has escaped from one set of difficulties, it has plunged into another' (p. 421). This comment relates to the three-year military training required of Germany's young men.

Baring-Gould was trenchant in his opinions. He viewed the crowning of Charlemagne as emperor as 'the greatest mischief [Pope Leo III] could do to Germany' (p. 79), and he described Pope Gregory VII as 'a carpenter's son, whose head had been turned by his elevation to the Papacy, and who was puffed up with pride and love of power' (p. 99). He thought Zwingli 'a man of more daring mind than Luther; his equal in intrepidity, and his superior in learning' (p. 22). There is much praise of Frederick the Great, a detailed account of the 'Battle of the Nations', near Leipzig, in 1813, but – as the present day is approached – Bismarck is mentioned only when he meets the defeated Napoleon III at Donchéry, though a fine portrait of him graces the opposite page (pp. 406-07). The immediate past does not appear in such sharp focus as, say, fifty or a hundred years previously.

The last book to claim our attention is Henrietta Elizabeth Marshall's large volume, brought out in 1913 in a style comparable with the gift-book editions of the Grimms, Andersen and *The Arabian Nights* and illustrated by such artists as Rackham, Nielsen and Dulac. Her illustrator, A. C. Michael, is, however, hardly in the same category. H. E. Marshall (born 1876), who concealed her gender behind the use of initials, was also the author of *A History of France*, *Our Island Story* and *Scotland's Story* and skilled in the art of popular history. Hers is not a textbook, any more than Baring-Gould's book is, but it was aimed at children in the absence of there being 'outside school books (and there are a few of these) no simple history of the German Empire . . . in the English language' (preface). Given what was to happen a year after her book appeared, her final paragraph in retrospect has an ironic tinge:

> In this time of peace and unity Germany has grown great. In commerce and manufacture it is now among the foremost countries in the world. In learning and science it has no equal. Peace has done for Germany far more than all the wars and conquests of the Holy Roman Emperors, and the Germans who love their country well know the value of that peace, and pray that it may long continue (pp. 448-49).

Like other writers, Marshall points out the dynastic connexions between Britain and Germany, noting with regard to Henry the Lion in the twelfth century that King George V was descended from him (p. 217). Her coverage of the varied aspects of German history is measured and seems to have no axes to grind. To a modern reader it may seem strange that the period up to 1493 occupies two-thirds of the book, whereas for the same period Baring-Gould uses about two-fifths of his space. Marshall has a narrower range of reference (for example, to literature, the arts and music) than Baring-Gould, but she provides a fluent narrative adapted to the interests of children.

One thing that stands out in all the histories apart from Pütz is the use of anecdotes and legends as keys to meaning. Several are quoted by more than one author; two were extremely popular. First comes the story of the women of the besieged castle of Weinsberg, whom Conrad III grants permission to leave unharmed with as much as they can personally carry; each of the women then appears carrying her husband on her back, whereupon peace terms are immediately proposed. This story is given by Corner (pp. 52-53), Paul (p. 115), SPCK (p. 61), Sime (pp. 73-74), Yonge (pp. 83-85), Baring-Gould (pp. 117-18), Marshall (pp. 198-99). The second concerns the legend that Frederick Barbarossa is asleep inside a mountain waiting for the moment at which he should awake and come once more to his country's aid. The legend has a certain appropriateness since Barbarossa died on the Third Crusade attempting to cross a river in Asia Minor. The mountain is usually stated to be the Kyffhäuser in the Harz (Paul (p. 129), Sime (pp. 77-78), Yonge (pp. 97-98), Baring-Gould (p. 124), Marshall (p. 219), but the SPCK book situates it in the Salzburg area, probably confusing it with a similar legend about the Emperor Charlemagne (p. 12).

Two of the authors cite the anecdote illustrating Fugger's wealth in burning a fire of spices and setting alight the bonds owed to him by the Emperor Charles V (Corner (p. 105), Yonge (p. 203)). Four refer to William Tell (Paul (pp. 184-86), Yonge (pp. 140-41), Baring-Gould (p. 151), Marshall (pp. 256-57)), though the latter two query the historicity of the apple-shooting episode. In more modern times the largest number of anecdotes focus on Frederick William I of Prussia and his son Frederick the Great. Perhaps the most striking of these is one about Frederick the Great and a soldier who wore chains and a seal attached to a bullet in place of a watch, which he could not afford. Frederick challenges him on the supposed watch, judging it to be foppery, and asks him the time. The embarrassed soldier replies: 'Sire, my watch points only to one hour – that in which I am ready to die for your majesty'. Frederick is so pleased at this reply that he gives the soldier his own watch (Paul (p. 411); Baring-Gould (p. 299)).[96]

These are not the only anecdotes and legends to make an appearance in the various histories, but they encapsulate some of the key values that are presented – woman's devotion to her husband, the willingness of the soldier to sacrifice his life or his money to the king or emperor; the monarch as the guardian, even in death, of his people.

It is interesting, too, to observe the attention paid to the stories of the Nibelungs in three of the histories. Paul mentions 'the famous "Niebelungenlied" in his brief account of medieval literature (p. 170), just a year before the publication of the first English translation of Germany's passionate and bloodthirsty heroic epic (followed by a second translation in 1850). Charlotte M. Yonge, with Wagner's *Ring* published in 1863, provides a story combining the youth of Siegfried taken from Norse (or Wagnerian) sources together with a summary of the *Nibelungenlied*, in order to fill the period between the end of the Roman Empire and the arrival of the Franks (pp. 31-38). Baring-Gould mentions the poem first in connexion with Attila (pp. 26-27) and summarizes the plot in his account of medieval literature. As was common at the time, he claims that this 'grand epic . . . may take rank beside the Iliad' (p. 143).

All the home-grown histories of Germany except Sime contain illustrations, Corner beginning modestly with four engravings by Davenport after paintings by Gilbert. These are narrative illustrations, focussing on dramatic episodes of history: the forced abdication of Henry IV, the murder of Albert I, Maria Theresa presenting her infant son to the assembled states. Paul's history offers fifty-six engravings that document places and personages, the latter usually on the basis of contemporary funeral monuments, statues and portraits. These are not nineteenth-century re-creations, but for the most part pictures of buildings and artefacts. That is true also of the 103 illustrations in Baring-Gould, which are largely taken from L. Stacke's *Deutsche Geschichte*. Yonge's history, again, is equipped with 86 illustrations, but these tend more to the imaginative than the documentary, so we find such subjects as 'St. Boniface felling the oak', 'Friedrich II. Putting on the crown of Jerusalem', 'Huss at Constance', 'Luther at Wartburg', 'Death of Wallenstein', 'Metternich and Napoleon'.

The SPCK's *Scenes and Narratives* reverts to the narrative dramatic style of

---

[96] This anecdote was so popular that it found its way into *Joe Miller's Jest-Book, with Additions* (London: Charles Mason, 1836), no. 709, pp. 127-28.

Corner's book. There are just six anonymous engravings including 'Luther before Charles V' and 'Gustavus kneeling in front of his army'. The ten colour-plates in Marshall are rather a disappointment, since A. C. Michael was not a distinctive artist. The plates are badly placed in relation to the text, and those depicting Wallenstein and Frederick the Great (patronizingly referred to in the text as 'the plucky little Prussian king') are in the wrong chronological order. Marshall, Baring-Gould and Yonge all have depictions of the new Kaiser Wilhelm I, bringing their story up to date. The focus on monarchs in all the histories reflects Germany's slowness to change in the exercise of political power. However, Baring-Gould at least does provide a picture of Bismarck.

The incidence of illustration can probably be related to the age-range of the books' target readerships. Thus, with their lack of illustration Paul, Pütz and Sime may be seen as aiming at the upper age-range. Paul was a Fellow of Exeter College, Oxford, before he became Vicar of St. Augustine's, Bristol, and both he and Sime were university-trained historians. It is odd that Corner is the only publication to provide a map of Germany. Perhaps the other authors assumed that their readers had access to helpful atlases. It is a pity that the illustrations in Corner are not more plentiful, but they may have cost too much to reproduce. Cheaper methods of reproduction allowed Paul and Baring-Gould to have a greater number, the character of which enabled their readers to envisage important places, personages and events more easily. Marshall's book, with its large format and colour-plates, was clearly designed for a privileged class of reader.

These eight books dealing with the history of Germany represent a variety of approaches and target readerships. The little SPCK book addresses the youngest age-range and does not pretend to be a systematic history: its main aim is the provision of moral and religious instruction through historical examples. Corner, Paul, Pütz and Sime fit unambiguously into the category of textbook. Chronologically they demonstrate an increasing refinement in the historian's craft. Sime may be regarded as the culmination in terms of accuracy, clarity, objectivity and analytical skill. Yonge may or may not have been intended as some kind of textbook. The advertisements appended to Sime list three further historical works by her – *Cameos from English History, European History Narrated in a Series of Historical Selections from the Best Authorities*, and *A Parallel History of France and England* – which are clearly textbooks, but she, like Corner, Baring-Gould and Marshall, is a popular writer rather than a professional historian.

Each of these eight books is an earnest endeavour to present the history of Germany from the earliest times to the present day. There is no serious disagreement between them about the important personages and events. The emphasis at the beginning on Hermann/Arminius mirrors Germany's need for a national hero who is successful in defending her against the threat of foreign powers. This focus goes back at least to the end of the seventeenth century with Lohenstein's massive novel *Grossmüthiger Feldherr Arminius*, which was followed in the eighteenth century by works from the pens of Wieland and Klopstock. In the nineteenth century the theme is documented above all by Kleist's anti-Napoleonic play *Die Hermannsschlacht* (1808, first published 1821) and the gigantic monument erected in the Teutoburg Forest and dedicated in 1875.

Between Arminius and the Carolingian era there are only fitful gleams of light, but from Charlemagne onwards there is a continuous history of monarchs, with a dual pull on our attention from the establishment of Prussia as a monarchy at the beginning of the eighteenth century and its rivalry with Austria. The United Kingdom's dynastic connexions with Germany do not appear to have brought about an engagement of strong British emotions with regard to the history of Germany. From the cultural point of view, the marriage of Prince Albert of Saxe-Coburg-Gotha to Queen Victoria was of greater significance than the accession of George I. The middle decades of the nineteenth century show an increasing interest in Germany and things German. In the four decades from 1870 this grows into admiration and a sense of kinship, a state of affairs that was totally changed by the First World War.

17. The Thirty Years War

Without any question the period of the Thirty Years War, from 1618 to 1648, was one of the most horrifying in the history of Germany. Not only were huge numbers of soldiers killed in battle in virtually every part of the Holy Roman Empire, but even greater numbers of the civilian population died in the conflict or through starvation or disease. Houses, churches, villages and towns were burnt and destroyed, and by the end of the war the population had been reduced from about sixteen millions to about four. Although the war took place on German soil, many foreign powers were deeply involved also – Denmark, Sweden, Poland, France and, to a much lesser extent, Britain. The soldiers on both sides came from all over Europe, with armies being composed of men from many nationalities. Scots in particular fought at every level, especially on the Swedish side, and on the Imperialist side Croats were notorious for their barbarity. If people in Britain today know anything about the Thirty Years War, it is most likely to reflect the sufferings of the common people and to be linked with the picture given in Brecht's *Mother Courage* (published 1949). The ins and outs of the struggles for political power between the Emperor and the princes are less well known.

The picture of the Thirty Years War that Britain had in the nineteenth century is dominated, as one might expect, by Friedrich Schiller (1750-1805). His position as a popular historian – he was appointed Professor of History at the University of Jena in 1788 – and as Germany's leading dramatist made him immensely influential. His *History of the Thirty Years War in Germany* appeared in an English translation by Captain Blaquiere in London in 1799 and in Dublin in 1800. While another translation by J. M. Duncan was published in 1828, Blaquiere's version was reissued by Charles Jugel in Frankfurt am Main in 1842 to satisfy the historical and cultural interests of the increasing numbers of British tourists to Germany, especially to the Rhineland. Schiller's trilogy *Wallenstein*, first published in Germany in 1800, was translated by Coleridge in the same year and reissued a number of times during the nineteenth century. Further translations of parts or the whole of the trilogy were made by G. Moir (1827), F. L. Gower (1830), E. Thornton (1854), W. R. Walkington (1862), J. A. W. Hunter (1885), C. G. N. Lockhart (1887) and T. Martin (1894), demonstrating a continually renewed interest in the play throughout the nineteenth century. Quotations from both the trilogy and the *History of the Thirty Years War* were used by both R. B. Paul in *A History of Germany, . . . on the plan of Mrs. Markham's Histories* (London: John Murray, 1847) and Samuel Rawson Gardiner in *The Thirty Years War 1618-1648* (London: Longmans, Green, & Co., 1874), two much used textbooks.

Apart from Schiller few notable German prose-writers or dramatists seem to have concerned themselves with the Thirty Years War. The greatest of contemporary reflections of the period, Grimmelshausen's protean novel *Simplicissimus* (1669), was not translated into English until 1912, and to my knowledge Conrad Ferdinand Meyer's *Gustav Adolfs Page* (Gustavus Adolphus's Page) (1882) was not translated into English at all. But for much of the nineteenth century British readers had the translation of a popular novel by Caroline Pichler, which appeared under a variety of titles – *Waldstein, or the Swedes in Prague* (1828), *The Swedes in Prague, or the Signal Rocket* (1839), *The Swedes in Prague* (London: James Burns, 1845) and *The Signal Rocket* (1878). Born in Vienna, Caroline Pichler (1769-1843) was a prolific Austrian writer, and it is interesting to note that the publisher James Burns, who was keenly committed to German writers, especially Fouqué and Hauff, also issued Pichler's *Quentin Matsys*. Pichler's novel is the only one translated into English to view the war from the Habsburg and Catholic side. Her Wallenstein, however, is the nephew of the great Wallenstein, and the setting is Prague at the end of the Thirty Years War. The novel centres on a complicated love-story involving the Catholic Wallenstein and the Protestant Helen, but ends with Wallenstein marrying another, worthier woman who turns out to be the daughter of Count Königsmark, while Helen eventually marries an aged nobleman in Sweden. There is less of religious *parti pris* in this novel than in the late nineteenth-century British Protestant stories to which we shall come in due course.

It is against this background that I want to turn now to look at how the Thirty Years War was dealt with in Britain in books for children. To begin with, there are the history textbooks or instructional books that we

The Thirty Years War 293

have looked at in another chapter for their general presentations of German history. The proportions of space allotted by them to the Thirty Years War are as follows:

> Julia Corner, *A History of Germany, and the Austrian Empire* (1841): 10 out of 270 pp.; 1/27th
>
> Robert B. Paul, *A History of Germany, . . . on the plan of Mrs. Markham's Histories* (1847): 40 out of 480 pp.; 1/12th
>
> Wilhelm Pütz, *Handbook of Modern Geography and History*, Part III (1850): 8 out of 312 pp.; 1/39th
>
> *Scenes and Narratives from German History* (SPCK, c. 1858-60): 51 out of 206 pp.; 1/4th
>
> Charlotte M. Yonge, *Aunt Charlotte's Stories of German History* (1878): 27 out of 344 pp.; 1/13th
>
> S. Baring-Gould, *Germany* (1886): 28 out of 427 pp.; 1/16th
>
> H. E. Marshall, *A History of Germany* (1913): 23 out of 449 pp.; 1/19th

The two extreme cases can easily be explained: Pütz deals with the whole of Europe, not merely Germany, so the ratio reflects that. The SPCK book, on the other hand, is highly selective in its coverage and focusses on only eight key figures or events in German history. Given the strongly Protestant tenor of the publishing house, it is not surprising that three of the eight sections centre on Protestant concerns and that two concern Wallenstein's role in the Thirty Years War and the Siege of Magdeburg.

Between them these seven books target a wide age-range of children and young people and display a variety of approaches to writing history. Pütz's account is extremely concentrated with little room for description, anecdote or interpretation, while Baring-Gould seems to be writing for a popular adult readership that would include the enquiring adolescent. Corner and Paul are more obviously textbooks, the former calculated for a slightly younger readership than the latter. The SPCK book targets the younger age range with an emphasis on incident, story and focal characters. By contrast, Yonge, though her title ends with the words 'for the little ones', would appear to have adolescents in mind as her readers. The same is true of Marshall.

Books for children and adolescents commonly aim at attracting their readers' interest through providing pictures and telling anecdotes. Pütz reveals the serious nature of his readership through his book's lack of illustrations, and Corner has none relating to this particular section on the

Thirty Years War. Paul has three engravings, depicting Wallenstein's castle of Friedland in Bohemia, the entry of Gustavus Adolphus into Munich, and the Swede's Stone, which marks the spot on the field of Lützen where Gustavus fell (1632). The SPCK book shows Gustavus kneeling in prayer before his army and a family leaving their burning home in Magdeburg. Yonge's book follows its author's focus on kings and rulers by providing portraits of Matthias, Friedrich V, Ferdinand II, Gustaf Adolf and Bernhard of Saxe-Weimar along with pictures of St. Vitus' church in Prague, the death of Wallenstein and the signing of the Peace of Westphalia. Baring-Gould gives portraits of Tilly and Wallenstein and reproduces a seventeenth-century view of Vienna. Marshall has a colour plate showing Wallenstein on the battlefield. Clearly, there are many personalities and incidents that offer an opportunity for illustration, and each serves its purpose in the different books. As it is impossible to deal with every aspect of the treatment of the Thirty Years War in these books, I shall concentrate on the three military leaders, Tilly, Wallenstein and Gustavus. What is particularly striking to note is the kind of stereotypes that emerge.

Count Tilly, the first leader of the Imperial forces, figures in only one illustration, but his physical appearance was such that none of the books except Pütz and the SPCK book can resist describing his hat with its long red feather and his green satin doublet. But whatever Tilly's genius as a military leader may be, no author can paint a sympathetic portrait of him. The siege of Magdeburg, with the horrifying destruction and plunder of buildings and the massacre of the greater part of its population, marks Tilly indelibly for his English authors and readers with a barbaric and cruel reputation, no different from the Croat soldiers who are everywhere depicted as the epitome of barbarism.

In the wake of Schiller the later Imperial leader, Wallenstein, is the central figure in all accounts of the war. His threat to take Stralsund even if it were bound with chains to heaven (an image that Schiller strikingly uses in *Wallenstein's Camp*) is retailed by Paul, SPCK, Baring-Gould and Marshall. His fascination with astrology is mentioned by Corner, Paul, SPCK and Yonge. The major interest, however, lies in Wallenstein's assassination. Corner deals with this in very general terms, mentioning no names. Paul devotes four pages full of detail to the subject, but points out that 'modern historians' do not give credence to the false oath story, though it was believed to be true in Schiller's time. The assassins are named as Gordon, Butler, Leslie and Devereux. Pütz with customary terseness simply declares: '. .

. on the 25th February, 1634, he was assassinated at Eger by some of his own officers' (p. 56). SPCK names the assassins, but gets their nationalities muddled, referring to Butler and Gordon as Scots, Leslie and Devereux as Irish (Butler was Irish, Leslie a Scot). Yonge merely refers to 'six Scottish and Irish officers of his guards' (p. 247). Baring-Gould gives the four names and describes the murder, commenting ambiguously: 'Though the treachery of Wallenstein is undeniable, his murder must ever remain as a stain on the history of Austria' (p. 256). Finally, Marshall depicts the event in some detail, but mentions neither the names nor the nationalities of the assassins. One may wonder whether Marshall, and Corner before her, did not want to clutter their readers' minds with names that were to occur only once in their histories, or whether they did not want them to know of the involvement of Scots and Irishmen in this murky event. There was not much sorrowing over the death of Wallenstein, but the assassins' actions certainly did not fit in with the ideals of honesty, courage and straightforwardness that would characterize a British hero.

Of course, for Protestant Britain the true hero of the Thirty Years War is Gustavus Adolphus, King of Sweden, everywhere lauded for his personal courage, sober frugality (a great contrast here to Wallenstein), modesty, Protestant piety and, not least, his handsome physique. Hezekiah Butterworth's *Zigzag Journeys in Northern Lands* (Boston: Estes & Lauriat, 1883) devotes almost all its space on Sweden to an ardent account of Gustavus' achievements. Corner simply calls him 'the renowned king of Sweden', while Paul declares:

> He was of gigantic height, with an open countenance, large blue eyes, and a mild but majestic bearing; presenting in his whole appearance a remarkable contrast to the gloomy Wallenstein, the ferocious Tilly, and most of the German princes, who affected a mysterious demeanour, to cover their low plans of personal ambition (pp. 337-38).

SPCK tells a similar story. Yonge concentrates on his Christian qualities, but Baring-Gould once more dwells on his physical qualities. Marshall alludes to his sobriquet of 'Lion of the North', explaining: 'And a lion of strength he looked with his mane of tawny hair and great broad shoulders' (p. 345). His physical appearance may be dealt with at length, but all the same for the British writers what matters more is the fact that Gustavus is exemplary in his Christian bearing, his simple piety and trust in God. However, as Marshall describes his corpse after the Battle of Lützen there are distinct echoes of Vergil's depiction of the dead Hector after the fall of

Troy: '... among the slain, his fair face trampled and disfigured, his yellow hair clotted and dark with the dust and blood of battle, lay the "Golden King of the North"' (p. 349).

It would be possible to look at other aspects of the various authors' treatment of the Thirty Years War, but they would not materially alter the picture so far given. Most of the accounts refer to the British connexion through the fact that Frederick, the Elector Palatine and 'Winter King', was married to and egged on by James VI and I's daughter Elizabeth. They also point to the participation of English, Scottish and Irish soldiers as volunteers, especially on the Protestant side. This is a matter of some importance in the fictional works dealing with the war. Though the English angle is slight in the historical works, most authors betray a sense of emotional involvement in at least some of the events they describe. Corner, for example, immediately after mentioning the sack of Magdeburg, states: 'I am not fond of dwelling on such scenes as this, nor of describing their horrors very minutely; but it is well, now and then, to read of, and reflect on, the dreadful miseries of war, that we may be thankful for the blessings of peace' (p. 124). The Jesuits come in for occasional comment, as when Paul reiterates the Bohemians' description of them as 'that hypocritical pestilent sect' (p. 325), but in talking about Frederick he also speaks of the 'stupid barbarism, which was at that time the distinguishing characteristic of the Calvinists' (p. 326). But what each of the various authors was trying to do was to give a picture of the war in the context of the whole history of Germany, and there was little space for detail.

For the more advanced student, and thus not intended for young children, the distinguished historian Samuel Rawson Gardiner produced a much fuller account in the series 'Epochs of Modern History' entitled *The Thirty Years' War* (London: Longmans, Green, and Co., 1874, already sixth edition 1884). This 'little book', in which Gardiner synthesizes the work of many German historians, he characterizes as

> an expression of the sympathy which an Englishman cannot but feel for the misfortunes as well as the achievements of his kindred on the Continent, and as an effort to tell something of the bygone fortunes of their race to those amongst his own countrymen to whom, from youth or from the circumstances of education, German literature is a sealed book (Preface, p. viii).

These history books, whether conceived as textbooks or written for a broader readership, show British writers grappling with the problem of introducing children and adolescents to the largely unknown history and culture of Germany. It may be coincidence that Julia Corner's history made its first appearance in 1841, the year after Queen Victoria married Prince Albert of Saxe-Coburg and Gotha, but the 1840s certainly mark a considerable growth of interest in Germany and in the translation of German literature. Crucially, this includes children's books, though it was not until the mid 1850s that a German fictional work dealing with the Thirty Years War was translated into English. This was Gustav Nieritz's *Siege of Magdeburg*, published in a collection of his *Tales for the Young* (Edinburgh: Paton & Richie, 1855). The German original, *Die Belagerung von Magdeburg*, had appeared in 1846. Nieritz was a prolific Protestant writer of children's books, many of which, like this, had historical subjects. Several were translated into English from about 1850 onwards and are dealt with in another chapter. Nieritz's procedure was generally to paint a graphic picture of a person struggling against deprivation, misery and injustice, only to win through in the end. The fictional account of the siege of Magdeburg in the SPCK book is conceived in similar terms. The horrors are recounted as affecting a family with four children, an apprentice and the children's nurse. Father and apprentice are killed, the family house burnt, mother and babe in arms are run through by a Croat's sword, while another flings the four-year-old boy into the flames of a burning house. Only the old nurse and the two older children survive.

The sack of Magdeburg and some indication of the role of Gustavus Adolphus are mentioned in the first English children's book to deal with the Thirty Years War, but they are not its focus. The book's significance for us is concealed by its title – *A Story about a Christmas in the Seventeenth Century* – which makes no reference to Germany or the war. It was written by Mrs Percy Sinnett (Jane Sinnett) and published by Chapman & Hall in 1846. The story centres on the problems faced by the family of a wealthy Protestant merchant called Merck in the Silesian town of Schweidnitz in the early period of the war. Events are set in motion through the refusal of Frau Merck's uncle in Sagan to send his ward to Wallenstein's new military school, an act that leads to his imprisonment. Merck sends Albert Thorn, a man whom the family is sheltering, to intercede with Wallenstein and be allowed to bring Merck's widowed sister-in-law and daughter back to Schweidnitz. Though Albert is subjected to trickery by the disagreeable Imperial Captain Gripenclau, whom Merck's sister-in-law has quartered on her, Wallenstein treats him generously, having seen and remembered

Albert's bravery on the opposing side at the Battle of the Dessau Bridge (1626), and grants his request. Later, however, Schweidnitz is occupied by Imperial forces, and Captain Gripenclau takes over the Mercks' house. Father and two sons are imprisoned, while mother and daughters take refuge in a hidden hermitage in the back garden. Eventually peasant forces led by the disguised Albert attack the Imperial soldiers, burn down a large house and release Merck and his companions from prison. The reunited Merck family then escape into the Giant Mountains and find refuge with other fugitive Protestants.

Although the book is written from a Protestant viewpoint, the author does not demonize the Catholics. In fact, she gives a particularly sympathetic role to Father Anselmus, a Franciscan friar, who not only comforts Frau Merck in her distress at her husband's imprisonment, but also promises to find asylum for the girls in a convent where his sister is abbess. Antagonism between the Imperialists and the Protestants focusses largely on the soldiery and peasants, whose actions are relentless and unrestrained. Once the Imperialists have taken Schweidnitz the townspeople are given eight days to renounce their Protestantism or be killed. Merck of course refuses and is imprisoned. The cruelty of the war is further illustrated by the fact that the Protestant Albert turns out to be the son of the Imperialist and Catholic Colonel von Hardenfels, who demands, but does not receive, his recantation. Obviously, the book attempts first and foremost to tell a story that will grip and also to some degree instruct its target readers, but within a small space it gives a good idea of major aspects of the Thirty Years War as viewed through the purported experiences of a single Protestant family.

It was not until the last quarter of the nineteenth century that children were provided with more independently written fiction based on the events of the Thirty Years War. First we find J. B. De Liefde's *The Maid of Stralsund* (1876), in later editions retitled *A Brave Resolve: or, the Siege of Stralsund*. It was followed by G. A Henty's *The Lion of the North* (1886), Deborah Alcock's *The King's Service* (c. 1890), Sarah M. S. Clarke's translation of W. Noeldechen's *Baron and Squire* (1892), Grace Stebbing's *Never Give In* (1890s) and a further novel by Henty, *Won by the Sword* (1900). This cluster may perhaps reflect increased British interest in the history of Germany following the unification of Germany under Prussia after the Franco-Prussian War. All the books of British origin engage their young readers through the simple device of having one or more of their leading characters British, more often Scottish than English. This is entirely plausible, since neither the Imperialist nor the Protestant side consisted solely of German stock. As already noted, Wallenstein's assassins were Scots or Irish, and Gustavus' army contained many Scots. Even Noeldechen's novel has a minor English character, a man in the service of Elizabeth, wife of the Elector Palatine.

Jacob B. De Liefde's *The Maid of Stralsund*, like Deborah Alcock's *The King's Service*, is written from a strongly Protestant viewpoint. It covers the period from April 1628 to the Battle of Lützen on 16 November 1632, beginning with the Siege of Stralsund. Like all the other fictional works, it provides a good deal of background information and narrative of the progress of the war. This is articulated in relation to a love-story centred on Helena, the daughter of the Calvinist pastor Hermann, her would-be husband Theodore Wechter, son of a wealthy magistrate and later defector to the Imperialist side, and her gallant English admirer, Harry Wyndham, of whom Theodore is viciously jealous. Towards the end of the siege Wyndham is taken prisoner by Wallenstein's troops and imprisoned in the fortress of Templin for two years. He escapes with the help of a gipsy and rejoins the Swedish camp. Gustavus sends him with a despatch to Stralsund, and en route he fights a party of Croats, but prevents their officer from being killed. Some time later Wyndham learns that Helena and her father are in Magdeburg, now about to be besieged. Disguised as an Imperialist, Harry helps them to escape, rather implausibly aided by the Croat officer who coincidentally turns up. Equally implausibly they are helped to cross the Elbe by an Imperialist officer who turns out to be the turncoat Theodore Wechter. Later still, in the stand-off between Wallenstein and Gustavus at Nuremberg, Wyndham meets Wechter the father again. He sends a message via a gipsy to Theodore, trying to induce him to join the Swedish army, but with no success. Finally, in the Battle of Lützen Wechter and his son are reunited, but both killed. Wyndham marries Helena and takes her to England.

While De Liefde's plot depends a lot on coincidences and unexpectedly renewed encounters, there is precedent for such things in Grimmelshausen's infinitely profounder narrative, *Simplicissimus*. In the gipsy figures who appear at several points in the story we have a minor diversion from the relentlessly middle and upper class characters who otherwise populate it. De Liefde points up the usual contrasts between Gustavus and Wallenstein, but he does not reproduce the grotesque picture of Tilly, treating him less emotively. The plot places the reader firmly on the Protestant side, and the defection of Theodore Wechter to the Imperialists may be read as a condemnation of the Imperialist position generally. Good deeds, acts of generosity towards individuals, of which there are several in the course of the novel, are reciprocated in later incidents. But Wechter the father and Theodore the son, in political (and religious) opposition to each other, can only be united in death on the battlefield. The effects of the war are poignantly shown in the destruction of family relationships between the central characters. Wyndham and the other Englishmen share the soldier's lot, but in the end we see the Englishman withdrawing from the fray that has not yet ended and taking his fatherless bride with him. Thus, German womankind is rescued by the help of the doughty, honest Englishman. The story ends at Lützen, but the war went on for another sixteen years, which are laconically summarized in half a dozen pages.

Ten years after De Liefde, George Arthur Henty dealt with the same period of the war in *The Lion of the North*. Henty had already devoted one book, *The Young Franc-Tireurs* (1872), to the Franco-Prussian War, looking at it from the French side, but the majority of his boys' stories focus on adventures in far-flung parts of the British Empire. Only in *The Lion of the North* and later *With Frederick the Great* (1897/98) and *Won by the Sword* does he turn to German or partly German subjects. Henty was particularly keen on getting the historical context of his adventure stories correct, and he spent a lot of time reading source material. This is quite apparent in *The Lion of the North*, which retails great slabs of factual information about the military operations and historical background. In his preface he records his indebtedness to James Grant's *Memoirs and Adventures of Sir John Hepburn* (Edinburgh and London, 1851).

The story is told through the experience of a young Scot called Malcolm Munro, who goes with his uncle to join the Scots in the service of Gustavus Adolphus. As is the case with Henty's novels generally, the boy hero achieves astonishing feats of military adventure through a combination of youthful vigour, a cool head, quick intelligence, steadfastness, courage and directness. Henty's ideal of military conduct also requires honesty, loyalty and modesty. His heroes fight for a cause they believe in and for a leader whom they can unreservedly admire. Gustavus fulfils this role perfectly. As Henty declares, he

> was indeed beloved as well as admired by his soldiers. Fearless himself of danger, he ever recognized bravery in others, and was ready to take his full share of every hardship as well as every peril.
> He had ever a word of commendation and encouragement for his troops, and was regarded by them as a comrade as well as a leader... He had

The Thirty Years War 301

an air of majesty which enabled him to address his soldiers in terms of cheerful familiarity, without in the slightest degree diminishing their respect and reverence for him as their monarch (p. 140).

Malcolm's actions in the siege of Mansfeld lead him into a warm relationship with the Count of Mansfeld's family and in particular with Thekla, his daughter. Later in the story, disguising her as a boy, Malcolm enables her to escape captivity in Prague, but has to leave her in Pilsen while he himself infiltrates Wallenstein's quarters as a clockmaker, a skill he had learnt whilst in Nuremberg. He learns about the conspiracy regarding Wallenstein and uses his knowledge to persuade Wallenstein to let him go to Oxenstierna to convince the latter of Wallenstein's desire to make common cause with him. Malcolm manages to take Thekla with him, and at the end of the book he marries her and returns to England. Such romantic episodes are always marginal in Henty's stories: the hero's personal adventures are his priority.

The Lion of the North covers the period from Gustavus' landing in Pomerania to the Battle of Lützen, but goes on to include the murder of Wallenstein and the Battle of Nördlingen. The siege of Magdeburg is passed over quickly:

> The ferocious Tilly had determined upon a deed which would, he believed, frighten Germany into submission: he ordered that no quarter should be given, and for five days the city was handed over to the troops. History has no record since the days of Attila of so frightful a massacre (p. 97)

But in the section dealing with the passage of the Lech Henty produces the stock account of Tilly, complete with the description of his hat with the large red ostrich feather (pp. 181-82).

In dealing with the murder of Wallenstein Henty emphasizes that his youthful hero, Malcolm, does not find his fellow Scot, Leslie, a 'cheerful companion'. A page later he calls him a 'treacherous officer' (p. 339). Leslie, Gordon, Butler and Devereux are all named and their treachery against Wallenstein condemned. Henty's judgement of Wallenstein is remarkably favourable:

> Wallenstein was no bigot, his views were broad and enlightened, and he was therefore viewed with the greatest hostility by the violent Catholics around the king, by Maximilian of Bavaria, by the Spaniards, and by the Jesuits, who were all powerful at court. These had once before brought about his dismissal from the command, after he had rendered supreme services, and their intrigues against him were again at the point of

success when Wallenstein determined to defy and dethrone the emperor. The coldness with which he was treated at court, the marked inattention to all his requests, the consciousness that while he was winning victories in the field his enemies were successfully plotting at court, angered the proud and haughty spirit of Wallenstein almost to madness, and it may truly be said that he was goaded into rebellion. The verdict of posterity has certainly been favourable to him, and the dastardly murder which requited a lifetime of brilliant service has been held to more than counterbalance the faults which he committed (p. 342).

In the preface to *The Lion of the North* Henty indicated his hope of writing another book about the latter part of the Thirty Years War, but it was not until 1900 that he published *Won by the Sword*. There are many parallels between the two books, since Henty's plots frequently recycled similar kinds of incident and his young heroes often ended up marrying the daughters of the aristocrats to whose aid they came. However, after the death of Gustavus Henty turned to the French side in the war in order to find suitably worthy leaders for his new young hero to serve and emulate. Once more we have another young Scot as hero, one Hector Campbell, who is fifteen at the outset of his adventures. His father has been killed at the siege of La Rochelle, and he becomes a lieutenant in the household of Viscount Turenne, performing tireless deeds of fortitude and ingenuity, which always seem to involve swimming across icy rivers in the dark. With each success he is promoted and eventually gains an estate and barony in Poitou, finally marrying the daughter of a widowed baroness and, because of hostility from the party of the Duke of Beaufort, departing for England. In the middle stage of his career Hector is involved with the Duke of Enghien, whose personal bravery is greatly admired, but whose impetuosity is not. Turenne is the preferred model of military conduct, disciplined, thoughtful, fair-minded, considerate of those over whom he has charge. *Won by the Sword* is of lesser import for those interested in the depiction of Germany in the Thirty Years War, because its focus is on France during the period of Mazarin.

Contrasting markedly with Henty's stories of young male adventure, Deborah Alcock's *The King's Service* is decidedly a girls' book. It covers the same period as *The Lion of the North* and, as one would expect of a book published by the Religious Tract Society, treats its subject from an emphatically Evangelical viewpoint. The whole book is underpinned by the antithesis Protestant = good, pious, trustworthy; Catholic = bad, deceitful, etc. Once more we have a Scottish dimension, with an initially feckless Scottish nobleman, Charlie Graham, being persuaded to fight along with Gustavus and taking his young nephew Hugh, aged twelve, and his older niece Giovana or Jeanie along with him to Germany. Their father is presumed dead, but the latter part of the story shows him alive and manipulated by the Jesuits; his son is tricked and abducted by a Jesuit symbolically called Krausman ('crooked man'). Meanwhile, Jeanie has become companion to a dispossessed Bohemian noblewoman called Gertrud von Savelburg, whose lands have coincidentally been granted to the children's father as a supporter of the Habsburgs. The book ends, of course, with the marriage of Gertrud and the Scottish father, who now turns away from Catholicism to Evangelical Christianity.

Another part of the story centres on a romantic relationship between Jeanie and August von Lübeling, the son of a noble family with whom Gertrud and Jeanie gain shelter in Nuremberg. August fights in the Battle of Lützen and is the page who attempts to conceal Gustavus' identity when the latter is killed. This is based on historical documentation, as a footnote in the book indicates. The incident is mentioned, but without the name, by H. E. Marshall (pp. 348-49). Henty also uses the incident in *The Lion of the North*, where he gives the page's name, more accurately, as Leubelfing (p. 254). The Swiss writer Conrad Ferdinand Meyer takes this occurrence as his point of departure in his novella *Gustav Adolfs Page*, but in making the page August's sister, who serves the Swedish king in male disguise, he contravenes the historical record. Nonetheless, he creates a work of literature that is far superior in every way to all the children's books here under discussion and to Caroline Pichler's romantic novel. Meyer's novella perhaps further influences Wilhelm Noeldechen's *Baron and Squire*, for there the page Leubelfinger is described as 'a remarkably handsome youth, but his features were almost too lovely and girlish for those of a soldier' (p. 159). Returning now to *The King's Service*, August von Lübeling – a further coincidence – dies later in the care of Charlie Graham. Uncle Charlie's life is totally changed through his training as a Protestant soldier, and he is made to declare at the end of the book: '"I have learned that godliness is the truest manliness, and the soldier of Christ the best of soldiers"' (p. 231).

Last among the children's books to be considered here is Sarah M. S. Clarke's *Baron and Squire*. It is a translation of Wilhelm Noeldechen's *Die Zwillingsbrüder. Eine Erzählung aus dem Zeitalter des 30jährigen Krieges für die deutsche Jugend* (The Twin Brothers. A Story for German Young People from the Period of the Thirty Years War) (Bielefeld: Velhagen und Klasing, 1892).

Noeldechen wrote around twenty historical books for children and some plays and verse between 1883 and 1908 and, unless *Die Zwillingsbrüder* was actually published earlier than the *Gesamtverzeichnis des deutschen Schrifttums* states, it was translated into English and published extraordinarily quickly. Sarah Clarke did a lot of translations from German as well as writing a couple of children's books of her own on German topics.

What is fascinating about *Baron and Squire* is the fact that this is a German view of the Thirty Years War, not a British adventure story set in the period of the war. Unlike the other story-books we have looked at, it does not single out a particular section of this lengthy war, but attempts to give an account of the whole through the life-stories of twin brothers who, after they reached the age at which they could join the forces of Gustavus Adolphus, soon found themselves separated and caught up on opposing sides in this long drawn out conflict. The brothers Berthold and Winfried embody the oppositions from the start, as they are the offspring of a Calvinist father and a Lutheran mother whose marriage was opposed by their respective fathers. As children they are playmates of the son of the Elector Palatine before Heidelberg is besieged by Tilly in July 1622, but they escape with their foster-mother and her English husband, who is devoted to Elizabeth, the Elector's wife and daughter of James VI and I. Later the boys and their mother flee to Naumburg, where they are given refuge by their maternal grandfather, who nonetheless remains emotionally alienated from their mother till she dies. After the Battle of Breitenfeld (1631) the brothers become separated and Winfried, wounded, is taken into the troops of Count Pappenheim. Berthold participates in the siege of the fortress of Marienberg, across the River Main from Würzburg, and joins the company of Duke Bernard of Saxe-Weimar. In the Battle of Lützen, in which Gustavus is killed, the brothers meet briefly and accidentally on opposite sides. Berthold continues with Bernard of Saxe-Weimar, while Winfried, who is a reluctant active soldier, becomes secretary to Wallenstein. A Jew, Simeon Ben Sina, who mistakes Winfried for his brother Berthold, facilitates Winfried's return to their childhood home at Wiesenbach, near Heidelberg, and here, after the Battle of Nördlingen (1638) the brothers meet again. Berthold continues with Bernard during the latter's involvement with Richelieu, as France takes a more active role in the war, while Winfried is forced back into soldiery by John of Werth on the Imperialist side. After the Battle of Rheinfelden the brothers are reunited, and Berthold joins the forces of Charles Lewis, the young Elector Palatine, his childhood friend.

Bernard takes the fortress of Breisach from the Imperialists, but dies not long afterwards. Berthold and Winfried regain possession of their ancestral castle of Dilsberg, not far from Heidelberg, and the war ends with the Treaty of Westphalia, signed in the cities of Münster and Osnabrück.

Noeldechen's book manages to combine a broad chronicle of the war with an adventure story focussed on the twin brothers. The latter's differences of personality reflect contrasting aspects of the war, Berthold being a committed soldier on the Protestant side, while Winfried is pushed hither and thither and forced into Imperialist service. Winfried's experience was a commonplace of the war. Soldiers changed sides not out of principle, but because circumstances such as defeat or capture dictated it. Noeldechen's viewpoint is nonetheless essentially Protestant, and he describes events largely from the perspective of his aristocratic twin heroes. The latter enjoy a certain privilege, but the roughness and brutality of the ordinary soldiers is evident in the experience of the brothers' foster-mother and her own elderly mother, who is suspected of witchcraft and viciously treated. The difference between Noeldechen and the British authors lies chiefly in the fact that the German writer regards himself primarily as a historian and keeps his other concerns in check. He does not present an idealized form of Protestantism, but reveals its harsh divisions and emotional consequences in the unyielding attitudes of the boys' grandfathers. Its cruelty is shown in the torture of the suspected witch. Nor is Noeldechen out to promote a particular kind of youthful military idealism in the way that is second nature to Henty. He is not writing from a soldier's (or would-be soldier's) viewpoint, but has broader, more humane objectives that look for tolerance and kindliness.

All the British fictional stories have an agenda that includes more than recounting a section of the Thirty Years War. Each looks at the war from the Protestant viewpoint; no sympathy is accorded to the Imperialist Habsburg side, and that is perfectly understandable, given the nineteenth-century Protestant culture of Britain and given the fact that James VI and I and to a lesser extent Charles I supported, however inadequately, the Protestant cause through the dynastic link with Elector Frederick of the Palatinate. De Liefde and Alcock give prominence to religious aspects of the war, and both attempt in this way to interpret the suffering and personal sacrifice involved in the war as something to be accepted for Christ's sake. Sinnett even sounds an eirenic note in having a Catholic friar actually help the Protestant Merck family. The roles of father and son Wechter in De Liefde and of the twin brothers in Noeldechen point to a view of the war as fratricidal, as tearing families apart, and this is the case also with Alcock. Henty is more concerned with specifically military aspects of the war, though he propounds clear standards of moral conduct that go beyond purely military situations. The endings to both his novels, and indeed to De Liefde and Alcock, are optimistic in that they picture the linking of nationalities through the institution of marriage. Every British hero marries a German wife. However, this is nowhere a marriage of equals: it reflects the power situation in both political and gender terms. The German women are *rescued* by marriage, and the British soldiers are in a position where they can withdraw from the war, having achieved proud success and demonstrated their virility.

Both the histories and the fictional accounts of the war place more weight on the presentation of facts than on the motives of the opposing parties or the constraints under which they operated. Of course, the histories have only a limited space for the Thirty Years War in their accounts of German history as a whole, and with the novels (apart from Noeldechen) history is a background rather than the prime purpose of the books. Even so, it is noteworthy that the British books make play with stereotypes and tend to simplify the issues. Their Protestant tenor leads to a playing down or a complete omission of the fact that Richelieu provided financial support for Gustavus. Julia Corner acknowledged this, commenting that it proved that Richelieu 'was more influenced by political than religious motives, since, in order to lessen the power of the House of Austria, he was ready to support the enemies of the Catholic church' (p. 126). Paul mentions Richelieu's support in the second part of the war, but makes no allusion to the Treaty of Bärwalde earlier. Pütz refers tersely to 'an alliance with the French' (p. 53). There is no mention of French support at all in SPCK, Yonge or Baring-Gould, while Marshall refers to it more or less as an afterthought (p. 353). Gardiner, by contrast, devotes a full paragraph to the Treaty (pp. 129-30). As far as the novels go, neither De Liefde nor Alcock have anything, while Henty, in *The Lion of the North*, states early on: 'it did not suit the interests of France that Ferdinand should become the absolute monarch of all Germany' (p. 23). A few pages later he explains:

> In January [1631] Gustavus concluded a treaty with France, which agreed to pay him an annual subsidy of 400,000 thalers on the condition that Gustavus maintained in the field an army of 30,000 infantry and 6000 cavalry, and assured to the princes and peoples whose territory he might occupy the free exercise of their religion (p. 42).

The suppression of information about the French support given to Gustavus is presumably due to the fact that the writers did not want to admit another dimension to Gustavus Adolphus' ambitions, but insisted in portraying him as a purely Protestant hero. The French connexion would have sullied his purity of motive and displayed more of the *political* complexity that characterizes the Thirty Years War. Perhaps some of the authors supposed this might have puzzled or misled their young readers, but the SPCK book reveals a bitter anti-French stance in its remarks about the Peace of Westphalia:

> . . . the country which profited most by the peace was the one which had had the least to do with the war – namely, France. The cunning ambassadors of that kingdom persuaded the Germans, with very little reason, to give them up the bishoprics of Metz, Toul, and Verdun, together with the province of Alsace, all of which were separated from Germany by treaty, and have been kept by France to this day (p. 412).

These comments in a book published around 1860 may be seen as capturing the mood that led to the Franco-Prussian War of 1870-1. But that is another story and told in another chapter.

18. Historical Tales and Adventure Stories

There is no hard and fast dividing line between moral and religious tales on the one hand and historical tales and adventure stories on the other. The moral and religious concerns of nineteenth-century children's writers do not disappear overnight: they simply become less prominent. The telling of a gripping story, the presentation of historical events and the description of distant places and unfamiliar human activities become more important than a simple didactic message. The lure of adventure is of course present in German children's books right from Campe's *Robinson der Jüngere* and the exploits of Baron Münchhausen and is swiftly expanded with Wyss's *Schweizerischer Robinson*. Campe also provided exciting historical and geographical material in his books about the discovery of Central and South America and about polar exploration. But it was not until the middle part of the nineteenth century that German authors focussed more strongly on the narrative rather than didactic potential of historical and geographical themes.

Both Christoph von Schmid and C. G. Barth situate some of their stories in periods of considerable historical interest, e.g. the aftermath of the French Revolution or the Siege of Belgrade, but they do not exploit the historical material: it is simply the background for a particular set of events. The writer who took this one stage further was Gustav Nieritz (1795-1876), a Protestant schoolmaster and prolific author of children's books, who spent most of his life in Dresden and its immediate vicinity. Nieritz was the author of nearly 120 books, the first of which appeared in 1829. He was always on the look-out for story material, which he took from many sources – his wide general reading, anecdotes, sermons and newspaper reports, visits to taverns, plays and operas. He acknowledged a debt to Salzmann, but in his youth he was also a keen reader of stories about robbers, knights and ghosts, which were then very much in fashion. Nieritz's Protestant background is readily apparent in the stories he wrote, but he did not write with a solely religious motive. Posterity has not been kind to him. He was a workmanlike writer who turned his hand to a multiplicity of themes, but was undemanding and undistinctive in style and literary form. But in his own day he was a popular and productive author and eventually received an order of merit from the King of Saxony. Two years after his death the city of Dresden erected a monument in his memory.

Of the many books that Nieritz wrote approximately a sixth were translated into English. The earliest to be published were *The Foundling, or the School of Life* (Edinburgh: Paton & Ritchie, 1850), published in German as *Der Findling, oder: Die Schule des Lebens* (1839), and *Duty and Affection* (Edinburgh: William and Robert Chambers, 1850), which appeared in German in 1838 as *Der junge Trommelschläger und der gute Sohn*. Paton and Ritchie were particularly interested in Christian literature, but William and Robert Chambers had a rather broader range of publications to their credit. However, with *Duty and Affection* they introduced into the annals of children's literature the non-existent author Gustav Moritz, to whom the book is assigned on the leaf after the title-page. This name presumably derives from a misreading of the name Gustav Nieritz in unfamiliar Gothic type. Unfortunately this ghost author now steps the pages of a number of respected reference works and bibliographies. A later edition by W. & R. Chambers (c. 1910) with a curiously inappropriate decoration by Mabel Lucie Attwell on the front cover removes all mention of any author. Another translation of the text, this time correctly attributed to Nieritz, was made by H. W. Dulcken with the more fitting title *The Little Drummer: or, Filial Affection. A Story of the Russian Campaign* (London: G. Routledge & Co., 1856; reprinted 1856 and 1859). The popularity of the story was demonstrated by a further edition entitled *The German Drummer Boy; or, the Horrors of War*, adapted from the German by Mrs Campbell Overend (Edinburgh: Oliphant, Anderson, & Ferrier, 1883). No other book of Nieritz's enjoyed so many editions over so long a time-span.

The Little Drummer (if we use Dulcken's title to stand for all the versions of Nieritz's story) centres on the period of the Napoleonic occupation of Germany and subsequent invasion of Russia. It was a period within Nieritz's own youth and early adulthood, so the events, figures and mood that the book reflects derive at least partly from personal memory and not wholly from historical records. The story concentrates on the experiences of a fourteen-year-old boy, Augustus, who is conscripted into the Napoleonic army, 'la grande armée', that marches into Russia wreaking havoc and destruction, but eventually retreats, decimated, in misery and ignominy. The boy's father had killed a French drummer for, as he thought, causing the death of his sick daughter, and was about to be executed by the soldiers when Augustus, following the Biblical injunction to lay down one's life for one's brethren, asks to be executed to save his father. Instead, Augustus is forced to be a drummer. The Russian expedition, the brutality and coarseness of the soldiers, the degradation and misery that they cause and are part of, are narrated from the shocked viewpoint of this boy who tries to put into practice what he has learnt of Christian forgiveness and loving one's neighbour. As is the case with the stories of Schmid and Barth, Nieritz's plot neatly produces reconciliations and positive outcomes for all the main characters, though Augustus himself suffers a broken leg in the battle of the River Berezina, and Sergeant Hoier, who is a kind of adoptive father to him in the army, loses several fingers.

The Christian message is important to Nieritz, but like so many writers of historical fiction for children – G. A. Henty is the prime example in later British boys' books – he was also concerned to give an authentic picture of key aspects of the Napoleonic campaign. Augustus experiences the full horrors of the Battle of Borodino (5-7 September 1812), in which fifty thousand died for what he refers to as 'a mound of earth and a ruined village', lamenting, 'What a price!' Nieritz concentrates on the miseries and sufferings of war as it affects both soldiers and ordinary people. He is not concerned with over-all military strategy or political aims or with celebrating military heroism in general. What he is prepared to celebrate is individual acts of kindness within the soldiers' exposure to extremes of bloodshed and physical deprivation.

Nieritz sees nothing to glorify in war and warfare as such, so it is not surprising to find among his other books one that centres on a particularly brutal and gory episode of the most destructive war that Europe experienced before the First World War – the Thirty Years War (1618-48). In 1846 Nieritz published *Die Belagerung von Magdeburg*, which was translated into English as *The Siege of Magdeburg* (Edinburgh: Paton & Ritchie, 1855). The sack and devastation of the Protestant city of Magdeburg by the Catholic Imperial forces under the direction of General Tilly had, for both contemporaries and later historians, a tremendous impact on their reactions to the war and the wanton destruction of ordinary human life that it entailed.

For British children Nieritz's books opened up new areas of historical and geographical experience. Not only did they deal with themes from the history of the Holy Roman Empire, but they also reached further afield to Tsarist Russia and early missionary activity in Greenland. Nieritz ranged widely in his search for suitable story material and provided German children with wholesome information and a strong moral and religious focus. Translations of his stories into English coincided with the period of Queen Victoria's marriage to Prince Albert, a period that saw a considerable growth of interest in German literature and culture generally as well as German children's books. Nieritz's work had the clear advantage of providing useful general information about important aspects of German history within the context of sound Protestant experience; and for all his books' easy use of stock themes and heart-tugging episodes they had a firm moral and religious core.

Among Nieritz's stories about Germany a few more deserve further comment. *The Exiles of Salzburg, and Other Stories*, translated by Mrs L. H. Kerr (London: Religious Tract Society, c. 1885), includes *The King of Prussia's Tall Soldier* and a very short piece called *The Belfry of Dresden* in addition to the title story. The English title of *The Exiles of Salzburg* probably alludes to the much reprinted *Elizabeth; or, the Exiles of Siberia* by the French writer Madame Sophie Cottin, first published in 1806. Nieritz's book appeared in German in 1843 with the longwinded title *Die protestantischen Salzburger und deren Vertreibung durch den Fürst-Erzbischof von Firmian* (The Protestants of Salzburg and their Expulsion by the Prince Archbishop von Firmian). It is concerned with the persecution of Protestants by the Archbishop of Salzburg and the Jesuits and their expulsion from his territory in 1732, followed by their welcome to Prussia and Berlin by King Frederick William I. Nieritz's story involves a young woman torn between two men who want to marry her and beset with problems arising from loyalty to her father when he is falsely accused of murder. Through and around this tale of personal distress and grief runs an account of the Bible-based Protestants' suffering at the hands of the Catholic authorities. Nieritz describes the solemn oath that a hundred delegates of the Protestant communities swore at Schwarzach to stick to their faith, symbolizing their union by each swallowing a portion of salt, as a result of which their action became known as the Salt Alliance (*Salzbund*). He has no sympathy for the Archbishop, but tries not to utterly blacken his character:

> The archbishop, who had not naturally a cruel heart, although imbued with the deepest fanaticism of the times, felt a truly paternal affection for his subjects, and was shocked when he reflected on what he called the error of their ways. The most exaggerated reports were repeated to him respecting the public defection of the heretics; and they operated on the weak mind of the prince so powerfully that he became much alarmed, not only for his own safety, but also for that of the Catholic part of the population (pp. 86-87).

Elsewhere, however, Nieritz does not spare us from details of the harsh conditions under which the Salzburgers had to sell their property and possessions before being driven into exile, of the burning of Bibles and Protestant books in the market square of the town of Werffen, of the violence and cruelty of soldiers towards them. The book thus becomes a story of Protestant martyrdom, with echoes of an exodus to the promised land, in this instance Prussia.

Nieritz was not, however, a blind admirer of Prussia – his loyalty as a citizen was in any case to Saxony – and in *The King of Prussia's Tall Soldier* he recounts the sad story of a rich Frankfurt merchant, Leo Librecht Hiebendahl, who, on account of his great height, is betrayed into the hands of Prussians looking for giants to be incorporated into King Frederick William's guard regiment. Librecht's treacherous book-keeper Blitterman increasingly takes over the business and household and dismisses all who are sympathetic to their former master. In this way Librecht's nephew Bertram is also dismissed. One day in September 1738 while on guard in Berlin Librecht catches sight of his nephew, but cannot follow him. He asks a handsome young man who comes out of the castle to help him contact Bertram. The young man happens to be the Crown Prince, the future Frederick the Great, and he does help him to find Bertram, who is given letters to various people in Frankfurt explaining Librecht's plight. A little later Librecht sees a newspaper announcement that Blitterman has married his wife. He absconds, but is captured two days later and condemned to run the gauntlet ten times. Before this can take place, a family whose son Librecht has saved from drowning in the River Spree intercede with the King and obtain mercy for him. He is discharged from the King's service and exiled from Prussia. Meanwhile, it turns out that Blitterman had inserted the wedding announcement before the event took place, and that Librecht's wife had refused to marry him. Librecht and his wife are thus reunited, and Blitterman drowns himself in despair. Nieritz requires a large number of coincidences and implausible events to construct his plot and bring the story to a satisfactory conclusion, but he certainly creates a gripping narrative. Frederick William I's regiment of giant grenadiers constitutes just one of the King's many unpleasant traits, and unscrupulous methods were necessary to find tall men to fill it. The regiment was disbanded after his death. Nieritz's cameo picture of the future Frederick the Great is testimony to the extraordinary number of anecdotes that his unique personality gave rise to, perhaps particularly as a reaction to the brutality and coarseness of his father.

Nieritz was, in many of his books, fierce against rulers and men in positions of authority who abused their power. He was tireless in using history to provide examples of the suffering that such misdeeds and wickedness brought about. His ideal was a state of order, mutual respect and an acceptance of mutual responsibilities, but he recognized that the world was imperfect and did not shun describing its harsher side. The dangers and temptations inherent in the wielding of political power form the subject of one of his most popular stories – *Alexander Menzikoff oder: Die Gefahren des Reichtums* (Alexander Menzikoff or the Dangers of Wealth) (1834). This cautionary tale tells how a man of humble birth becomes the favourite of Tsar Peter I and then prime minister, field marshal and prince. Having already divorced his wife, Menzikoff marries a second time. In the enterprise of founding St. Petersburg he is publicly berated and beaten by the Tsar for failures in bridge-building. Later, further corruption comes to light. On Peter's death he succeeds in naming Peter's widow, Catherine, as Empress and then himself becomes the virtual ruler of Russia. He betrothes his eldest daughter to the young Tsar, Peter II, but eventually Menzikoff's enemies succeed in having him arrested, stripped of his titles and possessions and exiled to Siberia. Menzikoff's second wife becomes ill and dies en route. His faithful servant, Micheloff, turns out to be his own son by his first marriage, and his mother is Menzikoff's first wife. Depressed and contrite, Menzikoff builds a new church, in which he and his first wife remarry.

Nieritz embroiders the life of the historical Alexander Menshikov (1673-1729) with picturesque details of his own, but the broad outline is true enough. As with his other books, the context corresponds to known historical facts, while the more intimate plot, not always entirely plausible or convincing, embodies details and characters of the author's making. There were at least three different editions of the book in English. The first bore the title *Alexander Menschikoff, the Founder of a Family* (Edinburgh: T. Constable & Co., 1855). A different translation appeared ten years later entitled *The Perils of Greatness: the Story of Alexander Menschikoff* (Edinburgh: William P. Nimmo, 1865). Neither edition identifies the translator. A third version, this time credited to Mrs Alexander Kerr, has the title *Menzikoff, or the Danger of Wealth* (London: Religious Tract Society, [1894]). The Nimmo edition gives the spelling 'Menschikoff' only in the title; in the text it is as with the other two editions and the German original. The modern English transliteration is now usually Menshikov. The RTS edition has the subtitle 'a story founded on fact', corresponding to the claim of the German that it was 'a true story, told to provide entertainment in family circles'. Nieritz was not content to be a purely fictional writer. He always seems to be happier when telling a story with a clear basis in historical and geographical reality, even if he has to invent characters and a plot to unfold within that reality. The books nonetheless abound with well-documented details that Nieritz derived from his extensive reading. He was not a particularly original writer, but his blend of factual information and a firm moral and religious outlook with a plot that can engage a young person's attention gave his stories great popularity in Germany. In Britain his readership probably had more of a religious character, but the expansion of such subject-matter to include German history, legend and culture should not be underestimated as interest in all things German grew in the second half of the nineteenth century.

As Gustav Nieritz was the chief writer of historical tales to be translated into English, we can also reckon Friedrich Gerstäcker (1816-72) to be the principal author of German adventure stories. His work follows in the wake of the various German Robinsonades and books about exploration by writers such as Joachim Heinrich Campe. Gerstäcker was born in Hamburg and began training as a merchant in Kassel, but then broke off and turned to agriculture. In 1837 he emigrated from Bremen to the United States of America and travelled widely there, taking work as a hunter, logger, cook, sailor, stoker, silversmith, farmer and hotelier before returning in 1843 to his mother in Dresden. In 1849 he set off on a world voyage to South America, California, Hawaii, Tahiti and south-east Australia, returning once more to Dresden in 1852.

From the mid 1840s onwards he wrote extensively about his travels and used his experiences as the basis for a large amount of adult and juvenile fiction. Several of his books were translated into English. Early works to be translated were *Der Deutschen Auswanderer Fahrten und Schicksale*, which D. Black translated as *The Wanderings and Fortunes of some German Emigrants* (London: D. Bogue, 1848), and *Die Flußpiraten des Mississippi* (1848), which was translated as *The Pirates of the Mississippi* (London, 1856). *Gold! Ein Californisches Lebensbild aus dem Jahre 1849* (1858) appeared a year later as *Each for Himself; or, the Two Adventurers* (London, 1859), while *Der kleine Goldgräber in Californien* (1858) took a little longer to be translated as *The Young Gold-Digger; or, a Boy's Adventures in the Gold Regions* (London, 1860). An Australian novel, *Die beiden Sträflinge* (1857) appeared in the same year as *The Two Convicts*. Further titles saw the light of day in the 1860s.

A more detailed look at one of Gerstäcker's novels perhaps gives a better idea of his attractions to a young reader.

His novel *Der kleine Wallfischfänger* (1856) was translated into English as *The Little Whaler: or, the Adventures of Charles Hollberg* and was illustrated by Harrison Weir (London and New York: G. Routledge & Co., 1857). Another edition was published in 1876. The 1850s were the decade of books about whaling, with both Herman Melville's *Moby Dick* and W. H. G. Kingston's *Peter the Whaler* appearing in 1851. Whether these books were a factor in Gerstäcker's writing is uncertain, since in any case *The Little Whaler* contains a great deal that links up with his own recent voyage to the South Atlantic and the Pacific. The book has very little by way of plot. The young German protagonist, Charles Hollberg, dejected about the prospect of undergoing training in a commercial firm in Hanover, goes on holiday with his parents to the island of Heligoland. He becomes friendly with an old sailor, Jahn, who takes him out in his boat and gives him a taste of the sea. On the final day of the holiday Charles, against all he has ever been told by his father, goes alone in a boat to look for Jahn and becomes fog-bound. He rescues from the water a man who turns out to be quite a villain, and soon afterwards the two are picked up by a whaler, which, coincidentally, Charles had seen being refitted in Hamburg. The rest of the book deals with the whaler's two-year voyage to the South Atlantic, the Falkland Isles, Cape Horn, Juan Fernandez, the Sandwich Islands (i.e. Hawaii), the North Pacific, Tahiti and Fiji. In Tahiti Charles stumbles across his sailor friend Jahn again, and the man he had rescued from the sea is arrested as a murderer. Charles returns home on a German brig and is reunited with his family.

The book is explicitly modelled at the beginning on the structure of *Robinson Crusoe*, which has formed a crucial part of Charles's early reading and childish play. Like Crusoe too, Charles disobeys his parents and as a

Historical Tales and Adventure Stories 317

result finds himself anxiously separated from them for a protracted period of time. But while Crusoe spends long years learning how to survive on a desert island, Charles's voyages may be seen as resembling, in a very distant fashion, those of Odysseus, for when Charles returns home it is the dog, Nestor, who first recognizes him, despite the fact that as a child Charles had tormented him by shooting arrows at him.

The young Charles's negative feelings about training for business and his subsequent travels around the world obviously pick up on Gerstäcker's own experiences. Charles's boyhood reading of Le Vaillant's *Hunting Adventures in Africa* and Cook's and Kotzebue's *Voyages in the South Seas* surely reflects what must have been available to Gerstäcker as a boy too. With the sight of Juan Fernandez Barthels, the older sailor who takes particular care of Charles on the whaler, explains the connexion with Robinson Crusoe through the fact that Alexander Selkirk, the real-life model for Crusoe, was marooned there for many years. The mention of Juan Fernandez may well combine literary and historical information with Gerstäcker's personal knowledge, since he travelled extensively in the Pacific.

In Hamburg Charles's attention is riveted by the many ships and boats he sees in the harbour, among them the *Kamehameha*, the rough-looking whaler that he will later find himself unexpectedly working on for two years. There too is a ship crowded with emigrants to the United States such as Gerstäcker himself would have sailed on. He paints a touching picture of the emigrants, the widely scattered parts of Germany that they come from, their mixed emotions at leaving their native country 'in all probability for ever'. Mrs Hollberg expresses sympathy with the poor people, but Mr Hollberg shrugs his shoulders, retorting, 'Why . . . poor people? It is all their own doing: no one forces them to go away. Why do they not remain here?' A tall, thin man standing close by asks him whether he has ever been hungry and makes the point that it is economic necessity that drives people to emigrate. German immigration into the American colonies had begun in the early eighteenth century, but the large-scale exodus from Germany that Gerstäcker is alluding to relates to the agricultural depression, crop failures and displacement of handicrafts that characterized the 1840s. By 1860 there were over a million German-born residents in the United States, about a quarter of the total number of foreign-born settlers. This cameo picture of a departing emigrant ship in *The Little Whaler* is just one of many episodes that demonstrate how the adventure story is firmly rooted in the reality of the day.

Like so many children's books, *The Little Whaler* begins with a holiday that then turns into an adventure. Charles's mother has been prescribed a regime of sea-bathing, and if it suits her the family will stay there a few weeks, but the holiday on the small island of Heligoland is a disappointment for the youthful enthusiast of Robinson Crusoe. Gerstäcker gives very little description of the island, since his chief purpose is simply to use it as the setting for Charles to learn how to use a boat and expand his knowledge through listening to Jahn's accounts of his voyages round the world. Heligoland, which had previously been a dependency of Holstein and thus subject to Danish rule, had been gained by Britain in 1807 and ceded to her in 1814. The inhabitants, however, were German and spoke Low German, their main links being with Hamburg.

British readers had been able to learn more about the island from a young woman who had spent four years there as a girl, her father having served with the regiment stationed there. *Heligoland: or, Reminiscences of Childhood*, by M. L'E[strange]. (London: John W. Parker, fifth edition, 1851), is a slim book, most of it centring on the author's heart-rending experience of losing both her mother and father to a fatal illness on the island whilst she was only a child. However, she does provide nearly twenty pages of description of the history, appearance, inhabitants and culture of Heligoland, and there are two attractive lithographs showing a view of the island from the sea and typical adult male and female costumes. The editor of M. L'Estrange's little book declares the existence of Heligoland to be almost forgotten in England, but it was obviously known to Gerstäcker as a holiday resort for the well-to-do in Germany.

As with *The Swiss Family Robinson*, a large part of *The Little Whaler* is taken up with providing detailed information about geography, natural history, climatology, astronomy and the like. There are sections devoted to explaining the trade winds, the formation of coral islands, the nature of icebergs, the habits of penguins on the Falkland Isles and, of course, the arduous job of whaling. The pursuit and slaughter of different species of whale, the dangerous task of extracting oil and dealing with blubber, the filth and stench that the process entails, the sailors' exposure to the elements and enforced continuous work once a whale has been caught – all this is recounted in copious detail. It is not a story for the squeamish, but any boy reading the book would come away armed with a mountain of facts, not only to do with the rigours of whaling, but also covering a wide range of interesting incidental information.

Gerstäcker was not the only German author of boys' adventure stories during the nineteenth century, though in the mid century he was the most widely read. With his tales of travel and daring deeds in America he was following in the footsteps of the Austrian Karl Anton Postl (1793-1864), who used the pseudonym Charles Sealsfield. Sealsfield's most famous book, *Das Kajütenbuch* (1841), was translated by S. Powell as *The Cabin Book; or, National Characteristics* (London, 1852), and another book, *Scenes and Adventures in Central America*, was edited by F. Hardman (Edinburgh and London, 1852). Though popular and admired in the German-speaking countries, Sealsfield never acquired a comparable reputation in Britain, though his American subject-matter proved more attractive to readers in the United States. Towards the end of the nineteenth century another writer of adventure stories gained a devoted readership in Germany. This was Karl May (1842-1912), whose books, especially those dealing with American Indians, are still widely read today. However, none of his books appear to have been translated into English during the period with which we are concerned, probably because there was an ample supply of the same kind of material from the pens of native British authors such as W. H. G. Kingston, R. M. Ballantyne, G. A. Henty and many more.

19. Picture Books

It is not possible within the scope of this book to deal with all the German illustrators whose work found its way into British children's books during the nineteenth century. That would really require a separate study. We shall note elsewhere Wilhelm Kaulbach's illustrations for *The Heroic Life and Exploits of Siegfried the Dragon Slayer* (1848), and his designs for Goethe's *Reynard the Fox* (1860) circulated much more widely. Ludwig Richter's illustrations to Bechstein's fairytales were used for both *The Old Story-Teller* (1854) and *As Pretty as Seven*. Julius Schnorr von Carolsfeld's pictures for the *Nibelungenlied* accompanied Lydia Hands's retelling of the story as *Golden Threads from an Ancient Loom* (1880). While these artists are of course famous in Germany, their names tend to be known only to specialists in Britain, and their illustrative work is simply an accompaniment to a significant text. There are, however, a number of German children's books whose reputations derive principally from their illustrations or from a marvellous coherence of their words and pictures.

In 1844 there appeared in England a book entitled *The Child's Picture and Verse Book: Commonly Called Otto Speckter's Fable Book*, with the original German and with French, translated into English by Mary Howitt (London: Longman, Brown, Green & Longmans). This is a book that requires some explanation. It is based on two German books – *Funfzig Fabeln für Kinder* (Fifty Fables for Children) and *Noch funfzig Fabeln für Kinder* (Another Fifty Fables for Children), both with pictures by Otto Speckter (Hamburg: Friedrich Perthes, 1833 and 1837). The author who provided the verses insisted at first on remaining anonymous, but was the Protestant pastor and teacher Wilhelm Hey (1789-1854), who had in 1832 just been appointed superintendent of Ichtershausen, near Erfurt, in Thuringia, and had married for the second time. Hey was very modest about his literary talents, but his fables were received very warmly and continued to be frequently reprinted in Germany up to the opening decades of the twentieth century. Each of the fables consists of two six-line stanzas skilfully crafted to the understanding of small children and expressing pleasure at the small things of daily life. Otto Speckter (1807-71) provided a lithographed illustration for each fable, and because only his name appeared on the title-pages it was often thought that he had also written the verses. It is understandable therefore that in Britain the fables were thought of as his book. Yet this first English collection of Hey's fables is not decorated with Speckter's original lithographs, but with engravings derived from those of Friedrich Wilhelm Gubitz (1786-1870), based on Speckter's lithographs and done for the French version published by Perthes in 1840. Speckter was himself invited to provide designs for new wood-engravings in 1850 and was apparently disgusted with those that had previously been done. In looking at both German and British editions of Hey's fables, therefore, we find that what is credited to Speckter may often be his only at a remove.

The translator of this first British edition was Mary Howitt (1799-1888), who, together with her husband William and their children, had just spent a protracted period in Germany and who was shortly to become of one the first translators of Hans Christian Andersen's tales into English. Mary Howitt was a prolific author of children's books, writing short stories, novels and verses throughout her long life. Though popular in her own day, few of them have survived into the twentieth century. Only the opening lines of her poem 'The Spider and the Fly', first published in 1834, are still remembered and quoted – '"Will you walk into my parlour?" said the Spider to the Fly, – / "'Tis the prettiest little parlour that ever you did spy..."' Her translation of Hey's verses keeps very close to the original.

A small selection of Hey's fables and their pictures was included in a collection of *Short Stories and Poems* (London: James Burns, 1846), the engravings being reversed from a Hamburg edition of c. 1845. The translation is a new one and nothing like as good as Mary Howitt's. The book is further witness to Burns's interest in German literature that we have noted elsewhere.

The next sight we have of Hey and Speckter comes a dozen years later with *Picture Fables drawn by Otto Speckter*, engraved by the Brothers Dalziel, with rhymes translated from the German of F. (*sic*) Hey by Henry W. Dulcken (London and New York: George Routledge & Co., 1858). The sequence of fables and pictures follows the 1833 German edition for the first twelve items, but then adopts a different pattern. The variations discernible between pictures in the various editions make it questionable to what extent we are really dealing with Speckter's designs. If we look, for example, at the illustrations to 'Bird at the Window', both Speckter's 1833 original and the 1844 Longman edition have a window with rectangular panes and a mother looking out alone, while the 1858 Routledge edition has diamond panes and a small child in front of the mother. It is instructive too to compare the verses for 'The Snowman':

> Seht den Mann, o große Noth!
> Wie er mit dem Stocke droht
> Gestern schon und heute noch!
> Aber niemals schlägt er doch.
> Schneemann, bist ein armer Wicht,
> Hast den Stock und wehrst dich nicht.
> (1833)

> See that man, O fly! quick! quick!
> How he threatens with his stick;
> Yesterday and still to-day!
> Yet his threatening is but play.
> Snowman! thou art a wretched elf,
> Armed, yet can't defend thyself.
> (Howitt)

> Look at him, O what a Guy!
> Who would not before him fly,
> Standing thus, with stick so stout,
> Threat'ning all his foes to rout,
> Did we not, from day to day,
> See him stand the self-same way?
> (Burns edition)

> Look at the man there! Run, boys, quick!
> See how he grasps his great thick stick;
> Two whole days he's been standing so,
> Yet he never hath struck one blow.
> Snow Man, poor man, I'd scorn to be,
> Holding a useless stick, like thee.
> (Dulcken)

Each of the translations keeps to the verse-form of the original and makes a good attempt at conveying the mood and content, but it is easy to see that verse translations cannot hope for strict accuracy. Mary Howitt's version has an echo of the old alphabet rhyme sometimes known as 'Tom

Thumb's Alphabet'. When she refers to the snowman as 'a wretched elf', she recalls 'U was a usurer, a miserable elf', where 'elf' doesn't have the sense of 'fairy', but is simply a derogatory term for 'creature'. Howitt's use of the forms 'thou' and 'thyself' may have a dialectal rather than a would-be 'poetic' resonance, as is possible for Dulcken's 'thee', but that may be used to get a convenient rhyme. Dulcken's 'hath', however, is a needless archaism.

Dulcken's translation was republished in 1868 with the title *One Hundred Picture Fables,* but there do not appear to have been any more British editions of Hey and Speckter's fable book. However, two further translations were made by S. Klingemann and published in Gotha by Friedrich Andreas Perthes, the son of the original Hamburg publisher, as *Fifty Fables for Children* (1867) and *Other Fifty Fables for Children* (1869). Speckter's name is known in Britain chiefly through his pictures for Hey, but he also provided designs for an edition of *Puss in Boots; and the Marquis of Carabas* (1844) and a translation of the Grimms' fairytale 'Brüderchen und Schwesterchen' called *The Charmed Roe* (1847), both published by John Murray.

Before we continue our consideration of books combining verses and pictures, we need to take a look at one of the most striking educational picture books of the mid century. Nicholas Bohny's *The New Picture Book; being Pictorial Lessons on Form, Comparison and Number for Children under Seven Years of Age* (Edinburgh: Edmonston & Douglas, 1858) consists of thirty-six large plates full of hand-coloured pictures calculated to appeal to and instruct a small child. Animals, birds, flowers, trees, butterflies, fungi, fish, soldiers, toys, household objects and so forth are presented both singly and in groups, providing an absorbing introduction to the larger world. Each set of images is provided with questions to capture and extend the child's interest. From a modern point of view the book is a rich and fascinating document of social history. This British version was popular enough to reach a sixth edition in 1873.

The original German work was written by the Swiss educator Niklaus Bohny (1815-56) and was designed for children from two-and-a-half to seven years old, to be used in families, nursery schools, institutions for the deaf and dumb and the first stage of elementary education. It was first published in 1848 by Schreiber and Schill in Esslingen, near Stuttgart, and was translated into many languages and disseminated widely in Europe and North and South America up to the 1920s. Anyone who sees a copy of this or the translation will marvel at the wealth of material presented and the detail of the engaging illustrations. The German book forms part of a tradition that goes back as far as Jan Amos Comenius's *Orbis pictus* (1658) and has as its most distinguished predecessor Friedrich Justin Bertuch's encyclopedic *Bilderbuch für Kinder* (Picture Book for Children) (1790-1830). Bohny, however, was not aiming primarily at scientific accuracy, but rather at providing an educational tool that would teach children basic concepts of form, number and comparison and stimulate them to increase their knowledge of the world. In this he appears to have enjoyed considerable success.

Returning now to the regular kind of children's picture book, we come to Oscar Pletsch (1830-88), a German artist whose work became well known in the latter half of the nineteenth century. At least seventeen books were published in Britain with illustrations by him, either exclusively or accompanied by others, in the period between 1862 and 1875. Their titles make it clear that they deal chiefly with scenes and events in the life of small children, so they very much follow the pattern set by Speckter, though reflecting the style of a later generation. *Buds and Flowers of Childish Life*, with illustrations by Oscar Pletsch, beautifully printed in colours (London and New York: George Routledge & Sons, 1870) is typical of Pletsch's work. The thirty-two colour plates were printed by Leighton Brothers in rich natural colours and present a delightful range of domestic scenes picturing mainly small children, occasionally also parents and servants. A number of outdoor scenes capture activities at different seasons of the year – sledging in the winter, digging in the garden, flying kites, pumping water. This is very much the idyll of middle-class family life with lots of happy children amusing themselves, sometimes unsupervised, other times with father or mother. One scene depicts parents with five children round the dining table and a maid bringing in a big tureen of something to eat. Another shows father, a soldier in uniform, playing with a little girl and her dolls. This is a book designed to give pleasure, and one can readily imagine the enjoyment that Pletsch got out of his drawing and successfully conveyed to his readers. He does include little childish squabbles and tantrums, but nothing that will spoil the mood for long. Simple verses accompany the pictures, but there is no indication of who composed them or whether they were meant as translations. That hardly matters, since the pictures are the main thing. Above all, the book is a world away from the moralizing that dominated the first half of the century.

Pletsch's books are essentially variations on the theme of a happy family at home. In 1861 he drew and engraved twenty-five pictures for an alphabet book that was published as *Wie's im Hause geht / Nach dem Alphabet* (A Domestic Alphabet) (Berlin: Weidmannsche Buchhandlung). Pletsch wrote the verses for each picture and cleverly included a number of items for each letter of the alphabet. He omitted J, which in the German gothic alphabet is identical with I, and combined X and Y in one picture. There is a separate drawing for the title-page. The illustration for P (*Papa*) is a self-portrait of Pletsch with his easel in the background and two children playing at his feet. The drawing for I shows a boy with two old soldiers, and the verses, which refer to the Battle of Leipzig in 1813, which freed Germany from Napoleon, show them to be *Invaliden* (invalids) with two shots in the arm and three in the leg. XY also has a picture of Pletsch and a verse telling the children he knows no words beginning with those letters. For the rest of the alphabet he has no problem in finding suitable objects within the range of a small child's understanding.

This engaging book was turned into English as *Little Lily's Alphabet* (London: Frederick Warne and Co., [1865]), and new verses were written by a person identified only by the initials S. M. P. The pictures do not all correspond to the same letters of the alphabet in English, so there had to be a skilful reassignment for about half of them. The illustration for P (*Papa* in German) is changed into D for Dolly, taking up the little girl's doll in the picture as its focus instead. Similarly, the picture for N (*Naschkatzen* or children always nibbling at sweet things) becomes V for Very naughty children. *Naschen*, looking for nice things to eat between meals, seems to be regarded as a particularly widespread bad habit in nineteenth-century German children's books, but it is almost the only negative piece of behaviour in Pletsch's alphabet. We might perhaps add the picture for T in German, which shows two little girls trying to shut the door to keep out their brother so that they can play by themselves. T stands for *Tölpel*, 'blockhead', *Thunichtgut*, 'good-for-nothing' and *Thür*, 'door'. This is converted into N, which apparently stands for Nelly, the name of the older girl, and naughty, which is how Nelly describes her brother. Apart from this, the rest of the illustrations depict typical scenes of family life inside and near the home. Pletsch's designs portray significant events in a child's daily life and are full of interesting detail. They contain a wealth of social observation.

Another book of Pletsch's is *Happy Child Life*, with rhymes for mothers and children by Mrs Charles Heaton (i.e. Mary Margaret Heaton) (London and New York: George Routledge & Sons, 1875). There is also an undated edition with the same title published by Frederick Warne. The book originally appeared in English with the title *Happy Spring-Time* (1874). The twenty-two colour plates closely resemble those in *Buds and Flowers of Childish Life* in character, providing a mixture of indoor and outdoor scenes, the latter being very obviously German in their townscapes and mountain scenery. One picture that must have elicited a good deal of boyish glee shows a little girl playing an upright piano with a boy sitting turned away from her with his hands covering both ears. Mrs Heaton's verses display no particular distinction and generally anglicize proper names, though she does allow a dog to retain the typically German name Spitz.

Little Lasses and Lads (London: Seeley, Jackson & Halliday, 1869) is in a larger format than *Happy Child Life* and *Buds and Flowers of Childish Life*, but Pletsch's nine illustrations are of a very similar character. They are larger in size and printed in rather subtle muted colours on a rectangular beige ground. Some bear the date 1867 and were presumably done for a German book. Here, however, they are used for a long story, divided into eight chapters, about life on an English farm, though no author's name is given.

Pletsch's style and subject-matter clearly commended itself to several publishers, and his reputation as an illustrator is well deserved. His scenes of childhood and family life are cleverly structured and clearly reflect their day-to-day realities, especially the interplay of small children with their siblings. They have been looked at here as successors to Speckter and have taken us into the latter half of the nineteenth century. Now, however, we have to turn back to a completely different author and illustrator, who, though untrained and amateurish, nonetheless produced a picture book that has never been out of print since it was first published in 1845. The author is Heinrich Hoffmann, and the book is *Struwwelpeter*.

Like many other successful children's books, *Der Struwwelpeter* began its life as a parent's attempt to amuse one of his own children. Heinrich Hoffmann (1809-94), a young doctor in Frankfurt am Main, despaired of finding a suitable book to give his three year old son Carl for Christmas 1844 and returned from the shops with a blank exercise book, in which he proceeded to draw six stories in pictures and verses. Friends and relatives were so taken with what he had done that they urged him to get the stories published. There thus appeared, in time for Christmas 1845, a printed version entitled *Lustige Geschichten und drollige Bilder* (Merry Stories and

Funny Pictures), published in an edition of 3000 copies,[97] price 59 kreutzers, by Dr Löning at the Literarische Anstalt, Frankfurt. The author was named as 'Reimerich Kinderlieb', which translates roughly as 'the rhymester fond of children'. The six stories corresponded to what we know in English as 'Cruel Frederick', 'The Inky Boys', 'The Man that went out Shooting', 'Augustus who would not have any Soup', 'Little Suck-a-Thumb' and, finally, 'Shock-Headed Peter'. The book sold out in a month, so a second edition followed, this time attributed to 'Heinrich Kinderlieb', with two more stories – 'Harriet and the Matches' and 'Fidgety Philip'. With the third edition 'Shock-Headed Peter' appeared on the title-page. Only with the fifth edition did 'Shock-Headed Peter' move to the first position among the stories. Two further stories were added – 'Johnny Head-in-Air' and 'Flying Robert' – and the author finally identified himself fully as Dr Heinrich Hoffmann, thus completing his gradual emergence from pseudonymity to full and open acknowledgement of his authorship. These early, lithographically illustrated editions followed the author's original drawings very closely, but in 1858 they were redone as wood-engravings with some modifications in the pictorial form. This latter format is the basis of most subsequent editions, which now, in Germany, have passed the thousand mark. After Grimms' fairytales it is the most widely circulated German children's book.

An English-language version was first published in Leipzig in 1848 by Friedrich Volckmar and quickly became popular in England. The anonymous translation became the standard English version. Though other renderings were made later, none were able to supplant it. Indeed, when Blackie produced a new translation, an anonymous commentator in *The Times* (6 January 1910) went carefully through it and concluded: 'In every poem are changes, and all are for the worse. Although, as for that, the quality of the change is immaterial; it is the fact of change at all that is wrong. A few things are sacred still'. The original translation had become so familiar to generations of British parents and children that they quoted and recited it at the drop of a hat. Any divergence could only be experienced as alienating and not the real thing at all. This new translation, like all the others, including Mark Twain's *Slovenly Peter* (first published New York

---

97 In his *Lebenserinnerungen* (written in 1889-92) Hoffmann stated that the first edition consisted of 1500 copies, but Ulrich Wiedmann, quoting from a letter Hoffmann wrote in October-December 1845, has convincingly argued that it must have been 3000. See Ulrich Wiedmann, 'Fünfzehnhundert? Wer bietet mehr?' *Struwwelpost*, 4 (1998), pp. 13-16.

W w Winter is everywhere,
And bitter the north winds blow;
And look, they have made up there
A capital man of snow!
He has a pail on his head,
And a broom stuck in for a gun;
Let us go out—Willie said
There would be plenty of fun.

28. *Little Lily's Alphabet. With Rhymes by S. M. P. and Pictures by Oscar Pletsch* (c. 1865). W for Winter.

and London: Harper & Brothers, 1935), had little success in Britain.

The original translation, *The English Struwwelpeter or Pretty Stories and Funny Pictures*, naturally took over the lithographically reproduced pictures of the early German editions, which have attractive curlicues, leaves and branches linking the different phases of the pictorial representation of some of the stories. The pictures were hand-coloured. This format then gave way to that of the German editions of 1858 and afterwards, which has remained the standard up to the present day. Though some people may have certain verses imprinted indelibly in their minds, for the majority of readers it will be Hoffmann's pictures that have become part of their living memory. Struwwelpeter himself, with his bizarrely long finger-nails and gigantic Afro-style hair, is perhaps the most, though not the only, striking figure. Hoffmann's book, in whatever version, presents an inspired fusion of stories and pictures. The images are what have given the book its enduring appeal. Attempts at replacing Hoffmann's 'naïve' drawings and their often oddly proportioned figures with the work of other, professional artists have never succeeding in ousting them permanently. The originals and their 1858 successors have an untamable vitality that is aptly embodied in the figure of Struwwelpeter himself.

We now need to take a closer look at *The English Struwwelpeter* and examine how the German book was transplanted from one culture to another. What kind of changes were made, consciously or unconsciously, in the process? What was the nature of the book's appeal, and why did it become so popular?

Both the German and the English versions of the complete *Struwwelpeter* have twenty-four full-page lay-outs of pictures and verses, printed on only one side of the page. After the title-page Struwwelpeter himself occupies the next page and has a status equivalent to that of the portrait of the author that so often appears as a frontispiece in books of the period. Insofar as he has a 'story', this is concentrated in the one picture of the extraordinary boy, accompanied by the discarded scissors and comb. Each of the following items tells a proper story with several narrative stages and an appropriate series of pictures to accompany them. The verbal and pictorial narratives are closely correlated, and a small child would be able to follow the story from the pictures alone. The pictures are clear, packed with action and gesture, brightly coloured and conceived as a unity with the verses on each page. The balance of text and image is cleverly calculated. Some of the pages have structural links between the pictures in the form of plant or tree scrolls, but the more one examines the lay-out of each page, the more one admires Hoffmann's skill in varying the techniques that he uses for dividing the pages. In 'The Story of the Inky Boys', for example, the woolly-headed black-a-moor and the white boys, Edward, William and Arthur, are placed as it were north, south, east and west on a complex framework representing a garden, each of them engaged in a different activity. Each boy is separately delineated and stands out from the whiteness of the page, as do the flowers, shrubs and other ornaments that decorate the page and provide additional, but no distracting interest. The two pages that depict 'tall Agrippa' (the German 'der große Nikolas') each have the massive figure in his long red gown and tasselled cap dominating the page, with the respective verses squeezed into the small space left. For 'Little Suck-a-Thumb' there are four pictures, of which the first two and the last one occupy the left half of the page, while the frightening picture with the 'great, long, red-legg'd scissor man' dashing in from the right takes up the whole of the top half of the second page of the story.

The revised version of 'Flying Robert' (i.e. those following the German editions of 1858 and later) places the three illustrations within picture-frames and puts them alternately on the left, right and left sides of the page with the verses next to them. These can thus be seen to mimic the pattern of landscape paintings in which a human figure adds interest to the scene. They are the only illustrations in the book that have this character. Where there are landscape elements elsewhere, as in 'Cruel Frederick' and, to a lesser degree, 'The Man that went out Shooting', they have more in common with medieval paintings in which several chronological phases of a narrative are combined in a single picture. The sheer inventiveness of Hoffmann's technique in varying the lay-out of pictures and verses and in knowing precisely what impression he wants to give of the characters in his stories is a major factor in the book's enduring appeal. It is a book to which children (and parents) can return again and again, not only to enjoy this variety, but also because they are captivated or mesmerized by many of the images. The scissor-man is the most memorably terrifying of these images (many people have told me how frightened they were as children by this picture), but Harriet's blazing frock and Augustus's decline from being a 'chubby lad' to scarcely weighing as much as a sugar-plum, dying on the fifth day, are comparably stark.

Undeniably, several of the pictures, much more than the verses, have the capacity to scare small children. Some parents and educationalists, especially in recent times, have castigated *Struwwelpeter* for this very reason and regard the book as totally unsuitable for today's children. This position is misguided. The history of the transmission of fairytales is strewn with examples of editors and adapters who have bowdlerized such favourites as 'Little Red Riding-Hood', 'Hansel and Gretel' and 'The Juniper Tree' in the attempt to protect children from frightening or unsuitable material. Today's children seem to be more resilient with regard to horror than their parents. They do not require a diet that is all sweetness and light and never exposes them to pain or fear. Heinrich Hoffmann would have read the stories together with his three year old son and would have been able to reassure him in the event of anxiety or tears, but his intention was primarily to amuse, as the book's original German title, *Lustige Geschichten und drollige Bilder*, plainly indicates. We have to remember that cautionary tales and a strongly moralizing authorial viewpoint were the norm in both nineteenth-century Germany and Victorian Britain. Children were commonly regarded as having natural proclivities to thoughtlessness, disobedience and wickedness that had to be checked and controlled. It was Hoffmann's genius to have set his awful warnings firmly in a humorous context. The fact that the conclusion to every story is so over the top is meant to provoke laughter and be understood as a satire at the expense of the traditional moral tale. Twenty years later Lewis Carroll also cocked a snook at the habit of moralizing with the figure of the Duchess in *Alice's Adventures in Wonderland* (1865). Carroll uses parody and the absurd to make his point; Hoffmann relies on grotesque exaggeration.

By and large both formats of *The English Struwwelpeter* conform to their German models, though there are some small differences. The German original and the version of 1858 and later contain in 'Cruel Frederick' a chamber pot beneath the naughty boy's bed, to which he has to retire on being bitten by the dog. This is eliminated from both English versions. This seems to be a part of the universal squeamishness of the British about anything to do with the natural functions of the body. It affects the transmission of the stories of Till Eulenspiegel, which abound in scatological incident. Moreover, none of the nineteenth-century translators of the Grimms' 'The Fisherman and his Wife' could cope with the fact that in the Low German original the couple first lived in a chamber pot.

The differences between the earlier and later German editions are too numerous to go into in detail, but there is one that affects the accuracy of the English text. In both the original German and the first English edition of

'Harriet and the Matches', the girl is definitely wearing an apron, and this is explicitly mentioned in the English and German accompanying verses. The apron remains in the German editions of 1858 and later, but it has vanished in the later English editions, thus creating an incongruence between text and image. There had been a similar incongruence in the original German drawings for 'Der böse Friedrich', since the text says that the dog had brought the whip with him and was carefully looking after it when he was scoffing the food originally meant for Friedrich. There is, however, no sign of the whip in the picture, but later versions correct the mistake. The first English version likewise has no whip, but the later versions do.

Translating verse from one language to another is trickier than translating prose. The anonymous English translator of *Struwwelpeter* followed the rhythms and rhyming patterns of the German very closely. The verses consist almost wholly of four-beat rhyming couplets, mainly with a monosyllabic rhyme, with a very few short lines for special effects. The English version uses a few more lines for eight of the eleven pieces (including the title-page) and abbreviates one. This gives a total of 365 lines as against the German 321. Obviously, a number of changes were necessary to make the book suitable for an English readership. The German proper names were changed into English ones. The title held firm to 'Struwwelpeter', but in the verses he becomes 'Shock-headed Peter'. 'Friedrich' becomes 'Frederick', and the anonymous dog 'Tray'. 'Paulinchen' is re-christened 'Harriet', but Minz and Maunz, the cats, lose their names altogether. The German 'Ludwig', 'Kaspar'and 'Wilhelm' become 'Edward', 'William' and 'Arthur' in 'The Inky Boys'. 'Der große Nikolas', the descendant of St. Nicholas, who doles out presents and punishments to German boys and girls before Christmas and who looks like Tsar Nicholas I in the illustrations, has no place in British tradition, but is replaced by a menacing, equally untraditional 'Agrippa'. Konrad of 'Little Suck-a-Thumb' and 'Philipp', the fidget, get English spellings for their names. 'Suppen-Kaspar' is converted into 'Augustus who would not have any soup'. The familiar 'Hanns Guck-in-die-Luft' turns easily into 'Johnny Head-in-Air', while in the final story 'Robert' needs no change at all.

A number of other alterations point to changes for cultural reasons. In 'Cruel Frederick' the dog eats soup, pies and puddings (in the text) rather than the German cake, liver-sausage and wine, though the picture remains the same. Similarly, in 'Fidgety Philip' the German plate, bottle of wine and bread are replaced by 'Glasses, plates, knives, forks and all'. In 'The

Inky Boys' there is no mention of the German *Brezel* (pretzel) that Arthur still carries in his hand in the English book; it has no equivalent in British culture. The title-page verses have a rather different ring to them in the two languages. The English makes no reference to the Christ Child of the German, and while the verses begin with a list of how children are expected to be 'good', they go on to more specific detail about bad behaviour:

> Naughty, romping girls and boys
> Tear their clothes and make a noise,
> Spoil their pinafores and frocks,
> And deserve no Christmas-box.

Hoffmann's original contains no such negatives here. Such other differences as there are between the German and English texts are largely a matter of slight amplifications or contractions, usually supported by the illustrations. 'Harriet and the Matches' actually introduces a new figure into the story – Nurse, who, together with Mamma, had left the unfortunate girl alone. Father, who, so the cats point out, forbade Paulinchen to touch the matches, is entirely eliminated. Otherwise it is fair to say that the tone of the German original is very well kept.

Given the character of Hoffmann's book in both its German and its English manifestations, how do we evaluate it today? Clearly, patterns of child-rearing have changed dramatically since the mid nineteenth century. Many parents would now roundly condemn the bogy-man threats that figure in 'The Inky Boys' and 'Little Suck-a-Thumb'. The 'great, long, red-legg'd scissor-man' is indubitably the most disturbing of Hoffmann's creations, for girls as well as boys – we need not go into the possible fears of castration – but Hoffmann must have considered its relation to the habit of thumb-sucking as being as disproportionate and absurd as Robert being blown away in a storm no one knows where or Paulinchen (Harriet) being burnt to ashes through playing with the matches. Modern parents may disagree about the rightness or wrongness of the threat, but the image of the scissor-man remains immensely powerful.

The ten stories as a whole encapsulate timeless problems in children's behaviour. Parents still worry about children sucking their thumbs, get annoyed at them for refusing to eat certain things, fidgeting on their chairs at the dinner-table, failing to look where they are going, refusing to keep themselves neat and tidy. Like Cruel Frederick, children can be wilfully cruel to animals and other people, and they are apt to mock and bully other children who are not just like themselves. Children also still have to learn what things in the home and elsewhere are dangerous and may injure or even kill them. The enactment of these universal struggles between parents and children reflects the expectations and priorities of the mid nineteenth century, but it is surely clear from the first page that this is a book in which fantasy, not realism, prevails. What actual child could ever acquire those long fingernails and that bush of hair? What cruel boy could be displaced at the dinner-table by a dog so fastidious as to wear a napkin round his neck?

The world of *Struwwelpeter* is marked by extremes. It encompasses violence perpetrated by and on children. Danger and death are near at hand. Harriet is burnt to death through playing with matches; Augustus starves to death in five days through refusing his soup; Robert is blown to oblivion in a storm; Conrad has his thumbs cut off; Johnny is almost drowned; Frederick is bitten by the dog and confined to bed; Edward, William and Arthur are dyed black as ink. Yet in none of these instances is any punishment or retribution carried out by a parent. There are threats and prophecies, to be sure, but in the one instance where the parents are present – with Fidgety Philip – their actions are mild. Mamma first 'look'd very grave', then 'did fret and frown', while 'Papa made such a face!' Though Philip is 'in sad disgrace', his parents are not described as undertaking any punitive measures:

> Poor Papa, and poor Mamma
> Look quite cross, and wonder how
> They shall make their dinner now.

Critics might well point out, however, that the doctor in 'Cruel Frederick', Agrippa and the scissor-man are all displaced parent-figures. The doctor, indeed, is hardly a disguise, since that was Hoffmann's own profession.

The assorted children in these stories are all alone. This is what sets them apart from the majority of fairytale protagonists, from Marie and Fritz in E. T. A. Hoffmann's *Nutcracker*, from the four brothers in *The Swiss Family Robinson*, from the happy children in Pletsch's illustrations. Heinrich Hoffmann's child characters appear to be only children with no support from siblings or friends. Even the animals are lined up against them. One dog bites Cruel Frederick, and another knocks over Johnny Head-in-Air. The fishes laugh at the latter's discomfiture. The two cats warn Harriet of the danger of her disobedience. Everything seems weighted against the children. The only story that offers a different pattern – 'The Man that went out Shooting' – has an animal, the hare, in a situation of powerlessness that elsewhere characterizes the child. This is a nice example of role-

29. Heinrich Hoffmann, *The English Struwwelpeter. Pretty Stories and Funny Pictures for Little Children. Fifteenth Edition* (c. 1858) 'The Story of Fidgedy [sic] Philip'.

reversal, but the fact that Hoffmann transposes it into the realm of animals perhaps reveals his unwillingness to countenance a story in which a child might get the better of an adult. Most children reading this story, however, will instinctively recognize their identity with the hare and laugh at the huntsman's predicament and the shooting of his wife's coffee-cup and saucer. There is a slight sting in the tail when the hare's own child gets scalded by coffee from the cup. Was even this success of the hare/child too subversive to be left unalloyed?

Struwwelpeter, being written by a father for his little son, is naturally a very boy-centred book. Poor Harriet, the only girl, burns to ashes through her disobedience. Did that mean that little Carl Hoffmann was more easily able to accept the import of that story for his own behaviour? That is a story in which Mamma and Nurse are the authority figures, as Mamma also is in 'Little Suck-a-Thumb'. Her smug satisfaction at her son's loss of both his thumbs at the hands of the scissor-man links strongly with the grim silence she displays at the actions of Fidgety Philip. Mamma is a rather fearsome person, more so than Papa. Cruel Frederick's whipping of Mary, his Nurse, is his last vicious act before attacking the dog. But Mary surely deserves our sympathy.

The twenty-four pages of *Struwwelpeter* present an astonishing diversity of material. The book's strength and durability surely stem from the fact that it does not view everything from exactly the same angle. It breaks the mould of the deadly serious moral tales and rhymes that were a staple of both German and British children's books of the time. The moral messages are still present, but Hoffmann's use of fantasy, humour and extraordinary visual inventiveness are primary. His stories are anchored in everyday family life. That is their starting point, but the stories in every other respect transcend them.

The earliest English editions of *Struwwelpeter* were published in Germany, and it is not certain just when the first edition was published in Britain. Many were co-published with the original German publisher, Literarische Anstalt Rütten and Loening of Frankfurt, but it was rare for them to bear a date. The book became extraordinarily popular. Round about 1865 the firm of Routledge, Warnes and Routledge attempted to muscle in on this money-spinner and published a new edition, entitled *Struwelpeter* (sic), with new pictures and newly translated verses. This was in every way an inferior version. The alterations seem to have been calculated to avoid copyright problems, beginning with the different spelling of the title (with a single 'w') and the lack of any author's, illustrator's or translator's name. Although 'Struwelpeter' provides the book's name, there are no picture and verses about him, nor is there any equivalent to the German title-page. Moreover, the story of 'Suck-a-Thumb' is also omitted. The eight stories retained are presented in an entirely different order from the original complete editions and are given different titles. The characters are for the most part given different names as well. The pictures are based on Hoffmann's, but drawn in a different style and printed with less variety in colour. However, as the verses are printed on separate pages and rarely on the same double spread as the pictures, the book completely lacks coherence.

There are too many differences from the English original for all to be noted, so the following must suffice. 'Johnny Head-in-Air' is now called simply 'Bob', and his writing-case (German 'Mappe') is wrongly given as an atlas. In 'The marvellous Story of the Sportsman and the Hare' the hare's child is misinterpreted as a little pig, which results in the following conclusion to the hare's shooting of the hunter's wife's coffee cup:

> The spoon which dropp'd beside the well,
> A little pig pick'd it up as it fell,
> And, knowing 'twas silver by the smell,
> He ran with it to a Jew to sell.

Several changes are made to 'The Surprising Story of the Three Boys and the Blackamoor'. The naughty boys are called Tom, Walter and Master Jack', and Agrippa ('der große Nikolas') becomes 'the wise and good Magician Hum', who is depicted wearing a blue gown with a red lining and yellow facings that comes only just below his knees. The blackamoor is shown, not with bare torso and red shorts as in the original, but with calf-length striped trousers, a blue jacket, red waistcoat and a straw hat, cutting a rather dandified figure. In 'The Surprising Story of Alfred and his Bread and Milk' Augustus is the only character to acquire a surname as well as a new first name; he becomes Alfred Jones. On the fifth day of refusing his bread and milk (not soup) he becomes 'lighter than a feather' and dies. While the verses in this edition keep to the general sense of the original, they are often metrically and syntactically awkward. Given all the inadequacies of this edition, affecting pictures, verses and lay-out, it is not surprising that it made no headway.

While there were a number of American translations of *Struwwelpeter* during the nineteenth century, beginning as early as 1849, they are outside the purview of this book as none of them, to my knowledge, made it across the Atlantic. The only exception is Mark Twain's *Slovenly Peter*, composed in 1891, but not published until 1935 (New York: Limited Editions Club, The Marbanks Press; also New York and London: Harper & Brothers). Several other British translations were made, but copies are not easy to locate. Among them are *The Magic Lantern Struwelpeter* (London: Frederick Warne, 1896; possibly related to the Routledge, Warnes and Routledge edition): *Struwelpeter of Today* (London: Dean, c. 1900); *Shock Headed Peter and Other Funny Stories*, by Dr Hoffmann (*Books for the Bairns*, no. 68, October 1901); *The English Struwwelpeter* (London: Dean, 1905; a rag book); *Struwwelpeter, or Merry Stories and Funny Pictures* (London: Blackie & Son, c. 1909).

The *Books for the Bairns* edition is radically different from the others in that the format is much reduced in size and thus both verses and pictures are spread out over more pages. The pictures are modelled on those of the earliest hand-coloured editions, but rely solely on line without any colour. The characters' dress is mainly brought up to date, but Johnny Head-in-Air wears what looks like a kilt rather than the trousers he has in the post-1858 editions. Some of the characters are renamed, so in 'The Very Sad Story of the Matches' Paulinchen (Harriet) becomes Katie, while the cats are called Tib and Tab. In 'The Story of the Black Boys' the white youngsters are called Bobby, Tom and Will, and the tale is anglicized enough for Will to carry a Union Jack. The wife of the man who went out shooting is burlesqued as 'Mrs Nimrod'. Little Suck-a-Thumb remains as Conrad, but Augustus is converted into Jack and refuses to eat porridge rather than soup. The verses are a largely independent translation with occasional phrases reminiscent of or perhaps lifted from the first English version. This *Books for the Bairns* edition was very modest in format, but it was actually among the twenty-five items from the series that was reissued by Ernest Benn in 1926.

The Blackie and Son edition has already been alluded to on account of the negative reaction to the translation by a writer in *The Times*. As is the case with several of the other editions, this indulges in a certain amount of renaming of the characters. Although the verses call the eponymous hero 'shock-headed Peter', the title above the stock picture has 'Untidy Peter'. Poor Harriet is called Pauletta, and the cats (as in the *Books for the Bairns* edition) are Tib and Tab. In 'The Story of the Little Black Boys' the 'pitch-black nigger-boy' is referred to as 'inky Sambo', the name no doubt being an allusion to Helen Bannerman's hugely popular *Story of Little Black Sambo*, first published in 1899. The white boys are called Arthur, Charlie and William, and the pretzel is described as a 'curly bun'. The boy who sucked his thumbs is here called Jimmy, while the boy who wouldn't eat his soup is Tommy. Curiously, in the pictures for the latter the cross for his grave is still marked 'Augustus'. The pictures for this edition are the traditional ones; only the verses have been redone. Later editions published by Blackie and Son reverted to the well-worn verses.

The amazing thing about *Struwwelpeter* is the fact that once Heinrich Hoffmann's book had got off the ground it spawned all manner of imitations. While the firm of Rütten and Loening zealously defended its copyright of Hoffmann's pictures and verses in the German-speaking countries, his humorous approach to the cautionary tale was quickly adopted in both Germany and Britain. The firm of Dean and Son round about 1858 brought out a 'New Series of English Struwelpeters, or, Amusing Stories, with Comic Engravings. Fit for little boys and girls'. It started off with 'No. 1. *English Struwelpeter*. Translated from the original German, with the original cuts'. The booklets that followed varied the themes relentlessly. We find verses on 'The Dainty Little Boy', 'The Little Boy who Bit his Nails', 'The Girl who Sucked her Fingers' (no. 2, *Comic Crumbs to Feed Little Ones*), 'The Little Boy who would not be Washed', 'The Boy who Played with Fire', 'The Girl who would not Comb her Hair' (no. 4, *Naughty Boys and Girls*). If we trawl through the series of ten booklets, we gain a virtually complete inventory of childish misbehaviour, but few of the fates narrated display much of the fantasy combined with grotesque comedy that is Hoffmann's hallmark. Some of the verses may amuse, but they are chiefly designed to instil obedience through warning examples. They rub in their messages with unnecessary admonitions as if their readers might otherwise fail to see the point.

One of the more attractive examples of these *Struwwelpeter* derivatives was a German book entitled *Lachende Kinder*, with pictures by Theodor Hosemann (Frankfurt am Main: Literarische Anstalt Rütten & Loening, 1850). The verses were by Adolf Glassbrenner, whose name, however, does not appear on the title-page. This book is one of the few derivatives that have enjoyed a considerable life of their own. A seventeenth impression was published as late as 1913. The book contains ten tales and an ABC, all illustrated in a style similar to Hoffmann's, but displaying the obvious skill of one of Germany's most distinguished illustrators. It was translated into English by Madame de Chatelain as *A Laughter Book for Little Folk* (London: Cundall & Addey, 1851), the ABC being omitted. The ratio of female to male protagonists is more evenly balanced than in Hoffmann's

Struwwelpeter: there are four girls to six boys. We have 'Slovenly Kate', 'Tell-Tale Jenny', 'Headstrong Nancy' and 'Screaming Annie' to line up against 'Envious Tom', 'Untidy Tom', 'Charley, the Story-Teller' (i.e. the fibber), 'Sammy Sweet-Tooth', 'Ned, the Toy-Breaker' and 'Prying Will'. Sammy Sweet-Tooth is the reverse of Augustus who would not eat his soup: he grows so fat 'He cannot waddle – much less run'. The verses continue:

> Still, like a bubble filled with air,
> He swells enough to make one stare, –
> And, should the worst come to the worst,
> To-morrow he will surely burst!

'Headstrong Nancy' is very much in the tradition of tales like the Grimms' 'King Thrushbeard' and Bechstein's 'The Two Bones of Contention', in which an unruly female is tamed. Nancy's three dollies first warn her one night about her headstrong ways, but on getting no satisfactory response plant a moustache over her lips and take their leave for better children. All her close relatives do the same, and the moustache sticks firmly to her ever after. Proper behaviour is thus strictly gender-related, but it is a sad conclusion that being headstrong is somehow acceptable in a male, though not in a female. Hosemann's illustrations are deftly amusing, but they don't pick out the particularities of each character in the way that Hoffmann's do.

Hoffmann, probably unconsciously, but certainly serendipitously, touched such deep places in the human psyche that his characters and their misfortunes resonated with readers long after they had exchanged juvenile anxieties and pleasures for sober adulthood. The result was that, from the late nineteenth century onwards, *Struwwelpeter* provided a model for all kinds of political and social satires.[98] The pictures and verses were so well known that they could be taken for granted and pressed into service for other ends. In Germany Henry Ritter's *Der politische Struwwelpeter* (Düsseldorf: Buddeus, 1849) can be seen as the most accomplished of the early adaptations, here focussed on the political upheaval of the 1848 revolution and its aftermath. It is perhaps not so remarkable that Hoffmann's children's book gave rise to such satires in Germany, but it is extraordinary that there were several in Britain at the end of the nineteenth and beginning of the twentieth centuries. *The Political Struwwelpeter*, by Harold Begbie, with illustrations by F. Carruthers Gould (London: Grant Richards, 1899),

---

98 See David Blamires, 'Some German and English Political Travesties of *Struwwelpeter*', in *Connections: Essays in Honour of Eda Sagarra on the Occasion of her 60th Birthday*, edited by Peter Skrine et al. (Stuttgart: Hans-Dieter Heinz, 1993), pp. 19-27.

centred on the problems of the British Empire in South Africa and Ireland, went into a second edition within a month and was followed by *The Struwwelpeter Alphabet* by the same pair and the same publisher in 1900. The earlier book depicts the British Lion as Struwwelpeter and declares:

> See the British Lion pose,
> Wildly groping for his foes!
> Men who tinker up the laws
> Never manicure his claws:
> And you will observe with pain
> No one ever crimps his mane;
> Seeing that he's so neglected
> Do you wonder he's dejected?

These books are an amazing confirmation of how widely known the English *Struwwelpeter* was. The satire would have had little resonance without it. In 1914 it served once more as the starting point for *Swollen-headed William. Painful Stories and Funny Pictures after the German!* (London: Methuen & Co.). The text was by E. V. Lucas, drawings by Geo. Morrow. This was just one of many satirical attacks on the Kaiser. During the Nazi period *Struwwelpeter* was used again to attack Hitler and his henchmen in three further parodies – *Truffle Eater. Pretty Stories and Funny Pictures*, by Oistros (pseudonym for Humbert Wolfe) (London: Arthur Barker, 1933); *Struwwelhitler. A Nazi Story Book by Doktor Schrecklichkeit*, by Robert and Philip Spence (London: Haycock Press, 1941); and *Schicklgrüber*, by Robert Colling-Pyper and Margaret Stavridi (Calcutta: Thacker's Press and Directories, 1943).

In addition to these political satires there were some others, more in the nature of burlesques, that focussed on social or cultural themes. *The Egyptian Struwwelpeter* (London: H. Grevel & Co., [1896]) was a translation of *Der Aegyptische Struwwelpeter* (Vienna: Carl Gerold's Sohn, 1895), of which the manuscript was originally done in 1894 by Fritz, Magdalena and Richard Netolitzky as a present for a friend of the family.[99] The Austrian edition had to be withdrawn because of infringements of Rütten & Loening's copyright, but the English edition escaped these problems. The transposition of Hoffmann's stories and pictures to an ancient Egyptian setting is very engagingly achieved. Next came two independent British parodies. *Petrol Peter*, by Archibald Williams, illustrated by A. Wallis Mills

---

99 See Adelheid Hlawacek, 'Der Aegyptische Struwwelpeter – ein Kuriosum der österreichischen Kinderliteratur?', in *Struwwelpeter-Hoffmann gestern und heute*, edited by G. H. Herzog et al. (Frankfurt am Main: Sinemis, 1999), pp. 88-106.

(London: Methuen & Co., [1906]), is a satire on the very recent introduction of the motor car on to the road, while *The Marlborough Struwwelpeter*, by A. de C. Williams (Marlborough: The 'Times' Office, [1908]) adapts the theme to public school life.[100] No other countries apart from Germany and Britain have given rise to such an abundance of translations and satirical adaptations of Hoffmann's masterpiece.

The enthusiasm with which *Struwwelpeter* was received in Germany led Hoffmann to compose a number of other children's books in a similar style, but none came anywhere near *Struwwelpeter* in popularity. Only one of them was translated into English. This was his Christmas fantasy *König Nußknacker und der arme Reinhold. Ein Kindermährchen* (Frankfurt am Main: Literarische Anstalt Rütten & Loening, 1851), which was deftly rendered into English by J. R. Planché as *King Nut-Cracker or the Dream of Poor Reinhold. A Fairy Tale for Children* (London: ? William Tegg, 1855). The idea of children interacting with toys coming to life goes back, of course, to E. T. A. Hoffmann's *Nußknacker und Mausekönig* and had often been re-used in Germany. Clara Fechner had included in *Die schwarze Tante* (Leipzig: F. A. Brockhaus, 1848) a story entitled 'Nußknaker und Zukerpüppchen', which had appeared in English as *Nut-Cracker and Sugar-Dolly*, translated by Charles A. Dana (London: Joseph Cundall, 1849). Robert Reinick also used the idea in *Die Wurzelprinzessin* (1848).

Heinrich Hoffmann's *King Nut-Cracker* lacks the bite and memorable verses of *Struwwelpeter* and the structural complexity and shimmering perspectives of his namesake's subtle story. It is, in fact, a sentimental tale of a poor, sick boy who is taken by an angel one Christmas Eve into a delightful world of living toys, from which he awakes the next morning restored to health and happiness and with a Christmas tree and all kinds of toys to entrance him. Hoffmann's verses are more varied and ambitious than those he wrote for *Struwwelpeter*, but they have less impact. The main interest of the book lies in the extended opportunity for illustration that its thirty-two pages provided. The scene depicting market stalls set out on the Römerberg in Frankfurt and the picture of the trumpeter are the most striking images in the book, but we have to note, towards the end, the reappearance of Struwwelpeter and his companions in a procession that properly ends with the thread-thin Augustus who would not eat his soup. Reinhold is a slightly older boy than the children in *Struwwelpeter*; he is

---

100 See David Blamires, 'Social Satire in English *Struwwelpeter* Parodies', *Princeton Library Journal* 62, 1 (Winter 2000), pp. 45-58.

six or seven in the German original, but Planché does not indicate his age. The English version did not enjoy the commercial success of *Struwwelpeter*. It does not appear to have been republished after its first appearance, and consequently copies are now scarce and very expensive when they come on to the market.

King Nut-Cracker is a genial, but superficial piece of writing, completely lacking the ambivalence that makes *Struwwelpeter* so powerful in its psychological impact. The author to whom we now turn, Wilhelm Busch, shares some of that ambivalence and power, but operates in a different context and with different aims. For one thing, Busch was a professional artist, while Hoffmann was an amateur, and for another, Busch's target audience was not only or principally small children, but more general and included adults. Even his child readers were older than the three to six year olds for whom *Struwwelpeter* was written. He worked on a much broader front than Hoffmann.

Wilhelm Busch (1832-1908) was born in Wiedensahl, a village in the kingdom of Hanover, but not far from Westphalia. It was a place that he was greatly attached to and returned to frequently as an adult. He studied first at the Polytechnic in Hanover, then went to the Academy of Art in Düsseldorf and later to Antwerp and Munich. From 1859 he contributed to the satirical *Fliegende Blätter* and the *Münchner Bilderbogen*, both highly popular publications. In 1865 he published his best known work, *Max und Moritz*, but both before and after there came from his pen a steady stream of humorous stories in pictures and verse that constitute his claim to lasting fame. Alongside this Busch also was a serious painter, much influenced by the seventeenth-century Dutch school, but alert too to the contemporary work of the French Impressionists. Busch's paintings and drawings reflect his abiding interest in the people, daily life and landscape of his boyhood home. Their skill and strength, however, have never gained the public recognition accorded to his other work.

Busch's most famous work, *Max und Moritz*, presents a sequence of seven tricks played by the eponymous pair of boys on various people in their village – Widow Bolte, Tailor Böck, Schoolmaster Lämpel, Uncle Fritz, the baker and Farmer Mecke. Max and Moritz are pranksters in the lineage of Till Eulenspiegel, makers of mischief for its own sake. They kill and steal Widow Bolte's hens and cock. They lure Tailor Böck on to a footbridge from which they have sawn the supports so that he falls into the water. They fill Schoolmaster Lämpel's pipe with gunpowder and cause an explosion.

They put cockchafers into Uncle Fritz's bed. After this things change somewhat. Falling down the baker's chimney, they are made into huge loaves and baked in the oven. Although they manage to eat themselves out of the bread, in the last episode Farmer Mecke takes them in sacks to the mill, where they are ground into little pieces and eaten by the miller's fowls. The pranks thus form a circular sequence, beginning and ending with domestic fowls, but with reversed results. Meanwhile, everyone in the village rejoices that they will be plagued no longer by the troublesome pair.

The book begins with tricks in which the reader is expected to identify with the two boys. From a child's point of view the widow, tailor, schoolmaster and Uncle Fritz are legitimate targets, and their discomfiture is amusing, though they have done nothing to deserve Max and Moritz's attentions. But then the tables are turned, and in the last two episodes the boys get their come-uppance, after which the village reverts to adult control and quiet. From the adult point of view there is no lasting harm, but from the child's point of view it is clear that the pranks cannot be tolerated. Max and Moritz are disposed of in a way every bit as drastic as Paulinchen (Harriet), Suppen-Kaspar (Augustus) or Flying Robert. But while the characters in *Struwwelpeter* have parents close at hand, Max and Moritz are curiously alone and independent. They are free agents, free from parental control and with no apparent home. It's not clear whether they are friends or brothers, though to judge from their divergent pictorial appearances the former is more likely. In any case, they are always together and function as a unit. Possibly Busch took their names from Glassbrenner and Hosemann's *Lachende Kinder*, in which there are two stories entitled 'Vom neidischen Moritz' (Envious Moritz) and 'Vom unordentlichen Max' (Untidy Max). Busch's boys, however, do not have any distinguishing traits of behaviour.

Busch is often thought of as an ancestor of the comic strip, and rightly so. His stories are essentially visual in character and full of lively incident. Beginning with the two boys, the one with a round face and shock of hair, the other with a pointed chin and three odd tufts of hair, the various actors in Busch's drama are caricatures. Widow Bolte is fat and plain, with a dumpling of a nose, while Böck wears a bizarre red hat and Lämpel is grotesquely tall and thin. Like many another of Busch's comic male figures, Uncle Fritz has laughably thin legs and buttocks. But even though the cartoon-like pictures carry the story, Busch matches them with his deft and witty verses. He is a master of the rhyming couplet, whether it stands alone or forms part of longer narrative unit.

The first translation into English was actually an American edition entitled *Max and Maurice. A Juvenile History in Seven Tricks*, by William Busch, translated from the German by Charles T. Brooks (Boston: Roberts Brothers, 1871). Unlike the original, which has coloured illustrations, this edition contents itself with black and white, but since Busch's emphasis was on line rather than colour there is little loss. A few changes were made to proper names. Widow Bolte becomes Widow Tibbets (with a convenient rhyme on 'exhibits'), Tailor Böck is changed to Buck, while Lämpel and Uncle Fritz remain the same. Busch does not name the baker, and Brooks deals similarly with the farmer. This translation was reissued in 1895 by the same publisher, then again in 1899 and 1902 by Little, Brown, and Co. of Boston. Meanwhile, the original publishers in Munich, Braun & Schneider, published another translation in collaboration with A. N. Myers and Co. of London in 1874. Here the title was given as *Max and Moritz. A Story in Seven Tricks*. This translation was reissued, re-set, by Siegle, Hill and Co. of London in an undated edition. The copies I have seen of both editions have coloured illustrations. Now we have a Widow Bolt, Snip the tailor, Doctor Whackem as the teacher, Uncle Fritz as ever, an unnamed baker and peasant Meck. With these names the characters slide away from their German origins into a more generalized comedy setting. The dog, however, as in the American version, keeps the name of Spitz. A third translation, rather free and using a quite different metre, was made by Arundell Esdaile and issued in a larger format (London: George Routledge & Sons, [1913]. Four of the characters bear different names again – Widow Poppletops, tailor Lambkin, Dr. Potts the teacher and Uncle Toby. It is worth noting that the British editions, following the pattern set with *Struwwelpeter*, remove the chamber-pot that the German editions show underneath Onkel Fritz's bed. Esdaile's version was not the last English translation: further ones have appeared at later dates in the twentieth century.

While *Max and Moritz* is Busch's best known work, it was not the first to be translated into English. It was preceded by a small collection of tales entitled *A Bushel of Merrythoughts*, described and ornamented by W. Harry Rogers (London: Sampson Low, Son, & Marston, 1868). Rogers's contribution is the English verses and a title-page decoration to each of the four items; Busch's illustrations remain. The first item is 'The Fearful Tragedy of Ice-Peter' ('Der Eispeter'), the story of a boy who is frozen into spikes of ice after extricating himself from a fall into the water while out skating. Brought home to thaw in front of the stove, his body melts into 'the soft consistency of pap' and is scooped up into a pan:

> And lastly, in the well-stocked cupboard, where
> Preserves are kept in pots of earthenware,
> One jar, which most the curious fancy tickles,
> Is PETER, stored among the jams and pickles.

The ending resembles that of *Max and Moritz*, and Peter's fate is a worthy counterpart to that of Paulinchen (Harriet) in *Struwwelpeter*.

'The Terrible Punishment of the Naughty Boys of Corinth' ('Diogenes und die bösen Buben von Korinth') tells how two unnamed boys (avatars of Max and Moritz) tease the philosopher Diogenes, but come to grief when they roll him in his barrel. Their clothes catch on the nails, they are pulled along and squashed flat underneath it. In 'The Exciting Story of the Cat and Mouse' ('Katze und Maus') Busch gives free rein to his hostility towards cats, as everything goes wrong in the cat's pursuit of the mouse through a series of domestic obstacles. The mouse escapes and rejoices, while the cat has to be pulled out of a boot in which it has got stuck (the boot has a hole in the foot through which the mouse escaped). When the cat attempts its own escape, the man servant squashes it in the kitchen door.

The final item in the book is called 'The Disobedient Children who Stole Sugar-Bread' and is Busch's adaptation of the fairytale 'Hänsel und Gretel'. This is not exactly the story we are familiar with from the Grimms. The children are told by their mother not to go into the wood, but they catch sight of a hare and follow it, then come across a trap for children and are captured by an ogre and a witch. The picture shows the trap baited with *Brezeln*, which is turned into 'sugar-bread' in the English, but the story is hardly one of disobedient stealing. The children are both placed in a cage while the witch stokes the fire in preparation for putting them in the cauldron, but when she pulls Gretel out of the cage, Hänsel escapes and pushes the witch into the cauldron herself. The ogre picks her out with a pitchfork, but she is dead. When he next turns to the children and attacks them, he gets caught in the cage, is imprisoned there and pushed into a deep bog. The children return home with half-eaten *Brezeln* in their hand, but they see their mother ready for them with a birch. This is a considerable twist on the fairytale, giving Hänsel rather than Gretel the leading role is disposing of the witch and depicting the children as naughty at the outset and the conclusion rather then as innocent victims of their mother.

This collection of cautionary tales was reprinted in different order by W. T. Stead as no. 48 of his *Books for the Bairns* (February 1900). He acknowledges the original British publishers and slightly adapts their title as *A Book of Merry Thoughts*. Because of the different format the illustrations are not always printed in the same size, so the tales do not have the careful unity of scale that Busch intended.

The 1870s seem to have been the prime decade for English versions of Busch's tales. *Pious Jemima. A Doleful Tale*, freely translated by John MacLush (Edinburgh: William P. Nimmo, 1872), is a long biographical story, recounting the protagonist's wilfully naughty childhood and youth, her progress to marriage and final decline into alcoholism. After a typical set of mischievous pranks with which Jemima torments her aunt and uncle, the main target of the book's satire is sanctimony, false religiosity cloaking secret sins. This English version is astonishingly up-to-date, since the German original, *Die fromme Helene*, was first published in the same year. The first seven chapters, dealing with Jemima's youth, end with an episode redolent of 'Cat and Mouse', in which Jemima disturbs two romping cats, slams the door on master Tom's tail, wraps paper and sealing wax round it and sets it alight. There is a quite sadistic streak in Busch's imagination, but at least up to this point the story centres on a young person and the manifold ways in which she tests the patience of her aunt and especially her uncle. However, when Jemima enters the realm of matrimony with John Plum and becomes a pious churchgoer, her adult life seems hardly calculated to be of interest to a young reader. The book moves from juvenile comedy to serious satire, as Busch changes horses midstream in the tale and addresses a different kind of reader. Busch's humour is rarely, if ever, completely carefree. He was interested in human folly at every age, and though his stories and pictures were designed to amuse, they would also prod many readers to reflect. John MacLush's adaptation was quickly reissued with the title *Naughty Jemima: a Doleful Tale* (London: Ward, Lock & Co., [1874]), but there do not appear to be any later reprints.

1872 also saw another of Busch's stories appear in English. This was *Buzz a Buzz; or, the Bees*, done freely into English by the author of *My Bee Book* (i.e. W. C. Cotton) from the German (London: Griffith & Farran; Chester: Phillipson & Golder). This was a version of *Schnurrdiburr oder die Bienen* (1869), a series of comic adventures centring on a beekeeper and his anthropomorphized bees, a young lady, a lover and, of course, a boy who gets up to no good. For Busch amorous relations between the sexes are always a matter for comedy, especially when the couple concerned make romantic assignations. The pictures, organized into ten chapters, are what carry the various episodes, but Busch's German verses are cast in more varied metres than usual and make play with both classical allusions and Low German dialect speech. The English version can hardly be claimed as a translation. Indeed, the author himself admits that his German was very limited and that he wrote his verses on the basis of the pictures.

Many of Busch's short picture tales were published in collections rather than as separate items. Fourteen of these smaller items were presented to the English public under the title *Fools Paradise with the Many Wonderful Adventures there as seen in the Strange Surprising Peep Show of Professor Wolley Cobble* (London: John Camden Hotten, [1872]). Unlike *Pious Jemima* and *Buzz a Buzz*, this book has the illustrations printed in colour. Among the items is a different version of 'The Troublesome Boys and Diogenes the Wise' from the one we have already noticed, but the rest are new to the British readers. Several merely take a simple idea and expand it, as we see in 'The Music Master' ('Ein Neujahrskonzert'), which consists of caricatures of different styles of playing the piano. 'The Merry Sledge Party and their Marvellous Slide' ('Die Rutschpartie') depicts a rollicking youth bumping into or picking up a series of unlikely passengers as his sledge careers down a hillside. 'Sixteen Startling Scenes in a Monkey's Life' ('Der Affe und der Schusterjunge') is a sequence of pictures showing how a monkey gets the better of a boy who has been teasing him. 'The Laughable Goings on, and Goings off, of the Comical People of Noseyland' is a visual fantasy about people with noses a foot or two feet long and all the problems and opportunities that this causes. 'The Woeful Panorama of the Toothache' ('Der hohle Zahn') turns what must have been a terrifying experience in the days before anaesthetics into a boisterous comedy. These are just a few of the ways in which Busch created fun and laughter out of the events of ordinary life. The village is the main setting of these scenes – Busch seems to have little to say about the world of industry or commerce. He is most at ease when he is depicting small-scale events in human intercourse, exaggerating and fantasizing, but still reflecting and poking fun at recognizable human types and situations. A later edition of *The Fool's Paradise* (London: Griffith & Farran, [1883]) mentions that the contents are taken from Busch's contributions to the *Münchener Bilderbogen*.

Another selection from Busch's shorter tales was translated by H. W. Dulcken under the title *Hookeybeak the Raven, and Other Tales* (London and New York: George Routledge & Sons, [1878]). The title-piece is taken from

Hans Huckebein, der Unglücksrabe (1867), the story of a boy who catches a young raven and of the havoc that the raven causes in the household before it finally strangles itself. Dulcken was not the most adroit of translators, and what he does with the German names is disconcerting. The German boy Fritz lives with his Aunt Lotte, which Dulcken turns into an implausible Tommy Tit and Aunt Matilda Tabitha. The dog Spitz, which we have noted time and again as the most common German dog's name, becomes the utterly bizarre 'Tooticums, who was a Poodle Pup', while the tomcat is the equally odd 'Bouncibell the Cat'. Dulcken provided versions of seven more tales in the book, including 'The Pea-Shooter; or, the Tragedy in a Country Garden' ('Das Pusterohr') and 'The Story of the Worrying Bluebottle; and of the Gentleman who lost his Temper', which Busch with admirable concision simply called 'Die Fliege' (the fly).

At the end of the 1870s A. B. Westmacott did separately published versions of three of Busch's short tales – *Diogenes and the Two Naughty Young Corinthians*; *Cousin Freddy's First and Last Donkey-Ride* ('Vetter Franz auf dem Esel'); and *The Power of Sound; or, the Effect of Music* ('Der Virtuos') (London: Alfred Hays, 1879). This seems to mark the end of new material in English by Busch, although, as we have seen, there were later reissues of previously published tales. There were also several more translations of Busch in the United States, but they lie outside the scope of this book.

The quantity of Busch's graphic work and verses is extensive enough to fill six volumes in a modern edition. Only a small proportion of it was adapted into English during the late nineteenth century and first published in a period of about a dozen years. The illustrations were reproduced intact except for a very few instances in which English words were substituted for German ones where they actually cropped up in a picture. But Busch's verses, calculatedly spare, mordantly witty and adroitly rhymed, did not fare as well. They never achieved the memorable status of the first *Struwwelpeter* translation. While the majority of Busch's tales were designed to appeal to children, their sardonic view of human nature, especially smugness and social pretensions, addresses adults as well. His drawings are caricatures of human frailty and surely popular with children because his child characters indulge every temptation that well-behaved children are taught to resist. Max and Moritz may become chicken feed at the end of their adventures, but they've had a lot of fun beforehand. Moreover, Busch's story world is largely lacking in parents, so children have a much freer time of it. The role of parent is usually taken by an aunt or uncle, and they are thus placed at a safer (if not entirely safe) distance for the children. What is perhaps more disturbing for the modern reader is Busch's unfeeling attitude towards animals. There is none of the sentiment or sentimentality that characterizes present-day attitudes. The more one reads of Busch, the more one recognizes these recurring patterns in his stories. But the last word has to be with his masterly technique as a graphic artist. His skill at creating images imbued with vitality, quirkiness and plausibility looks effortless. His style is unmistakable, and the pictures make their appeal regardless of the questionable character of some of the so-called translations.

20. Siegfried and the *Nibelungenlied*

One of the commonest patterns in the history of children's literature is the way in which traditional tales, medieval epics and romances become part of children's reading. Some of them then survive principally as children's books, though they started out as entertainment for the whole community. This was how British children became the primary consumers of the tales of Guy of Warwick, Robin Hood and Valentine and Orson. The same was true in Germany, as Goethe attests in a well-known passage in book 1 of his autobiography, *Dichtung und Wahrheit* (Poetry and Truth). Two of the works he mentions – *Fortunatus* and *Eulenspiegel* – had already made their mark in sixteenth-century England, the latter with the English name *Howleglass*, as works for adult reading.[101] Over the centuries both underwent abridgement or adaptation so that by the mid nineteenth century they were considered in Britain as essentially stories for children. However, the rediscovery of medieval German heroic epic and romance did not begin until the mid eighteenth century and took fifty years or more before it spread outside the ranks of scholars and the litterati.

Knowledge of the impact of various Germanic peoples on the Roman empire and, more especially, the defeat of Varus and his three brigades at the hands of the German Arminius in a momentous battle in the Teutoburg Forest in AD 9 goes back to the Renaissance and the first printed editions of Tacitus. A cult of Arminius or Hermann, as the Germans usually called him, gathered momentum in the eighteenth century and became a focus of national consciousness. It culminated in 1875 in the dedication of the

---

[101] For details of their reception in England see David Blamires, Fortunatus *in his Many English Guises* (Lewiston, Queenston, Lampeter: Edwin Mellen Press, 1996) and 'Eulenspiegel in englischer Sprache', *Eulenspiegel-Jahrbuch*, 29 (1989), pp. 51-66.

massive statue of Hermann, the Hermannsdenkmal, near Detmold, when Germany had at last become a united modern state under Prussia. The significance of Arminius as the first famous German to emerge from the mists of pre-history is emphasized in all histories of Germany, and he is celebrated too in the textbooks of German history that began to be written in English in the 1840s. Hermann, however, had not been the subject of oral or traditional German tales, and the poems and dramas of high literature did not lend themselves to adaptations for children's books. It was another figure and other stories to which we have to look to fill this gap. That figure was Siegfried, and the stories were those of the *Nibelungenlied* and other related works.

The *Nibelungenlied* is the finest of the many German heroic epics that centre on the exploits of legendary and historical figures from the Age of Migrations. Of anonymous authorship, it was composed around the turn of the twelfth to the thirteenth century and remained enormously popular to the end of the Middle Ages. Like most other medieval literature, however, it sank into oblivion in the sixteenth century.

The story of the *Nibelungenlied* centres on the fateful involvement of two mythical or fairytale figures, Siegfried and Brünhild, with a brother and sister of the royal house of Burgundy with its seat at Worms, Gunther and Kriemhild. As a youth Siegfried gains possession of the treasure of the Nibelungs, the sword Balmung and a cloak of darkness that makes him invisible and gives him the strength of twelve men. In addition, through bathing in the blood of a dragon he acquires a horny skin that is impenetrable except at one point between the shoulder-blades, where a lime-leaf has fallen on him. Brünhild, queen of Iceland, also has tremendous physical strength and is only prepared to marry the man who can beat her at three different tests of strength. Though Siegfried and Brünhild would thus seem to be made for each other, Siegfried falls in love with Kriemhild and wins her through helping Gunther, by trickery and the use of his cloak of darkness, to defeat and gain Brünhild. Brünhild's lingering suspicion that something is amiss in her defeat eventually brings about a quarrel between the two queens which quickly leads to Siegfried being murdered by Hagen, Gunther's terrifying, loyal vassal. After thirteen years of mourning Kriemhild marries Etzel, king of the Huns (the historical Attila), and after another thirteen years she invites her brothers and their vassals to a feast, at which she takes a ghastly revenge by murdering Gunther and Hagen and in the process slaughtering almost all the Burgundians.

This story of passion, deceit and revenge, which follows a geographical course from the Lower Rhine to Worms, and then from Worms to the Danube and right into the area of modern Hungary, became a potent nineteenth-century German myth, in which Siegfried was seen as the brave, generous, innocent young hero, capable of being killed only by treachery (Hagen stabs him in the back when he least suspects it). The *Nibelungenlied* became virtually a symbol of Germany's growing self-awareness, a foundation document in its acquisition of a venerable literary tradition. Not only were many editions of the medieval poem, modern German translations and adaptations published, but it became a stimulus for many new works, plays, poems, operas (though Wagner's *Ring* uses mainly Norse rather than German sources), paintings and engravings. When William and Mary Howitt visited Germany in the early 1840s, it was Julius Schnorr von Carolsfeld's frescoes of the *Nibelungenlied* in the Neue Residenz in Munich that caught their attention, rather than the poem itself.[102]

Britain owes its acquaintance with the *Nibelungenlied* in the first instance to the enquiring and independent minds of two Scottish men of letters. The first account of the poem was given by Henry William Weber in Weber, Jamieson and Scott's *Illustrations of Northern Antiquities from the Earlier Teutonic and Scandinavian Romances* (London and Edinburgh, 1814).[103] This lengthy abstract was followed in 1831 by a seminal article in the *Westminster Review* by Thomas Carlyle, who did more in the nineteenth century to promote the knowledge of German history, culture and literature than any other British man of letters. Carlyle's article not only gave an accurate epitome of the poem, together with verse translations of selected passages, but it also captured something of the poem's vigour and tone.[104] However, it was not until 1848 that the first complete translation into English verse was published by Jonathan Birch as *Das Nibelungen Lied; or, the Lay of the Last Nibelungers* (Berlin; reprinted 1878, 1887, 1895).[105] It seems odd that this was published in Germany rather than in Britain, but two years later there followed William Lettsom's home-grown product, *The Nibelungenlied: the Fall of the Nibelungers, otherwise the Book of Kriemhild* (London, 1850;

---

102 William Howitt, *The Rural and Domestic Life of Germany* (London: Longman, Brown, Green & Longmans, 1842), pp. 319-21.
103 For a detailed discussion of the reception of the *Nibelungenlied* see Francis E. Sandbach, *The Nibelungenlied and Gudrun in England and America* (London: David Nutt, 1904). Weber's work is treated on pp. 82-83.
104 Thomas Carlyle, 'The Nibelungen Lied', in *Critical and Miscellaneous Essays*, 4 vols. (London: Chapman & Hall, 1870), vol. 2, pp. 220-63.
105 Sandbach, *The Nibelungenlied*, pp. 39-44.

reprinted 1874, 1903), also in verse.[106] Four more translations came much later in the century – by Auber Forestier (1877, prose), A. G. Foster-Barham (1887, verse, reprinted 1891, 1893), Marguerite Armour (1897, prose, reprinted in Everyman's Library 1908) and Alice Horton (1898, verse).[107] This copious supply of English versions puts the *Nibelungenlied* into much the same category as Goethe's *Werther* and *Faust*, Fouqué's *Undine* and the fairytales of the Brothers Grimm and Wilhelm Hauff, as far as nineteenth-century English translations are concerned.

Given this pattern of British acquaintance with the *Nibelungenlied*, it is a little surprising that the first children's book relating to the theme was published in the same year as Birch's translation. This was *The Heroic Life and Exploits of Siegfried the Dragon Slayer: an Old German Story* (London: Joseph Cundall and David Bogue, 1848). No author's name is given, but the book had eight illustrations by Wilhelm Kaulbach (1805-74), one of Germany's leading illustrators. It would have been impossible for Cundall to commission Kaulbach simply for a British publication. What he had to do was to take over illustrations that had already been used on the Continent. The book that provided him with *Siegfried* was *Der hürnen Siegfried und sein Kampf mit dem Drachen, eine altdeutsche Sage* by Guido Goerres, with plates by Wilhelm Kaulbach (Schaffhausen, 1843). *Siegfried the Dragon Slayer* was one of Cundall's special books in a larger format. Perhaps he co-published with Bogue to share the costs of what was obviously an ambitious publication.

The content of the book is aptly summarized in the fourteen 'adventure' headings:[108]

1. Of King Siegmund and of heroes, Dwarfs, Giants, and Dragons of Ancient Times.
2. Of Siegfried the Swift, how he grew up to be a hero, and of his throwing the Spear.
3. Of the Emperor Otnit and Wolfdietrich, and how Siegfried asked permission to go out into the World.
4. How Siegfried the Swift went through the Wilderness, and what he encountered there.
5. Mimer relates the Adventures of Wieland, the best of all Smiths and Armourers.
6. How Siegfried brings an Urochs to the Smiths.

---

106 Sandbach, pp. 44-54.
107 Ibid., pp. 55-74, 76-79.
108 Ibid., pp. 131-32.

7. How Siegfried learns to be a Smith, and how he was sent by the treacherous Mimer to the Dragon.
8. How Siegfried fights with the Dragon, and bathes himself in his blood.
9. How Siegfried comes again to the Smithy, and settles accounts with Mimer.
10. Siegfried sees the great Dragon, and meets a King of the Dwarfs.
11. Siegfried's fight with the faithless Giants under the Drachenstein.
12. Of the great Wonders which Siegfried saw in the Dragon's Rock.
13. How Siegfried first sees the King's Daughter, and is received by her.
14. Siegfried's fight with the Dragon.

These are stories told about the young Siegfried that circulated separately from the *Nibelungenlied*. Drawing on a variety of sources, the nineteenth-century German author fitted them into this particular sequence. Adventures 10-14 are based on the late medieval German poem, the *Hürnen Seyfrid* (Horny Siegfried), which Friedrich Heinrich von der Hagen translated as *Hörnen Siegfried* and published as the first item in the first volume of *Der Helden Buch* (Book of the heroes) (Berlin: Johann Friedrich Unger, 1811). The giant (just one) is called Kuperan, the king of the dwarfs is Eugel, the king's daughter Kriemhild. Adventures 5, 7 and 9 derive ultimately from Norse sources, i.e. from *Thidrek's Saga*, of which von der Hagen, again, had provided a translation in his *Nordische Heldenromane* (Norse tales of the heroes) (Breslau, 1814-28). It is only in this form of the stories that the smith is called Mimer. Adventure 3 is taken from the medieval German epic of Ortnit and Wolfdietrich, of which there was an edition in von der Hagen and Alois Primisser's *Der Helden Buch in der Ursprache* (Book of the heroes in the original language), volume 1 (Berlin, 1820).

Siegfried the Dragon Slayer is thus a composite work. That is most clearly demonstrated in the ballad form of the tales of Otnit and Wieland. The practice of compilation, of including additional motifs and stories that have little or nothing to do with the principal story being related, runs through all the English versions of the story of Siegfried and the Nibelungs to a greater or lesser degree. It is foreshadowed already in Carlyle's *Westminster Review* article, since he incorporates summaries of the stories of Ottnit (his spelling), Hugdietrich and Wolfdietrich, the rose-garden of Worms and King Laurin before he embarks on a discussion of the *Nibelungenlied* itself. It is basically only at the opening and the close of Cundall's book

358 *Telling Tales*

that a connexion is made with the events narrated in the *Nibelungenlied*, as is the case with the *Hürnen Seyfrid* too. What is most important is the focus on Siegfried as the hero of a variety of amazing exploits. While the *Nibelungenlied* lapsed from general consciousness by the end of the sixteenth century, the figure of Siegfried persisted. Editions of the *Hürnen Seyfrid* are known up to 1642,[109] after which the story underwent a thoroughgoing adaptation, being turned into prose and modernized and emerging afresh as *Eine Wunderschöne Historie von dem gehörnten Siegfried* (A delightful story of horny Siegfried) (Braunschweig and Leipzig, 1726). The giant is now known as Wulffgrambähr, the king of the dwarfs as Egwald and the princess as Florigunda. New editions of this prose version continued to be printed up to the middle of the nineteenth century. There is, therefore, a long literary tradition of the exploits of a mythical or fairytale Siegfried separate from his role in the *Nibelungenlied*. What happens with the English children's versions of the *Nibelungenlied* is that they are contaminated, to a greater or lesser degree, with these stories of the young Siegfried or with other material that is not found in the medieval *Nibelungenlied*.

Since the next children's book dealing with Siegfried and the *Nibelungenlied* was not published for more than thirty years after *Siegfried and the Dragon Slayer*, this seems an appropriate place to look at some of the other ways in which British children may have come across them. The first of these is through history books, the second through travel guides.

The first reference to the *Nibelungenlied* in a young people's history of Germany occurs one year before the publication of Cundall's book. It is to be found in R. B. Paul's *A History of Germany . . . on the Plan of Mrs. Markham's Histories* (London: John Murray, 1847), where, in a brief passage dealing with medieval literature, the author declares: '. . . the most surprising work of that period was the famous "Niebelungenlied", in which a poet, whose name is unknown to us, has collected together the finest of the old German heroic legends' (p. 190). A school history book dealing with the whole of German history from Roman times to the present day cannot be expected to give details about matters of literature, so it is remarkable to have the poem highlighted. It is a measure of the importance attached to the poem in Germany that British children were now told about it. It is remarkable too that the reference comes before any English translation was available.

Much more detail is given in a history published some thirty years

---

109 K. C. King, *Das Lied vom Hürnen Seyfrid. Critical Edition with Introduction and Notes* (Manchester: Manchester University Press, 1958), pp. 6-7.

Siegfried and the Nibelungenlied 359

30. *The Heroic Life and Exploits of Siegfried the Dragon Slayer. An Old German Story. With Eight Illustrations Designed by Wilhelm Kaulbach* (1848).

later. In *Aunt Charlotte's Stories of German History for the Little Ones* (London and Belfast: Marcus Ward, 1878) Charlotte M. Yonge has a whole chapter, bizarrely headed 'The Nibelonig Heroes', which fills the gap between her accounts of the Romans and the Franks. Yonge tries to combine Norse and German versions of the medieval stories, but her confused chapter is marred by misstatements and misspellings. She explains her inclusion of the story here 'because two real personages, Attila the Hun and Theuderick of Verona, come into it, though there is no doubt that the story was much older than their time, and that they were worked into it when it was sung later' (p. 38). This is not a view that can be substantiated.

Only a few years later the prolific popular writer Sabine Baring-Gould gives more reliable information in his volume on Germany in 'The Story of the Nations' series published by T. Fisher Unwin (1886). The *Nibelungenlied* is mentioned first in connexion with Attila, but a more extensive account is given in a chapter on 'How the Germans wrote Romances' (pp. 143-45). Baring-Gould also mentions the other cycles of Germanic heroic legends centred on Gudrun, Beowulf and Laurin the Dwarf, but he reserves his enthusiasm for the *Nibelungenlied*, which he characterizes as 'a grand epic in two parts, which may take rank beside the *Iliad*' (p. 143). The comparison with the *Iliad* is not Baring-Gould's own idea: it goes right back to Johann Jacob Bodmer in the mid eighteenth century[110] and has been a persistent theme in literary discussion.

If we now turn to travel books about the Rhine, we can see a similar growth in awareness of certain figures and episodes from the *Nibelungenlied* in the second half of the nineteenth century. British travellers were supplied with a considerable variety of guide-books from the post-Napoleonic period onwards. Many of these were translations of German books and were published in major cities such as Frankfurt, Mainz and Cologne. They tend to concentrate on the part of the Rhine between Cologne and Mainz, so Worms rarely figures in them. The Drachenfels, of course, always comes in for a story, but the earliest tradition is of a maiden being sacrificed by two pagan princes and protecting herself against the dragon by holding a crucifix in front of her. This is the most persistent tradition, but in the second half of the century there are occasional allusions to Siegfried. Murray's celebrated *Handbook* of 1860 remarks rather cautiously: 'The traveller is shown . . . the cave of the Dragon (from which the mountain was named)

---

[110] Mary Thorp, *The Study of the Nibelungenlied* (Oxford: Clarendon Press, 1940), p. 3.

killed, as it is reported, by the horned Siegfried, the hero of the Niebelungen Lay'.[111] Some twenty years later the American children's author Hezekiah Butterworth, in *Zigzag Journeys to Northern Lands. The Rhine to the Arctic* (Boston: Estes & Lauriat, 1883), states quite baldly: 'It is said that Siegfried killed the Dragon there' (p. 174), but then proceeds to give a version of the traditional Christian story.

Murray's *Handbook* is more informative about Worms, which is described as 'partly the scene of the Nibelungenlied'. A footnote explains:

> This fine old German poem was written towards the latter end of the 12th century, but the traditions on which it is founded appear to have been handed down, probably in popular lays, from very remote times, and to have been common to all the tribes (German, Saxon, and Scandinavian) of the Teuton race. No less than 20 poems of the Edda, which, as it has been satisfactorily shown, must have been composed prior to the year 863, contain the same tragical story of the mythic-heroic personages who figure in the Nibelungen (p. 525).

While Murray provides background information rather than any account of the content of the poem, Butterworth attempts to tell the 'Story of Siegfried and the Nibelung heroes' in connexion with his description of Worms. His account of what he calls the Nibelungen Lied is more Norse than German, there is no mention of Brünhild, and Siegfried is said to have been stabbed on the hunt 'by a conspirator employed by Hagen' (p. 152) rather than by Hagen himself. This intermingling of Norse and German material is endemic in English-language accounts of the Nibelung story, but in this instance it may have something to do with James Baldwin's *The Story of Siegfried* (New York: Charles Scribner's Sons, 1882), which incorporates a vast amount of Norse mythology. We shall return to Baldwin in due course.

There are several books of German origin dealing with the many legends that have grown up around places on the Rhine. Since they concentrate on the Romantic stretch of the river, few have anything to say about Worms. However, F. J. Kiefer's *The Legends of the Rhine from Basle to Rotterdam*, translated by L. W. Garnham (Mayence: David Kapp, n.d. – a German-language fourth edition is dated 1876), deals with Siegfried at some length in connexion with Worms and his supposed birthplace, Xanten, in the region of the Lower Rhine. The Worms section summarizes the plot of the *Nibelungenlied* from Siegfried's arrival at Worms up to his murder

---

111 *A Handbook for Travellers on the Continent: being a Guide to Holland, Belgium, Prussia, Northern Germany, and the Rhine from Holland to Switzerland*, thirteenth edition, corrected (London: John Murray, 1860), p. 263.

in the Odenwald. (One manuscript of the poem has Siegfried murdered in the Forest of the Vosges, but another has, as here, the Odenwald.) Under 'Xanten' we are presented with a jumble of Young Siegfried stories derived from Norse and German sources. The giant is called Wolfgrambär, which provides us with a rare example of a detail taken from the prose *Wunderschöne Historie von dem gehörnten Siegfried*.

All of these travel books apart from that by Hezekiah Butterworth were written for adults. So too were the translations of the *Nibelungenlied* that we have already noted in the last quarter of the nineteenth century. There were also two substantial retellings of the poem in books designed for readers with a serious interest in medieval heroic literature. A vigorous, simplified account was given by E. H. Jones in G. W. Cox's and E. H. Jones's *Popular Romances of the Middle Ages* (London: Longmans, Green, & Co., 1871), and it was reprinted in the same authors' *Tales of the Teutonic Lands* (London: Longmans, Green, & Co., 1872). Another version, including the Young Siegfried adventures from Norse sources and the *Hürnen Seyfrid*, was made by M. W. MacDowall and published in *Epics and Romances of the Middle Ages*, adapted from the work of Dr. W. Wägner and edited by W. S. W. Anson (London: Swan Sonnenschein & Co., 1883; fifth edition 1889). If we add to these the first publication of Wagner's *Der Ring des Nibelungen* (1863) and William Morris's *Sigurd the Volsung* (1876), both admittedly dependent largely on Norse sources, we can readily understand how several more children's books appeared during this period.

Golden Threads from an Ancient Loom. Das Nibelungenlied, adapted for the use of young readers by Lydia Hands (London: Griffith & Farran; New York: E. P. Dutton, 1880), actually provides the fullest story of all the children's versions with which we are concerned. Hands retells Young Siegfried adventures, the events leading to Siegfried's murder and Kriemhild's revenge. The book's pretentious title mirrors its ambitious format, the most important feature of which is the fact that it contains fourteen wood-engravings by Julius Schnorr von Carolsfeld (1794-1872). These had been executed nearly forty years previously for a German edition of *Der Nibelungen Noth* (1843). Schnorr's designs are full of movement and interest, and his technique of dividing a full page horizontally into three, with different events occupying each level, was followed later by Frank C. Papé in illustrating another version of the *Nibelungenlied*.

Lydia Hands dedicates her book to Carlyle, acknowledging his essay and Karl Simrock's modern German translation as the stimulus for her work. In nine chapters she covers the high points of the poem, weaving in threads occasionally from other sources. Following Carlyle, she alludes to the story of the rose-garden of Worms, from the *Heldenbuch*, in which twelve heroes each from the followers of Siegfried and Dietrich von Bern (the historical Theodoric) fight over Criemhild's rose-garden, which is protected simply by a thread of silk. She also includes the adventures of Siegfried with Mimer and the dragon, which Carlyle mentions in outlining the adventures of the young Siegfried. From her own imagination Hands introduces a 'trusty chamberlain' called Fridolin, who accompanies Siegfried. Probably this has some purely personal significance; perhaps it was the name of a German boy Hands knew. Another of her innovations is a helpful female spirit incongruously called Hermione, whom Siegfried meets in the forest!

Chapter 3 returns to matters found in the *Nibelungenlied*, simplifying all the time. However, Siegfried is given an early visit to Isenland on which he meets, but rejects, Brunhild, before undertaking the adventures by the Rhine which equip him with the Nibelung treasure, the sword Balmung and the cloak of darkness. When he goes to Worms to woo Criemhild, he does not challenge the Burgundians, but is simply welcomed by them. Hagen here is not a vassal, but the uncle of Gunther and his brothers. Siegfried's magical powers are enlisted for the wooing and taming of Brunhild, but the sexual aspects are eliminated. The ensuing quarrel between the two queens in concerned solely with the respective status of their two husbands. It leads ineluctably to the murder of Siegfried at the fountain in the forest.

After a long period of mourning Criemhild agrees to marry Etzel, persuaded by Rudiger that Etzel's power may provide the possibility of her taking revenge. After her departure Hagen sinks the treasure in the Rhine. In the *Nibelungenlied* this occurs soon after Siegfried's murder, so its position here looks as though Hands had forgotten about it and just slipped it in when she remembered it again.

The second part of the *Nibelungenlied* is structurally and psychologically much simpler than the first, so Hands is easily able to omit the Burgundians' stays at Passau and Bechelaren (the modern Pöchlarn). She focusses on Hagen's encounter with the mermaids in the 'blue Danube' (picking up on Johann Strauss the Younger's famous waltz of 1867), together with the testing of their prophecy that no one will return from the journey except the chaplain. Hagen attempts to drown him in the river, but though the chaplain cannot swim he miraculously manages to get ashore. At the court of Etzel and Criemhild Hagen confesses to being Siegfried's murderer, and bloody conflict ensues. Dankwart, Hagen's brother, kills Blödel, here 'one of Criemhild's knights' rather than Etzel's brother, and Hagen himself kills Ortleben, the son of Criemhild and Etzel (his name should be Ortlieb). Then comes the burning of the hall in which the Burgundians have been housed, their drinking blood to quench their thirst, the death of Rudiger in battle, the taking captive of Gunther and Hagen, the beheading of Gunther, Criemhild's killing of Hagen and her own death at the hand of Dietrich of Berne's man, Hildebrand. In this last section Criemhild is depicted as being possessed by 'feverish joy' and with 'her eye glittering with the light of madness'. As in the *Nibelungenlied* itself, Hagen brands her as 'devil's wife'. At the end of the story, then, the terrible nature of Criemhild's revenge is portrayed as sickness, lunacy and marriage to the devil. Nothing worse can be envisaged. The spelling of her name in this text with an initial C (rather than the usual K) suggests to the English-language reader an association with 'crime' that is now horrifically realized.

Only a couple of years later another version of the material was published – James Baldwin's *The Story of Siegfried* (1882), which was popular enough to be reprinted in 1888 and 1931. This was very different from Lydia Hands's adaptation, concentrating on the figure of Siegfried and excluding the revenge story. The author was so deeply interested in the mythological approach to Siegfried that he used the framework of his story to recount a large number of other tales from Norse mythology that have no specific connexion with him. Not only do we have the usual items taken from the *Edda*, the *Saga of the Volsungs* and *Thidrek's Saga*, but we have such additional tales as Thor's encounter with the Midgard serpent, the goddess Idun and her apples, and the story of Balder embedded in the narrative. While the author of the *Nibelungenlied* had played down the mythological aspects of Siegfried's story, Baldwin does the opposite. When Siegfried first goes to Burgundyland (the name of Worms is never mentioned), he is thought possibly to be Odin or Thor or Balder. We have been told previously how he was brave enough to ride through the wall of fire to awaken the sleeping Brunhild. Any shadow of sexual involvement with Brunhild either here or in Burgundyland is expunged; there is no question of Siegfried needing to tame her in bed for Gunther. Siegfried has to be pure, blameless and superhuman in strength. Baldwin, given his mythological preoccupations, cannot resist making the (spurious) link between the Odenwald, where Siegfried is murdered, and the god Odin.

Siegfried and the Nibelungenlied 365

And the queen cried out in answer:—

"Base deceiver, yet shalt thou not strip me of all. The sword that my Siegfried wore, when he left me for the fatal hunt, I will have whether thou wilt give it me or not.

So saying, with a sudden rush towards him, she drew it from the scabbard, and Hagen, sorely wounded as he was, had no power to resist.

Brandishing the weapon with both hands, Criemhild

31. *Golden Threads from an Ancient Loom. Das Nibelungenlied. Adapted to the Use of Young Readers* by Lydia Hands. Engravings by Julius Schnorr, of Carolsfeld (1880). 'Criemhild's Frenzy'.

A great deal of Baldwin's energy is devoted to viewing Siegfried's story as part of the well-documented mythology of the northern peoples. When the dead Siegfried is burnt on a funeral pyre rather than buried, the intention is to link, perhaps even equate, Siegfried with the god Balder. In the notes appended to his narrative Baldwin makes a further connexion between Hagen and Hoder, the blind brother who unwittingly killed Balder with the mistletoe. Like many of his contemporaries, Baldwin was indebted in his views to those scholars who interpreted virtually all myths in terms of battles between summer and winter, night and day, thunder and lightning. Such interpretations appear simplistic today, but they were taken very seriously at the time. They do not intrude unacceptably on the various tales that are woven together in this book. Baldwin is fond of his digressions, but he keeps the story of Siegfried moving too. But with Richard Wagner and William Morris as the most recent literary models, Baldwin's Siegfried is certainly more Norse in character than German.

The same is true of S. Baring-Gould's *Siegfried* (London: Dean & Son, 1904), described on the title-page as a romance founded on Wagner's operas *Rheingold*, *Siegfried* and *Götterdämmerung* and running to 351 pages. The illustrations by Charles Robinson are in the same vein as those he did a few years previously for Fouqué's *Sintram*. Wagner was, again, the source for the two volumes *The Rhinegold and the Valkyrie* and *Siegfried and the Twilight of the Gods* (London: Heinemann, 1910 and 1911), their chief attraction being the colour plates by Arthur Rackham.

The Edwardian period seems to have been strongly drawn to the story of Siegfried, to judge by the number of children's books on the theme. The next one to which we turn is *The Linden Leaf; or, the Story of Siegfried* (London, Edinburgh, and New York: Thomas Nelson & Sons, 1907). No author's name is given, but the eight colour plates are signed 'Waugh' in the bottom right-hand corner. The book was reprinted a number of times. The narrative goes no further than the period immediately following Siegfried's murder and takes the main events of the *Nibelungenlied* as its basis. The Young Siegfried stories, extremely briefly dealt with, are motivated by his mother's falling into some unexplained disfavour and having to wander in the forest with the baby Siegfried. The quarrel of the queens is solely related to the supposed vassal status of Siegfried; Gunther's humiliation in the bedroom and Siegfried's subsequent taming of Brunhilda are entirely omitted. Kriemhilda declares instead that it was Siegfried, not Gunther, who overcame Brunhilda in the games, and this sparks off the plot to murder him, in which Gernot is also involved, while Giselher takes Siegfried's side. The location of the forest in which the hunt takes place is not given. The guarded nature of the narrative as a whole obviously points to a young readership.

At virtually the same time there appeared in the 'Told to the Children' series *Stories of Siegfried*, by Mary Macgregor (London: T. C. & E. C. Jack; New York: E. P. Dutton & Co., c. 1908), which had eight colour plates by Granville Fell. Macgregor has Siegfried brought up by the blacksmith Mimer, a dwarf, and the dragon that he kills is named as Regin, Mimer's brother. Immediately after this Siegfried goes to Isenland, where he meets Brunhild, but has no wish to conquer her for his bride. Instead he takes away her magic horse, Gana (this seems to be jumbled from Grani, the name of Sigurd's horse in the *Edda*). These details come from Norse sources, but for the most part Macgregor adapts the *Nibelungenlied*. She includes Kriemhild's prophetic dream and the battles with Kings Ludegast and Ludeger, but she makes Hagen into the uncle rather than the vassal of Gunther, Gernot and Giselher (in the Norse sources he is their half-brother). Siegfried plays the role of Gunther's vassal in Isenland, and it is there that he robs Brunhild of her ring and favourite girdle. The episode in which Siegfried tames Brunhild in Gunther's bed is omitted. The story then proceeds to Siegfried's murder in an unnamed forest and Hagen's sinking of the Nibelung treasure in the Rhine. In just a few lines Macgregor mentions Kriemhild's marriage to Etzel and her subsequent revenge on the Burgundians.

About the next book to appear on the scene not a great deal need be said. *The Heroic Life and Exploits of Siegfried the Dragon-Slayer. An Old Story of the North* (London: George G. Harrap & Company, 1910) is, as its title suggests, a retelling by Dora Ford Madeley of Cundall & Bogue's 1848 book. The decorations at the head of each chapter are, however, the only thing taken over unchanged from the earlier publication. The text is fairly thoroughly adapted, modernized and put into twelve rather than fourteen chapters, but it is the same story. Kaulbach's engravings are replaced by twelve attractive colour plates by Stephen Reid (1873-1948), which are similar to Rackham's in colouring and tone, but avoid his tendency to grotesquerie. Reid illustrated several other children's books with historical or legendary backgrounds about this time.[112] The combination of illustrations, modernized text and

---

112 Brigid Peppin and Lucy Micklethwait, *Dictionary of British Book Illustrators: the Twentieth Century* (London: John Murray, 1983), p. 248.

design make this book a very agreeable production.

The last book that I propose to devote extended attention to was, like *The Linden Leaf,* also published by Nelson and sticks very closely to the plot of the *Nibelungenlied*, with only rare details that can be traced to other sources. It too was anonymous in terms of authorship. However, the two texts are quite different in scope and approach. *Siegfried and Kriemhild. A Story of Passion and Revenge* (London, Edinburgh, Dublin, and New York: Thomas Nelson & Sons, 1912) forms part of a series entitled 'The World's Romances'. As one might therefore expect, it places a good deal of interest on the love-story element. Rather unusually, Kriemhild is depicted initially as extremely religious, wanting to be a nun, and when Siegfried first sees her she looks 'lovely, as a saint drawn in gold and silver and rich colours in a holy book, such as kings buy at a great price'. The whole narrative is conceived in strong visual terms, and the scenes of emotional tension and danger are frequently highlighted with symbols such as storms, lightning and sinister crows. Hagen, we are told, is always dressed in black. The author has some striking things to say about Iceland, which is stunningly depicted as snow-covered when Gunther, Siegfried, Hagen and Volker (not Dankwart) go to woo Brunhild. We are told earlier about Siegfried's sword Balmung that it was 'forged in ancient days by the earth-smiths dwelling in Iceland, where the smoke from his furnace still reeks from the mountain-top of Hecla, though the smith no longer labours at his weapon-making'. In addition to possessing this marvellous sword, Siegfried is equipped with a 'Tarn-Helm' rather than the traditional cloak of darkness. Most likely this comes from Wagner.

The story of *Siegfried and Kriemhild* is presented as though told by minstrels at the hostelry of the 'Dragon's Head' at Worms in the year 1460. It is an excellent adaptation of the *Nibelungenlied*, keeping faithfully to the key points in the plot and taking the story right through to the slaughter of the Burgundians at Etzelburg. While Baldwin determinedly mythicized his narrative, the author of *Siegfried and Kriemhild* romanticized it. The book has eight colour plates by Frank C. Papé (1878-1972),[113] whose work looks rather old-fashioned in comparison with Stephen Reid's. His technique is to use a decorative frame of leaves and branches within which there is a central square main picture, a kind of tympanum above and a small long oblong below. It is a similar pattern to that of Schnorr von Carolsfeld's engravings in Lydia Hands's *Golden Threads*.

---

113 Peppin and Micklethwait, *Dictionary*, pp. 225-26.

These books do not exhaust the children's versions of the Stories of Siegfried and the Nibelungs that were written in English up to c. 1920. The Rev. A. J. Church included a section on 'The Treasure of the Nibelungs' based on the translations of W. N. Lettsom and Alice Horton in his *Heroes of Chivalry and Romance* (London: Seeley & Co. Limited, 1898), and Thomas Cartwright similarly devoted a substantial part of his *Sigurd the Dragon-Slayer* (London: W. Heinemann, 1907) to 'The Lay of the Nibelungs'.[114] There may be others that I have missed. Each of the adapters takes a different line with the material, so that apart from the Cundall book and Madeley's retelling of it no two versions provide even the same plot. The *Nibelungenlied* is central to Hands, Baldwin, Macgregor and the two Nelson volumes, but each author uses a different approach and spices it with additional materials. From a purist point of view, none of the authors is completely faithful to the *Nibelungenlied*, but all have tried to make a coherent story suitable for their target readership.

Siegfried is just one of the many heroes of ancient tradition, myth and legend whose story was presented to children from the early nineteenth century onwards. Of course, Greek mythology was there from the start, and so was Robin Hood (though not a supernatural hero). It is interesting that the first children's book to deal with Norse mythology, Annie and Eliza Keary's *The Heroes of Asgard* (London: David Bogue, 1857), came after *Siegfried the Dragon Slayer* and was published by Cundall's partner in that enterprise. A children's *Beowulf* comes very late on the scene, though an English translation of the original poem had been made by John M. Kemble as early as 1837. The first children's versions of *Beowulf* would seem to be by A. J. Church in his *Heroes of Chivalry and Romance*, mentioned above, and by C. Thomas, *The Adventures of Beowulf*, translated from the Old English, and adapted to the use of schools (London: H. Marshall & Son, 1899). But then the first modern edition of *Beowulf* was not published until 1815, some sixty years after the discovery of the *Nibelungenlied*. However, James Baldwin did mention Beowulf *en passant* in *The Story of Siegfried*.

The Siegfried of the *Nibelungenlied*, quite apart from his supernatural accoutrements and capacities, is a rather more complex figure than what we find in these children's books. His provocative stance towards the Burgundians on his first arrival at Worms, his several deceptions of Brünhild and, especially, his gift of Brünhild's girdle to Kriemhild after

---

114 Judith St. John, *The Osborne Collection of Early Children's Books 1476-1910. A Catalogue* (Toronto: Toronto Public Library, 1975), vol. 2, pp. 572, 577.

taming Brünhild in bed, all show a darker side that the children's versions ignore. In medieval German tradition the lime leaf is symbolic of love, so Siegfried's vulnerability is not just a matter of a chink in his physical constitution. The children's versions simplify and idealize him. He is a match for all opponents – a dragon, dwarfs and giants, the Saxon and Danish armies, the amazing strength of Brünhild – so that he can only be overcome by treachery. The epitome of youth, courage, strength and beauty, Siegfried has to be blameless too. The pity is that he is so naïve, so unsuspicious, so lacking in psychological awareness. But he is so great an ideal because in many ways he is still so much a child. That must surely be a factor in his popularity as a hero in so many children's books.

21. The Franco-Prussian War

During the last three decades of the nineteenth century the number of new German children's books that were translated into English declined, although earlier books continued to be reissued. Germany did not cease to be of interest, but the interest was expressed in different ways. What I want to discuss in this chapter is the way in which British writers dealt with contemporary Germany through novels centred on the Franco-Prussian War (1870-71). This may seem an unlikely subject for British children's books, since Britain was not directly involved in the war. But there are at least ten books written between 1871 and 1910 that present aspects of the war in fictionalized form. Their authors include four of the foremost children's writers of the day – Hesba Stretton, G. A. Henty, Evelyn Everett-Green and F. S. Brereton. Two of the books were written as immediate responses to the war, while a third followed a mere four years later. The remaining books appeared at longer intervals. In chronological order the authors and titles are as follows:

Hesba Stretton, *Max Krömer. A Story of the Siege of Strasbourg* (London: The Religious Tract Society, [1871])

G. A. Henty, *The Young Franc-Tireurs and their Adventures in the Franco-Prussian War* (London: Griffith & Farran, 1872)

Annie Lucas, *Léonie; or, Light out of Darkness: and Within Iron Walls: a Tale of the Siege of Paris. Twin-Stories of the Franco-German War* (London: Thomas Nelson & Sons, 1875)

Lillias Lobenhoffer, *Fritz of the Tower. A Tale of the Franco-German War* (London and Edinburgh: The Religious Tract Society, [1887])

M. E. Clements, *Eagle and Dove. A Tale of the Franco-Prussian War* (London: Thomas Nelson & Sons, 1889)

G. A. Henty, *A Woman of the Commune. A Tale of the Two Sieges of Paris* (London: F. V. White & Co., 1895). This novel was also published with the titles *A Girl of the Commune*; *Two Sieges of Paris*; *Two Sieges*; and *Cuthbert Hartington*; of which the last seems the most appropriate.

Herbert Hayens, *Paris at Bay* (London and Glasgow: Blackie & Son, [1897])

Evelyn Everett-Green, *The Castle of the White Flag. A Tale of the Franco-German War* (London, Edinburgh and New York: Thomas Nelson & Sons, 1904)

Evelyn Everett-Green, *Ringed by Fire* (London, Edinburgh and New York: Thomas Nelson & Sons, [1904])

F. S. Brereton, *A Hero of Sedan. A Tale of the Franco-Prussian War* (London, Glasgow, Dublin, Bombay: Blackie & Son, 1910)

Several of these books were reprinted a few years after the first editions, so the historical context remained significant right into the Edwardian period. The books vary considerably in their target readership, which ranges from pre-pubertal children of both sexes to adolescent boys, adolescent girls and young adults. They also cover different phases and locations of the war and are narrated from a variety of standpoints. But while each of them tries to be faithful to the facts and experience of the war, each has its own sub-text and moral agenda.

The first of the books to appear was *Max Krömer*, so titled after its eponymous narrator, a fourteen year old boy of mixed English and French parentage. This device of having one or more leading characters with a partly or wholly English background is used in all the books except Annie Lucas's *Léonie*. It provides a means whereby the young reader is drawn into identifying with the events in the stories, and it also gives an international context to the narrative. When *Max Krömer* appeared in 1871, Hesba Stretton (1832-1911) was at the peak of her career as a writer of Evangelical stories for children. Her first story had been published by Dickens in *Household Words* in 1859, but her name will always be connected with two enormously successful books – *Jessica's First Prayer* (1867) and *Little Meg's Children* (1868). Hesba Stretton (whose real name was Sarah Smith) had lived in northern France with her sister Lizzie, so she had some personal experience of French life on which to build. But *Max Krömer*, as she indicates in her preface to the book, owes its origin to something more specific. She explains how, on returning home from Switzerland, she had seen distraught fugitives and children in Basle, Karlsruhe and Mannheim and that in writing her story she was 'softening down, rather than heightening, the horrors of the siege of Strasbourg' (p. 6). Clearly, she was writing under the immediate impact of the war upon herself.

The story-line is simple. Max and his ten-year-old sister Sylvie are living with their paternal grandmother in Strasbourg while their French father is with a party of explorers in central Africa. Their English mother had died two years previously. Part of the house is occupied by a young mother, Lisbeth, and her five-year-old daughter Elsie, who is knitting a birthday present for the Christ Child. When hostilities break out and refugees flood into Strasbourg, Max brings a little girl called Louise to shelter in their house. They also have Sergeant Klein and three soldiers billeted on them.

As bombardments continue, their house is struck and they have to retreat to the cellar. A sick elderly man in their building dies of shock. The refugee girl Louise is killed while at school. They learn of the siege of Metz and the fall of Sedan. Lisbeth, having lost her home, entrusts Elsie to Max's care and goes to nurse the wounded. A school friend of Max's finds a way of getting Sylvie, now ill, out of the city into safety. Sergeant Klein is killed. When Strasbourg eventually capitulates, Dr Krömer reappears and settles them in new lodgings. Sylvie is found in Basle. Little Elsie completes her knitted vest, which Dr Krömer insists on keeping as a memento of this six-week siege of Strasbourg. Finally, the family, together with the reunited Lisbeth and Elsie, move to London.

In common with so many children's books the parent generation is wholly absent from the narrative's main events, so the action is seen through the eyes of the children. From the innocence and spontaneity of childhood they are exposed to physical danger, material deprivation, conflict and violence between boys desperate for food, the deaths of neighbours and friends. They learn at first hand the horrors of war and the fact that there is no glory in it. Only little Elsie remains untouched in her unspoilt goodness of heart.

The war is viewed through the eyes of a young teenage boy and the other children around him, so its political dimensions are barely in evidence. At the outset of the action Max explains:

> Here were we, French citizens, with a French garrison and a French governor; when only a mile or so away was Germany. We spoke German too, and we had dear friends who were in the habit of coming to visit the people of Strasbourg, and whom they visited in return. There was not any enmity between us, any more than there is between the English and the Scotch, who live close and good neighbours on the borders, with

only a line on the map to separate them. That was how we were living together up to the middle of July last year. I suppose the Emperor and the King and their statesmen knew that there was mischief brewing; but none of their townspeople knew (p. 14).

Max's initial response to the Emperor's declaration of war is to say to Lisbeth, '"War brings glory!"' She has been weeping at the thought of her German friends suffering from a French invasion and says to Max:

'I should like to know why the Emperor and the King could not go to law about their quarrels, as they make us poor folks do. They will not let us settle our disputes by fighting; and I ask you, Max, which is the worse – for two men to fight, or two hundred thousand?' (p. 19).

Max exults at the German blowing up of the Rhine bridge at Kehl, shouting, '"the Germans know we shall conquer"', and of course the French expectation at that time is that the French will advance to Berlin.

Hesba Stretton's story is strongly coloured by Christian themes. Max, for example, regards Christ as 'both my Brother and my Captain', and when he takes home the abandoned child Louise, it is because he asks himself: 'What else would the Lord have done, if he had been a boy in Strasbourg?' (p. 44). Another telling incident centres on Max's intervention in a struggle between two hungry boys over a half-rotten turnip. Max protects the smaller one, but on realizing that the other boy, too, is starving, he takes him to the baker's and gives him a little loaf. The Krömers' maid upbraids Max for his action. Towards the end of the book, when the populace is attempting to surrender, Max sees a picture of Christ on the cross, still hanging in the ruins of their old house, and feels that Christ is being crucified afresh in Strasbourg.

Stretton aims to evoke compassion through the graphic depiction of the realities of ordinary people's lives. She shows how food becomes scarce and prices rise, how hunger forces people into violence. The destructiveness of the war affects the family's own home. They encounter at first hand the death of their elderly neighbour, while that of little Louise, to whom they have given refuge, is reported to them rather than directly experienced. Stretton is skilful at making the results of the war real to her child readership.

The wider context of the war is only given in broad outline. The French victory at Saarbruck is mentioned, only to be followed immediately with General MacMahon's retreat to Saverne. From the attic of the Krömers' house the German camp can easily be seen:

It was not till the 17th of August, nearly three weeks after the siege

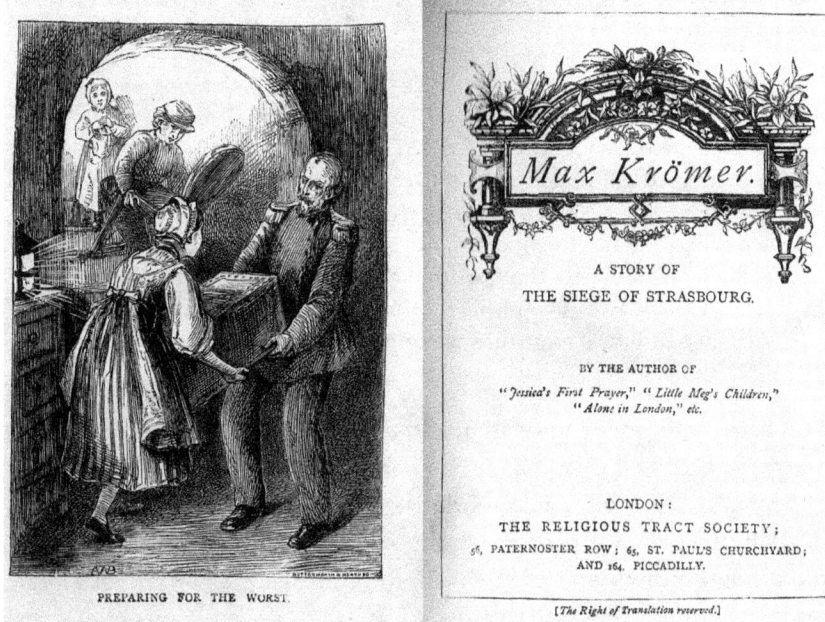

32. Title-page and frontispiece of *Max Krömer. A Story of the Siege of Strasbourg* [1871].

was proclaimed, that the enemy's circle was completed, and we were fairly shut in. Now there could be no more coming in or going out of Strasbourg until Marshal Bazaine came to our aid, or General Uhrich and his brave garrison drove the invaders back to their own side of the Rhine. The worst of it was that they were the Baden troops that surrounded us; the people who had been our friends and neighbours for many a quiet year. Even now we did not feel any hatred towards them; everybody said they were only doing what the Emperor and his army had intended to do to them. We could scarcely believe it was all true (p. 47).

On 21 August they experience the first shell. The cathedral becomes a place of refuge, dear also to Protestants (the Krömers have to be Protestants for the English readers and the Evangelical author). Later in the story their hopes of relief are shattered when they hear that Marshal Bazaine is 'shut up in Metz and cannot get out'. Worse still is what they think must be a Prussian boast: 'They say the Emperor and General MacMahon have been beaten at Sedan and given themselves up; them and all the army, and gone prisoners into Germany, while the Prussians are marching on to Paris' (p. 114).

General Uhrich is reluctant to raise the white flag and surrender, but the people weep with mingled joy and sorrow when it happens. The German response is swift:

> The Germans entered Strasbourg the next morning, bringing with them wagon-loads of provisions, which had been prepared in readiness against the surrender of the city. You should have seen the crowds of all sorts of people thronging round the wagons, with glistening eyes, eager to snatch away the first thing put into their hands. Our old friends across the Rhine had not forgotten us, nor had they turned into enemies. The soldiers themselves, who had been doing all they could to destroy us, were now ready to share what they had with us. The suddenness of the change was almost more than we could bear . . . (pp. 132-33).

The book ends with the symbol of Elsie's knitted vest for the Christ Child being interpreted in relation to the alabaster box of ointment poured on Jesus's head, so it is kept as a remembrance rather than given away.

Hesba Stretton's book is carefully structured, despite having little that can really be called a plot. Its strongest message is concerned with the brotherhood of man and Christ's suffering presence as a brother among those who suffer. Above all, the book is a call to the emotions with many incidents calculated to move the reader to tears. As it focusses almost exclusively on the French civilian population, very little is said about the Germans. Until the very end, when they bring provisions into the defeated Strasbourg, they are an impersonal military force and more or less off-stage, though their bombs and military might wreak havoc on the city and its inhabitants.

Hot on the heels of *Max Krömer* came a very different sort of book by an exact contemporary, George Arthur Henty (1832-1902). *The Young Franc-Tireurs* was only Henty's second book for boys, following *Out on the Pampas*, published in 1871, but written in 1868. Like Hesba Stretton, Henty was writing here from personal experience. After serving in the army for some years and experiencing the Crimean War, he had eventually turned to journalism and was correspondent for the *Standard* during the Franco-Prussian War and the period of the Paris Commune. He was always concerned about the authenticity of the historical events in his stories. In the preface to *The Young Franc-Tireurs* he declares: 'Many of the occurrences in this tale are related almost in the words in which they were described to me by those who took part in them, and nearly every fact and circumstance actually occurred according to my own knowledge'. A few lines before this he had also stated: 'The names, places, and dates have been changed, but circumstances and incidents are true'. Even in this early book Henty had an unerring way of weaving an exciting adventure story involving teenage boys into the broader context of important historical events. In this instance it was contemporary history.

The geographical setting of Henty's novel is wider than Stretton's. It begins in Dijon and moves then to the Vosges; there is an episode in Mainz and along the Rhine, followed by a long trek to Tours, an adventure mission to Paris, return to Tours, a cross-country escape back to Dijon, with a final attack on the Germans, after which the boy heroes learn of the general defeat of the French. While Stretton deals with the war in terms of its victims, Henty, the military man, depicts it as a set of adventures, full of daring and danger, in which two English boys join the volunteers known as *franc-tireurs* and engage in a variety of glorious exploits.

The boys are, of course, idealized and come from a moderately privileged background. Ralph and Percy Barclay, nearly sixteen and fifteen years old respectively, are the sons of Captain Barclay, wounded in one of the Indian wars, and his French wife. Now living in France, they have been two years each at school in England and Germany, so they are fluent in three languages. The family lives comfortably on Captain Barclay's half-pay, a small private income and his wife's little fortune. The boys have two cousins, Louis and Philippe Duburg (an oddly spelt surname – Dubourg would be more plausible), who play a minor role in the story. The fact that Philippe is wounded in a desperate fight near Mutzig and returns to Dijon with Louis effectively demonstrates that the English are always better than anyone else. This superiority is further shown when, in the initial excitement of joining the franc-tireurs in Dijon, the boys rescue an Irishman, Tim Doyle, from the crowd's suspicion that he is a spy. Thereafter he becomes the boys' comic servant, and yet another stereotype is hammered into place. The figure of the comic Irishman coalesces with that of the despised, ridiculous Jew when Tim objects to being disguised as 'a haythin Jew' in order to escape from German captivity. His reaction provokes 'screams of laughter' from Ralph and Percy. The disguise is not adopted on this occasion, but when the two boys later undertake a spying expedition through the German lines into Paris on behalf of General Gambetta, it is as stereotypical Jewish traders that they disguise themselves:

> 'We intend to go as German Jews', Ralph said. 'The Prussians strip all the clocks, pictures, and furniture of any value from the villas they occupy, and send them back to Germany. There are a number of Jews who follow the army, and either buy these stolen goods from them, or undertake to convey them back to Germany at a certain price. . . .'

Henty is not one for subtlety in his portrayal of character, which in any case is rarely sought for in adventure stories. His moral values are military, conservative and born of an unquestioned conviction of English superiority.

Henty, like Hesba Stretton, tells his story from the French viewpoint, but this does not mean that he glorifies the French. When the Barclay boys go to visit a party of *franc-tireurs* after Ralph has been wounded and General Cambriels has retreated to Besançon, they are worried at the *franc-tireurs'* lack of discipline, and rightly so, as they are then surprised by Prussians and taken prisoner. The French lack of discipline and organization is a recurring theme in novels about the war. An incident of treachery is given a very high profile. When, on their first spying mission, the Barclay brothers accidentally learn that the French schoolmaster in Grunsdorf has betrayed the franc-tireurs to the Prussians, the eventual result is that the *franc-tireurs* return to the village, capture the schoolmaster and hang him. There is, however, no such sense of outrage when the boys are helped to escape from the lodgings to which they have been paroled in Mayence (Mainz) by the daughter of the house.

As a military man, Henty can admire the Germans' organization, but he provides at least two episodes in which they are shown in a bad light. One day Ralph encounters an old peasant taking vengeance, who explains:

> I had a nice farm near Metz; I lived there with my wife and daughter, and my three boys. Someone fired at the Prussians from a wood near. No one was hit, but that made no difference. The black-hearted scoundrels came to my farm, shot my three boys before their mother's eyes, ill-treated her so that she died next day, and when I returned – for I was away at the time – I found a heap of ashes where my house had stood, the dead bodies of my three boys, my wife dying, and my daughter sitting by, screaming with laughter, mad – quite mad! I took her away to a friend's house, and stayed with her till she died too, a fortnight after; then I bought this gun and some powder and lead with my last money, and went out to kill Prussians. I have killed thirteen already, and, please God', and the peasant lifted his hat devoutly, 'I will kill two more to-day'.

In another, slightly later episode Henty describes how a brutal Prussian major forces one of his young lieutenants to shoot some *franc-tireurs* and peasants in cold blood. After considerable argument the lieutenant finally obeys, declaring he has done his duty, but then blows his own brains out.

The Young Franc-Tireurs was frequently reprinted by a variety of publishers. Despite many implausibilities in the boys' adventures, Henty's careful embedding of the story in the broad sweep of the war, with due attention to geography and the names of leading French generals, commands a certain respect. It is clear all the same that Henty's underlying purpose in this, as in all his books, was the presentation of models of courage, decency and honourable conduct for English boys to follow.

With Annie Lucas's *Léonie. A Tale of the Franco-German War and of the Siege of Paris* (1875) we encounter yet another way of looking at the war. It has links with *Max Krömer* in that it is full of Evangelical piety, but in structure it presents two strangely connected love-stories, told in a rather long-winded fashion. The first part of the novel, entitled 'Light out of Darkness', is set near Belfort in the south of Alsace and narrated in the first person by its heroine, Léonie. The second part, called 'Within Iron Walls', provides another first-person narrative, this time by a young woman called Renée, which is set in Paris and introduces, towards the end, characters that have first appeared in Léonie's narrative.

Unlike Stretton and Henty, Annie Lucas is a minor figure among nineteenth-century authors of children's books, She wrote some seven books between 1875 and 1900, two of which, in addition to *Léonie*, deal with aspects of German-speaking Europe. What is interesting about *Léonie* is the fact that it has more of a plot than either *Max Krömer* or *The Young Franc-Tireurs* and that the characters are French and German, without any English blood to mediate the story to its readers. The main thrust of the novel, which is really a romance, is to show how the war affected two contrasting families, both part of the decayed minor aristocracy. An Evangelical Christian message is apparent from the start, and the author's intention is clearly to demonstrate how French and German can be reconciled through a mutual devotion to Christ. It is the Protestant Evangelicalism that constitutes the unspoken English factor in the book, pointing the way to success.

Léonie is the only child of a rationalist French father and an originally Protestant German mother, who died when she was nine. The mother had been a governess at the neighbouring castle, had fallen in love with the son of the family, but was prevented from marrying him. She had been forced to adopt the Catholic faith and eventually submitted to a loveless marriage to Léonie's father. When war breaks out, Léonie's father is taken ill. Noisy German soldiers are billeted on them, but in their officer in charge Léonie finds a courteous helper and protector. He turns out to be Conrad von Edelstein, the nephew of Léonie's father's dearest German friend, bearing the same name and closely resembling him in appearance. Conrad speaks words of Evangelical comfort to Léonie, tells her about his sister Thekla and loans her the German Bible which he has received from his mother. When he and his men depart from the castle, Léonie and Conrad, despite their opposing national backgrounds, have become friends in both an emotional and a religious sense. Conrad later returns with a new Bible for Léonie and learns that her father is listening with eager interest to what she reads from it. He eventually dies with the word 'Jesus' on his lips. Meanwhile, Conrad is attacked and wounded in the woods near the castle, as a result of which he too dies. The two are buried side by side. French soldiers put up a last-ditch resistance, but the house is attacked and destroyed, and Léonie decides to go to Paris to care for the sick and wounded. One day she lends her Bible to a wounded soldier and in so doing discovers that Conrad was a friend of his. He turns out to be Karl Erhardt and is betrothed to Thekla. Eventually they marry, and Léonie goes to live with them in Munich, continuing to work in hospitals and supposing her 'service to [God] to be the lowly unmarked ministry of household love'.

At this point the book turns to a second, contrasting first-person narrative that tells the fortunes of a large family from Brittany whose father died in the Mexican War of 1862. Their mother is ill from April 1870 onwards, dying on 18 December and in some measure symbolizing France. There are five children – Renée, who tells the story in retrospect, Léon, Augustine (oddly given the English form of his name rather than the French Augustin), Victor and Arnaud. In addition there is an orphan distantly related to the family – Nina, to whom Léon is secretly devoted, but who appears unconcerned about him. Léon articulates the commonplace view that France is unprepared for war and that the Germans are better organized. From the battle-front he sends news of the death of his friend, Henri de l'Orme, and mentions words of comfort given by a German officer, who, it later turns out, must have been Conrad von Edelstein. It is at first assumed that Léon has perished in the desperate struggle at Sedan, but he turns up at the end of the book, being looked after by Léonie St. Hilaire, and eventually marries Nina at a simple Protestant wedding.

Augustine is originally destined for the priesthood, but after a period of agnostic disenchantment becomes a 'Christian'. Victor is first wounded and then killed on the battlefield, where he is found by Augustine. As Hesba Stretton had used the figure of the child Elsie to symbolize innocence and hope, so Annie Lucas invents a little English girl who is attempting to care for her sick mother during the siege of Paris. Her name, Lilian, evokes the purity of the lily, and when her mother dies, she says 'she is with Jesus'. Lilian is taken into the French family, where her simple faith in Jesus converts Nina from despair and Augustine from agnosticism. Peace is signed on 1 March 1871, and in due course the old family estate near Rennes is restored to the family and Léon and Nina move there.

It would be easy to criticize Annie Lucas for her tear-jerking scenes and her facile use of coincidence, but her story is not meant primarily as a realistic account of the war, but as a paradigm of life and death as interpreted by Evangelical Christianity. It is particularly interesting that the leading German characters, being good Evangelicals, are heavily idealized: Conrad's surname, Edelstein, 'jewel, precious stone', is typical of the symbolism of names. His sister Thekla gets her name from one of the most famous first-century saints, the first woman martyr, who according to legend came from a noble family. The French, on the other hand, are either misguided Roman Catholics or Deists. The events of the war and the cross-connexions between the characters are designed to demonstrate that Christian discipleship transcends and reconciles otherwise divided nations. It would therefore be otiose to look for any military or political account of the war. The most important aspect of Lucas's book is her location of true Christianity among the Germans.

A dozen years later a book was published that actually told a story of the Franco-Prussian War as it affected a German family. This was *Fritz of the Tower* (1887) by L. Lobenhoffer (the initial L concealed the name Lillias). It is the only book to focus on German experience of the war, and the detail that it provides about the Black Forest, especially the village of Maulbronn, and its use of German words lead one to surmise that the author herself was German. She certainly writes warmly and knowledgeably about many aspects of ordinary German life. The story opens with the village doctor acclaiming the patriotic enthusiasm of a group of students:

> We shall have fine stirring times. Well, so much the better. It is time that Germany asserted herself. One common defensive war will settle the jealousies of all our petty states, will do away with our insane dislike for everything North German (or Prussian, as we call it), and create that national union which till now has seemed to be an impossible dream.

The professor at the theological seminary, standing next to him, is mournful at the prospect, and in fact his two sons eagerly join up and both die in the hostilities. The doctor's nephew, Herr Walther, reluctantly leaves his wife and child in straitened circumstances, but before he goes husband and wife place their betrothal ring in the baby's dress. After his departure things get worse and the poverty-stricken Frau Walther is turned out of her home. She leaves Maulbronn and is found some days later in the forest by a couple of fiddlers, who think she is dead, but take the child and deposit it with a couple who guard the church tower in a nearby town. The boy is regarded as a gift of God from the childless couple, and he becomes known as Fritz of the Tower. Meanwhile, Frau Walther is rescued by a charcoal-burner, recovers, eventually learns that her husband is ill in France and goes off to nurse him. Herr Walther had been appointed field preacher (i.e. army chaplain) and knew of the horrors of Weissenburg, Wörth, Sedan and Metz before going to Paris and being wounded at Champigny. When he recovers and returns to Germany he is offered a chair at the University of Königsberg. At a later date when coincidentally visiting the town in which Fritz of the Tower has grown up, he discovers his son and can confirm his identity through the betrothal ring that he wears round his neck. Fritz rejoins his parents, but keeps an affectionate contact with his foster-parents.

Fritz of the Tower is a book very much in the mould of C. G. Barth's religious tales. The setting of events in the Black Forest and south-west of Germany picks up the locations in which Barth himself lived, and the whole tone of the book, its primary religious focus, its emphasis on trusting in God whatever the circumstances, its use of coincidence and a token of recognition, reflect Barth's concerns and narrative devices. The actual fighting of the war takes place at a distance and is concisely reported as it affects the professor's sons and Herr Walther, but the main action of the book concerns the wife and child left behind. It is a story of separation, poverty and physical deprivation, but also one in which simple human kindness and Christian faith combine to bring about a happy conclusion in the reunion of husband, wife and child. The military side of the war is a backdrop; what matters here is the effect on those left behind in Germany.

The next book about the Franco-Prussian War to appear was Mary E. Clements's *Eagle and Dove* (1889), which returns the focus to the principal area of fighting in north-east France. In many ways, this is the most informative of the children's books about the war. Probably only about a quarter of the length of *Léonie*, it nonetheless manages to convey a variety of viewpoints with adequate detail about the war. It is rather like a history of part of the war presented in the form of fiction, but with not very much of a plot.

The setting is Metz, but an English connexion is made by means of the first-person narrator, an English girl called Nellé, who has been sent by

The Franco-Prussian War 383

her widowed mother to complete her schooling with Madame Briey, a long-time friend, in Metz. A German girl, Rose Breimar, joins the school after Easter, and Nellé becomes her closest friend. Rose has been sent there to separate her from her lover, Max Meyer, because of their youth. The political and military progress of the war occupies plenty of attention from the declaration of war on 15 July to the surrender of Metz on 27 October. Rose's elder brother, Ernst, comes immediately to visit; her brother Albrecht has suffered a bullet wound, while her brother Franz has been killed. Max Meyer has been heroic enough to receive the Iron Cross. Ernst shows his fondness for Nellé, but has to go with the Prussian army to Paris. On his return he and Nellé are betrothed, as Rose and Max were before them. The book ends with the two couples living only a ten-minute walk away from each other in Germany.

Like Stretton, Lucas and Lobenhoffer, M. E. Clements was a writer of Christian stories, but in this book the Christian message is largely implicit. The character of Madame Briey's great-uncle, Colonel Crévy, allows for a historical perspective on the decline of France from the great Napoleon to Louis Napoleon. In addition there is a Monsieur Gascon, who gives lessons in history and literature that provoke Rose's disagreement. Emphasis is placed elsewhere on France's unpreparedness for war. However, Metz in general and the schoolgirls are depicted initially as devoted admirers of the first Napoleon and loyal enthusiasts of Napoleon III, Metz being a garrison town and full of soldiers marching and exercising. M. Gascon explains the plebiscite called by the Emperor as an invitation to a vote of confidence in the constitutional changes made in the past ten years. The girls expect a confirmation of the Emperor, but Madame Briey has doubts which she is careful to conceal. She supposes that the people may simply want 'la tranquillité'.

One day M. Gascon gives the girls the benefit of his views on the present condition of Prussia, seen as a provocation to France on her northern boundaries:

> Prussia, puffed up with her little victories, won by some trick of improved fire-arms, or rather by the inferiority of the arms of her adversaries, dreams that by making herself dictator among the Germanic States she can erect herself into an impassable barrier on this our only open side. Shall she be permitted to do so? Shall not France, with her love of that liberty for which she herself has suffered so much, hasten to interfere on behalf of the smaller Germanic States, deliver them from the unwelcome dictatorship of the newly-aggrandized neighbour, and at the same time

chastise the arrogance of this parvenu among the nations? (pp. 31-32).

Nellé's comments indicate that the substance and tone of this outburst were shared by most of the French press at this time. A brief account is given of the Prussian candidacy for the Spanish throne and Prince Leopold's subsequent withdrawal. But the provocation to France was enough, and the Emperor declared war on 15 July. M. Gascon describes the German destruction of the Rhine bridge between Kehl and Strasbourg as 'an act of vandalism'. That evening Rose is too upset to go into the salon.

Clements uses the hindsight of history to provide a fuller picture of the war than could be gained from a small group of people in one locality. The German situation and viewpoint are more sketchily dealt with than the French, but a letter to Rose from her father, written just before war is declared, talks about his students 'singing "Die Wacht am Rhein" and cheering lustily for the Fatherland'. If Germany is invaded, writes Dr Breimar', there is nothing our young students so much desire as to rush at once to the frontier and exchange shots with the would-be invader'. That was also the mood reported by Lobenhoffer at the beginning of *Fritz of the Tower*. Dr Breimar regrets the students' attitude and comments: 'There is a season for everything – a season for valour without prudence, and a season when prudence is greater than valour; and to the latter season has come thy loving FATHER' (p. 35). However, Germany's state of preparedness, the mobilization of more than a million men as soldiers and the smooth operation of 'the splendid Prussian organization' are given to the reader in a quotation from Capt. H. M. Hozier's two-volume history, *The Franco-Prussian War; its Causes, Incidents, and Consequences* (1870-72). In ways like this Clements makes apparent her desire to document accurately the different aspects of the war.

M. Gascon represents the belligerent mood of the French towards the Prussians, while Col. Crévy, the seasoned soldier, voices early the fear that the French are unready and ill-equipped. He does this at the time of initial jubilation, when there is talk of the Emperor celebrating his fête day in Berlin on 15 August. In his proclamation to the army Louis Napoleon emphasizes that the way may be 'a long and severe one'; he looks worn and does not smile. Metz is in a different mood. In M. Gascon's report of the first French success in the taking of Saarbrück the girls hear how the young Prince Louis

> had sat unmoved upon his horse while the bullets were falling at his feet; how he had picked one up to keep as a souvenir of his first battle; and old

soldiers seeing him had wept with emotion as they rejoiced that another Buonaparte had arisen to lead the future armies of France to universal victory (p. 56).

By contrast, Madame Briey is incensed:

> For me, I find it somewhat undignified of his imperial majesty to seek to touch the emotions of his troops by exposing a child to danger and hardship. . . . Yes, it is very touching, no doubt, the enthusiasm of this Buonaparte child! It is touching; but it is not war (pp. 57-58).

When the storm breaks and Metz hears of French defeats at Wissembourg, Woerth and Forbach, with troops and civilians in flight, anger and hatred are expressed towards all Germans. Girls cold-shoulder Rose at school, and Nellé, as Rose's friend, finds herself included in this. However, one girl, who has lost her father at Woerth, sympathizes with Rose, wondering whether she too may now be an orphan. Many of the girls are now sent away from Metz to Belgium for safety.

Eagle and Dove is full of circumstantial detail about the progress of the war and changing patterns of life in Metz. The advance of the Prussian infantry, the retreat of the Emperor in a third-class railway carriage from Verdun to Chalons, the appointment of Marshal Bazaine to join MacMahon, the battles at Courcelle, Vionville and Gravelotte are all noted. Metz is surrounded, besieged, and ordinary people keep asking why Marshal Bazaine has not done such and such, but no satisfactory answers are forthcoming. Madame Briey ponders whether the troops' surrender would not result in less damage and slaughter, to which Col. Crévy, aghast, retorts that it would be dishonour and that the meanest soldier would prefer death by slow starvation. In another comment, taken from subsequent accounts, Clements reports that the Germans could have successfully bombarded Metz, provided it did not matter how many lost their lives, but that King William, shocked at the awful cost of the victories of Vionville and Gravelotte, ordered the avoidance of further sacrifice of life which, consistently with the purposes of the war, might be spared. The people of Metz are suspicious of journalists' stories about the capitulation of Sedan, but eventually have to come to terms with it. In the beleaguered city life concentrates on the care of the wounded and the decreasing supplies of food. There are both French and Germans to tend, the French being far more demanding than the Germans; the latter 'lay still, and suffered in grim silence' (p. 91).

M. Gascon is outraged at the terms for surrender, and when Nellé asks why they should wait until soldiers and citizens are worn out with privations, he explodes against the English. The surrender comes nonetheless, and the Prussians refuse General Changarnier's pleas to negotiate the terms. 27 October sees the streets of Metz full of 'impotent wrath' as the commandant, conquered by famine, has to yield. Prince Frederick Charles of Prussia accepts the surrender of men and arms, and on 29 October, a Sunday, Metz becomes a German town.

When Nellé first meets Rose's brother, she tells him she is entirely French in her sympathies; she does not want to appear to sympathize with 'the enemy'. Ernst, on learning she is English, dilates on the medical assistance given by the Red-cross Association, in which many English people are employed. Nellé is interested in this as an example of the 'brotherhood of mankind that centuries ago Christ's apostles preached, but men have not yet understood' (p. 133). Madame Briey, now dying of an unspecified illness, is one of the few who do understand this call to brotherhood.

While Stretton's and Henty's stories end with the main figures departing for a safer place in England, Clements's book provides a different symbolism. The named French characters have had their day: M. Gascon disappears from the story before the surrender; Madame Briey dies just after, and Col. Crévy dies just after the peace is made and is buried with military honours. The future of the younger generation lies in Germany, though it is a curiously vague entity. Rose's father is a professor of medicine at 'some German university with an unpronounceable name', while Rose and Max, Nellé and Ernst live in an unnamed town that has a 'simple, sociable life'. Nellé is now totally separated from France and her French school-fellows. She wonders whether as French mothers now they have taught their sons and daughters 'that in all the affairs of life, public and domestic, to speak the truth is a more important thing than that this or that impression should be made upon the mind of the hearer' (pp. 169-70).

The state of France seems to be mirrored in the fates of Louis Napoleon and his young son, the former dying in 1872 of 'the disorder which, even before the days of the war, was sapping his energies away', the latter dying 'in early manhood, in war, but not for France' (p. 170). The Prince Imperial died in Southern Africa, killed by Zulus in 1879. Much more sympathy is directed to King William of Prussia, proclaimed Emperor of a united Germany at Versailles, and his subsequent death in old age and honour. Then follows the tragically brief reign of Frederick III, while Clements speaks grandiosely of 'the firm utterances of our young Kaiser [William II], telling us that he is no unworthy son of that splendid line of soldier-kings, whose delight is not all in war and victory' (p. 172). Such it was possible to say in a book published in 1889. Sabine Baring-Gould was equally admiring of Germany in his history of 1886.

With our next title in the chronological sequence of books dealing with the Franco-Prussian War we return to Henty and *A Woman of the Commune* (1895). But as this is one of Henty's few books for adults and has very little about Germany in it, it need not detain us long. Its central character is Cuthbert Hartington, a young Englishman who goes to Paris to learn to paint and gets caught up in the siege and the subsequent events of the Commune. Germans do not figure as individuals in the book, but are portrayed at a distance as ruthlessly efficient. The French are divided into two categories – those on the same social level as Cuthbert are charming, but undisciplined, while the lower orders, fighting for social change, are dismissed as 'scum' and an unruly, mindlessly cruel mob. Henty is incapable of making his readers appreciate what it meant to be French during the Franco-Prussian War, still less what it meant to be German. He also displays his animus against independent-minded women in the figure of Mary Brander, who at the end of the book becomes Cuthbert's wife. Henty's deficiencies in plot and characterization in *A Woman of the Commune* detract from his attention to details of daily life during the siege and his accounts of the general background and particular stages of the siege. There he is in his wonted adventure story mode and is more convincing. But his picture is painted from an unremittingly middle-class viewpoint and has no sympathy of any kind for the Commune.

The actual war and period of the Paris Commune are dealt with in another book that was published only a couple of years after Henty, and some ideas seem to have been taken from him. This was *Paris at Bay* (1897) by Herbert Hayens, who wrote about a hundred adventure stories and history books between 1896 and 1933. Like Henty's *Young Franc-Tireurs* and Brereton's *A Hero of Sedan* (which we still have to look at), *Paris at Bay* is a boys' book, concentrating more on the military campaign and deeds of male bravery, at least to begin with. Once more we have an English protagonist, the young Geoffrey Townsend, nephew to the French colonel Gustave Humbert, who is the first-person narrator of the story. The first five chapters deal with the campaign in north-east France, focussing on Sedan, where Geoffrey's friend, Achille Devine, is killed and commends his sister, Marie, to him. In Paris Geoffrey teams up with another Englishman, the painter Stephen

Wilton – Henty's Cuthbert Hartington is also a painter! – and the rest of the book revolves around their joint experiences in Paris, the abduction of Marie in the Commune, their search for her and their encounters with leaders of the Commune. At the end of the story Geoffrey marries Marie, but Stephen is described as his 'more-than-brother'.

Henty and Hayens tell their stories from the French angle, sympathizing with the plight of both the French soldiers and the French civilians, praising their individual courage, but deploring their leaders' military insufficiency and lack of organization. Achille tells his friend:

> 'Bonaparte himself could not have extricated his army from this position; but then he would never have been drawn into it. The fact is, Geoffrey, we are out-generalled. The Prussians have the advantage over us in everything save pluck. On their side are better leaders, better artillery, and bigger battalions. They know just what they require, and go for it. To-morrow they will mow us down like sheep. We cannot stir, hand or foot. Geoffrey, this is a lost army' (p. 20).

The Germans appear in the story, whether at Sedan or round Paris, only in the mass, and there are no incidents that reveal any personal contact between them and the French. After the opening chapters Hayens is more interested in his adventure story of the Commune than in going more deeply into the progress and details of the war.

In the early Edwardian period we have two linked novels by Evelyn Everett-Green which, only at this late date, attempt to give some sympathetic treatment to German characters. *The Castle of the White Flag* and *Ringed by Fire* were both published in 1904. Their author, now largely ignored, was one of the most prolific girls' writers of the day, producing nearly three hundred separate books between 1879 and 1933. The two books about the Franco-Prussian War are clearly girls' books. Their standpoint is identical, international in spirit, as the cast of characters includes English, French, German, American, Canadian and Irish young people, all related to each other to some degree by blood or marriage, and all belonging to the aristocracy. The events of the war are thus depicted, in part at least, as affecting the members of a large extended family, each of whom is loved and respected by the others. Everett-Green (1856-1932) was of the same generation as Stretton and Henty, but writing more than thirty years after the end of the war, she provides a broader and less partisan picture.

The Castle of the White Flag centres on two families of cousins who go with their aunt to live in a castle near Haguenau, in Alsace, while their parents

The Franco-Prussian War 389

go to Australia. The fathers of the two families are brothers, one having married a French wife, the other a German. There are twelve cousins, aged between the early twenties and nine. Opposite the White Castle stands another, known as the Red Castle, in which live the de Selincourts, whose son Gustave is in the Imperial Guard in Paris. A twenty-year-old daughter, Renée (*sic*), lives at home in this Roman Catholic family. The twelve Seymour cousins are, naturally, Protestants. The novel purports to be told on the basis of diaries, letters and records made by all concerned at the time. As the two families settle in at the White Castle in mid March, they are aware of 'a sort of cat-and-dog feeling between France and Prussia, though Maidie, the rather German-looking eldest daughter of the family with the German mother, says 'it was really Prussia who had cause to quarrel with [France], not she with Prussia' (p. xxvii). The local people, however, hate Prussia. Eustace, one of the sons with the French mother, reacts boisterously about the prospect of war and hopes that 'it comes soon rather than late, so that we may see something of the fun. I don't care a hang which side licks the other; I only want to see a real good thundering battle' (pp. 19-20).

Visits from other cousins on both the French and the German sides of the family, together with a developing friendship with the de Selincourts, including both Gustave and his father, provide opportunity for sketching in the historical and political background. Otto von Degenfeldt, one of the German cousins, was at Sadowa in 1866 when the Prussians defeated Austria. His brother Eugen is with the Uhlans, involved in intelligence work (in another context it would be called spying), and meets the Seymours at an extended family visit to the Geissberg near Wissembourg/Weissenburg. This is in the nature of a lull before the storm and a pointing-up of the horrors of war, since the Geissberg is the scene of an early Prussian victory over the French. With their connexions with both sides in the war, the Seymours become involved everywhere. The White Castle is set up as a kind of military hospital for the wounded of both sides, Renée helping along with them. Keith and Duff, two sixteen-year-old cousins, become stretcher-bearers with the Germans. Walter and Eustace, Gustave de Selincourt and Paul Rellier, a French-American cousin, are with the French in Metz and Nancy. One day three of the youngest Seymours are walking in the woods near the White Castle and manage to prevent a group of Frenchmen from torturing and killing a Prussian soldier. They are then interrupted by the appearance of the Crown Prince, who presents them with an iron cross. Monsieur de Selincourt leads a last-ditch rally against the Germans from the Red Castle, in which he himself and Gustave are killed. Victor Rellier had also joined them out of 'misdirected patriotism' (p. 322), but he escapes. Two love-relationships accentuate the emotional tension: both Gustave and Otto are smitten with the shy, beautiful Deborah Seymour, while Walter is in love with Renée. The novel ends with Otto declaring that he wants to win Deborah.

Everett-Green's other novel, *Ringed by Fire*, is a partial sequel to *The Castle of the White Flag*. In fact, the relationship between the two is very similar to that between the two parts of Annie Lucas's *Léonie*. *Ringed by Fire* begins with a different set of leading characters, into which are introduced, in particular, Eugen von Degenfeldt and then, towards the end, various other characters from *The Castle of the White Flag*. The novel is set in Metz and abounds in romantic coincidences.

Its heroine is the twenty-year-old Cicely Varennes, whose English mother and French father are now dead. She has been convent-educated in Canada, but now joins her older brothers, Leon and Kingsford, and their millionaire grandfather, who is of noble descent and a financial genius. Cicely's task in Metz, where the events of the story take place, is to look after another orphan cousin, known as 'La Petite', who can charm her way into anything and who is a source of comedy in the novel. There is also another cousin, Maurice, who is 28 or 29 and in the army. He is in love with a mysterious young lady called Hilda St. Aiden, of Irish descent. This love is thwarted because of a feud between the Varennes family and the St. Aidens, partly because of a duel and partly because of some unexplained financial chicanery. However, the primary romantic interest in the story is provided by a young Prussian officer with an aunt in Metz, Eugen von Degenfeldt, whose English cousins are at present living in a castle in the Vosges. By the end of the novel Eugen is looking forward to gaining Cicely's hand in marriage. Walter Seymour, who had set his sights on Renée de Selincourt, loses his life in the process of saving Leon from being killed by a shell, and Leon instead is destined to become Renée's husband. Deborah Seymour becomes Otto von Degenfeldt's wife. The feud between Lady Geraldine St. Aiden, Hilda's mother, and M. Varennes is brought to an end to allow the marriage of Maurice and Hilda, but the way in which it is done is unpleasant. The financial débâcle that overtook the St. Aidens is retrospectively attributed to 'one beastly little Jew' (p. 303) and not the fault of any of the Varennes family. The anti-Semitic note can hardly be denied and blemishes the rather calculated scheme of international reconciliation.

Within her two novels Everett-Green provides plenty of information about the nature of the war in Alsace-Lorraine. She uses the national background of her English, French and German characters to give different perspectives on the action. She also engages in more explanation, which she must have felt was necessary given the amount of time that had elapsed sine the war was over. The novels present a good mix of adventure, romance, courage, suspense and even comedy (with 'La Petite'). The love stories ensure that each book ends on an up-beat, but three of the families have, nonetheless, lost one or more of their loved ones to the war. Everett-Green interprets the war in terms of an interconnected, interrelated set of families, and family values lie at the heart of these two novels – kindness, decency, mutual respect, willingness to risk one's life for others, readiness to help those in trouble. Eugen von Degenfeldt may be recognised in his reconnaissance work as being a spy, but he has become a friend to Cicely Varennes and 'La Petite' and is treated as such and not denounced. He is to become a closer part of the family at the end of *Ringed with Fire*. In 1904, then, Evelyn Everett-Green has a view of the leading powers of western Europe, England, France and Germany, as constituting one family. This, of course, very much reflects the situation of Queen Victoria's descendants, beginning with Victoria, the Princess Royal, father of Kaiser Wilhelm II, but including so many others who married into German princely families. This is a more optimistic view than any put forward by previous authors of children's books about the Franco-Prussian War. Ten years later it was completely shattered.

Everett-Green's two novels were not the last to take the Franco-Prussian War as their subject. Captain F. S. Brereton's *A Hero of Sedan* (1910) reverts to the mood and treatment that had been employed by his uncle, G. A. Henty, in creating *The Young Franc-Tireurs*, but his book is written with historical hindsight rather than contemporary journalistic experience. Yet Brereton (1872-1957) shares some of Everett-Green's attitudes in depicting the war as it affects three close friends – his English hero, Jack Carter, and his two friends, Louis Castiline and Carl Prunzen. Louis is the vivacious, brave and humorous 'little Frenchman', while Carl is a big Prussian, 'slow, and dull if left to himself'. Carl says, 'Yes, we shall always be friends. . . . Whatever happens, let us remember that'. And the novel predictably provides an episode in which Carl, though fighting on the opposing side to Jack, enables Jack to escape from being sentenced to death in a 'drumhead court martial'. Brereton's choice of surname for Carl is extremely unfortunate, since the verb *brunzen* means 'to piss'. Presumably he invented the name on the basis of a similarity with the word 'Prussian'.

A Hero of Sedan is set in the same geographical area as Everett-Green's books, and its hero belongs to an English family with property in the area. Jack's father has lived ten years in the area, but is 'still an Englishman to his backbone', and Jack is thus 'no Frenchman, though his sympathies were much with that charming nation' (p. 31). Like Henty, Brereton's aim is to present in his hero a model of English courage, decency, fair play and trustworthiness. Jack is the epitome of the young English gentleman who never loses heart and who, through clear thinking and common sense, finds a way out of every difficulty. The figure that provides the most striking contrast is the Carters' vindictive neighbour Von Veltenden, a German spy whom even the Germans find obnoxious. He is caught spying in Paris at the end of the book and is fittingly shot. Another dark figure is the coarse, bullying leader of a group of *francs-tireurs* whom Jack falls in with and whom he kills with a blow of his fists because he will not tolerate his brutality towards a group of Prussian prisoners. Brereton's animus is not against German or French, but against those who do not act fairly and decently regardless of nationality. There are a number of occasions when Brereton shows Prussian officers exercising mercy and respect for the gentlemanly English values he views as paramount. Indeed, the Prussian who admires Jack for his attack on Veltenden at the beginning of the story is described as 'Tall and slim, and looking every inch a soldier in his fine uniform, this German general had almost the appearance of an Englishman'. (p. 47).

The passage of nearly forty years from the conclusion of the Franco-Prussian War permits Brereton to furnish plenty of historical information. He mentions the long-standing antagonism of France and Germany, Buonaparte's crushing of Prussia in 1806 and his own defeat at the Battle of Leipzig in 1813, but he also writes admiringly of Bismarck's skill in bringing the northern and southern states of Germany together, increasing Prussia's power and importance while France remains much the same as before. While Brereton, like all his predecessors, emphasizes the bravery of the French soldiers and blames the unprepared state of the army on the Emperor, he cannot conceal how impressed he is by the Germans' organization of the fighting soldiers marching light and being supported by others carrying blankets and other equipment. By contrast, the individual French soldier carries a weight of personal equipment that makes his job more difficult. What is particularly interesting in Brereton's assessment

The Franco-Prussian War 393

of the build-up of German troops prior to the war is his comment on the present rivalry between Germany and Britain in 1910:

> Germany's huge army, her fast-increasing fleet, and her gain in wealth since 1870, place her second to no power in the world, but make her a keen rival of Great Britain. Her desire to be paramount, her marked jealousy of us may – who knows – plunge the two countries into a terrible conflict, and Germany will be ready for it – perhaps even willing (p. 89).

The life-and-death conflict was to begin only four years later.

In looking at these ten books we can see that each of the authors has a different agenda in treating aspects of the Franco-Prussian War. Each book, whatever section of the war it deals with, sticks closely to the documented historical facts, though attempts to interpret or analyse their political significance are less in evidence. It is fascinating to note how all of the books except Lucas's *Léonie* and Lobenhoffer's *Fritz of the Tower* manage to incorporate English or half-English characters to mediate the experience of the war, despite the fact that Britain was not involved in it. This does not by any means lead to a kind of detached or objective picture of events. On the contrary, there is a considerable variety of approach and emotional impact, and it is particularly interesting to register the changes in the portrayal of the Germans in general and the introduction of individual German characters into the novels.

It is a curious fact that few contemporary German children's books seem to have been translated into English in the period 1880-1914 apart from Johanna Spyri's *Heidi* and some of her other stories (and we must remember that Spyri was Swiss). Nonetheless, the passion for earlier German children's books such as the Grimms' and Hauff's fairytales, Fouqué's *Undine* and *Sintram*, Hoffmann's *Struwwelpeter* and even Schmid's *Basket of Flowers* continued unabated. What we appear to have instead of contemporary German children's books is an increasing number of books by British authors that deal with German history, geography and travel, together with works of historical fiction that focus on Germany. G. A. Henty, for example, produced *The Lion of the North* (1886) and *Won by the Sword* (1899) about different periods of the Thirty Years War and *With Frederick the Great* (1897) among his huge output of boys' adventure stories. Frederick the Great was a particularly popular king to figure in history books, and a chapter on him was included in *Men of Deeds and Daring. Stories of their Lives*, by the author of *Remarkable Men* (London: Dean & Son, c. 1860) as well as in *Leaders of Empires* (London and Edinburgh: Gall & Inglis, c. 1908), which also contains a long section on Prince Bismarck as well as Napoleon Buonaparte and Queen Victoria. The earlier book goes back further in history to include a section on John Frederic the Magnanimous, i.e. Johann Friedrich, Elector of Saxony, fighter for the Protestant cause against the Emperor Charles V in the sixteenth century. John Frederic is significant not only for that reason, but also for the fact that, as the account concludes, His Royal Highness Prince Albert is a descendant of the illustrious Elector. Historical accounts of great Germans and novels by British authors that are grounded in events from German history can thus be seen as an important part of the impact that Germany made on British children's books. They are relevant not only in their own right, but they are also firmly linked to the dynastic connexions between Britain and Germany that became prominent with Victoria's marriage to Prince Albert and with the marriages of several of their children and grandchildren to German princes.

22. German Books for Girls

In the English-speaking world the development of girls' stories is particularly linked with two American classics – Louisa M. Alcott's *Little Women* (1868) and Susan Coolidge's *What Katy Did* (1872) – after which the genre blossomed in both North America and the British Isles. L. T. Meade's most famous book was *A World of Girls* (1886), but that was simply one of more than 300 that she wrote. Only a little less prolific was Evelyn Everett-Green, whose first stories appeared in the 1880s. Two of her later books are of special interest in that they deal with aspects of the Franco-Prussian War. However, neither Everett-Green nor Meade produced books that are classics and reprinted today. The German-speaking countries also had many women authors who wrote principally for girls, but only one of them from the second half of the nineteenth century has achieved lasting fame, namely, Johanna Spyri with *Heidi* (1880-81). Spyri's predecessors, Amalia Schoppe (1791-1858), Marie Nathusius (1817-57) and Ottilie Wildermuth (1817-77), had some of their books translated into English during the nineteenth century, but none of them made a lasting impression on their readers. By contrast, Spyri's success with *Heidi* has been marked by countless twentieth-century reprints and adaptations right up to our own time.

Amalia Schoppe, writing in the first half of the nineteenth century, did not write specifically for girls, but she seems to be the first German woman writing for children whose work was translated into English and credited to her by name. For this reason alone she deserves our attention. As far as I can tell, only one of her many books for children was translated into English, and this was yet another of the stories about poor orphans that proliferated in both Germany and Britain during this period. *Heinrich und Marie oder die verwaisten Kinder* (Leipzig: Leopold Michelsen, 2. verbesserte

Auflage, 1839) was translated into English by Susan Cobbett with the title *Henry and Mary, or the Little Orphans* (Manchester: John Heywood; London: Simpkin & Marshall, & Houlston & Wright, [1860]). The German edition describes the book as 'a moving and instructive story for good children of both sexes from 8 to 12 years old', while the English subtitle merely says it is 'an interesting tale for young readers'.

The Henry and Mary of the story lose their father, a former soldier, to an accident with a horse, then their house and possessions are swept away in a flood, and their mother is abducted to be an unwilling housekeeper to counterfeiters in an underground forest den. The destitute children encounter both hostile and friendly adults, the most helpful being an elderly woman who earns her meagre living by drying and selling herbs. On her death the children are assisted by Mr Truelove, the druggist to whom she used to sell her wares. The children are then separated, with Henry being employed by Mr Truelove's brother. One night, while sheltering from a storm, Henry overhears the two counterfeiters talking about their activities as they wait, hiding in the same place, for an old Jew who buys their coins. This results in the counterfeiters being apprehended and the children's mother rescued. The family is reunited, and all gain suitable employment and a roof over their heads. These frightening events, which are little more than variations on stock motifs from moral tales and popular chapbooks, are interspersed with examples of Christian forbearance and trustfulness that lead to the story's happy conclusion. Both German and British writers of the day had an inexhaustible appetite for tales that exposed children to such wild fears – loss of parents and home, hunger and starvation, abandonment in the forest – only to end with reunion, hope and economic stability. Whether children enjoyed and profited from them in the way their authors intended is open to question.

Like Amalia Schoppe, Marie Nathusius built on the traditions of Christian stories exemplified by Christoph von Schmid, Christian Gottlob Barth and Gustav Nieritz, but her work was not as comprehensively translated into English as that of her male predecessors. The title story in *Christfried's First Journey, and Other Tales* (Edinburgh: Johnstone, Hunter, & Co., c. 1871) is typical of the optimistic Christian genre. As with Schoppe's *Henry and Mary*, this is not specifically a girls' book, but tells how Christfried, the fourteen year old son of a clergyman's widow, through his obliging, candid nature and trust that God will help him, gains financial backing to study to become a clergyman himself. The help comes from a nobleman who signs himself 'Frederick, Count of Renna'. The story is not credited to Nathusius, nor is any translator's name given. The other two equally anonymous tales in this little book appear to be by British writers. An eight-page list of other works published by Johnstone, Hunter, and Co. concentrates on similarly improving tales and includes Krummacher's *Alfred and the Little Dove, Gottfried of the Iron Hand: a Tale of German Chivalry* and *Cockerill the Conjurer; or, the Brave Boy of Hameln*, a story of the Pied Piper. Another form of Nathusius's story was published in *Max Wild the Merchant's Son, and other Stories for the Young* (London and Edinburgh: Nimmo, 1874) with the variant spelling *Christfrid's First Journey*. The title-story is by Franz Hoffmann. I have not been able to check whether the Nathusius translations, both anonymous, are identical or not.

Much more significant than *Christfried* is Nathusius's *Tagebuch eines armen Fräuleins* (1854), of which five different English translations were published in scarcely more than a dozen years. First came an anonymous American translation entitled *Louisa von Plettenhaus: the Diary of a Poor Young Lady* (Boston and New York: Francis, 1857). It was followed in 1860 by two British editions – *The Diary of a Poor Young Gentlewoman*, translated from the German by M. Anna Childs (London: Trübner & Co.) and *Step by Step; or, the Good Fight* (London: R. Bentley). In 1867 Tauchnitz published Miss Thompson's translation, *Diary of a Poor Young Lady*, in volume 12 of its 'Collection of German Authors', and the same title was given for Emily Ritzerow's translation in 1869. The number of translations is remarkable. *The Diary of a Poor Young Gentlewoman* is a full-length novel aimed at an adolescent (and probably also adult) female readership. Focussing on the experiences of an impoverished young Christian lady who is forced to become a governess, it comes, for British readers, in the wake of Anne Brontë's *Agnes Grey* (1847) and Charlotte Brontë's *Jane Eyre* (1847) and *Villette* (1853), though it does not have their power. Luise finds the experience of being a governess humbling because of her social station, but she also has to negotiate the problems of a household divided between a stern, religious younger brother, Mr von Schaffau, and a socialite, malicious older sister, Frau von Schlichten. She gains the friendship and support of various members of the family and engages in works of mercy among the poor of the neighbourhood. She is pursued by the rich, but unacceptable Mr von Tülfen. However, Mr von Schaffau is generally helpful and pleasant, but sometimes seems stern and displeased. Eventually, on Luise's birthday (26 March), Mrs von Schlichten dismisses her and sends her back home. The date is significant in being the day after the Feast of the Annunciation and also the Tuesday in Holy Week, so a promise of improvement is combined with further suffering. At this same time Luise's elderly aunt dies, and Plettenhaus, the ancestral home, has to be sold. The novel ends with Mr von Schaffau buying the property and marrying Luise. The narrative is conveyed in the form of Luise's diary interspersed with occasional letters, a first-person technique that encourages reader-identification with the heroine. The whole book centres on the heroine's Christian fortitude and humility, suffering patiently borne leading ultimately to redemption in the form of marriage and a return to home. The religious dimension is not insisted upon quite as strongly as one finds in other children's books of the period and later, but the ending appears formulaic rather than realistically convincing.

Ottilie Wildermuth was a more prolific writer of children's books than Marie Nathusius, but not many of them were translated into English. A version of *Die Ferien auf Schloß Bärenburg* was published as *The Holidays at Bärenburg Castle* in Mary Howitt's *The Golden Casket: a Treasury of Tales for Young People* (London, [1861]) and also William Howitt's *Luke Barnicott, and Other Stories* (London and New York: Cassell, Petter, & Galpin, [1866]). It is not clear whether the translation was made by Mary or William, both being proficient in German. Another translation was published in 1865 with the title *Midsummer Holidays at Castle Bärenburg*. Among Wildermuth's other books we find *The Home Queen; or, Unconscious Rule* (London and New York: Frederick Warne & Co., c. 1893) with the author's first name misspelt 'Ottalie'. This is most probably a translation of 'Eine Königin', a story included in *Von Berg und Thal* (2nd edition, 1861). Four other titles of books by Wildermuth are *By Daylight; or Pictures from Real Life* (1865), *Nurse Margaret's Two St. Sylvester's Eves* (London and Oxford: Society for Promoting Christian Knowledge, 1871), *Barbara's Christmas* (SPCK, 1873) and *The Little Sand Boy; or, Who is best off* (Edinburgh, 1877).

The Holidays at Bärenburg Castle is particularly interesting for the English reader on account of the detailed descriptions it gives of German life. The plot is simple: the son and daughter of a village schoolmaster travel fifteen miles, mainly on foot, to stay with their godmother, who is housekeeper at the castle of Bärenburg. There they meet the Princess Clotilde and her two children, who are slightly younger than themselves. The social distinctions are preserved, but the children become friends. One day when Prince Hugo gets into difficulties climbing, Fritz rescues him and Hugo gives him a beautiful ring with a red stone in recompense. The holidays come to an end, and the schoolmaster's children return home. Fourteen years later, Hugo unexpectedly becomes the ruler of the principality and passes through the village. Through catching sight of the ring he recognizes Fritz, who is now a young curate, appoints him to the living and thus helps him to care for the previous clergyman's widow, as well as his own schoolmaster father and sister. The story ends with the observation:

> The brother and sister, who continued to find their daily bread supplied in honour without any especial princely generosity, yet retained, from their early intercourse with their high-born playfellows, something of great value as a bright memento of the past – a living faith in the help of God at the right time.

The unexpected happy ending, which comes as a complement to some earlier spontaneous act of help, is a commonplace of Christian children's stories, but Wildermuth is skilful enough to place the primary interest of her tale elsewhere and not to overdo the explicitly Christian aspect. The descriptive details of rural life, the end of the school year, the furnishings of the castle, the lay-out of its gardens and Mrs Dote's role as housekeeper make the story a fascinating social document. There are also interesting comments on social roles and status, since Fritz calls the traditional expectations into question. His sister, Mina, thinks she might be frightened if she should meet the princess, to which Fritz boldly retorts: 'I shall not, . . .all men are equal before God, prince or peasant or nobleman; it makes no difference'. Their godmother, representative of the older generation, responds angrily:

> it is true that God created all men equal, but the Lord himself has appointed to each one his particular place; one in a lofty position, another humbler, and the humble must never fail in respect; and the lofty will one day be called to answer before the Lord for his stewardship, whether he have done well or evil, with that which was intrusted to him.

As a boy being prepared to become a clergyman, Fritz displays the questioning attitudes of the younger generation, but when he is a man and a curate he is suitably deferent towards the prince, waiting for the latter to recognize the ring rather than taking the initiative himself.

Either Mary or William Howitt might well have been drawn to translate this story because of their own residence and interest in Germany. Nearly twenty years previously William had written *The Rural and Domestic Life of Germany* for an adult readership, and Wildermuth's story provides a wealth of comparable material for children. Being of a progressive mind himself, he would have also appreciated the gentle questioning of social distinctions that Wildermuth expressed through her depiction of Fritz.

The stories of Nathusius and Wildermuth, though popular in Germany in their day, pale in significance in comparison with Johanna Spyri's *Heidi*, which deservedly enjoys classic status in both the German and the English-speaking world. A multitude of editions, translations and adaptations have rolled off the printing presses ever since its first appearance in 1880-81 and are still continuing to do so. Only a small proportion of the book's success thus lies within our period. Johanna Spyri (1827-1901) was over fifty when her masterpiece was first published in Germany in two volumes with the titles *Heidis Lehr- und Wanderjahre* and *Heidi kann brauchen, was es gelernt hat* (Gotha: Friedrich Andreas Perthes, 1880-81).[115] There was also a subtitle: *Eine Geschichte für Kinder und auch für Solche, welche die Kinder lieb haben*, which is particularly significant since it points to the book's dual readership – 'a story for children and also for those who are fond of children'. *Heidi* tends to be thought of as a girls' book, but this unjustly restricts its appeal. It has, undeniably, a central female character in Heidi and a preponderance of other female figures, but the male characters – the grandfather, Peter the goatherd, Herr Sesemann, the man-servant Sebastian and Dr Classen – all have serious roles to play. It is a pity to treat *Heidi* as a girls' book just because it has a central female character. In the same way it is a pity to treat *Heidi* simply as a children's book because it deals with the lives of children. The very title of the first volume – 'Heidi's years of learning and travel' – by its allusion to Goethe's novels *Wilhelm Meisters Lehrjahre* and *Wilhelm Meisters Wanderjahre* points to Spyri's sense of ambition. The title of her second volume – 'Heidi is able to make use of what she has learnt' – shows us the Swiss author with her sights on that most ambitious of German prose genres, the *Bildungsroman*, the novel that illustrates the development of character. *Heidi* is actually a novel that an adult can read with pleasure because it is true to the feelings of the children – Heidi and Peter especially, Klara to a lesser extent – who are its focus. It is both a story of childhood and a study of it, accessible to children and adults alike. Like so many nineteenth-century children's books, *Heidi* is the story of an orphan. Heidi enters the book as a little girl not quite five years old. We learn from her aunt Dete that Heidi's father was killed by a falling beam

---

115 For much of my discussion I am indebted to Peter Skrine, 'Johanna Spyri's *Heidi*', *Bulletin of the John Rylands University Library of Manchester*, vol. 76, no. 3 (Autumn 1994), pp. 145-64.

33. Title-page and frontispiece of *Ottilie Wildermuth, Nurse Margaret's Two St. Sylvester's Eves* [1871]

and that her mother was so severely affected by the event that she too died only a few weeks later. The one year old child was taken care of by Dete and her mother. Then Dete's mother died, and now Dete has the offer of a job in Frankfurt and cannot take Heidi with her. She unceremoniously offloads responsibility for the child on to Heidi's grandfather, a seventy year old widower who shuns contact with the people in the village and has a fearsome reputation among them. He lives in a mountain hut and is known as the Alm-Öhi, 'Alm uncle'. From such inauspicious beginnings Heidi and her grandfather gradually develop a warm, mutually supportive relationship. Heidi's innocent, open nature, uncomplicated by the fears and inhibitions of the adult world, eventually enables her grandfather to re-establish contact with the village and the people from whom he had been estranged.

Heidi's relationship with her grandfather is the most important one in the book, but she also develops loving relationships with two other grandparent figures – first, the blind grandmother of her friend Peter, the goat-boy, and secondly, Frau Sesemann, the grandmamma of her invalid friend Klara in Frankfurt. Peter's grandmother is the focus of Heidi's outgoing, helpful nature. Heidi is saddened at her blindness and poverty and does everything she can to alleviate it: she talks to her and later reads to her, especially Christian hymns and poems, and when she returns from

Frankfurt she brings material comforts for her. By contrast, Frau Sesemann provides Heidi with love and support when she is badly treated by Fräulein Rottenmeier, the Sesemanns' martinet housekeeper, and feels out of place and homesick. Frau Sesemann comes from Holstein, and it seems as though she and Heidi, coming from opposite ends of the German-speaking world, are kindred spirits. She is the epitome of the affectionate, understanding, commonsensical grandmother. She knows how to put Fräulein Rottenmeier in her place and counteract the regime of terror that she has inflicted on poor Heidi, who knows nothing of the niceties of middle-class social behaviour. Grandparents, whether blood relations or adoptive, are thus the most significant figures in Heidi's life.

Parent figures occupy a more shadowy role in Spyri's book. Heidi's aunt Dete resembles nothing so much as a Greek messenger of the gods. She has done her best for Heidi as a small child, looking after her with her mother and then farming her out to old Ursel when she gets a job as a chambermaid in Bad Ragaz. But when she gets an offer she can't refuse in Frankfurt, she has no compunction about abandoning the child to the strange, problematic figure of the Alm uncle. Then, just when it seems that Heidi is happily settled with her grandfather, Dete intervenes again by having the eight year old Heidi sent to Frankfurt to be a companion to the invalid, twelve year old Klara. Once Dete has managed to get Heidi into the Sesemann household, she disappears and virtually nothing more is heard of her. Heidi is delivered to the tender mercies of Fräulein Rottenmeier and the supercilious maid, Tinette, neither of whom has any understanding of or sympathy for her country background. Fräulein Rottenmeier insists on conformity to ritualized standards of bourgeois conduct; she cannot see anything below this rigid surface and thus makes Heidi's existence miserable. These are the figures that occupy the displaced mother role, none of them attractive.

Father figures are more positive. Klara's father, Herr Sesemann, is away on business when Heidi arrives in Frankfurt, but on his return he proves totally sympathetic towards her and instructs the daunting Fräulein Rottenmeier to deal kindly with her and not to regard Heidi's differences of behaviour as misdemeanours. Herr Sesemann's friend, Dr Classen, is another ally. It is he who diagnoses what lies behind Heidi's unhappiness and sleepwalking in Frankfurt and urges his friend to let Heidi go back home to Switzerland. Dr Classen is the first to visit Heidi there when Klara is not well enough to undertake the long journey. Heidi takes the place of his own daughter, who has just died, and Dr Classen moves his own residence to the mountains to be near Heidi and provide support alongside the Alm uncle. Sebastian, the Sesemanns' man-servant, is a further adult male supportive to Heidi. He is a complete contrast to Tinette, doing little acts of kindness for Heidi and accompanying her as far as Mayenfeld on her journey home.

After the Alm uncle the most important male figure in Heidi's little world is Peter, the goat-boy, who is eleven years old when Heidi is roughly deposited at her grandfather's hut. Peter has no father either, but lives with his mother and blind grandmother. In certain respects he is the most realistically portrayed and most complex character in the book. While Heidi's acts and reactions reflect a kind of primal goodness, honesty and spontaneity, Peter is altogether more ambivalent. His job is to take the villagers' goats up to the high pastures and take care of them. The Alm uncle teases him by calling him 'general of the goats', but Peter is not entirely reliable, nor is he very bright. Although he is eleven and Heidi five, they do not seem so very far removed in mental capacity. Peter hates going to school in winter and makes little progress until Heidi actually teaches him to read properly, though he says he's learnt before. Peter likes having Heidi to himself and is jealous when Klara comes to visit. As a result he destroys her wheelchair by furtively pushing it headlong down the mountain. Afterwards he is racked with guilt at what he has done, though no one knows who did it. When Herr Sesemann arrives in the village, Peter imagines he is the policeman come from Frankfurt to apprehend him, and he is terrified. However, Grandmamma Sesemann, insightful and sympathetic towards children as always, immediately realizes that Peter has punished himself quite enough with anxiety and guilt and needs reassurance rather than any further punishment from outside. She recognizes that the poor boy needs some kind of compensation for the fact that he is no longer Heidi's only friend and asks him what he would like as a present. Peter demonstrates his simplicity of heart by asking only for the smallest sum of money, and Frau Sesemann is the very embodiment of mercy in making this sum what Peter gets every week for a whole year.

With Heidi herself Johanna Spyri created a most engaging character, for Heidi is unusual in being admirable without being a goody-goody. She is a child of nature, spontaneous, kind and thoughtful. She blossoms under the care of her grandfather, who respects her abilities and choices and allows her freedom to develop. In turn, Heidi is the catalyst for her grandfather's gradual reintegration into village life. Without knowing what she is doing, she enables him to put the wrongs of the past and his soured relationships behind him, to help Peter's mother and grandmother in practical ways and eventually to become reconciled with the pastor and return to live in the village. In the hands of another writer Heidi might well have been portrayed as a sentimental and unbelievable example of Christian goodness, but Spyri avoids this trap by making her into a fully rounded figure. Heidi's goodness is natural rather than calculatedly Christian. But she is human and has her limitations. She cannot cope with the restraints of the city, the petty restrictions and rituals imposed by Fräulein Rottenmeier, the loss of contact with the mountains, the countryside and the sky. In Frankfurt and middle-class society Heidi wilts and becomes sad and depressed. Gaiety and spontaneity are gradually squeezed out of her so that she becomes emotionally as weak as Klara is physically. Spyri does not psychologize about Heidi's state, but gives her readers sufficient description for them to understand, according to their different ages, what Heidi must be experiencing. A lesser writer might have attempted to spell out and account for Heidi's feelings, but Spyri allows them to unfold through the events and actions of the story, largely free from authorial comment.

One of the most fascinating aspects of *Heidi* is the fact that the story takes place in a clearly identified geographical setting and that the setting is crucial for the story's meaning. Johanna Spyri locates the major part of the book in eastern Switzerland near the little town of Mayenfeld (now spelt Maienfeld) in the northern part of the large canton of Graubünden (Grisons), only a mile or two across the Rhine from the spa of Bad Ragaz in the canton of St. Gallen. The actual village is given the fictitious name of Dörfli ('little village'), but the Alm uncle specifically identifies two of the mountains that Heidi describes as the Falknis and the Schesaplana. The Prättigau is the area between Maienfeld and Klosters, and Domleschg, where the Alm uncle and Dete's mother come from, is south of Chur, the capital of Graubünden. The mountains and pastures, the snow-capped peaks that turn rosy in the setting sun, the meadows, the goats and wild flowers are constantly described and celebrated for their beauty, yet the harshness and poverty of the peasants' life is not glossed over. Admittedly Bad Ragaz provides Dete with a job as a chambermaid, but to get something economically more worthwhile she has to travel as far afield as Frankfurt, and that is where Heidi later has to follow her. The great city provides wealth, but not health. In the city Klara is an invalid and Heidi becomes emotionally and physically debilitated. Both recover in the pure air of the mountains of eastern Switzerland. Ironically, it is Peter's malevolent destruction of Klara's wheelchair that leads directly to her gradual acquisition of the strength to walk again and to the establishment of a new small community at Dörfli, where people from the city and the mountains can live together in health and harmony.

Spyri's *Heidi* came at an opportune time for British readers. Switzerland had opened up to a wider range of visitors with the extension of the railway system, and the enjoyment of an unpolluted environment was increasingly sought by those who were making their money in the expanding cities of the Industrial Revolution. Germany, Belgium and France provided a multitude of spas that promoted this quest for health, but Switzerland added a grander landscape, a large number of picturesque lakes and the thrill of the mountains for climbing, walking and breathing pure air. There had been travel books aplenty up to this time, most catering to an adult readership, but C. J. G. and F. Rivington published *Travels in Switzerland* in a format suitable for children as early as 1831. Every book on Switzerland mentioned its national hero, William Tell, and his story was immensely popular with children.[116] The tone had been set by Jean Pierre Claris de Florian, whose *William Tell; or, Swisserland Delivered* appeared in English translation as early as 1809. Other versions of the Tell story were published throughout the nineteenth century, reworking the traditional material in a variety of ways and focussing attention on the Forest Cantons, the ancient core of the Swiss Federation. Alongside the Tell story the idea of Switzerland was alive to British children through the protagonists of that most popular adventure story, *The Swiss Family Robinson*, first published in 1814, but printed in a large variety of formats and editions from then until the present day. *The Swiss Family Robinson* was not about Switzerland, of course, but it formed part of the awareness of Switzerland and Swiss history in nineteenth-century Britain. When *Heidi* was first published in English, rural Switzerland became visually and emotionally alive to new generations of child readers, especially girls. Florian had made the William Tell story more appealing to children through the invention of a sub-plot centring on Tell's son and his young girl friend, and we can see Spyri using a similar pattern with Heidi and Peter, though they were not to be future lovers. With *Heidi*, however, the emphasis is on the young female character,

---

116 David Blamires, 'Politics, Religion and Family Values in English Children's Versions of the William Tell Story', *New Comparison*, 20 (Autumn 1995), pp. 61-74.

in contrast to Florian, where the males dominate, whether it is Tell's son or Tell himself and his compatriots who are at the centre of action. Many generations of British children must have had their image of Switzerland first shaped by their enjoyment of Spyri's masterpiece.

The earliest translations of *Heidi* into English were American. The first, by Louise Brooks, was issued in two volumes with the titles *Heidi: Her Years of Wandering and Learning* and *Heidi: How she Used what she Learned*, corresponding to those of the German (Boston: De Wolfe, Fiske & Co., 1884). A British edition appeared in the same year, but with the different titles *Heidi's Early Experiences* and *Heidi's Later Experiences*. Fifteen years later a second American translation was published, this time by Helen B. Dole, with the subtitles *Heidi's Years of Learning and Travel* and *Heidi Makes Use of what she has Learned* (Boston: Ginn & Company, 1899). Further translations were made by H. A. Melcon (New York: A. L. Burt, [1901], and Springfield, Massachusetts: McLoughlin Bros., 190-?); Helene S. White (New York: T. Y. Crowell & Co., [1902]); and a translator whose identity is concealed behind the initials M. E. (London: J. M. Dent & Co., [1909]). This last translation enjoyed a wide circulation through being reprinted frequently in Everyman's Library. The number of different translations and publishers involved shows what a commercial proposition *Heidi* was in the English-speaking world in the period before the First World War, and its popularity has not waned since then.

The success of *Heidi* led to some of Spyri's other stories being translated into English too. In 1888 (though dated 1889) five stories were translated by Lucy Wheelock as *Swiss Stories for Children and Those who Love Children* (London, etc.: Blackie & Son). They are said to have been taken from a volume of *Kurze Geschichten* and are titled 'Toni', 'In Safe Keeping', 'Rosenresli', 'Lisa's Christmas' and 'Basti's Song in Altorf'. 'In Safe Keeping' was published separately by the same publisher in 1896. All five stories are set in the German Swiss Alps and focus on children below the age of ten. They are suffused with a similar piety to that we have encountered in many earlier books, but it is more marked than in *Heidi*. While all the stories end happily, they show a side of Alpine life that is hard and rugged. 'Toni' gives a moving account of a shy boy left with virtually no human society in a mountain hut, while his mother is forced to get work in a hotel in Interlaken. The boy's loneliness leads to his total inner withdrawal and inability to communicate, and he has to be sent to a hospital in Berne. There a lady from Geneva who has lost a son befriends him and helps him to do what he has always wanted – train to become a wood-carver. 'Rosenresli' has quite a lot in common with the section of *Heidi* that deals with Heidi's relationship with Peter's grandmother, for Rosenresli (i.e. little Theresa with the roses) establishes a mutually supportive relationship with a poor widow who is known as Mother Grief.

When Rosenresli is forced out of her own home, the widow's long lost son coincidentally returns home and takes care of her because of all she has done to help his mother. 'Lina's Christmas' centres on the loss of a pet lamb, which is found again in the local church just in time for Christmas. 'In Safe Keeping' concerns the rescue of a little girl who has fallen down a mountain precipice, while 'Basti's Song in Altorf' tells about two children who, when their mother is ill, try to earn money by singing in an inn. Their wholly inappropriate song provokes laughter, but then generous and continuing help from a group of young men once they realize the plight the children are in.

Spyri's short stories have obvious affinities with *Heidi*, but they can more easily be viewed as part of the long tradition of moral Christian tales that precedes her masterpiece. Her characters seem more real than, say, Amalia Schoppe's Henry and Mary because they are not all paragons of Christian virtue who always do the right thing. Lisa, who forgets to look after the pet lamb and fails to bring it back home, does not immediately tell her mother what she has done. She knows she has done something wrong, but when her mother voices her belief that Lisa couldn't have been the person who lost the lamb, she keeps silent through shame. Many readers will have identified with Lisa in her distress. We can recognize Spyri using commonplaces of story-telling like all the other nineteenth-century authors of moral tales, but she has many touches that ring psychologically true. Another example is Toni's catatonic depression deriving from the appalling situation to which he is subjected at home because of dire poverty. This is a situation analogous to Heidi's homesickness and sleepwalking in Frankfurt, where she feels truncated from her life with her grandfather. Alpine life is not always an idyll in Spyri's stories, however much it may be so at the end of *Heidi*. Some of the stories have been reissued and others published for the first time in the twentieth century, but Spyri's lasting reputation unquestionably rests on the appeal and distinction of *Heidi*.

23. Children's Books and the First World War

No war has been more exhaustively recorded in every kind of medium than what we now call the First World War. During the period 1914-18 itself writers of all kinds documented its impact in both public and private forms, through newspaper reports, propaganda items, works of literary ambition and expressions of personal experience. Painters, illustrators and photographers also bent their skills to the task. Both during and after the war for about twenty-five years poems and novels attempted to distil diverse areas of an experience that, for the soldiers in the trenches, was the most shattering and also the profoundest that they had had or would ever have. Some of the finest English poetry of the twentieth century stems from this personal experience. Though French and German writing of high quality also emerged from the war, it does not have a comparable weight in the literatures of France and Germany. It is a remarkable fact that even eighty years after the conclusion of the First World War the British reading public still devours the work of historians on the subject, sometimes in investigating a particular aspect, sometimes in providing a new angle of interpretation or a different way of contextualizing it. Responses to the war are immensely varied. They encompass simplistic forms of patriotism and xenophobia as well as deep compassion, revulsion, admiration, horror and tears. The catalogue of reactions is endless, but one that is particularly moving is articulated in the dedication to David Jones's long-gestated *In Parenthesis*, first published in 1937. *In Parenthesis* recalls and reinterprets Jones's experience as a private in the trenches and the battle of Mametz Wood, using an extraordinary combination of a painter's careful observation of things, people and events together with a wide range of literary, religious and cultural reference. The book transfigures, but does not deny or diminish the terrors of the war, and it holds together both pathos and humour. The book is dedicated to his friends, his fellow soldiers from London and Wales, but also 'to the enemy front-fighters who shared our pains against whom we found ourselves by misadventure'.

The poems and novels that came out of the First World War have a great lustre. Anthologies that place these great literary achievements alongside the personal outpourings of untutored men writing home or venting their emotions in traditional verse move us still. But what was written for children and teenagers about the war has virtually disappeared from awareness. Certainly, it has not survived as living literature for young people of today. Mary Cadogan and Patricia Craig have examined the subject in their book, *Women and Children First. The Fiction of Two World Wars* (London: Victor Gollancz, 1978), which looks at both popular books for adults and children's books and magazines. It is a very useful, briskly written account and provides a lot of detailed information. Naturally enough, it is chiefly concerned with Britain and British experience. It has very little to say about the Germans. That is not very surprising since the focus of everything written in Britain about the war was how it affected British people and interests. But Germans, both individual and *en masse*, do figure in children's books about the war, though they are rarely the centre of attention.

In what follows I want to look at three different types of material to see what pictures of 'the Germans' are to be found. Firstly, there are histories of the war, written as the war was proceeding. Secondly, there are books in which boys and girls or young soldiers have 'adventures' in the war situation. Thirdly, there are parodies (more directed at adults rather than children) in which popular books (including several children's books) provide the scaffold for swingeing satirical attacks on the Germans, especially of course on the Kaiser. Linked with this kind of material there are also popular verses not necessarily based on parody, but having a similar propagandistic aim.

Let us look first of all at histories of the war. Elizabeth O'Neill wrote a series of them as the war was continuing. I have copies only of volumes two and four, entitled *The War 1914-15. A History and an Explanation for Boys and Girls* (London and Edinburgh: T.C. Jack & E.C. Jack, 1915) and *The War, 1915-16. A History and an Explanation for Boys and Girls* (do., 1916). Volume 2, of course, deals with the second stage of the war, after 'the Germans saw that Calais was as difficult to win as Paris' (p. 3). O'Neill concentrates on what the British and the Allies had to do, but she notes that 'the Germans fought too with desperate courage' (p. 3). When she deals with the assault on Ypres she comments on the Bavarians' dislike of the Prussians (p. 11), but goes on to describe the Prussian Guard as 'a fine set of men' who were 'always thought of as being invincible' (p. 12). Then comes the 'terrible bombardment of the town which made it a mass of ruins', which she compares with the bombardment of Rheims as 'a crime committed in mere anger and spitefulness'. This leads to a condemnation that recurs a multitude of times in contemporary British views of the war: 'Though the Germans have boasted so much of their "culture," they have not shown any love for beautiful things for their own sake' (p.13). Towards the end of this account of the battle for the coast O'Neill again gives credit to the Germans:

> And in telling the tale of the victory of the Allies, though we cannot help being proud of the way our men fought, it must be remembered that the Germans fought bravely too, though they were not always well led. Every Briton must rejoice at the story of how the invincible soldiers of the Prussian Guard gave way at last before our men. But one cannot help feeling sorry for the companies of reserves, often mere boys, who rushed forward to their death singing the German patriotic song, "Die Wacht am Rhein," just as companies of Britishers pressed forward to the fight singing "Rule, Britannia!" (pp. 16-17).

One of the things that constantly comes through O'Neill's book is the fact that the Germans were not conducting the war according to previously established 'rules'. On 16 December 1914 the Germans shelled the east coast towns of Whitby, Scarborough and the Hartlepools. 'Only West Hartlepool', wrote O'Neill, can in any sense be called a fortified town, and the shelling of the others was quite against the rules of warfare, but no one by this time expected the Germans to keep those rules. [...] At Whitby the shells fell chiefly in a field behind the town, and it was thought afterwards that the German officer in command of the attack on that place did not like the work, and, though he had to obey orders, he took good care that the shells should do as little harm as possible (pp. 54-55).

With regard to Scarborough she quotes from Mr Winston Churchill's message to the mayor: 'Whatever feats of arms the German navy may hereafter perform, the stigma of the baby-killers of Scarborough will brand its officers and men while sailors sail the seas' (p. 55). This language is the emotive rhetoric of politicians, in which the deaths of children and women are outrages, while the slaughter of men in similar circumstances is of little account. A few pages on, O'Neill observes, 'It will be remembered how German airmen dropped bombs on Antwerp, Warsaw, Paris, and other places, and killed women and children without helping themselves on in the war at all' (p. 59).

The Children's Story of the War by Sir Edward Parrott (London, Edinburgh, Dublin and New York: Thomas Nelson & Sons, 1915), of which the first volume deals with the beginning of the war to the landing of the British Army in France, provides a full historical background, going back to the establishment of Prussia, Frederick the Great, the impact of Napoleon, the Franco-Prussian War and the boyhood of Kaiser Wilhelm II. The latter's militaristic education and attitudes, his arrogance and self-will are dealt with at some length. His declaration: 'I consider myself […] an instrument of Heaven, and shall go my way without regard to the views and opinions of the day' elicits Parrott's comment: 'Now to you and me such statements as this seem to be the ravings of a madman, and we wonder why the Prussians permit one man to lord it over them in this fashion. The explanation is that the Prussians have never known any other condition of things […]' (p. 135) The Kaiser's envy of Britain and his expansionist political ambitions form the focus of most of the satirical writing about the war, as we shall see later. When Parrott turns to the invasion of Belgium, he writes about the 'many black and shameful deeds done by the Germans', but is ready to 'honour them for their treatment of General Leman and the gallant twenty-five who fought with him to the end' (p. 239) in the defence of Fort Loncin on the west of Liège. Mainly, however, we are given accounts of the terrible destruction that the Germans inflicted, both on cities like Louvain and Malines and on the civilian population.

One incident figures in other books apart from Parrott's. It concerns Alsace rather than Belgium and illustrates the bitter opposition to German military might that was typical of Alsatians despite the fact that they spoke German too. The incident was told in a German newspaper in which 'the writer actually gloried in the dastardly crime that he there set forth. It seems that a German column was passing along a wooded defile when it met a French boy scout, who was seized, and asked where the French troops were. He refused to say. At this moment a French battery opened fire from a wood only fifty yards away. The Germans managed to get into cover, and took the boy with them. When they asked him if he knew that the French were in the wood, he did not deny it. They told him that they were going to shoot him, but he showed no fear. He walked with firm steps to a telegraph post, stood against it, and with the green vineyard behind him, smiled as they shot him dead' (p. 245). This story is also included in Nellie Pollock's short children's novel, *Belgian Playmates. Heroes Small – and Heroes Tall* (London: Gay & Hancock, [1914]) (pp. 79-80). It seems to be the most compelling story of a boy's courage in the war, as it crops up again, this time with the separate heading 'Faithful unto Death', in John Lea's collection of true stories entitled *Brave Boys and Girls in Wartime* (London, Glasgow and Bombay: Blackie & Son, [1918]). In the latter two examples the emphasis lies more on the French boy's heroism than on the cruelty of the German soldiers.

Understandably, British books about the war focus on aspects in which soldiers from Britain and the Empire were crucially involved. Germans tend to figure only as the undifferentiated enemy. The aim of the British books is to encourage their readers to identify with the values and aspirations of the Allies, so Mrs Belloc Lowndes's book subtitled 'A Child's History of the War', is called *Told in Gallant Deeds* (London: James Nisbet & Co., [1915]) and centres on deeds of exemplary bravery and compassion, especially where children or young people are personally involved. The kind of explanatory historical and political background provided by Sir Edward Parrott is hardly attempted, perhaps because Mrs Lowndes was targeting a younger readership. However, at this stage in the war she allows herself to relate a merciful exception to the pitiless way in which the war was being waged:

> One of these was the reconciliation on the battlefield between a French and a German soldier, who lay wounded and abandoned near the little town of Blâmont. They were there all through the cold, dark night, with only the dead about them. When dawn came they began to talk to one another, and the Frenchman gave his water-bottle to the German. The German sipped a little, and then kissed the hand of the man who had been his enemy. 'There will be no war in Heaven', he said (pp. 208-09).

This kind of episode finds a place in many of the British books about the war as a counterpart to the characterization of the Germans *en masse*, and especially their leaders, as cruel and barbarous. It is a rare reminder that the German soldiers were men with similar feelings to their opponents. But on the whole the historical accounts written for boys, such as Herbert Strang's *The Blue Book of the War* (London: Humphrey Milford, Oxford University Press, reprinted 1917), are more interested in military strategy on land and sea and in the air than in the Germans as a nation or as individuals.

The restraint shown by the history books is often jettisoned in fictions of the war, which tend to have a cruder approach to the Germans. Though the stories of F.S. Brereton and Charles Gilson were generally believed by their young readers to be authentic, their accounts of battle were, as Cadogan and Craig point out, 'often based on Boer war experiences and on ideas of wish-fulfilment rather than on the actuality of the Somme, the Marne and Passchendaele' (p. 72). Brereton, in *With the Allies to the Rhine. A Story of the Finish of the War* (London, Glasgow and Bombay: Blackie & Son, [1919], writes pretty indiscriminately about 'the unspeakable Hun' (p. 10), 'the Boche' (p. 11), 'Fritz' (*passim*), 'truculent, triumphant Germans' (p. 35), 'the Kaiser and his vandals' (p. 136), 'the Teuton' (p. 247). He declares roundly through the voice of his American soldier character, Dan: 'Fritz is a murderer and a barbarian. He's out to kill for the sake of killing, and he's out at the same time to kill the *moral* of the French people – as if anything that a German ever did or could do could kill that!' (pp. 38-39). The three soldier friends who are at the centre of Brereton's story have learned 'that violence is idolized by the German, that he makes of it a fetish, and that he made a deliberate display of it to spread terror wherever he went. The more helpless the people the more they were exposed to his violence' (pp. 42-43). The German is marked by 'ferocity', 'love of violence' and 'unscrupulousness' (p. 82). A young Prussian officer into whose hands the three soldiers are delivered is described as 'arrogant, fierce, and unsympathetic' (p. 68) and 'this bullying, swaggering, overbearing Prussian' (p. 70). Among other matters that Brereton criticizes strongly are the Germans' lack of mercy towards their opponents (p. 190) and their failure to deal out to their prisoners the treatment to which they were entitled (p. 224). Yet amidst all these strictures he can say of a German general at the end of the war:

> To speak the truth, four and a half years of terrible warfare, of death and wounds and killing, had satiated this Prussian's desire for slaughter. [...] His mind went back to his own little house somewhere on the Rhine in Germany, to his own home-circle, to the son who had accompanied him to the war in 1914 (p. 114).

In accounts of this kind we have to remember that the authors were writing boys' adventure stories, not histories of the war. They were following in the footsteps of G. A. Henty – Brereton was actually a cousin of Henty – and they used the staples of his stories, but transferred to the setting of the First World War. In these stories it was a quite typical procedure to paint the enemy black, but have a single enemy figure with some humane characteristics. But the main focus was youthful deeds of bravery against the odds, captures by the enemy followed by skilful escapes and plenty of robust action and fighting. Very often the hero would be wounded, but not too seriously. In this way the accusation of unrealism would be avoided.

The war often provided a setting for a spy story. Brereton's book contains an extraordinary German spy who masquerades as a Frenchman and tricks the British and American soldiers. He is called Monsieur Joseph, and he has a colleague called Paul Harn. Brereton may well have known the meaning of the latter's surname – it means 'urine' – since he uses a similarly scornful name in *A Hero of Sedan*; it was probably a tasteless joke. However, at the end of the book Brereton writes: 'And though we hesitate to do so, seeing that he was an unmitigated rascal, we must admit that Monsieur Joseph too had pluck, had resource, was filled with energy and decision' (p. 284).

Herbert Strang's *With Haig on the Somme* (London, etc.: Humphrey Milford, Oxford University Press, 1917) has a rather more disagreeable attitude towards spies. It tells a story about a few Australian soldiers who are pitted against the machinations of two naturalized Britons of German descent – Sir Julius Hoggenbach, a powerful man in the City, and Mr Montague Spurling (formerly Sperling) – who are working as spies in the German interest. The book ends with a laconic paragraph on the latter's disappearance:

> No one appeared to know what had become of them, though some suspected that Sir Julius had fallen a victim to the rage for interning men of enemy birth, however useful they might have shown themselves to their adopted country. Very few connected their disappearance with a brief paragraph that was printed one day in the papers – the bare official announcement that two spies, tried by court-martial and convicted, had been sentenced to death (p. 277).

The war at sea is the subject of Captain Charles Gilson's *Submarine U93*, subtitled 'A Tale of the Great War, of German Spies, and Submarines, of Naval Warfare, and all manner of Adventures' (London: 'The Boy's Own Paper' Office, c. 1917). As the author states, the story consists of 'fact blended with fiction' in dealing with the Battle of Dogger Bank, but its youthful protagonist has once again to contend with the machinations of a spy as well as the might of German naval power. The reader knows what poor Jimmy Burke is up against when he is confronted in New York with Rudolf Stork, 'a strange-looking man, with an exceedingly wrinkled face, and a sinister cast of countenance', who is instinctively distrusted by Jimmy's girl-friend. Stork speaks German, French, English and Dutch, was formerly an actor and once played Iago, so his malignant role can hardly be doubted. Towards the end of the book his venality rather than heroism or courage is underlined when he is described as 'the paid servant of the Wilhelmstrasse, the man who had served the Fatherland for gold'. The man from whom he has taken his orders, Baron von Essling, ends up in a prisoner of war camp at Wakefield reading the Prussian historian Treitschke. Stork's distasteful motives contrast strongly with those of Captain Crouch, who is 'cast in a most heroic mould'. Gilson roundly declares:

> In sinking one of the most famous of the U boats within range of the great guns of four of the most powerful of the German battle-cruisers, Captain Crouch accomplished a feat which was as much to his own credit as it was of service to his country (p. 251).

There are, of course, lots of other adventure books about the war, some aimed at adolescent boys, some at girls, and others at smaller children. The boys' books tend to be more specific about the details of the conduct of the war, but the emphasis everywhere is on the children or young people's adventures and escapades, for which the war is merely a context.

In addition to the history books and adventure stories there is a third category of material that links up with popular children's books. It forms part of the propaganda of the war, in which the popular press played a prominent role. Newspapers and magazines published cartoons and verses galore, encouraging those left at home and vigorously attacking the enemy. The *War Poems* of Jessie Pope (London: Grant Richards, 1915) were not designed for children, but they display in skilful verses many of the stereotypes that we find in the books that travesty children's classics. Heavy sarcasm is frequently to the fore, as in 'The Blackest Lie', which, after speaking of 'Poor little Germany, / Gentle land of peace', goes on to say:

> Hurry with the whitewash,
> Pour it out in streams!
> Bleach the ravaged country,
> Louvain, Antwerp, Rheims!
> Belgium concocted war,
> Thus deserves her fate!
> That's the blackest Teuton lie
> Published up to date (pp. 30-31).

This same line of bitter sarcasm is directed at the Swedish explorer

Sven Hedin (1865-1952), who notoriously took up a pro-German stance in the war and was prepared to whitewash whatever the Germans did. His gullibility was derided by E. V. Lucas in a book entitled *In Gentlest Germany* and attributed to 'Hun Svedend', supposed to be 'translated from the Svengalese' (London: John Lane, The Bodley Head, 1915).

Another kind of approach was taken by A. T. Mason in *The Book of Artemas*, which was sufficiently popular to have reached a 127th edition by 1918 (London: W. Westall & Co.). Its style and format is modelled on the Authorized Version of the Bible, and it begins by attacking the Kaiser in allegorical mode:

> 3. Now there was peace over all the land of Eur and amongst all the nations that abode there, it was a time of great content.
>
> 4. But Willi, who ruled over the men of Hu, was a crafty man and greedy, and *his ways* were devious.
>
> 5. And when he beheld the prosperity of the land and the industry of those that dwelt round about, and *that* they did live in peace, the one with the other, his heart grew black within him and his soul vomited envy.
>
> 6. *Moreover,* he was a proud man and ambitious withal. His covetousness was like unto a tree, that being planted in fertile ground, flourisheth mightily; and the independence of the peoples *was* as gall unto his vanity.
>
> 7. Now the son of Willi was a young man, and he was puffed out with pride and his mind was empty; in his living, he was vicious, and his name, *it was* Mud.

This kind of satire clearly sold well and gave rise to *The Second Book of Artemas* (2nd edition, 1918).

The Kaiser and the Crown Prince were natural targets of satire and propaganda, but the Germans as a nation were frequently portrayed as being of limited intelligence and human understanding. This is exemplified in connexion with the spy theme in Alfred Leete's *Schmidt the Spy and his Messages to Berlin* (London: Duckworth & Co., 1916), which shows the German spy constantly misinterpreting typical features of British life. Railway stations at St. Pancras, Euston and so on are identified as Zeppelin sheds; road works are interpreted as military preparations for the defence of London; Salvation Army women are thought to demonstrate the failure to raise an army of men, and, what's more, they have strange weapons and a peculiar war-cry of their own! The humour is rather simple-minded and has no greater aim that to raise a laugh at the expense of the stupid

Germans. It is not as clever as the criticism of heavy-handed German ways and notions of culture to be found in *Professor Knatschke. Selected Works of the Great German Scholar and of his Daughter Elsa* by the popular Alsatian author Hansi, translated into English by Professor R. L. Crewe (London: Hodder & Stoughton, 2nd impression, 1917). As the introduction says, the Germans had never been so wittily ridiculed, but as Alsace was part of the German Empire Hansi was arrested, tried and sentenced to fifteen months' imprisonment, but managed through the help of a friend to escape to Switzerland. The book caricatures the Germans' inability to understand why their 'reconquered brothers' (p. 55) in Alsace do not appreciate their incorporation into the German Empire. Professor Knatschke remarks:

> When you have once had the experience of observing how dull and joyless an Alsatian village is on the morning of the Kaiser's Birthday, and how, as soon as the 'Herr Gendarm' starts on his beat down the village street, flags and banners are at once displayed on every side, you will agree with me when I state that *he* it is who, in spite of the resplendent sublimity of our Art, contributes most to instil true and pure Germanism into the hearts of the Alsatian Folk (p. 70).

One of the fascinating features of British satire unleashed by the war is the plethora of parodies or travesties of children's books and nursery rhymes. *Nursery Rhymes for Fighting Times* was written by Elphinstone Thorpe and illustrated by G. A. Stevens (London: Everett & Co., Ltd., [1914]). It is dedicated 'To the children of all British heroes, whether on land or sea'. A considerable number of the rhymes focus on the Kaiser and the drubbing the British soldiers are going to inflict on him. A typical example is:

> Ride-a-cock horse, the frontier across,
> To see Puffing Billy astride a high horse –
> Blood on his fingers and shells for his foes,
> He shall be hated wherever he goes! (p. 14).

Stevens's cartoon has the Kaiser on a very large wooden horse facing a tiny hobby-horse (Belgium) only a few inches high. Around him are shells marked 'for babies', 'for libraries', 'for cathedrals and churches', 'for hospitals', 'for museums' and, finally, '2 tons for the contemptible British army'. The Kaiser's dismissal of the British army as 'contemptible' was to re-echo through countless pieces of British writing about the war. But the Germans more generally were also mocked in these parodies:

> Higgledy-piggledy, my Black Hun!

> She lays mines where the trade-ships run;
> Friends and foes she treats as one –
> Higgledy-piggledy, my Black Hun! (p. 22).

A little pamphlet issued at the end of the war presents just the same kind of picture. This was *Rhymes of the Times for War Babies of all Ages* by J. G. Russell Harvey and Charlie Thomas (Bristol: A. W. Ford & Co., Ltd., [1919]). It targets not only the Kaiser, but also Hindenburg (spelt 'Hindenberg'), Tirpitz, the Yanks and Lloyd George. Here we have yet another nursery rhyme travestied:

> Little Bill Kaiser, come blow up your horn,
> The fat's in the fire and hope is forlorn;
> Where's the old German Gott who looks after the Army?
> Peradventure he journeys, or sleeps, or is balmy (p. 13).

The most extensive use of nursery rhymes was made very early in the war in *The Crown Prince's First Lesson-book or Nursery Rhymes for the Times* by George H. Powell, with decorations by Scott Calder (London: Grant Richards Ltd., [1914]). The book is sarcastically dedicated to 'H.I.H. Frederick William / Crown Prince / of / "the most civilised nation in the world" / Worthy Son of Worthy Sire'. Fifty-one travesties of nursery rhymes and similar verse-forms treat a whole range of German figures and war-matters, not simply the Kaiser and the Crown Prince. No. XXX, entitled 'Ambition', reads as follows:

> There was a Pan-German
> And what do you think?
> He lived upon nothing
> But envy and ink.
>
> Bernhardi and Treitschke
> Were all of his diet,
> And so this Pan-German
> Could *never* be quiet! (p. 33)

A rhyming alphabet called 'The Alphabet of the War' opens with the lines:

> A was an Army that none could withstand.
> B were the British (contemptible band!).
> C is the Confidence Germans display, - till
> D, that is Doubt, is displaced by Dismay (p. 15).

George Powell demonstrates a very clever wit and turn of phrase in adapting a large variety of popular forms to satirizing the Germans.

To them we can add several other travesties. Grant Richards followed up Powell's verses with *The Rubaiyat of William the War-Lord* by St. John Hamund (1915), while Frederick Warne and Co. issued *The Book of William*, with apologies to Edward Lear, author of *The Book of Nonsense* (probably 1914). Horace Wyatt wrote a quite expansive travesty of *Alice in Wonderland* in prose and verse entitled *Malice in Kulturland* (London: The Car Illustrated, 1914). All of these books pillory the Germans in expected fashion, using a variety of popular classics and children's books as their point of departure.

To conclude I shall look at one of them more closely, since it was a travesty of Germany's most famous children's picture-book, Heinrich Hoffmann's *Der Struwwelpeter*, which had appeared in English in 1848 and quickly become an essential part of the English nursery. It has remained in print ever since. Its familiarity to the English middle class meant that its verses and pictures were so well known that it lent itself to travesties of the most amazing kind. There had already been two political travesties – *The Political Struwwelpeter* (1899) and *The Struwwelpeter Alphabet* (1900) – before the work we now turn to – *Swollen-headed William. Painful Stories and Funny Pictures. After the German!* (London: Methuen & Co., 1914). For this E. V. Lucas adapted the text and George Morrow the drawings of the Anglo-German nursery classic. It proved such a hit that the first edition of 1st October 1914 was succeeded by the second on 6th October. Each of the celebrated *Struwwelpeter* stories is adapted to deal with the Kaiser, so in addition to embodying the title-figure he takes on the roles of Cruel Frederick, Harriet in the story with the matches, the man that went out shooting, Conrad the thumb-sucker, Augustus who would not have any soup, Fidgety Philip, Johnny Head-in-Air and Flying Robert. In 'The Story of the Inky Boys' he is accompanied by Chancellor Bethmann-Hollweg and General Bernhardi. The opening section of 'The Story of Cultured William' is a typical example of Lucas's approach:

> Here is cultured William, see!
> An enlightened soul was he.
> He killed the doves and broke the chairs,
> And threw the Grey cat down the stairs,
> And, oh! far worse than all beside,
> He hurt his Mary till she cried.
> Such stores of 'Kultur' Will possessed,
> That he'd to spare for all the rest
> (Particularly dark Louvain
> Sunk in the barbarous inane),

And he vowed the world should be
Just as full of it as he.
Helped by Mr. Krupp of Essen,
Everyone should learn the lesson,
Spread by missionary Huns
Well equipped with bombs and guns.

The 'Grey cat' is the British Foreign Secretary, Sir Edward Grey, and 'Mary', who in Hoffmann's original is Cruel Frederick's nursemaid, is depicted in Morrow's drawing as Germania. In 'The Story of the Man that went out shooting' the hare is interpreted as Belgium.

It is obvious in *Swollen-headed William*, as in the many other travesties and satires, that the British public laid the whole responsibility for the war on the Kaiser, his ministers and generals and the Crown Prince. The ordinary German soldier barely figures in these tirades. By and large, the fighting soldier is seen as doing what he has to do, and he is criticized only when he acts unfairly or barbarously. Yet by the end of the war, with millions dead on either side, the German army and navy in the service of their masters brought about a sea-change in British attitudes towards Germany and the Germans, attitudes that the Nazi regime and the Second World War reinforced and that live on in the gutter press today.

The First World War marks the end of an era in the impact that Germany had had on British children's books for almost 140 years. Few new German children's books were translated into English after Johanna Spyri's *Heidi* (and that was Swiss rather than German, though published in Germany). The most concentrated period of British interest in German children's books, Germany and German history and culture was from around 1840 to about 1900, as this book has demonstrated. By the end of the nineteenth century Germany was increasingly regarded as a threat to Britain's supremacy in the world, and this clearly had an effect on children's literature. The Edwardian period saw the virtual demise of moral and religious books; of German material only Christoph von Schmid's *Basket of Flowers* survived.

However, several other German children's books established themselves as classics that are still read and loved today. The Grimms' fairytales stand pre-eminent, the most widely disseminated contribution of Germany to world literature. The only other fairytale author to have been reprinted throughout the twentieth century is Wilhelm Hauff, but his popularity lies a long distance behind that of the Grimms. At the beginning of the twentieth century Fouqué's *Undine* and *Sintram*, Chamisso's *Peter Schlemihl* and Hoffmann's *Nutcracker* testified to the continuing appeal of the Romantic tradition, but only the *Nutcracker* (and that most probably through Dumas rather than directly from Hoffmann) is known to today's children. Going back further in date, *Baron Munchausen* enjoys the most long-lasting fame of all, aided by a transposition into film as well as updated adaptations. Two of the other great survivors are Swiss – Johann David Wyss's *Swiss Family Robinson* and Johanna Spyri's *Heidi*.

The only other claim to classic status comes from Heinrich Hoffmann's *Struwwelpeter*, now more than 150 years old. Though waning in its appeal in Britain from the Second World War onwards, it has come to new life very recently through *Shockheaded Peter: a Junk Opera*, a captivating stage production by the Tiger Lillies that has proved an amazing success wherever it has been performed in Britain and Germany. The original English version of Hoffmann's *Struwwelpeter* has continued being reprinted at intervals, though nothing like as often as during its first seventy or eighty years. But the 'junk opera' shows how its virtually archetypal stories can unexpectedly catch fire and entertain a new public. They have a similar power to that of so many of the Grimms' fairytales, which are constantly being retold, adapted given new illustrations and formats.

These were books that had become a firm part of British children's literature well before the outbreak of the First World War. Their German origins were virtually irrelevant, sometimes not even known or obvious, so they survived without hindrance. It was contemporary German material that was excluded in the huge wash of emotional antipathy generated by the horrors of the war in which so many millions of soldiers (on both sides) lost their lives. Germany ceased to be 'our cousins' and became instead the stereotypical enemy of a multitude of boys' adventure stories, supplanting the multifarious indigenous peoples that the British Empire had spent its energies in conquering throughout the previous century.

Primary Texts

References are given only to the editions mentioned in this book, with minor exceptions. For many of the texts and authors dealt with a complete list would be impossible within the scope of this book. Short titles are used where practical. Place of publication is London unless otherwise stated.

1. The Adventures of Baron Munchausen

'M-h-sche Geschichten' and 'Noch zwei M-Lügen', in *Vade mecum für lustige Leute*, nos. VIII and X (1781 and 1783).

Baron Munchausen's Narrative of his Marvellous Travels and Campaigns in Russia. Oxford, 1786 [actually 1785].

Gulliver Revived. The third edition. G. Kearsley, 1786.

[G. A. Bürger], *Wunderbare Reisen zu Wasser und Lande . . . des Freyherrn von Münchhausen*. Göttingen: J.C. Dieterich, 1786.

The Surprising Travels. . . . A Sequel to the Adventures of Baron Munchausen humbly dedicated to Mr Bruce the Abyssinian Traveller. H.D. Symonds & J. Owen, 1792.

The Surprising Adventures of the Renowned Baron Munchausen. Abridged. Illustrated with 3 engravings. Glasgow: Chapman & Lang, 1802.

The Surprising Adventures. Edinburgh: W. & J. Deas, 1809.

Surprising Adventures of the Renowned Baron Munchausen, containing Singular Travels, Campaigns, Voyages and Adventures. Engravings by Rowlandson. Thomas Tegg, 1809 (another edition 1811).

The Surprising Adventures. Dean &Munday, 1810.

— Gainsborough: H. Mozley, 1814.

— Derby: H. Mozley, 1821.

The Life and Exploits of Baron Munchausen. Who outdid all other Travellers. Related by Himself. Glasgow: Richard Griffin & Co., 1827.

The Surprising Adventures. Newcastle upon Tyne: W.T. Fordyce, n.d.

— York: C. Croshaw, n.d.

424   Telling Tales

The Surprising Travels. Derby: Thomas Richardson, n.d.

— William Cole, n.d.

Baron Munchausen. Webb, Millington & Co., [c. 1860].

The Surprising Adventures of Baron Munchausen. Illustrated by William Strang and J.B. Clark, with an introduction by Thomas Seccombe. Lawrence & Bullen, 1895.

Tales from the Travels of Baron Munchausen. Books for the Bairns, no. 23 (January 1898).

John Kendrick Bangs, *Mr. Munchausen.* Grant Richards, 1901.

The Surprising Travels and Adventures of Baron Munchausen. Illustrated by W. Heath Robinson. Grant Richards, 1902.

2. A World of Discovery: Joachim Heinrich Campe

J.H. Campe, *Robinson the Younger.* Hamburg: C.E. Bohn, 1781-82.

— *The New Robinson Crusoe.* John Stockdale, 1788.

— *The New Robinson Crusoe.* E. Newbery, 1790; 1797.

— *Elementary Dialogues, for the Improvement of Youth.* Hookham & Carpenter, 1792.

— *Robinson the Younger.* Trans. from the German. Francfort on the Main: F. Wilmans,. 1799, 1807, 1824.

— *Robinson the Younger, or the New Crusoe.* Trans. by R. Hick. G. Routledge & Co., 1855, 1866.

— *The Discovery of America.* J. Johnson, 1799.

— *Columbus.* Sampson Low, 1799.

— *Cortes; or, the Discovery of Mexico.* J. Johnson, 1800.

— *Pizarro; or, the Conquest of Peru.* J. Johnson, 1800.

— *Pizarro.* Trans. Elizabeth Helme. Dublin: P. Wogan, 1800. C. Cradock & W. Joy, 1811; Baldwin, Cradock & Joy, 1819.

— *Polar Scenes.* J. Harris, 1821, 1822, 1823, 1825, 1829.

3. *Elements of Morality:* Salzmann and Wollstonecraft

C. G. Salzmann, *Moralisches Elementarbuch.* Leipzig: Siegfried Lebrecht Crusius, 1783; new improved edition 1785.

— *Elements of Morality.* Trans. Mary Wollstonecraft. J. Johnson, 1790, 1791, 1793, 1799, 1800; Dublin: William Porter, 1798; Edinburgh: Oliver & Boyd, 1821. The first edition by Johnson was illustrated by William Blake after Daniel Chodowiecki.

4. Musäus and the Beginnings of the Fairytale

J.K.A. Musäus, *Volksmährchen der Deutschen.* Gotha: C.W. Ettlinger, 1782-86.

Anon., *Popular Tales of the Germans.* John Murray, 1791.

Thomas Roscoe (ed.), *The German Novelists*, vol. 3. Henry Colburn, 1826; reprinted c. 1880. (The Dumb Lover).

The Odd Volume, pts 1 and 2, 1826 (The Elopement, The Legends of Number Nip).

Thomas Carlyle, *German Romance*, vol. 1. Chapman & Hall, 1827; reprinted 1858, 1897. (Dumb Love, Libussa, Melechsala).

John Oxenford and C.A. Feiling, *Tales from the German*. Chapman & Hall, 1844. (Libussa).

Select Popular Tales from the German of Musaeus. [Trans. J.T. Hanstein]. James Burns, 1845.

Popular Works of Musaeus. Trans. J.T. Hanstein. J. Neal & Co., 1865.

Legends of Number Nip and Other Tales. Joseph Cundall, 1845.

'Legends of Number Nip', in Leitch Ritchie, *Schinderhannes: the Robber of the Rhine*. Simms & M'Intyre, 1848.

Zytogorski, *The Nymph of the Well and The Barber's Ghost*. G. E. Nias, 1848.

Melechsala. Trans. W.S.M.E. Ramsgate: Thistleton, 1848.

The Stolen Veil; or, the Tale à la Montgolfier. Trans. W.S.M.E. Ramsgate: Thistleton, 1850.

Tales of Fairy Land; or Legends of the Olden Time. The Booksellers, 1852. (The Spectre Barber).

Mark Lemon, *Legends of Number Nip*. Macmillan & Co., 1864, 1872.

George G. Cunningham, *Tales and Traditions, chiefly selected from the Literature of Germany*. Edinburgh, London and Dublin: A. Fullerton & Co., 1854.

Francis Paul Palmer, *Old Tales for the Young*. George Routledge & Co., 1857.

Mary C. Rowsell, *Number Nip; or the Spirit of the Giant Mountains*. Swan Sonnenschein, 1884.

Andrew Lang, *The Brown Fairy Book*. Longmans, Green & Co., 1904.

The Enchanted Knights; or, the Chronicle of the Three Sisters. Trans. A. Sagorski. H. Cunningham, 1845.

M.G. Kennedy, *The Arm! – the Sword! – and the Hour! Or, the Legend of the Enchanted Knights*. Longman, Brown, Green & Longmans, 1850.

The Three Sons-in-law. Trans. A.F. Frere, 1861.

Mark Lemon, *Fairy Tales*. Bradbury, Evans, & Co., 1868.

Alfred H. Miles, *Fifty-two Fairy Tales*. Hutchinson & Co., 1892.

5. Discovering Germany

Lenglet du Fresnoy, *Geography for Children*, 16th edition. J. Johnson and E. Newbery, 1791. First publ. 1737.

A Lady, *Geography and History*, 5th edition. C. Law, J. Scatcherd, Longman & Rees & Darton & Harvey, 1803. 19th edition, 1843. First publ. 1790.

Sir Richard Phillips (pseud. J. Goldsmith), *A Grammar of General Geography*. Longman, Rees, Orme, Brown & Green, n.d. First publ. 1803.

Abbé Gaultier, *A Complete Course of Geography*. E. Newbery, 1795.

Barbara Hofland, *The Panorama of Europe*. A.K. Newman & Co., n.d. Firxt publ. 1813.

Isaac Taylor, *Scenes in Europe*. John Harris, 1818.

Priscilla Wakefield, *The Juvenile Travellers*. Harvey & Darton, 1824. First publ. 1801.

Abbé Gaultier, *Familiar Geography*. John Harris, 1826.

A Peep at Various Nations of the World. Dean & Munday; A. K. Newman, c. 1825-30.

Samuel Griswold Goodrich, *Peter Parley's Tales about Europe, Asia, Africa, America and Australia*. 3rd ed. Darton & Clark, c. 1839-40.

Anon., *Travels with Minna and Godfrey in Many Lands*. Smith, Elder & Co., 1839.

John Guy, *Geography for Children*, 75th edition. T.J. Allman, 1869. First publ. 1840.

Sir Francis Bond Head, *Bubbles from the Brunnens of Nassau*. Frankfort o.M.: C. Jugel, 1845.

John Olding Butler, *A New Introduction to Geography*. 18th edition. William Walker, 1860.

Murray's Handbook for Travellers on the Continent. 13th ed. John Murray, 1860.

M. Betham Edwards, *Scenes and Stories of the Rhine*. Griffith & Farran, 1863.

George Gill, *Descriptive and Pictorial Europe*. 1881

James Cornwell, *A School Geography*. 70th edition. Simpkin, Marshall & Co., 1882. First publ. 1847.

6. *The Swiss Family Robinson*

Johann David Wyss, *Der Schweizerische Robinson*. Herausgegeben von Johann Rudolf Wyss. Zürich: Orell, Füssli, 1812-13, 1826-27.

Le Robinson suisse. Traduit de l'allemand de M. Wiss par Isabelle de Montolieu. Paris: Arthus Bertrand, 1814.

[Johann David Wyss], *The Family Robinson Crusoe*. Trans. from the German of M.Wiss. M.J. Godwin & Co., 1814.

[Johann David Wyss], *The Swiss Family Robinson*. Fourth edition. M.J. Godwin & Co., 1820. The new title came with the second edition, 1818.

Johann Rudolf Wyss, *Schweizerischer Robinson oder der schiffbrüchige Schweizerprediger und seine Familie*. {Herausgegeben von Heinrich Kurz]. Zürich: Orell, Füssli und Comp., [1841/42].

Frederick Marryat, *Masterman Ready*. Longman, Orme, Brown, Green & Longmans, 1841-45.

The Swiss Family Robinson, second series. Sampson Low, etc., 1849.

The Swiss Family Robinson, new edition, combining the first and second series. Simpkin, Marshall & Co., 1852.

Adrien Paul, *Willis the Pilot*. C.H. Clarke, 1857. First publ. in Paris under the title *Le Pilote Willis*, 1855.

The Swiss Family Robinson. Halifax: Milner & Sowerby, 1859. 'Cottage Library'.

The Swiss Family Robinson. Halifax: Milner & Sowerby, 1862.

Mary Godolphin, *The Swiss Family Robinson in Words of one Syllable*. George Routledge & Sons, 1869.

The Swiss Family Robinson. Trans. W.H.D. Adams. Nelson & Sons, 1870. From the French of Mme Elise Voïart, first publ. Paris: Lavigne, 1841.

Pierre-Jules Stahl, *Le Nouveau Robinson suisse*. Paris, 1864.

The Swiss Family Robinson. Ed. and trans. John Lovell. Cassell, Petter & Galpin, [1869]. From the French of P.-J. Stahl.

J. Bonnet, *Der schweizerische Robinson*. Bielefeld: Velhagen & Klasing, 1870.

The Swiss Family Robinson. James Nisbet, 1877. Anonymously trans. from the German of J. Bonnett.

The Swiss Family Robinson. New and unabridged trans. by Mrs H.B. Paull. Frederick Warne & Co., n.d.

The Swiss Family Robinson. Trans. H. Frith. Ward, Lock, 1878.

The Swiss Family Robinson. A new trans. from the original German edited by William H.G. Kingston. George Routledge & Sons, 1879.

Johann Rudolf Wyss, *The Swiss Family Robinson*. New translation edited by Alfonzo Gardiner. Manchester: John Heywood, 1887.

The Swiss Family Robinson. Edited by Julia S.E. Rae. Trischler & Co, 1891.

The Swiss Family Robinson. Edited by G.E. Mitton. A. & C. Black, 1907.

The Swiss Family Robinson. J.M. Dent & Sons, 1910. 'Everyman's Library'.

7. Moral, Didactic and Religious Tales

Maria Joseph Crabb, *Tales for Children in a Popular Style*. Darton & Harvey, 1805.

[Gottlob Eusebius Fischer], *Gustavus; or, the Macaw*. Darton, Harvey & Darton, 1814.

Friedrich Adolf Krummacher, *Parables*. Trans. F. Shoberl. R. Ackermann, 1824.

— *Parables*. Trans. Miss F. Johnston. London and Brighton, 1839.

— *Parables for Little People*. Books for the Bairns, no. 121 (March 1906).

— *The Little Dove*. Trans. Ann Steinkopff. Harvey & Darton, 1828.

— *The Little Dove*. New edition. Dean & Son, c. 1854; Charles Gilpin.

— *Alfred and the Little Dove*. Edinburgh: Johnstone Hunter & Co., n.d.

Friedrich Wilhelm Krummacher, *The Infant Saviour; the Ransomed of the Lord; and the Flying Roll*. B. Wertheim, 1837.

[Franz Sales Meyer], *Little Swiss Seppeli*. Harvey & Darton, 1829.

Friedrich Wilhelm Carové, *The Story Without an End*. Trans. Sarah Austin. Effingham Wilson, 1834; repr.1840, 1864.

— *The Story Without an End*. Illustrated by E.V. Boyle. Sampson Low & Co., 1868; repr. 1874.

— *The Story Without an End*. Wells Gardner, Darton & Co., 1899.

— *The Story Without an End*. Illustrated by Frank C. Papé. Duckworth & Co., 1912.

Christoph von Schmid, *Little Henry*. Trans. from the French of M. Lambert. John Harris & Son, 1823.

— *The Stolen Child, or how Henry of Eichenfels came to the Knowledge of God.* Trans. J. Bachman and J.Miller. Harrisburg, Pa.: John Winebrenner, second edition, 1836.

— *How Little Henry came to the Knowledge of God.* New edition. Thomas Allman, 1853.

— *The Easter Eggs.* 1829.

— *Godfrey, the Little Hermit.* Milner & Co, 1853.

— *Louis, the Little Emigrant.* Baltimore, 1841.

— *Christmas Eve.* 1843.

— *Genevieve.* New York: Catholic Publication Society, c. 1872.

— *The Basket of Flowers.* Trans. G.T. Bedell. Philadelphia, 1833.

— *The Flower-Basket.* Trans. William E. Drugulin. Stuttgart: J.B. Müller; London: W.S. Orr, 1848.

— *The Basket of Flowers.* Trans. J.H. St A. Thomas Nelson & Sons, 1857.

— *The Basket of Flowers.* Anonymous trans. Frederick Warne & Co., 1866.

— *The Basket of Flowers.* Anonymous trans. Blackie, c. 1900.

C.G. Barth, *Setma, the Turkish Girl; and Woodrof, the Swedish Boy.* Darton & Harvey, 1838.

— *Setma.* Edinburgh: Paton & Ritchie, 1853.

— *The Swedish Shepherd Boy.* Religious Tract Society, 1850s.

— *The Juvenile Artist.* Trans. Samuel Jackson. Darton & Clark, 1838.

— *Gregory Krau; or the Window Shutter.* Trans. R. Menzies. Edinburgh: Paton & Ritchie, 1850.

— *Winter Evening Stories.* Darton & Clark, c. 1844.

— *Cuff, the Negro Boy.* Trans. R. Menzies. Edinburgh: Paton & Ritchie, 1848.

— *The Young Tyrolese.* Trans. Samuel Jackson. Darton & Clark, [1838].

— *Christmas Morning; or, the Little Ink Cask.* Trans. R. Menzies. Edinburgh: Paton & Ritchie, 1851.

— *The Raven's Feather.* Religious Tract Society, c. 1855; repr. 1878.

8. Friedrich de la Motte Fouqué: *Undine* and *Sintram*

Undine. Trans. George Soane. London, 1821.

The Seasons. [Trans. Thomas Tracy]. James Burns, 1843.

Undine. Anonymous trans. James Burns, 1845; repr. Edward Lumley, 1850s and 1860s.

Undine. Illus. Julius Höppner. Griffith, Farran, Okeden & Welsh, 1885.

Undine. Illus. Heywood Sumner. Chapman & Hall, 1888.

Sintram and his Companions and *Undine*. Introduction by Charlotte M. Yonge. Illus. Gordon Browne. W. Gardner, Darton & Co., 1896.

Undine. Trans. Sir Edmund Gosse. Illus. W.E.F. Britten. Lawrence & Bullen, 1896.

— Illus. Florence M. Rudland. Lawrence & Bullen, 1897.

Undine. Illus. Rosie M.M. Pitman. Macmillan, 1897.

Undine. Adapted by W.A. Courtney. Illus. Arthur Rackham. Heinemann, 1909.

Undine. Edited by Mary Macgregor. Illus. Katharine Cameron. T.C. & E.C. Jack, [1907].

The Story of Undine. Thomas Nelson & Sons, 1908.

The Story of Undine. Edited by Mary Macleod. Wells Gardner & Co., 1912.

The Story of Undine. The Sprite Maiden. Books for the Bairns, no. 163 (September 1909).

Undine. Edited by Gladys Davidson. 1908.

Sintram. Trans. Julius C. Hare. 1820.

— Trans. Julius C. Hare. Illus. Heywood Sumner. Seeley & Co., 1883.

Sintram. James Burns, 1842.

— Illus. H.C. Selous. James Burns, 1843; repr. Edward Lumley, n.d.

Sintram and *Aslauga's Knight*. Illus. Charles Robinson. J.M. Dent & Co., 1900.

Sintram. Trans. A.M. Richards. Illus. Anna Richards. Fremantle & Co., 1900.

Sintram. Trans. A.C. Farquharson. Illus. Edward J. Sullivan. Methuen, 1908.

9. Adelbert von Chamisso's *Peter Schlemihl*

Peter Schlemihl. [Trans. Sir John Bowring] from the German of Lamotte Fouqué. With plates by George Cruikshank. G. and W.B. Whittaker, 1824.

The Shadowless Man; or, the Wonderful History of Peter Schlemihl. Anonymous trans. James Burns, 1843; repr. 1845. Reissued. by Edward Lumley, c. 1860.

Peter Schlemihl. Bilingual edition. Trans. William Howitt. Longman & Co.

Peter Schlemihl. Adapted, in *Tales of Fairy Land; or, Legends of the Olden Time*. The Booksellers, 1852.

The Shadowless Man; or, the Wonderful History of Peter Schlemihl. G. Routledge & Sons, [1877].

Peter Schlemihl, Carové, *The Story Without an End*, and Novalis, *Hymns to Night*. Cassell, 1889.

Peter Schlemihl. Illus. Sir Philip Burne-Jones. George Allen, 1899.

The Shadowless Man, Peter Schlemihl. Trans. Sir John Bowring. Illus. Gordon Browne. Chatto & Windus, 1910.

Adelbert von Chamisso, *The Marvellous History of the Shadowless Man*, and Wilhelm Hauff, *The Cold Heart*. Illus. Forster Robson. Holden & Hardingham, [1913].

10. The Fairytales of the Brothers Grimm

[Edgar Taylor], *German Popular Stories, translated from the Kinder und Haus Märchen collected by M.M. Grimm, from oral tradition.* C. Baldwyn, 1823 (vol. 1); James Robins & Co.; Dublin: Joseph Robins Junr. & Co., 1826 (vol. 2).

Madame Leinstein, *Unlucky John and his Lump of Silver.* Dean & Munday, c. 1825.

A Lady, *Wishing; or, the Fisherman and his Wife; a Juvenile Poem.* Dean & Munday, c. 1825.

George G. Cunningham, *Foreign Tales and Traditions, Chiefly Selected from the Fugitive Literature of Germany.* Glasgow: Blackie, Fullarton & Co., 1828.

W.J. Thoms, *Lays and Legends of Germany.* George Cowie, 1834.

[Edgar Taylor], *Gammer Grethel.* John Green, 1839. Repr. 1849, 1888, 1897.

G[eorge] N[icol], *The Wolf and the Seven Kids.* W. Wright, 1839; 1841.

Household Tales and Traditions of England, Germany, France, Scotland, &c. 2 vols. James Burns, 1843-45.

John Edward Taylor, *The Fairy Ring: a New Collection of Popular Tales, Translated from the German of Jacob and Wilhelm Grimm.* John Murray, 1846. Enlarged 1847; repr. 1857.

The Charmed Roe; or, the Little Brother and Little Sister. Illus. by Otto Speckter. John Murray, 1847.

Papa's Present of Household Stories, from the German. Darton & Co., 1851.

Madame de Chatelain, *Fairy Folk and Wonderful Men.* Addey & Co., 1852.

Household Stories, collected by the Brothers Grimm. 2 vols. Addey & Co., 1853. Republ. by David Bogue, 1857; George Routledge & Co., 1862.

Madame de Chatelain, *Tales of the Fairy Folk.* Darton & Co., c. 1855.

Matilda Davis, *Home Stories.* G. Routledge & Co., 1855.

Grimms' Goblins. George Vickers, [1861].

Household Tales and Popular Stories. Ward & Lock, 1862.

Mrs H.B. Paull, *Grimm's Fairy Tales.* Frederick Warne & Co., 1862.

The Frog Prince. Illus. by Walter Crane. George Routledge & Sons, [1874].

Lucy Crane, *Household Stories from the collection of the Bros: Grimm.* Illus. by Walter Crane. Macmillan & Co., 1882.

Rumpel-stilts-kin. Illus. by George R. Halkett. Thomas de la Rue, 1882.

Margaret Hunt, *Grimm's Household Tales.* 2 vols. George Bell & Sons, 1884.

Clever Hans. Illus. by J. Lawson. Thomas de la Rue, c. 1884.

Mrs H.B. Paull and L.A. Wheatley, *Grimms' Fairy Tales and Household Stories.* Frederick Warne & Co., 1893.

Fairy Tales from Grimm. Wells Gardner, Darton & Co., 1894.

Grimm's Fairy Tales. Illus. by Ada Dennis. Ernest Nister, 1898.

Beatrice Marshall, *Grimm's Fairy Tales for Children and the Household.* Ward, Lock &

Co., 1900.

Edric Vredenburg (ed.), *Grimm's Fairy Tales*. Raphael Tuck & Sons, 1900.

Household Tales by the Brothers Grimm. J.M. Dent, 1906. 'Everyman's Library'.

Amy Steedman, *Stories from Grimm*. 'Told to the children'. T.C. & E.C. Jack, c. 1906.

Mrs Edgar Lucas, *Fairy Tales of the Brothers Grimm*. Illus. by Arthur Rackham. Constable & Co., 1909.

Grimm's Fairy Tales. Illus. by Charles Robinson. Ernest Nister, 1910.

Stories from Grimm. Blackie & Son, c. 1912.

Edith Robarts, *Golden Tales from Grimm*. Wells Gardner, Darton & Co., n.d.

Edric Vredenburg (ed.), *Grimm's Fairy Tales*. Raphael Tuck & Sons, 1914.

11. The Fairy Tales of Wilhelm Hauff

C.A. Feiling and J. Oxenford, *Tales from the German*. Chapman & Hall, 1844.

Popular Tales. Rugeley: J.T. Walters; London: James Burns, 1844.

Select Popular Tales from the German of Wilhelm Hauff. James Burns, 1845.

The King of the Swans and Other Tales. Cundall, 1846. Includes 'The False Prince'

Tales of Wonder; or, the Inn in the Black Forest. Cheap Repository Series, 1861.

Grimms' Goblins. George Vickers, [1861]. Includes versions of several tales by Hauff.

The Caravan. Trans. from the German of Wilhelm Hauff. Ward, Lock, 1862; repr. 1884.

M.A. Faber, *Tales by Wilhelm Hauff*. Leipzig: Tauchnitz, 1867.

Elizabeth S. Harrington, *The Storks and the False Prince*. Sotheran, 1875.

Percy E. Pinkerton, *Longnose the Dwarf and other Fairy Tales*. Swan Sonnenschein & Allen, 1881.

S. Mendel, *Tales by Wilhelm Hauff*. George Bell & Sons, 1886; repr. 1914.

The Cold Heart. Trans. Agnes Henry. Digby & Lang, 1890.

Andrew Lang, *The Green Fairy Book*. Longmans, Green & Co., 1892. Includes 'The Story of Caliph Stork'.

The Little Glass Man and Other Stories. T. Fisher Unwin, 1893.

Books for the Bairns, nos. 32, 57, 160. Retellings by W.T. Stead from 1898 onwards.

Andrew Lang, *The Violet Fairy Book*. Longmans, Green & Co., 1901. Includes 'The History of Dwarf Longnose'.

Hauff's Tales. Trans. and adapted by Cicely McDonnell. Dean & Son, 1903.

Andrew Lang, *The Crimson Fairy Book*. Longmans, Green & Co., 1903. Includes 'The Story of the Sham Prince, or the Ambitious Taylor'.

Hauff's Tales. Trans. Sybil Thesiger. James Finch & Co., 1905.

E.J. Cunningham, *The Caliph Stork*. Swan Sonnenschein, 1905.

L.L. Weedon, *Fairy Tales by Wilhelm Hauff*. Ernest Nister, 1910.

Caravan Tales and some others by Wilhelm Hauff. Freely adapted and retold by J.G. Hornstein. Wells Gardner, Darton & Co., n.d.

The Marvellous History of the Shadowless Man, by A. von Chamisso, and *The Cold Heart*, by Wilhelm Hauff. Holden & Hardingham, [1914].

12. The Folktale Tradition in Germany

Ludwig Bechstein, *The Old Story-teller. Popular German Tales*. Addey & Co., 1854.

— *As Pretty as Seven and other Popular German Tales*. John Camden Hotten, 1872; reissued Chatto & Windus, 1884.

Andrew Lang, *The Green Fairy Book*. Longmans, Green & Co., 1892.

— *The Pink Fairy Book*. Longmans, Green & Co., 1897.

Benjamin Thorpe, *Yule-Tide Stories. A Collection of Scandinavian and North German Popular Tales and Traditions*. George Bell & Sons, 1892.

Zoe Dana Underhill, *The Dwarf's Tailor and others. Fairy Tales from all Nations*. Osgood, McIlvaine, 1897.

Madame de Chatelain, *Merry Tales for Little Folk*. Cundall & Addey, 1851.

— *Fairy Folk and Wonderful Men*. Addey & Co., 1852.

Dinah Mulock, *The Fairy Book*. Macmillan, 1863.

The True Annals of Fairyland in the Reign of King Cole. J.M. Dent & Sons, 1909.

Anna Dabis, *Fairy Tales from the Isle of Rügen*. David Nutt, 1896.

Joseph Snowe, *Legends, Traditions, Histories of the Rhine*. Frankfort o.M.: Charles Jugel. 1847.

Robert Southey, *Poetical Works*, vol. 6. Longman, Brown, Green & Longmans, 1844.

Thomas Roscoe, *The German Novelists*. Henry Colburn, 1826.

Mary C. Rowsell, *Hatto's Tower; and other stories*. Blackie & Son, c. 1870.

Robert Browning, *Bells and Pomegranates*. 1842.

Kate Greenaway (illus.), *The Pied Piper of Hamelin*. Frederick Warne & Co., 1888.

Robert Buchanan, *The Piper of Hamelin*. William Heinemann, 1893.

Gustav Nieritz, *The Ratcatcher's Magic Whistle*, trans. C.W. Heckethorn. Ben George, c. 1873.

[Rachel Busk], *Household Stories from the Land of Hofer; or, Popular Tales of Tirol*. Griffith & Farran, 1871.

W. Westall, *Tales and Legends of Saxony and Lusatia*. Griffith & Farran, 1877.

Leitch Ritchie, *Schinderhannes, the Robber of the Rhine*. Simms & M'Intyre, 1848.

Francis Paul Palmer, *Old Tales for the Young*. George Routledge & Co., 1857.

Mary C. Rowsell, *Number Nip; or, the Spirit of the Giant Mountains*. Swan Sonnenschein, 1884.

Andrew Lang, *The Brown Fairy Book*. Longmans, Green & Co., 1904.

Alfred C. Fryer, *Fairy Tales from the Harz Mountains*. David Nutt, 1908.

Lady Maxwell Wallace, *Princess Ilse*. Bell & Daldy, [1856].

13. E.T.A. Hoffmann's *Nutcracker and Mouse King*

William Makepeace Thackeray, 'The History of Krakatuk', *National Standard*, 1833. Reprinted in: Lewis Melville and Reginald Hargreaves, *Great German Short Stories*. Ernest Benn, 1929, pp. 513-26.

Alexandre Dumas the Elder, *The History of a Nutcracker*. Chapman & Hall, 1847, Reprinted in: *A Picture Story-book*. G. Routledge & Sons, c. 1875.

E.T.A. Hoffmann, *The Serapion Brothers*. Trans. by Major Alexander Ewing. George Bell & Son, 1886.

— *Nutcracker and Mouse King*. Trans. from the German by Ascott R. Hope. T. Fisher Unwin, 1892.

— *Nutcracker and Mouse-King*. Adapted by E. Gordon Browne. Illus. by Florence Anderson. George G. Harrap & Co. 1919.

14. Lesser Fairytale Authors

Albert Ludwig Grimm, *Fairy Tales*. Illus. [Robert] Cruikshank. Charles Tilt, 1827.

— *Tales from the Eastern-Land*. Trans. H.V. Joseph Cundall, 1847. Repr. H.G. Bohn, 1852.

— *The Two Talismans*. Joseph Cundall, 1846.

— *The Water Fairy's Gift and Other Tales*. Joseph Cundall, 1846.

— *The Miller's Son*. Joseph Cundall, 1846.

The Playmate. A Pleasant Companion for Spare Hours. David Bogue, c. 1860.

A..L.Grimm, J.J. Rudolphi, Wilhelm Hauff and Ernst von Houwald, *The Christmas Roses and Other Tales*. Joseph Cundall, 1845.

The King of the Swans, and Other Tales. Joseph Cundall, 1846

[Robert Reinick], *The Donkey's Shadow and other Stories*. Addey & Co., c. 1856.

Robert Reinick, *The King of Root Valley and his Curious Daughter*. London, 1856.

— *The Root Princess. A Christmas Story*. Philadelphia: F. Laypoldt, 1865.

Richard von Volkmann-Leander, *Dreams by a French Fireside*. Trans. M. O'Callaghan. Chapman & Hall, 1886.

— *Dreams by French Firesides*. Trans. J. Raleigh. Adam and Charles Black, 1890.

The Diamond Fairy Book. Hutchinson & Co., 1897.

The Golden Fairy Book. Hutchinson & Co., n.d.

Zoe Dana Underhill, *The Dwarf's Tailor and Others. Fairy Tales from all Nations*. Osgood, McIlvaine, 1897.

John Ruskin, *The King of the Golden River*. Orpington: George Allen, 1851. Many reprints.

15. Clemens Brentano's Fairytales

Kate Freiligrath Kroeker, *Fairy Tales from Brentano*. T. Fisher Unwin, 1884. Repr. 1890, 1911, 1925.

— *New Fairy Tales from Brentano*. T. Fisher Unwin, 1887. Repr. 1902.

16. Learning about German History

M.E. Budden, *Hofer the Tyrolese*. John Harris & Sons, 1824.

Charlotte Maria Tucker / A.L.O.E., *The Life of Luther*. The Book Society, 1873.

Henry Mayhew, *The Boyhood of Martin Luther*. Edinburgh and London: Gall & Inglis, c. 1890.

Samuel Rawson Gardiner, *The Thirty Years' War*. Longmans, Green & Co., 1874.

L. Cecil Jane, *From Metternich to Bismarck*. (Oxford: Clarendon Press, 1910.

James Bryce, *The Holy Roman Empire*. Oxford: T. & G. Shrimpton, 1864.

Julia Corner, *A History of Germany, and the Austrian Empire*. Thomas Dean & Co., 1841.

[Robert B. Paul], *A History of Germany, from the Invasion of Marius to the Battle of Leipsic. On the plan of Mrs Markham's Histories*. John Murray, 1847.

Wilhelm Pütz, *Handbook of Modern Geography and History*, part III. Trans. R.B. Paul. Francis & John Rivington, 1850.

Anon., *Scenes and Narratives from German History*. SPCK, c. 1858-60.

James Sime, *History of Germany*. Macmillan & Co., 1874.

Charlottte M. Yonge, *Aunt Charlotte's Stories of German History for the Little Ones*. Belfast and New York: Marcus Ward & Co., 1878.

S. Baring-Gould, with the collaboration of Arthur Gilman, *Germany*. T. Fisher Unwin, 1886.

H.E. Marshall, *A History of Germany*. Henry Frowde & Hodder & Stoughton, 1913.

Richmal Mangnall, *Questions for the Use of Young People*. First publ. 1800.

17. The Thirty Years War

Friedrich Schiller, *History of the Thirty Years War in Germany*. Trans. Captain Blaquiere. London, 1799. Dublin, 1800. Repr. Frankfurt am Main: Charles Jugel, 1842.

Caroline Pichler, *Waldstein; or, the Swedes in Prague*. Editions with varying titles in 1828, 1839, 1845 (James Burns) and 1878.

Hezekiah Butterworth, *Zigzag Journeys in Northern Lands*. Boston: Estes & Lauriat, 1883.

Gustav Nieritz, *The Siege of Magdeburg*. Edinburgh: Paton & Ritchie, 1855.

Mrs Percy [Jane] Sinnett, *A Story about a Christmas in the Seventeenth Century*. Chapman & Hall, 1846.

J.B. De Liefde, *The Maid of Stralsund*. 1876. Reissued as *A Brave Resolve; or, the Siege of Stralsund*. Hodder & Stoughton, ninth ed. 1894.

G.A. Henty, *The Lion of the North*. Blackie & Son, 1886.

Deborah Alcock, *The King's Service*. Religious Tract Society, c. 1890.

Wilhelm Noeldechen, *Die Zwillingsbrüder. Eine Erzählung aus dem Zeitalter des 30jährigen Krieges für die deutsche Jugend*. Bielefeld: Velhagen und Klasing, 1892.

W. Noeldechen, *Baron and Squire*. Trans. Sarah M.S. Clarke. 1892.

Grace Stebbing, *Never Give In*. John F. Shaw, 1890s.

G.A. Henty, *Won by the Sword*. Blackie & Son, 1900.

18. Historical Tales and Adventure Stories

Gustav Nieritz, *The Foundling, or the School of Life*. Edinburgh: Paton & Ritchie, 1850.

— [wrongly attributed to the non-existent Gustav Moritz] *Duty and Affection*. Edinburgh: William & Robert Chambers, 1850.

— *The Little Drummer; or, Filial Affection. A Story of the Russian Campaign*. Trans. H.W. Dulcken. G. Routledge & Co., 1856; repr. 1856, 1859.

— *The German Drummer Boy; or, the Horrors of War*. Trans. Mrs Campbell Overend. Edinburgh: Oliphant, Anderson, & Ferrier, 1883.

— *The Siege of Magdeburg*. Edinburgh: Paton & Ritchie, 1855.

— *The Exiles of Salzburg, and Other Stories*. Trans. Mrs L.H. Kerr. Religious Tract Society, c. 1885. Including *The King of Prussia's Tall Soldier*.

— *Alexander Menschikoff, the Founder of a Family*. Edinburgh: T. Constable & Co., 1855.

— *The Perils of Greatness: the Story of Alexander Menschikoff*. Edinburgh: W.P. Nimmo, 1865.

— *Menzikoff, or the Danger of Wealth*. Trans. Mrs Alexander Kerr. Religious Tract Society, [1854].

Friedrich Gerstäcker, *The Wanderings and Fortunes of Some German Emigrants*. Trans. D. Black. D. Bogue, 1848.

— *The Pirates of the Mississippi*. London, 1856.

— *Each for Himself; or, the Two Adventurers*. London, 1859.

— *The Young Gold-Digger; or, a Boy's Adventures in the Gold Regions*. London, 1860.

— *The Two Convicts*. London, 1857.

— *The Little Whaler; or, the Adventures of Charles Hollberg*. G. Routledge & Co., 1857.

M. L'E[strange], *Heligoland; or, Reminiscences of Childhood*. John W. Parker, fifth edition, 1851.

Charles Sealsfield [Karl Postl], *The Cabin Book, or National Characteristics*. London, 1852.

— *Scenes and Adventures in Central America*. Ed. F. Hardman. Edinburgh and London, 1852.

19. Picture Books

[Wilhelm Hey], *Funfzig Fabeln für Kinder; Noch funfzig Fabeln für Kinder.* Hamburg: Friedrich Perthes, 1833; 1837.

[Wilhelm Hey], *The Child's Picture and Verse Book: commonly called Otto Speckter's Fable Book.* Trans. Mary Howitt. Longman, Brown, Green & Longmans, 1844.

[Wilhelm Hey], *Short Stories and Poems.* James Burns, 1846.

[Wilhelm Hey], *Picture Fables drawn by Otto Speckter.* Trans. Henry W. Dulcken. George Routledge & Co., 1858.

[Wilhelm Hey], *One Hundred Picture Fables.* 1868.

[Wilhelm Hey], *Fifty Fables for Children; Other Fifty Fables for Children.* Trans. S. Klingemann. Gotha: Friedrich Andreas Perthes, 1869.

[Charles Perrault], *Puss in Boots; and the Marquis of Carabas.* Illus. Otto Speckter. John Murray, 1847.

J. and W. Grimm, *The Charmed Roe.* Illus. Otto Speckter. John Murray, 1847.

Nicholas Bohny, *The New Picture Book; being Pictorial Lessons on Form, Comparison and Number for Children under Seven Years of Age.* Edinburgh: Edmonston & Douglas, 1858; sixth edition, 1873.

Oscar Pletsch, *Buds and Flowers of Childish Life.* G. Routledge & Sons, 1870.

— *Little Lily's Alphabet.* Verses by S.M.P. Frederick Warne & Co., [1865].

— *Happy Child Life.* Rhymes by Mrs Charles Heaton. G. Routledge & Sons, 1875.

— *Little Lasses and Lads.* Seeley, Jackson & Halliday, 1869.

'Reimerich Kinderlieb' [Heinrich Hoffmann], *Lustige Geschichten und drollige Bilder.* Frankfurt: Dr Löning / Literarische Anstalt, 1845.

[Heinrich Hoffmann], *The English Struwwelpeter or Pretty Stories and Funny Pictures.* Leipzig: Friedrich Volckmar, 1848.

Struwelpeter [sic], Routledge, Warnes & Routledge, c. 1865.

Mark Twain, *Slovenly Peter.* Composed 1891. First publ. New York: Limited Editions Club, 1935.

The Magic Lantern Struwwelpeter. Frederick Warne, 1896.

Struwwelpeter of Today. Dean & Son, c. 1900.

Shock Headed Peter and Other Funny Stories. Books for the Bairns, no. 68. October 1901.

The English Struwwelpeter. Dean & Son, 1905. Rag book.

Struwwelpeter or Merry Stories and Funny Pictures. Blackie & Son, c. 1909.

[Adolf Glassbrenner and Theodor Hosemann, *A Laughter Book for Little Folk.* Trans. Madame de Chatelain. Cundall & Addey, 1851.

Harold Begbie and F. Carruthers Gould, *The Political Struwwelpeter.* Grant Richards, 1899.

— *The Struwwelpeter Alphabet.* Grant Richards, 1900.

E.V. Lucas and Geo. Morrow, *Swollen-headed William. Painful Stories and Funny*

Pictures. Methuen & Co., 1914.

The Egyptian Struwwelpeter. H. Grevel & Co., [1896].

Archibald Williams and A. Wallis Mills, *Petrol Peter*. Methuen & Co., 1906.

A.and C. Williams, *The Marlborough Struwwelpeter*. Marlborough: The 'Times' Office, [1908]

J. R. Planché, *King Nut-Cracker or the Dream of Poor Reinhold. A Fairy Tale for Children*. ? William Tegg, 1855.

Clara Fechner, *Nut-Cracker and Sugar Dolly*. Trans. Charles A. Dana. Joseph Cundall, 1849.

Wilhelm Busch, *Max and Maurice. A Juvenile History in Seven Tricks*. Trans. Charles T. Brooks. Boston: Roberts Brothers, 1871.

— *Max and Moritz. A Story Book in Seven Tricks*. Trans. Anon. Munich: Braun & Schneider, London: A.N. Myers, 1874.

— *Max and Moritz*. Trans. Arundell Esdaile. G. Routledge & Sons [1913].

— *A Bushel of Merrythoughts*. Trans. W. Harry Rogers. Sampson Low, Son & Marston, 1868.

— *A Book of Merry Thoughts*. Books for the Bairns, no. 48, February 1900.

— *Pious Jemima. A Doleful Tale*. Trans. John MacLush. Edinburgh: William P. Nimmo, 1872.

— *Naughty Jemima*. Ward, Lock & Co., [1874].

— *Buzz a Buzz; or, the Bees*. Trans. W.C. Cotton. Griffith & Farran, 1872.

— *Fools Paradise*. J.C. Hotten, [1872].

— *Hookeybeak the Raven and Other Tales*. Trans. H.W. Dulcken. G. Routledge & Sons, [1878].

— *Diogenes and the Two Naughty Young Corinthians*. Trans. A.B. Westmacott. Alfred Hays, 1879.

— *Cousin Freddy's First and Last Donkey Ride*. Trans. A.B. Westmacott. Alfred Hays, 1879.

— *The Power of Sound; or, the Effect of Music*. Trans. A.B. Westmacott. Alfred Hays, 1879.

20. Siegfried and the *Nibelungenlied*

The Heroic Life and Exploits of Siegfried the Dragon Slayer: an Old German Book. Joseph Cundall & David Bogue, 1848.

Guido Goerres, *Der Hürnen Siegfried und sein Kampf mit dem Drachen*. Illus. W. Kaulbach. Schaffhausen, 1843.

James Baldwin, *The Story of Siegfried*. New York: Charles Scribner's Sons, 1882. Repr. 1888, 1931.

F.J. Kiefer, *The Legends of the Rhine from Basle to Rotterdam*. Trans. L.W. Garnham. Mayence: David Kapp, n.d.

438 Telling Tales

G.W. Cox and E.H. Jones, *Popular Romances of the Middle Ages*. Longmans, Green & Co., 1891.

— *Tales of the Teutonic Lands*. Longmans, Green & Co., 1872.

W. Wägner, *Epics and Romances of the Middle Ages*. Swan Sonnenschein, 1883, fifth edition, 1889.

Lydia Hands, *Golden Threads from an Ancient Loom. Das Nibelungenlied*. Griffith & Farran, 1880,

S. Baring-Gould, *Siegfried*. Dean & Son, 1904.

The Rhinegold and the Valkyrie. Illus. Arthur Rackham. W. Heinemann, 1910.

Siegfried and the Twilight of the Gods. Illus. Arthur Rackham. W. Heinemann, 1911.

The Linden Leaf; or, the Story of Siegfried. Thomas Nelson & Sons, 1907.

Mary Macgregor, *Stories of Siegfried*. T.C. & E.C. Jack, c. 1908.

Dora Ford Madeley, *The Heroic Life and Exploits of Siegfried the Dragon-Slayer. An Old Story of the North*. George G. Harrap & Co., 1910.

Siegfried and Kriemhild. A Story of Passion and Revenge. Thomas Nelson & Sons, 1912.

A.J. Church, *Heroes of Chivalry and Romance*. Seeley & Co., 1898.

Thomas Cartwright, *Sigurd the Dragon-Slayer*. W. Heinemann, 1907.

21. The Franco-Prussian War

Hesba Stretton, *Max Krömer. A Story of the Siege of Strasbourg*. Religious Tract Society, [1871].

G.A. Henty, *The Young Franc-Tireurs and their Adventures in the Franco-Prussian War*. Griffith & Farran, 1872.

Annie Lucas, *Léonie; or, Light out of Darkness; and Within Iron Walls: a Tale of the Siege of Paris. Twin Stories of the Franco-German War*. Thomas Nelson & Sons, 1875.

L[illias] Lobenhoffer, *Fritz of the Tower. A Tale of the Franco-German War*. Religious Tract Society, [1887].

M.E. Clements, *Eagle and Dove. A Tale of the Franco-Prussian War*. Thomas Nelson & Sons, 1889.

G.A. Henty, *A Woman of the Commune. A Tale of the two Sieges of Paris*. F.V. White & Co., 1895.

Herbert Hayens, *Paris at Bay*. Blackie & Son, [1897].

Evelyn Everett-Green, *The Castle of the White Flag. A Tale of the Franco-German War*. Thomas Nelson & Sons, 1904.

— *Ringed by Fire*. Thomas Nelson & Sons, [1904].

F.S. Brereton, *A Hero of Sedan. A Tale of the Franco-Prussian War*. Blackie & Son, 1910.

22. German Books for Girls

Amalie Schoppe, *Heinrich und Marie oder die verwaisten Kinder*. Leipzig: Leopold Michelsen, second edition, 1839.

— *Henry and Mary, or the Little Orphans*. Trans. Susan Cobbett. Manchester: John Heywood; London: Simpkin & Marshall, & Houlston & Wright, [1860].

[Marie Nathusius], *Christfried's First Journey, and Other Tales*. Edinburgh: Johnstone, Hunter, & Co., c. 1871.

— *Christfrid's First Journey*, in *Max Wild the Merchant's Son, and other Stories for the Young*. William P. Nimmo, 1874.

— *Louisa von Plettenhaus: the Diary of a Poor Young Lady*. Trans. Anon. Boston and New York: Francis, 1857.

— *The Diary of a Poor Young Gentlewoman*. Trans. M. Anna Childs. Trübner & Co., 1860.

— *Step by Step; or, the Good Fight*. R. Bentley, 1860.

— *Diary of a Poor Young Lady*. Trans. Miss Thompson. Leipzig: Tauchnitz, 1867.

— *Diary of a Poor Young Lady*. Trans. Emily Ritzerow. 1869.

Ottilie Wildermuth, *The Holidays at Bärenburg Castle*. Trans. Mary or William Howitt, in Mary Howitt, *The Golden Casket*. [1861].

— *The Holidays at Bärenburg Castle*. Trans. William Howitt, in *Luke Barnicott and Other Stories*. Cassell, Petter & Galpin, [1866].

— *Midsummer Holidays at Castle Bärenburg*. 1865.

— *The Home Queen; or, Unconscious Rule*. Frederick Warne & Co., c. 1893.

— *By Daylight; or Pictures from Real Life*. 1865.

— *Nurse Margaret's Two St. Sylvester's Eves*. SPCK, 1871.

— *Barbara's Christmas*. SPCK, 1873.

— *The Little Sand Boy; or, Who is best off*. Edinburgh, 1877.

Travels in Switzerland. C.J.G. & F. Rivington, 1831.

J.P.C. de Florian, *William Tell; or, Swisserland Delivered*. Sherwood, Neely & Jones, 1809.

Johanna Spyri, *Heidis Lehr- und Wanderjahre. Heidi kann brauchen, was es gelernt hat*. Gotha: Friedrich Andreas Perthes, 1880-81.

— *Heidi: Her Years of Wandering and Learning. Heidi: How she Used what she Learned*. Trans. Louise Brooks. Boston: De Wolfe, Fiske & Co., 1884.

— *Heidi's Early Experiences. Heidi's Later Experiences*. London, 1884.

— *Heidi's Years of Learning and Travel. Heidi Makes Use of what she has Learned*. Trans. Helen B. Dole. Boston: Ginn & Co., 1899.

— further translations by H.A. Melcon. New York: A.L. Burt, [1901]; by Helene S. White. New York: T.Y. Crowell & Co., [1902]; by M.E. J.M. Dent & Co., [1909] 'Everyman's Library'.

— *Swiss Stories for Children and those who love Children*. Trans. Lucy Wheelock. Blackie & Son, 1889 [actually 1888].

23. Children's Books and the First World War

Elizabeth O'Neill, *The War 1914-15. A History and an Explanation for Boys and Girls*. T.C. & E.C. Jack, 1915.

— *The War, 1915-16*. T.C. & E.C. Jack, 1916.

Sir Edward Parrott, *The Children's Story of the War*. Thomas Nelson & Sons, 1915.

Nelly Pollock, *The Belgian Playmates. Heroes Small – and Heroes Tall*. Gay & Hancock, [1914].

John Lea, *Brave Boys and Girls in War-time*. Blackie & Son, [1918].

Mrs Belloc Lowndes, *Told in Gallant Deeds*. James Nisbet & Co., [1915].

Herbert Strang, *The Blue Book of the War*. Humphrey Milford / Oxford University Press, 1917.

— *With Haig on the Somme*. Humphrey Milford / Oxford University Press, 1917.

F.S. Brereton, *With the Allies to the Rhine. A Story of the Finish of the War*. Blackie & Son, [1919].

Charles Gilson, *Submarine U93*. 'The Boy's Own Paper', c. 1917.

Jessie Pope, *War Poems*. Grant Richards, 1915.

E.V. Lucas, *In Gentlest Germany*. John Lane The Bodley Head, 1915.

A.T. Mason, *The Book of Artemas*. W. Westall, 127th edition, 1918.

— *The Second Book of Artemas*. W. Westall, second edition, 1918.

Alfred Leete, *Schmidt the Spy and his Message to Berlin*. Duckworth & Co., 1916.

Hansi, *Professor Knatschke. Selected Works of the Great German Scholar and of his Daughter Elsa*. Trans. R.L. Crewe. Hodder & Stoughton, second edition, 1917.

Elphinstone Thorpe, *Nursery Rhymes for Fighting Times*. Everett & Co., [1914].

J.G. Russell Harvey and Charlie Thomas, *Rhymes of the Times for War Babies of All Ages*. Bristol: A.W. Ford & Co., [1919].

George H. Powell, *The Crown Prince's First Lesson Book or Nursery Rhymes for the Times*. Grant Richards, [1914].

St John Hamund, *The Book of William. The Rubaiyat of William the War-Lord*. Grant Richards, [1915].

With apologies to Edward Lear. Frederick Warne & Co., [1914].

Horace Wyatt, *Malice in Kulturland*. The Car Illustrated, 1914.

E.V. Lucas and Geo. Morrow, *Swollen-headed William. Painful Stories and Funny Pictures. After the German*. Methuen & Co., 1914.

Select Bibliography

Note: This bibliography is restricted largely to general works of reference and bibliographical works. It does not include bibliographies of works dealt with in the main body of the book, nor does it attempt to provide secondary literature on particular texts and authors. Footnotes in the individual chapters of the book refer to secondary literature that has proved useful for particular points.

Allgemeine Deutsche Biographie (Leipzig: Duncker and Humblot, 1875-1912)

Alderson, Brian, *Grimm Tales in English*. British Library exhibition notes (London: British Library, 1985)

— 'Some Notes on James Burns as a Publisher of Children's Books', *Bulletin of the John Rylands University Library of Manchester*, 76, 3 (Autumn 1994), pp. 103-25

— and Tessa Chester, *Tall Stories of Baron Munchausen*. Bethnal Green Museum of Childhood exhibition book (London: Victoria & Albert Museum for the Bethnal Green Museum of Childhood, 1985)

— and Felix de Marez Oyens, *Be Merry and Wise: Origins of Children's Book Publishing in England, 1650-1850* (London: The British Library; New Castle, DE: Oak Knoll Press, 2006)

Ashton, Rosemary, *Little Germany: Exile and Asylum in Victorian England* (Oxford: Oxford University Press, 1986)

Baumgartner, Johannes in collaboration with Walter Sauer, Hasso Böhme and Karin Mayer (ed.), *Der Struwwelpeter. Ein Bilderbuch macht Karriere*. Teil 1 (Freiburg, 1996), Teil 2 (Freiburg 1998)

Binder, Alwin and Heinrich Richartz (eds.), *Joachim Heinrich Campe, Robinson der Jüngere* (Stuttgart: Reclam, 1981)

Biographie universelle ancienne et moderne. Nouvelle édition (Paris: A. Thoisnier Desplaces, éditeur, 1843)

Blamires, David, 'The Early Reception of the Grimms' *Kinder- und Hausmärchen* in England', *Bulletin of the John Rylands University Library of Manchester*, 71, 3 (Autumn 1989), pp. 63-77

— 'Eulenspiegel in englischer Sprache', *Eulenspiegel-Jahrbuch*, 29 (1989), pp. 51-66

— 'Some German and English Political Travesties of *Struwwelpeter*', in *Connections: Essays in Honour of Eda Sagarra on the Occasion of her 60th Birthday*, ed. Peter Skrine, Rosemary E. Wallbank-Turner and Jonathan West (Stuttgart: Verlag Hans-Dieter Heinz, 1993), pp. 19-27

— *Fortunatus in his many English Guises* (Lewiston, Queenston, Lampeter: Mellen, 1996)

— (ed.), *Children's Literature. Bulletin of the John Rylands University Library of Manchester*, 76, 3 (Autumn 1994)

— 'How and what Victorian and Edwardian Children Learnt about German History', *Paradigm*, 22 (May 1997), pp. 23-37

— 'German Children's Books in English 1840-1860', in *Das schwierige neunzehnte Jahrhundert. Germanistische Tagung zum 65. Geburtstag von Eda Sagarra im August 1998*, ed. Jürgen Barkhoff, Gilbert Carr and Roger Paulin (Tübingen: Niemeyer, 2000), pp. 559-65

— 'Social Satire in English *Struwwelpeter* Parodies', *Princeton University Library Chronicle*, 62,1 (Autumn 2000), pp. 45-58

— 'The Reception of Musäus's Fairytales in English up to 1900', *New Comparison*, 31 (Spring 2001), pp. 23-34

— 'The Meaning of Disfigurement in Wilhelm Hauff's *Dwarf Nose*', *Children's Literature in Education*, 33, 4 (December 2002), pp. 297-307

— 'A Workshop of Editorial Practice: the Grimms' *Kinder- und Hausmärchen*', in *A Companion to the Fairy Tale*, ed. Hilda Ellis Davidson and Anna Chaudhri (Cambridge: D. S. Brewer, 2003), pp. 71-83

— 'A Little Known English *Struwwelpeter*', *Children's Books History Society Newsletter*, 88 (August 2007), pp. 24-27

Bratton, J. S., *The Impact of Victorian Children's Fiction* (London: Croom Helm, 1981)

Briggs, Julia, Dennis Butts and M. O. Grenby (eds.), *Popular Children's Literature in Britain* (Aldershot and Burlington, VT: Ashgate, 2008)

The British Library General Catalogue of Printed Books to 1975 (London: Clive Bingley; London, München, New York, Paris: K. G. Saur, 1979-88)

Buchanan-Brown, John, *Early Victorian Illustrated Books: Britain, France and Germany 1820-1860* (London: The British Library; New Castle, DE: Oak Knoll Press, 2005)

Butler, G. P., 'Beckford and Musäus: a Likely Pair?', in Eoin Bourke, Roisin Ni Néill and Michael Shields (eds.), *Schein und Widerschein. Festschrift für T. J. Casey* (Galway: Galway University Press, [1999]), pp. 24-35

Butts, Dennis, 'Exploiting a Formula: the Adventure Stories of G. A. Henty (1832-1902)', in Julia Briggs, Dennis Butts and M. O. Grenby (eds.), *Popular Children's Literature in Britain* (Aldershot and Burlington, VT: Ashgate, 2008), pp. 149-63

Cadogan, Mary and Patricia Craig, *Women and Children First. The Fiction of Two World Wars* (London: Gollancz, 1978)

Carpenter Humphrey and Mari Prichard, *The Oxford Companion to Children's*

Literature (Oxford, New York: Oxford University Press, 1984)

Carswell, John, *The Prospector, Being the Life and Times of Rudolf Erich Raspe (1733-1794)* (London: The Cresset Press, 1950)

— (ed.), *Singular Travels, Campaigns and Adventures of Baron Munchausen, by R. E. Raspe and others* (London: The Cresset Press, 1948)

Catalogue générale des livres imprimés de la Bibliothèque Nationale (Paris: Imprimerie Nationale, 1910-81)

Darton, F. J. Harvey, *Children's Books in England. Five Centuries of Social Life*, revised by Brian Alderson (Cambridge: Cambridge University Press, 1982)

Darton, Lawrence, 'Books for Children and Young People: two Quaker Publishers', *Friends' Quarterly* (April 1988), pp. 82-90

— with editorial assistance and a preface by Brian Alderson, *The Dartons: an Annotated Check-list of Children's Books issued by two Publishing Houses 1787-1876* (London: The British Library; New Castle, DE: Oak Knoll Press, 2004)

Dartt, Robert L., *G. A. Henty: a Bibliography* (Cedar Grove, NJ: Dar-Web, Inc.; Altrincham: John Sherratt & Son, 1971)

Doderer, Klaus (ed.), *Lexikon der Kinder- und Jugendliteratur* (Weinheim und Basel: Beltz, 1979)

Dorson, Richard M., *The British Folklorists. A History* (Chicago: University of Chicago Press, 1968)

Elardo, Ronald J., 'E. T. A. Hoffmann's *Nußknacker und Mausekönig*. The Mouse-Queen in the Tragedy of the Hero,' *Germanic Review*, 55 (1980)

Ewers, Hans-Heino (ed.), *Kinder- und Jugendliteratur der Aufklärung. Eine Textsammlung* (Stuttgart: Reclam, 1980)

— (ed.), *Kinder- und Jugendliteratur der Romantik. Eine Textsammlung* (Stuttgart: Reclam, 1984)

— (ed.), *Ludwig Bechstein, Deutsches Märchenbuch* (Stuttgart: Reclam, 1996)

France, Peter and Kenneth Haynes (eds.), *The Oxford History of Literary Translation in English*, vol. 4, *1790-1900* (Oxford: Oxford University Press, 2006)

Gehrmann, Thekla, *Bilder & Bücher. Münchhausen-Illustrationen aus zwei Jahrhunderten. Sammlung Bodenwerder* (Stadt Bodenwerder, 1992)

Geils, Peter and Willi Gorzny (eds.), *Gesamtverzeichnis des deutschsprachigen Schrifttums (GV) 1700-1910* (München, New York, London, Paris: K. G. Saur, 1979-87)

Gibbs, Rowan, *The Swiss Family Robinson, Book Catalogue* (Wellington, New Zealand: Rowan Gibbs; Smith's Bookshop, 1997)

Göbels, Hubert (ed.), *Christian Gotthilf Salzmann, Moralisches Elementarbuch. Nachdruck der Auflage von 1785* (Dortmund: Harenberg, 1980)

Gottlieb, Gerald, *Early Children's Books and their Illustration* (New York: The Pierpont Morgan Library; Boston: David R. Godine, 1975)

Grenz, Dagmar, *Mädchenliteratur. Von den moralisch-belehrenden Schriften bis zur Herausbildung der Backfischliteratur im 19. Jahrhundert* (Stuttgart, 1981)

Gumuchian, *Les Livres de l'enfance du XVe au XIXe siècle* (London: The Holland Press, 1979)

Haase, Donald (ed.), *The Reception of the Grimms' Fairy Tales: Responses, Reactions, Revisions* (Detroit: Wayne State University Press, 1993)

A Handbook for Travellers on the Continent: being a Guide to Holland, Belgium, Prussia, Northern Germany, and the Rhine from Holland to Switzerland, 13th edition, corrected (London: John Murray, 1860)

Herzog, G. H., Marion Herzog-Hoinkis and Helmut Siefert (eds.), *Heinrich Hoffmann. Leben und Werk in Texten und Bildern* (Frankfurt am Main: Insel Verlag, 1995)

— and Marion Herzog-Hoinkis, Stephen H. A. Kaendler and Helmut Siefert (eds.), *Struwwelpeter-Hoffmann gestern und heute* (Frankfurt am Main: Sinemis, 1999)

Hill, Ruth A. and Elsa de Bondell, *Children's Books from Foreign Languages: English Translations from Published and Unpublished Sources* (New York: The H. W. Wilson Company, 1937)

Hillier, Mary, *Automata and Mechanical Toys* (London: Bloomsbury Books, 1988)

Hilton, Mary, Morag Styles and Victor Watson (eds.), *Opening the Nursery Door. Reading, Writing and Childhood 1600-1900* (London and New York: Routledge, 1997)

Howitt, William, *The Rural and Domestic Life of Germany* (London: Longman, Brown, Green & Longmans, 1842)

Hunt, Julia and Frederick, *Peeps into Nisterland: a Guide to the Children's Books of Ernest Nister* (Chester: Casmelda Publishing, 2006)

Hunt, Peter, *An Introduction to Children's Literature* (Oxford and New York: Oxford University Press, 1994)

Hürlimann, Bettina, *Three Centuries of Children's Books in Europe*, trans. and ed. by Brian Alderson (London: Oxford University Press, 1967)

Jackson, Mary V., *Engines of Instruction, Mischief, and Magic* (Lincoln: University of Nebraska Press, 1989)

Klotz, Volker, *Das europäische Kunstmärchen* (München: Deutscher Taschenbuch Verlag, 1987)

Knoepflmacher, U. C., *Ventures into Childland: Victorians, Fairy Tales, and Femininity* (Chicago and London: University of Chicago Press, 1998)

Lomax, Elaine, 'Telling the Other Side: Hesba Stretton's "Outcast" Stories', in Julia Briggs, Dennis Butts and M. O. Grenby (eds.), *Popular Children's Literature in Britain* (Aldershot and Burlington, VT: Ashgate, 2008), pp. 123-48

Maas, Jeremy, Pamela White Trimpe, Charlotte Gere and others, *Victorian Fairy Painting* (London: Royal Academy of Arts; Iowa: The University of Iowa Museum of Art; Toronto: The Art Gallery of Ontario, in association with Merrell Holberton, 1997)

McLean, Ruari, *Joseph Cundall. A Victorian Publisher* (Pinner: Private Libraries Association, 1976)

Masaki, Tomoko, *A History of Victorian Popular Picture Books: the Aesthetic, Creative,* and Technological Aspects of the Toy Book through the Publications of the Firm of Routledge 1852-1893 (Tokyo: Kazamashobo, 2006)

Michaelis-Jena, Ruth, The Brothers Grimm (London: Routledge & Kegan Paul, 1970)

Moon, Marjorie, John Harris's Books for Youth 1801-1843 (Cambridge: Marjorie Moon and A. J. B. Spilman, 1976)

— Benjamin Tabart's Juvenile Library (Winchester: St. Paul's Bibliographies; Detroit: Omnigraphics, 1990)

National Union Catalog Pre-1956 Imprints (London and Chicago: Mansell, 1969-81)

Newbolt, Peter, G. A. Henty 1832-1902: a Bibliographical Study of his British Editions (Aldershot: Scolar Press, 1996)

O'Sullivan, Emer, Friend and Foe: the Image of Germany and the Germans in British Children's Fiction from 1870 to the Present (Tübingen: Narr, 1990)

Pech, Klaus-Ulrich (ed.), Kinder- und Jugendliteratur vom Biedermeier bis zum Realismus (Stuttgart: Reclam, 1985)

Penzer, N. M., (ed.), The Pentamerone of Giambattista Basile (London: John Lane the Bodley Head; New York: E.P. Dutton & Co., 1932)

Peppin, Brigid and Lucy Micklethwait, Dictionary of British Book Illustrators: the Twentieth Century (London: John Murray, 1983)

Pressler, Christine, Schöne alte Kinderbücher. Eine illustrierte Geschichte des deutschen Kinderbuches aus fünf Jahrhunderten (München: Bruckmann, 1980)

Pörnbacher, Hans (ed.), Christoph von Schmid und seine Zeit (Weissenhorn: Anton H. Konrad Verlag, 1968)

Ranke, Kurt (ed.), Enzyklopädie des Märchens (Berlin and New York: de Gruyter, 1977-)

Renier, Anne, The Basket of Flowers by Christoph von Schmid. A Checklist of Copies in the Renier Collection. Signal Supplement, no. 1 (Stroud: The Thimble Press, 1972)

Richards, Jeffrey (ed.), Imperialism and Juvenile Literature (Manchester and New York: Manchester University Press, 1989)

Rölleke, Heinz (ed.), Brüder Grimm, Kinder- und Hausmärchen, Ausgabe letzter Hand mit den Originalanmerkungen der Brüder Grimm (Stuttgart: Reclam, 1980)

Roscoe, S., John Newbery and his Successors 1740-1814. A Bibliography (Wormley: Five Owls Press, 1973)

Rühle, Reiner, 'Böse Kinder'. Kommentierte Bibliographie von Struwwelpetriaden und Max-und-Moritziaden mit biographischen Daten zu Verfassern und Illustratoren (Osnabrück: H. T. Wenner, 1999)

St. John, Judith, The Osborne Collection of Early Children's Books. A Catalogue (Toronto: Toronto Public Library, 2 vols. 1975)

Sandbach, Francis E., The Nibelungenlied and Gudrun in England and America (London: David Nutt, 1904)

Schweizer, Werner R., Münchhausen und Münchhausiaden. Werden und Schicksale einer deutsch-englischen Burleske (Bern und München: Francke, 1969)

Seebaß, Adolf, *Alte Kinderbücher und Jugendschriften. Livres de l'enfance. Children's books*. Katalog 636 und 818 (Mansfield Centre, CT: Maurizo Martino, n.d.)

Shteir, Ann B., 'Priscilla Wakefield's Books "for the Instruction and Amusement of Young Persons"', *Friends' Quarterly* (April 1988), pp. 90-96

Stach, Reinhard, *Robinson der Jüngere als pädagogisch-didaktisches Modell des philanthropistischen Erziehungsdenkens* (Ratingen, Wuppertal, Kastellaun: Aloys Henn, 1970)

Stephen, Leslie, Sir, and Sir Sidney Lee (eds.), *Dictionary of National Biography* (London: Oxford University Press, 1949-50)

Sutton, Martin, *The Sin-Complex. A Critical Study of English Versions of the Grimms' Kinder- und Hausmärchen in the Nineteenth Century* (Kassel: Brüder Grimm-Gesellschaft, 1996)

Thorp, Mary, *The Study of the Nibelungenlied* (Oxford: Clarendon Press, 1940)

Vaughan, William, *German Romantic Painting* (New Haven and London: Yale University Press, 1980)

— *Romanticism and Art* (London: Thames & Hudson, 1994)

Warner, Marina, *Queen Victoria's Sketchbook* (London: Macmillan, 1979)

— *From the Beast to the Blonde. On Fairy Tales and their Tellers* (London: Chatto & Windus, 1994)

— *No Go the Bogeyman. Scaring, Lulling and Making Mock* (London: Chatto & Windus, 1998)

Wegehaupt, Heinz, in collaboration with Edith Fichtner, *Alte deutsche Kinderbücher. Bibliographie 1507-1850. Zugleich Bestandsverzeichnis der Kinder- und Jugendbuchabteilung der Deutschen Staatsbibliothek zu Berlin* (Berlin: Der Kinderbuchverlag, 1979)

Wegehaupt, Heinz, *Alte deutsche Kinderbücher: Bibliographie 1851-1900. Zugleich Bestandsverzeichnis der Kinder- und Jugendbuchabteilung der Deutschen Staatsbibliothek zu Berlin* (Stuttgart: Dr. Ernst Hauswedell & Co. Verlag, 1985)

— *Robinson und Struwwelpeter. Bücher für Kinder aus fünf Jahrhunderten* (Berlin: Deutsche Staatsbibliothek in der Stiftung Preussischer Kulturbesitz, 1991)

Werner, Hugo (ed.), *Wilhelm Busch. Das Gesamtwerk des Zeichners und Dichters in sechs Bänden* (Olten, Stuttgart, Salzburg: Fackelverlag, 1959)

Wesselski, Albert (ed.), *Deutsche Märchen vor Grimm* (Brünn, Leipzig: Rohrer, 1938)

Whalley, Joyce Irene, and Tessa Rose Chester, *A History of Children's Book Illustration* (London: John Murray with the Victoria & Albert Museum, 1988)

Wood, Sally, *W. T. Stead and his 'Books for the Bairns'* (Edinburgh: Salvia Books, 1987)

Woof, Robert, Stephen Hebron and Claire Tomalin, *Hyenas in Petticoats. Mary Wollstonecraft and Mary Shelley* (Grasmere: The Wordsworth Trust, 1997)

Wyss, Robert L., 'Der schweizerische Robinson. Seine Entstehung und sein Manuskript', *Stultifera Navis. Mitteilungsblatt der Schweizerischen Bibliophilen-Gesellschaft*, 12. Jahrgang, Nr. 3-4 (Oktober 1955)

Wunderlich, Werner, 'The Pied Piper of Hamelin in History and Literature',

Michigan German Studies, 19, 1 (1993), pp. 1-17

Ziersch, Amélie (ed.), *Bilderbuch – Begleiter der Kindheit. Katalog zur Ausstellung über die Entwicklung des Bilderbuches in drei Jahrhunderten* (München: Museum Villa Stuck, 1986)

Zipes, Jack, *The Brothers Grimm. From Enchanted Forests to the Modern World* (New York & London: Routledge, 1988; second edition New York and Basingstoke: Palgrave Macmillan, 2002)

– (ed.), *The Oxford Companion to Fairy Tales* (Oxford: Oxford University Press, 2000)

Index

Adams, W.H.D., 89
Addey & Co., 150n., 162, 165-66, 169, 171, 173, 177, 207, 211, 212, 252, 340
Adelung, Friedrich von, 140
Adventures of the Renowned Baron Munchausen, containing Singular Travels, Campaigns, Voyages, and Adventures, see also Münchhausen, K.F. Hieronymus von, 4, 5, 8-21, 23, 139, 422, fig. 1
adult books adapted for children, 1-2, 9-21, 27-28, 51-61, 121-33, 135-45, 263-74
Albert, Prince, 75, 229, 278, 290, 297, 312, 394
Alcock, Deborah, 298, 299, 302-03, 305-06
Alcott, Louisa M., 395,
Alderson, Brian, 79, 143n., 163
Alexander Menzikoff, 314-15
alienation, 135, 189, 191
A.L.O.E. ('A Lady Of England'), pseudonym of Charlotte Maria Tucker, 275
Alsace, 269, 278, 286, 307, 379, 388, 412, 418
Alsace-Lorraine, 391
Andersen, Hans Christian, 101-02, 135, 167, 168, 173, 181, 256, 257, 259, 267, 286, 322
Anderson, Florence, 203, 243-44
Andrews, Eddie J., 175
animals, attitudes towards, 42-43, 90, 92-93, 99
Arabian Nights, 16-17, 149, 182, 184, 194-95, 230, 232, 249, 286
Arabian Nights' Entertainments, 16
arme Heinrich, Der, 258

Arminius, 281, 290, 353-54
Armour, Marguerite, 356
Arndt, Ernst Moritz, 3, 211-14, 217, 221
Arnim, Ludwig Achim von, 264, 265
Attwell, Mabel Lucie, 175-76, 310
Aulnoy, Marie-Catherine d', 2, 52, 149, 166, 181, 218, 242
Ault, Norman, 202
Aunt Charlotte's Stories of German History for the Little Ones (*see also* Charlotte M. Yonge), 276, 284, 293, 360
Austin, Sarah, 102, 173

Baldwin, James, 361, 364, 369
Baldwin, Cradock and Joy, 35n., 88
Baldwyn, C., 149
Ballantyne, R.M., 319
Barbara's Christmas, 398
Barbauld, Anna Laetitia, 44
Baring-Gould, S., 171, 276, 285-89, 293-95, 306, 360, 366, 387
Baron and Squire, 298, 303-04
Baron Munchausen, fig. 3
Barth, Christian Gottlob, 114-18, 309, 311, 382, 396,
Basedow, Johann Bernhard, 23-24, 25, 39, 42, 51
Basile, Giambattista, 53, 59-60, 160-61, 265-66, 269, 272
Basket of Flowers, The (or Flower-Basket), 3, 7, 103, 106-14, 118, 254, 393, 421, fig. frontispiece, 13
Beaumont, Madame Leprince de, 43, 68, 149, 166
Bechstein, Ludwig, 3, 149, 205-11, 221, 245, 256, 263, 271, 321, 341
Beckford, William, 54

Bedell, Rev. G.T., 110-13
Begbie, Harold, 341
Belgian Playmates, Heroes Small – and Heroes Tall, The, 413
Bell, Robert Anning, 173
Belloc Lowndes, Mrs, 413
Bennett, Charles, 60
Beowulf, 369
Bergen, Fritz, 201
Bertall (pseudonym of Charles-Albert d'Arnoux), 168, 198, 199, 238-39, 242, 244
Bertuch, Friedrich Justin, 230, 325
bibliographical problems, 5, 88, 90-91, 266, 310
Birch, Jonathan, 355-56
Bishop Hatto of Mainz, 214-15, 274
Black Forest (*see also Tales of Wonder; or, the Inn in the Black Forest*), 69, 70, 114, 184, 185, 186, 198, 228, 381, 382
Blackie and Son, 113-14, 132, 173, 215, 274, 339-40, 372, 406, 413, 414
Blake, William, 45
Blanchard, Edward, 124
Blanchard, François, 15
Blaquiere, Captain, 291
Blue Book of the War, The, 413
Boccaccio, Giovanni, 182, 265
Bogue, David, 141, 165, 246, 316, 356, 367, 369
Bohny, Nicholas/Niklaus, 324-25
Bonnet, J., 90
Book of Artemas, The, 417
Book of William, The, 420
Books for the Bairns, (*see also* Stead, W. T.), 20, 98, 127, 176, 185, 192, 200-01, 247, 252, 339, 347-48
Botany Bay, 16
Bowring, Sir John, 140-142
Boyhood of Martin Luther, The, 275
Boyle, Eleanor Vere, 102
Brave Boys and Girls in Wartime, 413
Brecht, Bertolt, 291
Brentano, Clemens, 181, 245, 263-74
Brereton, F.S., 371, 372, 387, 391-93, 414-15
Brontë, Anne and Charlotte, 397
Brooks, Charles T., 346
Brooks, Louise, 406

Browne, Gordon, 124, 127, 132, 141-42, 203, 243
Browne, Hablot K., 166, 197
Browning, Robert, 214-15
Bruce, James, 17
Bryce, James, 275
Buch der Beispiele der alten Weisen, 208
Buchanan, Robert, 216-17
Budden, Maria Elizabeth, 275
Buds and Flowers of Childish Life, 325, 327
Bürger, G. A., 10
Burns, James, 54, 58-59, 123-24, 129, 131, 132
Busch, Wilhelm, 4, 344-51
Büsching, J.G., 150, 217
Bushel of Merrythoughts, A, 246-47
Busk, Rachel, 217, 221
Butler, John Olding, 67, 295, 301
Butler-Stoney, T., 216
Butterworth, Hezekiah, 185, 187, 295, 361, 362
Buzz a Buzz; or, the Bees, 348-49
By Daylight; or Pictures from Real Life, 398
Byfield, John, 155
Byron, George Gordon, Lord, 64

Cabin Book, The, 319
Cadogan, Mary, 410, 414
'Caliph Stork', 184, 194, 195-97, 198, 199, 200-201, 202
Cameron, Katherine, 126
Campe, Joachim Heinrich, 23-38, 309
Caravan Tales and Some Others, 190, 198, 201-02
Carlyle, Thomas, 56-58, 244, 355, 357, 362-63
Carové, F.W., 101-03, 118, 139, 144
Carroll, Lewis, 6, 124, 277, 332
Cartland, Dame Barbara, 126
Castiglione, B., 14
Castle of the White Flag, The, 372, 388-90
Catholicism, 101, 103-04, 105, 114, 117, 131, 279, 280, 292, 298, 301, 302-05, 306, 311-13, 379, 381, 389
Cervantes, Miguel de, 230-31
Chamber, William and Robert, 310
Chamisso, Adelbert von, 2, 121, 135-45, 203, 244, 263, 421-22

chapbooks, 1-2, 18-20, 67, 95, 135, 149, 157, 183, 206, 396
Chapman & Hall, 56, 57, 124, 185, 238, 255, 297, 355n.
Chapman & Lang, 18
Charmed Roe, The, 158, 324
Chatelain, Madame de, 151, 158, 197, 212-13, 220, 250, 340
children's adventure stories in the First World War, 410-16
Childs, M. Anna, 397
Chodowiecki, Daniel, 40, 45, 49
Christfried's First Journey, 396-97
Christmas, 96, 116, 128-29, 190, 218, 224-30, 233, 238-41, 254, 297, 327, 33-34, 343, 398, 406-07
Christmas Eve, 104, 106, 197, 229, 230, 238, 343
Christmas Roses and Other Tales from the German, The, 190, 246-47, 250-51
Church, A.C., 369
Clare, John, 2
Clarke, Sarah M.S., 298, 303, 304
Clements, M.E., 371-72, 382-87
Cold Heart, The, 199
Cole, William, 18
Coleridge, Samuel Taylor, 18n., 44, 64, 111, 122, 292
Comenius, Jan Amos, 325
Comical Creatures from Wurtemberg, 197
Contessa, Carl Wilhelm, 223
Cook, James, 16, 317
Coolidge, Susan, 395
Coppélia, 244
Corner, Julia, 276-79, 284-85, 287-89, 293-97, 306
Cornwell, James, 76
Coryat, Thomas, 63, 214
Cottin, Sophie, 312
Courtney, W.L., 125, 126
Coventry, Sir Francis, 46
Cowper, William, 111
Cox, James, 228
Crabb, George, 97
Crabb, Maria Joseph, 96, 97
Craig, Patricia, 410, 414
Crane, Lucy, 147, 163, 165n.
Crane, Walter, 147, 170-71, 177
Croker, Thomas Crofton, 155

Croshaw, C., 18, 423
Crown Prince's First Lesson-book, The, 419
Cruikshank, George, 21, 139, 141-42, 145, 147, 149-50, 155, 246
Cuff, the Negro Boy, 115-16
cultural differences, 4, 47, 55, 238-40
Cundall, Joseph, 58-60, 190
Cunningham, George, 59, 158-60, 162, 200-01, 214, 217, 219-20

Dabis, Anna, 213, 221
Dalziel Brothers, 322
Dana, Charles A., 343
Darton, F.J. Harvey, 255
Darton, firm of, 96, 97, 99, 101, 102, 114, 115, 117, 118, 124, 132, 158, 171, 179-80, 190, 202, 255
Davis, Matilda, 163, 165-66
De Liefde, J.B., 298-300, 305-06
Dean & Munday, 18
Dean & Son, 99, 185, 201, 202, 340, 366, 394
Deane, Margery, 61
Deas, W. & J., 18
Death of Abel, 2
Defoe, Daniel, 1, 22, 27-28, 30, 93
deformity, 112, 189, 192, 195
Dekker, Thomas, 135
Delibes, Léo, 244
Dennis, Ada, 172
Deutsche Sagen, 204
Diamond Fairy Book, 200, 257, 273
Dickens, Charles, 1, 166, 372
discovering Germany, 63-77
discovery, 15, 26, 32-37, 79, 87, 92, 147, 283, 309
Discovery of America; for the Use of Children and Young Persons, The, 23-38, fig. 5
Disney, Walt, 241
Dixon, Arthur A., 113, 202
Dole, Helen B., 406
Donkey's Shadow and Other Stories, The, 252-54
double address, 267n., 271
Doyle, Richard, 160, 260
Dreams by a French Fireside, 255
Drugulin, William E., 112
Dulac, Edmund, 147, 286

452   *Telling Tales*

Dulcken, H.W., 309-10, 322-24, 349-50
Dumas, Alexandre, père, 168, 238-44, 422
Duncan, J.M., 291
Dürer, Albrecht, 126, 129, 131-32
Duty and Affection, 310
'Dwarf Nose' (or *Longnose*), 182, 184, 187-90, 193, 195, 199, 201-02, 203, fig. 20

Each for Himself, 316
Eagle and Dove, 371, 382, 385
Easter Eggs, The, 103, 105
Edgeworth, Richard and Maria, 44
education, 3, 23-26, 28, 33, 37, 39, 43-45, 49, 76, 83, 85, 93, 95-119, 129, 144, 259, 283, 296, 324-25, 331-32, 412
Edwards, M. Betham, 74
Eichendorff, Joseph von, 121
Elementary Dialogues, 36
Elements of Morality, 39-49, fig. 6
Exiles of Salzburg, The, 312
Elizabeth; or, the Exiles of Siberia, 312
English-German connexions, 63-77, 266, 287, 290, 294
English Struwwelpeter, or Pretty Stories and Funny Pictures, 330, 339, 342
Enlightenment, 23, 42-43, 63, 98, 105, 301, 420
Epics and Romances of the Middle Ages, 362
Esdaile, Arundell, 346
Eulenspiegel, Till, 1-2, 4, 332, 344, 353
Evangelicalism, 110-11, 152, 379
Evans, Edmund, 113, 166
Everett-Green, Evelyn, 371, 372, 388-89, 390-92, 395
Ewing, Major Alex, 241
Ewing, Juliana Horatia, 241

Faber, M.A., 185, 198
fables, 1, 4, 43, 119, 156, 200, 208, 245, 247, 251, 321-24,
Fables of Pilpay, 208
Facardins, Les quatre, 52, 230-32, 234
fairies, 126, 160, 196, 247, 255, 267
Fairy Ring, The, 160-61
fairytales, 2-3, 5, 6-7, 43, 51-52, 84, 95, 139, 147-203, 203-14, 221, 230, 236,
244, 321, 328, 332, 245-74, 393, 421-22
Fairy Tales from Brentano, 264, 273
fantasy and reality, 136-37, 223
Faust, 2, 137, 147, 152, 218, 220, 356
Faustus, 2
Fechner, Clara, 197, 343
Feiling, C.A., 57, 185, 187, 190, 197, 198, 199
Fielding, Sarah, 43, 68,
film, 21, 422
fire, playing with, 96-97, 340, 391
First World War, 3, 6, 21, 103, 113, 127, 132, 133, 142, 145, 177, 200-03, 243, 290, 311, 406, 409-22
Fischer, Gottlob Eusebius, 97
Florian, Jean Pierre Claris de, 144, 405-06
folktales, 52, 137, 139, 147, 171, 205-21, 245
Fools Paradise, 349
Fordyce, W. and T., 18, 423
Forestier, Auber, 356
Fortunatus, 1-2, 135, 137, 191, 278, 353
Foster-Barham, A.G., 356
Foundling, or the School of Life, 310
Fouqué, F. H. de la Motte, 1, 121-33, 139-40, 141, 223
Franco-Prussian War, 6, 221, 255, 275, 283, 285-86, 298, 300, 307, 371-394, 395, 412
Frederick Barbarossa, 220, 281, 283, 287
Frederick the Great, 71, 275, 278-79, 286-87, 289, 300, 313-14, 393, 412
Freiligrath, Ferdinand, 264, 281
French Revolution, 104, 309
Frith, H., 90
Fritz of the Tower, 371, 381-84, 393
Frere, A.F., 60
Fryer, Alfred, 219-21

Gall and Inglis, 275, 294
Galland, Antoine, 52, 149, 230
Gammer Grethel, 155, 171-72
Gardiner, Alfonzo, 90
Gardiner, Samuel Rawson, 275, 292, 296, 306
Gaultier, Abbé, 67
Gemälde des Nordens, 26, 36
gender roles, 179, 306, 341

Genlis, Madame de (Stéphanie Félicité Ducrest de St-Aubin, comtesse de Genlis), 68
Genovefa, 103-04
Geography and History, selected by a Lady for the Use of her own Children, 65
German dictionaries, 7, 45-46, 161
German grammars, 7, 46
German geography, 55, 64-68, 75-77, 280, 393
German Novelists, The, 56, 214, 217, 220
German Popular Stories, 140, 149, 155, 158, 159, 175, 210, 211, 220, 250
Germany, 276, 293
Gerstäcker, Friedrich, 315-19
Gessner, Solomon, 2
Gill, George, 75
Gillies, Robert P. , 182
Gilpin, Charles, 99
Gilson, Charles, 414-16
girls' books, 44, 388, 395-407
Godfrey, the Little Hermit, 27, 104-07, 214, 428
Godolphin, Mary, 88
Godwin, Mary Jane, 82, 88-89
Godwin, William, 44-45, 82-85, 88
Goerres, Guido, 356
Goethe, Johann Wolfgang von, 2, 47, 52, 95, 110, 137, 140, 147, 151-52, 220, 237, 321, 353, 356, 400
Golden Fairy Book, The, 259
Golden Threads from an Ancient Loom, 321, 362, 368, fig. 31
Goldsmith, Revd. J., 66
Goodrich, Samuel Griswold, 71
Gosse, Sir Edmund, 125
Gould, F. Carruthers, 264, 276, 285-89, 293-95, 306, 341-42, 360, 366, 387
Greenaway, Kate, 216
Grimm, Albert Ludwig, 51, 192, 248
Grimm, Jakob and Wilhelm, 2-3, 5, 6, 13, 51, 52, 53, 57, 61, 125, 137, 139, 140, 147-180, 182, 184, 191, 192, 193-94, 196, 98, 202, 205, 206-7, 209, 210-13, 215, 217, 218-20, 227, 244, 245-47, 249, 250, 253, 255, 256, 260, 261, 263, 264, 265, 266, 271, 272-73, 286, 324, 328, 332, 341, 347, 356, 393, 421, 422
Grimmelshausen, H.C. von, 272, 292, 299
Grimms' Goblins, 165-68, 193, 194, 197, 199
Gubitz, F.W., 322
Gulliver's Travels, 1, 16
Gustav Adolfs Page, 292
Gustavus Adolphus, 292, 294, 295-96, 299-307
Gustavus; or, the Macaw, 97-98
Guy, John, 66

Haller, Albrecht von, 137
Hamilton, Count Antoine, 52, 230-32
Hamund, St John, 420
Handbook for Travellers on the Continent: being a Guide to Holland, Belgium, Prussia, Northern Germany, and the Rhine from Holland to Switzerland, 59, 74, 99, 219
Handbook of Modern Geography and History, 276, 280, 293
Hands, Lydia, 321, 362-64, 368
'Hänsel und Gretel', 150, 347
Hansi, 418
Hanstein, J.T., 54, 57-58, 60
Happy Child Life, 326-27
Happy Spring-Time, 327
Hardman, F., 319
Hardwick & Bogue, 141
Hardwicke, Robert, 141
Hardy, E. Stuart, 172
Hare, Julius C., 129, 132
Harris, John, 2, 26, 36, 67, 71, 104, 275
Hartmann von Aue, 258
Harvey, William, 102
Harvey, J.G. Russell, 419
Harz Mounains, 35, 53, 220-21
Hauff, Wilhelm, 3, 5, 61, 139, 143, 166, 181-203, 242, 244, 245, 246, 263, 264, 271, 292, 356, 393, 421
Haxthausen family, 13
Hayens, Herbert, 372, 387-88
Heckethorn, C.W., 216, 274
Heaton, Mary Margaret, 326-27
Hedin, Sven, 417
Heidi, 393, 395, 400-07, 421-22
Heine, Heinrich, 140, 252, 281
Heligoland, 316, 318
Helme, Elizabeth, 33-34

Henry, Agnes, 185, 199
Henry and Mary, or the Little Orphans, 396-97, 407
Henty, G.A., 6, 275, 298, 300-06, 311, 319, 371, 372, 376-79, 386-90, 392, 414
Hermann (or Arminius), 281-82, 290, 299, 353-54, 381, 390
Hero of Sedan, A (*see also* Brerenon, Captain F. S.), 372, 387, 391-92, 415
Heroic Life and Exploits of Siegfried the Dragon Slayer, The, 197, 207, 321, 356, 367, fig. 30
Hey, Wilhelm, 4, 321-22, 324
Hick, R., 27
High Dutch Minerva, 62
Hislop, A., 113
Histoire d'un casse-noisette, 238-39
historical anecdotes, 276-77, 278, 281, 283, 287-88, 293-94
histories of the First World War, 409-22
history books, 277, 281-84, 296-97, 358, 387, 393-94, 414-16, 413
History of a Nutcracker, 223-44, 254, 421-22
History of Germany, 276-77, 283-84, 287, 288, 289
History of Germany, A, 276, 279-80, 286-87, 289-95, 303, 306
History of Germany . . . On the plan of Mrs. Markham's Histories, 279-80, 284, 287-89, 292-96, 306, 358, fig. 26
History of Germany, and the Austrian Empire, A, 276-79, 284-85, 287, 288-89, 293-97, fig. 25
History of the Thirty Years War in Germany, 291
Hitzig, Julius Eduard and family, 140, 142, 223, 225-26, 238
Hockney, David, 147
Hodder & Stoughton, 276, 418
Hofer, Andreas, 236
Hofer, the Tyrolese, 275
Hoffmann, E.T.A., 3, 6, 96, 121, 136-37, 140, 168, 181, 203, 223-44, 245, 254, 255, 263, 281, 330-44, 397, 420-21
Hoffmann, Heinrich, 4, 97, 327, 328, 332, 335, 340, 343, 420, 422
Hoffmann von Fallersleben, August Heinrich, 281

Hofland, Barbara, 67-68
Hogg, J., 113, 274
Holidays at Bärenburg Castle, The, 398-99
Holy Roman Empire, 64, 65, 275, 277, 291, 312
Home Queen; or, Unconscious Rule, The, 398
Home Stories, 165
Honor; or, the Story of Brave Casper and the Fair Annerl, 264
Hookeybeak the Raven, and Other Tales, 347-48
Hope, Ascott R., 244
Höppner, Julius, 124
Hornstein, J.G., 190-91, 192, 193, 196, 202
Horton, Alice, 356, 369
Hosemann, Theodor, 197, 340, 341, 345
Hotten, John Camden, 155, 210-11, 349
Houlston and Son, 114
Household Stories. Newly translated, fig. 19
Household Tales, 148, 159, 171, 173, 176, 199
Household Tales and Popular Stories, 165-68
An Hour at Bearwood. The Wolf and the Seven Little Kids, 157-58, fig. 18
Houwald, Ernst von, 246
Howitt, Mary, 321, 322-24, 355, 398, 399
Howitt, William, 48, 142, 185, 399
Howleglass, 1, 353
Hozier, Capt. H.M., 384
Humboldt, Wilhelm and Alexander von, 25
Humboldt, Alexander von, 36, 83, 137
Hunt, Margaret, 165n. 167, 171, 173, 177, 199

illustration, techniques of, 203, 331, 351, 362, 368
In Parenthesis, 409
Industrial Revolution, 184, 405
Infant Saviour, The, 8
Irving, Washington, 150, 185
Italian fairytales, 265

Jack, T.C. & E.C., 410
Jack and the Beanstalk, 13, 149

Jacobs, Joseph, 144
Jacobs, S., 175
Jane, L. Cecil, 275
Jardine, David, 155
Jew(s), 42, 54, 74-75, 117, 138-39, 170, 182, 194-95, 215-16, 236, 242, 250, 270-72, 304, 338, 377-78, 391, 396
Johnson, Joseph, 26, 33, 39, 43-45, 49, 86
Jones, David, 409
Juvenile Artist, The, 115

Kafka, Franz, 136, 138, 147
Kaiser William II, 387, 391, 410, 412, 414, 417-19, 420-21
Kaulbach, Wilhelm, 321, 356, 367
Keene, Charles, 59, 219, fig. 7
Keightley, Thomas, 266
Kennedy, M.G., 60
Kerr, Mrs Alexander, 312
King Nut-cracker or the Dream of Poor Reinhold, 343-44
King of Prussia's Tall Soldier, The, 312-13
King of Root Valley and his Curious Daughter, The, 254-61
King of the Golden River, The, 160, 259
King of the Swans, and Other Tales, The, 192, 247-48, 251-52, fig. 23
King Solomon's Mines, 92
King's Service, The, 298-99, 302-03
Kingston, W.H.G., 316, 319
Kleist, Heinrich von, 290
Klopstock, 290
Kotzebue, August von, 39, 52, 317
Kroeker, Kate Freiligrath, 264, 266, 269-74
Krummacher, Friedrich Adolf, 397
Krummacher, Friedrich Wilhelm, 98-99
Krusenstern, Adam Johann von, 81, 89
Kurz, Heinrich, 84

La Condamine, C.M. de, 36
Lang, Andrew, 18, 59, 176, 187, 199
Lareyn, 217
Laughter Book for Little Folk, A, 197, 340
Laurin (or Lareyn), 217, 357, 360
Le Fanu, Brinsley, 20, 127, 200
Lea, John, 413
Legends of Number Nip, 54, 58-59, 219, fig. 7

Leete, Alfred, 417
legends, 53-55, 58-59, 73, 144, 150-51, 155, 159, 163, 168, 183, 197, 205, 206, 213, 214, 217-21, 274, 287-88, 358, 360-61
Leinstein, Mme, 157
Lemon, Mark, 58-60, 219
Lenglet du Fresnoy, 64-65
Léonie; or, Light out of Darkness, 371
Lessing, Gotthold Ephraim, 197
L'Estrange, M., 318
Lettsom, William H., 285n., 355-56, 369
The Life and Exploits of Baron Munchausen. Who outdid all other Travellers. Related by himself, fig. 2
Life of Luther, The, 275
Linden Leaf; or, the Story of Siegfried, The, 366, 368
Linné, Carl von, 137
Lion of the North, The, 295, 298, 300-03, 306, 393
Little Dove, The, 99-100, 397, fig. 11
Little Drummer, The, 310
Little Henry, 104-06
Little Lasses and Lads, 327
Little Lily's Alphabet, 326, 329, fig. 28
Little Sand Boy, The, 398
Little Swiss Seppeli; or Confidence in God Rewarded. A true story translated from the German, The, 100-01, fig. 12
Little Whaler, The, 316-18
Lohenstein, D.C. von, 290
Löhr, J.A.C., 230
Longman, Brown, Green, and Longmans, 60, 142, 214, 321
Loreley legend, 264, 274
Louis, the Little Emigrant, 104
Lovell, John, 89
Lucas, Annie, 371, 372, 379, 381, 383, 390, 393
Lucas, Mrs Edgar, 174
Lucas, E.V., 342, 417, 420
Lucian, 15
Lumley, Edward, 124, 131, 133, 143, 144
Lunardi, Vicenzo, 15
Lusatia, 218, 221
Luther, Martin, 63, 75, 275, 279-81, 286, 288-89, 304
Lützen, Battle of, 121, 294, 295, 299, 300-

01, 304

Magasin des enfans, 43
Macgregor, Mary, 126, 367, 369
Macleod, Mary, 127, 132
Magdeburg, 65, 59, 70, 281, 293, 294, 296-97, 299, 301, 311
Maid of Stralsund, The, 298-99
Malice in Kulturland, 420
Mangnall, Richmal, 277
Manheim, Ralph, 243
Margetson, W.H., 175-76
Marryat, Captain Frederick, 83
Marshall, Beatrice, 172-73, 177
Marshall, Henrietta Elizabeth, 276, 286-89, 293-96, 303
Mason, A.T., 43, 417
Masterman Ready, 83
Max and Moritz, 4, 344-51, fig. cover
Max Krömer. A Story of the Siege of Strasbourg, 371, 372-73, 376, 379, fig. 32
May, Karl, 319
Mayhew, Henry, 375
McDonnell, Cicely, 185, 190, 201
Meade, L.T., 395
Melcon, H.A., 406
Mendel, S., 185-87, 190, 193, 195, 199, 200-02, 203
Melville, Herman, 237, 316
Menshikov, Alexander, 314-15
Meyer, Conrad Ferdinand, 292, 303
Meyer, Franz Sales, 101
Milner and Sowerby, 88, 103, 114, 144
Mitton, Geraldine Edith, 90
Moby Dick, 316
Montolieu, Baroness Isabelle de, 80-89
moral and religious stories, 3-4, 83, 95-119, 167, 201, 289, 309, 312, 315, 421
moral education, 24, 95-119, 283
Moravians, 117
Montgolfier brothers, 15
More, Hannah, 55
Moryson, Fynes, 63
Moritz, Gustav, 310
Morris, William, 126, 362, 366
Morrow, George, 420
Mother Courage, 291
Mozart, Wolfgang Amadeus, 225

Mozley, H., 18
Mulock, Dinah, 212
Münchhausen, 4, 5, 8-21, 23, 139, 422, fig. 1
Münchhausen, K.F. Hieronymus von, 11, 20
Murray, John, 54, 59n., 74, 155, 158, 160, 161, 219, 276, 292, 324, 358, 361n., 367n.
Musäus, Johann Karl August, 3, 51-61, 137, 143, 197, 219, 263, 266, 271

Napoleon Buonaparte, 26, 99, 183, 211-12, 255, 271, 277-80, 286, 288, 290, 310-11, 326, 360, 383, 384, 386, 394, 412
Nathusius, Marie, 395-98, 400
Nelson, Thomas, and Sons, 89, 127, 175, 366, 368-369, 372, 412
Nesbit, E., 131
New Fairy Tales from Brentano, 264, 273, fig. 24
New Picture Book, The, 324
New Robinson Crusoe, The, 23-37, fig. 4
Newbery, Elizabeth, 26, 67
Never Give In, 298
Nibelungenlied, 6, 128, 210, 285, 288, 321, 352-70
Nicholson, W., and Son, 114, 144
Nicol, George, 157
Nielsen, Kai, 286
Nieritz, Gustav, 216-17, 297, 309-15, 396
Nisbet, James, and Co., 90, 413
Nister, Ernest, 172, 185, 189, 202
Noeldechen, W., 298-99, 303-06
Norse literature, 6, 121, 128, 284-85, 288, 355-57, 360, 361-69
Novalis, 139, 144
Nuremberg, 76, 140, 142, 233-34, 238, 254, 277, 299, 301, 303
Nurse Margaret's Two St. Sylvester's Eves, 398, fig. 33
Nursery Rhymes for Fighting Times, 418
Nutcracker, 3, 136, 168, 181, 203, 223-44, 254, 263, 335, 421-22
Nut-Cracker and Sugar Dolly, 197, 343-44
Nutt, David, 131, 213, 220, 285n., 355n.

O'Callaghan, M., 255
Oer, Theodor von, 254

Index   457

Old Story-Teller, The, 207, 209-11, 321, fig. 21
O'Neill, Elizabeth, 410-12
Orgel, Doris, 274
Original Stories, 43-44, 46
Otmar, 150, 155, 217, 220
Overend, Mrs Campbell, 310
Oxenford, John, 57, 185, 197

Pabke, Marie, 61
Palmer, Francis Paul, 59, 219
pantomimes, 124
Papa's Present of Household Stories, 179-80
Papé, Frank C., 102-03, 362, 368
Parables, 98-99
Paracelsus, 123
Paris at Bay, 372, 387
parodies, 12, 223, 332, 342-43, 410, 418
Parrott, Sir Edward, 412-13
Paul, Adrien, 89
Paul, Robert B., 276, 279, 293
Paull, Mrs H.B., 90, 165n., 168-70, 173, 177
Penrose, Elizabeth, 279
Perrault, Charles, 2, 51, 53, 138, 149, 159, 163, 166, 169, 175-77, 181, 208, 242, 247
Peter Parley's Tales about Europe, 71
Peter Schlemihl, 2, 135, 146, fig. 16
Peter the Whaler, 316
Phillips, Sir Richard, 66
Pichler, Caroline, 197, 292, 303
picture books, 170, 229-30, 235, 321-351
Picture Story-book, A, fig. 22
Pied Piper of Hamelin, 11, 215, 221, 397
Pilote Willis, Le, 89
Pinkerton, Percy E., 185, 187, 199
Pious Jemima, 348-49
Pirates of the Mississippi, The, 316
Pitman, Rosie M.M., 125
Planché, J.R., 343-44
Playmate, The, 197, 246, 250, 255
Pletsch, Oscar, 325-27
Poe, Edgar Allan, 122
Polar Scenes, 36-37
Political Struwwelpeter, The, 341, 420
Pollock, Nellie, 413
Pope, Jessie, 416

Popular Romances of the Middle Ages, 362
Popular Tales, 185
Popular Tales of the Germans, 54-56
Postl, Karl Anton, 319
Powell, George, 419-20
Powell, S., 319
Princess Ilse, 220
Professor Knatschke. Selected Works of the Great German Scholar and of his Daughter, 418
Protestantism, 24, 63, 98, 113, 114, 117, 149, 159, 178, 292, 293, 295-99, 302, 303, 305-07, 309-13, 321, 275, 379-80, 389, 394
Pütz, Wilhelm, 276-77, 280, 281, 284, 287, 289, 293-95, 306

Questions for the Use of Young People, 277

Rackham, Arthur, 125-26, 129, 132, 144, 147, 174, 176, 286, 366, 367
Rae, Julia S.E., 90
Raspe, Rudolf Erich, 9-21
Raven's Feather, The, 117
Recke-Volmerstein, Count von der, 99-100
Reformation, 63, 75, 277-79, 283
Reid, Stephen, 367-68
Reinick, Robert, 245, 252-55, 261, 343
religion, 1, 25, 38, 42, 63, 65, 73, 76, 111, 279, 281, 306
religious tales, 4, 95-119, 167, 178, 309, 382
Religious Tract Society, 115, 117, 118, 302, 312, 315, 371
Reynard the Fox, 2, 253, 321
Rhineland, 159, 214, 292
Rhymes of the Times for War Babies of All Ages, 419
Richards, A.M., 132
Richards, Anna, 132
Richards, Grant, 173, 341, 416
Richardson, Samuel, 44
Richardson, T., 18
Richter, Ludwig, 207, 321
Ringed by Fire, 372, 388, 390
Ritchie, Leitch, 58, 219
Ritson, Joseph, 215
Ritzerow, Emily, 397

Robins, James, & Co., 149
Robinson, Charles, 131, 172, 366
Robinson, W. Heath, 20
Robinsonades, 26-28, 79, 83, 104, 315
Robinson Crusoe, 1, 3, 27-28, 90, 317
Robson, Forster, 143, 203
Rochow, Friedrich Eberhard von, 23-24, 49
Romanticism, 3, 10, 24, 52, 56, 57, 64, 103, 121-22, 126, 129, 135, 137, 139-40, 145, 147, 171, 181, 245, 263-64, 274, 421-22
Root Princess, The, 254-55
Roscoe, Thomas, 56, 214, 217, 220
Rountree, Harry (also known as Rowntree), 176
Rousseau, Jean-Jacques, 24, 28
Routledge, George, and Sons, 90, 143, 165, 166, 176, 219, 238, 249, 310, 316, 322, 323, 325, 327, 339, 346, 349
Rowntree, Harry, *see* Rountree
Rowsell, Mary C., 59, 215, 219, 221, 274
Rubaiyat of William the War-Lord, The, 420
Rübezahl, 53, 54-55, 58-59, 61, 218-19, 220-21
Rügen island, 211-13
Rudolphi, J.J., 192, 245, 246, 250-52
Runge, Philipp Otto, 148, 265
Ruskin, John, 155, 160, 210-11, 259-61

Sagorski, A., 59
Salzmann, C.G., 23, 24, 36, 39-49, 95-96, 310
Sampson Low, Son, and Marston, 102, 346
Sandmann, Der, 227-28, 240, 244
Saxony, 60, 65, 68, 218, 221, 310, 313, 394
Scenes and Adventures in Central America, 319
Scenes and Narratives from German History, 276, 281, 293, fig. 27
Scenes in Europe, for the Amusement and Instruction of Little Tarry-at-Home Travellers, 71, fig. 8
Schiller, Friedrich von, 25, 95, 140, 197, 291-92, 294
Schlegel, August Wilhelm, 232
Schmid, Christoph von, 3, 7, 27, 103-19, 197, 254, 309, 311, 393, 396, 417, 421
Schnorr von Carolsfeld, Julius, 320, 355, 362, 368
Schoemwald, Franz-Anton, 228
Schoppe, Amalie, 395-96, 407
Schummel, Johann Gottlieb, 24-25, 51
Scott, Sir Walter, 181, 355
Sealsfield, Charles, 319
Selous, H.C., 131
Sendak, Maurice, 147, 243, 274
Serapion Brethren, The (Serapionsbrüder, Die), 223, 241
Setma, the Turkish Girl: and Woodrof, the Swedish Boy, 115, 117
sexuality, 58, 129, 152, 161-62, 169, 179, 189, 261, 348-49, 363, 364, 372
Shoberl, F., 98
Short Stories and Poems, 322
Shirley, Edward, 175
Siege of Magdeburg, The, 281, 293
Siegfried, 6, 121, 141, 174, 197, 210, 288, 353-70
Siegfried and Kriemhild, 368
Silver Fairy Book, The, 200
Sime, James, 276-77, 283-84, 286-89
Simpkin, Marshall and Co., 88, 90, 114, 396
Sinnett, Jane, 297, 305
Sintram and his Companions, 2, 121-33, 144, 244, 263, 366, 393, 421, fig. 15
Snowe, Joseph, 214
Snow-White, 53, 54, 147, 154, 168, 170, 172, 175-79, 261
Southey, Robert, 18, 64, 214, 274
Sowerby, Millicent, 173
SPCK, 276, 287-89, 293-95, 297, 306, 307, 398
Speckter, Otto, 4, 158, 321-25
spies, 377-78, 389, 391-92, 415-17
Spyri, Johanna, 393, 395, 400-07, 420, 422
St. A., J.H., 111-13
Stahl, Pierre-Jules (pen-name of P. J. Hetzel), 89
Stead, W.T., 20, 98, 127, 176, 185, 194, 200-01, 247, 348
Stebbing, Grace, 298
Steinkopff, Ann, 99
Stockdale, J., 23, 26, fig. 4

Stories of Siegfried, 367
'Story of Little Muck', 191-92, 195, 199
Story of Siegfried, The, 361, 364, 366, 369
Story without an End, The, 101-03, 118, 139
Story about a Christmas in the Seventeenth Century, A, 297
Strang, Herbert, 413, 415
Stratton, Helen, 173, 176
Stretton, Hesba, 6, 371-72, 374-76, 377, 378-80, 383, 386, 388
Struwwelpeter, 4, 5, 6-7, 327, 330-51, 420, 422, fig. 29
Struwwelpeter Alphabet, The, 342, 420
Submarine U93, 415
Sullivan, Edmund J., 132
Sumner, Heywood, 124, 129, 131
Swan Sonnenschein, 59, 185, 199, 201, 219, 362
Swedish Shepherd Boy, The, 115
Swiss Family Robinson, The, 3, 5, 16, 27, 79-93, 139, 168, 318, 335, 405, 422, fig. 10
Swiss Stories for Children and those who love Children, 406
Switzerland, 39, 60, 65, 69, 77, 79, 81, 83, 87, 93, 99, 101, 126, 219, 277, 373, 402, 404-05, 406, 418
Swollen-headed William, 342, 420, 421

Tacitus, 353
Tagebuch eines armen Fräuleins, 397
Tale of Gockel, Hinkel & Gackeliah, 274
Tales from the German, 58, 185, 190
Tales for Children, in a Familiar Style, 96
Tales from the Eastern-Land, 246, 249
Tales of the Teutonic Lands, 362
Tales of Wonder; or, the Inn in the Black Forest, 193, 197-98, 228
Taylor, Edgar, 149, 150, 155-56, 159-60, 163, 171-72, 173, 175, 176-77, 180, 197, 210-11, 220, 251
Taylor, Rev. Isaac, 71, 73, fig. 8
Taylor, J.E., 160-61, 170
Tchaikovsky, P.I., 241, 244
Tell, William, 144, 287, 405
Tenniel, John, 124
textbooks, 6-7, 64-69, 75-77, 275-77, 292-93, 296

Thackeray, William Makepeace, 237-38
Thesiger, Sybil, 185, 190, 193, 201
Thirty Years War, 6, 117, 211, 272, 275, 277, 281, 285, 291-307, 311, 393,
Thomas, Charlie, 419
Thompson, Miss, 397
Thoms, W.J., 159-60, 162, 170
Thorpe, Benjamin, 211
Thorpe, Elphinstone, 418
Thousand and One Nights, see *Arabian Nights' and Arabian Nights' Entertainments*
Three Bears, The, 157
Tieck, Ludwig, 56, 95, 138, 150
Tilly, Count, 281, 294-95, 299, 301, 304, 311
Tilt, Charles, 246, 248
Tirol, 217-18, 221
Told in Gallant Deeds, 413
'Tom Thumb's Alphabet', 323-24
Tott, Baron de, 49
toys and automata, 71, 224, 227-28, 230, 232, 234, 240-41, 254, 257, 324, 343
Tracy, Thomas, 123
traditional tales, 3, 12, 15, 51, 53, 138, 146, 155, 181, 182, 184, 199, 200, 205, 245, 251, 255, 262, 265, 353
translation, 1-6, 14, 26-27, 34, 36, 39, 41-47, 53-61, 81083, 85, 86-87, 89, 90, 96, 98-99, 102, 103-04, 108, 110-16, 122-27, 129, 131-33, 135, 139-43, 149, 151, 153-55, 156, 157, 159-161, 165, 169-73, 174, 176-77, 179-80, 182, 185, 186-87, 193-96, 198, 199-203, 207-09, 210-11, 214-15, 219, 221, 230, 232, 237-38, 241-42, 243, 244, 252, 255, 259-60, 266, 270, 271, 273-74, 285, 288, 291, 292, 297, 298, 299, 304, 310, 312, 315, 322, 323, 324-25, 328, 330, 338-39, 342, 343, 346, 349, 350-51, 355-57, 358, 360, 362, 369, 397-98, 400, 405-06
translation from French, 4, 26, 52, 80, 81, 82, 84-85, 86-88, 89, 91, 110-11, 149, 168, 278, 322
travel books, 6, 64, 68, 159, 214, 360, 362, 405
Travels in Switzerland, 405
Travels with Minna and Godfrey in many Lands. The Rhine, Nassau, and Baden,

73, 75-76, 214, fig. 9
Trease, Geoffrey, 91-92
Trimmer, Sarah, 43, 55
Tschuggmall, Christian, 228
Tuck, Raphael, and Sons, 175
Tucker, Charlotte Maria, see A.L.O.E.
Twain, Mark, 328, 339
Two Convicts, The, 316
Two Talismans, The, 197, 246, 249

Underhill, Zoe Dana, 211, 259
Undine, 2, 121-33, 135, 140, 143-454, 174, 201, 244, 263, 356, 393, 421
Unlucky John and his Lump of Silver. A Juvenile Comic Tale. Translated into easy verse by Madame Leinstein, 157, fig. 17
Unwin, T. Fisher, 185, 190, 199, 242, 264, 276, 285, 360

Valentine, Laura, 176
versification, 158, 170, 200-01, 210, 265, 322, 323-24, 327, 330-31, 333-34, 338, 340, 343, 345-46, 349
Verstegen, Richard, 215
Vickers, George, 165-66, 193
violence and cruelty, 43, 54, 90, 152, 163, 313, 335, 373, 414, 151-52, 163, 178, 214-15, 260-61, 274, 279, 298, 305, 313, 335, 373, 413-14
Voïart, Elise, 89
Volkmann-Leander, Richard von, 245, 255-59
Vredenburg, Edric, 175

Wagner, Richard, 6, 121, 174, 288, 355, 362, 366, 368
Wakefield, Priscilla, 68-73, 74
Wallenstein, 281-82, 288-89, 292-95, 297-302, 304,
Wallenstein, 292
Wanderings and Fortune of Some German Emigrants, 172, 316

Wanley, Nathaniel, 215
Ward and Lock, 114, 116, 166-67, 168
Warne, Frederick, 90, 112, 113, 114, 168, 169, 171, 176, 216, 326, 327, 398, 420
Weber, Henry William, 355
Wehnert, Edward H., 162-63, 165, 171, 207
Werther, 47, 110, 356
Wheatley, L.A., 168, 171, 177
Wheelock, Lucy, 406
Whittaker, G. and W.B., 88, 140
Whittier, John Greenleaf, 212-13
Wieland, Christoph Martin, 52, 266, 290, 356, 357
Wilde, Oscar, 267
Wildermuth, Ottilie, 395, 398-400
With Frederick the Great, 300, 393-94
With Haig on the Somme, 415
With the Allies to the Rhine, 414
Wollstonecraft, Mary, 39-49, 96
Woman of the Commune, A Tale of the Two Sieges of Paris, 372, 387
Won by the Sword, 298, 300, 302, 393
Wonderful Wizard of Oz, The, 21
Wordsworth, William, 1, 44, 64
Wright, W., 157, 396
Wyatt, Horace, 420
Wyss, Johann David, 16, 27, 79-93, 309, 422

Yonge, Charlotte M., 124-25, 127, 131-32, 276, 284-89, 293-95, 306, 360
Young Franc-Tireurs, The, 300, 371, 376-77, 379, 387
Young Gold-Digger, The, 316
Young Tyrolese, The, 115-17, fig. 14

Zadig, 182, 195
Zigzag Journeys to Northern Lands, 185, 361

OpenBook
Publishers

Open Book Publishers is an independent community interest company set up and run by academics for academics and for readers of academic work. We publish high quality, peer-reviewed monographs, collected volumes and lecture series in the humanities and social sciences.

Open Book speeds up the whole publishing process from author to reader by applying three recent technological advances: digital medium, the internet and print-on-demand. We thus offer all the advantages of digital texts (speed, searchability, updating, archival material, databases, discussion forums, and links to institutions' websites) together with those of the traditional printed medium.

Works accepted for publication, after the rigorous peer-review process, are published within weeks.

All Open Book publications are available online to be read free of charge by anyone with access to the internet, a point of high importance for those who wish to reach colleagues, students, and other readers around the world with poor access to research libraries.

For further information on our publishing enterprise, additional digital material related to our titles and to order our books please visit our website: www.openbookpublishers.com
or contact the Managing Director, Dr. Alessandra Tosi: a.tosi@openbookpublishers.com